HANDBOOKS

NICARAGUA

AMBER DOBRZENSKY

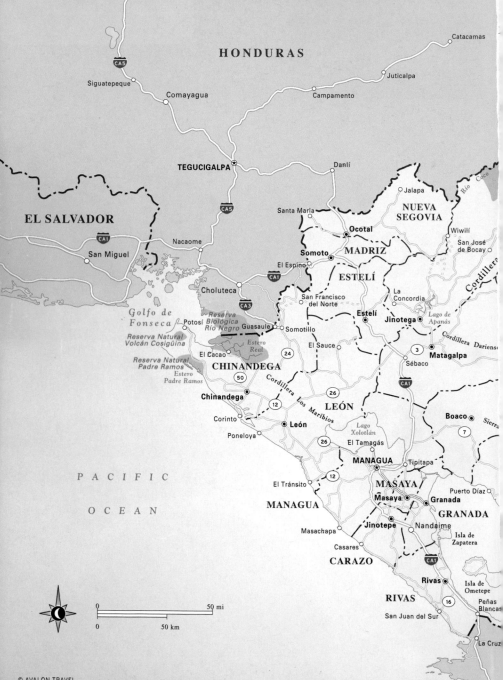

HONDURAS

Catacamas

Siguatepeque

Comayagua

Juticalpa

Campamento

TEGUCIGALPA

Danlí

Jalapa

EL SALVADOR

Santa María

NUEVA
SEGOVIA

Nacaome

Ocotal

Wiwilí

San Miguel

Somoto

MADRIZ

San José
de Bocay

El Espino

Choluteca

ESTELÍ

Reserva
Biológica
Río Negro

San Francisco
del Norte

La
Concordia

Cordillera

Golfo de
Fonseca

Potosí

Guasaule

Estelí

Jinotega

Lago de
Apanás

Reserva Natural
Volcán Cosigüina

Somotillo

Reserva Natural
Padre Ramos

El Cacao

Estero
Real

El Sauce

Cordillera Dariense

Estero
Padre Ramos

CHINANDEGA

24

Sébaco

Matagalpa

3

Chinandega

50

Cordillera Los Maribios

26

LEÓN

CA1

Corinto

12

Boaco

Sierra

Poneloya

León

Lago
Xolotlán

7

26

El Tamagás

PACIFIC

MANAGUA

Tipitapa

El Tránsito

12

OCEAN

MASAYA

Puerto Díaz

Masaya

Granada

Masachapa

MANAGUA

Jinotepe

Nandaime

GRANADA

Casares

Isla de
Zapatera

CARAZO

CA1

Rivas

Isla de
Ometepe

RIVAS

16

Peñas
Blancas

San Juan del Sur

La Cruz

0   50 mi

0   50 km

© AVALON TRAVEL

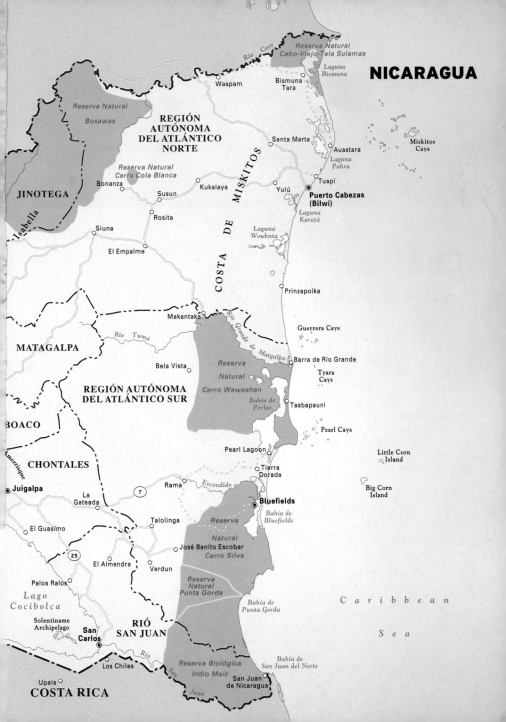

NICARAGUA

Reserva Natural
Cabo-Viejo-Tela Sulamas

Río Coco

Laguna
Bismuna

Waspam

Bismuna
Tara

Reserva Natural
Bosawas

REGIÓN
AUTÓNOMA
DEL ATLÁNTICO
NORTE

Santa Marta

Miskitos
Cays

Auastara

Laguna
Pahra

Reserva Natural
Cerro Cola Blanca

Bonanza

Kukalaya

Tuapí

Susun

Yulú

Puerto Cabezas
(Bilwi)

JINOTEGA

Rosita

Laguna
Karatá

Isabella

Siuna

Laguna
Wouhnta

El Empalme

Prinzapolka

Makantaka

Río Grande de Matagalpa

Guerrera Cays

Río Tuma

MATAGALPA

Bela Vista

Reserva
Natural
Cerro Wawashan

Barra de Río Grande

Tyara
Cays

REGIÓN AUTÓNOMA
DEL ATLÁNTICO SUR

Bahía de
Perlas

Tasbapauni

BOACO

Pearl Cays

CHONTALES

Pearl Lagoon

Little Corn
Island

Amerrisque

Juigalpa

Rama

Escondido

Tierra
Dorada

Big Corn
Island

La
Gateada

⑦

Talolinga

Bluefields

El Guasimo

Reserva

Bahía de
Bluefields

㉕

José Benito Escobar
Cerro Silva

Natural

El Almendra

Verdun

Palos Ralos

Reserva
Natural
Punta Gorda

Lago
Cocibolca

Bahía de
Punta Gorda

C a r i b b e a n

Solentiname
Archipelago

RIÓ
SAN JUAN

San
Carlos

S e a

Reserva Biológica
Indio Maíz

Río

Los Chiles

San Juan
de Nicaragua

Bahía de
San Juan del Norte

Upala

Juan

COSTA RICA

COSTA DE MISKITOS

Contents

Discover Nicaragua

A land of clay-tiled villages and soaring cathedrals, of volcanic heat and Caribbean cool, Nicaragua is as charming as it is diverse, enticing as it is unfathomable. Its seven million proud, outspoken inhabitants continue to reinvent themselves amid unending political, geological, and economic drama.

Nicaragua's volcanoes, lagoons, highlands, rivers, and valleys provide opportunities for hiking, paddling, and exploring. An endless network of dusty roads and mule trails carry curious travelers to country villages throughout the interior. The Atlantic coast is a remote labyrinth of mangrove swamps and classic Caribbean colors, while the Pacific side is a bold stretch of hills, plains, and pueblos, its bays and beaches washed by superb surf. Catch some waves, glide through cloud forest canopy, summit an active volcano—or just soak up a series of languid afternoons over home-cooked meals and the company of your Nica hosts.

What was once a nascent travel industry in a little-known, misunderstood nation is finally coming into its own. More than a decade of economic growth has catalyzed the slowly maturing Nicaraguan tourism industry, from resurfaced roads and new hotels to a panoply of chic clubs

and restaurants. Granada has blossomed into an ex-pat hotspot and tourist destination the international press can't keep quiet about, while San Juan del Sur's surroundings have become a patchwork of farmland, gated gringo communities, jungle hills, and a smattering of luxury resorts—a trend slowly creeping northward.

Still, travel in most of Nicaragua involves compromises you wouldn't be asked to make in more prosperous countries. Patience is key, and Nicaragua's greatest adventures require daring and imagination, not to mention some conversational Spanish (if your Spanish is rusty, enroll in one of the many excellent language schools, where you can brush up in beachfront classrooms and colonial cities).

Nicaragua is a place where independent spirits can easily fall off the map, live simply and witness life at a slower pace. Red beans and toasted corn tortillas cooked over a wood fire. A crisp night sky behind a volcano's silhouette. A simple, friendly exchange with a *campesino* in the town plaza.

There's something to see and learn around every corner.

Planning Your Trip

In general, destinations south of Managua are more developed for travelers, especially Granada and San Juan del Sur, whose exploding number of colonial hotels, upscale surf camps, and convenient shuttle services have drastically altered the tourism landscape. The rest of the country—north and east of Managua, and the Río San Juan in the southeast—is a different story. In these places, with some basic Spanish, patience, and persistence, you can pueblo-hop on public buses till the Chontales cattle come home. Basic room and board are found in even small pueblos, as are community homestay and rural tourism programs. Fancier hotels and restaurants are found in most department capitals, usually on or near the central plaza.

Most travelers begin in Granada and with good reason. It is smaller and more manageable

beachfront restaurant on San Juan del Sur

than Managua and you can get a shuttle directly to Granada from the airport (under one hour). Granada is a beautiful, tranquil place to get acclimated to the heat and pace of things, and provides access to numerous day trips.

Passengers, animals, and supplies are all welcome on the country's "chicken buses."

Watch out for crab traffic on Big Corn Island.

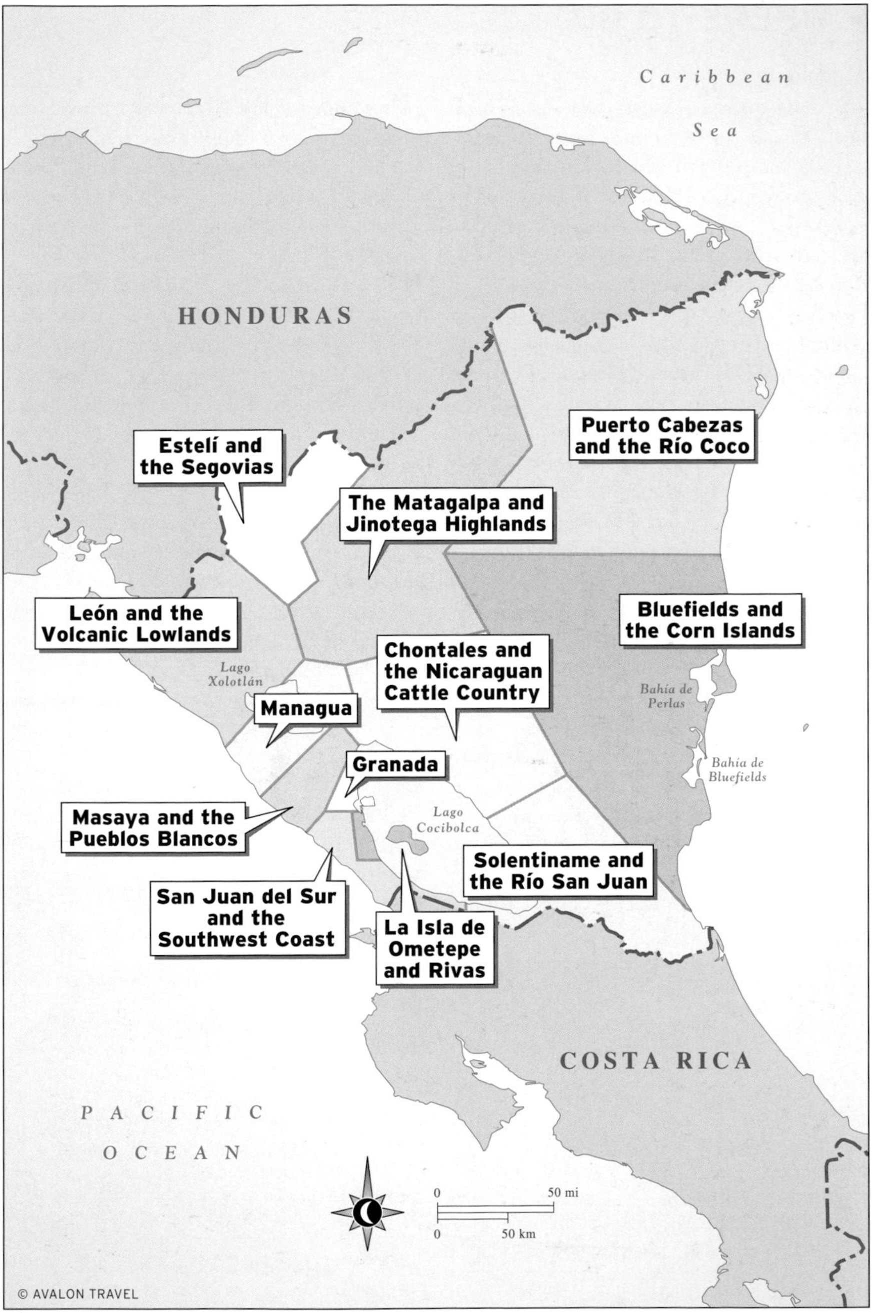

Caribbean

Sea

HONDURAS

Estelí and
the Segovias

Puerto Cabezas
and the Río Coco

The Matagalpa and
Jinotega Highlands

León and the
Volcanic Lowlands

Bluefields and
the Corn Islands

Lago
Xolotlán

Chontales and
the Nicaraguan
Cattle Country

Bahía de
Perlas

Managua

Bahía de
Bluefields

Granada

Lago
Cocibolca

Masaya and the
Pueblos Blancos

Solentiname and
the Río San Juan

San Juan del Sur
and the
Southwest Coast

La Isla de
Ometepe
and Rivas

COSTA RICA

PACIFIC

OCEAN

0   50 mi

0   50 km

© AVALON TRAVEL

▶ WHERE TO GO

Managua

The most chaotic of Central American capitals, Managua used to be a modern, cosmopolitan center until it was flattened by an earthquake in 1972, the first of a series of recent major disasters to strike the city. Today, amid an ongoing building boom and expansion of Managua's middle class, *la capital* can be a fun stopover if you're traveling through on business or pleasure. Though you could conceivably pass through Nicaragua without visiting Managua at all, its central location makes it an important transport hub and the place to go for services not available elsewhere. You can see Managua's small cadre of attractions in half a day, but if you're here on a weekend, consider staying to sample the vibrant nightlife.

Granada

The most colorful and comfortable of Nicaragua's cities, Granada has been charming travelers with its red-tiled roofs, grand cathedrals, breezy lakeshore, and drowsy lifestyle since the days of the Spanish, who used the city as their first Atlantic port (via Lake Cocibolca and the Río San Juan). Today, Granada is the undisputed hub of tourism in the country, and it's got the international cuisine and café culture to prove it. Many visitors opt to stay in Granada throughout their trip, as a tranquil base from which to explore the 365 *isletas* and the cloud forests of Volcán Mombacho, as well as Masaya, the Pueblos Blancos, and the Laguna de Apoyo.

Masaya and the Pueblos Blancos

Less than an hour south of the capital, Masaya and the dozens of villages that comprise the Pueblos Blancos are known for their residents' artistry. Start with a trip to Volcán Masaya, where you can peer into Nicaragua's fiery entrails, then visit the shaded stalls of Masaya's craft markets. Spend a lazy afternoon driving through the Pueblos Blancos and take a dip in the Laguna de Apoyo, the country's nicest swimming hole. You could easily devote two full days to this region, either by staying in Masaya or the Laguna, or by traveling here each day from Granada. The Pueblos make a nice diversion for those spending a longer time in Managua, as the hills are markedly cooler.

La Isla de Ometepe and Rivas

An old administrative city with a colonial history, Rivas may be worth a stop on your way to the beaches of San Juan del Sur or to Nicaragua's crown jewel: La Isla de Ometepe,

IF YOU HAVE . . .

- **ONE WEEK:** Visit Granada and San Juan del Sur.

- **TWO WEEKS:** Add La Isla de Ometepe and/or a side trip to León and the northwest beaches.

- **THREE WEEKS:** Add the Solentiname Islands and a trip down the Río San Juan. Take the time to hike a volcano or explore the Estero Reál. Or work your way up the Pacific coast, one beach at a time.

- **FOUR WEEKS:** Go deep. After visiting the above, get off the beaten track using Matagalpa, Jinotega, or Estelí as a base. Or spend a couple days camping in the more remote wildlife reserves of Matagalpa and the Río San Juan.

The bays near San Juan del Sur offer world-class surf.

Enjoy a traditional Nica meal in Granada.

a few kilometers across Lake Cocibolca. Visible from the entire southern highway, Ometepe's twin volcanic peaks—Concepción is hot and active, Maderas is dormant and forested—offer challenging, unique treks. Or stick to the lakeshore, enjoying island-grown coffee, lagoons, waterfalls, and the call of howler monkeys. The slopes of Maderas are home to an array of rustic, farm-based hostels, surrounded by old-growth hardwoods, petroglyphs, barnyard animals, and memorable views.

San Juan del Sur and the Southwest Coast

Nicaragua's favorite beach town is also the most popular with foreign tourists. In addition to a crescent bay lined with barefoot restaurants and sandy bars, San Juan del Sur offers a slow-paced, tranquil setting, fresh seafood, and charming guesthouses. Go fishing and sailing, try the canopy tour, or learn surfing and Spanish. From San Juan's bay, the Pacific coastline extends in both directions in a series of hidden beaches, hills, and wave-strewn coves. The southwest coast is an important habitat for the Paslama turtle—witnessing the hatching is breathtaking.

León and the Volcanic Lowlands

Lying at the feet of the imposing Maribio volcanoes, León and Chinandega are colonial cities in the arid lowlands of Nicaragua's Pacific northwest. León's importance as a political and economic center over the past four centuries has bequeathed it a rich history. Stop in at the baroque cathedral, the largest in Central America, or wander the indigenous Subtiava neighborhood, with a magnificent church of its own. Most travelers stroll León's streets, walk up (and ride down) Cerro Negro, and then head back south or east. With a week or more, you can work your way farther northwest. In addition to beaches near León, the Northwest Coast—including remote protected areas throughout the Cosigüina Peninsula—is home to numerous small fishing villages with

Matagalpa is characterized by verdant valleys and steep mountains.

great morning surf and fairly empty beaches (except during Semana Santa).

Estelí and the Segovias

Nicaragua's mountainous north is accessible by comfortable public transportation; its main city, Estelí, is only a few hours from Managua. Farther north, the peaks are some of the oldest in Central America, and they boast an unforgettable landscape with hardwood and pine forests, stony river valleys, and fields of tobacco, coffee, and corn. Spend a day at the Estanzuelas waterfall and Reserva El-Tisey, or head into the hills for a weekend in Miraflor Nature Reserve, a precious habitat for some of Nicaragua's rarest species of birds and orchids. Press farther northward to the small towns of the Segovias—Somoto and Ocotal—dry as dust but alive with history, legends, and lore.

The Matagalpa and Jinotega Highlands

Nicaragua's rugged interior is coffee country, where the unrushed traveler will find rough, undeveloped adventure. Green valleys and steep peaks define the landscape, and the hard-working, sometimes aloof residents define its character. Everyone's got a war story in these mountains, and hearing them adds texture to your travels. Matagalpa has steep streets, famous steaks, and long vistas; Jinotega is the gateway to the untrodden, as most of Nicaragua's landmass lies farther afield to the east. A guide in Matagalpa can take you trekking to summits, waterfalls, and forgotten gold mines. Spend a weekend in a rural lodge, tour coffee plantations, or participate in a village guest program for a closer look at *campesino* life.

Chontales and the Nicaraguan Cattle Country

The golden hillsides beyond the east shore of Lake Cocibolca fold upward into the rocky precipices of the Amerrisque Mountains, stomping grounds of the Chontal people during pre-Columbian times. Today, the area runs thick with cattle ranches that produce most of Nicaragua's cheese and milk. To the north and east, the roads dwindle to rutted tracks and old, rural encampments. It was here that the Chontal people carved their totemlike statues, a few of which are on display in the museum in Juigalpa. Most travelers speed through on buses bound for El Rama and the Atlantic coast, but spending a night in Juigalpa or Boaco, where the wild west vibe hasn't lost its edge, may lead you on to the area's hot springs, petroglyphs, horseback treks, and burly hikes.

Solentiname and the Río San Juan

Life moves slowly along the broad river that drains Lake Cocibolca to the Caribbean. This gorgeous, verdant lowland is Nicaragua's wettest, and its remoteness means you'll spend more time and more money getting around. The Spanish fort at El Castillo has watched over river traffic since the 17th century. Along the southern shore of Cocibolca, you'll find wildlife reserves and cultural curiosities. The Solentiname archipelago isn't easy to get to, but you'll be rewarded with an up-close look at the birthplace of liberation theology and a thriving colony of artists. Explore the wilds of Los Guatuzos, habitat for monkeys, birds, and amphibians, then set sail downstream for San Juan de Nicaragua, home to the bones of English pirates and more ghosts than residents.

Bluefields and the Corn Islands

The isolated Atlantic coast may as well be a country unto itself. Nicaragua's Caribbean is tough, muddy, and quite unlike any Cancún-tainted visions you may harbor. Most tourists fly straight from Managua to Big Corn, but a few hardy souls still visit Bluefields to experience Creole culture and crab soup. When you tire of Bluefields' grittiness, board a boat for Pearl Lagoon, the coastal fishing communities, Pearl Cays, or Reserva Silvestre Greenfields. Both Big Corn Island and Little

fishing on the coast for crab, shrimp, and lobster, as well as fish

The *guardabarranco* is Nicaragua's national bird.

Corn Island are Caribbean gems as gorgeous below the waterline as above. There are kilometers of coral reefs, a handful of hotels, and only one dive shop on each island. Little Corn has no roads, so the only sound you hear should be the wind in the trees.

Puerto Cabezas and the Río Coco

The northeast Miskito communities of Puerto Cabezas (Bilwi), Waspám, and the Río Coco are a far removed, embattled corner of the country, where resources go more toward fighting the drug trade and recovering from natural disasters than developing tourism. Still, there are basic services in Puerto Cabezas, including decent oceanfront accommodations and low-budget tour guides to take you to nearby rivers, beaches, and Miskito communities. Even farther north, Waspám is the commercial center for villages up the Río Coco, mostly indigenous communities where Miskito is still the first language and where foreign visitors may arouse more suspicion than hospitality.

► WHEN TO GO

Generally speaking, the best months—when the land is still green from the rains and the days are sunny and dry—are December, January, and February. June, July, and August are nice as well, with cooler temperatures, fewer North Americans, and more European travelers. March, April, and May are the hottest, driest months, prone to pervasive dust and smoke caused by agricultural burning; September–November are the wettest months, and also hurricane season, when you can expect periodic tropical depressions to raise the rivers.

Nicaragua's *invierno* (winter, or rainy season) lasts approximately May–October, and *verano* (summer, or dry season) lasts November–April. Rain during these months may mean just a quick shower each afternoon, or it may go on for days. As you travel east toward the Atlantic coast or down the Río San

A ripe coconut sits half-buried on the white sands of Little Corn Island.

Juan, the rainy season grows longer and wetter; in these areas, the dry season sometimes lasts only a month or two (around April).

Several fiestas are worth planning your trip around: the fiestas in Diriamba around January 19, the Palo de Mayo on the Atlantic coast (throughout May), the Crab Soup Festival on Corn Island (August 27–28), and the Fiesta del Toro Venado in Masaya (last Sunday of October). The first weeks of December, when Nicaraguans celebrate the Immaculate Conception with various *purísima* and *gritería* parades, are particularly lively in Granada and León.

▶ BEFORE YOU GO

Passport and Visa Requirements
Every traveler to Nicaragua must have a passport valid for at least six months following the date of entry. A visa is required only for citizens of the following countries: Afghanistan, Albania, Angola, Bangladesh, Bosnia and Herzegovina, Cameroon, Colombia, Cuba, Dominican Republic, Ecuador, Egypt, Ghana, Haiti, India, Iran, Iraq, Jordan, Kenya, Lebanon, Libya, Mozambique, Nepal, Nigeria, Pakistan, People's Republic of China, People's Republic of Korea, Peru, Romania, Somalia, Sri Lanka, Sudan, Syria, Ukraine, Vietnam, and Yemen. Everyone else is automatically given a tourist pass good for three months.

Vaccinations
Required: A certificate of vaccination against yellow fever is required for all travelers over one year of age and arriving from affected areas.
Recommended: Before traveling to Nicaragua, be sure your tetanus, diphtheria, measles, mumps, rubella, and polio vaccines are up-to-date. Protection against hepatitis A and typhoid fever is also recommended for all travelers.

Explore Nicaragua

▶ THE BEST OF NICARAGUA

Like other countries in the region, Nicaragua has a popular, carved-out tourist route based on its principal, most-developed attractions. Nicaragua's beaten path is made up of the Granada–Ometepe–San Juan del Sur circuit, which can be done in about one week; save time for tackling the northwestern lowlands and add the Atlantic coast or Río San Juan. Wherever you head, Granada is a good place to ease into things, with colorful surroundings, wonderful cuisine, and more creature comforts than elsewhere in the country.

Day 1

Arrive in the afternoon at Managua's International Airport. Transfer to a hotel in Granada, less than an hour's drive from the airport. Check into your hotel, get accustomed to the heat, and relax after your flight.

Day 2

Tour Granada, visiting museums, the cathedral, and enjoying the languid waterfront. Paddle to the nearby *isletas* or go hiking on Volcán Mombacho, whose heights above the city make for a cool day.

Day 3

From Granada, it's a short day-trip to visit the city of Masaya and its active volcano. Start early at Volcán Masaya National Park, then browse the handicrafts in the El Mercado Viejo Craft Market. Return to Granada that evening.

Granada's cathedral is one of the finest in the country.

Brig Bay on Big Corn Island

Masaya's active volcano

Days 4-6

Pack up and head south. Catch the boat at San Jorge to Ometepe. Spend 2–3 days exploring the island's unique getaways, or arrange a guide to take you to the top of one of the volcanoes for more adventurous travel.

Day 7

Catch the boat back to San Jorge and bus it south through Rivas to the beach at San Juan del Sur. Spend at least one night there, but tag on a few more if the surf's up or the turtles are laying eggs.

Days 8-10

Catch the early express bus to Managua, then transfer directly to Matagalpa; continue east to the village of San Ramón. It will take you the better part of a day to get here, so enjoy the afternoon and that plate of *gallo pinto* waiting for you in the mountains. Spend the next two days hiking to the mines and touring a coffee farm or two.

Days 11-14

Catch a ride to Managua and take the afternoon flight to Big Corn Island. Spend two days on Big Corn Island or brave the boat and make for Little Corn, soaking up sun, fresh lobster, island vibes, and perhaps a dive on the reef. Make your way back to Managua on the last day and fly home.

SURF'S UP

Playa Maderas is one of the most popular surfing beaches in the country.

Swells from South Pacific storms pound Central America during the North American summer months, especially in June and July. The shape of Nicaragua's long, isolated beaches and direction of the shoreline help form these pushes of water into perfect overhead barrels. On the southwest coast around San Juan del Sur, lake-generated offshore breezes often blow year-round. Waves are still being "discovered" and named. Old-school surfers compare Nicaragua to Hawaii's unspoiled North Shore in the 1970s.

Nicaragua, once a blank spot on the world's surfing map, now hosts international competitions and draws an increasingly well-informed crew of sponsored and nonsponsored shredders from across the planet. Meanwhile, a few young Nicaraguans have picked up the sport and caught the attention of surf journalists and documentary filmmakers, while small ecosurf camps spring up along the entire Pacific coast. In short, the secret is out.

Most surfers head straight to **San Juan del Sur** (a.k.a. Sin City) where they can get oriented, rent or buy a board, socialize, and arrange transport to breaks north and south of town. You'll find plenty of accommodations, guides, surf shops, and beach shuttles--none of which existed only a few years ago.

Start your research with **Nicasurfing** (www.nicasurfing.com), the first and only surf tour operator that is entirely Nica-owned. For photos and practical information, check out **Nica Surf Report** (www.nicaraguasurfreport.com), the longest-running online daily wave report in the country, which also offers a full complement of services for visiting surfers (rentals, equipment, transport, etc.). Another option, especially if you'd prefer to explore the north coast, **Rise Up Surf Tours Nicaragua** (www.riseupsurftoursnicaragua.com) offers fully guided surf tour packages to Nicaragua's Central and Northwest Pacific coast; the owners are surfers based in León.

Women surfers can check out the San Juan del Sur–based **ChicaBrava Surf Camp** (U.S. tel. 832/519-0253, www.chicabrava.com), the first all-female surf operation in the country. The second, **Surf with Amigas Surf and Yoga Retreat** (SuaveDulce@gmail.com, www.surfwithamigas.com), was opened in 2010 by pro surfer Holly Beck on the Nicaraguan north coast.

▶ THE GREAT GREEN NORTH

Nicaragua north of Managua is offbeat and little-traveled, and gives the creative traveler lots of opportunities. Pueblo-hopping through the Segovia Mountains and participating in the Ruta de Café will immerse you in an authentic and sublime world you won't soon forget. Each town has a swimming hole, local hike, or archaeological site that will beckon you further. Alternate legs include passing through San Juan de Limay and the back roads to León; or from Jinotega, looping through Yalí to Condega. This sample itinerary will give you a taste of what to expect.

Day 1

From Managua, head north to Estelí and spend the day walking the streets of this bustling commercial center, viewing the murals and markets, and enjoying cool weather.

Days 2-3

Take an early-morning bus to the El Salto Estanzuela waterfall; stay in a cabin on Reserva El-Tisey, where you can arrange hikes, horseback expeditions, and farm tours. Return to Estelí at the end of day three.

Days 4-5

From Estelí, go east and up, into the Miraflor Nature Reserve, where you can experience a rural homestay, photograph orchids, and try to spot elusive wildlife. Even if you don't find any quetzals or ocelots, the locals will regale you with legends and ghost stories. Spend the night, return in the morning, and grab a bus north.

Day 6

Stop in for lunch at one of the quiet northern agricultural towns like Condega or Palacagüina; press on to Ocotal, and spend the evening roaming the park and city center.

The northern forests are home to some of the most intact jungle in the country.

Matagalpa and the surrounding mountains

Day 7

Day trips galore await from Ocotal—seek out the ruins, or head northeast to Jalapa if you have the time. Otherwise, check out the humble church and exhibits in the Ocotal *casa de cultura* and hop an express bus back to Estelí.

Day 8

Leave Estelí in the morning and make your way through Sébaco to Matagalpa. Enjoy the city for the day, maybe even take a quick hike up Cerro Apante.

Day 9

Here's your chance to visit a coffee plantation and witness the process that brings us that magical beverage. You can stay in San Ramón, Finca Esperanza Verde, or in the cozy stone cottages at Hotel de Montaña Selva Negra.

Day 10

Enjoy a beautiful, fun-filled day of monkeys in the trees, hearty country dining, and a guided tour through the farm. Return to Managua, hopefully with a few pounds of freshly roasted coffee in your pack.

Hotel de Montaña Selva Negra

► DOWN THE RÍO SAN JUAN

The watery "Golden Route" through southern Lake Cocibolca and down the Río San Juan is tougher to access than it was when boat service was more frequent, so you'll need a minimum of 7–10 days to get there, get around, and get back. Once you reach San Carlos (by boat, bus, or small plane), public boat transportation is regular and cheap, but limited to a handful of boats per week. As a result, unless you drop a lot of cash to hire your own personal boat and driver, you may find yourself stranded on one of 36 Solentiname islands for three days, with nothing to do but go fishing or bird- and crocodile-watching in a dugout canoe. The Río San Juan is unquestionably worth a visit, especially the photogenic fort and river town at El Castillo.

Day 1

Fly from Managua to San Carlos in the early morning. If you really want the full-blown adventure, take the slow boat from Granada on Monday: You'll arrive Tuesday morning. Poke around San Carlos until the afternoon, when the boat leaves for Solentiname.

Days 2-3

Enjoy the island artist colony of Solentiname, set in a unique area of profound natural splendor. You can hire boats to take you among the islands, enjoy scarlet sunsets, and absorb the intense tranquility of the archipelago. Return to San Carlos Thursday morning to catch the boat to Los Guatuzos. If you'd rather go directly and bypass San Carlos, strike a deal with a local Solentiname boat owner.

Days 4-6

Hike and explore the fascinating tropical landscape of the Los Guatuzos Wildlife Reserve. A two-day stay will give you a taste for the reserve, but real outdoors enthusiasts

Kayaking is a fun way to explore the Río San Juan.

El Castillo is the main attraction on the Río San Juan.

will probably prefer to stay until the next boat (Tuesday, unless you make other arrangements). Arrival in San Carlos on Saturday means you are just in time to catch a boat downstream. Cast away and start your adventure down the mighty Río San Juan, bound for El Castillo.

Day 7

Start your day off in El Castillo early, so you can hear the sky fill with birds. Visit the old Spanish fort or rent a horse for a bush trip. Most travelers return to San Carlos for a flight to Managua at this point, but if the downstream horizon is beckoning, then keep on floating.

► EXTREME NICADVENTURES

Adrenaline junkies will certainly get their fix in Nicaragua. Surfing, canopy zip lines, rappelling, wake-boarding, ash-boarding, and bouldering opportunities will leave the most die-hard addicts exhausted but content. The growing number of extreme activities on offer cover Nicaragua from top to bottom, so you'll also have the chance to see and experience diverse landscapes, climates, *pueblos,* and colonial cities in this heart-racing dash across the country.

Day 1

Arrive at Managua International Airport and transfer via express shuttle to the small town of San Juan del Sur.

Day 2

After breakfast in the *pueblo*, drive or boat out to one of the many surf breaks in the area; most of the beaches near town are still secluded and wild, with world-class surf. If you've never surfed before, this is a great place to start, as San Juan's numerous surf shops offer lessons and tours to the surrounding beaches.

HIKING THE RING OF FIRE

Volcán Momotombo is a stratovolcano near the city of León.

Volcano hopping, anyone? Pack some sturdy boots and hike one or all of the more than a dozen ascents detailed in this book. Nicaragua's Maribio and Dirián mountain ranges contain both dormant and active cones, each one completely unique in scenery, difficulty, vegetation, and length. A few of these hikes have established, well-blazed trails (Mombacho and Masaya); most don't. In undeveloped-for-tourism areas, "hiking" means turning off the pavement, taking a poor dirt road to an even poorer one, and then entering the country's vast network of mule- and footpaths that have connected rural communities for centuries. You'll share the road with horses, cattle, and families walking to and from their fields, and you'll discover small adobe chapels, hidden shrines to the Virgin Mary, and cool watering holes.

Always hire a local guide, both as a way to both support the community and to not get lost, both respectable goals: León has an excellent selection of guides and tour services specializing in volcano treks.

- **Cerro Negro:** This relatively short, but stout and rewarding hike heats up with a quick descent via ash-boarding (page 180).

- **Cosigüina:** The dense vegetation inside Cosigüina's crater houses a rare scarlet macaw population (page 180).

- **Concepción:** This active volcano last darkened the skies in 2009 (page 121).

- **Las Casitas:** Although not as tall, La Casitas offers a better view of Managua and the lake than San Cristóbal (page 180).

- **Maderas:** Hike to a forested lake within the crater of this dormant volcano (page 121).

- **Masaya:** This gaping crater, only an hour from Granada, is guaranteed to impress (page 95).

- **Mombacho:** Mombacho looms over the colonial streets. The various ridge trails around its jungle craters make wonderful loops (page 279).

- **Momotombo:** Climbing Momotombo requires a 1,300-meter, eight-hour round-trip on horseback and foot (page 180).

- **San Cristóbal:** The granddaddy of volcano hikes, San Cristóbal stands active at over 1,700 meters as the highest peak in the country (page 180).

Pool-jumping is one way to explore the Grand Canyon of Somoto.

Day 3

Depending on your skill level, enthusiasm, and energy, you can hit the surf again or sign up with Aracne Rappel or Da Flying Frog for a rappel or canopy tour, which offer spectacular views of the town and surroundings.

Day 4

Make the relatively short trip to Granada, continuing on to Las Isletas, a maze of a tiny island with a lush, monkey-filled backdrop. Spend the day kayaking or wakeboarding at the base of Volcán Mombacho.

Day 5

Head north to León and spend the afternoon volcano boarding on Cerro Negro, an active volcano. "Ash-boarding" encompasses both sledding and boarding as a surefire way to get the blood pumping.

Day 6

Drive northeast to Somoto for rappelling, bouldering, or pool-jumping in the Grand Canyon of Somoto, the deepest canyon in Central America. Local outfit Namancambre Tours can arrange these adrenaline activities, or hire a local guide for a relaxing hike or horseback ride in the surrounding area.

Day 7

From Somoto, it's about a six-hour bus ride back to Managua. By this point, you should be tired enough to sleep through the journey and wake up ready for your plane departure. Otherwise, it may be time to see if you can change that return ticket.

MANAGUA

If Nicaragua's capital were a vehicle, it would be a battered 1960s school bus, dented and dinged on all sides, paint chipping through multiple layers of color, four bald tires rolling slightly akilter, but sporting a brand new $2,000 sound system blaring a merengue classic for its smiling passengers. Managua rarely impresses; its labyrinthine, unnamed streets are complicated to navigate, it is loud and architecturally uninspiring, and there's no city center to speak of. Though it's relatively safe, it doesn't *feel* that way, and its understated charms don't exactly jump out at you.

Home to nearly a quarter of Nicaragua's population, Managua sets the tone for the political and economic dialogue that shapes the nation's destiny. The story of Managua and Nicaragua are largely parallel, from earthquake to revolution to economic revival and onward, so the better you understand Managua, the better you will understand the history of Nicaragua itself.

Managua is also the best place in the country to get your gear repaired, visit a doctor or dentist, see a movie or show, and party like a salsa star; it has the nation's most varied selection of restaurants and night spots. You likely won't plan your trip around a visit to Managua, but neither should you necessarily avoid it, as Managua does have a covert appeal that will become apparent once you've spent a little time here. You may even discover you like the place.

As well as being a transport hub, Managua

© JOSHUA BERMAN

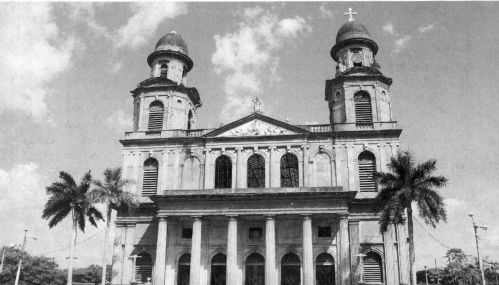

HIGHLIGHTS

◖ Plaza de la Revolución: Most of Managua's historical sights are clustered in this four-block area, still the cultural heart of Nicaragua's capital (page 34).

◖ Catedral Santiago de los Caballeros: This cathedral is standing testimony to the earthquake of 1972 (page 36).

◖ La Laguna de Tiscapa: Just one of the area's many volcanic lakes, this is the only one you can zip over while tethered to a steel cable; or just enjoy the view (page 37).

◖ Las Huellas de Acahualinca: This glimpse of Managua's mysterious past is haunting for the questions it raises, not the ones it answers (page 38).

◖ Chocoyero-El Brujo Nature Reserve: Located just south of Managua in a gorgeous patch of protected hillsides and ravines, this community-based tourism venture offers some wonderful day hikes (page 54).

LOOK FOR ◖ TO FIND RECOMMENDED SIGHTS, ACTIVITIES, DINING, AND LODGING.

offers easy access to nearby Pochomil and Masachapa, with some of the cheapest seafood and quietest beaches in the isthmus. If you prefer lush terrain to sand and sea, head to the Chocoyero or Montibelli nature reserves for a glimpse of some of the country's wildly varied flora and fauna.

HISTORY

Managua's modern layout is the very embodiment of its history, in a tale that leads inexorably from the water's edge in the direction of Masaya. Mana-huac ("the big water vessel") has been inhabited since 4000 B.C.; you can see the footsteps of some of the earliest inhabitants in

the Museum of the Footprints of Acahualinca at the city's western edge. The Nahuatls met the Spanish so fiercely there the Spanish retaliated by razing the city in the 15th century; the land remained abandoned for another 300 years. By the mid-1800s, when both León and Granada rivaled for political control of the nation, Managua was again a prosperous fishing village. The Conservatives and Liberals compromised by making Managua the capital, and the fishing village began to grow. But in 1931, by which time Managua was a small municipality of 10 square city blocks, an earthquake of 5.6 on the Richter scale leveled Managua and killed more than 1,000 people. For five years, Managuans rebuilt

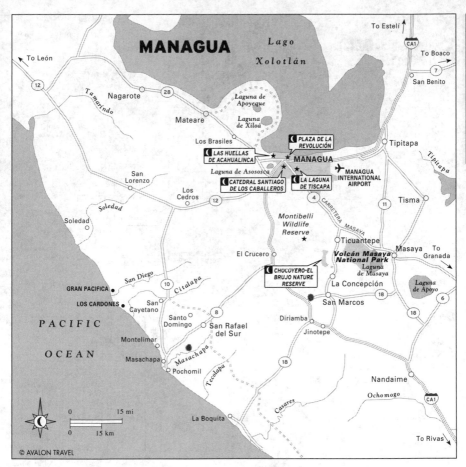

their city, only to see it consumed by flames in the Fire of 1936. Again, they rebuilt.

By the late 1960s, Managua was the most modern capital in Central America, home to nearly half a million inhabitants, with a modern center and two skyscrapers. But at 27 minutes past midnight on December 23, 1972, an earthquake of 6.3 on the Richter scale laid waste to the five square miles of the city. The quake killed 10,000 people, destroyed 50,000 homes, and reduced the city's entire infrastructure to rubble. Managua was left without water, sewers, or electricity, hospitals lay in ruins, and the roads were choked with debris.

This was a disaster from which Managua has never quite recovered, as little of the initial material aid arrived at its intended destination. President Anastasio Somoza Debayle saw to it that humanitarian assistance channeled through the "emergency committee" under his control ended up in his personal bank accounts. For Nicaraguans who'd lost everything, being forced to purchase donated relief items from the National Guard was the last straw: The revolution would fully erupt only seven years later. Today, the ruins of old Managua have been largely left to rot at the south shore

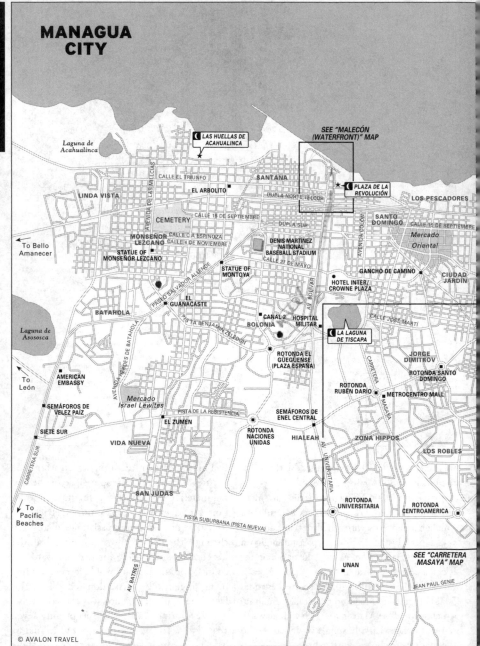

MANAGUA CITY

Laguna de Acahualinca

LAS HUELLAS DE ACAHUALINCA

SEE "MALECÓN (WATERFRONT)" MAP

CALLE EL TRIUNFO

SANTANA

LINDA VISTA

EL ARBOLITO

DUPLA NORTE TELCOR

PLAZA DE LA REVOLUCIÓN

LOS PESCADORES

CALLE 15 DE SEPTIEMBRE

CEMETERY

DUPLA SUR

SANTO DOMINGO

CALLE 15 DE SEPTIEMBRE

Mercado Oriental

To Bello Amanecer

MONSEÑOR LEZCANO

CALLE C A ESPINOZA

CALLE 4 DE NOVIEMBRE

STATUE OF MONSEÑOR LEZCANO

DENIS MARTÍNEZ NATIONAL BASEBALL STADIUM

CALLE 27 DE MAYO

GANCHO DE CAMINO

CIUDAD JARDÍN

PASEO SALVADOR ALLENDE

STATUE OF MONTOYA

HOTEL INTER/ CROWNE PLAZA

EL GUANACASTE

BATAHOLA

PISTA BENJAMÍN ZELEDÓN

CANAL 2

BOLONIA

HOSPITAL MILITAR

LA LAGUNA DE TISCAPA

CALLE JOSÉ MARTÍ

Laguna de Asososca

ROTONDA EL GÜEGÜENSE (PLAZA ESPAÑA)

CARRETERA MASAYA

JORGE DIMITROV

ROTONDA SANTO DOMINGO

AVENIDA DE LAS HÉROES DE BATAHOLA

To León

AMERICAN EMBASSY

Mercado Israel Lewites

ROTONDA RUBÉN DARÍO

METROCENTRO MALL

SEMÁFOROS DE VELEZ PAÍZ

PISTA DE LA RESISTENCIA

EL ZUMEN

SEMÁFOROS DE ENEL CENTRAL

SIETE SUR

VIDA NUEVA

ROTONDA NACIONES UNIDAS

HIALEAH

ZONA HIPPOS

LOS ROBLES

CARRETERA SUR

SAN JUDAS

AV UNIVERSITARIA

To Pacific Beaches

PISTA SUBURBANA (PISTA NUEVA)

ROTONDA UNIVERSITARIA

ROTONDA CENTROAMERICA

SEE "CARRETERA MASAYA" MAP

AV BATRES

UNAN

JEAN PAUL GENIE

AV BOLÍVAR

AVENIDA COLÓN

© AVALON TRAVEL

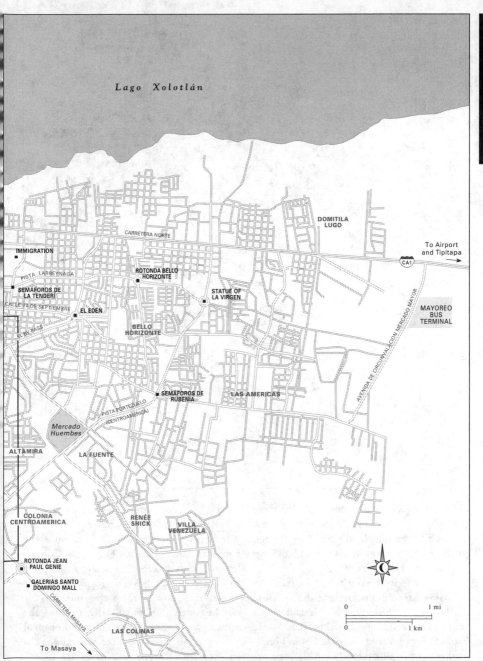

Lago Xolotlán

DOMITILA
LUGO

CARRETERA NORTE

IMMIGRATION

To Airport
and Tipitapa

CA1

PISTA LARREYNAGA

ROTONDA BELLO
HORIZONTE

SEMÁFOROS DE
LA TENDERÍ

STATUE OF
LA VIRGEN

MAYOREO
BUS
TERMINAL

CALLE 14 DE SEPTIEMBRE

EL EDÉN

EL BY-PASS

BELLO
HORIZONTE

AVENIDA DE CIRCUNVALACIÓN MERCADO MAYOR

SEMÁFOROS DE
RUBENIA

LAS AMERICAS

PISTA PORTEZUELO
(CENTROAMÉRICA)

Mercado
Huembes

ALTAMIRA

LA FUENTE

COLONIA
CENTROAMERICA

RENÉE
SHICK

VILLA
VENEZUELA

ROTONDA JEAN
PAUL GENIE

GALERIAS SANTO
DOMINGO MALL

CARRETERA MASAYA

0   1 mi

0   1 km

LAS COLINAS

To Masaya

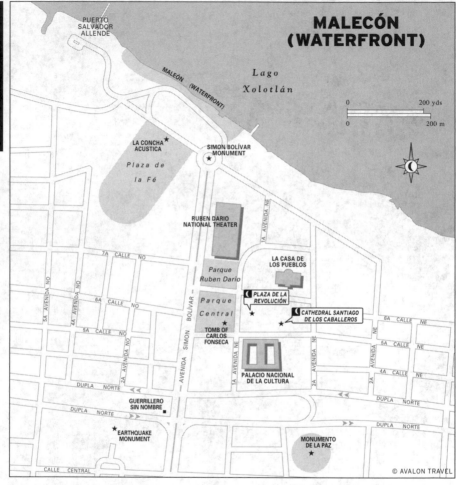

MALECÓN (WATERFRONT)

PUERTO SALVADOR ALLENDE

MALEÓN (WATERFRONT)

Lago Xolotlán

0   200 yds
0   200 m

LA CONCHA ACUSTICA

SIMON BOLÍVAR MONUMENT

Plaza de la Fé

RUBEN DARIO NATIONAL THEATER

7A CALLE NO

LA CASA DE LOS PUEBLOS

Parque Ruben Darío

PLAZA DE LA REVOLUCIÓN

5A AVENIDA NO

4A AVENIDA NO

6A CALLE NO

Parque Central

CATHEDRAL SANTIAGO DE LOS CABALLEROS

6A CALLE NE

AVENIDA BOLÍVAR

5A CALLE NO

TOMB OF CARLOS FONSECA

5A CALLE NE

5A AVENIDA NE

1A AVENIDA NE

4A CALLE NE

2A AVENIDA NE

AVENIDA SIMON

PALACIO NACIONAL DE LA CULTURA

DUPLA NORTE

DUPLA NORTE

GUERRILLERO SIN NOMBRE

DUPLA NORTE

EARTHQUAKE MONUMENT

MONUMENTO DE LA PAZ

CALLE CENTRAL

© AVALON TRAVEL

of Lake Xolotlán, a depressing reminder of the city's glory years. The old cathedral and several other buildings still remain standing, though squatters occupy many of the derelict buildings that were not cleared away.

When the city finally found its feet, the Sandinista revolution brought destruction, not healing, to the capital. Managua bore the brunt of the revolution's final battles. As the Sandinistas advanced, Somoza began bombing his own capital, concentrating his ire on the barrios of Riguera and El Dorado. Managua remained wrecked throughout Somoza's war against the Sandinistas, and once the Sandinistas took power, fighting the Contras left no money to rebuild Managua according to any sort of plan. It was during this time that Managuans shoveled themselves out, and the city began to grow organically, forming the twisting, homogenous neighborhoods of small houses and shanties that make Managua so difficult for foreigners to decipher today.

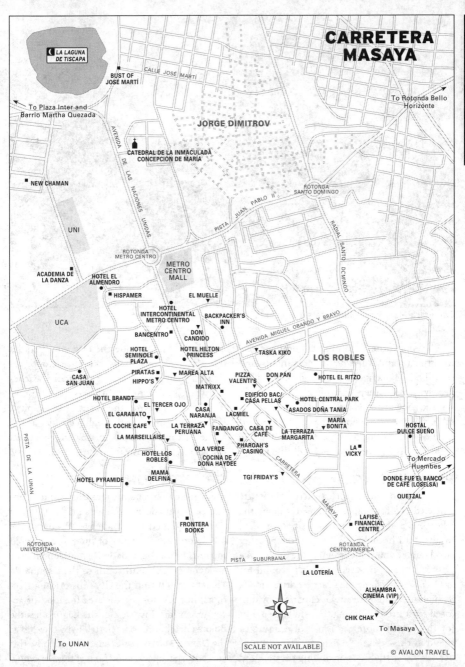

CARRETERA MASAYA

LA LAGUNA DE TISCAPA

BUST OF JOSÉ MARTÍ

CALLE JOSÉ MARTÍ

To Plaza Inter and Barrio Martha Quezada

JORGE DIMITROV

To Rotonda Bello Horizonte

AVENIDA DE LAS NACIONES UNIDAS

CATEDRAL DE LA INMÁCULADA CONCEPCIÓN DE MARÍA

NEW CHAMAN

ROTONDA SANTO DOMINGO

PISTA JUAN PABLO II

RADIAL SANTO DOMINGO

UNI

ROTONDA METRO CENTRO

METRO CENTRO MALL

ACADEMIA DE LA DANZA

HOTEL EL ALMENDRO

HISPAMER

EL MUELLE

UCA

HOTEL INTERCONTINENTAL METRO CENTRO

BACKPACKER'S INN

AVENIDA MIGUEL OBANDO Y BRAVO

BANCENTRO

DON CANDIDO

HOTEL SEMINOLE PLAZA

HOTEL HILTON PRINCESS

TASKA KIKO

LOS ROBLES

CASA SAN JUAN

PIRATAS

HIPPO'S

MAREA ALTA

PIZZA VALENTI'S

DON PAN

HOTEL EL RITZO

MATRIXX

HOTEL BRANDT

EL TERCER OJO

CASA NARANJA

EDIFICIO BAC/ CASA PELLAS

HOTEL CENTRAL PARK

EL GARABATO

LACMIEL

ASADOS DOÑA TANIA

EL COCHE CAFE

LA TERRAZA PERUANA

FANDANGO

CASA DE CAFE

MARÍA BONITA

HOSTAL DULCE SUEÑO

LA MARSEILLAISE

OLA VERDE

LA TERRAZA MARGARITA

HOTEL LOS ROBLES

PHAROAH'S CASINO

LA VICKY

To Mercado Huembes

COCINA DE DOÑA HAYDEE

MAMA DELFINA

CARRETERA

DONDE FUE EL BANCO DE CAFE (LOSELSA)

HOTEL PYRAMIDE

TGI FRIDAY'S

QUETZAL

MASAYA

FRONTERA BOOKS

LAFISE FINANCIAL CENTRE

ROTONDA UNIVERSITARIA

ROTONDA CENTROAMERICA

PISTA DE LA UNAN

PISTA SUBURBANA

LA LOTERÍA

ALHAMBRA CINEMA (VIP)

CHIK CHAK

To Masaya

To UNAN

SCALE NOT AVAILABLE

© AVALON TRAVEL

MANAGUA

© AMBER DOBRZENSKY

Carretera Masaya is Managua's main drag.

The end of the Sandinista era brought new investment capital and new opportunities, and since 1990 Managua has grown quickly and impressively. But rather than risk rebuilding in the seismic zone at the lakefront, new, upscale establishments stretch down the city's main road in the direction of Masaya, where they now form the city's Zona Rosa and nightlife hub.

PLANNING YOUR TIME

Managua's main historical attractions are clustered in a four-block-square area along the lakeshore, and you can easily visit all of them in about an hour by taxi, or reserve another two hours if you'd like to take one of the lake cruises. It pays, however, to stick around for an evening, as Managua's biggest attraction is its nightlife, and its beauty is enhanced by dim (or absent) urban lighting. For the intrepid or for those with more than just an evening to spend in the capital, Managua offers a number of other attractions, including theaters and

museums. Just outside the city you'll find a few excellent, usually overlooked outdoor activities. You can also visit the Pacific beaches and the Chocoyero–El Brujo Nature Reserve if you want to avoid the chaos of the capital. If you're just passing through, consider a stop at the Tiscapa crater for an amazing view that reveals just how many trees there are in the city.

ORIENTATION

Managua city has no obvious center and its unnamed streets do not follow a grid pattern, so staying oriented is a challenge. Focus on the following specific zones of interest and avoid the rest: From **Plaza de la Revolución** and the **Malecón** (waterfront) south to the **Laguna de Tiscapa** you'll find the city's historical attractions, but it's not a great area for food or accommodation. Just west of the Laguna lies the Bolonia neighborhood, referred to by travelers as the **Barrio Martha Quezada.** Historically, this area was a backpacker and budget traveler center,

FOLLOWING DIRECTIONS IN MANAGUA

Locating addresses in Managua is unlike any system you've ever seen, but with a few tips, some basic vocabulary, and a couple of examples, you'll master Managua in no time. Street names and house numbers are few and far between, and where they do exist, they are universally ignored. Addresses in Managua begin with a landmark (either existing or historical), which is followed by the number of *cuadras* (blocks) and a direction. Remember this: **North** is *al lago* (toward the lake); **east** is *arriba* (up, referring to the sunrise); **south** is *al sur* (to the south); and **west** is *abajo* (down, where the sun sets).

Some other key phrases to know are *contiguo a* (next door to), *frente a* (across from), *casa esquinera* (corner house), and *a mano derecha/izquierda* (on the right-/left-hand side). Also note that *varas* are often used to measure distances of less than one block; this is an old colonial measurement just shy of a meter.

Directions throughout this chapter are given in English for consistency's sake, but always beginning with the landmark exactly as it is referred to in Spanish. By studying the following examples, you should be able to find your way around with few hassles.

- *De la Plaza España, tres cuadras abajo, tres c. al lago, casa esquinera:* From Plaza España, three blocks west, three north, corner house.

- *De donde fue el Sandy's, 200 varas arriba, frente al gran hotel:* From where Sandy's used to be, 200 meters to the east, across from the big hotel.

- *De los Semáforos El Dorado, dos cuadras al sur, una c. arriba, casa lila:* From the El Dorado traffic light, two blocks south, one east, purple house.

- *Reparto San Juan, de la UNIVAL, 50 varitas al lago, edificio de cinco pisos:* In the San Juan neighborhood, just 50 meters north of the UNIVAL, five-story building.

and still houses the cheapest hostels in town as well as most international bus depots; however, the area has become increasingly unsafe to navigate on foot. South of the Laguna, the various neighborhoods that flank main street **Carretera Masaya** are where you'll find the bars, clubs, and restaurants that make Managua fun, and an increasing number of charming guesthouses, sandwiched between the Metrocentro and Galerías Santo Domingo malls.

SAFETY

Managua is still statistically less dangerous than other Central American capitals, but you should keep your wits about you, as minor crime from pickpockets and purse snatching to carjacking seems to be on the rise. The best way to stay out of trouble is to avoid areas where you'll find it. The safest and cleanest neighborhoods are **Los Robles, Altamira** along Carretera Masaya, plus **Reparto San Juan** (near the University of Central America), **Villa Fontana,** and **Santo Domingo** (south of the Galerías mall), all of which offer more upscale accommodations and bed-and-breakfasts.

Dangerous neighborhoods include Reparto Schick, Jorgé Dimitrov, La Fuente, San Judas, Villa Venezuela, Batahola, Las Americas, Bello Amanecer, Vida Nueva, Los Pescadores, Domitila Lugo, Santana, and Hialeah. You should be safe enough in and around the major shopping centers and the restaurants and clubs along Carretera Masaya, but in general you're better off staying in groups when possible—especially when traveling by taxi. Always pay close attention to your surroundings, and don't get into taxis where the driver is keeping his face obscured by a baseball cap. Solo female travelers should be especially wary of hailing taxis late at night; it's best to ride with a recommended driver, so ask at your hotel and plan pickups ahead of time.

Sights

Managua was not made for walking, a fact that is highlighted by a total lack of sidewalks. Organize your day into trips to different regions of interest, and resign yourself to getting around by car or taxi, as the buses are slow and can be dangerous, and walkers are at risk not only for petty crime but general harassment (not to mention heat stroke). Negotiate a rate with a recommended driver to take you around the sights (one hour is enough and should cost you about $10). Finish the driving tour at the Malecón, where you can enjoy a boat trip on Lake Xolotlán (Tues.–Sun.), then move on. Any middle or upper-range hotel can organize a guide and/or taxi to help you tour Managua. A taxi will cost around $25 per half day and a guide a similar amount.

MALECÓN (WATERFRONT)

The backsides of **Simón Bolívar,** hero of the Latin American liberation movement, and his horse greet you upon arrival (he's peering northward for impending Yanqui invasions, probably). It's an inauspicious welcome to one of Managua's more interesting quarters, though its full potential remains unmet for now.

Caution should be exercised when navigating this area on foot, even in broad daylight; the neighborhoods immediately east and west of here are unsafe for tourists.

Puerto Salvador Allende

It was a loudly decried pity that rather than capitalizing on Lake Xolotlán's windswept lakefront, Managuan mayors had instead chosen for decades to defile it. That has finally changed and the waterfront is now becoming a halfway decent place to spend some time. The Puerto Salvador Allende complex, just left of the Malecón, opened for business in 2008 and provides a safe area for eating and drinking. It's a popular watering hole on weekends, with most spots offering liter bottles of beer for only $2.

The port also offers tourist cruises (45 minutes round-trip) into the lake and around the Isla de Amor, an islet at Managua's western side (once used by the dictator for trysts), as well as longer tours across to the mostly underwhelming San Francisco Libre (famous for being the first village where illiteracy was eradicated in the 1980s). The lake is still polluted, mind you, but a Japanese-funded treatment plant that began operation in 2005 and an aggressive initiative to reroute city sewers have improved the lake's condition overall.

Note: At the time of publication, cruises around Isla de Amor and to San Francisco Libre from this port were suspended indefinitely (the ferry is undergoing maintenance).

Plaza de la Fé

The Plaza de la Fé (Plaza of Faith) was built in 1996 in tribute to Pope John Paul II's second visit to Nicaragua; former Managua mayor Herty Lewites built the adjacent **La Concha Acustica** (acoustic shell) stage here for live concerts. Both are used mostly for Ortega's political rallies these days, although the attractive Concha already appears to be crumbling.

◖ Plaza de la Revolución

The Plaza de la Revolución, ostensibly just an open area, has become a living monument to the incessant bickering of Nicaragua's political elite. Under Somoza, it was known as Plaza de la República. The rebel Sandinista movement assembled huge crowds there to manifest their outrage against the dictator, and upon overthrowing him, the Sandinista government

© AMBER DOBRZENSKY

Plaza de la Revolución

renamed it Plaza de la Revolución. Renowned Sandinista-hater President Alemán, upon taking power, was thus thrilled to punch a hole in the symbolic Sandinista chakra by building an audiovisual fountain in its center. So naturally when President Ortega returned to power in 2006 he wasted no time in demolishing Alemán's fountain and holding political rallies and celebrations here. Visit in the morning, when the breeze off the lake is cool, the trees are full of birds, and the traffic is momentarily silent. But avoid this area around the revolution's anniversary in mid-July, when the streets and plaza are crammed with booze-fuelled political supporters.

PALACIO NACIONAL DE LA CULTURA

On the south side of the Plaza, the attractive Palacio Nacional de la Cultura houses the **El Museo Nacional de Nicaragua** (in the Palacio Nacional de Cultura, tel. 505/2222-2905, 9 A.M.–4 P.M., $4), but at various times has also housed the Ministry of Housing, the treasury, the comptroller general, and the National Congress. Sandinista commandos raided the building in 1978 and held the entire Congress hostage, winning international recognition and the liberation of several political prisoners. It now highlights natural history, as well as pre-Columbian ceramics and statues from all over Nicaragua's territories. In addition to the national library, several murals and the Institute of Culture can be found here.

The first two floors of the old Gran Hotel (severely damaged by the quake in 1972) are now Managua's official cultural museum—look for the murals outside. The building hosts art exhibits, concerts, puppet shows, and dances. The second floor holds studios of prominent Nicaraguan artists. The hallways are lined with striking black-and-white photographs of old Managua, pre- and post-earthquake, and host handicraft fairs the first Saturday of each month. Sneak up to the roof to see how the upper floors of the old hotel were never replaced, yet another monument to the earthquake. There is a halfway decent café here as well, serving lunch only.

PLAZA DE LA CULTURA REPÚBLICA DE GUATEMALA

On the north side, the Plaza de la Cultura República de Guatemala celebrates Guatemalan author Miguel Angel Asturias Rosales, winner of the Nobel Prize in literature in 1967 for his colorful writings about national individuality and Native American traditions.

PARQUE CENTRAL

Set in the small green space of the Parque Central are several monuments of historical significance. An eternal flame guards the **Tomb of Comandante Carlos Fonseca,** father of the Sandinista revolution. Buried across from him is Santos Lopez, a member of General Sandino's "crazy little army" in the 1930s, who helped train latter-day Sandinistas in the general's ideology and the art of guerrilla warfare. The historical frieze that circles the **Templo de la Música,** a brightly painted gazebo, highlights the arrival of Columbus, Rafael Herrera fighting pirates, independence from Spain, Andrés Castro fighting William Walker, and more, but it's just as interesting for the antics of the sparrows in its arches.

PARQUE RUBÉN DARÍO
Parque Rubén Darío, dominated by a stark, white marble statue, is adjacent to the Parque Central and honors Nicaragua's most-beloved poet. Built in 1933, it was restored in 1998 with the help of the Texaco Corporation. At the bottom of the hill, the marble and brass **Teatro Rubén Darío** was designed by the same architects that created New York's Metropolitan Opera House. It was one of few surviving buildings in the 1972 earthquake and remains to this day a classy place to enjoy dance, theater, or musical presentations. Check the newspaper for performances, or visit online (505/2266-3630 or 505/2228-4021, www.tnrubendario. gob.ni) for upcoming events.

◖ Catedral Santiago de los Caballeros
Managua's most iconic and evocative landmark, the Catedral Santiago de los Caballeros in the Plaza de la Revolución, had barely been completed when the earthquake of 1931 struck. It survived relatively unscathed that time, but was all but destroyed by the 1972 earthquake that leveled Managua. Still standing but structurally unsound, the **Ruinas de la Catedral Vieja** (as it is now known) are a poignant testimonial to the destruction caused by the quake.

Until the late 1990s, the ruins of the cathedral were open to visitors, but due to continued structural degradation, it is no longer safe. You can still peer in, however, to appreciate its ravaged, sunlit interior—do so before the next quake finishes what the quake of '72 started.

Across the square, heading toward the lake, the lavishly decorated and brightly painted **Casa Presidencial** was built in 1999 by former president Arnoldo Alemán despite popular outrage over the unjustifiable expense in Hurricane Mitch's aftermath. President Ortega has since renamed it La Casa de Los Pueblos, or "the people's house."

Monumento de la Paz
Hugely representative of the peacemaking initiatives of former president Violeta Chamorro, the Monumento de la Paz celebrated a new era of peace. Beneath the concrete are buried the destroyed remains of thousands and thousands of weapons from the Contra war, many of which—including a tank—can be seen protruding through the cement. Almost directly across the street (just a bit west) is the unmistakable statue of the Guerrillero sin Nombre. This area was and may still be a favorite target for thieves. Despite continuous police presence now, play it safe: visit it only during daylight hours.

El Guerrillero sin Nombre
You can't miss this guy. The Nameless (and shirtless) Guerrilla Soldier grasps a pick-ax in one hand and an AK-47 in the disproportionately muscular other. This hulkish symbol of the revolution's aspirations is inscribed with one of Sandino's most treasured quotations: "Only the laborers and farmers will go to the end." Arnoldo Alemán's administration countered with a different statue just across the road, honoring the working class with two cowed and undernourished-looking figures, one representing a construction worker and the other a domestic servant, both representative

REVOLUTIONARY DRIVING TOUR

Historical trivia buffs, take note! A lot of Managua's most historically salient points are close to invisible, in stark contrast to the role they played in the lead-up to the 1979 revolution. None of these destinations has gotten the granite monument they deserve, but their importance is no less diminished, even as life goes on around them. If you have a rainy afternoon in Managua some day, hop in a taxi, and revisit history on this driving tour (about 30 minutes). Start at your hotel and go first to **Plaza de la Revolución.**

One block south of the Guerrillero sin Nombre, the southwest corner with a lone wooden telephone pole marks the site of journalist **Pedro Joaquin Chamorro's assassination** as he drove to his office on January 10, 1978. Although it was never officially determined who ordered the hit, Chamorro's death helped spark the revolution. Look for a concrete monument directly behind the telephone pole.

Turn south on to Avenida Bolívar. You'll pass some government buildings and basketball courts before coming to the **National Arboretum** (8 a.m.-5 p.m. Mon.-Sat., $0.50) on your left, home to more than 180 species of trees found in Nicaragua. It is practically unvisited except by local school groups, but is especially attractive in March, when the fragrant *sacuanjoche* (Nicaragua's national flower) blooms brightly; the scarlet flowers of the *malinche* tree blossom from May through August. The trees are planted atop the remnants of Somoza's Hormiguero (Anthill), a military base belonging to the National Guard and destroyed

in 1972 by the earthquake. Popular legend has it that this was the site where, on February 21, 1934, General Sandino was ambushed and assassinated after meeting with President Sacasa at his home on the Tiscapa Crater.

Turn left at Plaza Inter and head in the direction of the El Dorado neighborhood. The **monument to Bill Stewart** is one block west and two blocks south of the Semáforo El Dorado. Bill Stewart was a U.S. journalist for ABC in the 1970s. While reporting on the early days of the Sandinista insurrection, he was brutally attacked and killed by members of Somoza's National Guard. Stewart's cameraman filmed and published the whole thing, forcing the U.S. government to stop turning a blind eye to the excesses of Nicaragua's dictator.

A few blocks south in the same neighborhood, the **Iglesia de los Angeles** is a living monument to the revolution, painted on all sides in bright murals that tell the story of Nicaragua. Beautiful on its own, it can be better appreciated with a guide: Contact Solentiname Tours (tel. 505/2270-9981, zerger@ibw.com.ni) for an expert who will lead you through the story.

Finally, and in the opposite direction, just west of the petroleum refinery on the road leading west out of town is **La Cuesta del Plomo** (accessible from *ruta* bus 183), the ravine where Somoza was allegedly fond of making folks "disappear." Families whose loved ones didn't come home after a few days would go to this hillside to search for their bodies.

---

of Nicaragua's growing laborer community in neighboring Costa Rica.

Earthquake Monument

Across from the new *cancillería* (foreign affairs) building, where the old Iglesia de San Antonio used to stand, is the monument to victims of the earthquake of 1972. This touching statue, constructed in 1994, was the initiative of journalist Aldo Palacios and portrays a man standing amidst the wreckage of his home. It

is inscribed with the poem "Requiem a una Ciudad Muerta," by Pedro Rafael Gutierrez.

CARRETERA MASAYA
◖ La Laguna de Tiscapa

If you only have time to make one tourist stop in Managua, this is it. The **Parque Historica** occupies Managua's breeziest and highest point; follow the road immediately south of the Plaza Inter mall and Crowne Plaza Hotel, driving upward to get to it. The twin-towered monument halfway up the road is the **Monumento Roosevelt,** which delineated the southern terminus of the city pre-earthquake. Twenty meters farther up the hill is the statue of justice, sardonically decapitated ages ago. The **statue of Sandino** atop the crater lip is one of Managua's most recognizable symbols and is now a public park with impressive views of the old city and lake. The Sandinistas erected it atop the wreckage of Somoza's presidential mansion. A permanent exhibition of old photos of Sandino has been set up in the basement of the ruins. Just up the hill but closed to the public rests Las Mazmorras, a former prison in which Somoza tortured many political prisoners, including Daniel Ortega.

Older Managuans remember the Laguna de Tiscapa as a turquoise swimming hole and popular afternoon getaway. Under the Sandinista

© JOSHUA BERMAN

the zip line at Tiscapa crater

government of the 1980s it was turned into a sewer. A major cleanup began in 2005, including the diversion of sewer lines and a re-oxygenation plant to treat the waters, but it's still far from swimmable. See for yourself as you zoom across the lagoon on a zip line with **Tiscapa Canopy Tours** (tel. 505/8872-2555, 9 A.M.–5 P.M. Tues.–Sun., $15 for foreigners, $12 for Nicas).

Catedral de la Inmaculada Concepción de María

At the center of an immense field of young coconut trees along the Carretera Masaya, just a few minutes south of the Laguna de Tiscapa, is the new Catedral de la Inmaculada Concepción de María, constructed just two years after the conclusion of the civil war. Commissioned by American Thomas Monahan and designed by Mexican architect Ricardo Legorretta, this dynamic and open cathedral houses the Dutch bells of the old cathedral. Playing on the soaring forms of Spanish colonial architecture and using colors and materials of the Latin culture, the new cathedral is the pulpit of Nicaragua's famous and controversial Cardinal Miguel Obando y Bravo. Mass is celebrated Tuesday–Saturday at noon and 6 P.M. and Sunday at 11 A.M. and 6 P.M.

◖ LAS HUELLAS DE ACAHUALINCA

If you visit only one historical site outside of the city center, this is the one. Modest but intriguing, the site is a simple interpretation center built over the fossilized footprints of Managua's earliest known inhabitants who fished Lake Managua 4,000 years before Christ. The prehistoric footprints were found in the last century, four meters below the ground surface. Once thought to be the prints of people fleeing a volcanic eruption, forensic analysis now shows the walkers were unhurried. The women's prints are deeper, as they were carrying a heavier load, perhaps the children. The museum's exhibits on Nahuatl life and the volcanoes of Central America make clear that living in the shadow of imminent volcanic destruction is nothing new in town.

The museum (tel. 505/2266-5774, 9 A.M.–5 P.M. Mon.–Sun., $4) is a bit out of the way at the northwest end of the city, so call before going, and arrange for a taxi to take you there and back. The taxi will inevitably drive you through some of Managua's poorer lakefront neighborhoods, another statement about the continuity of experience in Managua.

Entertainment and Events

Dancing is a central part of the Managua experience. The music scene ranges from popular electronic to booty-shaking *reggaetón,* as well as plenty of salsa, merengue, and bachata. Managua has several places to learn salsa and merengue if you are in town for a longer period of time.

If you prefer something more low-key, there are lots of bars and clubs with atmospheres that range from sultry to suspect, but they change on an annual basis, as Managuans flock inexorably to the newest scene. For party and event listings, check online (www.bacanalnica.com).

NIGHTLIFE
Bars
The Galerías mall complex also houses several upmarket watering holes in its Zona Viva cluster of bars and eateries, of which **The Reef** bar and the extortionate, Miami-beach style **Palmeras Bar** are the most popular. Live music at The Reef (Wed.–Sun., cover charge from $5) often competes with the noise from next door's busy karaoke joint.

Another zone of tightly clustered fun spots where the bars serve food and the restaurants have a good bar scene is Zona Hippos off Carretera Masaya. **Piratas** on the corner opposite the Hotel Seminole, is always packed on the weekends, and a good place for cheap cocktails. **El Tercer Ojo** just down the road caters to a cosmopolitan, creative crowd, often hosting live DJs with an electronic, ambient, and international soundtrack. A few blocks east from here, just south of the Monte Olivos

landmark, **Santera Bar** is a central favorite for cheap, frosty beers.

Clubs
Moods in the Zona Viva, Galerías Santo Domingo mall, is probably the most upscale disco in town and is consistently popular for its swanky atmosphere, pumping music, and speedy bartenders (tel. 505/2276-5276, Wed.–Sun., cover charge from $5). You'll need to dress well to get in (no baseball caps, sneakers, or flip-flops) The city's bourgeoisie are upstairs in the VIP lounge, photographing themselves. Thursday is ladies' night, with varying specials. Less than five minutes south of Galerías on the Carretera Masaya you'll find **Hipa Hipa** (tel. 505/2263-7712, Wed.–Sun., cover charge from $5), young Managua's first club, which plays a mix of Latin rhythms and electronic beats, and also implements a strict dress-code.

The liveliest—and youngest—party in town is at the **Chamán** (no phone), a Mayan pyramid structure just south of the Laguna de Tiscapa and north of the UCA. Expect long lines, as Managua's youth have made this the place to be, especially on Thursdays when it's ladies' night (Wed.–Sun., cover from $5).

Two other discos are largely spurned by the trendy crowd; that makes them unpretentious, inexpensive, and still great places to dance. **El Quetzal** (a block from the Rotonda Centroamerica) and **El Mirador Tiscapa** are vintage Managua favorites, with a somewhat older crowd. The former is air-conditioned and

NICARAGUAN FOLK MUSIC AND THE HOUSE OF MEJÍA GODOY

In the wide, vast—and incredibly loud—sea of music flowing through Nicaragua's living rooms, bars, vehicles, and airwaves, music of true Nicaraguan roots is not the easiest to hear. However, once you get to know the distinctive 6/8 rhythms, the sound of the *marimba*, and the melodies that every single Nicaraguan knows by heart, you'll realize just how much Nicaraguan music is woven into its society.

Only a few musical remnants of Nicaragua's indigenous societies survived the conquistadores; these precious acts of dance, costume, and distinctive melodies are best observed today during the *fiestas patronales* of Masaya, Diriamba, and the various pueblos dotting the hills between them. These pre-Columbian fragments were further enriched by the different cultures they encountered along the way. Much of this influence was Spanish, and at some point, the African marimba traveled up the Río San Juan, landed in Granada, and found its home among the *folkloricos* of Carazo and Masaya.

Things are different in the northern hills of Nicaragua, where **Carlos Mejía Godoy** was born in 1943. The music there, he explains, is composed of *campesino* versions of the waltz, polka, and mazurka. Born and taught to play the accordion and guitar in Somoto, Carlos Mejía Godoy is neither the "father" nor "inventor" of Nicaraguan folk music, as some would have it. In fact, he is only one in a line of multiple generations of songwriting Nicaraguans. However, his love and passion for Nicaraguan culture, combined with his sheer talent as a musician, songwriter, and performer, have made Carlos Mejía and his long catalog of songs central in any discussion (or jam session) involving Nicaraguan music.

Don Carlos says he wishes he had two lives: one to learn all there is to be learned about Nicaraguan culture and a second to perform and use that knowledge. To most observers (and fans), it would appear he has done an adequate job at squeezing both into the one life he was given. Not only did he join the Sandinista Revolution in 1973 and proceed to compose its soundtrack, but throughout his life, Carlos Mejía has delved deeply into the *campo*, always in search of the regionally distinct riches of his country's cultural fabric. His songs are vibrant, colorful celebrations of everything Nicaraguan—from its geography, food, and wildlife to praise for the town gossip and shoeshine boy.

When asked about the Nicaraguita flower that inspired him to write the most famous song in the country's history ("Nicaragua, Nicaraguita"), Carlos Mejía quoted a passage titled "La Flor Escogida" (The Chosen Flower) by Profesor Carlos A. Bravo. In that passage, the rare variety of *sacuanjoche* (Nicaragua's national flower) is described as *"roja incendia, un clarinazo, listada de oro"* (burning red, a trumpet blast, with golden rays). Carlos Mejía called this "such a beautiful thing," and one is not sure if he was speaking of the flower or the lyrical words describing it—perhaps for him, there is no distinction between the two.

Pick up some of Carlos Mejía's music and learn his lyrics before you leave, but don't stop your discovery there. Carlos's brother, Luis Enrique, is a world-renowned salsa king, and they can both be found performing at their club in Managua, **Casa de los Mejía Godoy.**

glassy, the latter has an icy-cold VIP room and large terrace overlooking the crater. Both are recommended and open Friday–Sunday starting around 8 p.m., no cover charge.

Managua's Costeño crowd loves **Qweenz** (Rotonda Bello Horizonte, cover charge from $4), somewhat far away from the rest of town and a bit

grungy, but well-loved (and packed!). *Soca*, reggae, and country create the mish-mash soundtrack.

Live Music

Managua's music scene, both intimate and refined, shows a lot of local talent and energy. Without a doubt, the best traditional show in town is **Casa de los Mejía Godoy** (in front of the Hotel Crowne Plaza, tel. 505/2270-4928 or 505/2278-4913, fmejiago@cablenet.com.ni). Both brothers perform here regularly, Carlos on Thursday and Saturday, with or without his band Los de Palacagüina. Luis Enrique does Latin rhythm nights on Friday, and Sunday features other Nicaraguan or international performers. The brothers are born showmen and present a theatrical mix of stories, bawdy jokes, and famous songs. The club is expensive by Nica standards, but well worth it by any measure. Buy tickets the afternoon of the performance for $8–15; shows are Wednesday–Sunday only and start at 9 P.M. A few blocks north of here, alternative hotspot **El Caramanchel** is a riotous haunt playing everything from rock to reggae, and is the best place to catch local indie bands. Plan transport home ahead of time, as the bar is located in a somewhat unfavorable position opposite the Plaza Inter mall (Wed.–Sun., from $3 cover charge for live music).

The breezy, outdoor terrace of **La Ruta Maya** (150 meters east of the Estatua de Montoya, tel. 505/2268-0698, open Thurs.–Sat., $4–6) is a pleasant place to appreciate a wide variety of performers from singer-songwriters to reggae, jazz, and everything in between. Local talent includes names such as Macolla, Llama Viva, Dimensión Costeña, Elsa Basil, and Clara Grun, to name but a few.

THE ARTS

Managua's finest theater, **El Teatro Nacional Rubén Darío** (at the Malecón, tel. 505/2222-7426, www.tnrubendario.gob.ni) hosts top-name international acts. Check the website for performances. **La Escuela Nacional de Teatro** (Palacio Nacional de Cultura, tel. 505/2222-4449) is primarily a teaching facility that presents performances on weekends by students and small professional troupes from all over Latin America; call for a list of events, as they're not always published. The **Sala de Teatro Justo Rufino Garay** (from Montoya, 3 blocks west, 20 meters north, next to Parque Las Palmas, tel. 505/2266-3714, www.rufinos.org) is better frequented and offers similar fare on weekends only.

Located across from the UCA, **La Academia de Danza** (tel. 505/2277-5557) has frequent dance performances and concerts. The students deliver professional and talented renditions of traditional, folk, modern jazz, Brazilian, and ballet; call or drop by for a schedule of events, or if you're in town for the long haul, consider taking one of their dance classes to prepare you for the club scene.

Art Galleries

Managua's art galleries individually showcase Nicaragua's creative artists. The most traditional is probably **Galería Solentiname** (Colonia Centroamerica, one block north of Canal 23, tel. 505/2278-3998, call for an appointment), set in the home of Doña Elena Pineda, a native Solentinameña who has done a great job of promoting the works of painters from the famous archipelago. Related, the **Galería de Los Tres Mundos** (Los Robles, two blocks north of the French restaurant La Marseillaise, tel. 505/2267-0304, 9 A.M.–4 P.M. Mon.–Fri.) is Ernesto Cardenal's home base and showcases a variety of Solentiname artwork, from paintings to balsa work. More a cultural center than a museum, the **Códice Galería** (Colonial Los Robles *segunda etapa,* house #15, tel. 505/2267-2635, www.galeriacodice.com, 9 A.M.–7 P.M., sometimes later, Mon.–Sat.) displays changing exhibitions of contemporary sculpture, paintings, and ceramics. With a funky, star-studded exterior, the gallery stands out on its quiet, residential street.

The **Alianza Francesa** (tel. 505/2267-2811, www.alianzafrancesa.org.ni) in Los Robles is a multipurpose venue, with monthly changing art exhibitions, musical concerts, regular screenings of European films, and a lunchtime bistro menu.

MANAGUA

CINEMA

Managua's five main commercial centers each have a modern multiplex theater showing the same half-dozen films: mostly Hollywood fare, with some Spanish and Mexican films as well. Most central are the **Cinemark** (tel. 505/2271-9037 or 505/2271-9000) in the Plaza Metrocentro, **Cinema Plaza Inter** (tel. 505/2222-5090 or 505/2222-5122) on the third floor of the Plaza Inter mall (remember to take a cab at night; the neighborhoods west of the theater are no longer walkable at night), and the **Galerías Santo Domingo** shopping complex (tel. 505/2276-5065) on the Carretera Masaya just southeast of the Rotunda Jean Paul Genie. The **Alhambra VIP** (tel. 505/2278-7278 or 505/2277-4280), in the Camino de Oriente complex just off Carretera Masaya, brings luxury screenings to the city with enormous recliner seating. Dine while you watch, as hovering waiters whisk you mozzarella sticks and cold beer at your command.

Simply drop in to the theaters, or check out the *Revista Cinematógrafica* (a weekly bulletin distributed at most gas stations and some hotels and restaurants). Shows change every Thursday and cost about $3–5. Tuesdays and Wednesdays are often cut-price. Bring a jacket: Managua's theaters are glacially air-conditioned. In addition, Cinemark and Galería complexes host occasional film festivals with the support of the local embassies' cultural attachés.

Miercoles de Cine shows an artsy foreign flick each Wednesday at 7 P.M. at the Sala de Teatro Justo Rufino Garay (from Montoya, 3 blocks west, 20 meters north, tel. 505/2266-3714, www.rufinos.org, $3).

FESTIVALS AND EVENTS

Las Fiestas Patronales each August are when Managua celebrates its patron saint Santo

La Concha Acustica is often used for national celebrations and political rallies.

Domingo and are the highlight of the calendar year. On the first of the month, the saint (a diminutive little figure under a glass dome) is brought down from a small church in the hilly neighborhood of Santo Domingo and on the 10th he is returned. On both those dates, and for much of the time in between, Managua celebrates. Expect parades, horse shows, unlimited quantities of beer and rum, and a lot of fun and colors. INTUR sponsors a series of events during this time, like Las Noches Agostinas, featuring cultural presentations and live music throughout the capital.

Every **July 19th** since 1979, Nicaraguans have celebrated the final victory against Somoza during the Sandinista revolution. July 19th celebrations bring out the Sandinista party faithful, with a rally and presentations in Plaza de la Fé and a show choreographed by President Ortega's wife Rosario Murillo. The truly devout stay through Ortega's predictable and lengthy speech at the end, and carry on celebrating into the wee hours.

If you are in Managua during the first few weeks of December, be sure to catch the massive **INPYME** crafts fair on Avenida Bolívar—arts, crafts, and food from all over the country, plus a two-week carnival. **Expica** is a permanent farming-related exhibition site in Barrio Acahualinca (Casa Pellas, two blocks west and one block north, tel. 505/2266-9634) and where in August ranchers descend upon the capital to exhibit and sell breeding stock, and generally show off their latest SUVs, ill-concealed revolvers, and beer-swilling prowess on the bar stool. The Nicaraguan cowboy elite show hundreds of some of the most magnificent and beautifully tended specimens of Brahman cattle in this part of the world, as well as impressive displays of horsemanship in the saddles of pure-bred Spanish, Peruvian, and Ibero equines.

Shopping

ARTS AND CRAFTS

For a gorgeous selection of locally sourced leather goods and handmade jewelry, visit **Calle Mas Calle Artwear,** a funky boutique within the Tercer Ojo restaurant in Zona Hippos. The own-label belts, bags, and accessories are beautifully made—the quality is reflected by the prices (credit cards are accepted). Four blocks further south is **Mama Delfina** (tel. 505/2267-8288), where you can pick up a variety of crafts made by artisans from all over the country. Mull over your purchases on a breezy second-floor balcony, with a tall glass of icy cacao. Several blocks east of here towards Carretera Masaya, you'll probably smell the **Fabrica de Chocolate Momotombo** (8 A.M.–5 P.M. Mon.–Sat.) before you see it—the art of cocoa comes to life here. Artisanal products include fresh chocolate mixed with local ingredients (think mango, peanuts, and rum) as well as chocolate coffee beans and a variety of wrapped bars.

BOOKSTORES

The best bilingual selection of local and international books is **Frontera Books** (200 meters north of the Enitel Villa Fontana intersection, tel. 550/2270-2345); there's a great children's section, plus the latest maps and magazines.

Hispamer (Reparto Tiscapa, just east of the UCA, tel. 505/2278-1210) is the largest and oldest bookstore in the city. In the Centro Comercial, you'll find the **Librería Rigoberto López Pérez** (tel. 505/2277-2240), named for the poet who, for love of his country, assassinated Anastasio Somoza García.

MALLS

Managua has seen four U.S.-style malls built since 1998: **Plaza Inter, Plaza Metrocentro** on

Carretera Masaya, **Galerías Santo Domingo** farther south on the same road, and **Plaza Las Américas** in Bello Horizonte. At the upper end of the market, Galerías Santo Domingo sells luxury goods and a selection of European fashions; at the lower end Plaza Inter has made a go at cheaper-quality imported goods from Asia (the Plaza is wholly owned by Taiwanese investors). Plaza Las Américas falls somewhere in the middle. Metrocentro and Plaza Las Américas are the most recommended for satisfying travelers' needs, but at any of them you should be able to pick up a cell phone or cell phone chip, a clean shirt, new shoes, a Swiss Army watch, sunglasses, a digital camera, a sun hat, and similar items (these malls offer free wireless Internet as well).

The **Centro Comercial de Managua** is a pleasant open-air strip mall built in the Somoza era, offering a good selection of books, clothing, fabric, and sporting goods, plus two banks, an Internet café, and a post office—not a bad place to get some errands out of the way if malls aren't your cup of tea.

MARKETS

Mercado Roberto Huembes (7:30 A.M.–5 P.M. daily) is a fun market: It's full of the exuberance, color, and life that so typifies Nicaragua, and is tourist friendly and easily accessible. That's what makes it such a pleasant way to spend an afternoon in Managua, and you will be perfectly safe there while you shop. Although many Managuans rely on Huembes for lots of day-to-day stuff (chicken cutlets, toothpaste, socks), the market also has a splendid selection of hammocks, pottery, paintings, leatherwork, and other Nicaraguan artisan specialties. Only Masaya is a better place to shop.

Accommodations

Where you should spend the night in Managua depends a lot on your reason for spending the night here. If all you need is the cheapest possible bed before boarding an international bus to a neighboring country, the *hospedaje* scene in Barrio Martha Quezada is probably your best bet. But if you're overnighting in order to make an early morning flight, there are safer options elsewhere, especially if you're willing to spend a few extra dollars. You can catch an early-morning taxi to the airport from anywhere in the city, or you can roll out of bed at the Best Western La Mercedes and walk across the street to check in.

For comfort, safety, and peace of mind, expect to spend $50–100 per night for accommodations. (Fortunately, this price category has more options than can be printed here.) For this kind of money, expect hot water, cable TV, telephone, minibar, Internet, and probably airport pickup. Many of these hotels also have a small pool, which you will appreciate in Managuan heat.

CARRETERA MASAYA AND VICINITY
Under $25
Located in the shadow of the grand Hotel Intercontinental in central Managua, **Managua Backpacker's Inn** (Chaman Viejo, 75 meters south, house #55, tel. 505/2267-0006, www.managuahostel.com, contact@managuahostel.com, $8 shared dorm, $15 private room) blew away the competition as soon as it arrived a couple of years ago. It offers clean rooms, a friendly atmosphere, swimming pool, and breakfast bar ($3–5)—a great value in a safe neighborhood, all within walking distance of Metrocentro and Zona Hippos. It is very popular, so reserve (and even prepay) online.

$25-50
The **Hostal Dulce Hogar** on Altamira's Avenida principal (tel. 505/2277-0865, www.

hostaldulcehogar.com, $40) is a popular budget bed-and-breakfast with simple, tidy rooms. Hot water and air-conditioning are included in the price.

At about the same level of amenities as Posadita de Bolonia but situated in a safer area, **Casa San Juan** (Reparto San Juan Calle Esperanza 560, tel. 505/2278-3220, www.casa-sanjuan.net, sanjuan@cablenet.com.ni, $39 s) is quiet and close to the universities, offering wireless Internet, cable TV, and hot-water showers.

$50-100

◀ **Hotel El Ritzo** (from the BAC building Carretera Masaya, three blocks east, 25 meters south, tel. 505/2277-5616, hotelritzo@alianza.com.ni, www.hotelritzo.net, $76) is tastefully decorated, quiet, and gorgeous. (They've got a second hotel in Villa Fontana, which is slightly less convenient.) Nearby, the family-run **Hotel Central Park** (from Pizza Valenti's one block east, two blocks south, tel. 505/2270-2315, http://centralparkhotel.weebly.com, $65) offers great value for the money. Solidly built over four stories, the comfortable rooms offer rare views of the city that stretch down to the lakefront and beyond. The surrounding neighborhood is pleasant, walkable, and offers good bars and restaurants, as well as a prime central location handy for longer-stay guests.

A good option in this area is the **Hotel Colonnade** (Planes de Altamira, one block west and half a block north of Pharoah's Casino, tel. 505/2277-4838, www.hotelcolonnadenicaragua.com, $80 d) a family-run location with comfy rooms that gets consistently great reviews from readers.

◀ **Hotel Pyramide** (Reparto San Juan, del Gimnasio Hercules one block south, one east, 2.5 south, tel. 505/2278-0687, pyramide@ibw.com.ni, www.lapyramidehotel.com, $75) gets consistently favorable reviews for the attentiveness of the owner, who will make sure you are comfortable as soon as you get to the airport. Good value for the money, but just a bit hard to get to the restaurants from here: The owner will help you get taxis. In the same neighborhood, **Hotel Brandt** (Reparto San Juan, from Zona Hippos one block south, one block west, tel. 505/2270-2114, www.brandtshotel.com.ni, $75) is clean, safe, and friendly, and has been in business a long time. (They've opened a fancier branch closer to the Metrocentro mall).

Over $100

Casa Naranja (from Tip Top Chicken on Carretera Masaya, one block west, tel. 505/2277-3403, www.hotelcasanaranja.com, $118) gets consistently favorable reviews from travelers for its understated colonial style, shaded dipping pool, and cool green patio—a welcome respite from Managua's bustle. Further down Carretera Masaya in the Residencial Las Praderas, the **Hotel Contempo** (tel. 505 2264-9160, www.contempohb.com, $104) is a newer addition to the city's small luxury hotels. Smart and modern, with an expensive in-house restaurant, this city-outskirts location provides a good pit stop for travelers heading south to Masaya and beyond.

Managua's premium chain hotels cater to business travelers with expense accounts (and travelers who want to splurge at the end of their trip). Your safest bet in this category is ◀ **Intercontinental Metrocentro** (tel. 505/2271-9483, mga-metro@interconti.com, www.ichotelsgroup.com, from $160), with its convenient location next to the Metrocentro mall, and good service. Towering over the mall in one of the tallest buildings in the city, this branch has standard smallish rooms (club level are the nicest), a nice pool, event center, overpriced bar, and steakhouse restaurant.

Other options include **Hotel Hilton Princess** (Carretera Masaya, tel. 505/2255-5777, from $130). One block west and one block north of the Princess, and a short stroll from a dozen excellent restaurants, the **Hotel Seminole Plaza** (tel. 505/2270-0061, www.seminoleplaza.com, $150) is a popular pick for business conventions.

In the Los Robles area just west of Carretera Masaya, **Hotel Los Robles** (in front of Restaurante La Marseillaise, tel. 505/2267-3008, www.hotellosrobles.com, $120) blends colonial charm with business-minded amenities; their breakfast buffet is splendid.

LAS COLINAS AND VILLA FONTANA $25-50

Managua Hills Bed and Breakfast (Primera entrada Las Colinas, two blocks east, two blocks south, tel. 505/2276-2323, www.managuahills.com.ni, $46 d) is popular with readers for large double rooms and a decent breakfast (included in the price), set in a very safe neighborhood.

$50-100

In the residential Las Colinas area, **Boutique Hotel Villa Maya** (Residencial Las Colinas, Calle Los Laureles 105, tel. 505/2276-2175, villamaya.nic@gmail.com, $93 d) has elegant rooms set in an attractive house with a large garden and pool, choice of (included) breakfasts, Wi-Fi, and more.

Boutique Hotel Angel Azul (Villa Fontana 17, from Club Terraza one block east and half a block north, tel. 505/2278-2368, $76 d) has modern, spotless rooms set in a cool building with a handy onsite restaurant.

BOLONIA AND BARRIO MARTHA QUEZADA

Managua's former backpacker district, Barrio Martha Quezada is getting tougher to recommend to anyone but overnighters bound for an international bus line. The neighborhood that has hosted international budget travelers since the *sandalistas* (a nickname which pokes fun at the sandal-clad Sandinista supporters) poured south to support the revolution is run-down

and the worse for wear these days, and notoriously unsafe. Travel in groups, don't stray from the main roads, and always take a taxi, especially to the nearby Plaza Inter shopping center.

Under $10

The new and family-run **Hostal Dulce Sueño** (75 meters east of TicaBus, 505/2228-4125, www.hostaldulcesueno.com, hospedaje_dulcesueno@yahoo.es, $10 s) is clean and safe, with private bathrooms and laundry service. Traditional Nica meals are available for $2 per person (recommended). **Guesthouse Santos** (from TicaBus, one block north and 1.5 blocks west, tel. 505/2222-3713, $6) remains quirky, grungy, and handy for international bus departures. **Hospedaje El Dorado** (1.5 blocks north of Ticabus, tel. 505/2222-6012, $15 d) is plain but secure under the watchful eye of a very demanding proprietress. The remaining guesthouses in this neighborhood will not be around for much longer, as travelers increasingly pay more and go elsewhere.

$10-25

◖ **Hotel Los Felipe** (1.5 blocks west of TicaBus, tel. 505/2222-6501, www.hotellosfelipe.com.ni, $15 s with fan, $25 with a/c) is the best of the hotels in Barrio Martha Quezada. Rooms are clean and safe and have cable TV and phone; the hotel offers Internet, parking, pool, a shady patio area under a thatched roof, laundry service, and private baths. **Hotel Cisneros** (tel. 505/2222-3535, www.hotelloscisneros.com, $25 with fan, $40 with a/c), just opposite Guesthouse Santos, offers similar comforts but is slightly more expensive and not quite as pretty.

$25-50

Posadita de Bolonia (three blocks west of Canal 2, then 75 meters south, tel. 505/2268-6692, www.posaditadebolonia.com, $35 s) is a comfortable and quiet place offering cable

TV, Internet, hot water, and private showers. Breakfast is included. Other meals can be provided by arrangement. The hotel also offers a full range of tour and guide services.

$50-100

Hotel Mozonte (from the entrance to PriceSmart, 1.5 blocks north, across from the old French Embassy, tel. 505/2266-0686, www.hotelmozonte.com, info@hotelmozonte.com, $60 d) has pleasant, clean rooms, breezy common and sitting areas, and a gorgeous pool. Have them pick you up at the airport. Nearby, **Hotel Europeo** (75 meters west of Canal 2, tel. 505/2268-2130, www.hoteleuropeo.com.ni, $76) is a safe choice with a clean pool set in an attractive garden patio.

Over $100

The old pyramidal Hotel Inter at the base of the Tiscapa Crater is now the **Hotel Crowne Plaza** (located in Plaza Inter, tel. 505/2228-3530, from $100), a landmark since the Somoza days; its rooms afford supreme views of the lake.

AIRPORT

The **Camino Real** (U.S. tel. 505/2255-5888, www.caminoreal.com.ni, $100) is very close to the airport, just minutes away on Carretera Norte, and is adjacent to a casino. Also handy if you have an early flight is the **Best Western Las Mercedes** (tel. 505/2255-9910, $105), directly across from the airport. Decompress on the last night before your flight in a decent restaurant or with the mixed bag of travelers and diplomats lounging by the pool.

LONG-TERM ACCOMMODATIONS

Visiting students tend to gravitate to **Arcoiris** (Barrio Los Robles, two blocks south and one block east of Plaza del Sol, house #97, tel. 505/2278-0905, $350/month), a clean, family-run guesthouse in a safe neighborhood. The price includes breakfast, and minimum one-month stay applies. Internet is available, and laundry and other meals can be arranged. **Hostal Dulce Sueño** (75 meters east of TicaBus, tel. 505/2228-4125, hospedaje_dulcesueno@yahoo.es, www.hostaldulcesueno.com) offers similar services plus free laundry for $200 per month single or $320 per month for a couple. **Belinda's House** (Canal 2, two blocks north and 75 meters west, tel. 505/2266-3856, $20/night, $220/month) is a similar, cozy family-run long-term guesthouse.

At the higher end, several boutique hotels can accommodate long-stay visitors in luxury with full cable TV, Internet, laundry service, and similar amenities. **Hotel El Almendro** (from the Metrocentro rotunda, two blocks west, half block south, tel. 505/2270-1260, www.hotelelalmendro.com, almendro@cablenet.com.ni, $57 s, $60 d) specializes in long-term accommodations, offering studio suites with kitchenettes and parking; pricing depends on the length of your stay. Being able to cook your own meals once in a while is a huge advantage. **Los Robles** (one block west, two blocks south of the Hotel Intercontinental Metrocentro, tel. 505/2278-6334), in the same class, has 12 rooms at $1,500 per month.

Los Cedros (Km 13, Carretera Sur, across from the Iglesia Monte Tabor, tel. 505/2265-8340) has 30 furnished rooms ($200 per month single or $300 per month for a couple) in a fresh climate, all with bath, terrace, kitchen, pool, and plenty of green space.

If you're content living outside the city limits, several excellent long-term options line the far reaches of Carretera Masaya. **Hotel Campo Real** (Km 12.5, tel. 505/2279-7067, camporeal@ideay.net.ni, www.hotelcamporeal.com) has six fully furnished apartments with all the amenities to make you feel at home, from $60 a night, depending on how long you stay.

MANAGUA

Food

Keeping up with restaurants is a challenge in a city where most eateries thrive for a year and then vanish. Dining out is the mainstay of Managua's elite and they tend to abandon a place as soon as something newer and trendier comes along. But a few classics help hold the whole scene together. ¡Buen provecho!

The many branches of La Colonial and La Union not only stock their modern aisles with national and imported foodstuffs, they also sell clothing, sandals, books, CDs, cosmetics, and more. The easiest to reach from Barrio Martha Quezada is just up the road at **Plaza España** (8 A.M.–7 P.M Mon.–Fri., 8 A.M.–5 P.M. Sat., 9 A.M.–3 P.M. Sun.). If you're in the Carretera Masaya area, your best bet is La Colonia in the Metrocentro mall. Visit **La Familiar** (located across the street from Valenti's Pizza, 9 A.M.–10 P.M. Mon.–Sat., 9 A.M.–3 P.M. Sun.) for gourmet goodies, alcohol, and imported bulk items, including dark European beers (and crappy U.S. ones), shiitake mushrooms, and specialty olive oils and cheeses. There are several other supermarkets around the city, but most travelers will find what they need at one of the many smaller "mini-supers" and pulperías that populate the neighborhoods.

CARRETERA MASAYA AND VICINITY

La Terraza Peruana (one block west of the Tip Top Chicken, Carretera Masaya, tel. 505/2278-0031, $5–10) is a great Peruvian joint, with good ceviche and other seafood, as well as a huge array of appetizers, chicken, and beef dishes.

For home-cooked Nicaraguan cuisine in an upscale atmosphere, **La Cocina de Doña Haydee** (one block west of Casino Pharaoh, $3–7) has been around for ages and always gets good reviews.

Chik Chak (in the Camino de Oriente complex, on Carretera Masaya, tel. 505/2254-3527, $4–8) is a firm fixture for young Managua, with a Mediterranean-Nica menu and contemporary decor featuring recycled wine bottles (surely emptied by merry customers). Choose the outdoor patio if you're not a fan of arctic air-conditioning. There is also another branch at km 9 Carretera Sur.

On your way to Granada, **Sushi Itto** (tel. 505/2278-4886, $5–15), a Central American chain of upscale sushi restaurants, has two branches in Managua; the main one in the Galerías Santo Domingo's Zona Viva has a much livelier atmosphere. Meals start at $10, but you could just go for the two-for-one frozen margaritas. Other favored eateries in the Galerías cluster include the multiethnic **Savor Restaurant & Lounge** ($6–15), and the more budget-friendly **Tacontento** (from $6), which offers hearty Mexican dishes. **◖ Ola Verde** (entrance 1 to Las Colinas, in front of the Tip Top Chicken, tel. 505/2270-3048, 8 A.M.–close daily, lunch $8, more for dinner) features fresh juices, salads, soups, hummus, and babaghanoush on a pleasant and fresh menu of changing vegetarian and chicken dishes. Ola Verde also has a small shop of natural (local) products and is a popular meeting spot for foreigners; ask about upcoming cooking classes.

Opposite Ola Verde, **Pizzeria Rock Munchies** (tel. 505/2276-1141, $6–10) is a popular haunt for the rocker kids of Managua, with a 50 percent discount on your second pizza and delivery service to boot.

LOS ROBLES

Pizza Valenti's (Colonial Los Robles, two blocks east of Lacmiel, tel. 505/2277-5744, $6–10) is essentially a landmark—a family restaurant serving a variety of classic pizzas and cold beer. Their pizza is decent, though not gourmet, and cheaper than much of the competition. **Don Pan** (across from Pizza Valenti, $3–6) serves coffee, American-style breakfasts, sandwiches, and baked goods.

Taska Kiko (200 m east of the Monte Olivos funeral home, tel. 505/2270-1569, from $8) serves a Spanish menu including Ibero ham and a variety of garlicky dishes; the ranchito provides a romantic atmosphere (except during the rowdy screenings of Spanish soccer matches). **La Terraza Margarita** (one block east, one south, and 1.5 blocks west of Pizza Valenti, tel. 505/2277-1723, $4–7) is a nice alternative to pizza and local dishes, serving sweet and savory crepes as well as healthy salads and fresh-baked goods. Across the road, **Asados Doña Tania** ($5–8) is the evolution of a local *fritanga,* an authentic neighborhood staple for grilled meats, *cuajada* cheese, and fresh fruit *refrescos.*

Managua's premier coffee shop is ❰ **La Casa de Café** (half a block west and one block south of Pizza Valenti's, tel. 505/2270-0620, $3–8) with a selection of pastries, snacks, and Nicaraguan coffee all served on a gorgeous, second-story open terrace overlooking the street. Local artisanal chocolate Momotombo is sold at a counter downstairs. Visit for the strong coffee and free wireless Internet (they have branches in the commercial centers as well). **María Bonita** (1.5 blocks west of Distribuidora Vicky, tel. 505/2270-4326, $7) is another family favorite, serving Mexican and Nica classics in an open, romantic atmosphere.

Don Candido (from old El Chamán, 50 meters south, Los Robles, tel. 505/2277-2485, from $20) ranks high among the most expensive steak houses in the country, but their certified Angus beef is top-notch. The menu also features a long selection of wines, with some very expensive bottles. Otherwise, **La Plancha** (from the Semáforos Plaza del Café, 150 meters to the east, $5–10) serves tasty "ironed" steak with less imposing prices. Ask for the *parrillada* rack or just go for the grill, *a la plancha.*

El Muelle (one block east of the Hotel Intercontinental Metrocentro, $6–10) offers decent seafood cocktails and main courses.

ZONA HIPPOS

Zona Hippos lies just off the Carretera Masaya, starting south of the Hotel Seminole, and is thickly clustered with competing fast food-style restaurants, lively bars with open-air seating, and fine dining options. ❰ **El Garabato** (two blocks south of the Hotel Seminole Plaza, tel. 505/2278-2944, $5–9) is popular with locals for their variety of Nicaraguan classic foods and internationally inspired chicken and beef dishes. The pleasant indoor/outdoor environment gets a bit noisy later at night, especially when there's live music in the house. Opposite, **El Tercer Ojo** (tel. 505/2277-4787, $4–12) is a bar and restaurant with a good, eclectic menu including curry and sushi. The hip, multi-ethnic vibe sees live DJs on Thursday nights (go early if you want a table), and has inspired a soundtrack of local electronic music that you can buy from the bar. Half a block south, **El Coche Cafe** (tel. 505/2270-5443, $2–5) is the closest you'll find to a Starbucks in Nicaragua. Enjoy the best coffee milkshakes in town, while making use of the free Wi-Fi.

A long-standing seafood favorite in town, with a choice of outdoor seating and air-conditioning indoors, is **Marea Alta** (from Piratas bar, one block south, $6–12). The restaurant is the former residence of Chema Castillo, where in 1977 the Sandinistas took hostages of diplomats and government officials (Chema himself was killed). This "downtown" branch has become a core around which a dozen other restaurants have sprung up.

One of Managua's fanciest and oldest dining options, **La Marseillaise** (three blocks south of Hotel Seminole, tel. 505/2277-0224, from $10) is a city classic since before the war. It serves French cuisine, expensive wine, and stunning desserts in a converted house adorned with works of art. It's also one of the city's most expensive restaurants, so be prepared.

BARRIO MARTHA QUEZADA AND BOLONIA

The budget backpacker stronghold specializes in low-cost eating as well—nothing fancy, but the price is right. For breakfast, you can't go wrong at **Café Myrna** (one block west of TicaBus, lunch from 6 A.M. daily, $3.50) for eggs any way you like them, fresh juice, and the best pancakes in the country. If you prefer just a pastry, try **Cafetín Tonalli** (2.5 blocks south of Cine Cabrera, $2–5), a unique women's cooperative that produces extraordinarily good breads and cakes, and sells juice, cheese, coffee, and more (Swiss training!). Take out or eat in their enclosed outdoor patio. **Frutilandia** (a block and a half east of the Calle 27 traffic light, look for the colorful storefront, 7 A.M.–5 P.M. Mon.–Sat., $2–5) is where you'll find a fresh, delicious menu of fruit smoothies, shakes, and simple meals.

For Nicaraguan barbeque, head to **Fritanga Doña Pilar** (one block west and half a block north of TicaBus, 6–9 P.M. daily, $3–5). Only dinner is served; chicken, *gallo pinto, tostones,* fresh avocado, an icy glass of fruit juice, and some fried cheese will fill you up for a price that can't be beat, if you're comfortable eating at a plastic table, roadside.

CARRETERA SUR

On the road to the Pacific beaches, this well-to-do suburb refreshes with a cooler climate than the inner city, and several great choices when it comes to dining out.

The Diner (Km 8.5 Carretera Sur, tel. 505/2265-1837, $4–10) may be tucked into a cheerless lot just off the main road, but the

1950s style decor (old records, red vinyl booths, and a jukebox) provides a lively atmosphere. The menu features burgers, shakes, and chili fries true to the theme and unlikely to disappoint; they also serve classic breakfasts. Sit outside on the retro car seat, made from one of Somoza's old limos.

La Casserole (Km 13.8, tel. 505/2271-7789, $6–15) may be the newest of the southside restaurants, but its popularity seems unlikely to wane; if you plan to visit on a Sunday, you'll likely need a reservation. The family-run establishment, set in a thicket of green off the highway, features a fusion menu with fresh local ingredients prepared by a Cordon Bleu-trained chef, as well as sushi and a mean mango cocktail.

Casa Mia (Km 13, tel. 505/2271-7054, $7–15) is a contender for the best Italian in Managua, with thin-crust pizzas and tasty pasta. The atmosphere (and wine list) is surprisingly sophisticated, despite a roadside location.

ESTATUA MONTOYA

There are two reasons to eat in this part of town: one is that you plan on catching a show at the La Ruta Maya, a popular live-music venue; the second is convenient access to nearby accommodation. **Los Ranchos** (Carretera Sur Km 3, tel. 505/2266-0526, noon–11 P.M. daily, from $15) isn't cheap or well situated, but they've served a fantastic steak *au poivre* since the days of Somoza. A second branch, more easily accessible, is located opposite the Laguna de Tiscapa.

Managua's second-most popular vegetarian place is **Licuados Ananda** (half a block east of the Estatua Montoya, tel. 505/2228-4140, 7 A.M.–9 P.M. daily, $2–6), with whole foods and a menu of several dozen fresh fruit juices and smoothies, well recommended on a hot day.

Information and Services

BANKS

Banking hours in Managua are 8 A.M.–4 P.M. Monday–Friday, and 8 A.M.–noon on Saturday. Along Carretera Masaya, you'll find the **Banco de América Central** (BAC, in the tallest building in the country), **Bancentro** (in the LAFISE financial center), **Banco de Finanzas (BDF), Banpro, Banco Uno** and the first truly international bank, **HSBC** (in the Discovery Building, Villa Fontana). For travelers staying in Barrio Martha Quezada, the nearest bank is the BDF near the Hotel Crowne Plaza, and you'll find plenty of ATMs within the Plaza Inter Mall. Several other nearby banks are clustered around Plaza España, including BAC and Banco Uno, and branches of most can be found in all the main malls. You'll find shorter lines at Multicambios, on the south side of Plaza España.

Bancentro will change euros directly to local currency without first changing them to U.S. dollars (and taking another commission). In a pinch, *coyotes* (money changers) on the street (try outside Pizza Valenti's in Los Robles) offer reasonable exchange rates and will also change euros.

EMERGENCY SERVICES

Dial 118 for police, 115 or 120 for the fire department, and 128 for the Red Cross ambulance. There are several hospitals in Managua; the most modern are the private **Hospital Vivian Pellas** (outside of Managua on the highway to Masaya, www.metropolitano.com.ni) and **Hospital Salud Integral** (by the Estatua Montoya, www.hospitalsaludintegral.com.ni). For less serious ailments and stomach disorders, **Hospital Bautista** (Barrio Largaespada, near the main fire station, tel. 505/2249-7070) is accustomed to dealing with foreigners.

INTERNET

The cybercafés typically also offer VOIP (voice over Internet protocol) calling booths as well, but they are quickly losing ground to the free Wi-Fi spots in the commercial centers like Metrocentro. Otherwise, head toward the university area, across from the main UCA gates, where there are a half dozen Internet joints, all with the cheapest rates in the city, usually open till 9 P.M. during the week. Macintosh addicts can get their fix (or get their own Macs fixed) at the **Mac Center** (tel. 505/2270-5918, 8 A.M.–5 P.M. daily), tucked behind the UCA, a few doors down from Hispamer bookstore.

LAUNDRY

If you're roughing it, you'll have noticed most *hospedajes* have a *lavandero* (cement-ridged washboard). Buy a slug of bar soap ($0.30) at the local *pulpería,* roll up your sleeves, and scrub away like everybody else. If you don't want to get your hands dirty (or rather, clean), most hotels and hostels offer laundry services for a reasonable fee. Otherwise, try one of the **Dryclean USA** locations, such as behind the Tip Top Chicken on Carretera Masaya.

LIBRARIES

Managua's public library, **Biblioteca Dr. Roberto Incer Barquero** (behind the bank at Carretera Sur Km 7, tel. 505/2265-0123, 8:30 A.M.–4 P.M. Mon.–Fri.) was built in 1999 and houses a notable collection of newspapers from the war years. The old National Library is located in the Palacio de Cultura down by the waterfront. INHCA is a remarkable collection of historical and cultural resources housed within the UCA; accessing them requires a library card obtainable from the director by paying a $10 fee.

MAIL AND PHONE

The Palacio de Comunicaciones, located across the plaza near the ruins of the old cathedral, contains the central office of both **Correos de**

Nicaragua and **ENITEL,** with full mail, fax, telex, express courier, and phone services (in a beautiful, deco-style building). In the *palacio,* the *oficina de filatelía* sells stamps from previous editions beginning in 1991 (Nicaragua is well known among philatelists for having the most beautiful postage stamps in Central America), plus postcards and greeting cards (8 A.M.–5 P.M. Mon.–Fri., 8 A.M.–1 P.M. Sat.). More compact, easier post offices to deal with are found in the Centro Comercial, Altamira, and the airport.

For packages, **DHL** (tel. 505/2251-2500) has branches on Carretera Masaya in front of the Colegio Teresiano, and Carretera Norte, 800 m north of the Puente Desnivel. **Federal Express** (tel. 505/2278-4500) has been operating in Nicaragua since 2000. Find it on Carretera Masaya near Subway, and in Ofiplaza El Retiro, Suite 515 (150 meters south of Rotonda Los Periodistas, tel. 505/2278-4500). **UPS** (tel. 505/2254-4892) is close to Barrio Martha Quezada and can be found two blocks north of Plaza España.

TRAVEL SERVICES

Many travel agents operate just southeast of the Plaza España and are a short cab ride from Barrio Martha Quezada. **Viajes Atlantida** (one block east and half block north of Plaza España, tel. 505/2266-4050 or 505 /266-8720) is a renowned agency and the official representative for American Express in Nicaragua. **Turismo Joven** (tel. 505/2222-2619, 8:30 A.M.–5:30 P.M. Mon.–Fri., 8:30 A.M.–noon Sat.) is the local representative for the student travel association (STA), and offers students discounted airfare. Close to Barrio Martha Quezada, **Viajes MTOM** (adjacent to Optica Nicaragüense, tel. 505/2266-8717) is quite professional.

OPPORTUNITIES FOR STUDY

You can join classes in Latin dancing any time at **La Academia Nicaragüense de la Danza** (50 meters north of the UCA gates, tel. 505/2277-5557). Language courses are also available in Managua; for Spanish, try the **Viva Spanish School** (from the Shell Plaza Sol, 2 blocks south, tel. 505/2270-2339, www.vivaspanishschool.com) for intensive and part-time programs, and to arrange homestays with local families. French and Portuguese classes are offered at the **Alianza Francesa** (tel. 505/2267-2811, www.alianzafrancesa.org.ni) in Los Robles.

Getting There and Around

BY AIR

International flights all arrive and depart from the **Augusto C. Sandino** airport (www.eaai.com.ni) on Carretera Norte in Managua; these include flights from Miami, Houston, Altanta, Panama City, and San Salvador. Domestic flights depart from a small terminal attached to the main airport. From here, La Costeña (tel. 505/2263-2142, www.lacostena.com.ni) operates daily flights to and from Bluefields, Corn Island, Puerto Cabezas, Las Minas (Siuna, Bonanza, and Rosita), Waspán and San Carlos.

BY BUS

Four main bus terminals link Managua to the towns and cities of Nicaragua's farthest corners. In general, buses depart approximately every hour, 5 A.M.–5 P.M.

To Points North and East

Buses to Estelí, Matagalpa, Ocotal, Jinotega, Boaco, Juigalpa, El Rama, and San Carlos operate out of the **Mercado Mayoreo** bus terminal on the eastern edge of town. From the other end of Managua (i.e., Barrio Martha Quezada),

NOT YOUR TYPICAL COLLEGE TOWN

Nicaragua's next generation of leaders attend more than 30 Managuan universities, the three biggest of which are **La Universidad de Centroamerica** (La UCA, rhymes with "hookah"), **La Universidad Nacional Autónoma de Nicaragua** (La UNAN), and **La Universidad Nicaragüense de Ingeniería** (La UNI). Visiting the courtyards, soda shops, cafés, and bars on campus provides a great opportunity to mingle with up-and-coming revolutionaries and neoliberal capitalists alike. Find out about the latest student strike or tire-burning session in the fight for 6 percent of the national budget, cheaper tuition, and of course, a classless society without corruption, war, or unfair wages. Actually, with the Sandinistas once again in power, and one of their principal student firebrands, Jasser Martínez, now a deputy in the National Assembly, it's probably safe to assume that the students will stay obediently off the streets unless Daniel Ortega's government needs some agitation to intimidate the opposition.

The intersection in front of the UCA and UNI is a hotspot during student strife, and a huge social scene at all other times. The parking lot across from the main gate, called La UCA, is also a transportation hub, with minivans departing the city daily for nearby destinations.

you can take the 102 *ruta* bus to get there, but plan up to an additional hour's travel through Managua's heart; a taxi is much quicker and should cost no more than $3 for a solo traveler.

Expresos del Norte services the entire north of Nicaragua with express buses. Their fleet includes a few Scania luxury buses (a rare treat), and they have a posted schedule, ticket window, and office where you can call to check on times (tel. 505/2233-4729).

To Points West and Northwest

Buses to León, Chinandega, and Carazo depart from the **Israel Lewites** terminal (named for a Jewish-Nicaraguan martyr of the revolution but sometimes referred to by its post-Sandinista name, El Boer). The terminal is surrounded on all sides by a chaotic fruit market by the same name; watch your belongings and expect a slightly more aggressive crowd of *buseros*.

To Points South

Buses to Carazo, Masaya, Granada, Rivas, Ometepe, the border at Peñas Blancas, and San Juan del Sur depart from **Mercado Roberto Huembes** in south-central Managua. The taxi ride from Barrio Martha Quezada should cost no more than $2 a person. Before you get to Huembes, be sure to specify *parada de los buses* (bus stop) to your driver, as opposed to *el mercado de artesanía* (crafts market), located on the opposite side of the same market. This is a very busy terminal, serving thousands of commuters from points south, and its porters and bus assistants will swarm you as you get out of your taxi.

Fast, express minibuses known as *interlocales* are the best option for Jinotepe, Diriamba, Masaya, and Granada, and depart from a lot across the street from **La UCA.** Service starts around 6 A.M. and runs as late as 9 P.M. You can also get Carazo expresses at **Mercado Israel Lewites,** from *el portón rojo* (the big red door).

Finally, **Adelante Express** (tel. 505/8850-6070 or 505/2568-2083, www.adelanteexpress.com) offers fast, direct service between the Managua airport and San Juan del Sur for people looking to bypass Managua entirely.

GETTING AROUND

Managua is easiest to deal with by taxi, given the lack of street names, landmarks, and the lousy public transportation, and the addresses given in this book are written with that in mind. If you find yourself walking in Managua, which is rare as sidewalks are almost nonexistent, watch your step. As well as the multitude of uncovered manholes, seismic shifting, and other forces of nature (namely large trees with determined roots) have resulted in a cracked, lumpy terrain that begs for twisted ankles.

Taxis

Not to fear, if you even approach the edge of the street, Managua's 14,000 taxis will circle you like vultures, beeping for your attention. *Colectivo*-style, drivers will pick up other passengers along the way if they are headed in your direction. Be alert, as the next passenger to get in could easily be part of a taxi-jacking scam. Taxis will take you most places for $2–8, though the ride to and from the airport might cost you as much as $20 if you don't bargain well. Managua taxis have no meters, so settle on a price before getting in the vehicle! Hotel and guesthouse owners can usually arrange a reliable taxi driver upon request.

Near Managua

◖ CHOCOYERO-EL BRUJO NATURE RESERVE

Less than 28 kilometers away from downtown Managua is a little pocket of wilderness so vibrant with wildlife you'll forget the capital is literally just over the horizon. The Chocoyero–El Brujo Nature Reserve (tel. 505/2276-7810 or 505/2276-7811) is a 41-square-kilometer protected hardwood forest that provides nearly 20 percent of Managua's water supply (20 million gallons of water per day). In the midst of moist hardwood forest and pineapple farms are two 25-meter waterfalls separated by a rocky knife-edge. El Brujo was named The Warlock because, to the locals, the fact that no river flows out from the waterfall meant it must be enchanted. The other fall, Chocoyero, was named for the incredible number of *chocoyos* (parakeets) that inhabit the adjacent cliff walls.

In fact, this protected area is a naturalist's paradise, with five kinds of *chocoyos* and 113 other bird species (including several owls), plus 49 species of mammals, and 21 species of reptiles and amphibians. Sharp-eyed travelers may even spot small cat species, like *tigrillos* and *gatos de monte,* and you'll likely hear both howler and capuchin monkeys in the treetops. In addition to having well-kept hiking trails, Chocoyero–El Brujo is also one of the few places in Nicaragua that encourages tent camping, making it a great place to spend an evening in the wild. Conditions are simple: a rustic, wooden base camp where guides will meet you and walk you the remaining way to the falls. The two best times to see the *chocoyos* are around 5:30 A.M. when they leave their nests, and around 4 P.M. when the flocks return. To catch the morning commute, you'll obviously have to spend the previous night here.

The entrance fee for foreigners is $5; guides, available on weekends, charge a nominal fee ($5 for up to 10 people). This is a safe, pretty, and easily accessible area in which to camp for a night ($5). If you call ahead and make a reservation, they'll even cook you simple, traditional Nica fare ($3–5 per meal). The reserve is actively promoting low-ropes courses, envirocamps, and more to local schools and church groups.

Getting There

Unless you have rented a vehicle, you'll need to charter a sturdy taxi from Managua with a group to take you all the way there. Otherwise, take any bus leaving Managua's Huembes terminal bound for La Concepción (called La Concha for short); buses leave Managua every 15 minutes. Get off at Km 21.5, where you'll

© GRACE GONZALEZ

The pineapple fields of Chocoyero-El Brujo Nature Reserve are a world away from the bustling city nearby.

see a wooden sign for the park entrance, then stretch out for a good, long walk. The dirt road that travels seven kilometers southwest to the reserve will lead you down a series of volcanic ridges and across a broad valley to the falls. It's an easy two-hour walk, passing through fields of pineapples, bananas, and coffee. There also may be some buses from Ticuantepe that take you all the way in—ask around.

MONTIBELLI WILDLIFE RESERVE

This 162-hectare private reserve and award-winning sustainable tourism project is set within the biological corridor between Chocoyero–El Brujo and Volcán Masaya National Park. Over 155 bird species have been spotted here, including manakins, motmots, oropendolas, trogons, tanagers, toucans, and hummingbirds. This is one of the most accessible wildlife reserves in the country, making it really easy to escape from the city. In this setting, you'll find comfortable accommodations with private bathrooms and an ample deck perched on the edge of a valley—great for armchair birding. There are three trails to hike, with views of the Masaya Volcano and surrounding forest. The restaurant features family recipes and Sunday barbecues.

Getting There

To reach Montibelli Wildlife Reserve, drive south on Carretera Masaya, taking the turnoff through the town of Ticuantepe, then just after leaving town on Km 18.5 of the Ticuantepe–La Concha Highway, it's a 2.8-kilometer road to the main lodge, known locally as La Casa Blanca. By bus, find a microbus heading south to La Concha and get off at Km 18.5 where you can take a mototaxi. Better yet, arrange for transport by contacting **Illiana Hernandez in Managua** (tel. 505/2220-9801, info@montibelli.com, www.montibelli.com).

© RANGERSLINKY/WIKIMEDIA COMMONS

waterfall in Chocoyero-El Brujo Nature Reserve

XILOÁ AND APOYEQUE LAGUNAS

Less than a half hour from the capital on the highway to León, the Peninsula de Chiltepe protrudes into the southwestern shore of Lake Xolotlán, cradling two ancient volcanic cones drowned in clean rainwater. Part of the Maribios chain, the twin crater lagoons of Xiloá and Apoyeque are a fun day trip if you find yourself in Managua for more than a weekend and are anxious for some greenery.

Legend says the Xiloá lagoon was formed when an indigenous princess of the same name, spurned by her Spanish lover, went down to the lake's edge to cry. She cried so much that the valley filled with tears, and the lagoon formed around her.

Broader and more easily accessed, Xiloá was a popular swimming hole for decades, but former Minister of Tourism director Herty Lewites took the initiative to develop the site more completely, with thatched-roof ranchónes, concrete pads, parking areas, and lunch stands. In 1998, Hurricane Mitch submerged the facilities under a meter of water. Rather forgotten, the lagoon will probably be deserted except for yourself and the occasional marine biologist, scuba diving to study the lake's endemic species.

Getting There

Buses leave Managua's Mercado Israel Lewites infrequently and go directly to the water at Xiloá. It's easier to take any León-bound bus from the same market, get off at the top of the road to Xiloá, and walk (30 minutes). Pay $1 per person ($1 per vehicle) to enter the park facilities at the water's edge. Getting to Apoyeque is a more challenging hike, requiring good boots and some autonomy (compass, water bottles, etc.). Take the road from Mateare, which you can walk or hitch down until you reach the access road for the radio antenna. That road will lead you to the ridge, from where you'll have to painstakingly and carefully make your way into the crater.

PACIFIC BEACHES

Roughly 65 kilometers due west of the capital are a handful of easy-to-reach beaches, with facilities ranging from low-key, grungy hospedajes to all-out, all-inclusive resorts. In fact, the diversity along the coastline couldn't be greater. Pochomíl and nearby Masachapa attract the casual day-tripper and odd surfer, while Montelimar is a pricey but pleasurable all-inclusive resort. Farther north, Los Cardones is an ecofriendly, offbeat lodge popular with surfers that's a bit harder to get to but worth the effort. When you hear about all the foreign real estate investment in Nicaragua, much of it is happening right here, so watch for big changes over the next decade unless Ortega scares away the foreigners again.

Pochomíl and Masachapa

Pochomíl was named in the early 20th century by a farmer named Felipe Gutierrez, in reference to all the "pocho" (money) he hoped to earn from his ambitious duck and goat farm. These days it's a once-popular beach town left to stagnate and now in the midst of an economic revival, as wealthy investors are building beachfront estates and hotel complexes. Situated a few minutes north of the village, Masachapa feels like an extension of Pochomil and features another empty stretch of sand, fringed with seafood ranchos that overflow during Semana Santa.

Hotel and restaurant rates fluctuate wildly according to the calendar. Semana Santa and Christmas are the most expensive times of year to visit. In the wet season, prices become significantly more flexible; traveling with a group gives you sizeable leverage to bargain for a good deal at any month of the year. Travelers driving their own vehicles will pay a $1 fee to enter the complex. As competition among restaurant owners is fierce, expect to be assaulted by employees of a dozen restaurants (all trying to drag you into their establishments to eat and drink)

when making an appearance. No one place is any better than another; you can expect beachfront palm thatch huts, fried fish, and cold beer no matter where you go.

One of the longest-established places on the beach in Pochomil, **Hotel Altamar** (tel. 505/8692-7971, from $25 per room with private bath, $10 per room with shared bath) has 15 basic rooms and a pleasant restaurant overlooking the water.

The first stop in Masachapa is the **Hostal Real Masachapa** (tel.505/2266-8123, www.hostalreal.com.ni, from $55). Rooms and cabins have sea views, with air-conditioning and hot water, and allow for access to the dipping pool and seafood restaurant. Transportation may be organized through the sister hostals in Managua; visit the website for details.

At Km 70 on the road to Pochomil, you'll find the **Vista Mar Hotel** (tel. 505/2265-8099, www.vistamarhotel.com, from $70), also home to a conservation sanctuary with the first artificially incubated turtle eggs in the country. Tidy, air-conditioned rooms with private balconies are pleasant enough and offer access to the beachside pool and restaurant. Ask about volunteer opportunities at the turtle hatchery.

Buses leave Managua's Israel Lewites bus station for Pochomíl every 30 minutes all day until about 5 P.M. The last bus from Pochomíl back to Managua departs at 5:30 P.M. from the cul-de-sac.

Barceló Montelimar Beach

Somoza's former personal summer palace was converted into a resort in the 1980s, and since being purchased by Barceló Resorts is now **Montelimar Beach** (tel. 505/2269-6769 or 505/2269-6752, U.S. and Canada tel. 800/227-2356, www.barcelomontelimarbeach.com, $86–111 per person), an all-inclusive resort which claims to be five-star. It offers 88 double guest rooms and 205 bungalows with private bath, air-conditioning, TV, strongbox, and minibar (but no wireless Internet). The price

MANAGUA

includes 24 hours of unlimited feasting, drinking, swimming, and playing. Often crowded on weekends with visitors from Managua, it is more peaceful on weekdays when you can swim by yourself in the largest pool in Central America. The Montelimar compound is enormous, with multiple beachside bars, sports opportunities, and a spunky coed crew of "animators" to help you have a good time. Any bus to Pochomíl will also get you to Montelimar, and there are various tour operators that arrange for transfers from Managua.

Los Cardones Surf Lodge

Set on eight acres of organically managed land, **❰ Los Cardones** (tel. 505/8618-7314, info@loscardones.com, www.loscardones.com, $74 d plus tax per person) is a unique, peaceful, and highly recommended beach escape with direct access to consistent surf breaks nearly year-round. A half dozen simple but elegant bungalows made from wood and thatch have solar hot water, soft beds, no electricity, and communal composting toilets; all are waterfront. The restaurant's inspired and creative menu involves lots of fresh fish, and their commitment to both the local community and the ecosystem is admirable. Rent surf or boogie boards, collect shells on the beach, or hike to nearby pre-Columbian petroglyphs. Rates are all-inclusive—lodging, meals, drinks (including beer), and transportation. The lodge is also

involved in **Arte Acción,** which promotes social change through art classes, in a neighboring community. Many guests often join in and help the class.

Los Cardones will send a car to Managua for you. To get there by bus, take the bus to San Cayetano from Mercado Israel Lewites in Managua (leaves every 45 minutes 4 A.M.–9 P.M.) and get off at "California." Then walk or hitch 15 kilometers toward the ocean and follow the signs. To drive, take the Carretera Masachapa to Km 49, then take a left and follow the signs to the lodge (about 20 kilometers).

Gran Pacifica Resort

A gringo development with privately owned condos and villas are available to rent, Gran Pacifica Resort (tel. 505/8354-1104, www.lavidanica.com, from $130) is conveniently situated in front of the fiercest point break in the region. The restaurant has an expensive if far from gourmet menu, but it's a handy spot to grab a beer and watch the sun set over the point. Activities include horseback riding, golf, and world-class surf. Those visiting on a day trip from the city will have to pay an entrance fee ($5 per person) at the gate. To get here, take the same turnoff as Los Cardones on the Carretera Masachapa; veer right at the turnoff to Cardones and carry on (again, following the signs) until you hit the beach. Airport shuttles can also be arranged.

GRANADA

Arguably Nicaragua's most picturesque town, Granada is an easy place to love. Much of its colonial architecture is remarkably intact and is being painstakingly restored by a new generation of homeowners. The colorful facades lining old narrow streets practically glow in the late afternoon sun. It's sultry and tropical here, but a fresh breeze blows off the waters of Lake Cocibolca. The views from along the lakeshore's broad, undeveloped shoreline—and the ever-looming silhouette of Volcán Mombacho—make for easy photos and good memories.

Granada has always been important politically for Nicaragua, and it is the home of many of the country's economic and political elite. Most travelers eschew Managua and flock to Granada because of its charm and lethargic pace, making it their base for further exploration. Some decide to stay, as evidenced by the many real estate offices that have sprung up over the last decade.

Granada is pleasant to explore by foot or old-fashioned horse carriage. In the evening, the sky fills with stars and neighbors come out to chitchat on their front stoops; inside, even the most nondescript colonial facade is an open, private courtyard designed to capture the evening breeze. Granada's restaurants are varied and high quality, offering something for just about everybody. While Granada lacks the five-star luxury or business hotels of the capital and coast, it instead offers a wide selection of small,

© ROBERT LERICH/123RF

HIGHLIGHTS

◖ **Antiguo Convento San Francisco:** The towering stone statues displayed in one of the Convento's many courtyards are a stunning glimpse into the nation's pre-Columbian past (page 63).

◖ **The Waterfront:** Lake Nicaragua is spectacular in different ways throughout the day, and nowhere is it more beautiful than Granada's landscaped lakefront (page 66).

◖ **Iglesia La Merced:** Climb the bell tower for the best view in all of Granada (page 66).

◖ **Las Isletas:** Spend a lazy day swimming, picnicking, and relaxing among the hundreds of gorgeous islands that comprise Las Isletas (page 80).

◖ **Parque Nacional Archipiélago Zapatera:** The stunning alter-ego statues in the museums came from these islands; an exciting lacustrine day trip leads you into Nicaragua's prehistory (page 81).

◖ **Volcán Mombacho:** More than a gorgeous background for your Granada photographs, Volcán Mombacho has a first-class set of hiking trails, an ecolodge, a canopy tour, and a lot more (page 82).

charming guesthouses, bed-and-breakfasts, and colonial lodges.

Lying in close proximity to the chaotic capital, Granada is an undeniably more attractive jumping off point for southern destinations. From here, there are direct ferries to La Isla de Ometepe. Carrying on south along the Pan-American Highway will lead you directly to the city of Rivas—with further transport options for Ometepe—and the surf-dominated coastline from San Juan del Sur to Popoyo. To the east, the crafts and folklore of Masaya are easily reached in under 30 minutes, while the capital itself is less than an hour away. If the large businesses and the international airport aren't keeping you in Managua, Granada is a handsome alternative hub for travel within the country.

HISTORY

Granada has a history as long as colonial Nicaragua's, as it is in fact the oldest city in North America. Founded 1524 by Francisco Hernández de Córdoba on the edge of Lake Cocibolca, the Spanish built Granada strategically adjacent to the indigenous community of Xalteva, whose residents suddenly found themselves working for their new foreign "visitors." Granada grew quickly as a sort of trade hub; sailing vessels would navigate their way up the Río San Juan and across the lake to Granada. As a result, an affluent Spanish merchant class developed, largely of Veracruz, Cartagena, and La Habana origin. From its beginnings, Granada was a symbol of Spanish opulence, an unsubtle show of mercantile success in the

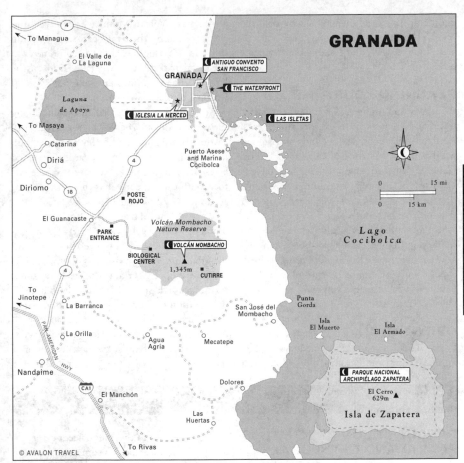

GRANADA

New World. The competing nations accepted the challenge, sacking and burning the city at every available opportunity (the English buccaneers were particularly effective).

After independence from Spain, Granada was the capital of Nicaragua each time the Conservatives took power (León was the capital when the Liberals won). As the Liberal-Conservative feud escalated, it was the Liberals who first called upon the American filibuster William Walker for support. He executed Granada's most ruthless sacking, even by pirate standards. Before he was eventually driven from

Granada, he finally burned the whole place to the ground, and buried a symbolic coffin in the central plaza under a wooden sign that read "Aquí Fue Granada" (Here Was Granada).

Despite the sackings and reconstruction, Granada remains little changed from its earliest colonial incarnation; if Córdoba were to rise from the grave today and walk the streets of La Gran Sultana, as it is sometimes called, he would find it eerily familiar. But these days, Granada is changing fast. Less influential than the old families these days is the influx of foreign capital, new ideas, and fast business. A decade ago, Granada was a "sleepy colonial jewel." The hum of the Internet cafés, chic eateries, tour services, and trendy hotels indicate it has woken up.

PLANNING YOUR TIME

A full day and night in Granada is the minimum and allows you to explore the streets, sleep somewhere interesting, and enjoy a good meal or two. But a lot of Granada's charm lies in the interesting excursions reachable if you use Granada as a base camp. Leave half a day for a boat ride in Las Isletas and another day for Volcán Mombacho. Most people devote another day for visiting the pueblos and markets in Masaya. While you could conceivably day-trip to the Laguna de Apoyo as well, the hotel options make it a fun place to stay (when was the last time you woke up inside a volcano crater?).

ORIENTATION

From Granada's central tree-lined plaza, a.k.a. Parque Central and Parque Colón, look south to the giant Volcán Mombacho. Just behind the cathedral on the park's east side, **Calle La Calzada** runs due east about one kilometer to the municipal dock on the lake. A lot of the lodging and restaurants lie along this street or within a block or two of it.

At the lake, a paved road runs south along the water's edge to **The Waterfront** (*malecón*), a would-be tourist complex that's emptier than it should be, but remains a peaceful, wooded lakeshore walking park. An easy taxi ride farther south finds the marinas that provide boat access to the *isletas* and Zapatera.

West of the plaza is the **Xalteva** (pronounced more or less with a hard "h") neighborhood, and eventually the cemetery and road to Nandaime. In this neighborhood, one block west of the Plaza, is **Calle Atravesada,** running north-south between the old 1886 train station to the bustling chaos of the municipal market. This is one of Granada's main thoroughfares and a modern commercial center, of sorts, for banks, movie theaters, and the like.

Sights

PARQUE COLÓN (CENTRAL PLAZA) AND CATHEDRAL

If Granada is the center of tourism in Nicaragua, then Granada's central plaza is the heart of it all. You'll pass through here dozens of times during your stay in Granada, and each time, sweat-drenched, you'll pause for something cold to drink. People-watchers will find it hard to leave, as the park is a steady stream of students gossiping, elderly men playing chess, and vendors hawking carved wooden toys, ceramics, jewelry, ice cream, and more. Order a glass of icy *fresco de cacao* at one of the corner kiosks, and enjoy the raucous bird-chatter in the treetops, and the hustle and bustle of life in North America's first city.

Cross the park to the magnificent cathedral on the plaza's east side. It's sometimes open to the public (even the bell towers). When the doors open for mass, it's worth a peek inside. The stone and wooden interior is dim and cool, and the bells echo overhead. Just outside the church's front step is the **Cruz del Siglo** (Century Cross), inaugurated January 1, 1900. Entombed in its cement are coins, pieces of art, and a gilded bottle from the 19th century.

LA PLAZUELA DE LOS LEONES

The pedestrian space guarded by the cannon off the northeast corner of the main plaza is where Henry Morgan once set 18 cannons

GRANADA

© GRACE GONZALEZ

Granada's Parque Colón is a great spot for soaking up local culture.

during his sacking of the city, and where, a century later, William Walker was sworn in as president of Nicaragua. On the Plazuela's eastern side is the **Casa de los Leones,** a colonial-era home whose lush interior has been transformed into an international cultural center. Don Diego de Montiel, governor of Costa Rica, built the Casa de los Leones in 1720. William Walker did not miss the opportunity to burn this place down, leaving nothing standing but the portal bearing the Montiel family crest (still visible). The unique, neoclassical colonnade facade was a product of the subsequent reconstruction. In 1987, the historical monument became the headquarters of the **Casa de los Tres Mundos Foundation** (tel. 505/2552-4176, www. c3mundos.org, 8 A.M.–6 P.M. daily), bearing an art and music school, museum, historical archive, library, concert hall, literary café, bookstore, and exhibition space which hosts resident artists from around the world.

◖ ANTIGUO CONVENTO SAN FRANCISCO

The Antiguo Convento San Francisco and its trio of bells (one block north and two east of the main cathedral, tel. 505/2552-5535, 8 A.M.–5 P.M. Mon.–Fri., 9 A.M.–4 P.M. Sat.–Sun., $2) were once famously blue. Inside, set around open courtyards festooned with palm trees, are centuries' worth of priceless artwork, and 30 alter-ego statues collected a century ago from Zapatera Island. The carved basalt shows human forms with the heads of jaguars, birds, and crocodiles whose spirits were thought to flow through humans' souls—a rare look into the cosmology of Nicaragua's pre-Columbian peoples. There is also a large to-scale replica of the city, and exhibits that represent the lifestyle of the Chorotega and Nahuatl peoples. The convent was first built by Franciscan monks in 1529 and lasted 150 years before pirate Henry Morgan burned it to the ground. Since then it has housed William Walker's troops, U.S.

GRANADA

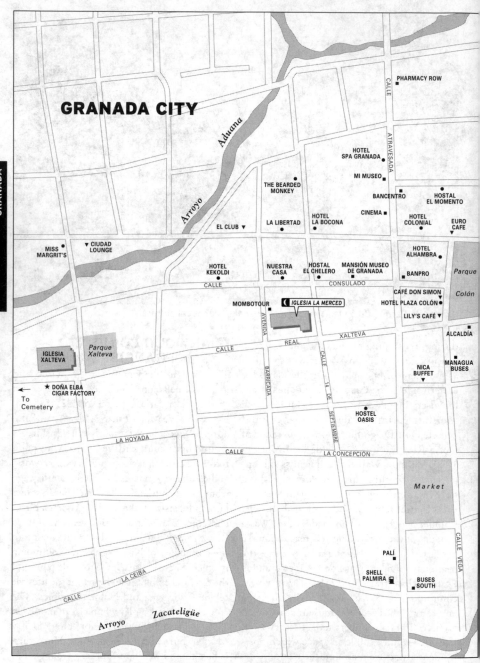

GRANADA CITY

Aduana

Arroyo

PHARMACY ROW

CALLE

ATRAVESADA

HOTEL
SPA GRANADA

MI MUSEO

BANCENTRO

HOSTAL
EL MOMENTO

THE BEARDED
MONKEY

CINEMA

HOTEL
COLONIAL

EURO
CAFE ▼

EL CLUB ▼

LA LIBERTAD

HOTEL
LA BOCONA

MISS
MARGRIT'S

▼ CIUDAD
LOUNGE

HOTEL
ALHAMBRA

Parque

HOTEL
KEKOLDI

NUESTRA
CASA

HOSTAL
EL CHELERO

MANSIÓN MUSEO
DE GRANADA

BANPRO

Colón

CALLE

CONSULADO

CAFÉ DON SIMON

MOMBOTOUR

☾ IGLESIA LA MERCED

HOTEL PLAZA COLÓN

LILY'S CAFÉ ▼

ALCALDÍA

AVENIDA

REAL

XALTEVA

IGLESIA
XALTEVA

Parque
Xalteva

CALLE

BARRICADA

CALLE
14
DE

NICA
BUFFET
▼

MANAGUA
BUSES

★ DOÑA ELBA
CIGAR FACTORY

To
Cemetery

HOSTEL
OASIS

SEPTIEMBRE

LA HOYADA

CALLE

LA CONCEPCIÓN

Market

CALLE
VEGA

PALÍ

LA CEIBA

CALLE

Arroyo   Zacateligüe

SHELL
PALMIRA

BUSES
SOUTH

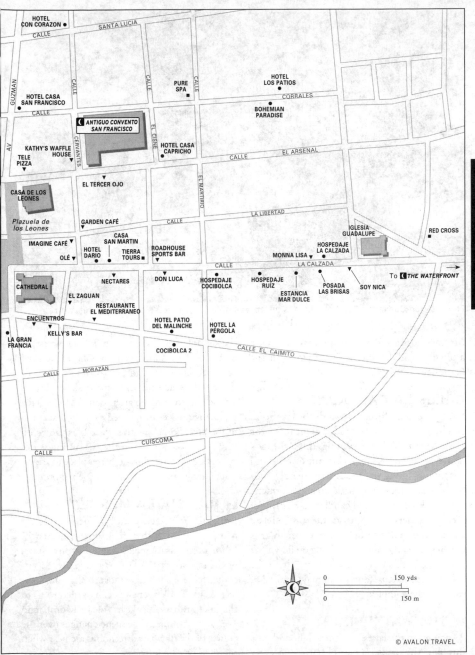

GRANADA

HOTEL
CON CORAZON
SANTA LUCIA
CALLE
GUZMAN
CALLE
CALLE
PURE
SPA
CALLE
HOTEL
LOS PATIOS
CORRALES
HOTEL CASA
SAN FRANCISCO
CALLE
BOHEMIAN
PARADISE
EL CISNE
ANTIGUO CONVENTO
SAN FRANCISCO
CERVANTES
HOTEL CASA
CAPRICHO
AV
KATHY'S WAFFLE
HOUSE
TELE
PIZZA
CALLE
EL ARSENAL
CASA DE LOS
LEONES
EL TERCER OJO
EL MARTIRIO
LA LIBERTAD
Plazuela de
los Leones
GARDEN CAFÉ
CALLE
IGLESIA
GUADALUPE
RED CROSS
IMAGINE CAFÉ
CASA
SAN MARTIN
HOSPEDAJE
LA CALZADA
OLÉ
HOTEL
DARIO
TIERRA
TOURS
ROADHOUSE
SPORTS BAR
MONNA LISA
LA CALZADA
CALLE
CATHEDRAL
NECTARES
DON LUCA
HOSPEDAJE
COCIBOLCA
HOSPEDAJE
RUÍZ
POSADA
LAS BRISAS
SOY NICA
To THE WATERFRONT
EL ZAGUAN
ESTANCIA
MAR DULCE
RESTAURANTE
EL MEDITERRANEO
ENCUENTROS
HOTEL PATIO
DEL MALINCHE
HOTEL LA
PÉRGOLA
LA GRAN
FRANCIA
KELLY'S BAR
COCIBOLCA 2
CALLE EL CAIMITO
CALLE
MORAZÁN
CUISCOMA
CALLE

0   150 yds
0   150 m

© AVALON TRAVEL

© AMBER DOBRZENSKY

The Antiguo Convento San Francisco is a fine example of Granada's colonial architecture.

Marines, a contingent of engineers surveying a possible canal route in the 1920s, and the National University.

CALLE LA CALZADA

Strolling east of the park towards the lakefront, you'll hit the heart of Granada's nightlife on the Calle la Calzada. In the evenings this is the liveliest strip in town, with a stream of bars and restaurants lining the pedestrian-friendly cobblestone street, buzzing with street performers, hammock salesmen, and candlelit tables full of merry travelers. The 17th-century **Iglesia de Guadelupe,** halfway down the street, marks the end of trendy eateries; carrying on down the palm-lined boulevard leads you directly to the *muelle* and *malecón* (dock and quay) and lakefront tourist complex.

◖ THE WATERFRONT

As you reach the lakeshore, turn right and pass through "the rooks" (a pair of statues) to enter the **Complejo Turístico,** a short row of restaurants and discos lining the lakeshore. None of the restaurants has a menu worth recommending, but the shady ambience and fresh lake breeze set the tone for languid afternoons (as long as the annoying no-see-ums, called *chayules,* aren't too numerous). Somehow this place fails to live up to its potential, and even the swimming is not good, but there remains no better place to appreciate Granada's gorgeous lacustrine panorama.

◖ IGLESIA LA MERCED

Built in 1534, sacked and burned by Henry Morgan in 1670, then rebuilt, the church itself is pretty, but ascend the tight spiral stairs of the bell tower (10 A.M.–6 P.M. daily, $1 entrance fee) for the single most spectacular view in the city. Look over an ocean of tiled roofs to the lake and *isletas,* with Volcán Mombacho over your shoulder. The scene changes over the course of the day; late afternoons are best when the shadows are long.

WILLIAM WALKER: GREY-EYED MAN OF DESTINY

The year was 1853, and Nicaragua's Liberals and Conservatives were once again at each other's throats in a fierce competition for political power. The León-based Liberals saw a chance to beat the Conservatives of Granada once and for all by hiring foreign mercenaries; so they invited a self-styled North American adventurer, white supremacist, and filibuster from Tennessee named William Walker to join them in battle in Nicaragua. He accepted, and within the year, they realized they'd created a monster.

Walker, the self-proclaimed Grey-Eyed Man of Destiny, arrived from Nashville with a band of 300 thugs and ruffians he'd rounded up in the tough neighborhoods of San Francisco. Walker and his men promptly led the Liberals to a rousing victory, but he had no intentions of going home. Two years later, he usurped power, arranged for elections that he rigged to his advantage, and declared himself president of Nicaragua. His goal was to make Nicaragua a slave state loyal to the American South's nascent confederacy.

The United States, at the brink of civil war, officially recognized Walker as president of Nicaragua. Walker reinstituted slavery and declared English the official language of the country. But Walker did what no Nicaraguan leader has been able to accomplish since: He united the people. In a rare moment of fear-inspired solidarity, the Nicaraguans temporarily forgot their differences, banded together, and with the help of the other Central American nations and some financing from Cornelius Vanderbilt (who'd lost his steamship company to Walker) defeated Walker at the Battle of San Jacinto on September 14, 1856, now a national holiday. Not long afterward, he was captured and executed by a rifle squad in Honduras. The Liberals fell into disgrace, and the Conservatives effectively ruled the nation for the next 30 years.

The scars Walker wrought on the nation run deep. As he and his men fled Granada, they paused long enough to burn the city to the ground. On the highway leading north from Managua to Estelí, a statue commemorates the victory over Walker's troops by a mobilized populace at San Jacinto. And deep inside every Nicaraguan, you'll find a distaste for loud, impudent North Americans with ambitious plans and a confident gait. William Walker's own account, *La Guerra de Nicaragua*, tells his story in no uncertain terms. Just be careful who sees you reading it. Or read *Tycoon's War* by Stephen Dando-Collins (Da Capo Press, 2008), a fascinating play-by-play, street-by-street account of William Walker's battles (and Cornelius Vanderbilt's ambitions).

GRANADA

FORTALEZA DE LA PÓLVORA

The old fort and powder storage facility is another seven blocks west of La Merced. Built in 1748 to secure Granada's gunpowder supply from marauding pirates, its medieval architecture speaks of simplicity and strength: five squat towers and one heavily guarded gate with two oak doors. In the 20th century, both the city government and later Somoza's National Guard used La Pólvora as a military garrison, and later a jail. These days it's a museum of arms or art whose exhibitions rotate regularly. Climb the towers for a breath of wind and a good perspective of the skyline. No entrance fee; watch your head and watch your step.

Adjacent, the 10-meter-high arched stone walls known as **Los Muros de Xalteva** were erected by the Spaniards in the mid-1700s to separate Spanish settlements from those of the locals. There is a relaxing park across the street with interesting stone shapes.

Located at Granada's southwest corner, Granada's **cemetery** of enormous marble tombs—bigger than the homes of many Nicaraguans—shelters the bones of several centuries of elite from Granada's heyday, including a half-dozen presidents. Note the column-lined Capilla de Animas and the replica of the Magdalena de Paris, both built between 1876 and 1922.

NICARAGUA BUTTERFLY RESERVA

Two kilometers down a dirt road and to the right of the cemetery is the Nicaragua Butterfly Reserva (tel. 505/8895-3012, www.backyardnature.net/nbr, $6). Tour the flight house and enjoy the butterflies flying around free outside on the lush grounds of an old fruit orchard. To get there, take a bus to Km 50 near the police station; it's less than a kilometer (an easy walk) from there. (Note that the track is too rough for cars at least half the year; travel by foot or bicycle.)

Sports and Recreation

BOATING AND SWIMMING

Getting out on the water is the right way to enjoy this beautiful corner of Nicaragua; watch weather conditions carefully since Lake Cocibolca gets choppy fast as the wind picks up. Taking a boat trip through Las Isletas is the best way to do that. The closest option for the active is a kayak tour from **Inuit Kayaks** (tel. 505/8691-0616, 2.5–4.5-hour tours $25–35 per person), in the Centro Turístico. Inuit assembles groups that caravan out through the closer *isletas,* a safe and fun way to explore. (There are a *lot* more options though.)

To beat the heat, use the swimming pool at the **Mombacho Beach Club** (Calle Atravesada, across from Bancentro, tel. 505/2552-4678, 10 A.M.–6 P.M. daily, $5 per person), located inside Hotel Spa Granada. You can make spa and beauty appointments there as well. Swim laps, cool off, enjoy cocktails and light snacks, or even check your email.

BICYCLING

If you start early before the temperature rises, a bike ride down the Peninsula de Asese can be excellent, and the birdlife present there will astound you. **Tours Opera Gioconda** (Calle Estrada 101, tel. 505/2552-2876, www.nicaragua-travel-guide.com) rents beater bikes (or a scooter, for the less athletic). Follow the signs for Balneario El Rayo, a small harbor out at the end of the Asese peninsula with a wonderful view of Ometepe. The road goes from bumpy to appalling over the course of the ride, but you should pedal slowly anyway so you can spot the animals (and so you don't get heatstroke). Bring lots of water and a bathing suit so you can cool off in the lake at the end.

SPAS AND MASSAGE

The three blind masseuses at **Seeing Hands Massage** (in the back of Euro Cafe, www.seeinghands.com, 9 A.M.–5:30 P.M. Mon.–Sat.) will give you a chair or full body massage (15-minute chair massage under $5). **Hotel Spa Granada** (Calle Atravesada, across from Bancentro, tel. 505/2552-4678) is the city's first full-service luxury spa. **Pure Yoga and Wellness Retreats** (Calle Corrales, 1.5 blocks east of the Convento San Francisco, tel. 505/2552-2304, www.purenica.com, open daily) offers a yoga and fitness studio with daily classes, full gym facilities, and a variety of treatments for both mind and body. Nearby, **Balance Spa and Medicina Alternativa** (in Hotel La Bocona on Calle La Libertad, tel. 505/2552-2888, $10–30) is sure to relax you with full body massages, acupuncture, reflexology and other alternative therapies.

Entertainment and Shopping

A concerted effort to raise Granada's profile, the annual February **Poetry Festival** is a knock-out, drawing not only Nicaragua's most acclaimed literati and musicians (Gioconda Belli, Ernesto Cardenal, Norma Elena Gadea), but an astonishing array of poets and artists from around the world as well. The event capitalizes on the open spaces of several Granada landmarks, including cathedrals, the San Francisco convent, and Granada's best plazas. If your trip coincides with this event, book your room early.

Throughout the rest of the year, the Casa de los Leones sponsors frequent events, including concerts by local musicians and visiting international artists. One block west of the plaza, Granada's humble movie theater, **El Teatro Karawala,** offers popular (often trashy) American movies.

BARS

Granada's most popular gringo watering hole, **Roadhouse Sports Bar** (noon–midnight daily), occupies a busy corner of La Calzada. There are half a dozen other bars within a stone's throw of this corner. The beer's cold at every one.

A loungier, more romantic scene is found at **El Tercer Ojo** (Calle El Arsenal across from Convento San Francisco, 11 A.M.–11 P.M. Tues.–Sun.), with swank tapas, wine, cocktails, and a popular happy hour (4–7 P.M.).

Charly's Bar and Restaurante (from Petronic, five blocks west and 25 meters south, tel. 505/2552-2942, 11 A.M.–11 P.M. Wed.–Mon.) is an old-time, schnitzel-flinging favorite on the western fringes of town, specializing in German cuisine, barbecue, and draft beer in a huge crystal cowboy boots. It's a bit far from the city center but worth the trip.

El Balcón (southeast corner of the central plaza, tel. 505/2552-6002, noon–10 P.M. daily), on the second floor of the grand, yellow-painted Gran Francia, offers the best aerial streetside balcony from which to watch the foot and horse traffic below as you sip your Centenario and enjoy the delicious bar menu.

CLUBS

Managua is still better for dancing, but a growing club scene exists in Granada. **Encuentros** (Calle El Caimito, www.encuentrosclub.com) is a newer venue. The enormous colonial building houses a daytime chill-out pool, a café, cinema, restaurant and wine bar, and hosts Latin salsa nights on the weekend. On Friday and Saturday nights, shuttles travel from here to sister venue **WEEKEND** (in the lakefront tourist complex, Thurs.–Sun., cover $3–5). Currently the hippest club in town, this Miami Beach—style party spot hosts banging fiestas where DJs spin electronic music for a raging crowd. More casual, cheaper, and rowdier is **Inuit Kayaks** (Fri.–Sat.), inside the Centro Turístico, serving cold beer and Latin rhythms. **Iguana's Bar,** in the Marina Cocibolca, is another drinking and dancing hotspot with a great lakeside breeze. For any club inside the Centro Turístico and Marina Cocibolca, take a cab there and back—this area is not safe at night and it's quite a hike from the Marina.

SHOPPING

Granada is not really the best place to shop for Nicaraguan handicrafts; most people save that activity for Masaya. But the steady volume of tourist traffic through Granada is slowly changing the picture. There are several gift shops around the plaza, as well as frequent street vendors. The municipal market is located one block south of the plaza, but spills up Calle Atravesada as well. It's geared more for the locals than for tourists, but is lots of fun to visit.

Soy Nica (Calle La Calzada in front of the

© JOSHUA BERMAN

At night, Granada's streets are a destination unto themselves.

Carlos Bravo School, tel. 505/2552-0234, www.soynica.dk, 9 A.M.–6 P.M. Mon.–Thurs., 9 A.M.–10 P.M. Fri.–Sun.) sells brightly colored leather goods in modern Scandinavian designs, crafted in the onsite workshop with Nicaraguan leather. Also worth a look is **Olé** (Calle La Calzada one block east of the park, 9 A.M.–7 P.M. Mon.–Wed., 9 A.M.–7 P.M. Thurs.–Sat., 10 A.M.–8 P.M. Sun.), a cute boutique with tropical clothing, jewelry, and accessories, as well as homemade gifts. Next door, the **Centro De Arte** (9 A.M.–4 P.M. Mon.–Fri., 11 A.M.–close Sat.) is a small gallery with pieces from local artists.

Granada is *guayabera* country, and there are several places to buy these elegant Latin shirts; the best (and most expensive) is **Guayabera**

Nora, right around the corner from the Bearded Monkey. At **Sultan Cigars** (Calle Vega or Calle La Libertad, tel. 505/8803-9569, eddyreyes78@ yahoo.es), Eddy Reyes and family can make you a custom-label case (your name on a cigar label) in a couple of hours; otherwise visit **Doña Elba Cigar Factory** (half a block west of the Xalteva church, tel. 505/2552-7348, www.el-bacigars.com, 8 A.M.–6 P.M. daily). Antique lovers will adore **El Anticuario** (tel. 505/2552-4457, open daily) a block north of the park on Calle Atravesada.

If you're looking for something to read, the **Lucha Libro** bookstore (Avenida Cervantes, tel. 505/2552-3584, 7 A.M.–9 P.M. daily) has one of the best selections of English-language books in the country.

Accommodations

Granada lodging runs from youthful backpacker hostels to refurbished colonial homes; much of the accommodations are located conveniently near Plaza Central. Interestingly, Granada has seen huge turnover in expat-owned places that appeared at the start of the real estate boom but then disappeared without a whisper. Locally owned places, on the other hand, have mostly weathered the storm. Expect higher rates during the high season (Dec.–Apr.).

UNDER $25

The Bearded Monkey (across from the fire station, tel. 505/2552-4028, $6 dorm, $14 for a private room) was for a long time the backpacker set's favorite, with dorm-style rooms and a laid-back, communal atmosphere. Cool music, an eclectic crowd, movie nights, and free Internet access marked this place apart from the rest. Nowadays, the service and the crowds are more hit-and-miss. The newer ◖**Hostel El Momento** (Calle el Arsenal 104, tel. 505/8457-6560, www.hostelgranadanicaragua.com, dorms $7, privates $12–28) has provided fierce competition. Amenities include new beds, pretty communal areas, an onsite spa, a bar and restaurant, and Wi-Fi; laundry service and bike rentals also available.

Hospedaje El Chelero (Calle el Consulado, two blocks west of the park, tel. 505/2552-5703, www.nahualtours.com, $5 dorm, $12–25 private rooms with fan or a/c) is locally owned and basic, housed in an unrenovated colonial home and sporting brand new beds. They can also organize bike rentals and tours through their sister company, **Nahualt Tours.**

Hostel Oasis (one block north, one block east of the market, tel. 505/2552-8005, www.nicaraguahostel.com, $9 dorm bed, $13–40 rooms) is one of the quietest accommodations in this range, with the bonus of a swimming pool, which matters. Travelers have reported surly staff and bedbugs here, so have a close look at the mattress before sealing the deal. **Hospedaje La Calzada** (tel. 505/8475-9229, $10 shared bath, $12 with private bath) has been around for more than a decade at least; what it lacks in decor and cleanliness, it makes up for in location.

Hospedaje Cocibolca (Calle la Calzada, three blocks east of park, tel. 505/2552-7223, hospedaje_cocibolca@yahoo.com, $16–26) has wireless Internet, friendly and professional service, and more than 10 years of experience.

Hospedaje Ruiz (Calle la Calzada, tel. 505/2552-2346, $20 with private bath) has been around longer than some of the competition; rooms are simple but well ventilated and are quite clean. Similar but less experienced is **Posada las Brisas** (Calle la Calzada, tel. 505/2552-3984 or 8754-5414, posadalasbrisas@gmail.com, $15–30 with fan or a/c); it's family-run, safe, and clean. Features include wireless Internet, refrigerator, and kitchen access. **Hospedaje La Libertad** (three blocks west of park on Calle la Libertad, tel. 505/2552-4087, www.la-libertad.net, hospedaje_libertad@gmail.com, $6 dorm beds, $15 s with shared bath) offers broad and well-ventilated dorms, with lockers, Internet, and access to the communal kitchen.

$25-50

◖**Estancia Mar Dulce** (Calle la Calzada, 3.5 blocks east of park, tel. 505/2552-3732, granadamardulce@hotmail.com, $30 with fan, $40 with a/c, includes breakfast) is locally owned, clean, and professional. It has large, pleasant rooms, cable TV, and a spacious interior courtyard with a landscaped swimming pool; poolside rooms are more expensive.

◖**Hotel Kekoldi** (3.5 blocks west of the

COMMUNITY TOURISM NEAR GRANADA

For those seeking a full-immersion cultural experience, the most obvious option is to sign up for a homestay with one of the many Spanish schools in Granada. This is a good option if you want to stay with a Nicaraguan family and still have access to Granada's many restaurants, Internet cafés, and other distractions. If you'd really like to get out there, then consider arranging a few days (or weeks) with the **Unión de Cooperativas Agropecuarias Tierra y Agua,** also known as the **Earth and Water UCA** (tel. 505/8896-9361 or 505/2552-0238, turismo@ucatierrayagua.org, www.ucatierrayagua.org). The office in Granada is located 75 yards to the west of the Shell Palmira and is open Monday, Wednesday, and Friday 8:30 A.M.–2 P.M. The UCA is an association of rural farmers on the slopes of Volcán Mombacho and Isla de Zapatera National Park who will be glad to be your hosts. You'll stay in primitive Nicaraguan lodging and eat typical food while getting to know your new neighborhood. Expect to pay about $5 per person per night for lodging in La Granadilla or Zonzapote, and about $3 per meal. Local guides will take you horseback riding, hiking, fishing, and more; cheap transport to and from Granada can be arranged.

Income generated by your visit goes directly to a cooperative collective fund to pay for meals, guides, maintenance, etc., and to distribute to families involved. The UCA also maintains a general fund for tourism, used for training and to make small loans for new tourist-related projects.

park on Calle El Consulado, tel. 506/2552-4106, U.S. tel. 786/221-9011, reservations@kekoldi.com, www.kekoldi-nicaragua.com, from $39) is spacious and colorful with well-planned architecture and plenty of open areas.

Hotel La Pérgola (three blocks east of the park on Calle El Caimito, tel. 505/2552-4221, lapergolanic@yahoo.com, www.lapergola.com.ni, $27–55) has 11 rooms with private bath, TV, air-conditioning, and access to a gorgeous open balcony (for which the hotel is named), plus tour service, Wi-Fi, and parking.

El Club (three blocks west of the northwest corner of the park, tel. 505/2552-4245, www.elclub-nicaragua.com, $45–65 high season, $25–90 low season) has a modern look with cozy, small, windowless rooms and the city's longest bar. **Hotel Casa San Martín** (Calle La Calzada, one block east of the plaza, tel. 505/2552-6185, reservaciones@hcasasanmartin.com, www.hcasasanmartin.com, $45–60) has eight rooms, all with gorgeous hardwood floors.

$50-100

Granada's midrange and upscale hotels offer remarkable value, each striving to offer an authentic but unique colonial experience with all the amenities. In this price range and above expect hot water, air-conditioning, private bathrooms, cable TV, artsy decor, and the ubiquitous open-air central patio with small swimming pool.

Casa San Francisco (kitty-corner to the Convento San Francisco, tel. 505/2552-8235, csfgranada@yahoo.com, www.casasanfrancisco.com, $45–90) is a charming colonial cluster of 13 decorated rooms with breakfast included. Run by a couple of dynamic and well-traveled ex–Peace Corps volunteer sisters, Casa San Francisco features a small pool and is located in a quiet and central neighborhood. You'll also find a great on-site restaurant and bar.

Hotel Spa Granada (in front of Bancentro on Calles Atrevesada, tel. 505/2552-4678, www.hotelspagranada.com, $70–200) is located in the largest intact colonial home in Granada, which also houses the Mombacho Beach Club's fabulous swimming pool. Quirkily decorated rooms and interesting artwork add to the visual element, although the rooms upstairs are not the best value for money. An onsite chocolate museum means this place always smells heavenly.

© RANDALL WOOD

Hotel Colonial

The delightful ☾ **Miss Margrit's** (two blocks north of the Xalteva church off Calle Libertad, missmargrits@gmail.com, www.missmargrits.com, no phone, from $60 s) has two large, luxurious rooms within a meticulously restored private home. The resplendent space offers a fine taste of Granada Colonial living, with the perks of a hotel including breakfast, laundry services, and a pool you don't have to clean.

A few blocks up Calle Corrales from Casa San Francisco, look for **Bohemian Paradise** (tel. 505/2552-0286, $60 s), a small, high-quality retreat in a surprisingly quiet neighborhood with a handful of excellent, über-comfortable rooms (guests rave about the quality of the mattresses and sheets) set around a small garden. Most basic services are available (including parking and laundry), except a bar and restaurant—the owners encourage guests to explore the city. This is a great option for small groups, and is gay friendly.

Hotel Patio del Malinche (Calle El Caimito, 2.5 blocks east of the central plaza, tel. 505/2552-2235, www.patiodelmalinche.com, $47–85) is Catalan-owned and very comfortable. Fifteen rooms surround a huge patio, bar, and pool.

Better for families in this price range is colorful and pleasant **Hotel Casa Capricho** (Calle El Arsenal, a block east of Convento San Francisco, tel. 505/2552-8422, www.hotelcasa-caprichogranada.com, $45–75), with 11 rooms, a kitchen, a dining room, and common areas.

☾ **Hotel con Corazón** (Calle Santa Lucia 141, tel. 505/2552-8852, www.hotelconcorazon.com, $64–100) has Scandinavian styling and a noble mission: In addition to a hotel, this is a foundation that invests heavily in the community, particularly in education. They have a cute little pool, 16 comfortable rooms with air-conditioning, ceiling fans, and TV, plus an on-site restaurant, making it hard not to recommend.

Also in this class are two legitimate hotels, not restored colonial houses. **Hotel Alhambra**

GRANADA

(northwest corner of the central plaza, tel. 505/2552-4486, www.hotelalhambra.com.ni, $70–90) was Granada's first luxury hotel and has the best spot in town, right on the park. Built around a gorgeous, landscaped patio, its 56 recently remodeled rooms (some with pleasing balcony views) have air-conditioning, TV, private bath, hot water, kitchenette, exposed wood beams, and tasteful decorations. The whole place has a classy, mahogany ambience. **⊠ Hotel Colonial** (20 meters west of the park's northwest corner, tel. 505/2552-7299, www.hotelcolonialgranada.com, $70–100) is newer, with 37 clean, well-appointed rooms surrounding an outdoor patio, pool, and bar.

OVER $100

At the top end of the boutique guesthouses in the country, **Hotel La Bocona** (Calle La Libertad, two blocks west of the park, tel. 505/2552-2888, $90–165, breakfast included) offers six impeccable rooms with king-size four-poster beds, sumptuous drapery and antique furnishings; the only drawback is that the bathrooms (while also luxurious) are shared. Guests can take advantage of the large pool, free gym membership, full concierge services, private parking, Wi-Fi, and a 10 percent discount at the onsite spa. Equally opulent, but with a more modern Scandinavian design, is **⊠ Hotel Los Patios** (Calle Corrales 525, tel. 505/2552-0641, www.lospatiosgranada.com, $105–175, breakfast included). Spacious rooms with private bathrooms are based around a courtyard pool and maze of relaxing areas for guests to enjoy. Amenities include a small spa, playing field, morning meals, Wi-Fi, and a wealth of

services and tours; ask about discounts for stays of more than two nights.

With a stately blue facade gracing Calle La Calzada, **Hotel Dario** (tel. 505/2552-3400, www.hoteldario.com, $80–125) has open walkways, gardens, and 22 rooms, which make artful use of the available space, all painted in bright and rather gaudy colors; request one of the rooms with a small balcony facing Mombacho.

One of Granada's first buildings (and one of the few that withstood the fire that consumed the rest of the city in the days of William Walker) has been painstakingly restored as **La Gran Francia Hotel** (southeast corner of the park, tel. 505/2552-6000, www.lagranfrancia.com, $80–175 includes tax and breakfast). A careful blend of neoclassical and colonial elements in hardwoods, wrought iron, and porcelain characterize La Gran Francia's every detail—down to the hand-painted sinks. Twenty-one rooms, some with balconies, are set around a courtyard and pool. The Duke's Suite, named after an 18th-century mystery man, is one of the few accommodations in Granada with a whirlpool tub.

Another class act is **Hotel Plaza Colón** (tel. 505/552-8489, www.hotelplazacolon.com, $105–230), whose 26 large, elegant rooms feature air-conditioning, hot water, cable TV, and ceiling fans. Six rooms have vast wooden porches looking straight across the central plaza to the main cathedral, a beautiful—but sometimes noisy—vista. The other rooms face a quiet street or the sculpted inner courtyards and pool. A restaurant, bar, and wine cellar are on the premises, and parking is available.

Food

The Granada dining scene is in constant rotation, with old favorites disappearing, new contenders appearing, and creative experimentation in between. Some favorite picks are listed, but you won't go hungry if you simply stroll down Calle La Calzada toward the lake, where the city's dining scene is at its most intense.

The two major supermarkets are the **Palí** (on Calle Atravesada just south of the market) and **La Colonia,** both open until 8 P.M. or so. As many of the lower priced *hospedajes* may offer a kitchen and fridge, you can stretch your travel dollars immensely by using these stores.

BREAKFAST

Garden Cafe (Calle la Libertad, one block east of central plaza, tel. 505/2552-8582, 7 A.M.–3 P.M. Mon.–Sat., under $5) is great for breakfast. Or try the orange-infused French toast at **Hotel Casa San Francisco** (kitty-corner to the Convento San Francisco, 7 A.M.–close daily, $4–7); ask for a table on the sidewalk. **Kathy's Waffle House** (across from Convento San Francisco, 7 A.M.–2 P.M. daily, $4) is a favorite for breakfast with its American-style pancakes, biscuits and gravy, eggs and bacon, omelets, and a lot more. Another greasy spoon–style breakfast joint is **Nica Buffet,** just south of the park, where you'll find both gringo breakfasts and heaping plates of *platano maduro* and *gallo pinto*. (Turn off your cell phone and behave if you don't want to end up on the owner's blacklist.)

CAFÉS

Euro Cafe (northwest corner of central plaza, 7:30 A.M.–9 P.M. daily, $5–10) serves homemade gelato, pastries, panini, fresh hummus, fruit juices, and strong coffee drinks; there's also free Wi-Fi. ◖ **Garden Cafe** (Calle la Libertad, one block east of central plaza, tel. 505/2552-8582, thegardencafe.granada@gmail.com, 7 A.M.–3 P.M. Mon.–Sat., under $4) is a wonderful respite from the heat, with a cool space to enjoy gourmet sandwiches, salads, smoothies, and coffee drinks. The artsy patio is a great place to crank the Wi-Fi.

Café Don Simon ($4–8), on the west side of the park, serves up burgers, sandwiches, roast chicken, and more. You can sample expertly prepared Nicaraguan classics at **Comida Típica,** just behind the cathedral. With a fine view of the park, the popular **Lily's Café** (next to Hotel Plaza Colón, tel. 505/2552-7266, 7 A.M.–7 P.M. daily, $2–9) serves fresh pastries, organic salads, gourmet sandwiches, and designer coffee.

ITALIAN

You'll find authentic pizza at **Monna Lisa** (Calle La Calzada, tel. 505/2552-8187, $7–10). The pizzas are better at **Don Luca's** (Calle La Calzada, tel. 505/2552-7822, $4–12), where they're baked in a wood-fired oven. Backpackers prefer the prices at **Telepizza** (Calle El Arsenal, 1.5 blocks east of Bancentro, tel. 505/2552-4219, 10 A.M.–10 P.M. daily, $6.50), with large pies and delivery available; the gigantic stuffed calzones ($3.50) may be one of the best deals in town.

UPSCALE

Lamb chops with fresh mint, top-notch filet mignon, and other inspired dinners are at **Imagine Café** (tel. 505/2552-4672 or 505/8842-2587, www.imaginerestaurantandbar.com, 4–11 P.M. Thurs.–Tues., $8–20), which also has a decent bit of live music some evenings. Meals are carefully handcrafted from local, and usually organic, ingredients; that said, several readers have reported poor service from moody staff.

◖ **El Tercer Ojo** (Calle El Arsenal across from Convento San Francisco, tel. 505/2552-6451,

GRANADA

11 A.M.–11 P.M. Tues.–Sun., $6–15) offers everything from Spanish tapas and sushi to gorgonzola pasta, kebabs, and fine wine in a gauzy lounge of candles and soothing music.

Head to **Villas Mombacho** (Marina Cocibolca, tel. 505/2552-8552, 10 A.M.–8 P.M. daily, $8–12) for the best local seafood around. In the breezy lakeside setting clients rave about the guapote fish, cooked up any way you like it. They also have bungalows and rent kayaks.

El Mediterraneo (Calle Caimito, two blocks east of the cathedral, tel. 505/2552-6764, Tues.–Sun., $7–15) is an elegant Spanish restaurant set in an airy garden patio adorned with colorful artwork—readers love this place.

El Arcángel Restaurant (tel. 505/2552-6000, 7 A.M. for breakfast, then noon–10 P.M. daily, $12–20), at La Gran Francia, features an exquisite fusion of Latin American ingredients with international cuisine. Entrées include whiskey-glazed steak, pasta, and banana and brown-sugar coated snapper fillet.

◖**El Zaguán** (noon–3 P.M. and 6 P.M.–close daily, $10–20), located directly behind the cathedral, is a hugely popular steakhouse grilling up some of the tastiest meat in the country over a huge open-flame pit. Satisfy your inner carnivore with anything from *churrasco* to filet mignon—as charred or as bloody as you like it. Large portions, a decent wine list, and attentive service are all good reasons to wait for a table.

The classiest eatery in town (and with the steepest prices) is **Ciudad Lounge** (five blocks west of the park on Calle La Libertad, tel. 505/2552-1543, 6 P.M.–midnight Thurs.–Sun., $10–35), presenting a daily-changing gourmet menu, world-class cocktails with premium liqueurs, an impressive wine list, and cigars from Estelí.

Information and Services

BANKS

Banco de America Central is on the southwest corner of the plaza, and Banpro and Bancentro are on Calle Atravesada, just a few blocks away. The sanctioned money changers are out in full force along this same section of Atravesada (they're on the street, waving wads of cash), and you'll find ATMs in most banks and at the Esso gas station on the edge of town.

EMERGENCY SERVICES

The police presence is pretty serious in Granada. You'll note an officer stationed full time in the park, and a lot of others patrolling to keep tourists safe. If you are a victim of crime, file a report online (webdenunciagr@policia.gob.ni) or visit the **police station** (on Calle Atravsesada by Parque Sandino, tel. 505/2552-2929). The biggest hospital is Bernardino Díaz Ochoa, a few kilometers out of town on the road toward Managua. On the same highway, a bit closer to town, is the **Hospital Privado Cocibolca** (tel. 505/2552-2907 or 505/2552-4092). For minor treatments, the section of Calle Atravesada just south of the bridge is occupied by more than a dozen clinics, blood labs, and pharmacies.

INTERNET

Internet cafés throughout the city usually offer service for $1–1.25 per hour and Internet phone service for around $0.10 per minute. Start at **Alhambra Internet** (across the street from Hotel Colonial, 8 A.M.–10 P.M. daily); they offer a variety of services and the shop is always air-conditioned. Also pleasant is the **Cafémail** (in the Casa de los Leones, 7 A.M.–10 P.M. daily, $1 per hr), offering a coffee-bar experience with a row of PCs and Wi-Fi. In fact, most restaurants and hotels have free Wi-Fi in Granada, so you'll have no problem with your laptop.

VOLUNTEERING IN GRANADA

Nicaragua has lots of potential and there are lots of ways to help. If you can commit more than a couple of weeks and have decent Spanish already, you can turn your vacation into something more than just travel by volunteering with one of the several Granada-based organizations that helps travelers make a difference. Yes, you'll miss out on some hammock time, but look at what you'll gain:

Building New Hope (BNH) (U.S. tel. 412/421-1625, in Granada, call Donna Tabor at tel. 505/8852-0210, www.buildingnewhope. org), based in both Granada and Pittsburgh, Pennsylvania, is a nonprofit organization offering a number of ongoing programs and volunteer opportunities. Start by purchasing a pound (or six) of Fair Trade-certified, organic, shade-grown coffee from their website, then mull over these options while sipping some hot Nica joe: BNH manages two neighborhood schools that welcome volunteer teachers' assistants. They often need mentors for young adult males attempting to enter the mainstream after life on the streets. BNH assists the community library and reading-in-schools program, and operates a veterinary clinic to help control the stray animal population in Granada, which is *always* looking for visiting veterinarians, vet techs, dog walkers, and vet students. BNH is also on the lookout for music teachers for their **Rhythm in the Barrios** project, physical education instructors, and other teachers (intermediate Spanish and one month minimum commitment).

Empowerment International (tel. 505/2552-1653 or 8678-3341, U.S. tel. 303/823-6495, www.empowermentinternational.org) runs a community-based educational program for impoverished and at-risk youth. Direct work with the families and community is an integral part of their methodology, as are art and photography projects. There are many ways to volunteer for EI both in Nicaragua and from afar. See their website for a list of needs and ways to help. Intermediate Spanish is a must, and there is a strong need for computer skills, psychology, and teaching experience.

Sisters of Madre Teresa de Calcuta in Barrio Sabonetta have a very organized school and residence for girls up to the age of 18. Most have been rescued from precarious conditions in their homes or were at-risk for drug use, prostitution, and other crimes. The school grounds are beautifully manicured and immaculate; the sisters welcome volunteers to teach music (guitar and voice), English, and art; conversational Spanish is a must.

La Harmonía (Carraterra Masaya, two blocks west of La Colonia supermarket, eeap_aman@yahoo.com) is an organization for mentally and physically challenged children and young adults. They accept volunteers with basic Spanish who can teach handicrafts, weaving, haircutting, sign language, or have experience in special education.

La Esperanza Granada (Calle Libertad #307, tel. 505/8913-8946, la_esperanza_granada@yahoo.com, www.la-esperanza-granada.org) focuses on education, especially with very young children. Volunteers work in public schools on the outskirts of Granada; they tutor and teach arts and crafts, sports, English, etc. Volunteer housing in the center of Granada is from $23 per week; preferred time frame is eight weeks with intermediate Spanish. No program fees or registration fee. They have experience with groups of international volunteers for short-term projects.

LAUNDRY

Mapache Laundry Service (Calle La Calzada, tel. 505/2552-6711, 8 A.M.–6 P.M. Mon.–Fri., 8 A.M.–4 P.M. Sat.–Sun.) will wash your duds in modern machines, with delivery and pickup service for about $10 per load.

Getting There and Around

GETTING THERE

Most tour operators offer exclusive shuttles to San Juan del Sur, León, the dock for Ometepe, and the airport.

By Bus

There are four places to catch a bus out of town. The easiest and most popular way to get to Managua (or Masaya, which is on the way) is to grab a **COGRAN** *expreso* (1.5 blocks south of the central plaza's southwest corner, tel. 505/2552-2954); these medium-sized buses leave every 15–20 minutes 4:30 A.M.–7 or 8 P.M. Monday–Friday (they stop service a few hours earlier on Sunday). Another fleet of minivans leaves from the Parque Sandino on the north side of Granada near the old railroad station, with regular departures 5 A.M.–7:30 P.M. Both services travel to La UCA in Managua. From there, the same vehicles leave for Granada every 15 minutes, 5:50 A.M.–8 P.M.

Regular bus service to Rivas, Nandaime, and Jinotepe works out of the **Shell Palmira,** on Granada's south side, just past the Palí supermarket. The first bus to Rivas leaves at 5:45 A.M. and takes 1.5 hours; service continues sporadically until the last one at 3:10 P.M. Nandaime buses leave every 20 minutes. Jinotepe *expresos* take a mere 45 minutes compared to the nearly two-hour *ordinario* trip through the pueblos. Around the corner, behind the Palí, is the bus terminal with service to Masaya (although any Managua-bound *expreso* will let you off in Masaya as well).

BY BUS TO COSTA RICA AND PANAMÁ

Avenida Arrellano, on the west end of Granada, is part of the San José- and Panama City-bound routes for Central American bus lines. The three offices are all located on the east side of the street, and reservations should be made at least two days in advance. The **TicaBus** terminal (tel. 505/2552-4301) is half a block south of the Old Hospital; be there at 6:15 A.M. for the 7 A.M. bus. **TransNica** (tel. 505/2552-6619) is three long blocks south of the Old Hospital, on the corner of Calle Xalteva; three daily south-bounders leave at 6:30 A.M., 8 A.M., and 11 A.M.; be there a half-hour before departure.

BY BOAT TO OMETEPE AND SAN CARLOS

Granada's crusty old ferry departs Granada's municipal dock (tel. 505/2552-4605) Monday and Thursday at 2 P.M., arriving in San Carlos around 6 A.M. When weather permits, the boat stops at Altagracia before cutting across to the eastern lakeshore and port calls in Morrito and San Miguelito. The adventure costs $10 for air-conditioning and padded benches upstairs or $4 for no air-conditioning and hard wooden benches downstairs. The boat can get crowded and uncomfortable, especially around Semana Santa when the lake turns *bravo* (rough) and the weather is hot. Get to the port early and be aggressive to stake your territory. During the rest of the year, the ride is usually languid and uneventful, and you may even be able to get some sleep on the deck.

GETTING AROUND

Most of what you'll want to visit or see lies in the kilometer between the lake and the plaza, and it's all walkable. That's really the best way to enjoy the city, but you'll be better off if you do your walking in the early morning when the sunlight is golden and the air temperature is still pleasant. Taxis are numerous and cheap if the heat really has you down. Better yet, hire a horse-drawn carriage from the west side of the plaza for an open-air local's view of town.

TOUR OPERATORS IN GRANADA

Most of the national tour operators have offices in Granada that provide all local trips and transfers. In addition, here are a few Granada specialists.

Amigo Tours (tel. 505/2552-7299, bernal@ amigotours.net, www.amigotours.net), connected to the lobby of the Hotel Colonial, provides a higher-end option for tours, plus travel agency services like national airline bookings, car rentals, and transfers to and from Costa Rica.

Leo Tours (tel. 505/8829-4372 or 505/8842-7905, leotoursgranada@gmail.com, leonica1971@yahoo.com), run by Leopoldo Castillo, a Granada native, tries to work in a more community-minded spirit that will connect you to Nicaragua rather than just show you the sights. They can take you around Granada, Ometepe, Laguna de Apoyo, and Mombacho, or show by bike tour how the "rest" of Granada lives.

Mombotour (next to BDF in the Centro Comercial Granada, tel. 505/2552-3297 or 505/8809-5143, www.cafelasflores.com) offers several different canopy tours starting at $30 per person, including their popular Tarzan Swing. You can be on belay in 30 minutes from

your hotel, and they pick you up. Also look for bike tours/rentals and canopy trips at the Cutirre Farm on Mombacho.

Tierra Tours (Calle La Calzada, two blocks east of park, tel. 505/2552-8723 or 505/8862-9580, www.tierratour.com) offers trips to Mombacho, Masaya, and Las Isletas, where they can coordinate kayak tours as well. They are also gaining traction as the go-to place for travelers—Spanish language students, usually—looking for longer-term homestays. In addition to local tours of Granada, Masaya, and Catarina, Tierra offers night tours of Volcán Masaya and overnight cabins and tent platforms at a nearby Butterfly Reserve and coffee farm ($55 pp for full-service camping trip). Ask about shuttle service to other parts of Nicaragua, including León, where they have a sister office.

Servitur (tel. 505/2552-2955, orvind@ hotmail.com) is connected to the Hotel Alhambra, offering travel agent services and a variety of local trips in the Granada area, including a horse-drawn-carriage city tour and fishing trips.

Car Rental

The **Budget** office (tel. 505/2552-2323, reserve@budget.com.ni, 8 A.M.–6:30 P.M. daily) is located in the Shell Guapinol gas station on the road to Managua. Cars rent from about $30–110 a day; they also rent cell phones. There is huge demand for their 28-vehicle fleet, so reservations are necessary, especially in the high season. Hotels also often maintain a list of trusted cars and drivers, and many tour operators have extra vehicles. For car rentals, drivers, transfers, and four-wheel drive, call Peter van der Meijs at **Armadillo Nicaragua** (tel. 505/8833-8663, info@armadillo-nicaragua.com, http://armadillo-nicaragua.com); from the Shell Guapinol gas

station, their office is four blocks north and 1.5 blocks west.

Horsedrawn Carriage Tours

Though Granada is easy to walk, the humidity will wear you down on the haul out to the lakeshore and back. Rather, explore Granada's narrow streets by enjoying a ride in horse and carriage. Find the carriages along the western, shady side of the plaza (prices vary, about $15–25 per hour). Please patronize only those drivers who seem to be taking good care of their animals (the situation is improving, but the occasional bag-o-bones with open saddle sores are still around). Not only is the tour pleasant, but it will help orient you for the rest of your stay in town.

Near Granada

ℂ LAS ISLETAS

This 365-island archipelago formed when Volcán Mombacho erupted some 20,000 years ago, hurling its top half into the nearby lake in giant masses of rock, ash, and lava. Today, the islands are inhabited by a few hundred *campesinos* and an ever-increasing number of wealthy Nicaraguans and foreigners who continue to buy up the *isletas* and build garish vacation homes on them. The natural beauty of the *isletas* is spectacular, and history buffs will enjoy the **Fortín de San Pablo,** a Spanish fort that was largely unsuccessful in preventing pirate attacks on Granada. The islanders themselves are interesting and friendly, maintaining a rural lifestyle unique in Nicaragua: Children paddle dugout canoes or rowboats to school from an early age, and their parents get along by fishing and farming—or by taking camera-toting tourists for a ride in their boats.

To visit Las Isletas, begin at either Cabañas Amarillo or Puerto Asese, both a seven-minute drive south of Granada at the end of the waterfront road (about $1 via taxi). Puerto Asese is more popular, while Cabañas Amarillo (fork left at the Asese sign) provides more shade and wider views—as well as kayak tours. At both docks, you'll find a restaurant, snack bars, and a plethora of boats vying for your business. Choose a *lanchero* (boatman) and don't expect to haggle over prices, as gasoline is expensive. You'll pay about $10 per person for a half-hour tour, more for longer or farther trips. Beef up your visit by asking to visit an island where a family can serve you lunch—or pull up and "refuel" at one of the mellow island bars before continuing your tour. You can also take a dip in the lake water or have your *lanchero* bring you to the cemetery, old fort, or monkey island.

Kayaking

Touring the islands in a *lancha* is not recommended for those seeking a quiet wilderness experience—the loud motors spew smoke and scare the birds away and keep you far up out of the water. Much more enjoyable is the sound of birdsong over your kayak as you cut silently through the glassy water. **NicarAgua Dulce** (Marina Cocibolca, tel. 505/2552-8827 or 505/8718-8407, www.nicaragaguadulce.com) rents rowboats, kayaks, and silent electric boats for a half or full day; all three can carry up to five persons.

Find tours in the Mombotour office (tel. 505/8388-2734 or 505/8809-5143) in Granada. The introductory class, which includes all equipment, sea kayaks, transportation, and tour of the Fortín San Pablo, costs $34 a person and lasts three hours. Special bird-watching kayak excursions run $20–30; Nica guides are available and for the full petroleum-free experience, try the bike-kayak combo tour.

Wakeboarding

A fun way to explore the isletas and to take advantage of the lake is with **Nica Action Sports** (at the Marina Cocibolca, tel. 505/8999-2427, www.nicaactionsports.com), the only wakeboarding operation in the country. Boats, wakeboards, kneeboards, Jet Skis, and tubes are available for rent; lessons can be provided for those without the skills.

Accommodations

The exclusive **Jicaro Lodge** (tel. 505/2552-6353, info@jicarolodge.com, www.jicarolodge.com, $380 for a three-day package for two people) is a spa, yoga, and wellness retreat with nine cabins. They will pick you up at the airport and feed you a classy, custom menu

COURTESY OF NICA ACTION SPORTS

GRANADA

Wakeboarding is one way to explore Las Isletas.

prepared on-site. Watch your step on the steep stairs at night. Travelers report that the islet is tinier than you might think, but appreciate the courteous staff.

◖ PARQUE NACIONAL ARCHIPIÉLAGO ZAPATERA

About 34 kilometers south of Granada, Zapatera is an extinct volcano surrounded by Isla el Muerto and a dozen or so other islets, all of which comprise 45 square kilometers of land; the whole complex is home for some 500 residents. Zapatera is a natural wonder, rising 629 meters above sea level. Its virgin forest is rife with myriad wildlife such as parrots, toucans, herons, and other waterfowl, plus white-tailed deer, and an alleged population of jaguars no one ever seems to see.

These islands were enormously important to the Nahuatl, who used them primarily as a vast burial ground and sacrifice spot. The sites of La Punta de las Figuras and Zonzapote are particularly rich in artifacts and have a network of caves that have never been researched. Also seek out the petroglyphs carved into the bedrock beaches of Isla el Muerto. An impressive selection of Zapatera's formidable stone idols is on display in the Convento San Francisco, but the islands' remaining archaeological treasures remain relatively unstudied and unprotected and (naturally) continue to disappear.

Officially declared a national park by the Sandinistas in 1983, the Zapatera Archipelago has never been adequately protected or funded. MARENA's thousand-page management plan document is just that—a document—while in reality, only one park ranger visits the islands a couple of times per month. It's no surprise then that inhabitants and visitors litter, loot the archaeological patrimony, hunt, and cut down trees for timber.

GRANADA

© RANDALL WOOD

petroglyph on Zapatera

Visiting Zapatera

Access the islands from Granada's Puerto Asese, where you can strike a deal with returning Zapatera islanders or hire a tourist boat. The most reliable way is to arrange a trip with **Zapatera Tours** (tel. 505/8842-2587, www.zapateratours.com), a small company that specializes in creative lake tours, including overnight camping trips, fishing, waterskiing, you name it. You can also inquire about Zapatera trips with any of the other Granada tour companies above. With a fast, powerful motor, it's a 20-minute trip from Granada, partly over a stretch of open water that can get choppy.

There are a scattering of places to stay around the island, including a cheap dormitory and homestay options in Zonzapote. Or book a room at **Casa Santa María** (tel. 505/2277-5299 or 505/8883-7533, katiacordova9@gmail.com, www.islazapatera.com, $95 pp room and board), where the Cordova

family's 120-year-old tile-roofed ranch house has been outfitted with six comfortably primitive double rooms with mosquito net, fan, and private bathrooms. Casa Santa María only accepts groups (minimum 8 people, maximum 24 with shared rooms). The hotel is on a relaxing sandy beach, looking north toward Isla el Muerto and Mombacho. The hotel will send a pickup boat to Granada for you ($180) or you can ask a *lanchero* at the Marina Cocibolca to take you for about the same price.

◖ VOLCÁN MOMBACHO

Mombacho is unavoidable; it towers over the southern horizon, lurks around every corner, creeps into your panoramic photos. In Granada, you are living in the shadow of a giant. Fortunately, this giant is gentle. Every bit of cool, misty, cloud forest higher than 850 meters above sea level is officially protected as a nature reserve. This equals about 700 hectares of park, rising to a peak elevation

GRANADA

This yellow flower grows in the Mombacho volcano and is typical of the rainy forest.

of 1,345 meters, and comprising a rich, concentrated island of flora and fauna. Thanks to the Fundación Cocibolca, the reserve is accessible and makes available the best-designed and maintained hiking trails in the nation.

Overgrown with hundreds of orchid and bromeliad species, tree ferns, and old-growth cloud and dwarf forests, Mombacho also boasts three species of monkeys, 168 observed birds (49 of which are migratory), 30 species of reptiles, 60 mammals (including at least one very secretive big cat), and 10 amphibians. The flanks of the volcano, 21 percent of which remains forested, are composed of privately owned coffee plantations and cattle ranches. Maintaining the forest canopy is a crucial objective of Fundación Cocibolca, since this is where more than 90 percent of Mombacho's 1,000 howler monkeys reside (the monkeys travel in 100 different troops, and venture into the actual reserve only to forage).

Visiting Volcán Mombacho

Although the majority of Mombacho's visitors arrive as part of a tour package, it is entirely possible to visit the reserve on your own, and it makes a perfect day trip from Managua, Granada, or Masaya. Start by taking a bus (or express minivan) headed for Nandaime or Rivas (or, from Granada, to Carazo as well); tell the driver to let you off at the Empalme el Guanacaste. This is a large intersection, and the road up to the parking lot and official reserve entrance is located 1.5 kilometers toward the mountain—look for the signs.

The walk to the parking lot is a solid half-hour trek, mostly uphill and in the sun. Water and snacks are available at the parking lot; be sure to drink lots of water before and during this first leg of your journey. Once you arrive at the parking lot, you'll pay the entrance fee and then board one of the foundation's vehicles to make the half-hour, six-kilometer climb up to the Biological Station. If you've got the time and the strong legs, feel free to hike all the way up the steep road yourself. (Allow a couple of hours—and lots of water—to reach the top).

The lumbering troop transports depart at 8:30 A.M., 10 A.M., 1 P.M., and 3 P.M. Thursday–Sunday, and return shortly after each climb up the hill (the last bus down is at 6 P.M.). If in your own four-wheel drive vehicle, you'll be asked to pay $13 in addition to the entrance fee.

The reserve is closed on Monday for maintenance, and usually restricts Tuesdays and Wednesdays to organized groups. From Thursday to Sunday, all are welcome. The entrance fee ($7.50 for foreigners, $5 for Nicas and residents, $4 for students and children) includes admission to the reserve, transport to and from the top of the volcano, and insurance.

Volcán Mombacho Biological Center

Volcán Mombacho Biological Center is located at the base of one of Mombacho's 14 communications antennas, on a small plateau called Plan de las Flores at 1,150 meters. The research station is also an interpretive center, *hospedaje, cafetín,* ranger station, and conference center; it was technically completed in 2000, but is still expanding.

Drinks and snacks are available here, including a simple meal ($3.50). There are 10 dormitory beds in a loft above the interpretive center; it costs $25 to rent out the whole *albergue* (hostel), which sleeps up to 10 people. The package deal includes dinner, a guided night hike (search for the famous red-eyed frog and Mombacho salamander), and breakfast; or pitch a tent ($15) and buy meals on the side. To make a reservation, contact the **Biological Station** (tel. 505/2248-8234/35 or 505/2552-5858) or **Fundación Cocibolca** in Managua (tel. 505/2278-3224 or 505/2277-1681, www.mombacho.org). Most tour companies will get you there; start with Mombotours or Tierra Tours.

Hiking

There is a short (half-hour) trail through the coffee farm at the bottom of the volcano, where you wait for your ride up. Once on top, there are two main trails to choose from. **Sendero el Cráter,** which encircles the forest-lined crater, features a moss-lined tunnel, several lookouts, and a spur trail to the **fumaroles** (holes in the ground venting hot sulfurous air). The fumaroles area is an open, grassy part of the volcano with blazing wildflowers and an incredible view of Granada and the *isletas.* The whole loop, including the spur, is 1.5 kilometers, with a few ups and downs, and takes a casual hour to walk.

The **Sendero la Puma** is considerably more challenging—a four-kilometer loop with several difficult climbs that lead to breathtaking viewpoints. It begins at a turnoff from the fumaroles trail, and you should allow a minimum of three hours to complete it (and lots of water).

Well-trained, knowledgeable local guides (some speak English) are available for the Sendero el Cráter ($5 per group, plus tip) and for the Sendero la Puma ($10). Note: Because of the altitude and the clouds, the visibility from these trails may be diminished on bad-weather days.

Canopy Tours

Put yourself on belay at the **Mombacho Canopy Tour** (tel. 505/8888-2566 or 505/8852-9483, gloriamaria@cablenet.com.ni, $30 pp), located up the road from the parking lot, just before the road passes through the El Progreso coffee mill. The 1,500-meter course involves 15 platforms and a 25-meter-long hanging bridge. Many tour operators offer a full-day Mombacho package that involves a visit to the reserve followed by a canopy tour on the way down, or you can arrange it yourself by calling Fundación Cocibolca.

On the opposite (east) face of Volcán Mombacho, cloud-forest coffee farm meets canopy tour at the Cutirre Farm. **Mombotour** (next to BDF, tel. 505/2552-4548, www.mombotour.com) offers a range of half-day trips, involving some combination of canopy tour, horseback ride, bird-watching hike, and coffee-farm tour. Trips include transportation to and from Granada and lunch ($55 per adult); add a kayak tour to make a full day out of it.

The 15-kilometer ride to the Cutirre Farm takes longer than you'd expect. The road turns into a river during the wet season, but the trip is worth it; once you arrive, the views from the lodge are spectacular, looking straight out at Isla de Zapatera, and behind it, the cone of Volcán Concepción. There is also a small but attractive insect museum, with a full butterfly farm in the works. Bird-watchers can take a walk through the plantation with guides experienced in spotting any of the 43 species observed here.

The canopy tour, suspended from 14 of the giant shade trees on the coffee farm, is a professional, safe system of 17 platforms, a hanging bridge, and 13 horizontal zip lines, ending with a 23-meter rappel from a massive ceiba tree. Show up at Mombotour's Granada office to arrange your trip, leaving at either 10 A.M. or 2 P.M. (arrive one hour prior), and returning you to Granada about three hours later.

Accommodations

The unique **Poste Rojo** (tel. 505/8903-4563, www.posterojo.com, $8–27) hostel skirts the base of the mighty Mombacho volcano, and draws nature-lovers and party animals alike with the lure of the Mombacho Treehouse. Accommodations consist of covered hammocks ($4), rustic dorms and private rooms with shared bath, casitas, and the honeymoon cabin (a half-hour hike from the rest, through fairly thick jungle), as well as space to pitch a tent ($3). The treehouse is accessed from the hangout bar and restaurant; a series of suspension bridges and platforms are attached to some large and very old trees that do a great job of providing a true canopy experience. To get here, hop on the free shuttle from Hospedaje la Libertad in Granada (daily departures at 12:30 P.M.).

MASAYA AND THE PUEBLOS BLANCOS

Masaya is a city of artisans, metalworkers, leatherworkers, carpenters, painters, and musicians. In fact, no other region of Nicaragua is as blessed with a sense of artistry and creativity as Masaya and the surrounding villages, called the Pueblos Blancos. Many of the handicrafts found in markets throughout the country are Masayan: handwoven hammocks, terra cotta pottery, musical instruments, and more. "The City of Flowers," as Rubén Darío christened the town a century ago (he was talking about the girls, not the flora), rarely garners more than a brief afternoon market visit for most travelers. It is a city relatively devoid of monuments, historical buildings, and traditional sights. As a marketplace, however,

it is unsurpassed, and wandering through the cool alleys of the crafts markets is a cultural tour through Nicaragua, a vivid expression of this people's vitality, passion, and creativity. If you are eager to come home from your trip with something special, this is the place to find it.

Adjacent, and an inextricable part not only of the landscape but of the culture, is Volcán Masaya. One of the world's most accessible volcanoes, one of only two on earth where you can drive up to the crater lip and look inside, and Nicaragua's most thoughtfully planned national park, Volcán Masaya is extremely active. You'll smell the sulphur when the wind is right. It's a rewarding and memorable experience well

HIGHLIGHTS

El Mercado Viejo Craft Market: The best handmade pottery, leatherwork, paintings, and more are all handsomely displayed in a professionally run market designed to showcase Nicaragua's finest (page 90).

Festival of San Jerónimo: Masaya's creative celebrations are in full bloom during this religious parade cum street party honoring the city's patron saint (page 92).

Volcán Masaya National Park: Peer into the gates of hell, wherein dwell demon parakeets—then visit the museum of this popular national park (page 95).

Laguna de Apoyo: Get away from it all in what might be the coolest swimming hole in the country, an enticing volcanic crater lake ringed with forest (page 96).

Catarina Mirador: This crater's lip patio terrace, with one of the best panoramas in Nicaragua, often offers live marimba music to accompany your beverage (page 99).

LOOK FOR **C** TO FIND RECOMMENDED SIGHTS, ACTIVITIES, DINING, AND LODGING.

MASAYA

worth your time, and possibly one of the top three things to do in Nicaragua.

To the south and west of Masaya, the charming Pueblos Blancos are artisan villages whose craftspeople produce what you find in the markets. It's easy to spend a day visiting their workshops or just enjoying the casual, friendly atmosphere of each town. In particular, the village of Catarina, perched on the crater lip above Laguna de Apoyo, enjoys one of the most spectacular vistas in all of Nicaragua. The Pueblos run into Carazo, another group of small towns, closer to the Pacific, with a pleasant climate and somewhat middle-class feel in a country of economic extremes. Its cooler temperatures

favor coffee production, often under the shade of beautiful hardwood trees. The towns of Diriamba and Jinotepe make delightful lunch stopovers on your way through from Managua to Masaya, but both have nice places to stay, and Jinotepe's open-air market is more manageable than most.

A regional turquoise jewel, the Laguna de Apoyo is probably the most pleasant freshwater swimming hole in the country, imbued with both a sense of tranquility and isolation that make more than just the cool lake water refreshing. It's an easy day trip from Granada, but many choose to stay the night as well, and a growing number of hotels and restaurants make

MASAYA

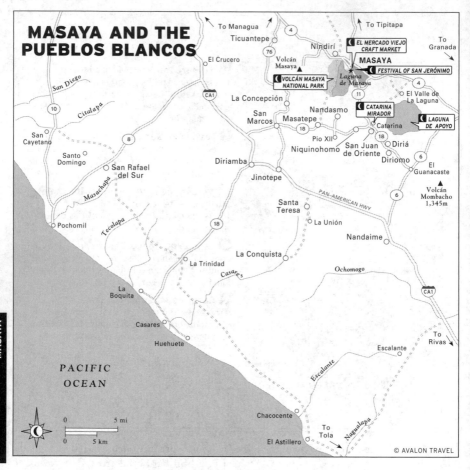

that possible. Unless you are truly water-averse, this delightful place should not be missed.

PLANNING YOUR TIME

Most people visit the craft markets, city, and volcano in one day, but if you are relying on public transportation, it may take longer. Naturalists more interested in the volcano can just as easily spend a long day on hiking trails, in the visitors center, and on guided tours. It's possible to make Masaya your base for excursions, but most travelers opt instead to stay in Granada, which has a better selection

of hotels and restaurants. On any trip to the Masaya craft market, be sure to allow for time to walk to the cliff-top lookout near the baseball stadium *(el malecón),* where you'll also find the hammock factories. You can also kill an hour or two at the Coyotepe fortress, where the views are pleasant and the wind takes the edge off the heat.

A trip through the Pueblos Blancos can occupy a full day, even if you're driving. It's fun to start at one end, work your way up to Catarina, have lunch, and then continue. You can visit the Pueblos Blancos by public transportation, as the buses run this route frequently throughout the day, but having the freedom of a vehicle will greatly facilitate your ability to pick and choose as you work your way through the villages. Lastly, though very few travelers stay the night in Masaya, consider doing so during one of the city's colorful festivals, when the town really comes alive.

Masaya City

Masaya (population 150,000) sprawls over a tropical plain nestled against the slopes of the volcano by the same name; at its western edge, paths carved by the Chorotegas trace the steep hillside down to the Laguna de Masaya. Twenty indigenous villages of Darianes used to cluster at the water's edge. Masaya was officially founded as a city in 1819 and has grown ever since. Several centuries of rebellion and uprising—first against the Spaniards in 1529 and later against William Walker's forces in 1856, the U.S. Marines in 1912, and in a number of ferocious battles against the National Guard during the revolution—earned the Masayans a reputation as fierce fighters.

Travelers find Masaya less picturesque than Granada, and it's true the streets and building facades in Masaya are less cared for. But the Masayans are a creative people with many traditions found nowhere else in Nicaragua, such as their solemn, mysterious funeral processions. Perhaps Masayan creative energy goes into its delightful arts and crafts instead of the architecture. Your best introduction to these delights is Masaya's Mercado Viejo (Old Market), which is so pleasant and compelling that many visitors choose not to stray beyond its stately stone walls. But it's well worth the money to charter a horse-drawn carriage to carry you to the breezy *malecón,* to see the crater lake 100 meters below.

Orientation

Masaya sits due south of the Managua–Granada Carretera along the east side of the Laguna de Masaya. The street that runs north along the plaza's east side is the Calle Central, and as you travel it toward the Carretera, it becomes increasingly commercial. One block east of the southeast corner of the park, you'll find the stone walls of the Mercado Viejo (Old Market). Walking six blocks west of the central park takes you to the hammock factories, baseball stadium, and *malecón;* traveling due south leads you to Barrio Monimbó; going five blocks north puts you in the heart of the Barrio San Jerónimo around the church of the same name, situated at the famous *siete esquinas* (seven corners) intersection. The heart of Masaya is easily walkable, but several hundred taxis, buses, horse-drawn carriages, and more exotic forms of transport will help you get out to the *malecón* or the highway.

SIGHTS

Masaya's central plaza is officially called **Parque 17 de Octubre,** named for a battle against Somoza's Guardia in 1977. Plenty of remaining bullet holes are testimony, plus two imposing command towers immediately to the west. The church in the northeast corner is La Parroquia La Asunción. The unremarkable, triangular **Plaza de Monimbó** park on the southern side of Masaya comes to life every afternoon at around 3 P.M. as the throbbing social and commercial heart of the mostly indigenous Monimbó neighborhood. The **Museo y Galería Héroes y Mártires** (inside the Alcaldía, 1.5 blocks north of the park, 8 A.M.–5 P.M. Mon.–Fri., donation requested) pays tribute to those Masayans who fought Somoza's National Guard during the revolution with a collection of guns and photos of the fallen, but the highlight is the unexploded napalm bomb Somoza dropped on the city in 1977.

MASAYA

MASAYA

◖ El Mercado Viejo Craft Market

All roads lead to El Mercado Viejo, built in 1891, destroyed by fires in 1966 and 1978, and refurbished in 1997 as a showcase for local handicrafts. Also known as El Mercado Nacionál de Artesanías, or simply the "tourist market," El Mercado Viejo is safe, comfortable, and geared toward foreigners. Here you'll find all manner of delightful leather, brass, iron, carved wood, and textile handicrafts, plus paintings, clothing, hammocks, and the best of what Nicaragua's talented craftspeople have to offer. It's the best reason to come to Masaya, and even if you don't buy anything, an enjoyable and colorful experience—of course you pay for the convenience in slightly higher prices. Right around the corner, **Chincheli** is a shop owned and run by talented local artists and former street kids. Not only do these artists sell high quality paintings, hammocks, and bracelets, they also teach other children, under the tutelage of nongovernmental organization (NGO) Los Quinchos.

El Malecón

Cool off after an intense morning in the market on the windswept *malecón,* a beautiful cliffside promenade with long views over the Volcán Masaya crater lake to the north and west. It's easily reached from the city center. Skip the taxi; charter a horse carriage instead, which makes for a nice ride through some quiet neighborhoods.

Artisan Workshops

Nicaragua's most treasured souvenirs, woven hammocks are handmade by scores of Masaya families, and take 2–3 days each to make. The most obvious place to purchase one is in the El Mercado Viejo Craft Market or in the market on the *malecón.* More fun than just buying one is to visit one of the many *fábricas de hamacas;* most are in people's homes, clustered on the same block near the southwest edge of town, across from the old hospital on the road to the

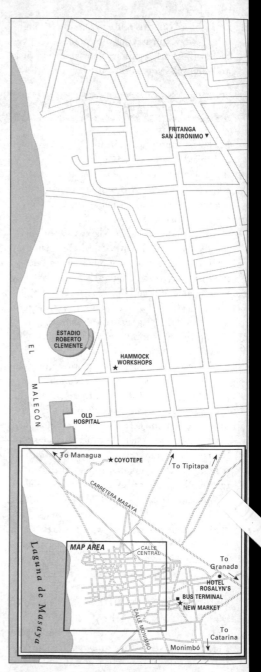

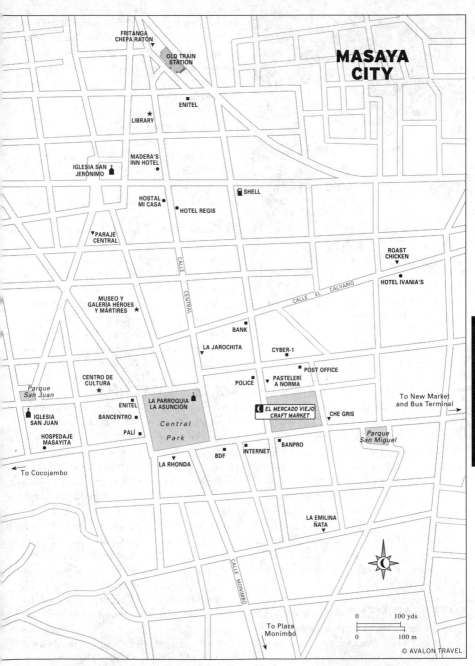

MASAYA CITY

FRITANGA CHEPA RATÓN

OLD TRAIN STATION

ENITEL

LIBRARY ★

MADERA'S INN HOTEL

IGLESIA SAN JERÓNIMO

SHELL

HOSTAL MI CASA

HOTEL REGIS

PARAJE CENTRAL

ROAST CHICKEN

HOTEL IVANIA'S

CALLE EL CALVARIO

CALLE CENTRAL

MUSEO Y GALERÍA HÉROES Y MÁRTIRES ★

BANK

LA JAROCHITA

CYBER-1

POST OFFICE

CENTRO DE CULTURA ★

Parque San Juan

POLICE

PASTELERÍ A NORMA

IGLESIA SAN JUAN

ENITEL

BANCENTRO

LA PARROQUIA LA ASUNCIÓN

Central

Park

EL MERCADO VIEJO CRAFT MARKET

CHE GRIS

To New Market and Bus Terminal

MASAYA

HOSPEDAJE MASAYITA

PALÍ

Parque San Miguel

To Cocojambo

LA RHONDA

BDF

INTERNET

BANPRO

LA EMILINA ÑATA

CALLE MONIMBÓ

To Plaza Monimbó

0   100 yds

0   100 m

© AVALON TRAVEL

© AMBER DOBRZENSKY

Hammocks here are some of the world's finest.

malecón and baseball stadium. There you'll find at least a half-dozen family porch-front businesses; all of these craftspeople will gladly show you how hammocks are woven.

Sergio Zepeda is a third-generation luthier (guitar builder) at **Guitarras Zepeda** (200 meters west of the Unión Fenosa, tel. 505/8883-0260, guitarraszepeda@yahoo.com). His shop is only a block off the Carretera Masaya, behind Hotel Rosalyn. Cheap children's and beater guitars start at $60 or so; professional hardwood instruments with cocobolo rosewood back and sides and imported red cedar, mahogany, or spruce tops can go for up to $800. Allow at least two weeks to order, or show up in his shop and see what's available.

ENTERTAINMENT AND EVENTS

Every Thursday 5–11 P.M., **Jueves de Verbena** consists of dance, theater, art expos, music, and more, all presented in the Old Market on one of several stages. Or rub elbows with the locals at the most popular local bar in town, **La Rhonda,** on the south side of the park, with beer, lots of space, and good appetizers.

If you're here on a weekend during baseball season (Nov.–May), be sure to catch the local team, San Fernando, who plays in **Estadio Roberto Clemente,** named for the Puerto Rico–born Pittsburgh Pirate who died in a plane crash in 1973 delivering aid to Nicaraguan earthquake victims. The tailgating scene atop the *malecón* may be one of the most scenic in the world. Tickets start at $0.50.

◖ Festival of San Jerónimo

The last week of September sees the fiesta of the town's patron saint, San Jerónimo. A religious procession that feels more like a street party runs throughout the town, honoring Saint Jerónimo. Exhibitions of folkloric dance with colorful costumes add a carnival quality to the festivities. The town also celebrates its *Hípica* during this week, where local cowboys show off dancing stallions in a day-long, alcohol-fuelled horse parade.

ACCOMMODATIONS

Along the highway and outside of town, Masaya's hotels tend to be pay-by-the-hour *auto-hotels;* nifty car park curtains hide your license plate to spying eyes. In town, lodging is reasonable but not nearly as varied or exciting as in Granada.

◖**Hotel Regis** (on Calle Central, 3.5 blocks north of the church on the main plaza, tel. 505/2522-2300, $5 pp) has a dozen neat, clean rooms (including some for groups and families), with shared bath and fan, and a respectable breakfast ($3). The couple that runs the place is friendly, knowledgeable about things to do in the area, and speaks some English; however, they are strict about running a clean shop, look down on partying, and close their doors at 10 P.M. There are several other options on the same block, including **Hostal Mi Casa** (tel. 505/2522-2500, $7 pp with shared bath,

MASAYA

A GUIDE TO MASAYA'S FIESTAS

Masayans celebrate all year long, observing various religious, historical, and indigenous rites with a wild collage of marimba music, traditional costumes, poetry, painting, food, drink, and age-old customs. Many of the dances are family traditions, in which certain roles—and their accompanying masks and costumes—are passed from generation to generation. Costumes are a key element of the festivals and are often elaborate and gorgeous.

September–December are peak fiesta months in Masaya. Pieces and parcels of Masaya's festivals are found in the various *fiestas patronales* of the many surrounding pueblos, each of which present their own peculiar twist to the events. In mid-June, for example, San Juan de Oriente's party involves "warriors" dancing through the streets and whipping each other with stiffened bull penises.

- **San Lázaro** (a few weeks before Easter): Believers promenade with their ornately costumed dogs to thank their patron saint for keeping their household animals in good health.

- **Festival of the Cross** (May): People exchange thousands of palm-thatch crosses in honor of La Señora de la Asunción. The virgin icon is carried to Monimbó in remembrance of the miracle that occurred there during the last eruption of Volcán Masaya's Santiago Crater, in which the virgin saved the city from hot ashes.

- *fiestas patronales* (Sept. 20): The *fiestas patronales* begin by honoring patron Saint Jerónimo.

- **Fiesta del Toro Venado** (last Sun. of Oct.): This extravagant fieta is similar to

the North American Halloween, but instead of ghosts and goblins, Masayans don disguises that poke fun at their favorite politicians, clergy, and other public figures.

- **Fiesta de los Agüisotes** (Fiesta of the Bad Omens, last Fri. in Oct.): In this nod to Nicaragua's darker side, folks dress up as scary figures from local legends, such as the *chancha bruja,* the *mocuana,* and the *arre chavalo* (a headless priest from León).

- **Procesión de San Jerónimo** (first Sun. in Dec.): This is perhaps the most stunning of Masaya's fiestas, as the statue of the city's patron saint is paraded through the streets amidst a sea of flowers. Look for the **Baile de las Inditas** (Dance of the Little Indian Girls), **Baile de Negras** (Dance of the Black Women), and the **Baile de Fantasía** (Dance of Fantasy). Every Sunday (Sept.–Dec.) features a folk dance, a competition between rival troops, or even dancers that go from house to house performing short dances to marimba music.

- **La Novena del Niño Dios** (Dec.): In this interesting ritual, small children are given pots, pans, whistles, and firecrackers and are sent into the streets at 5 A.M. to noisily call all the other children together for the 6 A.M. mass in celebration of the Christ child's birth.

- **Festival of San Sebastian** (mid-Jan.): The indigenous Monimbó barrio explodes with life and energy. The celebration's highlight is the **Baile de Chinegro de Mozote y Verga,** in which participants engage in a mock battle before finally coming together in a peace ritual. The *tunkún* drum (a Maya instrument) beats out the rhythm of the dance, along with a whistle called a *pífano.*

MASAYA

$20 room with fan) in a big, open, colorful space which includes the Fruti-Fruti smoothie bar and *cafetín.*

At ◖ **Madera's Inn Hotel** (two blocks south of the fire station, tel. 505/2522-5825, maderasinn@yahoo.com, $20–35) the 12 rooms occupy two floors set around a beautifully

furnished common room; some rooms have fan and shared bath, while more expensive ones have private bath and air-conditioning. You'll also find friendly service, Internet access, parking, tours, and laundry.

A well-run, modern option in central Masaya, **Hotel Ivania's** (from Calvario church,

3.5 blocks west, tel. 505/2522-7632, hoteliva-nias@hotmail.com, www.hotelivanias.com, $40–65 includes tax and breakfast) has 17 clean, plain rooms with air-conditioning, television, hot water, refrigerators, and tiled floors, all surrounding an attractive courtyard. Ask about the family suite and local tours.

FOOD
Comedores and Fritanga

Masaya is more famous for its street food than its restaurants, and nowhere will you find more authentic cuisine *de la calle* than at **El Tiangue,** an open-air, multivendor food market in barrio Monimbó. Vendors set up in the small triangular plaza across from the Don Bosco school. It gets going every evening around 5 P.M. when you'll find everything from standard finger-licking *fritanga* served on a banana leaf to hard-core snout-to-tail pig dishes and organ meat (featured on the Travel Channel's *Bizarre Foods with Andrew Zimmern*).

Countless small *comedores* line both sides of the main street from the central park all the way up to the old train station, all fine places to find out why Masayans refer to themselves as *"come-yucas"* (yucca eaters). You'll find all sorts of juicy, greasy, fried, and roasted treasures at one of several locally famous street grills: **Fritanga San Jerónimo,** a few blocks west of the church with the same name; or **La Emilina Ñata en el Barrio Loco** (5 P.M.–close daily), Flat-nose Emilina's in the Crazy Neighborhood, with its world-famous grilled beef. Still another savory sidewalk barbecue option is **La Chepa Ratona,** next to the old train station.

Cafés and Restaurants

Eateries close to El Mercado Viejo include **Repostería Norma** (20 meters north of the Old Market) for baked goods, juices, and snacks, and **Che Gris** (on the east side of the Old Market), which offers traditional cooking in an air-conditioned setting. A livelier,

more popular option is **❚ Jarochito's** (just north of the central park, tel. 505/2522-4831, 11 A.M.–10 P.M. daily, $3–8) for Mexican with a Nicaraguan twist. A bit farther up the main street is **Comedor La Criolla** (7 A.M.–5 P.M. daily, $2.50–$4), serving excellent local breakfast and lunch. It's a great place to sit and enjoy a fresh juice drink.

INFORMATION AND SERVICES

The INTUR office (tel. 505/2522-7615, closed for lunch) is open business hours and is located half a block south of the Old Market, but is of little use other than for upcoming events in the city.

Hospital Hilario Sanchez Vásquez (on the highway toward Granada, tel. 505/2522-2778) is the biggest facility in town, though you are much better off driving to Hospital Vivan Pellas, on the highway before you reach Managua.

The large blue **police station** (tel. 505/2522-4222 or 505/2522-2521) is half a block north of the Old Market across from Norma's bakery.

Besides the multiple ATMs within the Old Market, numerous banks are close by: Bancentro on the west side of the central park, BAC one block north of the Old Market, and Banpro on the southwestern corner of the Old Market. Several cheap and crowded Internet places line the south side of the central park. Both Correos de Nicaragua and a DHL Worldwide Express are available inside the Old Market compound to facilitate sending gifts and packages, and the ENITEL phone office is a block south of the old train station.

GETTING THERE

Nearly every southbound bus leaving Managua from Roberto Huembes passes Masaya, which is right on the highway, only 27 kilometers from Managua. Faster still are the Masaya- or Granada-bound *expresos* from the UCA leaving regularly 7 A.M.–9:30 P.M., arriving in Masaya's Parque San Miguel; from there, they depart for Managua 6 A.M.–8 P.M. The ride costs under $1.

Less recommended is the *expreso* service between Masaya's Plaza de Monimbó and Mercado Oriental in Managua, first leaving Masaya at 3 A.M. and running through 7 P.M. Ordinary bus service leaves and arrives at the main terminal in the parking lot of the Mercado Nuevo.

Near Masaya

VOLCÁN MASAYA NATIONAL PARK

An extraordinary and easy day trip from Managua, Masaya, or Granada, Volcán Masaya National Park (9 A.M.–4:45 P.M. daily, $5) is Nicaragua's most impressive outdoor attraction and premier tourist site. There are very few volcanoes in the world where you can simply drive up to the crater edge and look into what the Spaniards declared to be the very "mouth of hell": That's exactly what Masaya offers, but there's a lot more. One of the most visibly active volcanoes in the country, Volcán Masaya emits a nearly constant plume of sulfurous gas, smoke, and sometimes ash, visible from as far away as the airport in Managua. From one of its craters, you can sometimes glimpse incandescent rock and magma. A visitors center (where they'll ask you to park your car facing out "just in case") will help you interpret the geology and ecology of the site, as will the park's impressive nature museum. For the more actively inclined, hiking trails cover a portion of the volcano's slopes.

Volcán Masaya was called Popogatepe (mountain that burns) by the Chorotegas, who feared it and interpreted eruptions as displays of anger to be appeased with sacrifices, often human. In the early 1500s, Father Francisco Bobadilla placed a cross at the crater lip in order to exorcise the devil within and protect the villages below. Not long afterward, though, thinking the volcano might contain gold instead of the devil, both Friar Blas del Castillo and Gonzalo Fernandez de Oviedo lowered themselves into the crater on ropes to search. They found neither the devil nor gold, but probably singed their eyebrows.

The park is actually composed of several geologically linked volcanic craters: Volcán Nindirí, which last erupted in 1670, and Volcán Masaya, which blew its top in 1772. The relatively new Santiago Crater was formed between the other two in 1852, and is inhabited by a remarkable species of parakeet that nests contentedly in the rocky side of the crater walls, oblivious to the toxic gases and the scientists who had thought such a sulphurous environment would be uninhabitable. You might see these *chocoyos del cráter* (crater parakeets) from the parking area along the crater's edge.

As for the sensation of "just in case," the danger is quite real. In April 2000, the Santiago crater burped up a single volcanic boulder that plummeted to earth, crushing an unfortunate Italian tourist's car in the parking lot.

Visiting Volcán Masaya

The exhibits at the **Visitors Interpretation Center** and museum include three-dimensional dioramas of Nicaragua and Central America, models of active volcanoes, and remnants of indigenous sacrifice urns and musical instruments found deep in the volcano's caves; there is also a display of old lithographs and paintings of the volcano as the Spaniards saw it. Consider one of the several guided tours ($10 pp, sign up at the visitors center), including an exciting night tour beginning at sunset. Of special interest is the walk to the **Tzinancanostoc Bat Cave,** a lava tube passageway melted out of solid rock.

Though most visitors only snap a few photos from the crater's edge before continuing, the park also contains several **hiking trails** through a veritable moonscape of lava formations and

MASAYA

MASAYA

© GRACE GONZALEZ

the crater of Volcán Masaya

scrubby vegetation, making it easy to spend at least half a day here; carry lots of water and sunscreen (there is little to no shade); the trails are well worth your time and offer good opportunities to cross paths with some of the park's wildlife, including coyotes, deer, iguanas, and monkeys. The Coyote Trail will lead you east to the shore of the Laguna de Masaya.

COYOTEPE

Just south of Volcán Masaya on a hill overlooking the highway, the battlements of this fort (8:30 A.M.–5 P.M. daily, $2) overlook the city of Masaya. Take a cab or hike up the road—the view of Masaya, its lagoon and volcano, both great lakes, and the far-reaching surrounding countryside is worth it; that's before you even descend into the dungeons. Built at the turn of the 20th century, this site witnessed a fierce battle between national troops and U.S. Marines in 1912. Somoza rehabilitated it as a particularly cruel prison. Today, Coyotepe is in

the hands of the Nicaraguan Boy Scouts, who will accompany you through the pitch-black underground prison facilities in exchange for a small fee. (For special attention, or at least a smile, greet your guide with the three-finger Scout salute and their motto in Spanish: *Siempre Listo,* Always Prepared.)

NINDIRÍ

Just north of the highway between the entrance to Volcán Masaya National Park and the city of Masaya, Nindirí was the most important and densely populated of the indigenous settlements in the area—up to 1,500 years before the arrival of the Spanish. Its name in Chorotega means Hill of the Small Pig, and its principal attraction is the 1,000-artifact collection in the **Museo Tenderí** (named after a local cacique) that celebrates pre-Columbian culture. Also, ask around about the Cailagua site, with petroglyphs overlooking the Laguna de Masaya. During the last week of July, the festival for patron saint Santa Ana employs many of the ancient dance, costume, and music rituals popular to the whole Masaya and Carazo region.

◀ LAGUNA DE APOYO

Nicaragua's cleanest and most enticing swimming hole is Laguna de Apoyo, just outside of Masaya. Actually a lake that formed in the drowned volcanic crater of the long extinct Apoyo Volcano, the lagoon floor reaches 200 meters in depth—the lowest point in all of Central America. Considering how easy it is to reach the lagoon, it is surprisingly untouristed. Despite its continued seismicity—a minor earthquake in 2000 under the crater-rim town of Catarina caused Apoyo's water to slosh back and forth like a teapot and wrecked a few homes—for the most part the volcano is considered dormant, and a thick green forest has grown up the slopes over the years. These slopes harbor a few hiking trails and are protected from further development by law. The crater

LA LAGUNA DE MASAYA

The peaceful waters of the Laguna de Masaya belie the violent origin of the lake. Long before the first Chorotegas settled in 20 small villages around its perimeter, the lake was one of Volcán Masaya's gaping craters, choked off long ago by shifting channels of magma beneath the surface of the earth and abandoned to slowly fill up with rainwater. These days, the most impressive views of Laguna de Masaya are from the 100-meter-high vantage points of the *malecón* in the city of Masaya, or from the res-taurants that line Carretera Masaya, just west of the city. It's one of Nicaragua's bigger crater lakes: 8.5 square kilometers set at the foot of Volcán Masaya and 73 meters deep in the center. It's also one of the country's most polluted with sewage and trash. While several trails, some of which were made by the Chorotegas themselves, lead the intrepid hiker down to the water's edge, this is no swimming hole. Dip your heels in nearby Laguna de Apoyo instead.

hosts a few fish species found nowhere else on earth; scientists at the Proyecto Ecologico are studying them. If you hike through the forests, expect to observe species of toucan, humming-birds, blue jays, howler and white-face monkeys (which are prone to fling their feces at you if you approach), and rare butterflies. You will find very few places on earth quite like this charming, isolated community.

Accommodations and Food

The number of places to eat or lodge along the western shore of the crater lake is slowly increasing and diversifying, despite local grumbling about illegal development of the waterfront. At any establishment of those listed, expect to pay $4–10 to stay for the day and enjoy the docks, inner tubes, hammocks, and other facilities. The area has no stores or shops and few services, so either pack your essentials before coming, or count on one of the local hotels or restaurants. Most hotels offer cheap shuttles from Granada, or you can hire a taxi or take a bus.

The **Monkey Hut** (100 m north of the tri-angle, tel. 505/8887-3546, info@themonkey-hut.net, www.monkeyhut.net, $12 dorm, $25 d with shared bath and fan, $50 cabañas) is a well-liked retreat on a beautiful and terraced piece of land at the water's edge, with a small selec-tion of rooms and a fully equipped kitchen. Soft drinks, water, wine, and beer can be purchased at the hut; all other supplies need to be packed in. Next door, **Hostal Paradiso** (no phone, www.paradisolaguna.com, $10 pp dorm, $25–32 private room) is also geared toward budget travelers, offering terraced patios, waterside bar, floating dock, and free kayak use for guests. Use the open kitchen or opt for meals at the restau-rant. There is Wi-Fi, and local crafts are for sale. Arrange transport here through the Oasis Hostel in Granada ($10 return).

The **Proyecto Ecologico Spanish School and Hostel** (tel. 505/8882-3992, www.gaiani-caragua.org, $11 pp shared dorm, $21 d with fan and shared bath, breakfast included), a non-profit research station and Spanish school, is one of the oldest operations in the crater. They organize bird-watching, hikes, scuba div-ing expeditions ($60 for two tanks), and the chance to participate in a volunteer reforesta-tion brigade; all-inclusive Spanish school pack-ages start at $220 per week. There is nowhere better to speak with knowledgeable ecologists who can help interpret this unique region. The home-cooked meals ($5) are recommended.

At "Grandma's" **Posada Ecologica La Abuela** (tel. 505/8880-0368, info@posadae-cologicalaabuela.com, $70 d includes break-fast) you'll find a series of wooden docks, rocker swings for splashing around in the water, and

MASAYA

great views. The wooden *cabañas* are very comfortable and well appointed, with air-conditioning, private bath, nice mattresses; there are also great facilities for groups.

Neither hostel nor hotel, **Guest House La Orquidea** (tel. 505/8872-1866, www.laorquideanicaragua.com) is a stylish two-bedroom house, fully equipped for a relaxing stay; features include a gorgeous balcony, boats, and water toys. Rates run $120 a night for 4–7 guests and a healthy breakfast is provided; there is also a separate room for $40.

On the opposite end of the road, ◖ **San Simian Eco-Resort** (tel. 505/8850-8101, sansimianlodge@gmail.com, www.sansimian.com, $45–55 includes large breakfast) is a lovely waterside group of five private bungalows, each of which has a slightly different theme built from natural materials like thatch and bamboo. The tasteful, rustic rooms have bamboo beds with comfy mattresses, mosquito nets, fans, and fun outdoor showers and gardens. Amenities include great on-site meals, a bar, and a relaxing dock with water toys. Nearby trailheads lead up into the jungle and along the shore.

New management has taken over **Norome Resort and Villas** (tel. 505/2552-8200, U.S. or Canada tel. 760/494-7331, www.thevillasatapoyo.com, $88–190) and is bringing the property's 66 Caribbean-style villas back to glory. Apartments and suites (1–3 bedrooms) have hot water, bathtubs, air-conditioning, TV/DVD, and kitchenettes. The restaurant ($6–12) and bar perched over the water are stunning; Wi-Fi

is available. Relax by the lakeshore and swimming pools, book a massage, or go boating, biking, and hiking. Day-trippers are welcome with a $5 minimum purchase at the restaurant.

Getting There

Laguna de Apoyo is about a 20-minute ride from either Masaya or Granada, and about an hour from the airport in Managua. There are two paved roads that go up and over the crater lip and down to the water's edge; one originates on Carretera Masaya, at a spot called *el puentecito;* the other branches off the Masaya–Catarina road. They join just before passing through the village of Valle de Laguna, where you'll turn right at the T, then make a quick left to begin your descent (pay a $1 entrance fee if driving). The road winds downward until the paved section ends exactly at the gate to former president Alemén's vacation home.

Regular backpacker shuttles leave Hostel Oasis and the Bearded Monkey in Granada, charging about $10 return. Or share a taxi from Granada or Masaya for about $20. Public buses headed for *bajo al plan* (i.e., lakefront) cost under $1 and leave the main Masaya market terminal at 10:30 A.M. and 3:10 P.M.; or you can hop one of the hourly buses for Valle de Laguna, then walk (30 minutes downhill) or wait for a stray taxi. Mototaxis run between the *puentecito* and Valle de Laguna. Three public buses can get you back up the hill, leaving at 6 A.M., 11:10 A.M., and 4:40 P.M. (3 P.M. on Sunday is the last bus).

The Pueblos Blancos and Carazo

Escaping the heat of Managua or Granada is as easy as a 40-minute bus ride to the Pueblos Blancos and Carazo, two regions that occupy a breezy 500-meter-high *meseta* south of Managua and are thus far cooler and more relaxing. The Pueblos Blancos, or White Villages, are named for the purity of color of their churches (some of which, naturally, are now other colors). They are separated to the north by the Sierras de Managua, to the east by the slopes of Volcán Masaya, to the south by the Laguna de Apoyo and Volcán Mombacho, and to the west by the dry, desolate decline toward the Pacific Ocean. Each town is well known for something particular—bamboo craftwork, wicker chairs, black magic, folk dances, Sandino's birthplace, crater lakes, beaches, or interesting festivals. Visiting the pueblos is an easy day trip best appreciated if you have a car, which permits you to tour furniture workshops, coffee plantations, or outdoor plant nurseries.

In nearby Carazo, the January celebration of San Sebastián is a dramatic and colorful festival not to be missed. Diriamba is home to Nicaragua's national soccer team, but baseball is given equal attention; games are exciting and fun. This is also the gateway to several Pacific beaches quieter than their more developed neighbors.

ORIENTATION

Renting a car or taxi is the best way to visit the Pueblos, but you can get around almost as easily with the *expreso* minivan system. No more than 10 or 12 kilometers separate any two towns, all of which are easily accessible from Masaya, Granada, and Managua. Buses to the Pueblos Blancos leave from Huembes, continue south on the Carretera Masaya, and then turn west into the hills at various points, depending on the route. The Carazo buses—to Jinotepe and Diriamba—travel via Carretera Sur and leave from the Mercado Israel Lewites and from a lot across from the UCA.

◖ CATARINA MIRADOR

This hillside pueblo clings to the verdant lip of the spectacular Laguna de Apoyo crater lake. The Mirador is a blustery cliffside walkway and restaurant complex at the edge of the crater with one of the best panoramic views in Nicaragua—look for the distant red-tiled roofs and cathedral spires of Granada, broad Lake Cocibolca behind, and on a clear day, the twin volcanic peaks of Ometepe. Roaming marimba and guitar players will serenade you for a small fee (negotiate before they begin playing). Locals visit Catarina for its ornamental plant nurseries and the wares of local artisans and basket makers whose shops begin at roadside. Vehicles pay $1 each to enter the Mirador.

The fancy hotel in town is **Hotel Casa Catarina** (tel. 505/2558-0227, hotelcasacatarina@hotmail.com, www.hotelcasacatarina.com, $45–75 including breakfast), a modern and well-liked three-star hotel with 15 clean rooms set over four floors. The on-site bar and restaurant serves simple dishes as well as pizza. More popular with travelers is the ◖ **Hotel Cabañas** (150 m west of the Rotonda Catarina, tel. 505/2558-0484, $30–35), offering six simple cabins (sleeping up to four people) equipped with a/c, Wi-Fi and cable TV, and set in an unruly green garden. Meals are available upon request.

The eateries overlooking the lagoon serve similar plates of *fritanga* fare ($5), but none stand out from the rest. The best meals in the area are served on the road to Catarina at ◖ **Mi Viejo Ranchito** (Km 39.5 Carretera Masaya–Catarina, tel. 505/2558-0473, $4–15). Set in a green park that encompasses not only the restaurant, but also a pretty crafts market and a thicket of shade-providing trees, this family-friendly

MASAYA

MASAYA

© AMBER DOBRZENSKY

The Pueblos Blancos are known for fine bamboo craftsmanship.

spot dishes out upscale *comida típica* such as *vigorón* and *indio viejo,* as well as fantastic *quesillos* made with artisanal cheese. Try the lasagna *campesina,* made with refried beans, shredded chicken, fresh cream, string cheese, and tortilla; wash it down with some tropical juice.

Plant Nurseries

The road to Catarina hosts a plethora of plant nurseries which are half garden, half jungle, and a great place to learn about tropical flora. The **Ecovivero La Gallina** (tel. 505/8872-7181) is a botanist's heaven. Passionate owner José Ruiz knows virtually every leaf on the property, and is happy to give tours ($5 per person) of the eight manzanas, or to arrange one in advance with an English-speaking guide. The nursery is home to numerous birds, monkeys, more than 20 types of orchids, and a seemingly endless number of rare tropical plants—the pink-colored cacao here doesn't appear in any field guide in the world!

SAN JUAN DE ORIENTE

San Juan potters craft attractive ceramic vases, pots, plates, and more, in both a proud celebration of pre-Columbian styles and modern inspirations. Shop at one of the small cooperatives along the entrance to town, or in the many tiny displays in people's homes as you walk through the narrow streets. Many artisans are glad to invite you back into their workshops for a tour.

Opened with the aid of several nonprofit agencies, the **Centro de Visitantes** (one block north and one block east of the bus stop, tel. 505/2558-0456, 8 A.M.–5 P.M. Mon.–Sat., $0.75) for the Apoyo Lagoon offers tourists some information on the area. The center provides a geological analysis of the lagoon and crater, information on the local flora and fauna, a ceramics exhibition, and background on local folklore; it's well worth a look. The center can also help arrange hikes and visits to private farms in the area. The attached **Cafetín La Estación** sells decent cups of joe as well as snacks.

DIRIÁ AND DIRIOMO

Named for the indigenous Dirian people and their leader, Diriangén (the famed rebel cacique and martyr whose spilled blood at the hands of the conquistadores is immortalized in Carlos Mejía Godoy's anthem, "Nicaragua Nicaragüita"), Diriá and Diriomo face each other on both sides of the highway. Both towns are well loved for their unique celebrations throughout the year, mixing elements of pre-Columbian, Catholic, and bizarre regional traditions (like the "dicking" festival in which participants smack each other with dried-out bull penises, sometimes practiced in San Juan de Oriente as well). Diriá, on the east, has a *mirador* smaller and less frequented than the more famous one at Catarina, as well as additional trails down to the Laguna de Apoyo. Across the highway, Diriomo is renowned for its sorcery: The intrepid traveler looking for a love potion or revenge should seek out one of the pueblo's *brujos* (or at least read the book *Sofía de los Presagios*).

NIQUINOHOMO

"The valley of the warriors," in Nahuatl, produced a famous warrior indeed: Augusto César Sandino, born there at the turn of the 20th century. Sandino's childhood home off the northwest corner of the park has been restored as a library and museum. A 4,000-pound, solid bronze statue of the man, with the famous hat and bandolier of bullets around his waist, stands at attention at the east side of town. Niquinohomo's 320-year-old church is also worth a look.

MASATEPE

Masatepe (Nahuatl for "place of the deer") is a quiet pueblo of about 12,000 that explodes in revelry the first Sunday of every June during its famous **Hípica** (horse parade). Stick around after the festivities for a steaming bowl of Masatepe's culinary claim to fame—*sopa de mondongo* (cow tripe soup), served hot in front of the town's gorgeous, architecturally unique church. The Hípica is just one part of the *fiestas patronales* in honor of La Santísima Trinidad, the black Christ icon a Chorotegan found in the trunk of a tree during the years of the Spanish colony. Find other meals in the Bar Sarapao or Eskimo shop on the north side of the park.

Outside of the city, both sides of the highway are lined with the workshops of the extraordinarily talented Masatepe carpenters, whose gorgeous, handcrafted hardwood and rattan furniture is prized throughout the country. You'll wish you could fit more of it in your luggage (a set of chairs and a coffee table go for about $100), but console yourself instead with a comfortable, old-fashioned hardwood rocking chair. They'll disassemble and pack it down to airline-acceptable size for you for a small fee.

If driving to Masatepe from the south, save time for a meal at **Mi Teruño Masatepino** (on the east side of the road, just north of the turnoff for Pio XII and Nandasmo), a delicious open-air restaurant featuring Nicaragua's traditional country cuisine.

SAN MARCOS

San Marcos is sort of the hub of the Pueblos Blancos and hosts Nicaragua's best (and most expensive) university, the **Ave Maria College of the Americas** (three blocks south of the park, www.avemaria.edu.ni), a Catholic, bilingual, four-year liberal arts university with about 400 students and a sister campus in Ann Arbor, Michigan. Before 1998, its modern facilities belonged to the University of Mobile (Alabama). Ave Maria is one of the beneficiaries of Catholic conservative and Domino Pizza founder Thomas Monaghan. Not much to see here other than the church and town square, both of which are lovely. There's one very nice hotel: **Hotel Casablanca** (two blocks east of the church's southeast corner, tel. 505/2535-2717, $46–55, $10 extra for a/c), with Wi-Fi, hot water, breakfast included. There are several small restaurants; **La Casona** (near the park) is particularly recommended for its food and pleasant owner.

MARIPOSA ECOHOTEL AND SPANISH SCHOOL

Tucked into the forest off the road to the village of San Juan de la Concepción (a.k.a. La Concha, 12 kilometers west of Ticuantepe, under an hour from Managua), this unique hideaway has spurred a stream of rave reviews from readers. Mariposa Ecohotel and Spanish School (tel. 505/8869-9945, www.spanish-schoolnica.com) uses part of its revenue to fund a range of grassroots environmental and community projects. Guests are invited to help with the projects, from reforestation and raising chickens to literacy, education, and animal rescue. The hotel and rooms have excellent views of Volcán Masaya, use solar and wind power, and there is an organic farm with coffee, bananas, free-range eggs, and lots of fruit. Meals are typical Nicaraguan breakfast, buffet-style lunch (salads, meat, and vegetarian), and family-style dinner. The rooms are decorated with local handicrafts, each with their own bathroom and fan. There is a fully stocked library, quality one-on-one Spanish school, and the manager, Paulette Goudge, PhD, offers a three-month course in the "Politics of Development." This is a great place for families. There are volunteer and homestay opportunities as well. Rooms are $25 per night including breakfast, or look into their all-inclusive Spanish school packages ($300 a week in low season).

JINOTEPE AND DIRIAMBA (CARAZO)

Jinotepe

Jinotepe (Xilotepetl, or "field of baby corn") is a sometimes-sleepy, sometimes-bustling villa of 27,000 set around **La Iglesia Parroquial de Santiago** (built in 1860) and a lively park shaded by the canopy of several immense hardwood trees. Thanks to a branch of UNAN, Jinotepe's student population keeps things youthful and lively, and its outdoor market is fun. Don't miss the beautiful two-block-long mural on the nursing school (three blocks west of the park's northwest corner) and the towering statue of Pope John Paul II in front of the church. While you're there, enjoy an icy, chocolaty *cacao con leche* in the kiosk under the shade trees of one of Nicaragua's shadiest parks.

ACCOMMODATIONS

The **Hotel Casa Mateo** (one block north of the park and two blocks west, tel. 505/2532-3284, $50–85) has 40 rooms with TV, private bath, hot water, and fan; there's also laundry service, a guard for your car, a restaurant (Jardín de los Olivos), conference room, and Wi-Fi. This is a nonprofit hotel run by Glenn and Lynne Schweitzer, pastors and missionaries from Maryland, to help fund Quinta Esperanza, a home for abused and orphaned children,

preschool, and vocational center. They offer special group rates ($15–20 pp).

The town's only backpacker accommodation is the **Basecamp Hostel** (from Banpro one block west, 1.5 blocks south, tel. 505/8336-9755, www.basecamphostels.com, dorms $10, privates from $25), offering spotless new dorms and private rooms all with shared bathrooms; ask for the private room upstairs, where the connecting terrace offers sunshine, fresh air, and roof-top views. The living room, outdoor patio, and large communal kitchen are standard hostel fare; Internet and laundry services are provided. Staff can give you tips or help arrange exploration of the area.

FOOD

There are dozens of small, decent eateries, but Managua expats actually drive here to enjoy ◖ **Layha Bistro and Lounge Bar** (from Banpro, three blocks south, one block east and half a block north, tel. 505/2532-2440, Tues.–Sun., $5–15). At Layha's, you must ring the doorbell before being ushered through the front door and into a series of living rooms filled with quirky objects and set for a dinner party. A beautifully presented menu of fusion flavors includes avocado spring rolls, local roast lamb, and coconut curried shrimp. Weekend reservations are recommended.

Pizzería Coliseo (one block north of Bancentro, tel. 505/2532-2150 or 505/2532-2646, 12:30–9 P.M. Tues.–Sun., $6), a legitimate Italian restaurant run by Rome *originario* Fausto, has been preparing delicious pizzas and pasta in Jinotepe for more than 20 years. For simpler dining, **Terry's Diner** (opposite the BAC bank on the main square, 7 A.M.–6 P.M. daily, $3–5) specializes in all-day breakfasts, including waffles, pancakes and a wealth of egg dishes; or you can get your diner fix with decent burgers and shakes. The outdoor seating overlooks the central park and main square—perfect for soaking up the local scene.

Masks and costumes are an essential part of the Saint Sebastián celebrations.

Diriamba

Diriamba's **Festival of San Sebastian** in the third week of January is an annual religious, theatrical, folkloric celebration uninterrupted since colonial days. Featuring both pagan and Catholic elements, it is without rival in western Nicaragua, comparable perhaps only to Bluefields' Palo de Mayo.

Visit the **Museo Ecológico de Tropico Seco** (tel. 505/2422-2129, Mon.–Fri.) for background on much of the region's unique dry tropical ecosystem. The MARENA office here ministers some of the local turtle-nesting refuges.

Hospedaje Diriangén (one block east, half block south of the Shell Station, tel. 505/2534-2428, $7 pp with private bath and fan) is clean enough and safe.

Outside of town on the road to Managua, the ◖ **Eco Lodge El Jardín Tortuga Verde** (tel. 505/2534-2948 or 505/8905-5313, rorappal@turbonett.com.ni, www.ecolodgecarazo.com, $25–45) is Carazo's self-proclaimed "ecolodge." Based just off the highway, the dense greenery of vegetation here provides a decent buffer from the sound of passing freight trucks. Accommodations are set within the Tortuga Verde (green turtle) gardens and nursery, which are quirkily dotted with unusual sculptures. Rustic wooden cabins (from $25) are equipped with fan, Wi-Fi and cable TV—not quite "eco," but comforting and useful. The chained monkey in the garden also dampens the "eco" cred, but as the owner explains, it was rescued from animal dealers and would be poached (and dangerous to humans) if set free.

Getting There

Sleek, comfortable *interlocal* minibuses leave for both Jinotepe and Carazo from the UCA in Managua until 10 P.M. and much slower *rutas* leave from Terminal Israel Lewites.

From Jinotepe, buses leave from the COOTRAUS terminal—a dirt lot along the Pan-American Highway directly north of the park—at all hours for Managua, Masaya, Nandaime, and Rivas. Microbuses to Managua leave from the unofficial Sapasmapa terminal on the south side of the Instituto Alejandro, 4:45 A.M.–7:30 P.M. ($1). Your most comfortable choice is one of the *interlocales* to Diriamba and San Marcos queued up on the street in front of the Super Santiago—only the front one will load passengers, departing when the van is full.

From Diriamba, a fleet of *interlocales* run to and from Jinotepe for about $0.25, 6 A.M.–9 P.M. daily from a spot right next to the clock tower.

Walk east and take your first left to find microbus *expresos* to Managua's Mercado Israel Lewites and the UCA for $1, 5 A.M.–7 P.M. A little farther east at the first *caseta* (booth) on the left, you can ask about all the buses that pass from Jinotepe (Managua: 4:30 A.M.–6 P.M.; Masaya: 5 A.M.–6 P.M.).

MASAYA

THE FESTIVAL OF SAINT SEBASTIÁN

Every pueblo's *fiestas patronales* have something that make them unique, but Diriamba's celebration of the Holy Martyr San Sebastián stands above the rest as Nicaragua's most authentic connection to its indigenous roots. Many of the dances, songs, and costumes are true to traditions that predate the arrival of the Spanish by hundreds of years. But this is no nostalgia act—indeed, the integration of pre-Columbian ritual with Catholicism and the telling of modern history is as fascinating as the colors, costumes, and music.

This celebration is actually three fiestas for the price of one, since icons of San Santiago of Jinotepe, San Marcos of San Marcos, and San Sebastián of Diriamba have been observed together since the three of them first traveled from Spain, landing at nearby Casares beach. The icons are still believed to have the special bond they formed during their journey, and they get together to celebrate this three times a year during the fiesta of each of their towns. Santiago and Marcos meet up at the *tope* (end of the road) in Dolores on (or around) January 19, where they are danced around the village to a bombardment of cheers and homemade fireworks. The next day they reunite with their pal, Sebastián, in Diriamba, where the town has been partying for four days in preparation.

The following day is the peak of activities, the actual **Día del Santo,** marked by special masses and sometimes groups of tourists who come to view the long, raucous procession, famous for its theatrical dances and costumes. The following are the most important acts:

The Dance of Toro Huaco is of indigenous ancestry and features peacock feather hats and a multigeneration snake dance, with the youngest children bringing up the rear and an old man with a special tambourine and whistle up front. **El Güegüense,** also called the **Macho Ratón,** is recognizable for its masks and costumes depicting burdened-down donkeys and the faces of Spanish conquistadores. The Güegüense (from the old word *güegüe,* which means something like grumpy old man) is a hard-handed social satire with cleverly vulgar undertones that depicts the indigenous peoples' first impression of the Spanish—it has been called the oldest comedy act on the continent. **El Gigante** is a dance that depicts the biblical story of David and Goliath, and **La Danza de las Inditas** is a group act, recognizable by the white cotton costumes and the sound of the marimba. Most of the dancers are carrying out a family tradition that has been kept for dozens of generations, and each usually has a grandma-led support team on the sidelines to make sure their costumes and performances are kept in order.

A true believer will tell you that Diriamba's fiesta begins not on January 19, but on February 2 of the previous year, when the official *fiesteros* apply for roles in the upcoming celebration; they then begin more than 11 months of preparation, all of which is seen as a display of faith and thanks to their beloved San Sebastián. Those that don't show their devotion by dancing or playing music do so by carrying the icons or fulfilling promises to walk a certain number of blocks on their knees, sometimes until bloody.

Leave plenty of room on your camera's memory card, and be sure to try the official beverage of the festival: *chicha con genibre,* a ginger-tinted, slightly fermented cornmeal drink. Most of the masks and costumes in the productions are also for sale, as are homemade action figures depicting the various dance characters.

CENTRO ECOTURÍSTICO LA MÁQUINA

This is one of the "private wild reserves" protected by MARENA and managed by the landowners; La Máquina (sunrise–sunset Tues.–Sun., $1) remains almost completely unvisited by tourists. The views from the waterfall are gorgeous and the area is great for hiking and camping. There is a cheap food stand and a shallow bathing area; short hiking trails lead through the forest. La Máquina is located halfway (15 minutes) between Diriamba and the ocean, around Km 58. Buses pass the entrance all day long in both directions.

© AMBER DOBRZENSKY

The beaches of Carazo are still clustered around small fishing villages.

CARAZO BEACHES

La Boquita and Casares are 35 kilometers due west of Diriamba. The road ends at the coast where you'll turn right to reach humble, run-down **La Boquita** tourist center (you'll pay a small admission fee to enter). Left takes you to **Casares,** a fishing village to the south. These beaches attract mostly Nicaraguan families on picnics and outings and the odd foreigner in search of fresh fish dishes. On a big swell, the surf can be up at both places, and you'll likely be the only gringo in the lineup (rental boards sometimes available). Note that this area—particularly La Boquita—is probably best avoided during Semana Santa and New Year's Day when they are overrun by drunken mobs.

Rent some shade under one of the *ranchos,* where you can order drinks, food, and wandering musicians. The area is more accustomed to day-trippers, so there's not a lot of accommodations. Try **Hotel y Restaurante Suleyka** (tel. 505/2532-8161, from $15 with fan, from $25 per person with

a/c) right on the beach, where the nicer rooms have air conditioning and private bathrooms; the large room ($80) can sleep a family of 10, with bunk beds. Otherwise at La Boquita, there are a handful of interchangeable *hospedajes* with basic (occasionally filthy) rooms for under $15.

Just down the coast, the beach at Casares is uncomfortably short on shade—but it's also short on crowds, has a decent hotel if you choose to stay, and features a long, wide beach great for watching the fishing boats coming in and out. **Hotel el Casino de Casares** (on the beachfront, tel. 505/2532-8002, www.nicaraguabeachhotel.com, $25 d with fan, $35 with a/c) has 12 tidy rooms on the second floor of a modern beach mansion; ask for beachfront rooms with better views. The restaurant below looks straight out at the anglers hauling in the day's catch, which makes up the bulk of the menu. Trips with local anglers, as well as excursions to all local sights, can be arranged.

On the drive between La Boquita and Casares,

seek out **El Pozo del Padre,** a self-contained rocky bathtub that's loads of fun at high tide.

Public transportation leaves from the main market on the highway east of the clock tower. Express microbuses leave every 20 minutes for the 40-minute, $0.75 ride to La Boquita 6:20 A.M.–6 P.M. Regular buses take 90 minutes and leave between 6:40 A.M. and 6:30 P.M. From the beach at La Boquita the first bus leaves at 5 A.M., the last one at 6 P.M.

LA ISLA DE OMETEPE AND RIVAS

South of Managua, the land crumples into high cloudy ridges and the windblown peak of Las Nubes (934 meters), then falls off slowly until it spills into southwestern Nicaragua's plains. Here Lake Cocibolca presses the land into a narrow belt that barely separates the lake from the Pacific Ocean. In fact, geological evidence suggests that at one point it didn't separate them at all, and Lake Cocibolca once flowed across this slim margin of land to the west, draining into the Pacific near the fishing community of Brito rather than down the Río San Juan into the Atlantic Ocean, as it does today.

The isthmus of Rivas is replete with history. Although known as the land of Nicarao, the area was first inhabited by the Kiribisis tribe, whom the more powerful Chorotegas pushed aside. The Nicaraos came afterward, and by the time the Spanish "discovered" the region, had been residents here for at least seven generations. Rivas, a languorous colonial town of traders and farmers, watched hundreds of thousands of passengers traveling between New York and California pass through its streets in horse-drawn carts between San Jorge and San Juan del Sur; this was the only dry-land crossing of the entire gold rush journey. At about the same time, one of filibuster William Walker's first military defeats took place here.

These days, Rivas draws less attention than the coastal community of San Juan del Sur or La Isla de Ometepe, but retains a colonial

HIGHLIGHTS

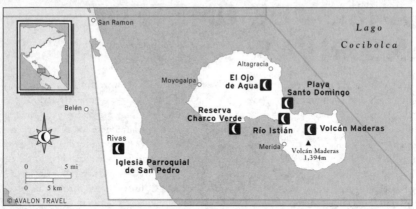

© AVALON TRAVEL

LOOK FOR 🌙 TO FIND RECOMMENDED SIGHTS, ACTIVITIES, DINING, AND LODGING.

🌙 **Reserva Charco Verde:** Verdant and cool, this lovely little ecosystem with a sandy lakeshore beach in the shadows of tall trees is, in a word, gorgeous (page 116).

🌙 **El Ojo de Agua:** The only place you can swim other than in the lake, the waters of El Ojo de Agua are crystal clear from the mountains, and bracing. Enjoy a languid afternoon in a garden setting (page 119).

🌙 **Playa Santo Domingo:** This sweeping crescent of black sand is nestled on the "bridge" between the two volcanoes (page 119).

🌙 **Río Istián:** Paddling a kayak through these still waters early in the morning or during sunset is breathtaking (page 120).

🌙 **Volcán Maderas:** Even casual hikers will find plenty to do here: dip into hot springs, enjoy the beach, tour coffee farms, or visit ancient petroglyphs (page 120).

🌙 **Iglesia Parroquial de San Pedro:** Rivas's historic church witnessed the entire gold rush of the 19th century, and emerged unscathed. (page 127).

charm appreciated by many. Still, it's hard to compete with La Isla de Ometepe for attention. The magnificent twin-peaked Ometepe rises like a crown from the center of Lake Cocibolca. An intensely volcanic island steeped in tradition and mystery, Ometepe was the ancestral home of the Nahuatl people, and today is an alluring destination for travelers, with its sandy beaches, swimming holes, hiking trails, and of course, two breathtaking volcanoes: one hot, one cold (the former remains quite active).

Southwestern Nicaragua does not suffer the same intense, grinding heat prevalent in the drier lands of the north and west. It rains more in the south, and the rivers flow nearly year-round. The volcanic soils on Lake Cocibolca's western shore are rich and productive. Cattle graze lazily in immense, lucrative ranches and sugarcane fields drape the valleys south of the foot of Mombacho, one of Nicaragua's most picturesque peaks.

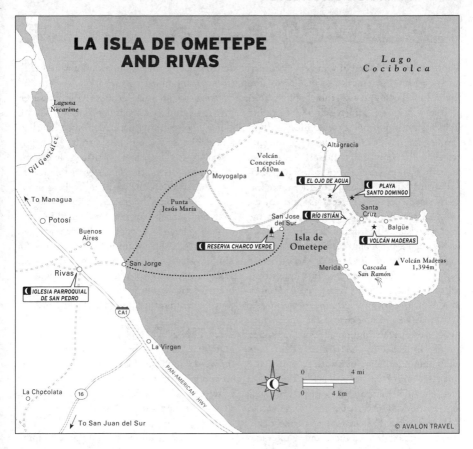

PLANNING YOUR TIME

You will probably visit Rivas on the way to and from San Juan del Sur; half a day is acceptable to walk around the historical sites, appreciate the cathedral, and perhaps take in a museum. Travelers with a more leisurely schedule can easily spend another half day enjoying the lakeshore in San Jorge before continuing to Ometepe.

La Isla de Ometepe should not be missed on any but the shortest trips to Nicaragua, offering in a nutshell a little of everything Nicaragua has to offer, from history to waterfalls, volcanic trekking, and

horseback riding, all in an environment travelers routinely rave about as relaxing and delightful. You could feasibly travel to and from the island in a single day, but such a short trip would be folly. Rather, allow at least two days and two nights (and an extra day and night if you'd like to hike a volcano, which is a full day activity in itself).

Note that travel in this region requires careful coordination of transport, as you can easily lose up to a half day waiting for boats and buses. Traveling around Ometepe is never easy; local transport is slow and erratic (especially on Sunday) and renting vehicles can be expensive.

La Isla de Ometepe

The twin-peaked island of Ometepe (Nahuatl for "two hills") is remarkably insulated from the rest of the country by the choppy waters of Lake Cocibolca. Ometepe's 38,000 proud residents live a mostly agrarian lifestyle, harvesting plantains, rice, tobacco, sorghum, sugarcane, corn, honey, and coffee on the slopes of the twin Cenozoic volcanoes. The two principal towns, Moyogalpa and Altagracia, are formerly sleepy commercial centers, port towns, and transportation hubs enjoying an upswing in ecotourism and accommodation.

Nicaragua's pre-Columbian history may have begun on and around Ometepe. According to legend, the Nahuatl people in modern-day Mexico fled the stronger Aztecs, guided southward by a vision of two volcanoes in the middle of a broad lake. Long before the Spanish arrived, the islanders considered Ometepe sacred ground, inhabited by gods of great power; even today the island remains awash in myths and legends, some of which date back to the days of the Nahuatl. Today's islanders prefer their home to what they call "over there." In 1957, as Volcán Concepción rumbled and threatened to erupt, the government ordered the islanders to evacuate Ometepe; they flatly refused, preferring to die on their island than live anywhere else.

At night, the slopes of the volcanoes echo with the deep roar of howler monkeys, and by day the air is filled with the sharp cry of the thousands of parakeets and *hurracas* (bright blue jays that scold you from the treetops). Ecologically, the island of Ometepe has been called the edge of the tropics, as a dividing line between tropical and dry falls right between the two volcanoes: Volcán Maderas is an extinct volcano whose crater is filled with a shallow lagoon and whose slopes are carpeted with more tropical and humid species, including actual cloud forest at the top. Concepción is an active volcano whose slopes are covered with tropical dry forest species like *guacimo* and *guanacaste*. Underneath the greenery, however, is fire. Beginning December 8, 1880, Volcán Concepción erupted with such force that lava and smoke flowed out of the crater for nearly a year. It was this eruption that created some of its more distinctive features visible today, like the Lava de Urbaite, Peña Bruja (a broad cliff visible from Altagracia), and Peña de San Marcos. Concepción erupted again in 1883, launching large rocks from the crater, and again in 1889 and 1902, ruining crops in Rivas. In 2005, Volcán Concepción rumbled, fumed, and ejected tons of volcanic ash, smoke, and debris in spectacular, frightening eruptions. There were also mini-eruptions in 2007 and 2009.

GETTING THERE

Note that Lake Cocibolca can get rough when the wind is high, at which times the larger boats are more comfortable. Avoid the roughest seas by traveling early morning and late evening, and sit near the center of the ship where the rocking is slightest. Don't worry—when you pull into port, the men climbing the rails and jumping aboard are not pirates, they are taxi drivers in San Jorge or bag porters in Moyogalpa.

The construction of a runway began in 2011, amidst concerns of Ometepe's residents that the island is as yet ill-equipped to deal with larger volumes of tourists. Set to open in late 2013, the Ometepe airport plans to receive flights from Managua as well as Costa Rica, opening the door to an ever-increasing number of visitors. Check online (www.visitaometepe.com) for current news regarding flights.

By Boat from San Jorge

Boats from San Jorge on the mainland sail to Moyogalpa daily. Thankfully, a few new safer

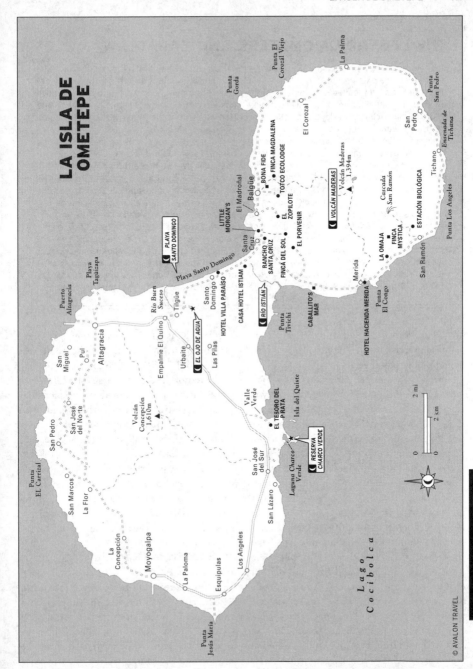

LA ISLA DE OMETEPE

© AVALON TRAVEL

THE LEGEND OF OMETEPE AND ZAPATERA

It is said that long ago, neither Lake Cocibolca nor the islands existed. In their place was a broad green valley called Caopol, inhabited by animals that lived in thick forest. Not a single human lived in the forested valley, but the Chorotega, Chontales, Nagrandan, and Niquirano tribes all inhabited the edges of the valley, where they fought battles between tribes.

In the Niquirano tribe there was a lovely Indian maiden by the name of Ometepetl, who caught the eye of the young Nagrandan warrior named Nagrando. He fell deeply in love with her, and she with him. Their love remained a secret because the Niquiranos and Nagrandans were sworn enemies. The day Ometepetl's father learned of the illicit romance, he grew furious and swore he would chase Nagrando to his death rather than see his daughter marry a Nagrandan. Ometepetl and Nagrando fled to the valley, where they hid in the forest to escape the fury of Ometepetl's father. There they decided the only way they'd ever be able to have peace would be to die together. Ometepetl and Nagrando slit their wrists with a sharp blade and died in each others' arms.

Ometeptl, as death overcame her, leaned backwards, and her breasts swelled. The sadness that overwhelmed the valley caused the sky to darken and an intense rain to fall. The valley began to flood, and her breasts became the twin peaks of Concepción and Maderas. Nagrando grew into an island as well, the volcanic island of Zapatera, located halfway between the lands of the Nagrandan people and his love Ometepetl. Ometepetl's father and the men who accompanied him in the search to kill Nagrando all perished in the flood. They became the Isletas de Granada and the Solentiname archipelago.

boats have joined the old, junky fleet. They compete to transport the island's plantain crop in addition to passengers.

The *Ferry Ometepe,* a big steel boat with radar and life jackets and from whose roof you can travel in the fresh air, is one of the better old ships. A newer, larger, cheaper, and faster option than the old junk ferries is *El Che Guevara* (departure from San Jorge to Moyogalpa 7 A.M. and 4 P.M.; departure from Moyogalpa to San Jorge 8:30 A.M. and 5:30 P.M.). *El Che* charges $16.50 to bring a small pickup truck; motorbikes cost less than $3.

Rey de Cocibolca, a 1,300-passenger, four-story boat built in the Netherlands, now plies the waters of Lake Nicaragua between San Jorge on the mainland and San Jose del Sur on Ometepe, a little town soon to become a big town thanks to the traffic. A one-way trip costs $2.50, any deck. This boat departs from San Jose del Sur to the mainland at 7:30 A.M. and 3:20 P.M.; from San Jorge to the island at 9:30 A.M. and 5:00 P.M. Bringing your vehicle

costs less than $14 and the driver goes for free. For more information on the boat schedule, call tel. 505/8691-3669 or 505/8833-4773.

The rest of the old San Jorge fleet ride lower to the water and thus provide a bumpier ride. These boats are independently owned, and unfortunately, rarely give honest information about the others; so if you're told, "The next boat doesn't leave for four hours," keep asking. Each company posts a sign with its own schedule; there is no main sign listing all the different times. **Volcano Lake Tours** (office near the port, tel. 505/8827-7714) will give you reliable information about the schedule.

By Boat from Granada and San Carlos

The **Empresa Portuario de Nicaragua (EPN)** ferry leaves Granada on Mondays and Thursdays at 3 P.M., arriving in Altagracia between 5 P.M. and 7 P.M. The ship then continues onward to San Miguelito on the southeastern lakeshore, arriving in San Carlos

© AMBER DOBRZENSKY

Volcán Concepción is a mile high and very active.

around dawn. You can usually stay on the boat until the Río San Juan boats begin operating at 6 or 7 A.M. (instead of having to get a room). An upper-deck ticket costs a couple dollars more and earns you more room to hang a hammock.

On the return trip, the ferry leaves San Carlos on Tuesdays and Fridays at 2 P.M., passes Altagracia at 11 P.M., and arrives in Granada at sunrise. The price for a one-way passage between Granada and Ometepe is $3, but when seas are high, the ship will skip Ometepe altogether, preferring to hold tight to the lee shore of the lake.

GETTING AROUND

Getting around the island is difficult, no matter how you slice it. You can take a slow, rickety, and infrequent bus on the worst roads you've ever seen for under a buck, or you can shell out $25–40 for a taxi or microbus to take you to the sites. You can also rent a motorcycle or scooter, but aside from a few motor-rickshaws or scoring a ride by hitchhiking, there's not

much in between. Once you've accommodated your stuff at your hotel, biking can be an enjoyable, cheap, and relatively fast way to get around the island if you take it easy, drink plenty of water, and don't mind riding a clunker. If you're traveling with a cell phone and speak Spanish, it can be helpful to get your taxi driver's number so you can call later and make arrangements yourself.

A popular way to get around and see the island is on one of **Hari's Horses** (tel. 505/8383-8499 or 8384-9578, email harishorses@gmail.com). Tours include a half-island trek (seven hours, $50 pp) on well-behaved and well-fed animals. Hari also has some cabins for rent beyond Santa Cruz ($25 d per night with tour, $30 for walk-ins).

By Bus

Be very aware that buses are few and far between, especially on Sundays, which remain a tough day to get around the island in anything but a rented car, taxi, or by availing yourself of the services of your hotel.

In general, there's a bus in Moyogalpa to meet every boat. For the most up-to-date schedule, ask around the dock, or look for a posting in the tour offices or El Indio Viejo in Moyogalpa. Fully 90 percent of the buses leave the Moyogalpa dock, travel straight up the hill along the main street, stop at the park, then head east out of town on the road to Altagracia; the other 10 percent turn left, passing through La Flor and San Marcos on their way to Altagracia.

From Altagracia, buses depart for Moyogalpa and for the small towns of Maderas (Merida, San Ramón, Santa Cruz, and Balgüe). If you board a bus in Moyogalpa that's heading to Maderas, remember you'll pass through Altagracia first, where you'll spend 30 minutes waiting for more passengers before continuing to Maderas. From Moyogalpa to Altagracia, it's approximately one hour, and from Altagracia to Balgüe it's another hour. The island is bigger than you think.

Three daily buses leave Moyogalpa for Merida at 8:30 A.M., 2:40 P.M., and 4:30 P.M.; from Altagracia buses depart at 7 A.M., 10:30 A.M., and 2 P.M. (these buses continue to San Ramón, returning the following day starting at 5:30 A.M.). From Merida to Moyogalpa, buses leave at 4 A.M., 8:30 A.M., and 3:30 P.M.

By Car

Either arrange a transfer with your hotel beforehand or call **Berman Gómez** (tel. 505/8816-6971, ometepeisland@hotmail.com), whose clients include the BBC. Berman specializes in (bilingual) tours and is very tapped in to tourism in the region; seek him out to arrange travel and transport, or for larger projects. Most hotels will gladly help to arrange tours as well, getting you up the volcanoes or on waterfall hikes, horseback rides, kayaking excursions, and other area attractions. CITOMETEPE, the island's tourism commission, offers overview information at www.visitaometepe.com.

MOYOGALPA

Moyogalpa (Nahuatl for "place of the mosquitoes") is Ometepe's largest commercial center, and though it's not that buggy, it is a bit bland. There are plenty of fine accommodations here, but it's better to base yourself outside of the town to experience the more isolated sides of the island.

Sights

At the top of the hill, Moyogalpa's **Catholic church** is charming, with a bell tower just high enough over the tree line to afford you a great view of the town, coastline, lake... and the statue of a boy urinating.

La Sala Arqueológica (or El Museo), located towards the top of the main street, has a small but interesting collection of pre-Columbian artifacts found on the island over the years. Owner and amateur historian Herman García and his wife, Ligia, are very knowledgeable about island history and lore, and can point you to local artisan communities. The store in front of the museum sells contemporary works. Get oriented at the office of **Fundación Entre Volcanes** (across the street from the Moyogalpa ENITEL office, www.fundacionentrevolcanes.org), a small NGO involved in several community projects across the island; staff may be able to help you find ways to volunteer your time while on the island. They also have some representative handicrafts of the region on display.

Entertainment and Events

Long-running disco **Johnny's Bar** (just north of the dock) attracts some of the rowdy dance crowd on the weekends, while the rest head to **Flor de Angel**'s (next to the Landing hotel on the main drag) sweaty dance floor.

The town of Moyogalpa celebrates its patron saint, Santa Ana, on June 23–26. The **Baile de las Inditas** is performed in much the same way as the indigenous dance it replaced, with traditional costumes and the resonant sound of the marimba.

Accommodations

Be sure to consider a homestay in Moyogalpa

© AMBER DOBRZENSKY

Moyogalpa is the busiest dock on the island.

and the surrounding villages. Around Moyogalpa, the best budget option is ◖ **Hospedaje Soma** (tel. 505/2569-4310, www.hospedajesoma.com, dorms $7, rooms $22–29)—even if the location opposite the J.R. Smith school is not quite central. The spacious dorm with private bathroom is a bargain; the large, newly built rooms and lovely private cabanas ($40–50) are also a good deal and include a hearty breakfast. For a better location, try **The Landing Hotel** (100 m north of the dock, tel. 505/2569-4113, www.thelanding-hotel.com, $6 dorm, private rooms $15–40), which has comfortable and clean sleeping arrangements to suit most budgets. Wi-Fi, a green garden, meals, and tours are also available.

The Cornerhouse B&B (tel. 505/2569-4212 or 505/8755-7840, www.thecornerhouseom-etepe.com, $20 s, $30 d), three blocks from the dock on the main drag, has four rustic-chic rooms above a café. The friendly owners will make you feel right at home, and a stay here includes your choice of their famous breakfasts—the eggs Benedict is not to be missed.

Hotelito Aly (a few blocks up from the dock on the left, tel. 505/2569-4196 rooms $7–10 with shared or private bath, from $45 with a/c) has 11 rooms set around a garden patio and a decent restaurant that serves three meals. Still, it's not quite as nice as the competition on this strip, and several readers have complained about poor service.

Easily recommendable is ◖ **Hotel Ometepetl** (a few blocks up from the dock on the right, tel. 505/2569-4276, $12–25 private bath and a/c), whose friendly staff can help you with the logistics of preparing your trip (guides, cars, etc.). There is a gift shop on-site and the hotel accepts credit cards. The newer **American Café & Hotel** (100 meters up the hill on the right, tel. 505/8645-7193, $35) has five spotless and spacious rooms with high ceilings, hot water, and gringo-style breakfasts.

Food

All of the suggested accommodations serve

LA ISLA DE OMETEPE

food; the nicest restaurant is found at the **Hotel Ometepetl** (a few blocks up from the dock on the right, tel. 505/2569-4276, $5). **La Casa Familiar** ($7–12) serves traditional Nicaraguan meals. **La Esquinita Caliente** ($4–7), one block east of the Cornerhouse, serves huge, inexpensive plates of comida típica for lunch and dinner. It is madly popular on game nights when the TV draws a large local crowd.

◖**The Cornerhouse** (www.cornerhouseometepe.com, Mon.–Sat., $7) is one very good reason to hang around in Moyogalpa. Aside from fantastic coffee and breakfast ($2–4), you'll find tropical-fruit smoothies, salads, and huge grilled sandwiches, largely made up of the island's fantastic organic produce (and conveniently available as a packed lunch for volcano hikers). Dinners are set to be included in the menu. All this, plus homebaked snacks and wireless Internet, draws expats, tourists, and locals alike to the best café in the Rivas department.

Pizzeria Buon Apetito (one block east of the dock on the main street, 11 A.M.–11 P.M. daily) is a favorite among locals and Peace Corps volunteers; its huge menu features surprisingly good pizza sold whole ($5–10) or by the slice, as well as calzones and pasta.

Information and Services

One of the few places that accepts travelers checks is Hotel Ometepetl (minus 10 percent). The ENITEL office is located 1.5 blocks east of the main street and is closed on Sundays. The Moyogalpa **hospital** (tel. 505/2569-4247) is three blocks east of the park along the highway out of town. For Internet access, go to the **Arcia Cyber Café** (8 A.M.–8 P.M. daily), which is air-conditioned, or continue up the main street and use one of the computers at the museum.

NEAR MOYOGALPA
San Marcos

Just northeast of Moyogalpa, along the "back way around the island," is the small community of San Marcos, home to a women's group that makes and sells ceramic pieces, including authentic replicas of pre-Columbian art. Ask around in town for the *taller de artesanía*.

Punta Jesús María

The long, sandy peninsula of Punta Jesús María is lovely for swimming and relaxing in the dry season, and submerges in the rainy season. This is a good place to watch the sun set or enjoy a meal after a swim in the lake. The restaurant here will give you a beer to take with you on your walk up the kilometer-long sandbar with waves lapping at both sides. Owner Joaquín Salazar may let you set up your tent on the beach and spend the night with the crickets. The entrance is a long driveway just north of the town of Esquipulas that takes 15 minutes to walk. Take the bus and ask to get off at the picturesquely named **Punta de la Paloma** (Dove's Point).

Mueso El Ceibo

Before reaching Puerto San Jose, follow the signs toward the waterfront to reach the Mueso El Ceibo (tel. 505/8874-8076, www.elceibomuseum.com, tours $4 each or $6 for both facilities). A visit here provides some insight into the indigenous customs and heritage of the island. The museum is split into two buildings, one of which is Nicaragua's sole "money museum," a vast collection of Nicaragua's currency as printed during different political and presidential regimes. The second building houses a vast collection of ceramics, almost entirely excavated from within the finca, dating from 3000 B.C. to A.D. 1550. More than 1,500 pieces are on display in a pleasantly air-conditioned building, including tools, petroglyphs and jewelry.

◖ Reserva Charco Verde

At Charco Verde you can swim in the lake accompanied only by the call of the monkeys in the treetops and the whir of colorful birds. This is still a relatively wild area, with enough tall

THE LEGEND OF CHICO LARGO

Over the years, this famous legend has taken two forms. In the first version, an old man by the name of Chico Largo lives in the wetlands of Charco Verde. There he appears to people at night and offers to make a deal with them: wealth and prosperity during the entirety of their lives, in exchange for their souls, which upon death he converts into cattle. Many of the cows on the island, then, are the souls of Ometepe's previous generation, which opted for a life of decadence instead of hard work.

In the second version, the cacique Nicarao is buried with his throne made of solid gold along the edge of the Charco Verde. In this version, Chico Largo is a descendant of Nicarao and roams the area guarding and protecting Nicarao's tomb. Chico Largo, since he is already guarding the tomb, has now taken it upon himself to guard the forest, animals, and fish as well, and is the primary protector of Ometepe's wildlife.

---

trees remaining to harbor some very exciting wildlife. The entire area has been cordoned off to prevent development, leaving this cove an oasis of peace to be shared by you and the monkeys (who, incidentally, do their own part by throwing excrement from the trees at intruders). Walk along the Charco Verde Nature Reserve (entrance $0.50), a short trail where you may see (or at least hear) howler monkeys, birds, and other wildlife. Bring bug spray.

There are three local hotels each owned by a different Riveras sibling. Each rents horses and offers boat and kayak trips along the shoreline, fishing trips, and outings to Isla de Quiste. The family owns a cattle farm just up the beach you can also visit. **Hotel y Restaurante Charco Verde** (tel. 505/8887-9302, www.charcoverde.com.ni, $43–68) is next to the reserve with easy trail access; a cute cabana with private bath and air-conditioning includes tile floors, oodles of windows, and a front porch. If you've been in-country a while, you'll appreciate the bedside reading lamps. Reservations are recommended during the high season.

Up the beach toward Moyogalpa, Ruben Riveras runs **Hotel Finca Venecia** (tel. 505/8734-4190, $25–50 with breakfast), a family-style guesthouse on the beach. Rooms are simple but pleasant, as are the meals served on-site. From here, it's an easy walk along the shore to the Charco Verde reserve. Right next door is **La Posada de Chico Largo** (tel. 505/8886-4069, chicolargo@yahoo.com, $5 dorm beds, $15 d). Despite their nickname, "Los Diablos" are accommodating hosts and their restaurant is good. Ask about the La Mirador del Diablo trail.

Isla de Quiste

Really just an islet, Quiste is overgrown and vacant, and a scant 100 meters long—a perfect place to pitch a tent and camp. Many Moyogalpa hotels will help you make arrangements with someone with a small boat. Otherwise, in Charco Verde, **Rubén Riveras** will drop you off on the island in his motorboat and pick you up again later (or the next day) for about $15, depending on the number of travelers. But you can just as easily strike a deal with any of the locals in the small communities to the north of Moyogalpa, like Barrio de los Pescadores.

Valle Verde

The pirate's treasure is, in this case, an isolated retreat on a wide, black-sand beach rather off the beaten track. Reach the cove by hiking through the Charco Verde reserve or by getting off the bus at the entrance just beyond the community of San José del Sur, then walking

15 minutes or so from the highway, following the signs. **El Tesoro del Pirata** (tel. 505/8832-2429) is located just far enough off the beaten track to encourage the local wildlife to whoop it up for you. The view is excellent, as is the swimming and boating, and several readers claim they serve the best-tasting fish on the island. Pay $25 for a cabana with air-conditioning and private bath, and $2 per person to camp, with a $6 tent rental. Group discounts are available.

ALTAGRACIA

The second-largest community on Ometepe and an important island port, Altagracia is more picturesque than Moyogalpa, but definitely plays second fiddle with regard to attractions and services. In 2000, *National Geographic* filmed a documentary about vampire bats here—and while there are indeed many vampire bats, they are a threat only to the local chickens, which the bats like to suck dry by hanging from the chickens' nerveless feet.

Sights

El Museo Ometepe (9 A.M.–5 P.M. daily, $1) has a few exhibits of the flora, fauna, and archaeology of Ometepe, including statues and ceramic pieces unearthed around the island. The church courtyard makes for a peaceful retreat with a few interesting pre-Columbian stone idols for added irony. You might get yelled at by a group of bright green parakeets that make their home in the roof of the dilapidated old church (next to the freshly painted new church). Across the street in the central park, you'll find the *artesanía cooperative*, composed of eight local artisans who take turns working in the shop. Some of the pieces are original and exhibit the pride that the islanders have for their home.

From the park, walk east down a sandy road about 30 minutes to the bay of **Playa Tagüizapa,** a fine sandy beach for swimming. You can pick up supplies in town for a picnic

and make a lazy day of it. Located three kilometers north of the town of Altagracia, the port has boat service between Granada and San Carlos (Río San Juan). The road that leads to the port is shady and makes a nice, short walk—allow about 45 minutes each way. On the way, you'll pass **Playa Paso Real,** an out-of-the-way bathing beach you'll likely have all to yourself. If you're heading to the port to catch the boat to Granada or San Carlos, it's worthwhile to speak with the owner of Hotel Central. They offer pickup truck service to the port, so you don't have to carry all your luggage that far. Be aware that when the water is too rough, the boat may not show up at Altagracia, preferring to hug the eastern shore of the lake.

Entertainment and Events

Altagracia's *fiestas patronales,* in celebration of San Diego, are held November 12–18. In addition to the traditional festivities, the **Baile de las Ramas** (Dance of the Branches) is a major component of the celebration. The dancers tear off smaller branches of the *guanacaste* tree and hold them to their heads while dancing to imitate the worker *zompopo* (leaf-cutter) ants carrying leaves off to the ant hills.

Accommodations and Food

Less touristy than other parts of the island, Altagracia nevertheless has reasonable options for lodging and food if you find yourself here for the night. All the hotels here serve meals; or try **Los Bocaditos** ($7), located two blocks north of the central park, for traditional Nicaraguan dishes.

Altagracia's accommodations are all located within a block of each other, so feel free to walk around and compare before settling in. One of the cheapest and friendliest choices is **Hospedaje Ortiz** (a block or so from the central plaza, $2–5), recommended by several readers. More popular ◖ **Hotel Central** (two blocks south of the park, tel. 505/2552-8770) is a traveler favorite, with a nicely furnished reading room, small garden, and friendly staff (though some have complained of overpriced tours and basic services). Expect to pay $6 per person for a private bath and fan, slightly less for a shared bath, and $7 per person for a private cabin out back. **Hotel Castillo** (tel. 505/8475-7455, $4 pp shared bath, $10 private bath) is similar and sports one of the nicer bars in town.

Across from the park, **Posada Cabrera** (tel. 505/8664-2788, www.posadacabrera.com, $5 pp) has a pleasant feel, nice staff, and a green backyard. The rooms, however, are extra small, and not as private (the walls don't go all the way up to the ceiling).

Try a homestay with a local family, courtesy of **La Peñita** (tel. 505/8972-6299, famrampaiza@yahoo.es, $3.50 pp). The friendly owner has bikes to rent and will take you on a guided tour of the island. To get there, take the bus from Altagracia to El Quino (at the fork for the isthmus) and walk 300 meters north. This is about as close as you can stay to El Ojo de Agua.

Information and Services

The Camara de Turismo in the park has decent information about the island. The ENITEL phone office and the post office are found diagonally across from the park on the same corner as the Museo Ometepe. The **Casa Cural,** located on the south side of the park, has six computers and Internet service (Mon.–Fri.). There's also one computer at Tienda Fashion, a block south of the park. You'll have no privacy there, as the computer is located in the middle of the store, but it's open late and on weekends. Check out the crafts while you're waiting.

The small **Centro de Salud** (on the southeast corner of the park) can treat patients 24 hours a day, but for serious injuries go to the hospital at Moyogalpa (get the owner of your hotel to take you in a vehicle).

C EL OJO DE AGUA

Located near the town of Tilgue, on the northern part of the isthmus, El Ojo de Agua consists of crystal clear spring-fed waters captured in two natural stone pools set in the middle of a gorgeous and colorful botanical garden. Swim in the revitalizing waters the way the Nahautls probably did, then climb out to drip-dry in the sun. It's essentially the only swimming hole on the island other than the lake itself, and the water is the cleanest you'll find anywhere. Your $2 entrance fee helps with maintenance, as does whatever you pay to take home some organic herbal tea. Snacks are available at the little bar/shop, but nothing fancy.

C PLAYA SANTO DOMINGO

Playa Santo Domingo is the narrow wedge of land that connects the volcanoes of Concepción and Maderas, the product of rich volcanic soil that washed down from the slopes of both volcanoes over millennia, gradually connecting the two islands. The several-kilometer-long stretch of black sand on the northern part of the Istián Isthmus has some of Ometepe's most upscale (relatively speaking) accommodations. The swimming can be nice, but with the near-constant onshore breeze, the water is usually choppy and it can get windy. If there are loads of *chayules* (gnats) when you visit, consider staying on another part of the island, away from the water, where these harmless but annoying little bugs are nearly nonexistent. Also note that in the rainy season water levels rise and the sandy beach all but disappears.

Accommodations and Food

Rent a charming stone cabin at C **Villa Paraíso** (tel. 505/2563-4675, www.villaparaiso.com.ni, $63–72). Rates are double for rooms with private bath and air-conditioning; suites feature air-conditioning, fridge, satellite TV, and hot water. The breezy waterfront restaurant is fabulous. Call early for reservations as the place fills up quickly, especially on weekends and holidays. Next door, **Hotel Finca Santo Domingo** (tel. 505/8927-2019, $25–30) is less

© GRACE GONZALEZ

Playa Santo Domingo is one of the island's most picturesque beaches.

exciting, and rooms are simple and uninspired, though some are air-conditioned.

Two kilometers farther down the beach toward Maderas, **Casa Hotel Istiam** (tel. 505/2569-4276) provides enormous value, and its beach is clean and pleasant. The rooms are so-so but cheap ($5 pp shared bath, $8 pp private bath) and the location is spectacular, with an impressive view of both volcanoes from the second-floor deck. There is one $25 double room with air-conditioning and private bath. The service is friendly and the restaurant good. Make reservations in Moyogalpa at Hotel Ometepetl as they sometimes fill up. Camping is possible.

◖ RÍO ISTIÁN

The paddle trip in a kayak or canoe up the Río Istián is best early in the morning or during sunset but is worthwhile at any time. You slip into the still waters of a marshy isthmus deep with shadow from the tree canopy and raucous with the sounds of birds, all under the reflection of two volcanic peaks. **Caballito's Mar** (5 km from Santa Cruz, turn right at the signs and follow the dirt road to the lake, fernando@caballitosmar.com, www.caballitosmar.com, tel. 505/8842-6120) rents kayaks by the hour and offers a fun three-hour guided trip ($20) in which they'll point out the kingfishers, white herons, turtles, and *caimanes* (crocodiles). You can easily stay in their basic dormitory ($5 pp) or just have a traditional Nicaraguan meal (lots of lake fish, about $3). You can also rent kayaks at Hacienda Mérida or Charco Verde ($5/hr). Allow half a day for the adventure, and bring sunscreen, snacks, and plenty of water. The shorter paddle to Isla el Congo, just offshore, is nice as well, but beware the monkeys!

◖ VOLCÁN MADERAS

Maderas is officially a national park, which will hopefully encourage preservation of the thick forests. Maderas is a pleasant volcano to climb, since you hike in the shade, and is

HIKING OMETEPE'S VOLCANOES

Ometepe's twin peaks are a siren's call for many an intrepid backpacker, and hiking one or both is an intimate way to get to know the island. But do not underestimate the difficulty of the challenge before you: Both peaks are equally dangerous, for different reasons.

Volcán Concepción (1,610 meters) is the more arduous climb, and large parts of the hike are treeless, rocky scrambles. Don't be surprised if the volcano is off-limits the day you arrive, as Concepción is a quite active volcano, and has spewn gas and ash on several occasions in the past five years, as recently as December 2009. As such, the authorities prohibit climbs when the seismologists show the conditions aren't safe.

As you reach the volcanic cone, the wind that buffets you is cold until you reach the crater lip, where the volcano's hot, sulphurous gas pours forth (the clash of hot and cold air is responsible for the almost permanent cloud cover at the top of the volcano). On the off chance the clouds thin, the view from the peak is unforgettable.

Most travelers hike Concepción by way of the towns La Concha or La Flor, and there is an eastern approach from Altagracia that takes you through an impressive amount of monkey-inhabited forest before hitting the exposed section. Allow a full day for the hike: five exhausting hours up and four knee-shattering hours down. Take plenty of water, food, sun protection, and good shoes and socks to protect your feet.

Volcán Maderas (1,394 meters) is more accessible, and the volcano is dormant, if not extinct (in fact, there's a forested lake within the crater). It is thus more frequently hiked, but remains equally dangerous and is responsible for at least two deaths since 2005. Volán Maderas is a national park above 400 meters, and for good reason: It's really beautiful up there. When you reach the crater lip, the final descent down to the mist-swept crater lake requires a rope and should not be attempted without proper safety equipment—make sure your guide packs one.

The most commonly used trail to the top starts at Finca Magdalena; if you're not staying at the Finca Magdalena, you must pay a trail fee to enter and pass through the coffee plantations. You'll pass a petroglyph or two on the way up. The trail, unfortunately, has seen better days. Lack of appropriate maintenance has made a knee-deep mud pit out of much of the upper stretch. Allow four hours to go up and two or three to come back down, and count on spending an hour at the crater lake (58 minutes of which you'll spend deciding whether or not to jump in the cold, mushy-bottomed *laguna*). The other, more strenuous ascent leaves from Mérida. The first three hours are an almost vertical ascent, leveling off into the upper reaches that one hiker calls "enchanted." Hotel Hacienda Mérida offers this excursion, and can arrange transport back from Magdalena if you choose to descend the other side.

On either peak, a guide is *required,* and for very good reason: The "trails" as such are unmarked, and branch off dozens of times. One death on Maderas was an experienced hiker who got lost in the crevices of the volcano's middle slopes and succumbed to dehydration. It is recommended to use a trained guide from the **Union Guias de Ometepe** (tel. 505/2569-4243 or 505/8827-7714, volcanolaketours@gmail.com). Forming a professional collective has enabled the local guides to share knowledge, formalize their training, and get some sharp-looking uniforms to boot. You can hire a guide for $10-20 per group of five people, enriching your trip, giving something back to the community, supporting conservation efforts, and oh yeah, getting back down again safely.

less demanding than its truly active twin, but a guide is now obligatory since a pair of hikers got lost and eventually perished on the mountain. But even if you're not a peak bagger, there's lots to do here, starting with a visit to the fields of old petroglyphs, a relic of the island's Nahuatl past; dipping into the natural springs at Ojo de Agua; sunning and splashing at the beach at Santo Domingo; mountain biking down the rutted roads to take a coffee tour, horseback ride, or kayak trip. In addition, a host of unique places to stay (many based on working farms, some using permaculture and principles of environmental sustainability) are fun and interesting.

From Mérida to San Ramó are some 250 families who fish and farm on Ometepe's least-visited shoreline, but it remains the "dark side of the moon"—little visited but equally, if not more, compelling. Beyond San Ramón, the lonely east coast of Maderas is one of the most isolated spots in Nicaragua, connected tentatively by a poor excuse of a road with no bus service. The locals are not used to receiving guests. It's potentially feasible to circumnavigate the entire volcano on foot or on a mountain bike (about 12 or 6 hours, respectively). The coast of Tichana hides lots of unexplored areas, including, reportedly, caves full of paintings as well as some petroglyphs near Corozal.

A rigorous and none-too-obvious trail leads up to Maderas's crater lagoon from Mérida; you can go down the way you came, or you can descend to the other side and emerge at Finca Magdalena or Finca Zopilote. But you absolutely must hire a guide, bring food and water, and get an early morning start—this a serious hike for pros only.

Santa Cruz and El Madroñal

A location at the intersection of two main roads makes **Rancho Santa Cruz** (tel. 505/8884-9894, santacruzometepe@gmail.com, www.santacruzometepe.com) an excellent base from which to explore in either direction, as your chances of catching a bus or taxi on this transportation challenged island double. Spacious rooms go for $3–20, nice dorms with good air circulation are $5 per person. The restaurant serves granola, yogurt, and pancake breakfasts ($2); a selection of vegetarian options ($4–7) include pastas and curries for lunch and dinner. You can also rent bikes ($5 a day) and they can arrange horseback riding on request.

Let the lapping waves of Lake Cocibolca rock you to sleep at ◖ **Little Morgan's** (tel. 505/8611-7973, www.littlemorgans.com, dorms $8, privates $25–35), named after the charismatic Irish owner's young son. Chill to the satellite tunes, play a game of pool, or simply hang out in one of the *rancho*'s dreamy hammocks. Little Morgan's is waterfront on the main road, about 200m past Santa Cruz on the road to Balgüe.

A 10-minute walk up the trail from the village of El Madroñal leads to **La Finca Ecológica El Zopilote** (tel. 505/8369-0644, www.ometepezopilote.com, $2.50–10 pp for camping, dorm beds, and private cabins), a hillside cluster of thatch huts and platforms run by a few peace-loving Italians and their pack of hound dogs. Meals are not provided, rather fix your own in the open-air communal kitchen; the compound has compost toilets, an artisan's workshop, and a clay oven for bread and pizza. Check out the organic products in the gift shop, from coffee to liqueur, and enjoy the permaculture plantation throughout the grounds. Tents for camping are also available. Volunteers willing to work on the farm for at least a week get a 20 percent discount and all the fruit they can eat.

Balgüe

Balgüe is your base for hiking Volcán Maderas, a worthwhile endeavor, but it has increasingly good lodging of its own. The stalwart of course is Finca Magdalena up on the skirts of the volcano itself, with petroglyphs and a compelling

NAHUATLS AND THE PETROGLYPHS OF OMETEPE

Catligüe, the goddess of fertility; Ecatl, the god of air; Migtanteot, the god of death; Tlaloc, the god of soil; and Xochipillo, the goddess of happiness. The Nahuatl gods were all-powerful and vindictive, and spent their days in the land where the sun rises doing what all-powerful gods do best—feeding on human blood.

The concept of a soul was an important part of the Nahuatl belief system, as were the concepts of an afterlife and some form of reincarnation. Their calendar consisted of 18 months of 20 days each, for a total of a 360-day calendar year. They believed in a cycle of catastrophic events that recurred every 52 years, and according to that cycle the Nahuatls would store grains and water, in case this was the year.

Scattered around the island of Ometepe, but principally on the north and northeastern slopes of Volcán Maderas, are the statues and petroglyphs, carved around the year A.D. 300, that paid homage to the Nahuatl gods. Spirals are a consistent theme, representing perhaps calendars or the Nahuatl concept of time and space. It has been suggested the spirals may also represent the islands themselves, or that the twin-spiral shape of Ometepe gave the island even more significance to the islanders, as it fit in with their ideas about the cosmos. More mundane images can also be identified in the carved rocks: monkeys, humans hunting deer, and a couple in coitus, suggesting Nahuatl wishes for prosperity and fertility, or just a bit of monkey business.

Ometepe petroglyphs

In the days of the Nahuatls, Volcán Maderas was called Coatlán, "the place where the sun lives," and Concepción was known as Choncoteciguatepe, "the brother of the moon," or Mestliltepe, "the peak that menstruates." In the lush forests of the lower slopes of the two volcanoes, the Nahuatls performed complicated rituals in honor of many different gods:

history, but various international newcomers are providing a much greater range of options.

Worthy of a look is the **Bona Fide** farm near Finca Magdalena, a huge, multilevel permaculture project that began with reintroducing biodiversity to the region. It is thought to house one of the largest botanical collections in Central America, and has become a mecca for volunteers. Bona Fide also supports various projects here, including Mano Amiga, Balgüe's community center, where locals have access to a library, computer lab, sewing co-op, a community kitchen, and classes. Bona Fide lies on the road to Finca Magdalena, about 50 meters from the main road. Contact the farm online (www.projectbonafide.com) to find out more about internships, homestays, and volunteer opportunities.

ACCOMMODATIONS

◖ **Totoco Eco-Lodge** (1.5 km up a steep hill from the secondary school in Balgüe, tel.

505/8425-2027, www.totoco.com.ni, cabins $20–25 per person, includes breakfast and dinner) is an ecologically sensitive master-piece. The property sits on a working 15-acre organic farm and was crafted of drought-resistant plants, compost toilets, passive cooling, and solar power. If "off the grid" means nothing to you, consider the awe-inspiring view of cloud-shrouded Volcán Concepción from your bedroom window. Private accommodation consists of four quirky cabins with private porches, quality mattresses, and hot water; the budget minded can stay in the open palm-roofed dorms for $12 per bed. The restaurant serves delicious three-course meals and provides excellent service.

In the same spirit, but smaller scale and homier, are the cabanas at **Finca del Sol** (tel. 505/8364-6394, www.hotelfincadelsol.com, $40–50). The whole place is sun-powered and ecofriendly, including the composting toilets—the Finca is overall a bit less mainstream. Better yet, let your welcoming hosts Cristiano and Sheri tell you over a home-cooked meal about constructing the place by hand with natural materials, all without use of a vehicle.

Así Es Mi Tierra (tel. 505/8717-2486 or 505/8923-2264, www.mitierraometepe.com, $10–15), in the town of Balgüe proper, is a family-run *hospedaje* with seven clean rooms. Fernando and his family can rent you a mountain bike ($1/hr) or a horse ($4/hr), and can easily arrange transportation to all the local hot spots in their minibus.

Just uphill from the town of Balgüe is the famed **Finca Magdalena** (tel. 505/8498-1683, www.fincamagdalena.com, $3 hammock or camping, $3.50 raised platform in a dorm, rooms $5–25, private cabins $40), a 24-family coffee cooperative established in the 1980s. The place tends towards austere, but is welcoming and sincere. Everyone showers in the same bracing cold water piped directly from a spring up the slope, and the evening meal is cooked over a wood fire. Horseback rides and coffee and petroglyph tours (45 min., $8 pp) are all available. You can also purchase fresh-roasted coffee and fresh honey—a good way to help support the farm. Magdalena is on the way up the trail to Volcán Maderas; guided trips leave pretty much every morning. To get to Finca Magdalena, take the bus to Balgüe and follow the signs along the 20-minute walk up the road to the farm (arrive before dark), or take a taxi or minibus. Five daily buses depart the dock in Moyogalpa, the last at 3:30 P.M.

FOOD

While you're in the neighborhood, stop by **(Café Campestre** (just before Balgüe's church, $4), which at first glance is just a simple roadside eatery. Don't be fooled by the simple exterior; the ever-changing menu offers treats like homemade hummus or chicken liver pâté with organic salad.

At **Eduardo's Comedor** (located at the entrance to the elementary school, $2–5), both vegetarians and meat lovers find fresh meals filled with love.

Mérida

Hotel Hacienda Mérida (tel. 505/8868-8973 or 505/8894-2551, www.hmerida.com, $6 dorm, $20–28 d with private bath, $3 pp campsite, plus tax) is a sprawling lakeside compound where second-floor balconies have views of the volcanoes and lake. They rent bikes and kayaks ($15 for the duration of your stay) and can arrange hikes, fishing trips, and horseback riding; breakfast and dinner buffets ($4.50 and $5.75 pp plus tax) are crafted with whole foods, many from the garden. Internet is available. The Nicaraguan owner, Alvaro Molina, speaks perfect English and is both a passionate advocate for and walking encyclopedia of Ometepe social causes; but if you're not on his wavelength, he may rub you the wrong way.

For more privacy and more money, try **La**

© JOSHUA BERMAN

Cascada San Ramón is worth the hike.

Omaja (300 meters past Merida, tel. 505/8885-1124, laomaja@hotmail.com, www.laomaja.com, $25–45). A bit isolated, it offers characterless cabins with panoramic lake views and all kinds of activities and services available.

For an even greater sense of isolation and relaxation, continue 20 minutes down the road to the organically constructed **K Finca Mystica** (tel. 505/8751-9653, www.fincamystica.com, $25). Monkeys roam the treetops here, right up to the dining *rancho* and the four beautifully crafted bottle cabins, which are all a 10-minute walk to the waterfront. A favored chill-out retreat, Mystica's restaurant offers an eclectic menu of home-baked goods and local produce, which means you're likely to leave the property only when hiking the volcano (by a direct private trail) or cooling off in the lake. Reservations are necessary, and transportation can be arranged in advance—convenient, considering the buses will only take you as far as the Santa Cruz turnoff, a good hour's hike away.

Despite the shabby exterior, travelers give good reviews of the food at **Restaurante El Pescadito,** just outside Hacienda Mérida. Huge plates of fresh fish or pasta will set you back $3–4. Service can be slow as this is a one-man band. The friendly owner has been known to take repeat diners out on his boat to snag the catch of the day and then cook it up.

Cascada San Ramón

The most popular attraction by far on Ometepe's south side is the stunning 180-meter Cascada San Ramón waterfall. The signs describe it as a three-kilometer trail, but it's likely more than that; allow three hours minimum, as the three kilometers are vertical. You can drive a four-wheel drive vehicle part way up to the water tank to skip past the exposed water pipes and head straight to the prettiest section of the hike. Otherwise, walk through avocado, mango, and lemon trees and up to a small parking area and hydroelectric plant. Once you enter the lush canyon, the humidity rises. You may have to scramble over some river rocks, and at times the trail seems to disappear before it emerges a few meters ahead. At the waterfall you can bathe in a shallow pool.

Maderas Rainforest Conservancy

Four kilometers up the road from Mérida, in the tiny village of San Ramón, the Maderas Rainforest Conservancy (formerly the Ometepe Biological Field Station, Miami tel. 305/666-9932, info@maderasrfc.org, www.maderasrfc.org) is a facility visited by student groups and researchers from all over the world. In addition to being active in numerous forward-thinking conservation projects in surrounding communities, MRC operates a field school on the volcano's slopes for undergraduate and graduate students in primatology, ecology, bat ecology, botany, and other biological sciences. Tourists are welcome to sample the restaurant or stay at the station for a small fee.

LA ISLA DE OMETEPE

ALTERNATIVE TOURISM ON LA ISLA DE OMETEPE

HOMESTAYS AND COMMUNITY TOURISM

Comunidad Indígina Urbaite-Las Pilas (Las Pilas, tel. 505/2569-4180, ask for Ulises Hernández). Live with local farmers and go on guided walking or fishing tours. Private lodging arrangements are available ($4 per person).

Escuela Hotel Teosintal (Moyogalpa, tel. 505/2569-4105, tecuilturismo@intelnett.com, contact Migdalia Tórrez, $10 pp). The hotel arranges tours around the island or can connect you with a network of agricultural cooperatives.

Pueblo Hotel (Moyogalpa, tel. 505/2617-1405, contact Danelia López Ponce). A network of 25 women from various communities on Ometepe who produce organic fertilizer, conduct workshops on domestic violence, and host tourists in their homes. The cost of a stay in one of the houses ($12 per person) includes three meals per day.

Puesta del Sol (La Paloma, tel. 505/8619-0219, www.puestadelsol.org). For $15 a night, visitors receive three home-cooked meals, filtered water, and stories of *campesino* living to tell the folks back home. Guests should speak basic Spanish.

VOLUNTEER OPPORTUNITIES

There are several projects on the island that lend a hand to youth at risk; a high level of Spanish is recommended, as this can be frustrating, difficult work (and equally rewarding, of course).

¡Sí a la Vida! (Yes to Life, Altagracia, U.S. tel. 619/593-9567, vccmueller@hotmail.com, www.asalv.org). International volunteers can expect to work with ex-street kids in sports, arts, handicrafts, and tutoring, as well as specialized services. Volunteers accompany Nicaraguan staff on field trips to the streets and markets of Managua. A commitment of six months or more is usually required.

Nuestros Pequeños Hermanos (NPH, San Lázaro, www.nphamigos.org). This orphanage is run by Our Little Brothers and Sisters, who provide "a Christian family environment." Adopt a godchild, come for a visit, or go online to apply to their volunteer program.

Fundación Entre Volcánes (Santa Cruz, tel. 505/2569-4118). This organization runs projects all over Volcán Maderas. Contact Raúl Mayorga (Moyogalpa, tel. 505/8882-5562) or Martín Juarez (Los Angeles, Ometepe) for details.

Ometepe Bilingual School (tel. 505/8868-8973, contact Alvaro Molina, alvaronica@gmail.com, www.hmerida.com). This free English-language school is a before- and after-school program which children attend on their own initiative, in addition to their five-hour days at the public school. The school also provides oatmeal and granola porridge for all of the kids after classes, and hosts international volunteers, student groups, and individuals come from around the world.

Maderas Rainforest Conservancy (near Merida, Miami tel. 305/666-9932, info@maderasrfc.org, www.maderasrfc.org). The Conservancy manages numerous conservation projects in surrounding communities and operates a field school for birding groups and research students. Tourists are welcome to stay at the station for a small fee.

AGRITOURISM

Finca Bona Fide (about 300 meters past Finca Magdalena, tel. 505/8616-4566, www.project-bonafide.com). A beautiful farm with 18-day organic agriculture workshops (free for locals), a nutritional kitchen in Balgüe, and farm-work internships and volunteer opportunities. Rustic lodging includes three meals a day ($5-8).

La Finca Ecologica El Zopilote (tel. 505/8419-0246, www.ometepezopilote.com). Volunteers stay for at least a week and receive a 20 percent discount on lodging.

Fincas Verdes (www.fincasverdes.com). A network with the lowdown on the various agricultural and conservation ventures offered on the island.

Rivas

Southern Nicaragua's most important town center, Rivas is a commercial center whose small population (under 50,000) helps it retain an old-world charm. Few visitors travel specifically to Rivas as a destination proper, but it remains an important companion town for San Juan del Sur, providing a better selection of medical, banking, and shopping services. Rivas is also the site of a Costa Rican consulate, in case you have immigration issues. Don't discount it as inconsequential however; it's one of Nicaragua's more pleasant cities, charismatic and enjoyable in its own right, and not lacking in historical sites worth visiting.

Rivas is often hot because of its low altitude, but a cool lake breeze from Lake Cocibolca makes it bearable. Rivas is known as Ciudad de los Mangos due to the abundance of the trees in and around the city; swarms of chatty *chocoyos* (parakeets) feast on the fruit, their calls filling the skies around sunset. Rivas was known as Valle de la Ermita de San Sebastián until 1717, when a delegation of pious villagers traveled to Guatemala, the capital of the republic at that time, to request their little town be declared a villa with the name of La Pura y Limpia Concepción de Nuestra Señora la Virgen María. Capitán General del Reino Francisco Rodríguez de Rivas granted the request, and to thank him, the villagers modified the name to La Villa de la Pura y Limpia Concepción de Rivas de Nicaragua. Thankfully for travelers and mapmakers, over time the name contracted to something shorter.

SIGHTS

Rivas is the birthplace of several presidents of the republic, including Máximo Jérez (Liberal, governed from June 8, 1818–August 12, 1881), Adén Cárdenas (Conservative, governed from March 1, 1883–March 1, 1887), and Violeta Barrios de Chamorro (Coalition, governed from April 25, 1990–January 10, 1997). Chamorro's childhood home is located across the street from the Iglesia Parroquial de San Pedro's south side. Several direct descendants of William Walker also continue to reside in Rivas.

At the southeast end of town not far from the road to La Chocolata, the Rivas **cemetery** is set on a little hill with a nice view of town and the surrounding hillsides. It's worth visiting in the late afternoon, as Rivas sunsets are often blazing washes of red and orange, thanks to the humidity from Lake Cocibolca.

◖ Iglesia Parroquial de San Pedro

Rivas's obvious centerpiece is a well-loved historical monument. Built in the 18th century and repainted in 2007, the Iglesia Parroquial de San Pedro has witnessed the California gold rush, William Walker, the Sandinista revolution, and the 21st-century real estate boom. As you take in the details of the church's pleasing colonial design, remember that every single gold rush–bound passenger that traversed Nicaragua in the days of Cornelius Vanderbilt's steamship line passed under its shadow. It is today, as always, a peaceful place to seek refuge; mass is held evenings around 6 P.M.

Iglesia de San Francisco

Four blocks west of the park at the town's center, the Iglesia de San Francisco was built in 1778 and was the first convent of the Franciscan friars. A beautiful statue commemorates the devotion of the friars to both God and their work. When they began construction of the nearby Bancentro, an underground tunnel was discovered that linked the Iglesia de San Francisco with the plaza (the open area adjacent to the central park's north side); the tunnel passes beneath the library (one door east of

LA ISLA DE OMETEPE

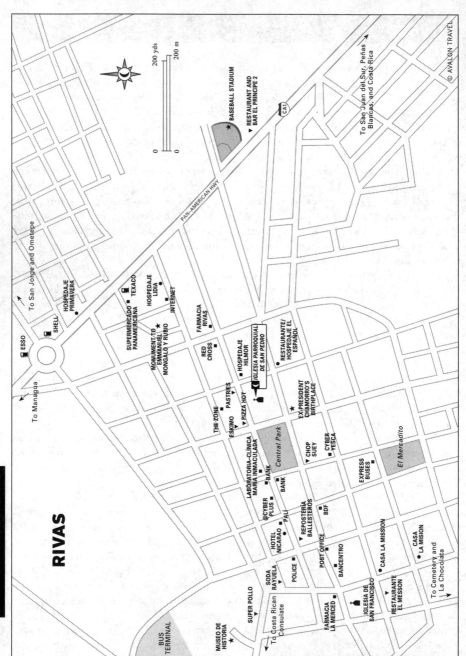

RIVAS

BUS TERMINAL

MUSEO DE HISTORIA ★

SUPER POLLO

To Costa Rican Consulate

SODA RAYUELA

POLICE

FARMACIA LA MERCED

IGLESIA DE SAN FRANCISCO

RESTAURANTE EL MESSON

To Cemetery and La Chocolata

To Managua

To San Jorge and Ometepe

ESSO

SHELL

HOSPEDAJE PRIMAVERA

PAN-AMERICAN HWY

SUPERMERCADO PANAMERICANA

TEXACO

HOSPEDAJE LIDIA

INTERNET

MONUMENT TO EMMANUEL MONGALO Y RUBIO

FARMACIA RIVAS

RED CROSS

HOSPEDAJE HILMOR

IGLESIA PARROQUIAL DE SAN PEDRO

RESTAURANTE/ HOSPEDAJE EL ESPAÑOL

PASTRIES

THE ZONE

ESKIMO

PIZZA HOT

EXPRESIDENT CHAMORRO'S BIRTHPLACE

CYBER YESCA

CHOP SUEY

Central Park

El Mercadito

LABORATORIA-CLINICA MARIA INMACULADA

BANK

BANK

CYBER PLUS

PALI

HOTEL NICARAO

REPOSTERIA BALLESTEROS

BDF

EXPRESS BUSES

POST OFFICE

BANCENTRO

CASA LA MISSION

CASA LA MISION

BASEBALL STADIUM

RESTAURANT AND BAR EL PRINCIPE 2

CA1

To San Juan del Sur, Peñas Blancas, and Costa Rica

© AVALON TRAVEL

200 yds
200 m

0
0

The Iglesia Parroquial de San Pedro witnessed the California gold rush.

Bancentro). Researchers speculate it was probably dug at the same time as the church, meaning it was in place and probably used during the Battle of Rivas, when the plaza was the site of a military barracks.

Museo de Historia y Antropología de Rivas

Rivas has its own history museum, the Museo de Historia y Antropología de Rivas (8 A.M.–noon and 2–5 P.M. Mon.–Fri., mornings only Sat., foreign travelers $1), set on the western side of town in a 200-year-old house that was once part of a cacao and indigo plantation. Once known as the Casa Hacienda Santa Úrsula, on June 29, 1855, William Walker and his men were defeated here in a heroic battle Nicaraguans are still proud of. The Battle of Rivas, as it became known, was one of the first manifestations of Nicaragua's growing sense of independence in the late 19th century; in fact, the people of Rivas claim that "nationalism

began in Rivas." The museum has a healthy collection of pre-Columbian pottery, as well as domestic utensils from the 18th and 19th centuries including kerosene lamps, silverware, and hand tools. The building itself evokes the lifestyle of the old farming community; more exciting are several old maps of the region. Some books are for sale.

Emmanuel Mongalo y Rubio Monument

The Monument to Emmanuel Mongalo y Rubio marks the final resting place of a young Rivas teacher who lived here in the mid-1800s. Mongalo y Rubio gained his fame during the Battle of Rivas by setting fire to the Mesón (the museum building) where Walker and his men had sought refuge; as they abandoned the blazing building, they were captured or shot.

Biblioteca Pública de Rivas

A museum piece in its own right, the Biblioteca

Pública de Rivas, next to Bancentro, is one of the oldest still-standing buildings in Nicaragua, dating back to at least the early 17th century. Among its various incarnations, it was a secondary school founded in 1872 by Máximo Jérez and El Colegio de la Inmaculada Concepción. Still easily visible in the building is a stray bullet hole incurred during the Battle of Rivas.

ENTERTAINMENT AND EVENTS

The **Restaurante y Disco El Principe Numero Dos** (next to the baseball stadium on the highway to the border) is Rivas's most popular dancing nightspot, especially on Saturdays when you likely won't see any other gringos. The city's best bar is **The Zone** (1.5 blocks east of the Red Cross), serving appetizers and drinks starting at 5 P.M. Sports fans will particularly enjoy this bar, which fills to bursting if there's a good game or fight being screened here.

No one enjoys **baseball** as much as the people of Rivas; at last count, there were 138 officially registered baseball teams and more than 3,900 registered players in the municipality, with stadiums or makeshift diamonds in every village in the department! Attending a Sunday afternoon game in Rivas's main stadium on the highway is a great way to experience the city and the energy of its people; tickets are $1, and in lieu of chili dogs, there are plenty of *vigorón* (fried pork and yucca) and enchiladas in the grandstand.

ACCOMMODATIONS

Few travelers find a reason to spend the night in Rivas, and the Ometepe-bound tend to prefer the lakeside places in San Jorge. But if you're visiting from San Juan del Sur, there's no reason not to spend the night.

For budget travelers, **Hospedaje Lidia** (half a block west of the Texaco station, tel. 505/2563-3477, $8 pp shared bath, $12 private bath) is the most popular option with a dozen clean rooms, including large rooms for up to five people, although some tourists have complained

that the staff here are unhelpful. At the southeast corner of the church is a good, cheap alternative, **Hospedaje Hilmor.** Basic rooms with paper-thin walls set you back $12, while dorms at half the price will work in a pinch.

Hospedaje Primavera (next to the Shell station, $5 pp private bath) is a bare-bones dump catering mostly to working Nicaraguan expats on their way to and from Costa Rica. If you get stuck, you'll find a handful of similar, unremarkable but inexpensive ($5–7 pp) places to stay within a block or two of Primavera.

Hotel Cacique Nicarao (a block west of the park, tel. 505/2563-3234, www.hotelnicarao-inn.com.ni, $69 includes tax and breakfast) is efficient and modern with cable TV, air-conditioning, Wi-Fi, a guarded parking lot, pleasant lobby, and attentive staff. You can arrange rides to San Juan del Sur and other parts here.

Casa La Mision (a block south of the San Francisco church, tel. 505/2563-0384, www.casalamision.com, $30–60) is the prettiest hotel in Rivas, set in a converted colonial home resplendent with polished wood, cool tiled floors, and a lovely green courtyard. The 10 large, high-ceilinged rooms all have a/c, private bathrooms, cable TV, and Wi-Fi, and breakfast is included in the price.

FOOD

Buy fresh pastries and juice at **Repostería Don Marcos,** a block east of the park, an easy breakfast en route between San Juan del Sur and the boat to Ometepe. The best coffee in town can be had at **Repostería Ballesteros** (across from the Nicarao Hotel), where the outdoor seating lends itself to some quality people-watching and their pastries are a nationwide sensation.

Possibly the lowest-price lunch in town is **Soda Rayuela** (7 A.M.–10 P.M. daily, $1–4), serving sandwiches, burgers, and other dishes. Across the street from the Iglesia San Pedro is **Pizza Hot** (Tues.–Sun., $4–9) with outdoor tables and an **Eskimo** ice cream parlor next door

the local market in Rivas

for dessert. In the same price range is **Hotter's Pizza** ($4–10), around the corner from the Texaco, with outdoor seating and karaoke some Wednesdays. During the evening, a number of typical *fritangas* set up shop in the plaza, and most of the bars have reasonable food as well.

Pollo Dorado (closest to the center of town, $3–7) and **Super Pollo** (near the market, $3–7) sell chicken your way. On the southwest corner of the park is **Chop Suey** ($5–7 a plate), a Chinese place not far off the mark, though all the dishes have been subtly adapted to suit the Nicaraguan palate.

◀ **El Messon** (south side of Iglesia de San Francisco, $4–9) serves a tasty Nicaraguan buffet lunch as well as *caballo bayo*, a hearty stew. The most upscale restaurant in Rivas is in the **Hotel Cacique Nicarao** (a block west of the park, tel. 505/2563-3234, www.hotelnicaraoinn.com.ni, $6–12).

INFORMATION AND SERVICES

The **Costa Rican Consulate** (7 A.M.–5 P.M. Mon.–Fri., 7 A.M.–noon Sat.) in Rivas offers help with immigration issues for Costa Rica–bound travelers. It's located about one kilometer west of town.

Several well-stocked pharmacies in town make Rivas a good service stop for the San Juan del Sur beach crowd. **Farmacia María Inmaculada** (right across from the park on the side of the plaza, 7:30 A.M.–7:30 P.M. daily) has a well-respected doctor on staff (consultation 2–4 P.M. Mon.–Fri.) and professional massage therapists. Another well-stocked pharmacy is the **Farmacia Rivas** (two blocks east of the park at the intersection of the boulevard, tel. 505/2563-4292).

The **post office** (7:30 A.M.–4:30 P.M. Mon.–Fri., 7:30 A.M.–noon Sat.) is a block south of the police station and has fax service. Of the many Internet cafés in town, two of the most popular ones are one block south of the park.

There are several banks in town including BDF, Bancentro, Banpro, and BAC, all of which operate essentially on a schedule of 8:30 A.M.–4:30 P.M. Monday–Friday and 8:30 A.M.–noon Saturday.

GETTING THERE AND AROUND

Rivas is small and easy to get around; a pedal-powered *triciclo* (about $1–3 dollars per hour) can carry you around town among the different attractions.

Buses leave Managua's Roberto Huembes terminal for Rivas every 30 minutes. Several express buses depart in the early morning before 8 A.M. Express buses to San Juan del Sur and the border at Peñas Blancas will let you off on the highway at Rivas. They leave Huembes at 5 A.M., 8 A.M., 9:30 A.M., and 3:30 P.M.

A good way to reach Managua, Masaya, Carazo, and the Pueblos Blancos (such as Catarina) is to take one of the express minibuses, which leave from El Mercadito on the south end of town about once every hour ($2.50). Regular buses leave from the market on the northwest side of Rivas: every hour for Jinotepe and Granada, every 25 minutes for

LA ISLA DE OMETEPE

Nandaime, Masaya, and Managua. The last bus for Managua leaves from the Texaco station on the highway at 6 P.M. Four daily buses go to Belén and six for Las Salinas (9 A.M., 11 A.M., 12:40 P.M., 2:30 P.M., 4 P.M., and 4:30 P.M.).

To and From Costa Rica

Bus service to Peñas Blancas and the border begins at 5 A.M. and continues every 30–45 minutes. The last bus leaves Rivas at 5:30 P.M. (the ride takes less than an hour and costs less than a dollar). You can also share a *colectivo*. On the highway in the Supermercado Panamericana (next to the Texaco station), you can buy tickets for the TicaBus, which passes by Rivas each morning bound for Costa Rica between 7 and

8 A.M., and between 3 and 4 P.M. every afternoon bound for Managua. Buy your tickets the day before ($10–12 to San José, Costa Rica).

Taxis to San Jorge and San Juan del Sur

To San Jorge and the ferry to Ometepe, a taxi should cost you no more than $1 per person, whether you take it from the highway traffic circle or from Rivas proper. Ignore any taxi driver that tries to charge $2 or more, unless you're traveling after 10 P.M., when taxi prices go up. Taxis from Rivas to San Juan del Sur cost around $8 per person, or $1 if it's a *colectivo,* which only run during daylight hours.

Near Rivas

NANDAIME

Just south of where the highways from Granada and Carazo join to continue on to Rivas and the border, you'll pass by the midsize city of Nandaime, located on the Pan-American Highway in the shadow of Volcán Mombacho. This is a humble, unassuming pueblo with the most basic of traveler's amenities, a small-town tranquility, and a passion for music. Nandaime's most famous son is Camilo Zapata, a key founder of the Nicaraguan folk style, who composed the song "El Nandaimeño." Nandaime is also home to three *chichera* groups, ragtag bands composed of a bass drum, a snare, cymbals, a sousaphone, and loud, clashing brass. Known as "orchestras," they participate frequently in parades and bullrings, and their music is happy, loud, and scrappy.

Just south of Nandaime, the private **Domitila Wildlife Reserve** (tel. 505/2637-0101 ext. 169 or 505/2563-3722, www.domitila.org) sits on 230 hectares of tropical dry forest and lakeshore. There are tree nurseries, hiking trails, and oodles of wildlife. At time of publication,

accommodations were undergoing extensive remodeling; call or check the website for the latest information and prices. The reserve entrance is located five kilometers south of Nandaime (Km 72) on the road to Rivas; turn off the highway onto a dusty dirt road, which will lead you 10 kilometers past the Lagunas de Mecatepe to Domitila.

SAN JORGE

A traditional village with a strong Catholic spirit, San Jorge is primarily a port town and farming community that produces plantains. Nearby Popoyuapa, true to its Nahuatl-sounding name, cultivates cacao, the tree whose seed is used to produce cocoa and eventually chocolate; it was once used by the Nicarao people as a form of currency.

The tiny lakeside port of San Jorge is your access point to La Isla de Ometepe and as such, most travelers breeze straight through it on the way to catch a boat. If you have an hour to kill before your ferry departs, there's no reason to spend it dockside sitting on your luggage. Some travelers even find San Jorge a pleasant place to spend a night, and the locals are turning out increasingly acceptable hotel accommodations (mostly targeting the backpacker set) hoping that's exactly what you'll do.

Be advised that at certain unpredictable times of the year, a southern wind brings plagues of *chayules,* small white gnats that swarm the lakeside in San Jorge and eastern shores of Ometepe. They neither bite nor sting, but are relentless and always seem to wind up in your mouth.

Sights

Halfway down the long road to town, you'll pass under **La Cruz de España,** a graceful concrete arch that suspends a stone cross directly over San Jorge's main drag. This main street runs through town down to the water's edge and the docks. The monument commemorates—and is ostensibly built over the very place where—on October 12, 1523, Spanish conquistador Gil González Dávila and indigenous cacique Nicarao-Calli first met and exchanged words.

Across the street from the base of the arch is a **mural** commemorating the same event, with the words attributed to Nicarao: *"Saben los Españoles del diluvio, quien movía las estrellas el sol y la luna. Dónde estaba el alma. Cómo Jesús siendo hombre es Dios y su madre virgen pariendo y para qué tan pocos hombres querían tanto oro."* ("The Spanish know about the flood, who moved the stars, the sun, and the moon. Where the soul was found. How Jesus, a man, is God and his virgin mother giving birth, and why so few men wanted so much gold.") Many believe that the Spanish went on to refer to Nicaragua as The Land of Nicarao, which over time evolved into the modern word Nicaragua.

The squat **Iglesia de las Mercedes** is one of Central America's earliest churches. Built around the year 1575, it was renovated and repainted a bright yellow in 2001. Most tourists

© JOSHUA BERMAN

LA ISLA DE OMETEPE

In San Jorge, all signs point to the great lake.

keep their bathing suits packed until they get to Ometepe, but San Jorge's kilometer-long **beach** is hugely popular among Nicaraguans, who flock there during Semana Santa to enjoy the lake and the awesome view of twin-peaked Ometepe on the horizon.

San Jorge celebrates its *fiestas patronales* in honor of their eponymous saint every year April 19–23 (the date changes to accommodate Semana Santa when necessary), at which time you can expect the beach to be packed. San Jorge usually has a parade or two during the celebrations, and there are performances of traditional dances, including **Las Yeguitas** (The Dance of the Little Mares) and **Los Enmascarados** (The Dance of the Masked Ones).

Accommodations and Food

If you missed the last boat to La Isla and don't feel like backtracking to Rivas, book one of the rooms at ◖ **Hotel Las Hamacas** (tel. 505/2563-0048, www.hotelhamacas.com, $30 d with private bath and fan, $40 with a/c, includes breakfast), no more than 100 meters west of the dock. Also consider **Hotel California** (on the main street, one block before Hotel Hamacas, tel. 505/2563-2046, $26–47),

where the 12 comfortable rooms are equipped with a/c, cable TV, and Wi-Fi.

You won't go hungry in San Jorge's numerous food-and-drink joints lining the beachfront, but neither will you be surprised by the menu: chicken, beef, fish, fries, burgers, and sandwiches.

Getting There

Many tour operators in Granada now run shuttles straight to the dock for about $15. From Managua, take any southbound bus from the Huembes bus terminal to Rivas and get off at the traffic circle on the highway at Rivas. From the traffic circle in Rivas to the dock at San Jorge is four kilometers, accessible by Rivas buses once an hour ($0.25); they pass the traffic circle approximately 20 minutes after the hour. Unless you happen to be there right at that moment, however (or are traveling on an extraordinarily tight budget), take a taxi to San Jorge for $1.50 per person—ignore anyone who tries charging more. There is one Managua–San Jorge express, departing Huembes at 9 A.M., arriving in San Jorge at 10:50 A.M. The same bus departs San Jorge evenings at 5 P.M., arriving in Managua at 6:50 P.M.

SAN JUAN DEL SUR AND THE SOUTHWEST COAST

San Juan del Sur's crescent-shaped beach washed with the gentle, warm waves of the protected harbor have been attracting travelers for a long time.

In the 1850s, this quiet fishing village experienced its first brief boom as a transport hub for gold rush pioneers crossing the peninsula on Cornelius Vanderbilt's passenger route. Here, North American travelers boarded the sailing ships to take them up the Pacific coastline to California and onward. This was also where many of William Walker's glory-seeking soldiers disembarked to join his ill-fated adventure. After the gold rush, the town sank into obscurity and tropical lethargy, where it remained for a century-and-a-half.

At the turn of the 21st century, San Juan del Sur again grew in international popularity to the steady drumbeat of high-profile international press coverage declaring the area a real estate hot spot. The area attracted a frenzy of property pimps, land sharks, and a flock of checkbook-toting prospectors scouring the coastline for a piece of the pie.

Some of these investment led to progress, new establishments, and healthy relationships between foreign investors determined to make money *and* a positive impact for their Nicaraguan colleagues and beneficiaries. But the economic growth was not without scuffles.

Meanwhile, sunsets continue to paint the silhouettes of fishing vessels in crimson, and

© AMBER DOBRZENSKY

HIGHLIGHTS

LOOK FOR ◖ TO FIND RECOMMENDED SIGHTS, ACTIVITIES, DINING, AND LODGING.

◖ **Surfing:** San Juan del Sur has become a major surf center, drawing shredders and groms from all over. There are waves for all levels out here, and plenty of places that will give you your first lesson (page 137).

◖ **Sunset Cruise:** San Juan del Sur's sunsets are spectacular year-round, and there's no better place to enjoy one than on the water with a dozen friends and a glass of wine (page 138).

◖ **La Flor Wildlife Refuge:** Even if you miss the spectacular nighttime turtle-nesting events, a simple walk along this protected beach and up the forested river is remarkable (page 150).

◖ **Playa Marsella:** A gentle wave and a secluded beach make for all sorts of opportunities (page 151).

the mood in San Juan del Sur is low-key and fun. The noon sun is scorching, so life is languorous and measured, spent swinging in breezy hammocks, enjoying fresh fish and cold beer at seaside, or splashing about in the surf.

San Juan del Sur

San Juan del Sur proper is a relatively small town; you could walk every street in a single morning. Most visitors spend at least two days and a night here, and if you start exploring the surrounding beaches and coves, beach lovers can stretch it into a full week, as can surfers. At a minimum, count on one full day wandering around town, one trip north to a nearby beach, and another trip south to Playa el Coco or La Flor Wildlife Reserve; plan an extra half day for a canopy or rappelling tour, sportfishing, or sailing excursion.

SPORTS AND RECREATION

Of course, the main show in town is the brightly colored day's end over the languid

SAN JUAN DEL SUR AND THE SOUTHWEST COAST

© AVALON TRAVEL

harbor waves; San Juan sunsets can go on for hours. Make sure you're on the beach as the setting sun drapes the fishing boats in shadow and the rock face of El Indio dims behind the evening. But there's a lot to do before day's end.

Next to the Casa de Cultura on the main beach drag are volleyball and soccer facilities, with league games on weeknights. During the rest of the day, the **Sports Park** is open for (often competitive) pickup games. Otherwise, expect soccer games to be played on the hard sand beach at low tide on either end of the bay.

🌙 Surfing

Most surfers make base camp in San Juan del Sur and then drive or boat out to the better breaks, though a lot of beaches are now also developing accommodations of their own. Many of the best breaks are accessible only by boat. **Rana Tours** (tel. 505/2568-2066) runs shuttles to the beach at Majagual in an authentic *panga,* leaving at 11 A.M. and returning at 4:30 P.M. ($10 round-trip, seven person minimum) and fishing and snorkeling expeditions ($35/hr, eight-person boat). Sign up at the kiosk in front of Hotel Estrella. But you can just as easily strike a deal with any local boat operator for a water taxi out to the other beaches.

An adequate selection of new and used surfboards is easy to find in San Juan. Local shredders Byron and Kervin López can be found in their shop, **Arena Caliente** (www.arenacaliente.com), next to the market. They'll rent you a board, drive you out to the beach, and teach you the basics for $32; you can also rent rooms ($6 per person). **Baloy's Surf Shop** (a block east of El Gato Negro, tel. 505/8956-9230) is owned by a pair of Nicaraguan brothers who learned to surf on a secondhand board left behind by a tourist. They can arrange boards, gear, transportation, and lessons. **Action Tours** (tel. 505/8668-4407) runs private surfing, fishing, and chilling charters. The $250 full-day trip includes lunch.

Good Times Surf Shop (across from the casino, tel. 505/8675-1621, www.goodtimessurfshop.com) sells handcrafted boards manufactured in Nicaragua using renewable materials, and can help you arrange for a repair if you ding your board. They also offer boat trips to local surf breaks starting at $25 per person.

Chicabrava (tel. 505/8894-2842, www.chicabrava.com) is the first all-women's surf camp in Nicaragua, with both nightly and weekly rates at their beach house in town (drop in for a day's lesson and gear rental) and high-end, all-inclusive packages that cover lodging, food, equipment, six days of instruction, and transportation. You can also stay at their flagship "cloud farm" nature retreat, with many activities available.

◖ Sunset Cruise

San Juan Surf & Sport (20 meters west of the market, tel. 505/2586-2022 or 505/8984-2464) offers a sunset cruise in a fancy *panga* for $16 per person. Expect great photo ops, a merry crowd, and just a bit o' booze. Keep in mind that San Juan Surf & Sport can also take you fishing: Darío and his laid-back crew provide the equipment and will show you how to cast; you can keep any fish you catch.

Sailing and Diving

Gypsy Sailing (tel. 505/8608-9498, justin@rootsengineering.com, $30–40 pp) offers all-inclusive half or full-day trips, or you can charter the *Pelican Eyes* yacht for an all-day jaunt (tel. 505/2563-7000, www.piedrasyolas.com, $90 pp) including lunch on a deserted beach and an open bar.

The Pacific lacks the visibility of the Caribbean waters, but fish are plentiful and there's a sunken Russian shrimp boat offshore, so it can be fun. The expert divers at San Juan's Nicaraguan owned and operated dive shop, **Neptune Watersports** (tel. 505/2568-2752, www.neptunenicadiving.com), will rent you gear and take you underwater ($90 for two tanks, $350 for open-water certification) if you already have your license and are an experienced diver.

Canopy and Rappel Tours

Da Flyin Frog (tel. 505/8613-4660 or 505/8611-6214, daflyingfrog@yahoo.com, $30 pp, closed Sun.) is a 17-platform, two-kilometer canopy tour through the trees with great views of the ocean. It's located just outside town on the Chocolata road; arrange free transportation directly from the company.

For climbers and adrenaline junkies, **Aracne Rappel** (tel. 505/8887-6255, www.aracnerappel.com, $30 per person, minimum four people) offers two daily tours. Start with a 30-minute hike, rappel a 100-meter cliff, splash about in the ocean below, and then cruise back to town while sipping your (included) beverage.

Hiking

The statue of **Jesús de la Misericordia,** a 15-meter fiberglass thank-you note for the restored health of the gentleman who built Pacific Marlin, is easily reached via the gated

SAN JUAN DEL SUR

To El Pacifico Hotel

FOOTBRIDGE

CRAZY CRAB DISCO

Río San Juan del Sur

To La Virgen and Rivas →

16

BAMBU BEACH CLUB

ARRIBAS BAR

TEXACO

ADVENTURA LODGE

HOSTAL CASA AMARILLA

HEALTH CLINIC

To Ostional and Remanso

ESKIMO ICE CREAM

BALLENA NEGRA

PAN DE VIDA

BALOY'S SURF SHOP

Bahía San Juan del Sur

BIG WAVE DAVE'S

EL GATO NEGRO

SECRET COVE INN

HOSPEDAJE DON WILFREDO

HOTEL ROYAL CHATEAU

IGUANA BAR

BANK

CYBER M@NFRED

ARENA CALIENTE SURFING

RESTAURANTE EL TIMÓN

HOSTEL BEACH FUN

PELICAN EYES PIEDRAS Y OLAS RESORT

MAURICIOS PIZZERIA 2

GOOD TIMES SURF SHOP

SURF & SPORT

MARKET/ BUS STOP

LAUNDRY

HOTEL CASA BLANCA (ATM)

CENTRAL

AZUL PITAHAYA

MI BARRIO CAFÉ

HOTEL VILLA ISABELLA

CALLE

HOTEL COLONIAL

EL POZO

LIBRARY

JOSSELINE'S

HOTEL ESTRELLA

NICA SURF

CASA ORO

POSADA PUESTA DEL SOL

Central Park

CHURCH

SJ SPANISH SCHOOL

POSADA AZUL

HOSTEL PACHAMAMA

BANK

ALCALDÍA

REBECCA'S INN

MAURICIOS PIZZA

EL COLIBRÍ

NICASPANISH SCHOOL

ZEN YOGA

HOSTAL ESPERANZA

CASA ARIKI

HOTEL ENCANTO DEL SUR

SPORTS PARK

CASA DE CULTURA

TOWN DOCK

FRESH FISH

HOTEL VICTORIANO

EXPOMAR

ENITEL/ POST OFFICE

POLICE

SCALE NOT AVAILABLE

© AVALON TRAVEL

driveway past the Pacific Marlin neighborhood or the ladder that winds its way from about 500 meters around the rocks on the northern point of the bay. The steep walk takes about 30 minutes each way and leads to one of the best overlooks of the bay. You can walk 90 percent of the way for free; pay $1 to access the summit. Beware the snarling dog. For a panorama from the **antennas,** take a bus toward Rivas and ask the driver to let you off at Bocas de las Montañas. From there, head through the trees and pastures to the breezy and beautiful *mirador* (lookout)—an hour each way.

Some 1,700-year-old **petroglyphs** are accessible via a 90-minute round-trip countryside walk beginning east of the Texaco station. Consider asking for a local guide. Take a left (north), pass the school, and walk through a gate after about 500 meters; find the farmhouse and ask permission to cut through. Follow the water pipes and the river until you find the

AFTER THE GOLD RUSH: THE FOREIGNER EFFECT IN SAN JUAN DEL SUR

From about 2003-2008, San Juan del Sur saw an explosion in foreign investment, property development, and tourism expansion that had no precedent. Old properties were scooped up, hotels and vacation homes constructed, and restaurants opened. Throughout the southwest corner of the country, scrublands were turned into investment properties and gated retirement communities under the mantra of "Nicaragua is the next Costa Rica!"

Then it ended with a whimper. In 2009, amid a global recession and increasing uncertainty about Nicaragua's direction, the mood was sour and the verdict still out as to whether it was all worth it. The wave of investment was followed by foreclosures, half-built properties, and bitterness on both sides—Nicaraguans and foreigners.

On the Nicaraguan side are campesinos who hastily sold their undeveloped land at rock-bottom prices. They then watched as their homesteads were turned into multimillion dollar investment properties. Some Nicas now work as guards and maids at the new places; others have taken advantage of the short construction boom. But not all of them. Meanwhile, to encourage tourism, the mayor's office criminalized the raising of livestock and chickens within city limits: reasonable at first glance, except that it's a law that impacts a lot of San Juan del Sur's poor right in the belly, and they're not happy about it.

On the North American side are the people who bought land during the frenzy but whose developments have not turned out as planned. In some cases, developers never connected water or power, nor built the roads they'd promised. Others blame the Nicaraguan government for suddenly enforcing forgotten taxes and the coastal law that prevents construction within 50 meters of the high-tide mark. Still others fell victim to contractors who ran off with prepayments without finishing the job and others whose workmanship was suspect. Many investors have found that, far from being the next Costa Rica, Nicaragua was just too difficult to do business in, and they picked up and left.

The tension has boiled over in proxy battles, one of which was the case of Eric Volz, an American expat who was accused of killing his Nicaraguan ex-girlfriend, Doris Jimenez, in 2006. Evidence placing Volz in Managua at the time of the crime was rejected by the Sandinista judge in what observers called a "kangaroo court," while FSLN-organized mobs surrounded the courthouse bellowing for justice. Volz, who originally came to Nicaragua to edit a magazine called El Puente ("the bridge," as in bridge between Nica and gringo cultures) was declared guilty and was sentenced to 30 years—the maximum—in prison. After eleven months in the horrific Tipitapa prison, he was released and fled the country (Eric Volz tells his story in the book Gringo Nightmare, Saint Martin's Press, 2010).

For the moment, it seems both Nicaraguans and foreigners live in an uneasy detente, as some foreigners decide to pursue other interests and some have redoubled their efforts to be part of the local community. To the casual traveler, most of this will go unnoticed. But under the surface, the forces of globalization ensure that the battle between the haves and the have-nots will continue to be important.

—Jean Walsh contributed to this story.

---

stone with the carvings. Continue upstream to the (rainy season only) waterfall.

Gym and Yoga

Buena Vida Fitness Center (half block from El Gato Negro, www.buenavidafitness.com, Mon.–Sat., closed for lunch) offers mellow yoga flow on Tuesday and Thursday ($5), fitness and

dance classes, and an assortment of free weights and machines. Find shiatsu massage ($20/hr), acupuncture, or chiropractic work at **Elixir** (next to the Casa de Cultura on the beach, tel. 505/8971-9393, Mon.–Sat.).

The central **Zen Yoga** (opposite the Pizzeria, 20 m south of the park, tel. 505/8465-1846, www.zenyoganicaragua.com) offers classes

CRUISE SHIPS: *LOS CRUCEROS* COMETH

In 1998, the Holland America Line added San Juan del Sur as a port of call on several of their cruises. The announcement sparked hope in the people of San Juan del Sur, who began preparing their sleepy town to receive the thousands of cruise ship passengers scheduled to disembark.

After several years of regular biweekly stops, however, whether or not *los cruceros* have benefited San Juan del Sur depends entirely on whom you ask. The well-to-do Careli Tours company, which enjoys a monopoly on the buses and guides who whisk passengers straight from the dock in San Juan to day trips in Granada or Masaya, isn't complaining. These passengers never set foot in San Juan proper, and the few hundred who decide to remain in town do not spend money in restaurants or hotels. A few bars have made a good business catering to thirsty crewmembers, but passengers themselves don't do much onshore imbibing or eating. The *ciclo* taxis and their drivers that cart passengers to and from the dock are imported from Rivas and few of the crafts vendors that display along the tree-lined beachfront strip are Nicaraguan. In fact, the majority of San Juaneños have not gained a dime from the arrival of the cruise ships and would only notice their absence by the lack of tinted-window bus convoys rumbling past their doors every two weeks.

Concerned cruise passengers should attempt to leave some dollars behind for someone other than their ship-sponsored tour operators, whether in San Juan del Sur or in other Nicaraguan cities they visit—and if you like what you see, come back and spend a night or two.

with monthly or drop-in passes ($8). In the hills outside of town, **Nica Yoga** (tel. 505/8696-9885, www.nicayoga.com) offers daily yoga classes, individual guest accommodations, all-inclusive yoga retreats, and custom packages that include yoga and surfing (starting at $700) in Nicaragua's first and only yoga community. Packages include fine food, San Juan's largest outdoor wooden yoga floor, and a saline lap pool open to guests. The **Casa Tranquila Day Spa** (tel. 505/2563-7000, reservations@piedrasyolas.com), in the Pelican Eyes resort, offers skin care, nail care, and salon services; an hour-long massage is $50. Call for appointments.

ENTERTAINMENT AND EVENTS

San Juan del Sur's mellow, year-round party scene picks up around Christmas, New Year's Eve, and Semana Santa when the town is flooded with visitors. Managuan club owners set up beach discos during the high season. The rest of the year, the town's discos—**Crazy Crab** (at the north end of the beach; take a taxi home at night) and **La Ballena Negra** (a block north of Iguana)—are open Thursday–Sunday (Saturday night is best). San Juan del Sur's busiest bar is still upstairs at **Iguana,** catering to locals and foreigners alike. A bit farther down the strip is another enjoyable waterfront bar, **Arribas** (open daily) with a chiller vibe.

A mellow bar with eclectic music, darts, and a great menu including a monster Philly cheesesteak, **Big Wave Dave's** is open early for breakfast, then serves bar food ($4) and drinks all day long. It's a good place to hang out at the ample horseshoe bar and chat with your compatriots.

San Juan del Sur's *fiestas patronales* are June 16–24, with bull riding, pole climbing, greased-pig catching, and Coca-Cola chugging contests, followed by **Procesión de la Virgen del Carmen** on July 17. Locals parade the icon, the Patron Saint of Fishermen, through town and to the docks where waiting boats take her (and as many locals as possible) for a lap around the bay. On **September 2** the town commemorates the tidal wave of 1992, a 62-foot monster that swept across main street, destroying many structures (and farther up the coast, entire villages, like El Tránsito).

SHOPPING

During weekends, holidays, and cruise ship arrivals, street vendors—from Masaya and as far as Guatemala and Argentina—work the beachfront opposite El Timon. **Vastu** (a few doors down from Pan de Vida, closed for lunch) is an interesting shop featuring recycled art made from beach-found garbage and driftwood; it's kitschy, retro, and environmentally friendly. Most everyday items, including fresh vegetables and those dollar flip-flops you've been looking for, can be purchased in or around the **Municipal Market** (center of town, 7 A.M.–7 P.M.). On Saturdays an **organic farmers market** sets up at Big Wave Dave's.

ACCOMMODATIONS

San Juan's lodging runs the gamut from grungy to luxe. The cheapest *hospedajes* are near the center of town, are Nicaraguan owned, and are usually extensions of someone's home. You may not encounter much of a "scene" at these places and a knock on the front door may be necessary if you return late at night. The beachfront road has a few nicer hotels and many of San Juan's restaurants and bars. It is safe to assume that nicer hotels have backup generators and water tanks, but you should still ask unless you don't mind the occasional candlelit bucket bath. Note: During the high season (New Year's and Easter) hotel prices double or even triple.

Under $25

Surfers like to stay above **Hostel Beach Fun** (tel. 505/2568-2441, $8 pp shared bath, $37 d with TV and a/c). The 16 rooms are small, but the owners are nice and the place is centrally located. You can rent a quad bike or ATV (don't even think of driving it on the beach) for $25 per hour and arrange rides to local beaches and trips to La Flor.

◀ **Hospedaje Don Wilfredo's** (25 meters east of El Timon, tel. 505/2568-2128, www.hospedajedonwilfredo.com, $6 pp with fan and private bath, $25 d with a/c) is a terrific value. The hostel is centrally located just steps from the beach. Ask for a room upstairs for good natural light and airflow.

Constructed in 1929, **Hotel Estrella** (located where the market road meets the beach, tel. 505/2568-2210, hotelestrella1929@hotmail.com) was the first hotel in San Juan del Sur. Less glamorous now than in its glory years, Estrella is still the only place in town where you get an oceanfront balcony for $8 a person (so make sure you get one). Drawbacks include a surly manager, bats, and having to walk downstairs to use the 1929-era bathroom. Next door is the **Hostel Esperanza** (tel. 505/8754-6816, www.hostelesperanza.net, $9), a chill work in progress right across from the ocean. Expect a thin mattress in a dorm room, use of the kitchen, and free Internet.

Casa Oro (tel. 505/2568-2415, www.casaeloro.com, $8 dorms, $25 d with private bath) is the oldest hostel in town, just west of the central park. They run three convenient beach shuttles daily, undercutting the competition Wal-Mart-style to the chagrin of the smaller tour operators and taxi drivers. Guests love the daily surf report and travel info, lockers, TV lounge, and free make-your-own-pancakes on the weekends.

Close to the beach, in a large wooden house, is ◀ **Hostel Pachamama** (Calle Principal, two blocks west of the church, tel. 505/2568-2043,www.hostelpachamama.com, dorm $8, private rooms $20–30). Trendy backpackers gravitate towards these colorful walls to take advantage of everything on offer, including ping pong, free skateboard and bike use, movies and board games, an open kitchen, on-site bar, and ubiquitous hammocks.

Find a warm welcome, kitchen, and parking at **Rebecca's Inn** (25 yards west of the park, tel. 505/8675-1048, martha_urcuyo@yahoo.

es, $16–25), run by Martha, who grew up in this house and can tell you about the local lore in English. All rooms come with private bath. Across the street, **Posada Puesta del Sol** (tel. 505/2568-2532, lalacard98@yahoo.com, $15–20 d) has five simple rooms and gives deals to students studying Spanish in town. **Mama Rosa** ($10 per person with fan and shared bath) has been welcoming foreigners into her home for eight years, mostly students from nearby Spanish schools. Clean, simple rooms have decent mattresses and newish sheets.

Stay at **El Encanto del Sur** (75 meters south of the park, tel. 505/2568-2222, $20 d with fan, $30 with a/c) for a traditional hotel on a quiet street with plenty of privacy. Private bathroom, TV, Wi-Fi, and tax are included.

Another central option is the **Hostal Casa Amarilla** (half a block west of the Texaco on the entry street, tel. 505/8882-7471, dorm $10, private rooms $25) with an open kitchen, breezy second-floor balcony, and meals on request. These homey rooms are popular with long-term guests and are not always available; call ahead and ask for monthly rates. The creative young owner also runs her own-brand **Turquesa Boutique** from here, so guests can peruse the handcrafted jewelry and trendy beachwear at their leisure.

$25-50

Royal Chateau Hotel (one block east of the market, tel. 505/2568-2551, www.hotelroyal-chateau.com, $50–80) is Nica-owned. Their friendliness, the security of the compound, private parking, a big wooden porch with traditional adobe-tiled roof, and a filling breakfast makes the Royal Chateau an easy pick for midrange hotels.

Across from Gato Negro, the **Secret Cove Inn** (tel. 505/8672-3013, rjesq@aol.com, www.secretcoveinn.com, $26–31) is a little American-owned bed-and-breakfast with Wi-Fi, bicycles, and services like massage and manicures and pedicures for guests. One of the owners is a

yoga instructor and can help you find classes; they also offer sailboat tours and weekly rates.

Azul Pitahaya (above the Barrio Cafe, one block west and one block north of the park, tel. 505/2568-2294, www.hotelazulsanjuan.com, $36–46) offers six spotless, brightly colored rooms with cable TV, air-conditioning, and private bath with hot water; breakfast is included.

The peaceful **Casa Ariki** guesthouse (2.5 blocks south of the market, tel. 505/2568-2629, www.casaariki.com, $30–35) has four spotless private rooms, most with shared bath, where you are sure to get a good night's sleep.

Hotel El Pacifico (tel. 505/2568-2557, www.el-pacifico-hotel.com, $20 d with fan, $46 d with a/c, plus tax) is located across the river in the wealthy neighborhood of Barrio El Talanguera, well removed from the hustle and bustle of the city. The nine remodeled rooms are comfortable, with private bath, parking, pool, Wi-Fi, cable TV, restaurant, and bar. Get there via the Chocolata road turnoff at the entrance to town or walk about 15 minutes across the Golden Gate–esque suspension bridge at the north end of the beach.

$50-100

Every listing in this category includes breakfast and free wireless Internet; you can also expect hot water and a private bathroom, air-conditioning, and a TV in your room. **Hotel Villa Isabella** (across from the northeast corner of the Catholic church, tel. 505/2568-2568, http://villaisabellasjds.com, $75 d) has large rooms with private bath, air-conditioning, TV, heated pool, and family-friendly condos ($175, six people). This pristine, 13-room bed-and-breakfast is two minutes from the beach, and offers business services, full wheelchair accessibility, a huge selection of DVDs, and free calls to the U.S. or Europe. Their breakfast is no meager continental affair—homemade waffles, cinnamon rolls, banana pancakes, breakfast burritos, fresh fruit, and great coffee.

Hotel Colonial (half a block from the park, tel. 505/2568-2539, www.hotel-nicaragua.com, $54 d) has 12 rooms and decent parking; the lush interior garden is a lovely place to relax.

◖**La Posada Azul** (half a block east of BDF bank, tel. 505/2568-2524, www.laposadaazul. com, $80–120) has lovely rooms and a small pool. Tasteful decor, lazily spinning wicker ceiling fans, and classy wood-grained ambience echo the remodeled building's 90-year history.

A short taxi ride outside of town, in the Las Delicias neighborhood on the road to the southern beaches, is **Aventura Lodge** (tel. 505/8903-7622, www.aventurasanjuan. com, $70). Pretty but dark rooms have somewhat cheap mattresses and border a whimsical pool and lush garden courtyard. Beds in the quirky treehouse *palapa* are $20 a night and "jungle suites" start at $55; rates include a self-serve breakfast of yogurt, granola, and fruit. Mind the resident parrot, who can be delightful or annoying depending on what time you hit the sack.

Over $100

Pelican Eyes Hotel and Resort (tel. 505/2563-2110, www.pelicaneyesresort.com, $207–368) was one the first high-end resorts of its kind in Nicaragua, built on the hill above town and offering fully equipped homes with kitchenettes and outdoor decks. Despite ongoing property disputes and management changes, the place trucks on. There are two bars, a world-class restaurant, and three infinity pools overlooking the ocean. Their **Bistro La Canoa** is one of the best places in town to enjoy a sunset; go for happy hour, otherwise a margarita can set you back $7. There's also an on-site spa and sailboat to charter.

The cocktails are cheaper and the pool is just as nice at **Villas de Palermo** (tel. 505/8672-0859, www.villasdepalermo.com, from $159), in the hills outside of town. Stay the night in a handsome villa or just drop in for the day to

take a swim and have a drink at the poolside bar and restaurant.

Built in 1902, then restored and splashed across the *New York Times* travel section, the ◖ **Hotel Victoriano** (tel. 505/2568-2006, www.hotelvictoriano.com.ni, $120–140) has 21 rooms, giant four-poster beds, and all the amenities—shampoo bottles, bathrobes, nice lobby, pool, air-conditioning, TV, hot water, private parking, and Wi-Fi. The hotel is located on the waterfront at the south end of town.

Long-Term Accommodations

Weekly or monthly rentals are easy to arrange, both in San Juan proper and in the hills surrounding the city. For the low budget set, most Spanish schools in town have packages combining lessons and a homestay, which can be arranged (whether or not you are attending class) for around $10 per day including three meals. Most places will cut you a deal if you stay more than a few nights.

For something fancier see **Vacation Rentals Nicaragua** (www.vacationrentalsnicaragua. com), **Vacation Rentals by Owner** (www. vrbo.com), or **Home Away** (www.homeaway. com), or stop by **Aurora Beachfront Realty** (tel. 505/2568-2498, U.S. tel. 323/908-6730). A fully furnished two-bedroom place goes for $800–1,200 per week and a big house is double that. Nearly all homes come with swimming pools and sweeping ocean views.

FOOD

Fear not the municipal market: You can eat three tasty and filling *corriente* meals a day at one of the four counters inside for under $3. Evenings, try Juanita's *fritanga* on the street where the buses leave or walk to the southwest corner of the park for **Asados Vilma,** a.k.a. the Chicken Lady, with grilled meat, mountains of *gallo pinto,* and delicious *frescos* from $3. Nearly every *hospedaje,* hotel, and beach restaurant makes a variety of breakfasts, usually for $3–5. Locally owned *sodas* offer Nicaraguan standards for under $5.

Bakeries and Cafés

El Gato Negro (7 A.M.–3 P.M. daily) serves freshly roasted organic espresso and good breakfasts, including bagels and cream cheese, in a bookstore setting. There's free Internet, but be warned—paying customers will be stung over a dollar to charge up their laptops here. **Barrio Café** (one block west of the bus stop, $3) makes first-rate espresso drinks and serves breakfasts with coffee and orange juice; there's free Wi-Fi too.

For freshly baked breads, cookies, brownies, and the like, head to **Pan de Vida,** a block west of the Texaco on the entry street. Ask about their group pizza-making nights, when you can pummel your own dough and create the monster pizza you always dreamed of.

Seafood

A long row of virtually identical thatched-roof rancho restaurants runs along the central part of the beach, serving fresh fish dishes ($5) and shrimp and lobster dishes ($10–14) until 10 P.M. Josseline's, at the southern end, offers delicious fish dishes, a notable vegetarian soup, and a pleasant atmosphere. El Timon is a longtime favorite of Nicaraguans and tourists alike. Some say it has the best service of all the *ranchos;* it's also one of the most expensive.

At the south end of the bay, just before the dock, you can buy grouper, swordfish, or red snapper fresh from the boat (they will fillet it for you), particularly on Wednesday and Saturday when the boats return from the sea.

Bambu Beach Club (located at the far north end of San Juan del Sur's main beach, tel. 505/2568-2101, www.thebambubeachclub.com, $6–10) is a Mediterranean-influenced restaurant with stylish decor and cool bathrooms.

© TAMARA MONTENEGRO

There are plenty of places to eat in town, from casual hole-in-the-walls to fancy restaurants.

Serving seafood *bocas,* sandwiches, and entrées, it's also a full bar, relaxed beach hangout, seaside cinema, and acoustic concert space.

Italian

Ⓒ Mauricio's Pizzería (next to El Timon, tel. 505/2568-2295 for delivery, 5 P.M.–close daily, $5) is easily one of the most popular restaurants in town, with great pasta and real Italian pizza. Ask Mauricio for a shot of his homemade *limoncello* after your meal. He's got another branch, just west of the playground at the municipal park, where the dining is more informal and you can grab pizza-to-go by the slice.

Upscale

Bar y Restaurante La Cascada (in Pelican Eyes Hotel, tel. 505/2568-2511, $12–25) offers tables set above the village with a prime view of the ocean and sunset. Breakfast and lunch start at $7; or just sample from the exotic tropical drink menu. (Prices are in dollars, if that tells you anything.)

Ⓒ El Colibrí (one block south of the east side of the church, tel. 505/2568-2861, Tues.–Sun., $8–15) offers a reasonably priced assortment of delicious Mediterranean specialties in an unbeatable outdoor ambience. The menu ranges from paella to polenta to chicken breast stuffed with walnuts, raisins, and basil in a red wine sauce—don't miss the sangria. Reservations for large parties during the high season are recommended. Credit cards are not accepted.

INFORMATION AND SERVICES

From home, start at **www.sanjuandelsurguide. com,** where many businesses listed here post their updated rates. The **Municipal Tourism Commission,** at the northwest corner of the park, can provide information on activities. Free maps and flyers around town advertise local goings-on. Pick up a free copy of *Del Sur News,* a weekly bulletin of community news and events in English and Spanish, at many places around town.

The few pharmacies in town have limited supplies; for medical needs, the **Centro de Salud** provides free consultations 8 A.M.–7 P.M. Monday–Saturday and 8 A.M.–noon Sunday. However, for any serious medical concerns, plan a trip to Rivas, as the Centro is typically understaffed and crowded.

Nearly all of the nicer hotels (and some restaurants) accept major credit cards, but the three banks in town all have ATMs. BDF, located half a block from the Casa de Cultura; Banco ProCredit, one block west of the market; and Bancentro, next to Big Wave Dave's, all offer similar services, but none will cash your travelers checks.

San Juan's handful of Internet cafés are slightly more expensive than other places in Nicaragua ($1 an hour), but are plentiful and easy to find. **Cyber M@nfred,** on the corner of the main street into town, has a generator and charges 50 percent more if you absolutely have to check Facebook while the power is out. Most hotels offer free Wi-Fi.

Most of the nicer hotels provide laundry service, as will the inexpensive hotels if you strike a deal. If you'd rather go to an independent *lavandería* (laundry) with modern machines, you'll find **Gaby's** (tel. 505/8837-7493) uphill from the market, charging $5 per load (wash, dry, fold). Gaby also gives massages.

GETTING THERE

The trip from Managua takes about 2–2.5 hours in your own vehicle or on the express bus, but is nearly four hours in an *ordinario.*

From Managua, the absolute fastest way is by express shuttles that leave from the airport. **Adelante Express** (tel. 505/8850-6070, www.adelanteexpress.com) charges about $45 one-way, cheaper per person for groups. For guaranteed service make your reservation at least 24 hours in advance. **Nica Express** (tel. 505/2552-8461, info@nica-adventures.com,

VOLUNTEERING IN SAN JUAN DEL SUR

© JOSHUA BERMAN

Bring a Spanish-language book for San Juan del Sur's lending library.

If you'd like to spend some time working with the community, the environment, or the children of San Juan del Sur, there are numerous options.

Barrio Planta Project (BPP, barrioplantaproject.org). The project aims to help local children find their voice; kids now come from all over town to participate in the numerous programs, which have included poetry writing and hip-hop workshops.

Comunidad Connect (CC, tel. 505/2568-2731, www.comunidadconnect.org). This local nonprofit is dedicated to supporting sustainable economic and community development in the area; they invite voluntourists like yourself to help with their projects. CC can arrange an all-inclusive homestay with a local family, volunteer projects, Spanish lessons, and excursions to their organic coffee farm.

Fundación A. Jean Brugger (tel. 505/2563-7000 ext. 861, www.fundaciona-jbrugger.org). This organization provides scholarships, uniforms, school supplies, and job training for promising local students. It also supports recycling and antilitter campaigns and a community art gallery, runs baseball camps for area youths, and hosts a popular monthly luncheon for senior citizens. Financial contributions are always needed, and materials such as school supplies are appreciated as well.

San Juan del Sur Biblioteca Movil (www.sjdsbiblioteca.com). Located across the street from the park, this is the first lending library in Nicaragua and serves as the town library. Besides helping monetarily, tourists can volunteer by teaching English, organizing books, and reading to youngsters, or joining the staff on a visit to one of the rural schools. There is a formal volunteer program for librarians, library school students, and others held twice a year. Book donations are always welcome.

www.nica-adventures.com) also has comfortable, scheduled shuttles from San Juan to other cities.

Regular express buses leave from Huembes market ($3–5 pp) about every hour around the middle of the day; the best and last one leaves at 4 P.M. Slow, crowded, *ordinario* service to Rivas from Huembes market in Managua operates 5 A.M.–5 P.M. The handlers at the Huembes bus terminal are unusually aggressive. They will grab your bags out of the taxi, push you onto a slow Rivas bus, claim it's an express, and then demand a tip. Read the windshield of the bus and ask the other passengers to verify.

Once in Rivas you can take a *colectivo* ($1.50 pp) or taxi ($10) the rest of the way to San Juan del Sur. *Colectivos* don't run after dark and taxi prices double because not even the most skilled drivers can see the potholes at night. And from Granada there are several shuttle services worth taking, all of which cost more than the bus but more than compensate in saved time and frustration.

To Managua and Rivas

Express buses leave from the corner in front of the market at 5 A.M. (this is the nicer *lujo* bus), 6 A.M., and 7 A.M. *Ordinarios* to Rivas and Managua leave every hour 5 A.M.–5 P.M. You can also catch a *colectivo* taxi to Rivas from 4 A.M. to about 3 or 4 P.M. and then catch any northbound bus toward Managua. The trip to and from Rivas takes about 30 minutes in a car; 45 minutes in a bus ($1).

To and From Costa Rica

From the Costa Rican border at Peñas Blancas, buses for Rivas leave every half hour. Get off at **Empalme la Vírgen** and flag a bus, taxi, or ride going between Rivas and San Juan del Sur. The beach is 18 kilometers due west of La Vírgen; taxis from the border to San Juan charge $15–25.

To the border at Peñas Blancas, get a ride to La Vírgen in a bus or taxi, then catch a lift south; the first Rivas–Peñas Blancas bus passes at 7:30 A.M. Or book a ticket with TicaBus (tel. 505/8877-1407) in Rivas. Also check with shuttle services.

GETTING AROUND

You won't need a taxi to get around town (you'll only see them trolling for passengers to Rivas and the beaches): From one end of town to the other is just a 15-minute stroll. Elizabeth's Hospedaje near the bus stop rents bikes.

To travel up and down the coast, you'll need a sturdy and preferably four-wheel drive car or a decent mountain bike and some stamina. Taxi drivers lounge around the market and can take you up and down the coast, but if you are going surfing for the day, you're better off catching a ride with one of the surf shops, or with the "gringo shuttles" from Casa Oro. Water taxis operate from in front of Hotel Estrella. Hotel Casablanca, on the central part of the beach, rents Alamo cars.

Arrange a car and driver in advance by contacting **Ricardo Morales** (2.5 blocks south of Hotel Villa Isabella, tel. 505/8882-8368, richardsjds@hotmail.com or transporte.gaby@gmail.com), a San Juan native with a few four-wheel drive vehicles and a great deal of local contacts and knowledge; he'll pick you up at the airport or in Granada.

NICARAGUA'S ROCKY RELATIONSHIP WITH COSTA RICA

Costa Rica is a wealthier, more politically stable country than Nicaragua. In his 1985 travelogue *So Far From God,* Patrick Marnham called Costa Rica "the most European of the countries of the isthmus." To keep it that way, the Costa Rican economy is wholly dependent on low-cost Nicaraguan laborers for harvesting their sugarcane and coffee and filling the ranks of the construction workforce in urban centers. In an effort to control immigration, Costa Rican officials conduct regular roundups of illegal aliens, returning as many as 150 to Nicaragua daily. If you travel south into Costa Rica, you can expect patrolmen to stop and search your bus several times for illegals. Some estimates put the number of Nicaraguans living in Costa Rica at more than a million, but with the constant flux and large percentage of undocumented Nicas, no one knows for sure. The real number might be half that.

The tense relationship between these incongruous Central American neighbors loosely parallels the relationship between the United States and Mexico: namely, a massive flood of poor immigrants crosses the border into a more prosperous and stable nation and is subsequently accused of driving down wages, taking all the jobs, and straining social services without paying taxes. As the immigrants are darker-skinned and easy to distinguish, they're easy to blame. Ask most Ticos (as Costa Ricans call themselves) about the issue and you'll likely get an earful of racist comments about Nicaraguans being "lazy, no-good, poor, and dirty." Oh yeah, they're "*Indios*," to boot.

Nicaraguans, for their part, generally mistrust Ticos and don't appreciate their arrogance.

"The truth is," wrote none other than Carlos Fonseca, founder of the FSLN, from exile in San José in 1960, that Costa Rica "doesn't even seem to be located next to Nicaragua–it is so totally different.... And even though this country is different from Nicaragua, and I am longing for a different Nicaragua, Costa Rica doesn't appeal to me, and I wouldn't want the Nicaragua of the future to be anything like Costa Rica."

Cultural tensions predate these new immigration issues; in fact, only 50 years ago, Ticos used to emigrate to Nicaragua to work on cattle farms. A hundred years before that, after helping to defeat William Walker's army in Rivas, Tico soldiers occupied southern Nicaragua, withdrawing only after being granted the Guanacaste Peninsula in an 1858 treaty. During the 1980s, U.S.-backed Contra forces illegally based operations in Costa Rica, prompting an irritated Costa Rican President Oscar Arías Sanchez to help negotiate an end to Nicaragua's conflict.

Costa Rica continues to press for a resolution to Nicaraguan immigration issues. Too much blustery rhetoric from Managua regarding other issues, like the sovereignty of the Río San Juan, may tempt the Ticos to crack down even more on illegal immigrants, something Managua would very much like to avoid. Even today, Nicaraguan immigrants have reported irregular and inhumane incarceration by Tico authorities, often for weeks at a time without formal charges (and sometimes without daylight, toilets, and food).

Rhetoric aside, the two neighbors desperately need each other. Perhaps pragmatism will win out over politics in the end.

Beaches South of San Juan del Sur

Between San Juan del Sur and Ostional on the Costa Rican border are a number of excellent beaches, and the Ostional bus will take you there, if you can afford to wait; otherwise, do like everyone else and bum a ride with someone with a vehicle, including the several shuttle options leaving from San Juan del Sur center. You'll first pass through Barrio Las Delicias, which includes San Juan del Sur's stadium and cemetery, followed by a fork in the road known as El Container. Turn right here to get to **Playa Remanso,** about a kilometer down a path

BEACHES SOUTH OF SAN JUAN DEL SUR

To La Virgen and Rivas
16
Bahía San Juan del Sur
San Juan del Sur
El Carrizal
Playa Remanso
Playa Tamarindo
Playa Hermosa
Escamequita
Playa Escamequita
GATE
Playa Yanqui
PACIFIC OCEAN
Playa El Coco
LA FLOR WILDLIFE REFUGE
Playa La Flor
To Tortuga
0   2 mi
0   2 km
© AVALON TRAVEL

of the new developments when the owner decided to build a "viewpoint" going out into the sea. An effort by local surfers and activists prevented the construction, and for now, this break remains one of the best in the area. Look for a sign at a fork on the main road before you get to the Yankee Beach development; go right and then left at another sign, then over a hill for a photo-worthy view of what awaits. Park at the small house on a hill at the south end of the beach for $3 to prevent theft. At low tide you can park right on the beach.

Places to stay in this area are limited. Carol and Alan rent out three cozy rooms at their charming bed-and-breakfast, **Latin Latitudes** (www.latin-latitudes.com, $40–80). They've landscaped with native plants, used local construction materials, and installed solar panels on the roof. **Orquidea Del Sur** (tel. 505/8984-2150, $180, three-night minimum) is a high-end retreat with a luxurious pool perched atop the hills. Reservations must be made in advance for both.

PLAYA EL COCO

Eighteen kilometers south of San Juan, this jewel of a beach is great for swimming, fishing, and access to the turtles at La Flor; this is where you'll find **Parque Marítimo El Coco** (tel. 505/8999-8069, www.playaelcoco.com.ni), an extensive compound on a wide beach with a popular restaurant called **Puesta del Sol** (8 A.M.–8 P.M. daily, $7). Accommodations range from furnished apartments to fully equipped bungalows and houses; prices start at $100 and rise to hundreds of dollars per night. Weekend packages are very reasonable with a group of people. Houses have air-conditioning, satellite TV, hot water, and kitchen, and sleep up to eight people. You should come prepared with supplies; there is an on-site minimarket, plus bike rental, Internet, and a conference facility.

◖ LA FLOR WILDLIFE REFUGE

One of the two Pacific turtle nesting beaches in Nicaragua, the park at La Flor is managed

infamous for robberies: Don't go alone. It'll take about 25 minutes to get there on rough dirt roads. This slow surf break is great for beginners, so expect to share it with all the new friends you met over beers last night. There's a shady outdoor bar right on the sand where you can purchase snacks and drinks at inflated prices. At low tide, look for bat caves, tidepools, blowholes, and various wildlife.

Walking 30 minutes south around the rocks brings you to **Playa Tamarindo,** followed by **Playa Hermosa** just under an hour later (it's a 20-minute walk from the bus stop at El Carizal, farther down the road toward Ostional). Ask in the surf shops in town about safety precautions and public access to these beaches.

A 30-minute drive south of town is **Playa Yanqui.** This powerful and fast wave that rolls into a giant beach was almost destroyed by one by the governmental environment agency MARENA. Make sure you catch one of the nighttime *arribadas,* or mass nesting events, that occur during the crescent moon from July–February. **Casa Oro** (tel. 505/2568-2415, www.casaeloro.com) in San Juan del Sur runs shuttles during the season. Foreigners pay $10 per person to enter, another $25 for group camping (bring your own gear).

OSTIONAL

This picturesque bay and community at the extreme southwestern tip of Nicaragua is still more of a fishing town than a tourist destination, but curious visitors can seek out the rural tourism cooperative, **Community Tours** (tel. 505/8846-2272, communitytours@yahoo.es), for tours of the area and nearby bays—along with simple accommodations. All trips are about four hours and have a local guide, whether by boat or horseback. A portion of the profits goes toward 30 university scholarships for promising youths of the community. Buses from Rivas to Ostional pass through the San Juan del Sur market at 1 P.M., 4 P.M., and 5 P.M. (two hours to Ostional). They depart the center of Ostional

La Flor Wildlife Refuge is a great place to watch *arribadas* (turtle nesting sites).

at 5 A.M., 7:30 A.M., and 4 P.M., but confirm with the driver and anyone else you can find waiting around.

Beaches North of San Juan del Sur

To get to Maderas or Marsella, stop by any of the surf shops in San Juan. Rides cost $5 round-trip. If you're driving, access these beaches via the road to Chocolata, just east of the Texaco station. Much of this road served as the old grade for a railroad that was never built. Seven kilometers along, turn left at Chocolata to a fork in the road: left goes to Marsella and Maderas, right to Majagual. It'll take you about 20 minutes to reach either beach.

PLAYA MARSELLA

This pleasant, breezy beach is one of the closest to San Juan del Sur and you can drive right up to the sand, making it a popular day trip for Frisbee throwers and sunset watchers. On the weekends a small restaurant on the beach serves ceviche, fried fish, and cold beer.

The well-liked **Elmpalme a Las Playas** (tel. 505/8803-7208 or 505/8994-9013, www.playamarsella.com, $50–85 with breakfast) is still more visited by passing

© GRACE GONZALEZ

TURTLES

The Olive Ridley (or Paslama) sea turtle (*Lepidochelys olivacea*) is an endangered species well known for its massive synchronous nesting emergences. These seasonal occurrences, called *arribadas*, occur several times during each lunar cycle in the July-February nesting season, and at their peak (August-October), result in as many as 20,000 females nesting and laying eggs on a single beach.

In Nicaragua, the two beaches that receive the most turtles are **Playa Chacocente** and **Playa La Flor,** both on the southwestern Pacific coast. Playa La Flor, located about 15 kilometers north of the Costa Rican border and 18 kilometers southeast of San Juan del Sur, is a 1.6-kilometer-long beach that has been protected as part of a wildlife preserve. Hatchings have been less successful every year. Fly larvae, beetles, coyotes, opossums, raccoons, skunks, coatimundis, feral dogs, pigs, and humans all prey on Olive Ridley sea turtles in one form or another. High tides and beach erosion sweep away other eggs, and once they emerge from their shells, they are pounced on by crabs, frigatebirds, caracara, vultures, and coyotes before they can reach the sea. Once in the water, they must still battle a host of predatory fish.

In general, females lay two clutches of eggs per season and remain near shore for approximately one month. The mean clutch size of the females differs from beach to beach but averages about 100 eggs; incubation takes 45-55 days, depending on the temperature, humidity, and organic content of the sand.

The *arribadas* and hatching events both occur during the night and witnessing these phenomena is an unforgettable experience. Tourism can protect the turtles, as it provides an incentive to continue protection efforts, but it can just as easily be disastrous (since the first edition of this book was published, the rangers have been permitting people to "swim with the turtles," an injurious practice). It is too easy to harass, injure, or frighten the turtles if you're not careful. Don't count on park rangers to tell you what's acceptable; use your common sense to respect this inspiring natural process and *please* pay close attention to the following rules during your expedition to the beaches of La Flor or Chacocente.

TURTLE-VIEWING ETIQUETTE

- Do not use your camera's flash when taking pictures of turtles coming out of the sea, digging a nest, or going back to the ocean—the light can scare them back into the ocean without laying their eggs. The only time that you can take a picture of them is when they are laying eggs; the flash will not disturb them as much, as they enter a semitrance state.

- Keep your flashlight use as minimal as possible; use a red filter over the lens or color it with a temporary red marker. If the moon is out, use its light instead.

- Do not dig out any nests that are being laid or are hatching.

- Do not eat sea turtle eggs, whether on the beach or in a restaurant. Despite their undeserved reputation as an aphrodisiac, the raw eggs may carry harmful organisms and their consumption supports a black market that incentivizes poaching.

- Do not touch, attempt to lift, turn, or ride turtles.

- Do not interfere with any research being performed on the beach (i.e., freeing hatchlings from nest boxes).

- If camping, place your tents beyond the vegetation line so as not to disturb the nesting turtles.

  —Shaya Honarvar, PhD, Department of Bioscience & Biotechnology, Drexel University, contributed to this piece.

BEACHES NORTH OF SAN JUAN DEL SUR

To Rivas

Arena Blanca

Playa Ocotál   MORGAN'S ROCK RESORT

La Chocolata

Bahía Majagual

Playa Maderas

PACIFIC

Playa Nacascolo

DA FLYIN FROG CANOPY TOUR

To La Virgen

16

Bahía San Juan del Sur

San Juan del Sur

OCEAN

To La Flor

0   1 mi

0   1 km

© AVALON TRAVEL

A short walk north is **Hideout Surf Camp** (ddwysdwy@hyahoo.com, $10 pp dorm, $20 private room), followed by, another five minutes north along the beach, **Matilda's** (tel. 505/2456-3461 or 505/8818-3374, camping_matildas@hotmail.com, $5 for a perma-tent, $8 dorm, $30 d private room with bath) right on the beach, perfect for swimming. **Buena Vista Surf Club** (tel. 505/8863-4180 or 505/8863-3312, www.buenavistasurfclub.com, $130 d including breakfast and dinner) leans towards luxury and gets good reviews, located in the hills above Maderas, from where you can watch the waves while doing yoga on an incredible wooden deck. About 1.5 kilometers from the beach, **Mango Rosa** (tel. 505/8403-5326, www.mangorosanicaragua.com, $95 d) has a pool, volleyball court, hammocks, restaurant, and bar under a shady *rancho*. They've built with an environmentally friendly sewer system and are careful about energy use.

howler monkeys and toucans than anything else. Rustic bamboo cabins with mosquito nets, private bathrooms, and breezy hammock-strung decks are set in a true jungle garden a mere 15-minute walk to the pristine Marsella beach.

PLAYA MADERAS

One of the most consistent, easy-to-access surf breaks from San Juan, Maderas is enjoyed for its medium-speed hollow wave that breaks both right and left, best on incoming tides. There's parking right on the beach, and the place turns into a popular hangout around sunset. Surf shops bring groups here several times a day, so you won't be surfing solo.

Hospedaje los Tres Hermanos, a simple wooden bunkhouse with a kitchen, offers lodging right on the beach for $7 per person and cheap meals ($2 breakfast, $5 lunch), and rents boards by the hour. There's no phone here, so it's first come, first served.

BAHÍA MAJAGUAL

Twelve rough kilometers from San Juan del Sur, this beautiful beach was formerly a peaceful backpacker-surfer retreat; it was purchased by investors and is now home to a 15-foot-tall cement wall surrounding their private property. The beach remains accessible, but the charm is gone.

MORGAN'S ROCK HACIENDA & ECO LODGE

Playa Ocotál is the home of a much-hyped ecolodge at the vanguard of Nicaragua's upscale tourism market. ◼ **Morgan's Rock Hacienda & Eco Lodge** (tel. 505/8670-7676, info@morgansrock.com, www.morgansrock.com) is an exclusive resort surrounded by a 1,000-hectare reforestation project and an 800-hectare private nature reserve; its 15 elegant, hardwood cabins are built into a bluff above the crashing surf on the beach below (which means lots of stair climbing). As few trees as possible were felled during construction, so you'll have to walk a 110-meter-long suspension

The beaches north of San Juan have great waves for beginners and pros alike.

bridge through a lush canopy to reach your cabin, which is the most luxurious and beautiful tree-house your childhood fantasies ever dreamed up. The structures—as well as the main lodge, which features a gorgeous infinity pool—were designed with all local materials and feature ingenious architecture and attention to detail.

You're on vacation here, so no phones or Internet, but there's plenty to do: sunrise kayak tours of the estuary, tree-planting excursions, and tours of their shrimp farm and sugar mill, where they brew their own Morgan's Rum.

More than 70 workers are employed to grow and produce much of the restaurant's vegetables, dairy products, herbs, and other needs; a noble idea, although some readers have been a bit let down by the meals here. A cool $255 per person per night gets you a cabin, three meals, all you can drink of local, nonalcoholic beverages, and two tours a day. Prices vary by season, and cheaper packages are available, so call or email to reserve your room. The facilities and services are for guests only; sorry, no day-trippers.

Tola and Pacific Beaches

Ten kilometers west of Rivas is the agricultural community of Tola, gateway to the steadily improving shore road and a string of lonely, beautiful beaches that make up thirty kilometers of Pacific shoreline. The word is out and land prices are rising, but the beaches west of Tola are still far less developed than San Juan del Sur and retain some of their fishing village character.

In Tola proper, many travelers have stayed and worked with Doña Loida (an influential Sandinista leader, elected mayor in 2004) of **Esperanza del Futuro** (tel. 505/2563-0482), who can help arrange cheap room and board from a week to six months. Her foundation provides education to local *campesinos* and provides a library, sewing co-op, and gardens; classes in guitar, agriculture, herbal medicine, and computers are offered. Find them on the road that leads from the park to the baseball field/basketball court, about 100 meters past the baseball field. There are a few decent eateries in Tola, the most popular of which is **Lumby's.**

PLAYA GIGANTE

North up the coast from San Juan del Sur, and an hour outside Rivas, Gigante is the first beach you come to after Tola and is named after the Punta Pie de Gigante (the Giant's Foot), the rock formation you'll see on the left side of the beach. The community of Gigante consists of a beautiful crescent beach, a few dozen poor homes occupied by about 500 locals—mostly fishermen—several restaurants and a few surf camps. Avoid

Tola's beaches are more remote and less crowded than those near San Juan del Sur.

© AMBER DOBRZENSKY

this beach during Semana Santa, when it gets crowded with locals who camp out on the beach, get phenomenally drunk, and run cockfights.

Accommodations

Options for drop-in accommodations in and near Playa Gigante are rapidly growing. **Hotel Blue Sol** ($10 with fan) rents out a few rooms right at the beach but should be your last resort unless you like bedbugs. The restaurant is said to have the best tacos in town.

Giant's Foot Surf Lodge (www.giantsfoot. com) rents out two adjacent beachfront lodges with air-conditioning, fan, and private bathroom; full capacity is 12 guests. Amenities include table tennis, a fire pit, hammocks, DVDs, books, and board games. Weeklong packages cost about $1,300, with everything included except your airfare; discounts are available in the off-season.

At **Dale Dagger's Surf Lodge** (Playa Gigante, tel. 505/8360-7508, speak@NicaSurf. com, www.nicasurf.com), $1,895 a week (high season) gets you cushy digs, a ride from the airport, all meals, and unlimited trips to some of the best and least-known breaks in Nicaragua, returning to the luxury of air-conditioning, wireless Internet, and running hot water.

At the top end of accommodations in the area is the ecoluxe ◖ **Aqua Wellness Resort** (tel. 505/8849-6235 or U.S. tel. 917/512-3977, www. aquawellnessresort.com, $150–450 seasonally). Elaborate wooden treehouses and villas with stylishly detailed rustic interiors are set in a rolling patch of jungle sloping down to a pristine beach. The facilities—full spa services, an organic restaurant, an oceanside yoga platform, and watersports rentals—are sure to have a positive effect on your wellness, although the same can't be said for your wallet. Be prepared to splash out.

Camino del Gigante (tel. 505/8712-8888, www.cominodelgigante.com, dorms $10, private $30 d) is the best budget option in the bay, with a variety of accommodations from dorm beds, hammocks, and camping to private

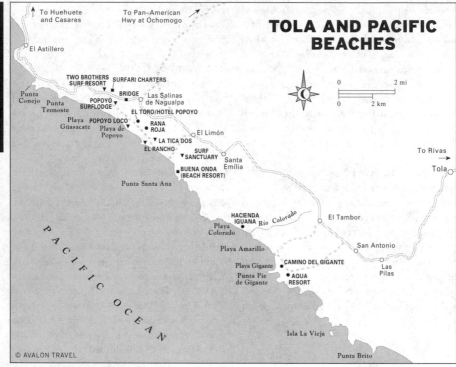

TOLA AND PACIFIC BEACHES

rooms and a fully equipped rental home. There's a relaxed beach bar and restaurant on site that's popular with travelers and local expats, and a variety of activities on offer including the area's only half-pipe skate park.

Food

Two big, airy *ranchos* sit right on the beach: **La Gaviota** ($4–11) is famous for its *plato típico de Gigante* featuring seasonal seafood. **El Mirador** prepares popular breaded fish nuggets *(deditos de pescado)*. Buy fresh seafood in the mornings from three local *acopios* (storage houses) and buy everything else from the well-stocked **Pulpería Mena.**

Getting There

It's really best to have your own vehicle to reach Gigante. Otherwise, take the Las Salinas bus from Tola or Rivas and get off at the first entrance

to Gigante. You'll have to walk or hitch about four kilometers to reach the beach. Taxis are few and far between, but anyone driving a pickup will probably let you hop in back. At the time of publication, only one bus a day went all the way to Gigante; on the way home, a school bus departs in the morning for Rivas at around 5:30 A.M. ($2).

LAS SALINAS DE NAHUALAPA

Las Salinas is a humble fishing community whose lovely beach is popular among surfers. **La Tica** is its restaurant and *hospedaje,* where spartan rooms cost about $5 per person. Nearby hot springs are worth exploring if you get sick of the beach (ask at La Tica for directions) but are also used by local families to wash clothing, so they're not exactly pristine.

The Surf Sanctuary (tel. 505/8894-6260,

www.thesurfsanctuary.com, $70 room, $100–150 house) is an upscale surf camp with restaurant, bar, TV, Internet, movies, and the works. Guests have a choice of rooms or varying private

houses, the latter of which have 1–4 bedrooms with a/c, bathrooms with hot water, and private porches, all scattered around the *rancho* and pool.

Guasacate and Popoyo

Guasacate, a huge stretch of gorgeous and mostly remote shoreline, is beautiful by any standard, and for the moment, mostly undeveloped. Many of the restaurants and hotels in this area are European-owned, unlike mostly gringo San Juan del Sur, and relative to Playa Gigante, there's a better range of accommodations from weekly surf camps to midrange hotels to cheap crash-pad *hospedajes*. The entrance to Guasacate is 5–8 kilometers down the first left-hand road after crossing a bridge in Las Salinas. The road runs along the ocean until it dead-ends at Playa Popoyo, with a handful of hotels and restaurants sprinkled along the 12-kilometer stretch. If you're here, you're probably here to surf; in case of disaster, take your board to **Popoyo Ding Repair/La Tiendita** (tel. 505/8464 9563), a cute shop that repairs, rents, and sells boards and other handmade items, 200 meters down the road.

ACCOMMODATIONS
Under $25
At the budget end of the spectrum is **❰ Popoyo Loco** ($5 per person), a funky surf shack right on the beach, offering a bed in a dorm with a thin mattress, fan, and shared bath. You won't find Internet or phone here, but feel free to use the kitchen. **La Tica Dos** (end of the road on the east side, $7 per person) is a two-story affair catering to surfers; accommodations include a basic room with fan, shared bath, and a few grunts from the unhelpful owner.

$25-50
South of Popoyo on Playa Santana, **❰ Buena**

Onda Beach Resort (tel. 505/8973-0101, www.buenaondabeachresort.com, $29–79) is the best deal in the area for midrange travelers. The resort offers a chill-out *rancho* restaurant, pool, and variety of lodging options. Four minimalist, comfortable rooms with ceiling fans and shared or private bathrooms, and one $12 dorm, occupy the main lodge. A separate building houses three deluxe rooms equipped with a/c, minifridge, satellite TV, and private porches; or you can rent one of two luxury villas that sleep up to six people ($150–200, minimum 3 nights). Exclusive surf packages, board rentals, boat trips, and local excursions can all be organized here, but the beach and surf out front mean you don't have to go far to get exactly what you came here for.

Over $50
On the left side of the road at the end of a short driveway, behind El Toro, sits **Hotel Popoyo** (tel. 505/8885-3334, www.hotelpopoyo.com, $50 s, $70 d). Spacious rooms include a king-size canopy bed, plenty of windows, bamboo roof, air-conditioning, and cable TV (including tax and breakfast); ask about the $15 dorm (low season only). There's a pool out back and a few hammocks slung under the *rancho*. Hotel Popoyo is closed the month of October.

Surf Lodges
Popoyo Surf Lodge (surfnicinc1@hotmail.com, www.surfnicaragua.com) pioneered the local surf scene in the 1990s. The owner, JJ, is a ripping, born-again surfer who also preaches at the local church. Reservations and

packages are available online; drop-ins (no surf pun intended) are accepted in the off-season. A 10-minute walk from the beach, **Surfari Charters** (tel. 505/8880-4318 or 505/8874-7173, www.surfaricharters.com) specializes in all-inclusive surf and fishing trips with expert guides; check their website for more information and captivating photography. Next door, **Two Brothers Surf Resort** (tel. 505/8877-7501, www.twobrotherssurf.com) offers more luxury, comfort, and security. Villas range $100–200 a night plus tax; the big villa fits up to six people. The resort features a pool, lounge, hand-carved Indonesian temple doors and archways, locally crafted Granada floor tiles, fully equipped kitchens, air-conditioning, ceiling fans, and indoor and outdoor showers.

FOOD

The most popular eatery in Guasacate is **El Toro** (behind Hotel Popoyo, east side of the road, tel. 505/8885-3334, $7–12), with an airy dining area and a great selection of meatless treats such as gazpacho, hummus, pasta, and veggie burritos. Just past El Toro, **Rana Roja** (6–10:30 P.M. Tues.–Sun., $5–10) serves wood-fired pizza in an atmospheric *rancho*.

At the end of the road, **Los Amores del Sol** (breakfast, lunch, and dinner, $3–10) or simply "el rancho," is a well-liked beachfront restaurant with a full bar where you can watch the waves roll in or just enjoy the meticulously landscaped grounds.

GETTING THERE

At least one bus a day leaves Roberto Huembes market in Managua bound for El Astillero via Ochomogo (not Tola). From San Juan del Sur or Costa Rica, you'll be driving through Rivas and Tola, following the signs to Rancho Santana, then continuing past this development's gates until you reach Las Salinas. Buses depart Rivas about every hour. A taxi to Guasacate from El Astillero costs $7, from

Rivas $30. The road to the beach will take you past several austere salt flats, from which the nearby town of Las Salinas gets its name.

EL ASTILLERO AND BEACHES TO THE NORTH

Most of the little deserted beaches in the 10-kilometer strip between Las Salinas and El Astillero don't even have names. El Astillero itself is a fishing village full of small boats and is, in fact, the first safe boat anchorage north of Gigante. North of El Astillero, the road turns inland away from the coast. Accessing the beach anywhere along this area requires a boat and a lot of dedication. Ask around in El Astillero. There are plenty of underemployed sailors and anglers that would be glad to strike a deal with you if you're interested in exploring the coastline.

Hostal Hamacas (tel. 505/8810-4144, hostalhamacas.com, $25–65) is a friendly little place. Clean, basic rooms (some with a/c) have firm mattresses and are cheerfully painted; there's also a separate apartment for rent (from $55). Close by, French-run ◖ **Las Plumerias** (tel. 505/8979-7782, www.lasplumerias.com, $70 s, $55 d, includes three meals) has four pretty bungalows and a bar and restaurant *rancho* that has garnered rave reviews. Surf packages, tours, and rentals are also available.

REFUGIO DE VIDA SILVESTRE RÍO ESCALANTE-CHACOCENTE

One of the only Nicaraguan Pacific beaches where the Paslama turtle lays its eggs, Escalante-Chacocente Wildlife Refuge is a protected wildlife area whose beach provides habitat for numerous species, including white-tailed deer, reptiles, and many interesting types of flora. Getting to Chacocente isn't easy, which, for the sake of the turtles, is just as well. Management of the reserve has been inconsistent, so arrange a tour through local co-operative **Cosertuchaco** (tel. 505/8839-7564, turismo.chacocente@gmail.com), who organize transportation to the reserve and provide guided walks of the area, turtle-spotting tours, and homestays with local families.

Peñas Blancas and the Costa Rica Border

Peñas Blancas is the official border crossing into Costa Rica. A major effort is underway, with financing from the United States, to make this border crossing a bottleneck and entrapment point for drug traffickers headed north. Many of the buildings you see in the compound are inspection points for the hundreds of tractor-trailers that cross the border every day. Needless to say, this is one place you don't want to be caught smuggling furs. Sniffing dogs are common.

Border hassles can last anywhere from 1–10 hours! The longest waits happen at times when the hundreds of thousands of Nicaraguans living across the border are traveling to and from their country—this happens a week before and after Christmas, Easter, and any Nicaraguan election. The best time of day to cross is during early evening; usually you can squeeze through in under an hour.

CROSSING THE BORDER
Hours and Fees
The border is open 6 A.M.–10 P.M. Monday–Saturday; on Sunday it closes at 8 P.M. There is a fee for exiting ($2–5) and entering ($10–13) Nicaragua.

Inside the customs and immigration compound, find a branch of Bancentro (with an ATM) which can help you change money if necessary. Its schedule is generally tied to that of the border post itself.

Paperwork
Just a passport and some cash is all that's required of North American and European travelers, but don't forget to get stamped on both sides of the border to avoid subsequent headaches! To enter Costa Rica, Nicaraguan citizens must have a Costa Rican visa from the consulate either in Rivas or Managua. Upon entering Nicaragua, most North American and European travelers are granted a 90-day visa, with the exception of Canadian and Japanese citizens, who for some reason are given only 30 days.

By law, folks entering Costa Rica must have a ticket to leave the country. They usually don't check, as long as you're dressed like you have money. If they do check, you lose your place in line and go to the table outside, where Transportes Deldu will sell you an open-ended ticket from San José to Peñas Blancas for $11.

Entering Nicaragua with Your Vehicle
If you are driving your own vehicle, the process to enter Nicaragua from Costa Rica is lengthy but usually not too difficult (rental vehicles cannot cross the border). You'll present your title *(Titulo de la Propiedad)*, as well as your driver's license and passport, and will pay a $17 vehicle entry fee. Get proper stamps from Hacienda (Timbres de Hacienda), and a property certificate from Hacienda. Also make sure you have a current tag and Tico insurance; all of this can be taken care of in the town of Liberia, just to the south. You will be given a temporary (30-day) permit to drive in Nicaragua that will cost $10—should you lose the permit, you will be fined $100. Travelers driving their own vehicles north from the border will be forced to pass through a dubious "sterilization process" on the Nica side, in which the exterior of the vehicle is sprayed with a mystery liquid to kill porcine and bovine diseases; it costs $1 and takes five minutes unless the line is long. Roll up the windows.

Getting There

International bus services like TicaBus are popular ways to get across the border easily and comfortably, the best service being the new TransNica Plus, since you travel with 30 instead of 55 passengers. In many cases, the bus has a helper who collects your passports and money and waits in line for you. The disadvantage is that the bus won't pull away from the border post until every single traveler has had their papers processed, which can be time-consuming in some cases (waits up to four hours are not unheard of). More confident travelers like to take a Nicaraguan bus to the border, walk across to Costa Rica, and take a Costa Rican bus to San José, which is often faster. Express buses from Managua to Peñas Blancas depart Mercado Huembes at 5 A.M., 8 A.M., 9:30 A.M., and 3:30 P.M. Buses and microbuses leave the market in Rivas every 30–45 minutes. On the Costa Rican side, the last bus leaves the border bound for San José at 10 P.M. (about a six-hour ride).

ENTERING COSTA RICA

After crossing the border, you've got two choices: Buy a ticket to San José from the TransNica booth across from customs ($10 pp); the ride takes 6–8 hours, with departures daily at 5 A.M., 7 A.M., 9 A.M. direct, 10 A.M., 1 P.M. direct. Or get a Liberia–Pulmitan bus (tel. 506/2256-9522) to Liberia ($3 pp, two hours, last bus at 5:30 P.M.). From Liberia, 14 daily buses go to San José (3–5 hours); buses leave every 20 minutes to the Nicoya Peninsula and its beaches. Liberia, the capital of Guanacaste, is also a good base for Santa Rosa National Park (where William Walker and company were resoundingly defeated) and Rincón de la Vieja National Park, with impressive volcanoes. In fact, Guanacaste used to belong to Nicaragua and some say it still feels connected, or at least socially and physically independent of Costa Rica proper. Many locals still have family in Nicaragua, and this is the only department with its own flag.

LEÓN AND THE VOLCANIC LOWLANDS

Northwest of Managua are broad plains of peanuts, corn, beans, sorghum, and sugar-cane. The fecund soils that make this the most agriculturally productive region in Nicaragua are a gift from the Maribio volcanoes, an uncommonly active and exposed chain of peaks and cones stretching from Lake Xolotlán to the Gulf of Fonseca.

Fire gives way to water, and the Pacific northwest coastline of Nicaragua includes some of the longest, most isolated stretches of sand in the country. There are coastal islands, endless estuaries, and virgin mangrove stands rich in marine life and waterfowl. Large tracts of this region are still difficult to access, but progress and paved roads are slowly creeping up on them.

You can't help but feel itinerant in León and Chinandega. Blame it on the heat—this is the driest, most scorching corner of the country. Volcanism seeps from the land in boiling mud pits, geothermal vents, and the occasional rumble. The ruins of León's first incarnation are a testament to the area's impermanence. This region suffered tremendously during Hurricane Mitch in 1998, when more than two meters of rain fell in three days. Nowhere in Nicaragua was the destruction as intense, and the still-visible landslide at Las Casitas is a silent reminder of the worst of it. For this, Leóneses and Chinandeganos know that life can be short and even violent, and should thus be enjoyed.

León is the principal city of the northwest,

© GRACE GONZALEZ

LEÓN

HIGHLIGHTS

© AVALON TRAVEL

LOOK FOR 【 TO FIND RECOMMENDED SIGHTS, ACTIVITIES, DINING, AND LODGING.

【 **León's Museums:** Begin your art immersion at La Casa de Cultura and then continue around the corner to the fabulous Centro de Arte Fundación Ortiz-Gurdián (page 166).

【 **Volcano Boarding on Cerro Negro:** Whether you go sitting down on a toboggan or standing up on a modified snowboard, hurling yourself down a steep pitch of tiny black pebbles on an active volcano is a scream (page 171).

【 **Las Ruinas de León Viejo:** As old as Nicaragua's colonial history, this legitimate archaeological dig exposes the bones of Spain's earliest settlement (page 178).

【 **Las Peñitas:** Relaxing and peaceful accommodations at the ocean's edge offer easy access to the impressive Isla Juan Venado (page 181).

【 **Padre Ramos Wetlands Reserve:** If you're into isolated beaches and protected bird-filled estuaries, the bouncy trip north is worth it (page 194).

a colonial town with the architecture and languid lifestyle of centuries past. This bastion of liberal thought in Central America has narrow streets lined with cathedrals, universities, and cafés. For five hundred years, León's political history has consisted of long stretches of peace, punctuated by the staccato call of uprising, resistance, and war.

In contrast, Chinandega, Nicaragua's most northwestern city, is the agribusiness capital of the country, center for both the sugarcane and shrimp industries. Chinandega Department is also home to the Padre Ramos

Reserve and the Cosigüina peninsula, whose beaches and surf are just beginning to be visited by foreigners.

PLANNING YOUR TIME

León is one of the few Nicaraguan cities with more attractions than you can see in a day. Plan on at least two to visit the museums and cathedrals of the city; another if you plan to hike a volcano, and another if you head to the shore. Las Peñitas, Isla Juan Venado, Padre Ramos, and other points outside León require more effort to get to but are excellent destinations for

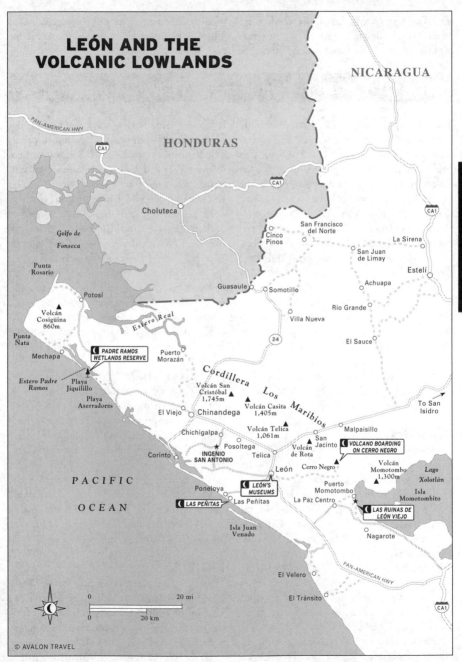

LEÓN AND THE VOLCANIC LOWLANDS

NICARAGUA

HONDURAS

PAN-AMERICAN HWY

CA1

CA1

CA1

Choluteca

*Golfo de
Fonseca*

San Francisco
del Norte

Cinco
Pinos

La Sirena

San Juan
de Limay

Estelí

Punta
Rosario

Potosí

Guasaule

Somotillo

Achuapa

Río Grande

Villa Nueva

Volcán
Cosigüina
860m

Estero Real

El Sauce

Punta
Nata

24

Mechapa

((PADRE RAMOS
WETLANDS RESERVE

Puerto
Morazán

*Estero Padre
Ramos*

Playa
Jiquilillo

Cordillera

Volcán San
Cristóbal
1,745m

Los

To San
Isidro

Playa
Aserradores

El Viejo

Chinandega

Volcán Casita
1,405m

Maribios

Chichigalpa

Volcán Telica
1,061m

Malpaisillo

Corinto

★
INGENIO
SAN ANTONIO

Posoltega

Telica

San
Jacinto

Volcán
de Rota

((VOLCANO BOARDING
ON CERRO NEGRO

PACIFIC

León

Cerro Negro

Volcán
Momotombo
1,300m

*Lago
Xolotlán*

OCEAN

Poneloya

((LEÓN'S
MUSEUMS

Puerto
Momotombo

Isla
Momotombito

((LAS PEÑITAS

Las Peñitas

La Paz Centro

★
LAS RUINAS DE
LEÓN VIEJO

Isla Juan
Venado

Nagarote

El Velero

PAN-AMERICAN HWY

El Tránsito

CA1

0   20 mi
0   20 km

© AVALON TRAVEL

those traveling on a slightly slower schedule. It's worth slowing down, in fact, so you can paddle boats through the estuaries and observe the wildlife (like nesting turtles on Juan Venado). There is plenty to do, whether you come for two days or two weeks.

City of León

The principal metropolis of the low-lying Nicaraguan northwest, León has had several incarnations over the centuries. The Spaniards first built the city along the shores of Lake Xolotlán; they picked up and moved when Volcán Momotombo shook the ground beneath their feet. Modern León is at once a dusty provincial capital and an architectural delight; traditionally designed colonial homes, churches, universities, and an immense cathedral stand shoulder to shoulder in a tropical torpor that keeps city life to a low but exciting hum. León is an easily walkable city, with a plethora of interesting cafés and restaurants, Latin America's largest cathedral, and an ambience quite unlike anywhere else in Nicaragua. Its longtime political rival, Granada, may have more fresh paint and international adoration, but León remains an irreverent, unique city where tourism is merely an afterthought, not a necessity.

HISTORY

The short-lived first city of León was a Spanish settlement founded by Francisco Hernández de Córdoba next to the indigenous village of Imabite on the shore of Lake Xolotlán in 1524. The Spanish were lousy neighbors. They immediately began to enslave the Imabite and doled out cruel punishments: Many natives met their ends at the jaws of the Spanish attack dogs. The old city was abandoned in 1610 when Volcán Momotombo erupted. They relocated alongside the indigenous village of Subtiava, which over the centuries was subsumed by the growing commercial center of León.

León was the capital of Nicaragua during Liberal governments several times before 1852. It has also been both a university town and a hotbed for leftist thought since colonial times. The Sandinistas found ready supporters here in the 1960s and '70s, and Somoza retaliated ferociously, even torching the central market and strafing peaceful demonstrations.

In September 1978, Sandinista forces attacked key locations in León, including National Guard installations at the famous XXI building. In response, Somoza bombed the populations of both León and Chinandega, and tortured or executed anyone suspected of sympathizing with the Sandinistas. Sandinista troops took León on June 4 after two days of a vicious battle whose bullet holes remain to the present, as does local sympathy for the FSLN.

ORIENTATION

León is laid out in the traditional colonial grid system with the central park and cathedral at the center. It sprawls impressively in all directions. The main bus terminal and market are nearly a kilometer northeast of the main plaza, and Barrio Subtiava is 12 blocks due west. A *zona rosa* of sorts is developing along 1 Calle SO as it extends westward from the southwest corner of the plaza. Most of the town's nightlife is condensed here; university campuses are primarily just north of the plaza.

SIGHTS

The shady and pleasant **Parque Rubén Darío** (also known as Parque de los Poetas), a block west of the central park, pays tribute to four famous Nicaraguan writers, all sons of León: Azarías H. Pallais (1884–1954), Salomon de la Selva (1893–1959), Alfonzo Cortéz

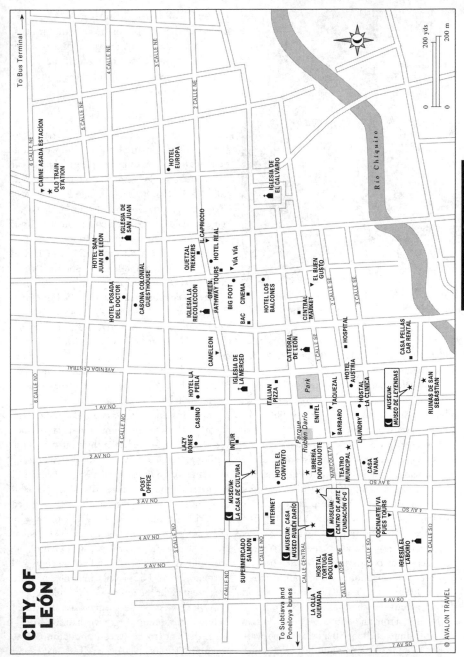

CITY OF LEÓN

LEÓN

To Bus Terminal →

To Subtiava and Poneloya buses →

Río Chiquito

Carne Asada Estación
Old Train Station
Hotel San Juan de León
Iglesia de San Juan
Hotel Europa
Iglesia de El Calvario
Capriccio
Quetzal Trekkers
Hotel Real
Vía Vía
Green Pathway Tours
Big Foot
Cinema
BAC
El Buen Gusto
Hotel Posada del Doctor
Casona Colonial Guesthouse
Iglesia la Recolección
Hotel Los Balcones
Central Market
Cameleon
Iglesia de la Merced
Catedral de León
Casa Pellas Car Rental
Hotel la Perla
Casino
Lazy Bones
Italian Pizza
Park
Taquezal
Hotel Austria
Hostal la Clínica
Museum: Museo de Leyendas
Ruinas de San Sebastián
Intur
Entiel
Parque Rubén Darío
Barbaro
Laundry
Post Office
Hotel el Convento
Librería Don Quijote
Marcoleta
Teatro Municipal
Casa Ivana
Museum: La Casa de Cultura
Internet
Museum: Centro de Arte Fundación O–G
Cocinarte/Vía Pues Tours
Museum: Casa Museo Rubén Darío
Supermercado Salmon
Hostal Tortuga Booluda
Iglesia El Laborio
La Olla Quemada

Avenida Central
6 Calle NE
5 Calle NE
4 Calle NE
3 Calle NE
2 Calle NE
6 Calle NO
5 Calle NO
4 Calle NO
3 Calle NO
2 Calle NO
1 Calle NO
2 AV NO
1 AV NO
3 AV NO
4 AV NO
5 AV NO
Calle Central
Calle José de
2 Calle SO
3 Calle SO
6 AV SO
7 AV SO
1 Calle SE
2 Calle SE
3 Calle SE
3 AV SO
4 AV SO
Hospital

200 yds
200 m
0
0

© AVALON TRAVEL

LEÓN

© GRACE GONZALEZ

León's many churches are one reason to visit the city.

(1893–1969), and of course, the beloved Rubén Darío (1867–1916).

León's **Old Train Station,** built in 1884, was Nicaragua's first and most majestic. It has been rebuilt since being gutted by fire in 1956, now housing a boisterous market.

The creepy yet captivating **El Fortín de Acosasco** sits on a grassy hill just south of the city, providing phenomenal views of the entire Maribio volcano chain. Conservative president Sacasa built it in 1889 to keep an eye on the Liberals that would overthrow him four years later. Abandoned until Anastasio Somoza took interest and rehabilitated it, El Fortín has since served as both a military base and jail. It is presently abandoned once again, though the city has invested a small amount to seal off the dangerous dungeons and to slap on some fresh paint. From the Subtiava church, it's an easy 45-minute walk or $6 by taxi (don't walk alone): Go one block east and head due south

up the hill along the shady dirt road. The panorama of the city is worth the walk (or taxi), though the stench and smoke from the nearby abandoned landfill can be a drag if the wind is blowing the wrong way (the city promises to cover it up soon).

◖ Museums

León's museums are exceedingly eclectic, covering the political, natural, and all things cultural. Start at **La Casa de Cultura** (from the Iglesia San Francisco, one block north, 20 meters east, tel. 505 /2311-2116, 8 A.M.–noon and 2–7:30 P.M. Mon.–Fri., until 6 P.M. Sat.–Sun.), housed in an old colonial home; enjoy a collection of artwork that includes a disparaging painting of Ronald Reagan and Henry Kissinger. Entrance is free. This is a good place to find out about all kinds of cultural classes and activities.

La Casa de Rubén Darío (tel. 505/2311-2388, 8 A.M.–noon and 2–5 P.M. Tues.–Sat., 8 A.M.–noon Sun.) is a glimpse into León in the 19th century. Nicaragua's favorite son lived here with his aunt and uncle until the age of 14. Fellow poet Alfonso Cortéz later inhabited the same house as he battled insanity (the room he inhabited still has the iron bars he bent during one attempted escape). Darío's bed and the rest of the furnishings of the museum are typical of middle-class León in the late 19th century, as is the building itself, built from adobe with a clay-tile and cane roof. On display are original copies of his most famous works translated into several languages and copies of a magazine he published in Paris. The silver crucifix given to him by Mexican poet Amado Nervos, correspondence from when Darío was the consul to Argentina and ambassador to Spain, and period coins and currency are also displayed; donations of $1–2 are accepted for the upkeep of the building.

A block west of the Parque Casa de Rubén Darío and occupying two facing buildings, the **Centro de Arte Fundación Ortiz-Gurdián** (10:30 A.M.–6 P.M. Tues.–Sat. and

A WALKING TOUR OF CHURCHES AND RUINS

La Catedral de León is the largest cathedral in Central America and the modern city's focal point. The cathedral was constructed in 1747 at the request of Archbishop Isidoro Bullón y Figueroa and inaugurated in 1860 as a basilica by Pope Pius XI. It's an imposing and majestic baroque structure whose grandeur is magnified by the open space of the park in front of it. You can observe elements of late Gothic and neoclassical architecture, primarily from inside. Check out the paintings of the stations of the cross and the 12 apostles. The **Tomb of Rubén Darío** is a notable element of the cathedral—look for the golden statue of a lion. The cathedral holds the mortal remains of the musician José de la Cruz Mena and several religious figures. Look for the famous *Cristo de Pedrarias*, a painting that once hung in the cathedral of León Viejo. The particularly beautiful **Patio de los Príncipes** is a small courtyard of Andalusian design, with a fountain in the center and colorful beds of flowers.

Iglesia de la Merced, 1.5 blocks north of the main cathedral, is the church considered most representative of León in the 1700s. It was originally built in 1762 by the Mercedarian monks, the first order of monks to arrive in Nicaragua during the years of the conquest.

The **Iglesia de la Recolección,** two blocks east along 2 Calle NE on the north side, has the most perfect baroque style of the León churches and a massive, functional bell tower. It was built in 1786 by Bishop Juan Félix de Villegas and is the only church in León constructed using carved stone.

Picturesque **Iglesia de San Juan,** north of the Iglesia de la Recolección, was built 1625–1650 and rebuilt in the 1700s. The Iglesia de San Juan's architecture is a modern interpretation of neoclassicism. The surrounding neighborhood of León will give you a good feel for what León was like in the 1700s.

The **Iglesia del Calvario,** four blocks south on the left side, is set at the top of broad steps on a small hill overlooking one of León's narrow streets. Renovated in the late 1990s, Calvario was built 200 years previous in a generally baroque style, but with neoclassical ornamentation in the front that reflects the increasing French influence in Spain in the 18th century. Inside are two famous statues: *El Buen y el Mal Ladrón* (The Good and the Bad Thief).

La Iglesia y Convento de San Francisco, three blocks west of the park on the north side, contains two of the most beautiful altars of colonial Nicaragua. The church was built in 1639 by Fray Pedro de Zuñiga and rebuilt and modified several times afterwards, notably in the mid-1980s to restore the damage done to it during the revolution.

Iglesia de San Juan de Dios, one block south, was built in 1620 as a chapel for León's first hospital (now gone). Its simplicity and colonial style reflect the wishes of Felipe II when he designed it in 1573.

Iglesia del Laborío, two blocks further south and slightly west, is a graceful, rural-feeling church in the old mixed neighborhood of El Laborío. This church, one of León's earliest, formed the nucleus of the working-class neighborhood that provided labor to León's wealthy class in the 17th century. The street from Laborío east to the Ruinas de la Ermita de San Sebastián is known as **Calle la Españolita** and was one of the first streets built in León.

The **Ruinas de la Ermita de San Sebastián** consist of the shattered remnants of the outer walls, and inexplicably, the intact bell tower. The Ermita was built in 1742 on a site long used by the indigenous people for worship of their own gods. It suffered major damage in 1979 during Somoza's bombardment of León.

LEÓN

LEÓN

© JOSHUA BERMAN

on the roof of León's cathedral

9 A.M.–5 P.M. Sun., $0.75 admission, free on Sun.) has reputedly the best collection of Latin American artwork in Nicaragua, with an emphasis on colonial America.

El Museo de Tradiciones y Leyendas (Barrio Laborío, 8 A.M.–noon and 2–5 P.M. Mon.–Sat., 8 A.M.–noon Sun., $1) celebrates Nicaragua's favorite folktales: the golden crab, La Carreta Nagua, the pig-witch, and La Mocuana. The building itself is the former XXI jail and base of the 12th Company of Somoza's National Guard. Built in 1921, XXI meted out 60 years of brutal torture. The mango tree that now shades this museum was planted by a prisoner and watered from the same well that was used for electric shock and water-boarding sessions.

Murals

Many of León's colorful murals are products of the 1980s that have been painstakingly maintained. Other new ones still spring up each year. Perhaps the most famous is located across

from the north side of the main cathedral—a long, horizontal piece telling the history of a proud and turbulent nation. Starting on the left with the arrival of the Nahuatl, the mural traces the planned interoceanic canal, the exploits of William Walker, Sandino's battle with U.S. Marines, the revolution of 1979, and a utopian ending image of a fertile, peaceful Nicaragua; flanking a doorway across the street, Sandino steps on Uncle Sam's and Somoza's heads. One block to the west the CIA, in the form of a thick serpent, coils through the Sandinistas' agrarian reform, literacy campaign, and construction efforts, to strike at a Nicaraguan hand at the ballot box. The trend seems to be reviving in the 21st century; to wit, the intricate anticorruption mural on the basketball court.

Barrio Subtiava

The indigenous neighborhood of Subtiava (Maribio for "land of the big men") retains a trace of both its cultural identity and political autonomy. Besides the thrill of walking the streets of a village predating Columbus, note several interesting ruins here. Just about any of the microbuses that circulate through León will take you to Subtiava if you're not up for the 12-block walk.

La Catedral de Subtiava, beautiful in its aged simplicity, is second only to the Catedral de León in size and is the keystone of the community. Construction began in 1698 and finished 12 years later, but the indigenous inhabitants of Subtiava kept worshiping their own gods despite Spanish proselytizing. In an effort to get the locals into the church, the Spanish mounted a carved wooden image of the sun representing the local god on the church ceiling, a compromise that left everyone satisfied, even if during a church service the Spanish and locals were simultaneously worshiping different gods. The beautifully crafted sun remains, as do the immense wooden columns that evoke the kind of forest that surrounded León three hundred years ago. Next to the cathedral is the Casa Cural, which predates the cathedral of Subtiava by 160 years but was rebuilt in 1743.

Across the street from the cathedral on the north side is the **Museo Adiact** (8 A.M.–noon and 2–5 P.M. Mon.–Fri., 8 A.M.–noon Sat., $1–2 donation), a run-down but captivating museum that houses many of the area's archaeological treasures. Sadly, some of the better idols and statues were stolen in the late 1980s and sold to foreign museums.

Five blocks east of the cathedral's southern side is a small park dedicated to the last cacique of Subtiava, Adiact, and his daughter, Xochilt Acalt. From the cathedral of Subtiava, three blocks south and two blocks west is **El Tamarindón,** an enormous, gnarled tamarind tree from whose branches the Spanish hanged the last cacique.

There are two sets of ruins in Subtiava, **Las Ruinas de Veracruz** (one block west of the cathedral, set in high weeds) and **Las Ruinas de Santiago** (one block north of the cathedral on the other side of Calle Central, look for a small sign). The church at Veracruz was Subtiava's first, built sometime around 1560 and abandoned in the late 1700s due to its small size. The eruption of Volcán Cosigüina in 1835 caused its subsequent collapse. The church at Santiago, constructed in the early 1600s, is significant because its small square bell tower remains intact.

ENTERTAINMENT AND EVENTS
Nightlife

It's no surprise that a university town like León would have a thriving nightlife. And it's not just poor students here—there is plenty of money in town to support a semiupscale nightlife. For student-centered beer gardens, roam the university area in the two blocks north of the main plaza. The nicest *discotecas* and bars are clustered on a single block called the *zona rosa* (a tongue-in-cheek swipe at Managua's more impressive and similarly named hot spot), located on Calle 1 SO between Avenida 1 and Avenida 2. Walk west from the southwest corner of the main plaza.

Start at **Bar Baro** (one block west of the southwest corner of main plaza, tel. 505/2315-2901 or 8820-4000, 8 A.M–midnight Mon.–Fri., 8 A.M–2 A.M. Sat.–Sun.), a lively, high-ceilinged tavern where you can choose between a romantic lounge area, a quiet coffee patio, or a convivial bar-restaurant. The drink menu is very long, the food is excellent, and you can actually have a conversation with your friends without shouting!

For dancing, the mood depends on where the crowd gathers. Start with **Oxigeno** (the sign says O2, 8 P.M.–close Wed.–Sat.), and see if there's anyone on the dance floor. If not, the **Don Señor** complex, across from Parque La Merced, houses a disco (8:30 P.M.–close Tues.–Sat., $3.50), restaurant, downstairs dive, and upstairs patio lounge with a view of the nightlife and attracts the college crowd as well as foreigners. The disco usually has a small cover

LEÓN

THE LEGEND OF ADIACT AND THE TAMARIND TREE

Several competing versions of this tale have been passed down over three centuries of Nicaraguan history. When Subtiava was still a rebellious Native American village and the Spanish were trying to subdue its inhabitants, victory appeared in the form of a young woman named Xochilt Acalt (Flower of the Sugarcane). Her father was Adiact, the cacique of the Subtiava people and a ferocious warrior renowned for his victories in battle with the Spanish. But legend goes that Xochilt fell in love with a young Spanish soldier. Some say the Spanish took advantage of the love affair to capture and hang Adiact; others say that when he learned of the illicit relationship, he hanged himself in shame. Xochilt Acalt disappeared from town, and legend has it she too committed suicide (though some say she banished herself to Poneloya, where another tribe took her in). Either way, everyone agrees that the 300-year-old tamarind tree that still stands proudly in the center of Subtiava is where Adiact was hanged. To modern Subtiavans, the tree still represents the rebelliousness of the indigenous people and is a source of much community pride.

charge; the restaurant and the bar are open for lunch and dinner, and close late on Saturday. Opposite here, **Bohemios** is another hip hangout frequented by foreigners and locals alike. For late-night boozing, the after party is always at **Cameleon** (one block west of La Iglesia de la Recolección), where a sweaty dance floor heaves with the best of the die-hards.

Live Music

Several bars and cafés host a weekly live music night. Friday nights at **Vía Vía** are a must; for current listings, check with the folks at CocinArte (across from the north side of La Iglesia el Laborío). On Wednesday, go to **La Olla Quemada** (a block west of Rubén Darío's House Museum, $2 cover), a low-lit bar with a nice atmosphere and variety of performing artists. **Tequetzal** (half a block west of the central park) hosts live music on Thursday nights.

Cinema and Theater

León's small but modern cinema is in the Plaza Siglo Nuevo shopping center (from the cathedral, one block north, one block east, tel. 505/2311-7080). Look for the *cartelera*

(schedule) at shops around the city for show times; tickets cost $4.

El Teatro Municipal José de la Cruz Mena (one block south of the southwest corner of the central park, tel. 505/2311-1788) is the cultural heart of the city, open to the public for half-hour theater tours during the day with all kinds of events at night. Some big-name performers prefer León over Managua.

Festivals and Events

June 1 is the celebration of Somoza's defeat in León and August 14 is **La Gritería Chiquita,** when devout Catholics celebrate being spared from Cerro Negro's frequent eruptions. The first week of December is huge, with loud, firework-festooned celebrations of the Immaculate Conception. León celebrates its *fiestas patronales* on September 24 and the weeks surrounding it.

León's **Semana Santa** celebrations are acclaimed throughout Nicaragua as the nation's most lively. In addition to tons of food and drink, local artisans craft religious scenes in beds of colored sawdust worked painstakingly by hand.

LEÓN

© GRACE GONZALEZ

León's streets are still bustling at night.

SHOPPING

You won't find much in the way of traditional Nicaraguan crafts in León. For that, you still have to make it to the Huembes market in Managua, or to Masaya. You will, however, find plenty of used American clothes and old books, León's specialties. For books (and old Sandinista money), look for the sidewalk vendors near the plaza. The best shop is **Librería Don Quijote** (two blocks west of the park, 8 A.M.–7 P.M. Mon.–Sat.), an interesting new and used bookshop that sells many old Sandinista titles. For crafts, **Kaman** (9 A.M.–6 P.M. Mon.–Sat.), just off the southwest corner of the plaza, has bead-making materials, bags, and textiles from around Latin America, artsy postcards, and body piercing. There's a sprawling market near the bus terminal, or a smaller one immediately behind the cathedral with a selection for local shoppers, but not many crafts.

SPORTS AND RECREATION
Baseball

León has won more baseball championships than any other city in Nicaragua. Catch a game during the season (Jan.–May). Ask any taxi driver when the next game is and if they will take you to the stadium on the edge of town.

◖ Volcano Boarding on Cerro Negro

Careening down the black sands of Cerro Negro volcanic scree on a modified snowboard is León's most exciting outdoor adrenaline rush, and with reason: the slope is a full 40° in places, and the ride is fast and hot. Stand-up boards get bogged down, but sitting down, you can build up some serious speed (Bigfoot has clocked clients at over 80 kph). Wear sturdy shoes, long pants, and long sleeves. Plan on a 60-minute climb and a 45-second descent in a hot, rugged landscape. Half-day trips run about $30 per person. The **Bigfoot** hostel runs

boarding Cerro Negro

daily trips, which include an orange jumpsuit, goggles, gloves, and pads. **Vapues Tours** and **Tierra Tours** also make daily trips to Cerro Negro with experienced guides, and can pick you up and drop you off at your hotel.

At the entrance to Cerro Negro you will find a small information center, a *ranchón,* some bathrooms, and a friendly and informative local tourism cooperative called **Las Pilas-El Hoyo.** The $5 entrance fee goes to support conservation efforts and pays a portion of the members' salaries. Cooperative guides can take you on other hikes in the area, including the two taller volcanoes—El Hoyo and El Pilas—a nearby swimming hole, and a larger reservoir with some of the best views in the country.

ACCOMMODATIONS

Dozens of hotel options range from backpacker hostels to midrange and luxury hotels, and increased experience with foreign tourists

is bringing the quality and the service up. You will sleep well here.

Under $25

The cheapest flop houses, often labeled *Abierto 24 Horas* (Open 24 Hours) are located near the main bus terminal and are universally dismal in a potentially dangerous area; avoid them without hesitation.

Casa Ivana (across from the Teatro Municipal's south side, tel. 505/2311-4423, $16 d) is the best Nicaraguan-owned option, with seven clean, quiet, safe rooms with private baths along a long garden in a family house. Around the corner, **Hostal La Clinica** (tel. 505/2311-2031, $6 in a dorm with fan, up to $25 with a/c) is another low-key, friendly, Nicaraguan-owned *hotelito* with a veritable jungle growing in the central patio. For a more Nicaraguan family-oriented, less meet-other-travelers vibe, check out ◖ **Casona Colonial Guesthouse** (half a block west of the Parque San Juan, tel. 505/2311-3178, $20 per person). Its eight rooms—with queen bed, private bath, hot water, and a fan—represent one of the best bargains in León, complete with high ceilings, flower-filled courtyard, and beautiful wooden furniture.

The city's many international-oriented hostels each cater to a slightly different style. **La Tortuga Booluda** (1.5 blocks west from the San Juan de Dios church, tel. 505/2311-4653, www.tortuga-Booluda.com, dorms $7, private rooms $12–40) offers a breezy courtyard and has common hangout areas and a communal kitchen excellent for meeting other travelers. La Tortuga feels homey; features include a nice book exchange, billiards, coffee, Wi-Fi, and common-use kitchen. The only meal they serve is free pancake breakfasts for guests, a fun morning ritual.

Enter ◖ **Vía Vía** (75 meters south of the Servicio Agrí cola Gurdián, tel. 505/2311-6142, www.viaviacafe.com, dorms $6, private rooms $18) through its popular multicultural café and information area, then continue walking into a quiet, colonial-style patio where a small selection of dorms and private rooms surround a gorgeous garden. The building was reportedly built in 1760 by an Italian for his Nicaraguan mistress and her servants. Ask about Spanish classes and salsa dance lessons; also, expect your hosts to encourage you to get out and explore the area, as if you needed the encouragement.

Bigfoot Hostel (from Banco Procredit, half a block south, tel. 505/8917-8832, www.bigfootnicaragua.com, $6 dorm, $15 d) caters to backpackers, surfers, and anyone else who enjoys sipping a delicious mojito while seated in a small, footprint-shaped swimming pool. This is the biggest hostel in León, so expect a lively scene, but it doesn't get too crazy and is quiet after 10 P.M. The halls branch into multiple dormitories, common areas, and a snack bar. Bigfoot offers lockboxes, a shared kitchen, laundry service, plus sign-up lists for volcano boarding and ecocentric tours through Green Pathways.

Centrally located two and a half blocks north of Parque de los Poetas, **Lazy Bones** (tel. 505/2311-3472, www.lazybonesleon.com, dorms $8, private rooms $19–28) offers dorms and a handful of private rooms with fan, some with shared bath. The kicker here is the pool, still a rarity in León hotels. Lazy Bones seems to be a quieter option in this price range, offering free lockers, breakfast, billiards, computers, and lounge space.

$25-50

Hotel San Juan de León (on the north side of the Plaza Iglesia San Juan, tel. 505/2311-0547, www.hsanjuandeleon.com, $35–65) has 20 smallish rooms with fan and private bath (a bit more with a/c) on two floors surrounding a tasteful courtyard and kitchen for guests' use. Breakfast is included. Another excellent, friendly family option in this range is **Hotel Real** (tel. 505/2311-2606, www.hotelrealdeleon.net, hotelreal.leon@gmail.com, $38–45, breakfast included), with 14 well-equipped rooms in a nicely furnished, comfortable home with Wi-Fi. Be sure to compare several rooms to see what you prefer, and don't miss the lookout point upstairs.

The imposing 30-room compound of **Hotel Europa** (from the Iglesia San Juan, one block south and one east, tel. 505/2311-6040, europaleon@yahoomail.com, $35 d) has been around since the 1960s, when it catered to the train passenger crowd. A fairly recent remodeling has updated the clean rooms. The hotel also offers a restaurant, lounge areas, Wi-Fi, and guarded parking.

$50-100

◖ **Hotel Posada del Doctor** (one block west of Parque San Juan, tel. 505/2311-4343, www.laposadadeldoctor.com, $45–85) offers 11 lovely, fully equipped rooms around a very bright and pleasant garden. Expect old colonial stateliness in the 20 wood-adorned rooms at ◖ **Hotel Los Balcones** (three blocks east of the cathedral, tel. 505/2311-0250, www.hotelbalcones.com, $35–85). Upstairs rooms have small balconies overlooking the street, plus standard amenities: TV, air-conditioning (discount if you don't use it), hot water, and Wi-Fi. In the center of León, **Hotel Austria** (from the cathedral, one block south and half a block west, tel. 505/2311-1206 or tel. 505/2311-7178, www.hotelaustria.com.ni, $45–90) is a practical hotel with 35 spotless, modern, and air-conditioned rooms of varying sizes with TV, phones, and hot water; amenities include a Continental breakfast and guarded parking for your vehicle. There is an on-site restaurant and comfortable space for relaxing or meetings.

Over $100

Hotel El Convento (next door to the San Francisco Church, tel. 505/2311-7053, www.hotelelconventonicaragua.com, $90–180) offers bathtub-equipped rooms with lots of space and history. Parts of the hotel were built with stones used in the convent's original 1639 construction. From the beautiful centerpiece garden and fountain to the long, cool corridors adorned with art and antiques, El Convento impresses. In addition, the hotel offers business and conference services, a ballroom, a restaurant, and local tours for guests.

The rooms at ◖**Hotel La Perla** (1.5 blocks north of Iglesia de la Merced, tel. 505/2311-3125, www.laperlaleon.com, $93–180) are among the classiest anywhere in Nicaragua, combining old-style elegance and antiques with modern comforts like plasma screen TVs and Wi-Fi. This 150-year-old home was lovingly restored by owners with a passion for architecture and history. The two presidential suites sport mirrored dressers, king beds, and mini-bars; both are on the second-story balcony with superb views of León's tiled roofs and churches. Hotel La Perla is also a veritable museum of fine art. There is an excellent breakfast and a small pool for guests, plus a restaurant with hearty fajita and pasta dishes.

Long-Term Accommodations

A college town, León caters easily to those looking to stay on longer. "Room for Rent" posters are found around the universities and on the bulletin boards of the main hostels. In general, expect to pay $150–200 a month for a room with shared kitchen and up to $400 a month for furnished apartments. Check with **Jordan Clark** (tel. 505/8672-3566, www.nicaraguarealestateleon.com) or **Green Pathways Tours** (www.greenpathways.com); both keep lists of long-term rentals in León and shared houses on the beach.

FOOD

León is slowly shedding its reputation for uninspired cuisine and lackluster restaurants. Though most Leónese eateries cater to the student crowd—i.e., *típica* (traditional), burgers, and pizza—new restaurants are starting to diversify the city's menu. León is hot, so ice cream takes on new significance. Start with any **Eskimo** outlet (or bicycle cart) in town for popsicles and cones.

Of the several huge supermarkets, the most central is **La Union** (a block east of the cathedral, 7:30 A.M.–8 P.M. Mon.–Sat., 8 A.M.–6 P.M. Sun.).

Fritanga and Comida Típica

The best finger-lickin' *fritanga* in town is **El Buen Gusto** (a couple blocks east of the cathedral's south side, 10 A.M.–10 P.M. Mon.–Sat., under $4); order a mix and match from their sidewalk smorgasbord and hubcap grill. The *carne asada* at the **Estación** offers strong competition for León's best *fritanga* crown. You'll find several large grills serving mountains of *gallo pinto*, plantains, and fried cheese to an appreciative crowd. When in doubt—or on a Sunday evening when everything else is closed—head to the food grills behind the main cathedral.

Comedor Lucía (across from Vía Vía, $4) specializes in the usual, but its solid traditional Nica dishes are well done.

Italian

Enjoy pizza and pasta at **Restaurante Italian Pizza** (half a block north of the cathedral, tel. 505/2311-0857 delivery, 9 A.M.–9 P.M. daily, $10). The pizza at **Hollywood Pizza** (located in the movie theater complex, tel. 505/2311-0636, 11:30 A.M.–9:30 P.M. Mon.–Fri., open later Sat.–Sun., $5–9) is less exciting, but the air-conditioning provides a good respite. Both pizzerias deliver.

Il Capriccio (tel. 505/2311-6339, 9 A.M.–12:30 P.M. and 2–7 P.M. daily), located across from Quetzal Trekkers, offers some of the best Italian desserts and Nicaraguan coffee in town, plus a menu of sandwiches, salads, and pasta.

Upscale and International

For central dining, **Bar Baro** (one block west of the southwest corner of main plaza, tel. 505/2315-2901 or 8820-4000, 8 A.M.–midnight Mon.–Fri., 8 A.M.–2 A.M. Sat.–Sun., $6–15) is a remarkable restaurant with old wooden beams, ceiling fans, and three different-themed dining areas in which to eat and lounge. The name comes from the common Nica expression *"¡Qué bárbaro!"* which means (more or less) "How awesome!" The ambitious menu offers both Nica and international comfort food with a flair—steak and chicken dishes, burgers, bar appetizers, and pizza. Prices are reasonable and the drink menu of coffee and cocktails is the longest in the city.

The restaurant and coffee shop at **CocinArte** (across from the north side of La Iglesia el Laborío, tel. 505/8854-6928, 11 A.M.–10 P.M. Wed.–Mon., $6–8) has an incredibly varied and creative menu, including Indian and middle Eastern dishes found nowhere else in Nicaragua, plus a small selection of chicken and traditional dishes for your carnivorous friends. The reading and lounging space boasts chessboards and tasteful art.

INFORMATION AND SERVICES
Tourist Information

The government **INTUR** office (from the central park, one block west and 1.5 north, tel. 505/2311-3682) has brochures, postcards, and updated bus schedules, but will shrug their shoulders if you ask about anything beyond that. Go instead to the student-run **Information Office** (near the northeast corner of the plaza, tel. 505/2311-3992), which also offers mounds of brochures, plus a gang of eager UNAN co-eds waiting to help you with local information and maps—and practice their English. Both offices operate Monday–Saturday during normal business hours, including a two-hour lunch break. Also check in the Casa de Cultura for local tour services and classes, and nearly all the youth hostels maintain up-to-date bulletin boards.

Banks

Bancentro is only a block north of the cathedral, and most of the other banks in the city are clustered in the same area. ATMs are located one block east of the cathedral in the BAC (open 24 hours with guard, *córdobas* or dollars), at La Union Supermarket, at gas stations, and in Plaza Siglo Nuevo shopping center.

Internet

Internet cafés in León are too numerous to list; odds are you're standing within a block of one as you read this. But the better ones have backup generators to deal with power failures; it's worth asking if you are doing anything you can't afford to lose. Of note, **CompuService** (across from Policlinica la Fraternidad, 8 A.M.–9:30 P.M. Mon.–Sat., 9 A.M.–6 P.M. Sun.) is air-conditioned with all kinds of fast services, including docks for laptops and cold beer from the restaurant next door. Also excellent, spacious, and well cooled is **Club en Conexion** (from the cathedral, three blocks north, half

LEÓN

LOCAL GUIDES AND TOUR OPERATORS IN LEÓN

In addition to being rich in history, museums, cathedrals, and natural wonders, León is also blessed with an intelligent young crop of guides and creatively conscious tour operators, both locals and *extranjeros* who enjoy sharing their knowledge and love of the land. Most accommodations can also recommend a guide or company, but here are a few options to let you know who's doing what.

For city tours and day trips to nearby sites like León Viejo, San Jacinto Hot Springs, Isla Juan Venado, and others, you can start with **Julio Tours Nicaragua** (Calle Rubén Darío, one block east of the San Francisco Catholic Church, tel. 505/8625-4467, info@juliotoursnicaragua.com.ni, www.juliotoursnicaragua.com.ni). Julio's has received rave reviews for his relaxed, homespun services.

Started by Barbados-born biology major Phillip Southan, **Green Pathways Tours** (tel. 505/2315-0964 or 505/8333-0898, greenpathways@gmail.com, www.greenpathways.com) is a self-described "association of naturalists and travelers" who constantly ask the question, "Are the actions of my travels making a positive impact on the people and environment of the places I visit?" They focus on outdoorsy activities like volcanoes, local tours, and whale-watching (January–March); there is also a mouthwatering list of expeditions to far-flung corners of the country, including a kayak trip down the Río San Juan. They also offer important traveler services

like TicaBus tickets (office open 10 A.M.–6 P.M. daily) and beach house rentals.

Vapues Tours (Costado Norte, from Iglesia del Laborío, in front of Casa Cural, tel. 505/2315-4999, info@vapues.com, www.vapues.com), with an office across from the Iglesia del Laborío, offer a huge range of reasonably priced trips, plus shuttle services to other cities across the country. They can take you to Cosigüina, to Selva Negra, or to Granada and points south. They are also tied in with some community-based tourism efforts. **Tierra Tours** (1.5 blocks north of Iglesia de la Merced, tel. 505/2311-0599, tierratour@gmail.com, http://tierratour.com) has offices in Granada and León, and are highly recommended, along with Vapues Tours, for any number of trips. Both can take you on volcano or history tours and also offer countrywide all-inclusive packages, international bus tickets, and domestic flight booking. They also both produce excellent local maps you can pick up around town.

For more eccentric, community-immersion tours, let Harrie from Holland, founder of **Nicaragua Así Tours** (tel. 505/8414-1192, www.nicasitours.com) take you to a cockfight, cow ranch, cooking class, or history tour. He likes to show visitors "more of Nicaragua than you can imagine exists." This generally means interacting with everyday Nicas, witnessing interesting community events, and giving you many opportunities to practice your Spanish.

a block east, 7:30 A.M.–9:30 P.M. Mon.–Fri., 7:30 A.M.–7 P.M. Sat.).

Mail and Phone

The **post office** (two blocks west and 1.5 north of Puerto Café Benjamin Linder, 8 A.M.–5 P.M. Mon.–Fri., 8 A.M.–noon Sat.) deals with faxes as well as snail mail. **Agencia de Viajes Premier** (across from the Rubén Darío park, tel. 505/2311-5535) is León's only authorized UPS agent. International calls are extra cheap in León and can be made from most any Internet café.

Medical Services

The hospital is in the center of León, one block south of the cathedral, though you're probably better off in one of the two private clinics with emergency rooms. On the block west of Café Puerto Benjamin Linder, **Policlinica la Fraternidad** (tel. 505/2311-1403) and **Policlinica Occidental** (tel. 505/2311-2722) face each other from opposite sides of the street. Even there, on weekends and after normal business hours, they may not have a doctor on-site.

Travel Agents

Viajes Mundiales (from the cathedral, three blocks north, half a block east, tel. 505/2311-6263 or 505/2311-5920, viajesmu@ibw.com. ni, 8 A.M.–noon and 2–6 P.M. Mon.–Fri., until 1 P.M. Sat.) is a full international agency and official representative of major airlines. Two blocks west is an authorized **TransNica** agency (tel. 505/2311-5219) with bus service to Costa Rica, Honduras, and El Salvador. **Agencia de Viajes Premier** (by the Iglesia San Juan, tel. 505/2311-5535) is the authorized agent for La Costeña airline tickets, to plan your flight to the Atlantic coast or Río San Juan.

GETTING THERE

From Managua, take an express *interlocal* from Mercado Israel Lewites; they cost about $1, take less than two hours, and depart every 40 minutes 5 A.M.–7:30 P.M. In León, the main bus station (La Terminal) is in the northeast corner of the city grid, where you'll find transportation to most points (except Poneloya and Las Peñitas—buses to these beaches depart from their own terminal in Mercadito Subtiava). Big yellow buses and small white *interlocales* depart all day long for both Managua and Chinandega, 4 A.M.–7 P.M. Traveling to Managua, you'll arrive at the UCA (best for Masaya and Granada connections) or Mercado Israel Lewites. There are also a few daily expresses to Estelí between 4 A.M. and 3:10 P.M. (depends on when they fill up) and to Matagalpa between 4:20 A.M. and 2:45 P.M.

If you'd rather not muck around with public transport, ask the tour providers and hostels in town about shuttle transport to Granada, San Juan del Sur, and other destinations.

Most Central American bus routes include a stop in León. **TicaBus** (two blocks north of the San Juan church in Viajes Cumbia travel agency, tel. 505/2311-6153, www.ticabus.com) offers buses to most Central American capitals and Mexico.

GETTING AROUND

Taxis charge $0.75 during the day and $1.50 at night anywhere within the city. Small city buses and converted pickup trucks crisscross León and charge about $0.25; ask about your destination before getting on.

Don't miss León's answer to London's double-decker bus tours: **El Bus Pelón** (The Bald Bus, 5–10 P.M. Sat.–Sun.) runs 30-minute rides around the city, and sometimes features live *chichero* music. Line up at the southwest corner of the central park with your own booze. The locals love it.

Car Rental

The only official rental agency in León is **Dollar** (tel. 505/2311-3371), run out of the Casa Pellas dealership in the southern part of town. You'll need a four-wheel drive if you're driving up to Cosigüina or on surf safari to coastal roads. Dollar can order up special cars from Managua or Chinandega, if you give them time, for roughly $100 per day. You can also find individual cars and drivers for rent by inquiring through the main tour operators and at your hotel.

LEÓN

Vicinity of León

SOUTH OF LEÓN
◖ Las Ruinas de León Viejo

The sleepy ruins of Spain's first settlement in Nicaragua make for an easy and worthwhile day trip from León. Francisco Hernández de Córdoba founded the first León in 1524 and Pedrarias Dávila governed it. After two years, for reasons unknown, Dávila had Hernández de Córdoba decapitated in the town square. In 1610, Volcán Momotombo erupted, burying the site under ash. But León may have already been abandoned following a series of premonitory earthquakes that convinced the settlers to look elsewhere for a place to call home. (Momotombo has erupted several times since then, most recently in 1905.)

Dr. Carlos Tünnerman and a team from the National University (UNAN) first uncovered the ruins of old León in 1966; in 2000, archaeologists found the remains of both Córdoba and Dávila and placed them in an on-site mausoleum. León Viejo is now a UNESCO World Heritage Site. The Nicaraguan Culture Institution has completed fascinating excavations and has trained many local guides to take you around, most of whom are friendly, enthusiastic, and speak passable English.

Las Ruinas de León Viejo (8 A.M.–5 P.M. Mon.–Sat., 8 A.M.–4 P.M. Sun., $3) is located just adjacent to Puerto Momotombo; turn off the highway at La Paz Centro (at the statue of an indigenous warrior). Note that visiting hours are strictly observed by bribe-resistant guards. Most visitors go on tours organized by their hotel or via tour companies in León, but you can do it by yourself as well. Catch

Las Ruinas de León Viejo

© HELMUT HAEFNER/WIKIMEDIA COMMONS

a bus from León to La Paz Centro, then take either an 8 A.M. or 11 A.M. bus to the ruins; the last return bus from the ruins is at 3 P.M. For more information, contact the Palacio Nacional de la Cultura (505/2222-2905, ext. 112) in Managua.

Volcán Momotombo and Momotombito Island

Volcán Momotombo is the most challenging Pacific volcano to climb, and it is one of Nicaragua's more active volcanic peaks. While the small town of El Cardón, on the other side of Volcán Momotombo is closer, the town itself is difficult to get to from the highway.

Momotombo's little sibling, the island of Momotombito was once a pre-Columbian religious sanctuary, when the islet was called Cocobolo. Today, it is an uninhabited natural reserve of tropical dry forest. First, head to the town of Puerto Momotombo, where for the right price, many fishermen would be eager to transport you the 25 kilometers along the north shore of Lake Managua to the island. Bring water and supplies to last two days in order to camp on the island, and don't pay your boatman until he returns to take you off the island. The island reportedly contains petroglyphs and the faintest remnants of the previous civilization, who would be horrified to see what has become of their precious lake.

Nagarote

About halfway between Managua and León is the historic village of Nagarote (Chorotega for "the road of the Nagarands"), whose claim to fame is an enormous old *genícero* tree dating to the time of Columbus; its broad branches shade the small market. The tree and a statue of Diriangén are two blocks north and one block west from the central park. The **Casa de Cultura** is located one block south of the tree. Nagarote is also nationally renowned for its *quesillos,* a snack of mozzarella-like string

cheese, sour cream, and onions wrapped in a hot tortilla. Enjoy them at any of the roadside restaurants that cater to León–Managua travelers, many of whom plan their trips around a stop in Nagarote for cheesy goodness.

WEST OF LEÓN
Rancho Los Alpes

Exactly halfway to the coast from León, look for the turnoff for **Rancho Los Alpes** (Km 99, León–Poneloya Road, tel. 505/8803-7085 or 8845-6341, www.ecolodgelosalpes.com, dorms $12, private rooms $35–45 with breakfast), an old-style ranch house with nice rooms filled with handmade furniture and interesting antiques, as well as large dorm rooms in the lodge next door. This is an excellent spot for groups, with service and tour opportunities, and good food and barbecues. The well-run community tourism project here offers visits and volunteer opportunities in the surrounding area, as well as horseback riding and unique trips to beaches and volcanoes. In 2012, the lodge opened León's first zip line, where three sturdy cables whiz you across an artificial swimming hole.

Poneloya

Only a 20-minute drive toward the coast from León, Poneloya has been a playground of the Leónese elite for generations. The road from León splits when it reaches the coast, the right fork placing you in Poneloya. The *estero* here is safer than the ocean, a fact not overlooked by lots of children who come to splash around. However, Poneloya has a vicious undertow that makes it dangerous for casual swimmers— bathers die here every year.

ACCOMMODATIONS AND FOOD

Hotel La Posada de Poneloya (150 m west of the entrance on the right-hand side, tel. 505/2317-0378, posadadeponeloya@yahoo. com, $30 d) is the only hotel in town, remodeled in 2010 and now offering 15 rooms with

LEÓN

HIKING THE MARIBIO VOLCANOES

There is nowhere better to feel the force of Nicaragua's volcanic strength than on the hot slopes of its volcanoes. Start early and bring a minimum of three liters of water per person. None of these hikes should be attempted without a guide. Choose from a range of independent guides and well-established, insured tour companies like like Tierra Tours and Vapues Tours. One freelance option is Flavio Parayón, whose **Knowing Nicaragua** guide service (tel. 505/8880-8673, or 505/2311-4383, fparayon2003@yahoo.es) can get you there. **Quetzal Trekkers** (1.5 blocks east of Iglesia de la Recolección, tel. 505/2311-6695, leon@quetzaltrekkers.com, www.quetzaltrekkers.com) is a remarkable organization that specializes in volcano hikes.

- **Momotombo** (1,300 meters, 8 hours round-trip): Momotombo is climbable, but it's not easy, especially when you hit the loose volcanic gravel that comprises the upper half of the cone. But your reward will be the views of Lago Xolotlán. From the Ruinas de León Viejo, head out of town to the main highway and turn right (north) along the highway. Follow that to the geothermal plant, where you'll have to convince the guard to let you through to hike.

- **Telica** (1,061 meters, 5-7 hours round-trip): Despite its tendency to spew ash, Volcán Telica makes for a good climb. Take a bus from León to Telica, then follow the road to the community of La Quimera and keep going until the road disappears beneath and becomes the volcano.

- **Cerro Negro** (675 meters, 2 hours round-trip): Cerro Negro rises from the landscape completely free of vegetation and scorching hot when there is no cloud cover. A road takes you from León to the base; from there, follow the makeshift "trail," part of which will have you scrambling over awkward rocks and fighting surprisingly strong wind. The trail loops around the steaming crater, which the brave may enter at their own risk. You can also

descend into the second crater accessible from the summit, again at your own risk. Getting out of this one is much harder and much hotter, so make sure you are in good shape. There are a number of approaches; the most common heads due east from León, near the town of Lechecuago. Leave early in the morning to beat the heat and avoid the afternoon thunderstorms.

- **La Casitas** (1,405 meters, 8 hours round-trip): Access here can be very difficult because of property issues. Near the top of the climb, guides will lead you into the saddle between La Casita and San Cristóbal and then to the peak of La Casita itself. There are some radio towers here, and the terminus of an access road damaged during the landslide. Though it's also possible to hike to the top along the slide itself, it's a treeless, sun-baked hike.

- **San Cristóbal** (1,745 meters, 8 hours round-trip): This is the granddaddy of volcano hikes in the region; it's long, but the grade is moderate and even easy compared to some of these other hikes. You'll need a guide to help you wend your way through the myriad fields, farms, and fences that obstruct the path upward. Enrique Reyes is experienced at leading trips up San Cristóbal; he can be found in the Barrio Pellisco Occidental, across from the Escuela Hector García. Horses cost $2 a day, and you should pay the guides at least $8 per group.

- **Cosigüina** (860 meters, 6-11 hours round-trip): Start walking from Potosí or rent horses. Head back along the road toward the community of La Chacara, where the slope of Cosigüina is most amenable for climbing. From the edge of the crater, you can see across the Gulf of Fonseca into El Salvador. Luís Mejía Castro (El Viejo, from the Cine Imperial, two blocks west, tel. 505/8886-5477) knows the Reserva Natural. Be careful: Hikers have died on this volcano.

private bath, fan, and air-conditioning, plus a pool for guests. It's simple and not quite on the beach, but essentially clean. A better option is a five-minute boat ride away, on Isla Los Brasiles. There, the **Surfing Turtle Lodge** (tel. 505/8640-0644, www.surfingturtlelodge.com, $10 dorm, $30 d rooms, $40 cabin) has one dormitory and several rooms, plus surfing lessons and rentals, horseback riding, biking, yoga, massage, fishing, and salsa dance lessons. Note that during Semana Santa, hotels swell to capacity and double their rates.

For food, **El Pariente Salinas** is the only restaurant in the middle of Poneloya. A better option is to walk north up the beach to La Bocana, where you will find a group of restaurants, all of which let you choose a fish to be fried whole. The last one, **El Chepe,** is the best, and the only establishment in the area that accepts credit cards.

GETTING THERE
Buses for Poneloya leave every 45 minutes from the Subtiava Mercadito, from early in the morning until 6 P.M. They stop first in Poneloya, idling for 10 minutes, then continue to Las Peñitas; the trip to the end of the road at Barca de Oro takes about 30 minutes with the new road. You'll save time if you take a taxi from León (about $10–12, not bad if you have three or four people to split the cost). The last bus back to León leaves Barca de Oro at 6:30 P.M., so you can easily do a day trip and end up back in your colonial room in León for dinner.

◖ Las Peñitas
Nearby Las Peñitas is better developed for foreign travelers who come looking for beginner surfing waves and nature excursions into the Isla Juan Venado Wildlife Reserve. The waves are a bit mellower and there are many boards for rent. It's a rare exception along this stretch of Nicaragua's Pacific shoreline, where the waves are less forgiving than the beaches

around San Juan del Sur; they break faster and with more force, and the currents are stronger.

ACCOMMODATIONS AND FOOD
Traveling several kilometers south along the coast will bring you to a series of accommodations that make up Las Peñitas, presented here in order from north to south. **Playa Roca** (three miles south of Poneloya, tel. 505/2317-0224, www.playaroca.com, $7 dorm, $25–45) has two dormitories, eight cozy rooms, and a popular bar-restaurant open till midnight on weekdays and until 2 A.M. on weekends. The view of the rocks and the waves is one of the best on the beach, and the large *pasillo* (patio) is ideal for reading, playing pool, and watching the sunset.

Hotel Suyapa Beach (tel. 505/2317-0219 or 505/8854-2698, www.suyapabeach.com, $53–65) is a modern, well-kept hotel and restaurant with 22 rooms around a small pool. The food and service here is reportedly the best on the beach.

French-owned **Hotelito El Oasis** (tel. 505/8839-5344, www.oasislaspenitas.com, $7 dorm, $20 d) has reasonable rates, spacious rooms, and slow service. But what's the rush? Rooms have fans and private baths. Enjoy the small *rancho* and hammock area with a great second-story view of the beach. Like most other places on the beach, they rent surfboards and can arrange tours of Isla Juan Venado or Spanish lessons ($4/hour). Around the corner and past the local bars of Los Cocos and El Calamar, you'll find the Canadian-owned **La Samaki.net** (tel. 505/8640-2058, $25 d), with simple concrete rooms, a small pool, Wi-Fi, and nice kite-surfing instruction and rentals. They serve different vegetarian options, including Indian curry. **Restaurante y Cyber Manojito** (no phone, reynercalderon@yahoo.es) offers seafood, cocktails, surf lessons, and local tours.

At the end of the road, ◖**Hotel de la Playa Barca de Oro** (tel. 505/2317-0275, tortuga@ibw.com.ni, www.barcadeoro.com) remains the clear favorite among travelers with its range of accommodations from $7 dorm to $25 double cabanas; includes fan, mosquito net, and private bath (you can fit up to four people in a $30 cabana). Food is fantastic. La Barca looks directly out to the northern tip of Isla Juan Venado, only 100 meters away across a protected lagoon. They can help you arrange all kinds of local (and inland) excursions. You can also rent kayaks, horses, sportfishing guides, and locals for a massage or pedicure.

Note that during Semana Santa, hotels swell to capacity and double their rates.

GETTING THERE

Buses for Las Peñitas leave every 45 minutes from the Subtiava Mercadito, from early in the morning until 6 P.M. They stop first in Poneloya, idling for 10 minutes, then continue to Las Peñitas; the trip to the end of the road at Barca de Oro takes about 30 minutes. The last bus back to León leaves Barca de Oro at 6:30 P.M. A taxi from León costs about $10–12.

Isla Juan Venado Wildlife Reserve

The 21-kilometer strip of tropical dry forest, mangroves, and inland estuary south of Las Peñitas provides habitat for hundreds of species of migratory birds, as well as crocodiles and other wetland creatures, and is also an important nesting beach for sea turtles. The park is named for a man who, in colonial times, made his living hunting deer on the island and selling the meat in the market of Subtiava.

Many León-based tour operators run trips to Isla Juan Venado, but you can just as easily strike a deal with one of the many boatmen in Las Peñitas to explore the endless, tree-lined channels. Arrange your trip at least one day in advance, especially if you plan on a sunrise excursion, when you'll see the most wildlife (late afternoons are good, too). Take sun protection and lots of water. You'll need to purchase tickets at the ranger station/youth club ($2 pp includes life vest), a two-story house

100 meters down the beach from Barca de Oro. The youth club helps with reforestation of the mangrove forests, turtle monitoring, and other types of ecological research in cooperation with the organization FUNDAR. Like many protected areas in Nicaragua, Isla Juan Venado is co-managed by the local community and LIDER, a nongovernmental organization (NGO). This is one of the most successful examples of the COMAP (co-management) program in Nicaragua, and the ranger station can be a good source of information on this topic, as well as other issues concerning the flora and fauna of the reserve. They can also arrange boat trips to the island for $50 per group of up to 14 or $20–30 for a smaller boat with one of the community members. Also available are nighttime turtle-viewing trips (seasonal, $10) and mandatory guided camping ($10). Some of the hazards in the reserve include caimans, bees, snakes, and crab and turtle egg hunters frustrated by poverty, so bringing a local guide is a really good idea.

Puerto Sandino

This nondescript fishing village and port town, about 45 minutes southwest of León, receives both Hugo Chavez's oil shipments and a tiny trickle of surfers seeking local waves. Infrastructure for tourists is extremely limited (there is one hotel in town, a few eateries, and 80 percent unemployment).

El Velero and El Tránsito Beaches

Local surf information (there are several world-class waves in the region) is fiercely guarded by those in the know. Beaches south of Puerto Sandino have enormous potential for tourism, and a few surf tour providers operate out of nice homes along the coast. One of those is **Surf Tours Nicaragua** (tel. 505/8438-4522 or 8844-4807, surftoursnica@gmail.com, www.surftoursnica.com), offering all kinds of activity-based, all-inclusive packages.

South from León, the gorgeous two-kilometer stretch of white-sand beach known as El Velero (The Sailboat) has tremendous tourist potential but instead is simply occupied by summer homes for wealthy Leóneses. Buses for Puerto Sandino and El Velero leave from the station at León. The limited options for travelers are not cheap and have fallen into total disrepair, an ignoble end to one of Herty Lewites's more ambitious tourism projects in the 1980s. It's better to visit for the day.

A quiet fishing community 60 kilometers from Managua along the old highway to León, El Tránsito was devastated by the tidal wave of December 1992. The Spanish helped them recover and built what is now the new town on the hills above the old one, which was at the shoreline. The swimming here can be a bit tricky, as there's a strong undertow that will pull you north along the cove, but walk south along the shoreline to see the rock formations and popular swimming holes behind them. These rocks run parallel to the shoreline and buttress the full blow of waves. Splash around in one of them at high tide, when the waves strike the rocks and rush up and over in an exhilarating saltwater shower. Ten minutes' walk north along the shoreline takes you to the wreckage of **El Balneario,** an old abandoned vacation spot. Enjoy cheap, cold beer and fresh fish on the south end of the village. Buses leave Managua every afternoon from Mercado Israel Lewites at 11:15 A.M., 12:40 P.M., and 2 P.M. Buses leave El Tránsito every day at 5 A.M., 6 A.M., and 7 A.M.

NORTH OF LEÓN
Los Hervideros de San Jacinto
On the southeast flank of 1,060-meter Volcán Telíca, Los Hervideros de San Jacinto (7 A.M.–5 P.M., $1) are a warren of boiling mud pits and thermal vents which have formed a veritable Martian landscape not far from León. The vents testify to the region's geothermal electric potential, an opportunity that has not gone unnoticed by potential foreign investors—some Israeli—that continue to explore the idea of producing energy from the vast reserves that are forming the vents. One visitor called it "Yellowstone without fences," and loved interacting with the children guides; others find it boring. The entrance is marked by an enormous arch and a posse of women and children selling "artifacts" from the hot springs. The boys will offer to guide you around for $1 or less—which is worth it, considering the danger of falling into a scalding mud bath.

To get there, take a bus from León bound for Estelí, San Isidro, or Malpaisillo and get off at the town of San Jacinto (approximately 25 kilometers from León).

El Sauce
In the foothills of the Segovia Mountains, about a 90-minute drive northeast of León, the village of El Sauce (rhymes with WOW-seh) was once the eastern terminus of the railroad that received inland-grown Nicaraguan coffee bound for the port at Corinto. In the 1800s, caravans of mules lumbered into town laden with thousands of pounds of coffee beans. El Sauce has since faded into a sleepy cowboy village whose pride and joy is a breathtaking colonial church built in 1750 in tribute to the patron saint, El Cristo Negro de Esquipulas (the Black Christ). El Sauce celebrates its *fiestas patronales* on January 18 and attracts a massive pilgrimage (as many as 25,000 people!) from all over Nicaragua to view the Black Christ icon.

El Sauce makes a fine first stop on pueblo-hopping routes toward Achuapa, San Juan de Limay, and Estelí. There are a couple of places to eat in town, and several simple *hospedajes* for lodging: try **Hotel Blanco** (tel. 505/2319-2403, $11 s, $20 d) or **Hotel El Viajero** (tel. 505/2319-2325, $8 s with private bath and TV).

If you're gong to stay here though, a better option is to sample El Sauce's unique community-based tourism project, administered by the **Associación Turística de El Sauce** (one block west of the bus station, tel. 505/2319-2213 or 505/8907-9645, visit.elsauce@gmail.com). They rent bicycles ($5 a day, $2 for two hours) and provide local history tours by teenagers who are forming their own company, Sauce Tours. Ask to see the church, the railroad line (with great views), swim holes in the river, and farm tours. They also manage the **Casa Huespedes** guesthouse program, where you can stay in a local home for $16 a night (three meals included) or $11 a night with just breakfast.

Their most spectacular offering is an overnight excursion to **Los Altos de Ocotal** (a local mountain peak, not the northern town of Ocotal), run by a rural tourism cooperative in Las Minitas. One reader writes that "the most spectacular view I've seen so far in Nicaragua" is from El Ocotal. Los Altos is about 17 kilometers from El Sauce along a steep road; it takes about an hour, and a four-wheel drive vehicle is necessary. For more information, contact Los Altos (505/2319-2213 or 505/8907-9645, altos.de.ocotal@gmail.com). Stay with a host family for about $12 a night (includes room and full board). There are hiking trails, horseback riding, and different tours to learn about the *campo* lifestyle, coffee production, and forest conservation, all in gorgeous pine forest (tours are only $3–5 per person). Pick up some organic coffee and export-quality pine needle baskets.

Chinandega

Chinandega, a provincial capital grown out of the agriculture business, is the last major town before the Guasaule border with Honduras, and also the gateway to Nicaragua's distant corner of the Gulf of Fonseca. It's a town you'll get to know well if you are stocking up for a visit to the desolate coastline or the unvisited crater wall of Volcán Cosigüina. It's also the undisputedly hottest corner of the nation.

The same threatening volcanoes that loom over the city of Chinandega and its surrounding plains are also responsible for the high fertility of the soil. This attracted the Nahuatl, who called their new home Chinamilt ("close to cane"). Chinandega suffers the same poverty as the rest of the nation, but also boasts a prosperous community of old and new money, based primarily in sugar, bananas, peanuts, sesame, soy, and shrimp. Cotton used to be the number one cash crop in the 1960s, but the deforestation and agrochemicals essential to its production caused monumental environmental damage, like poisoned aquifers and toxic soil, still affecting life to this day. The agricultural activity of the region and proximity to the northern borders and Port of Corinto make Chinandega Nicaragua's most important agribusiness center.

Did I mention that it's hot in Chinandega? It's so hot, expect to break a sweat in the shower. This is what it feels like to be a rotisserie chicken. You can easily see Chinandega's colonial churches and central market in a couple of hours before stopping to catch your breath. Keep your wits about you, as the areas south of center can be a bit dangerous.

SIGHTS AND ENTERTAINMENT

Chinandega's two hubs of activity are the area surrounding the Mercado Bisne (from the English word business), and the town center, or simply *el centro*. The Mercadito is located two blocks north of the central park, and the Central Market a few blocks east of the park, along the Calle Central.

For dancing, especially on Saturdays, the **Dilectus Disco** (located just east of town on

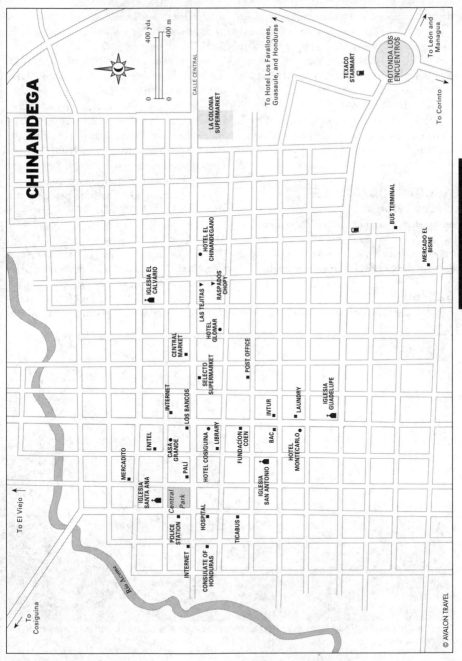

CHINANDEGA

LEÓN

© AVALON TRAVEL

To El Viejo

To Cosigüina

Río Acome

To Hotel Los Farallones, Guasaule, and Honduras

To León and Managua

To Corinto

ROTONDA LOS ENCUENTROS

TEXACO STARMART

CALLE CENTRAL

LA COLONIA SUPERMARKET

BUS TERMINAL

MERCADO EL BISNE

IGLESIA EL CALVARIO

HOTEL EL CHINANDEGANO

LAS TEJITAS
RASPADOS CHOPY

CENTRAL MARKET

HOTEL GLOMAR

SELECTO SUPERMARKET

POST OFFICE

INTERNET

LOS BANCOS

IGLESIA GUADELUPE

ENITEL

CASA GRANDE

INTUR

LAUNDRY

MERCADITO

PALÍ

HOTEL COSIGÜINA

LIBRARY

FUNDACION COEN

BAC

IGLESIA SANTA ANA

Central Park

IGLESIA SAN ANTONIO

HOTEL MONTECARLO

POLICE STATION

HOSPITAL

TICABUS

INTERNET

CONSULATE OF HONDURAS

400 yds
400 m
0
0

the road to León) is popular with well-off locals, but also overpriced and ridiculously loud. Next door, **Cacique** caters to a large crowd with two floors for boozing and jiving. If you prefer a looser, younger crowd and still want air-conditioning, try **Montserat** on the highway to Guasaule (Wednesday is mariachi night) or better still, **La Terraza** (on the road to El Corinto), which has an open-air *rancho;* it's very pleasant, with dancing on the weekend, decent food, and a clean swimming pool!

ACCOMMODATIONS
Under $25
Hotel Glomar (a block south of the central market, tel. 505/2341-2562, from $20) has 13 bare-bones doubles; a few rooms have air-conditioning and cost more. The place is clean enough.

$25-50
Hotel El Chinandegano (tel. 505/2341-4800, hotelchdgano@turbonett.com.ni, $25 d) offers 11 rooms with air-conditioning, private bath, breakfast, phone, and Wi-Fi, as well as laundry services and parking. Centrally located 75 meters north of *la esquina de los bancos,* **Hotel Los Balcones** (tel. 505/2341-8994, www.hotelbalcones.com, $40–70 including breakfast) is an excellent option. Another very central option is the **Hotel Montecarlo** (just north of the Guadalupe church, tel. 505/2341-0071, www.hotelmontecarlochinandega.com, $40–65 including breakfast). The 15 newly constructed rooms all have private bathrooms, hot water showers, a/c, cable TV, and Wi-Fi access.

Over $50
The fanciest digs in the city center are at **Hotel Cosigüina** (located half a block south of *la esquina de los bancos,* corner of the banks, tel. 505/2341-3636, $55 plus tax) with air-conditioning, hot water, private bath, Wi-Fi,

The San Cristóbal volcano lords over Chinandega, occasionally powdering it with a layer of white-gray ash.

© RYAN BALLANTYNE/WIKIMEDIA COMMONS

LEÓN

and breakfast included. Hotel Cosigüina also rents cars and serves food and drinks in the Fumaroles Restaurant. Newer **Hotel Los Fallarones** (on the Panamerican Highway, about four blocks east of La Colonia supermarket, tel. 505/2342-9160, www.hotelfallarones.com, from $60) has the plushest rooms and facilities in town, including a huge pool and swanky bar/restaurant. Upstairs rooms are deluxe suites with icy a/c, private bathrooms, cable TV, Wi-Fi, king-size beds and private balconies that catch a minimal breeze.

FOOD

You won't go hungry in Chinandega, with choices ranging from every type of street food imaginable staring at you from thousands of coolers, stands, and baskets all over town, to the *comida corriente* in any of the markets (meals for less than $2) to a host of expensive restaurants. Good Salvadoran *pupusas* are found in the central park. Or head to Calle Central, seven blocks east of the park, to **Las Tejitas** (open evenings). Sit outside on the sidewalk and enjoy a heaping plate of juicy roasted chicken, *gallo pinto, tajadas* (fried plantain chips), and any number of deep-fried delicacies, all for under $5, drink included. Another good *fritanga* is **La Parrillada** (about 100 meters south of Palí, tel. 505/2341-3745, open daily) with free delivery and buffet, grill, fry, and rotisserie options. For a large buffet of *comida típica,* head to local favorite **El Granadino** (Reparto 12 Septembre, Carretera Guasaule, tel. 505/2341-4094, Tues.–Sun., from $4). Huge portions are topped with specialties like *punche,* a delicious stuffed crab you're unlikely to find elsewhere.

If you can find **Raspados y Soda "Chopy"** (located around the corner from El Chinandegano), the sugar buzz from the traditional shaved ice might snap you out of the heat coma. Many fancier restaurants abound along the highways in and out of town, including **Restaurante Los Vitrales** at Hotel Los Volcanes (Km 129.5, Carretera a Chinandega, tel. 505/2341-1000, 6 A.M.–11 P.M. Sun.–Thurs., 6 A.M.–midnight Sat.–Sun., $8–15). Options include juicy bacon-wrapped filet mignon and other fare. Less expensive but equally tasty is the **Bar y Restaurante El Paraiso** (opposite the Hotel Fallarones on the Panamerican Highway, Tues.–Sun., $3–10), which offers hearty plates of upscale *comida típica* served in a huge open *rancho*, that is also a popular watering-hole on the weekends.

There are two fully stocked supermarkets: **El Palí,** in front of the park, and **El Selecto,** 3.5 blocks farther east.

INFORMATION AND SERVICES

INTUR (in front of the BAC bank, tel. 505/2341-1935, chinandega@intur.gob.ni) maintains an office full of brochures and has a staff who are surprisingly helpful as long as you sign in.

ATMs can be found at Banco America Central (BAC), as well as at StarMart and On the Run. Money changers work the streets near the central market, and most of Chinandega's banks are clustered on *la esquina de los bancos* (corner of banks), two blocks east of the park.

The police occupy the entire block along the west side of the central park, and the hospital is right across the street to the south.

The post office is three blocks east of the park and 1.5 blocks north. Also, the TicaBus agent will send FedEx packages via their Managua office. The ENITEL phone office is one block east of the park—look for the giant red and white tower.

Chinandega's abundant cybercafés are in constant flux, though you'll want to seek out the ones with air-conditioning, such as the one located one block north of the corner with all the banks. For laundry, head to **Lavamatic Express** (half a block north of Iglesia Guadelupe, tel. 505/2341-3319, 7 A.M.–9 P.M. Mon.–Sat., 8 A.M.–5 P.M. Sun.).

LEÓN

International Consulates

The **Honduras Consulate** (tel. 505/2341-0949, 8:30 A.M.–4:30 P.M. Mon.–Fri.) is across from ENITEL. The **Costa Rica Consulate** (tel. 505/2341-1584, 8:30 A.M.–5 P.M. Mon.–Fri., until noon Sat.) is located half a block north from Banpro.

Volunteering

Stop by the office of **Fundación COEN** (tel. 505/2341-2906, www.fundacioncoen.org), half a block south of INISER, where arrangements can be made to work with children with disabilities or with chemotherapy patients.

GETTING THERE

The main bus station is at Mercado Bisne, just past Rotonda los Encuentros. From La Rotonda, highways run north to Somotillo and the border with Honduras at Guasaule, southeast to León and Managua, south to Corinto, and three daily buses to Matagalpa. Bus service to Managua, León, and the border runs 4 A.M.–7 P.M. daily.

A second bus station located at El Mercadito (just north of the central park) provides service to all points north: El Viejo, Jiquilillo, Potosí, Cosigüina, and Puerto Morazán.

Car rentals start at $35 a day and are available at the Avis office in the Hotel Cosigüina and at Budget in Hostal Las Mañanitas. There is also a Dollar office at Casa Pellas.

Even though there is a TicaBus agency in town, those traveling north into Honduras or El Salvador will have to go to Managua to catch the bus, which no longer stops in Chinandega. Be advised: Any foreigner who enters El Salvador must have a visa. Get yours at the Salvadoran Consulate.

GETTING AROUND

La Rotonda los Encuentros and the Texaco StarMart are both important reference points you'll pass on your way into town. Everything is walkable, but drink lots of water. Taxis are plentiful and cost $0.40 within city limits; *ruta* buses are $0.10.

Near Chinandega

EL VIEJO

Only a few kilometers west of Chinandega, El Viejo is a cheerful town of some 50,000 Viejanos. Less service-oriented than its big neighbor, El Viejo can still launch you on your next adventure. El Viejo is much older than Chinandega. Originally an indigenous community called Tezoatega, for the fierce cacique who once ruled it, the town was renamed for the old Spaniard who arrived in 1562 carrying a sacred image of the Virgin Mary. According to legend, when the Spaniard tried to sail back to Spain, the Virgin created a hurricane so that she would be returned to her new home in Nicaragua. The old man complied, and the image soon became the most important Virgin Mary in the country. Her fame

has lasted through the centuries, and in 1996 the Pope himself recognized her when he came to declare El Viejo's church a Basilica Minor. The church is impressive and worth your time to visit.

Entertainment and Events

Nightlife in El Viejo is exciting and sometimes downright rowdy. Local volunteers say it's all "beer and bark" though, and everyone makes up and shakes hands the next day. Just north of the basilica is the clean and well-liked **Tezoatega** (well known even in León), with good food and service, lots of music (including mariachi night Thursdays). **La Piscina,** two blocks north of the basilica and half a block east, is almost as good, with dancing

© AMBER DOBRZENSKY

El Viejo's Basilica Inmaculada Concepción de Maria is a Basilica Minor.

Thursday–Saturday. Their swimming pool costs $0.75 to use all day.

El Viejo's *fiestas patronales* are the week of December 6, with firework-spitting bulls every night, culminating in the **Lavada de la Plata,** when even the president and national ballet often show up to help wash the church silver. There is no lodging in El Viejo save a few motels of ill repute: Stay in León instead.

Getting There

Buses arrive half a block north of the basilica, across the street from the market, where you'll find the cheapest eats. Buses called *interlocales* back to Chinandega leave from the basilica, one block west of the park, and run until about 11 P.M.

CHICHIGALPA

Set in the middle of hundreds of square kilometers of sugarcane, Chichigalpa's **Ingenio San**

Antonio is Nicaragua's largest and most powerful sugar refinery, and more importantly, the Compañía Licorera, Nicaragua's alcohol monopoly and source of all the Toña, Victoria, Flor de Caña, and Ron Plata you've been drinking. The two companies belong to the wealthy Pellas family, who founded the sugar refinery in 1890 and have produced sugar and liquor ever since (except 1988–1992, when the Sandinista government briefly expropriated it—the Chamorro government subsequently returned it).

As alcohol is a mainstay of Nicaraguan culture and legend, the refineries and distilleries have been important parts of Nicaraguan life for more than a century. Arrange a tour of the cane processing facilities and **Flor de Caña distillery** by calling the plant in advance (tel. 505/2343-2344, try asking for Simón Pedro Pereira) and requesting a guided tour. At the moment, there is no charge for the tour, but neither are there free samples.

CORINTO

Nicaragua's primary port complex is the reason for Corinto's existence, linking Nicaragua with the shipping lines of the Pacific. Corinto is 20 kilometers southwest of Chinandega, with a couple of halfway decent beaches and a small range of simple hotels and seaside restaurants. Corinto's 20,000 inhabitants live on 49 square kilometers of what is actually a barrier island, connected to the rest of Nicaragua by two small bridges.

The Spanish first made use of the harbor in the 1500s, but didn't completely conquer the region until 1633, when an armada of 26 ships, 500 Spaniards, 227 horses, and 2,000 slaves arrived, swiftly defeating Tezoatega's troops and taking many of them as additional slaves. The original port, placed at El Realejo (which still exists as a faint shadow of its former self), was transferred closer to the ocean at Corinto in 1858 after mangroves and sediment had choked the waterways.

In 1875, Corinto's wooden pier linked to the railroads transporting coffee from El Sauce to Corinto. At the harbor, ships took it to the

LEÓN

LEÓN

VOLCÁN CASITAS AND HURRICANE MITCH

On October 30, 1998, the quiet municipality of Posoltega (whose Nahuatl name, Posoli-tecatl, means "neighbor of the boiling place") was catapulted into a horrendous sort of fame as the site of one of the worst naturally caused disasters in Nicaragua's history. After Hurricane Mitch dropped two meters of rain in just three days, the southwest flank of Volcán Casitas transformed into a gigantic wave of mud and rock more than three meters high and nearly 1.5 kilometers wide. The communities of El Porvenir and Rolando Rodríguez were instantly consumed by the very soil on which they were built. Some 2,500 people immediately lost their lives, and those who were not buried lived through the horror of losing nearly everything and everyone in their lives. Immediate relief efforts were held up by the political shenanigans of President Alemán, who stalled help to the Sandinista leadership of Posoltega.

A survivor told one Witness for Peace volunteer, "You should have seen how the children, the little ones, fought to survive. People were pulling themselves up out of the mud naked, completely covered in mud. They looked like monsters in a horror movie. All you could see were their eyes. Children didn't even recognize their own parents. For days we could hear the ones who were still half-buried crying for help."

More than a decade later, the slide is still clearly visible from the León-Chinandega highway. International efforts helped construct several new communities for survivors, despite reports of disappearing relief funds reminiscent of Somoza's postearthquake "emergency committee." The new suburban communities, however, provided no means of production for a people accustomed to living off the land. Many were psychologically devastated and eventually made their way illegally to search for work in Costa Rica.

The entire slide area has been declared a national monument, and a memorial plaque personally delivered by U.S. President Bill Clinton can be visited in the Peace Park on the highway, near the turnoff for Posoltega.

United States and elsewhere. A railroad constructed during Zelaya's presidency further expanded the port and its strategic significance.

In 1912, nearly 3,000 U.S. Marines landed in Corinto in response to Benjamin Zeledón's revolution, beginning what would be a 20-year occupation of Nicaragua. In October 1983, CIA operatives stole into the harbor under cover of night, where they mined the harbor and blew up several oil tanks on the docks. The economic and psychological damage strained an already suffering Sandinista government, but the "covert" operation, when publicized later, earned the Reagan administration international condemnation and the ire of the American public.

From 2000–2001, the Alemán administration revitalized the port and dredged the harbor with project financing from the World Bank in order to increase export production. Corinto remains a vibrant coastal community with all the headaches and spice of a port town.

Sights

Playa Paso Caballo is located on the northern tip of the island, and all buses from Chinandega pass by here before continuing to the center of town. Be careful, as the rip currents are notoriously strong, and keep a close eye on your possessions on these beaches. Several *ranchos* on the beach provide shade, food, and alcohol, but a growing number have succumbed to the beach erosion that began when a spooky, wrecked tanker that had been there for years was finally scrapped.

In town, what was once the **Old Railroad Terminal and Customs House** is now a museum in tribute to the old train, well worth a visit.

Entertainment and Events

If you are in the neighborhood around the weekend that falls closest to May 3, don't miss the **Féria Gastronómica del Mar** (Seafood Festival, 10 A.M.–3 P.M. Sat.–Sun,), where you can try more than 100 different Corinteña recipes with fresh fish, shrimp, and other local delicacies. The festival takes place in the central park.

Accommodations and Food

As the few accommodation options here are not very pleasant, you're probably better off bedding down in nearby Chinandega. In a pinch, the **Hospedaje Vargas** (a block south of the bus terminal, tel. 505/2340-5814, $15 d) is cheap but clean.

For dining, you'll want to try some of the freshest seafood in the country. For some of the best *mariscos* in town, head to the ◖ **Restaurante Costa Azul** (tel. 505/2342-2888, from $5) set in a pleasant, breezy, open-air *rancho* with views of the harbor and islands. Another good dining option is on the main road to Chinandega, near the bridge (from which you can jump into the water)—it's called **El Español** and the owner makes a mean sangria.

Practicalities

Corinto Online (half a block north of the park) will connect you to the Internet for $2.50 per hour. Getting to and from Corinto is a snap from Chinandega's Mercado Bisne, or by hitching from the Rotonda.

Northwest Coast and Cosigüina Peninsula

This magnificent volcanic knuckle juts into the Golfo de Fonseca, providing stunning scenery, untouched wetlands, long unspoiled beaches, and massive peanut farms. This part of the country was too hot and isolated for most tourists until very recently, when parts of the main access road were improved and foreigners began investing in land and hotel projects. Although a trip to the scenic crater that makes up the highest point of Reserva Natural Volcán Cosigüina is the center point of a trip to this area, you can also ride horseback, explore, fish, or just lounge on the beach.

Access this area on the Nic-12 highway, most of which was paved with financial support from the American government in 2009. There's no real coastal road to area beaches, only side spurs from Nic-12. Some of the side roads are in better condition than others. Four-wheel drive is still necessary to explore this area. Buses to Cosigüina's scattered northern villages and beaches leave from Chinandega's Mercadito and make stops in El Viejo before continuing

northwest. Many of these destinations only have bus service once a day, which means you'll be making an overnight trip if you don't have your own wheels. Most visitors either rent a vehicle or arrange a transfer with their hotel.

VOLCÁN COSIGÜINA NATURAL RESERVE

Not only does this nationally protected reserve provide incredible views from the volcano's rim, but the dense vegetation inside the crater is home to a rare scarlet macaw population. Most hikes and horseback trips to the rim begin 15 kilometers past Potosí in the community of El Rosario; the park's official ranger station, co-managed by a nonprofit organization called LIDER, sits below the volcano and is the best place to begin your exploring. LIDER links tourists with a community tourism organization called Centro Ecoturístico de Aguas Termales, which offers two-day, one-night all-inclusive visits to the reserve during which you will take a horse ride up to the crater rim, take boat rides past mangrove forests, go on hikes, and cook (yourself) in the hot springs—all for $60, which goes to support the community and the co-managed conservation efforts. Contact Irving Caballeros at the **LIDER office** in El Viejo (tel. 505/8625-4607, turismocosiguina@yahoo.com).

Potosí

This poverty-stricken coastal village on the east coast of the peninsula was a trading port with El Salvador until the Contras blew it up in the 1980s. Authorities have yet to reestablish regular El Salvador–Nicaragua ferry service. If you can find a local licensed captain, you can make your own way to El Salvador, either to the port city of La Union or the tourist beach at Tamarindo, where you can find hotels, basic services, and buses to the capital. You'll need to stop by the lonely immigration office at the end of a dirt path to get your passport stamped and pay the exit fee. The

ride takes less than an hour and should cost less than $25 per person.

On the road toward Potosí you'll find the gorgeous █ **Hacienda Cosiguina** (tel. 505/2341-8448, www.haciendacosiguina.com, $25 per person including breakfast), which has remained in the hands of the Gasteazoro family for almost 300 years. The main farmhouse, once a cheese-making facility, has five rooms all lovingly restored by the owners. The enormous Guanacaste tree in the garden is home to more than 20 iguanas and two species of owl. A variety of excellent tours ($35–50 per person) are offered, from volcano visits to a wetlands horseback tour (have you ever ridden a swimming horse?). Call several days in advance, as reservations are required.

Further down the road, at the tiny village of La Piscina, is a community-based tourism effort called **VaPues Tours Leon** (tel. 505/2315-4099), located near a cemented-in hot springs.

The dock in Potosí offers an alternative route to visit El Salvador.

VaPues provides primitive wood-and-thatch huts; inexpensive meals also available. This is for adventurous, open-minded travelers who want to enjoy a tranquil, natural setting.

A few more kilometers up the road, as you enter Potosí, look on your right for the very reasonable, locally owned **Hotel Brisas del Golfo** (tel. 505/2231-2238, $15 d) with five clean, private rooms with fan at a very reasonable price. Don Rafael Castro and his wife can prepare you three meals a day and help organize your volcano expedition or onward travel to El Salvador.

If you're on the peninsula in May, ask about the three-day festival on Meanguera, an El Salvadoran island that allegedly allows unchecked passport access during the fiesta. You can reach Potosí at the end of a three-hour bus ride from Chinandega; about six buses leave daily and cost under $2 each way.

El Hostal Hato Nuevo Private Nature Reserve and Ranch

North of El Viejo, just past the community of El Congo but before you reach the volcano is El Hostal Hato Nuevo (tel. 505/2341-4245 or 505/8865-9683, www.hatonuevo.com, dorm $15, $40 d); look for a steep driveway on the right. This totally unique, elegant stone home in the middle of the forest has seven comfy rooms and an old-ranch feel with plenty of shade and hammocks. The owner, Mareano, is a native of Chinandega who has studied art in London and Mexico City and whose custom-crafted paintings and furniture fill the place. He's a wonderful cook too, so even if not spending the night, try calling ahead for a relaxing meal. Located on a 600-plus-acre natural reserve, there are nature trails, horseback riding, and wetlands, beach, and volcano expeditions available.

Mechapa Village and Redwood Beach

This tiny fishing village on the Pacific coast of Volcán Cosigüina fronts a long, gorgeous, nearly empty beach that stretches northwest to the cliffs at Punta Ñata (travel to the cliffs by horseback or car at low tide only). Ask for Captain Odel Yoel Gaitán, an experienced sailor who'd be happy to take you fishing or surfing in his *panga*.

There are few services in the area and only one place to stay: **Redwood Beach Resort** (tel. 505/8996-0328, U.S. tel. 800/583-4289, info@rbrmechapa.com, www.redwoodbeachresort.com, $150–170), an isolated, American-owned beach retreat especially popular with foreign diplomats and well-off Nicaraguans. The rate includes three solid meals, most of which are fresh from the sea; cheaper rates with fewer meals or during low season are available. The eight cabanas are wood-constructed, elevated one-room structures with fan, optional air-conditioning, private bathroom, and comfortable porches only meters from the pounding surf. Redwood Beach Resort has the only Wi-Fi service for miles around. You can laze around the beach, hunt *moro* crabs, and a lot more.

One bus leaves Chinandega daily at 1:30 P.M. for the three-hour ride to Mechapa; the bus departs the village the following morning at 4 A.M. A more pleasant option is to travel by vehicle to Jiquilillo, then arrange with the Redwood folks to be picked up by boat.

JIQUILILLO AND PADRE RAMOS

Less than a one-hour bus ride from El Viejo, **Playa Jiquilillo** is on a northwest-pointing peninsula of beaches, which make this area either a beautiful day trip or an extended, lazy stay, paddling through the wetlands and lazing on the beach. The area remains deserted and undeveloped, but is best avoided during Semana Santa, when it's overrun. Five buses make the daily round-trip from Chinandega to Jiquilillo, starting at 7 A.M.; the last one is at 4:30 P.M. The bus to Jiquilillo continues up the coast, through the Los Zorros barrio, and arrives at the end of the road in the community of Padre Ramos.

A simple fishing village of some 150

LEÓN

dispersed families, Padre Ramos is the gateway to the neighboring protected wetlands, and consequently the site of several grassroots tourism projects. Lately, high tides have been washing away large chunks of the gorgeous beach up and down the peninsula. The best local cooks are Doña Widia and Don Pablo—just ask for them. In peaceful, rural Padre Ramos, you can dine at **Bar Zulema** or **Don Roque's** traditional *ranchos* on the water's edge. You can get a quick boat ride to the community of Venecia across the estuary, where you'll find long stretches of utterly deserted beach. The entire area is a breeding ground for sea turtles, the eggs of which hatch between November and January.

◖ Padre Ramos Wetlands Reserve

Relax in the gentle waters of this protected estuary, laze in a hammock under the shade of a nearby *palapa,* or be lulled to sleep on a deserted starlit beach. Padre Ramos is a little-visited part of Nicaragua that will reward you with an expanse of serene coastline and an overflowing supply of hospitality, wilderness, community, and culture.

The estuary is a decidedly mellower place to swim than the ocean and is home to all the wildlife—especially birds—you could hope to see. Check out the visitors center when you arrive to ask about fishing and boat trips into the wetlands.

One of the best, most silent ways to explore Estero Padre Ramos is by sea kayak, paddling amongst the birds, sea turtles, and mangroves that inhabit this rich environment. **Ibis Exchange** (tel. 505/8961-8548, U.S. tel. 415/663-8192, www.ibiskayaking.com) has safe boats, professional guides, unique expeditions, plus delicious meals, kayak gear, and camping equipment for day tours and overnight adventures. Day trips cost $40–60 per person. A number of local and longer, farther-afield tours are available at much higher prices; see the website for detailed packages. All ages and skill levels are welcome.

© AMBER DOBRZENSKY

Explore Cosigüina's wetlands via horseback.

Guides

For guide services, **Eddy Maradeaga** (tel. 505/8371-6761, email Alduvil21@yahoo.es) is available for mangrove tours by boat, hiking, or horseback riding. Eddy is one of the most engaged community members and is very knowledgeable about the local ecosystem and conservation efforts. He is working with a group of local students to develop a community-based tourism program for Padre Ramos.

Accommodations and Food

Things are still quite basic in this area. ◖ **Rancho Esperanza** (tel. 505/8680-0270 or 505/8879-1795, rancho.esperanza@yahoo. com, www.rancho-esperanza.com, $7 dorm, cabins from $18) is a unique, community-centric operation offering a cluster of bamboo huts and dormitories with sand floors and grass mats; only $5 to pitch a tent or hammock. There is electricity and fans, lockboxes, books, surfboards, a community garden, and games.

Experience low-impact natural living with projects that actively benefit the village like a kids' club and community center. Ask about special rates for volunteers (two-week minimum, some Spanish required). The hostel offers great local food ($3–4 per meal) and will organize excursions to nearby Padre Ramos estuary and Volcán Cosigüina.

A more upscale option, down the beach from Rancho Esperanza, is **Monty's Beach Lodge** (tel. 505/8424-4087 or 505/8949-1952, www.montysbeachlodge.com, daily all-inclusive rates for one person $85), catering to the surf package crowd. Cabins and rooms are modern beach-rustic, with private bathrooms. The property also offers a dining *rancho* (which may be flooded at high tide) and chill-out balcony. You can rent surf and boogie boards, or arrange local excursions. Daily rates are also available; the more roommates you have, the cheaper it gets.

A bit farther up the beach, **Rancho Tranquilo** (tel. 505/8814-2245 or 8968-2290, $7 dorm, $20 private hut) has beachside bamboo-thatch huts with cement floors, mosquito nets, and shared toilets and showers. Features include a good learning beach for surfing, open *rancho* bar and restaurant right at the waterline, and primitive veggie living. Ask about English-teaching and Spanish-learning opportunities.

PUERTO MORAZÁN AND ESTERO REAL

Here's a chance to forge a trail on your own: The decrepit inland port town of Puerto Morazán is the gateway to the magnificent and sinuous Estero Real Wetlands Reserve, whose mangrove-filled estuary provides habitat for countless marine species and birds. The estuary is gorgeous, even if its "protected" status has been largely ignored by both government officials and the shrimp industry over the years. Morazán has not always been so poor. During World War II, Morazán's port, railway terminus, and customs office saw the movement of tons of cargo bound for European and North American destinations. When the war ended, so did Morazán's brief prosperity, and when Volcán Chonco erupted, damaging the railroad tracks, the final nail was put in Morazán's coffin. During Hurricane Mitch, Morazán flooded so severely that only the church steeple appeared over the surface of the water. Shortly after Mitch, the community rebuilt itself on its original site, disregarding the humanitarian assistance community's plan to relocate the community to higher ground.

Take a bus from El Viejo and ask around for a local guide or boat driver. The mayor's office may help guide you in the right direction. You won't be disappointed by the extraordinary variety of wildlife, nor by the amazing view of Volcán Cosigüina.

PLAYA LOS ASERRADORES

Playa Los Aserradores is quiet and desolate, with impressive surf good only for experienced wave-shredders. Beginning surfers will have better luck at nearby Aposentillo and Bahía Nahualapa.

Accommodations run the gamut from wallet-wincing to budget-backpacker. Surfers continue to flock to **(Hotel Chancletas** (tel. 505/8868-5036, www.hotelchancletas.com, $10 dorm, privates with or without a/c $35–90) despite attempts to keep this location off the map. A mere three-minute walk from the beach, Chancletas offers a variety of clean rooms plus casitas for long-term rental. Surfboard rentals and tours can also be organized at the *rancho,* which is also equipped with Wi-Fi (perfect for checking the surf forecast). Miami-born owner Shay O'Brien, a long-time resident here, is a great source of information and can advise you on all the surf breaks in the area.

North of Chancletas, just a short stroll from the beach, you'll find the ecoresort **El Coco Loco** (tel. 505/8999-8662, www.elcocolocoresort.com, $50–85), which also hosts Holly Beck's all-female surf camps. The

© AMBER DOBRZENSKY

Bahía Nahualapa has softer waves for less-experienced surfers.

all-inclusive rates cover three meals a day, accommodation in rustic cabins (sleeping up to four people with shared eco bathrooms), and access to the pool, restaurant, yoga *rancho,* volleyball court, and soccer field, plus all the rum you can drink. To reach El Coco Loco, from the highway take the sign-posted Aserradores turnoff. After about five kilometers, turn right at the hand-painted sign and head towards El Manzano Uno.

Farther from the action, but offering great value is the ◖ **Al Cielo Restaurant and Cabañas** (tel. 505/8993-4840, www.alcieloni-caragua.com, cabins $20–60, meals $8–13), run by two French surfers—one of whom is a trained chef—as passionate about food as they are about the waves. The acclaimed *rancho*-restaurant draws faithful clients from across the country with dishes like gourmet pizza and the fisherman's catch of the day, as well as homemade rum infusions. The sprawling hill-top property is scattered with eight cabins (two

with private bathrooms), a *veranera*-framed pool, and Nicaragua's only *petanque* pitch, all of which offer impressive views across the countryside and down to the beach. Wi-Fi, horseback riding, surf/beach/fishing/kayak trips, and airport transfers are also available. To reach Al Cielo Restaurant and Cabañas, from the highway take the sign-posted Aserradores turnoff. Turn right at Km 162 and continue for about a kilometer until you see two blue posts on your left.

Travelers on a tight budget will find a warm welcome at **Joe's Place** (tel. 505/8469-5687 or 505/8464-3824, www.nicaraguasurfhotel.com, $7 per person), in front of the Jose de la Cruz school. Three basic and clean rooms sleep up to four people each, with fan and private bathroom. Construction is underway to complete several more; check the website for updates.

This area is also home to Nicaragua's only luxury yacht-docking option. **Marina Puesta del Sol Resort** (www.marinapuestadelsol, from $185) is an incongruous multimillion-dollar, 600-acre development with posh suites and a dockside restaurant, all with stunning views over the estuary to the San Cristóbal volcano. They have a beach area and pool for events. The Marina hosts the Flor de Caña International Fishing Tournament during the first weekend of December.

There are two daily Los Aserradores buses, leaving from the Mercadito in Chinandega. Buses leave Chinandega at 12:30 P.M. and 3 P.M. for this area and return the next day at 5 A.M. and 7:30 A.M.

HONDURAN BORDER AT EL GUASAULE

Located about 1.5 hours north of Chinandega, El Guasaule is the principal Pacific-side border crossing with Honduras. It is six kilometers beyond the town of Somotillo, where you'll find a large number of trucker and traveler services. At the actual border, there is a Bancentro branch and some basic food services. Reach the migration office at Guasaule by calling 505/2346-2208.

El Guasaule is open 24 hours, and there is always heavy truck traffic and road repair problems on the Nicaraguan side. It costs $2 to leave Nicaragua and $7 to enter the country. Just a passport and some cash is all that's required of North American and European travelers.

If you are driving your own vehicle, the process to enter Nicaragua is lengthy, but usually not difficult. You must present the vehicle's title, as well as your own driver's license and passport. You will be given a temporary (30-day) permit to drive in Nicaragua, which will cost you $10—should you lose the permit, you will be fined $100.

There are numerous and regular buses traveling between the Bisne Terminal and El Guasaule, and the main international bus lines (TicaBus, etc.) heading to Honduras and El Salvador pass through Chinandega on their way to the border.

LEÓN

ESTELÍ AND THE SEGOVIAS

As you travel north and up out of the sultry Pacific lowlands, your introduction to Nicaragua's hilly interior begins with the Sébaco Valley, green with rice, carrot, and onion fields. From there, the Pan-American Highway struggles upward to the pleasant city of Estelí, "Diamond of the Segovias," then continues through mountains and valleys dotted with rural villages whose inhabitants are proud to call themselves *norteños*. Most folks here get along by subsistence farming and ranching, while cash crops like tobacco and coffee also define the land; a few communities boast talented artisans in pottery, leather, and stone. Underneath the north's gentle exterior of pine trees and tended fields are minor ruins of ancient cities, deep pools and cascades, and rugged communities of farmers and cowboys.

The north of Nicaragua suffers acutely from drought, poor soils, and deforestation: Nowhere else is the six-month dry season so intense. The challenging living conditions, however, make for a hardy and hardworking people, quick with a smile or a story. The curious and unrushed traveler will not regret breaking away from the highway and going deep into this northern countryside.

This region offers a huge variety of flora and fauna—from the chilly cloud forest of Miraflor to the gaping Grand Canyon of Somoto—and is ripe with hiking opportunities. In addition to the Grand Canyon of Somoto, the Reserva

HIGHLIGHTS

((Estelí Cigar Factories: Cigar aficionados know Nicaragua better than most, and the local factories are proud to invite you in for a glimpse at the smokes that rival even Cubans (page 202).

((Custom Cowboy Boots: They're custom made from high-quality leather, so don't leave Estelí without a pair for long rides into the wild or just dancing, northern-style (page 208).

((El Salto Estanzuela and Reserva El-Tisey: Visit Estelí's premier swimming hole and ecolodge, where you can hike, ride horses, or just jump in for a swim (page 212).

((Miraflor Nature Reserve: This is the best place in Nicaragua to get back to nature and spot the elusive quetzal or other exotic wildlife (page 215).

((San Juan de Limay: Rumble over the mountain pass and down into the valley to seek out one of the famous soapstone workshops (page 221).

((Iglesia de Nuestra Señora de la Asunción: Ocotal's church has seen it all, and even withstood the world's first air-raid bombing in the 1930s (page 222).

((Grand Canyon of Somoto: The nicest swimming hole north of Estelí is also a great example of responsible community-run tourism (page 229).

LOOK FOR ((TO FIND RECOMMENDED SIGHTS, ACTIVITIES, DINING, AND LODGING.

El Tisey offers trails that lead to a stunning waterfall and swimming hole, while the stretch of highway between Ocotal and Jalapa holds endless (and relatively unexplored) peaks to ascend.

HISTORY

The Spanish conquistador Francisco Hernández de Córdoba personally founded the city of Segovia on the banks of the Río Coco where it met the Jícaro, and the first settlers began exploring for veins of gold in the nearby hillsides. But the Spanish abandoned this original settlement and moved farther north along the Río Coco. Here, the Xicaque, Miskito, and Zambo tribes attacked the new settlement with growing ferocity, strengthened and emboldened by shiny new firearms from the British. English pirate Henry Morgan later sailed up the Río Coco and further reduced the city to rubble. The Spanish moved west to the present village of Ciudad Antigua, which became the Segovian capital despite continued attacks. Not until the early 19th century did the little village of Ocotal begin to assume any importance, when the Catholics transferred valuable religious artifacts to the new church of Nuestra Señora de la Asunción. The faithful followed the relics westward, and Ocotal began to grow.

ESTELÍ AND THE SEGOVIAS

HONDURAS

0   10 mi

0   10 km

Teotecacinte

Jalapa

Murra

Santa
María

Las
Manos

Cerro Mogotón
2,107m

Cordillera Dipilto y Jalapa

Santa Clara
Ciudad Sandino
Susucayan

San Fernando

Macuelizo
Ocotal

Ciudad Antigua

**IGLESIA DE NUESTRA
SEÑORA DE LA ASUNCIÓN**

Totogalpa

Quilalí

**GRAND CANYON
OF SOMOTO**

Telpaneca

San Juan del
Río Coco

PAN-AMERICAN HIGHWAY

Somoto

Palacagüina

El Espino

Yalagüina

Río Coco

CA1

Ducualí Grande

Pueblo Nuevo

Las Sabanas

Condega

San Sebastián de Yalí

Cinco Pinos

San José de
Cusmapa

CA1

**MIRAFLOR
NATURE RESERVE**

San Rafael
del Norte

La
Concordia

San Francisco
del Norte

Río Estelí

**SAN JUAN
DE LIMAY**

La Sirena

CUSTOM COWBOY BOOTS

ESTELÍ CIGAR FACTORIES

Estelí

Jinotega

Somotillo

Achuapa

**EL SALTO ESTANZUELA
AND RESERVA EL-TISEY**

Santa Cruz

Villa Nueva

Río Grande

La Trinidad

San Isidro

To Matagalpa

San Nicolas

El Sauce

Sébaco

To Chinandega

CA1

To Léon

To Managua

© AVALON TRAVEL

ESTELÍ AND THE SEGOVIAS

In the early 1930s, General Sandino and his men were firmly entrenched in the mountains north of Ocotal, and the American government, intent on capturing him, sent in the Marines. Based in Ocotal, they scoured the countryside around Cerro Guambuco and built the country's first airstrip in Somoto, from which they launched strikes on the city of Ocotal, the first city in the history of the world to experience an air raid. During the 1980s, much of the conflict between Sandinistas and Contras took place in the same area, fiercely punishing outpost towns like Jalapa.

PLANNING YOUR TIME

If you've only got a day and a night, spend them in the city of Estelí, Nicaragua's capital of tobacco, to sample world-renowned cigars and admire the town's inspiring collection of murals. With a second day, the bird-watcher, hiker, and historian should focus on nearby attractions like the Estanzuela waterfall, the lodge and trails at Tisey, or the orchid-rich broadleaf forest reserve of Miraflor. With a little more leisurely pace, however, you can easily spend another day exploring Miraflor. Or spend it getting a feel for the *campesino* lifestyle by spending a lazy afternoon in any of the small northern towns off the Pan-American—like Condega, La Trinidad, or Pueblo Nuevo—or find yourself in the highland border towns of Ocotal or Somoto. If you're really curious, go deeper still, by traveling long loops eastward to Jalapa and Quilalí, or to Cusmapa, the highest town in Nicaragua.

City of Estelí

Spread across a flat valley 800 meters above sea level, Estelí is an unassuming city whose 110,000 merchants, ranchers, artists, and cigar rollers are prouder than most. In Nahuatl, Estelí means something like "river of blood," an apt moniker for an area so saturated with Sandinista rebels in the days that led up to the 1979 revolution that Somoza carpet-bombed the city (ask locals where to find *la bomba,* a relic from the air strikes). But these days, most Esteliános live a bucolic life of farming and commerce.

ORIENTATION

Buses to Estelí will deposit you in one of the two bus terminals (Cotran Sur and Cotran Norte) on the east side of the highway, and express buses bound farther north for Ocotal and Somoto will drop you off at the nearby Shell Esquipulas. In either case, take a cab to the central park ($0.50) to start your exploration. Estelí is quite possibly the only city in the country to name avenues (north-south) and streets (east-west), a system ignored in lieu of the tradition of counting blocks from known landmarks.

The two avenues that border the park, and one additional avenue on either side, make up the bulk of the commercial district. Avenida Central, on the west side of the park, hosts the greatest number of businesses and restaurants.

You're essentially safe in Estelí, but exercise care here as you would elsewhere. In the barrios east of the highway and west of the river be especially cautious.

SIGHTS
El Parque Central

Estelí's central park is a hub of mellow activity and a magnet for local characters. Buy an ice cream cone, kick back on a bench, and watch it all swirl by. The **Iglesia de San Francisco** was built in layers starting in 1823. It began as nothing more than a humble adobe chapel with a straw roof. Rebuilt in 1889 to a grander scale and given a roof of clay tiles with a baroque

© AMBER DOBRZENSKY

The streets of Estelí are easily walkable.

facade, the church was later redesigned as a modern building, with stately columns, a neoclassic facade, and twin bell towers topped with crosses.

La Galería de Héroes y Mártires

La Galería (tel. 505/8419-3519 or 505/2713-7763, 9 A.M.–4 P.M. Mon.–Fri., donations accepted), located half a block south of Iglesia de San Francisco, is only one of the projects of the Association of Mothers of Heroes and Martyrs of Estelí, a support group of 300 women who lost children during the battle against Somoza's National Guard. The museum offers Spanish classes for individuals or for families; call ahead if other times are needed for groups or speak to Guellermina "Mina" Meza. The gallery itself is a single room in what was once one of Somoza's jails, filled with memorabilia from the days of the revolution—photos of Estelí as an urban battleground, quotes from Sandino and Che Guevara, weaponry and shell casings, and portraits of young men and women killed

in action, sometimes accompanied by uniforms and other personal effects.

Connected to the Galería, you'll find the less powerful but still interesting **Museo de Historia y Arqueología,** with a small display of petroglyphs, artifacts, and revolutionary photos.

Still in the same building, on the south side, the **Casa de Cultura** offers a series of music, art, and dance classes to the public; the Casa often has a display of local artists in its spacious lobby. The entire block used to belong to a prominent Estelíano family before it was confiscated by the Sandinistas.

◖ Estelí Cigar Factories

In the past, Estelí cigar factories were often closed to the casual visitor unless you sought permission from distant owners. Today, many offer tours either to individuals or to those with a local specialized tour guide; the local INTUR office and the information desk at Casa Estelí can provide a comprehensive list of factories offering tours. A simpler option is to contact **Leo Flores** (tel. 505/8415-2428, leoafl@yahoo.es), a certified tour guide and expert in the cigar making process. Make sure to call Leo in advance to arrange the tours.

Empresa Nica Cigars (around the corner from the COTRAN Sur, tel. 505/2713-2230) also allows curious visitors to come inside and take pictures of their rollers. You'll smell the tobacco from blocks away. They are famous for the *padron,* a cigar manufactured using organic tobacco that has received international awards and acclaim.

Tabacalero Santiago (from the old Cine Nancy 1.5 blocks west, tel. 505/2713-2230) gained fame with endorsements from Arnold Schwarzenegger, Bruce Willis, and Charlie Sheen—and a contract to provide cigars to the Playboy mansion. The owner's family won its first cigar factory in a poker game in Cuba shortly after World War II. Now with a factory in Panamá as well as Estelí, Don Francisco provides Churchills, Figurados, Magnums, El Presidentes, and other brands to a global market.

Tabacalera Perdomo (Km 155 Pan-American Hwy., 300 meters west, tel. 505/2713-5486, www.perdomocigars.net) is an aficionados favorite, with brands such as Lot 23 and Patriarch. Nearby, **Joya De Nicaragua** (Km 149 on the Pan-American Hwy., tel. 505/2713-2758, www.joyadenicaragua.com.ni) produces popular local cigars such as My Uzi Weighs a Ton, Antano 1970, and Cabinetta Serie.

Tobacos de Estanzuela/TESA (two blocks west of El Buen Sabor, tel. 505/2714-1800 or U.S. tel. 205/265-6703, www.tesacigars.com) can offer a close-up view of a small family-run operation which also specializes in carpentry. Kick back, spend some time, and hear the stories from Alan Arguello Kuper, the owner and designer of the furniture.

For an all-inclusive package where you can stay as close as possible to the production facilities, you may try contacting **Drew Estate** before you travel (U.S. tel. 786/581-1810, www.drewestate.com). They have a small all-inclusive hotel with a pool and fine views, and provide Cigar Safari tour packages. Drew Estate is known for producing more eclectic types of cigars with names such as Acid, Ambrosia, Chateau Real, and Isla del Sol.

Others in the area which may or may not be available for tour with a local guide and advanced notice are **Oliva, Plasencia,** and **My Father Cigars** (tel. 505/2713-3494).

As with a fine cigar, if you choose to take a tour or venture out on your own, make sure not to rush. The process of producing a well-made cigar is as enjoyable as smoking one. Make sure to block out lots of time and head in with a "go with the flow" attitude. Most establishments have been making cigars for many generations and are very proud to share their stories for all truly interested.

ENTERTAINMENT AND EVENTS

Estelí's festival season is clearly December. Practically the whole month there is some sort of activity, including the famous *Hípica* (horse parade) and Purisima celebrating the Virgin Mary with free takeaways at every house.

Estelí has quite an eclectic nightlife considering it is far from any beaches or larger cities. It has a little something for everyone from dive bars, mixed local and foreign crowd scenes, salsa, and live music.

El Punto de Encuentro (40 meters west of the northwest corner of the central park) features a mellow hangout in the hidden patio/garden for enjoying cheap eats and drinks. In the same area you will also find the very popular **Rancho Bar El Semáforo,** which is perfect for large groups and especially lively on Saturday, when its two large dance floors attract a mixed crowd. Just before Semáforo is **El Chaiman,** also large with a thatched roof and a jungle motif, live music every once in a while, and definitely more of a local crowd.

For good local live music and great food, try

ESTELÍ AND THE SEGOVIAS

ESTELÍ AND THE SEGOVIAS

CITY OF ESTELÍ

To Jinotega

■ PULPERIA MIRAFLOR BUS STOP

↑ To Miraflor

■ TEXACO STARMART

↖ To Somoto, Ocotal, and Honduras

CA1

■ MONUMENTO DEL CENTANARIO

■ CASA ESTELI

SHELL

SOCCER STADIUM

5 NE

4 NE

3 NE

2 NE

1 NE

■ LIBRARY

UCA ★ MIRAFLOR

■ HOTEL PURO ESTELI

■ CAFÉ-NET

▼ CAFÉ LUZ

● HOTEL EL MESÓN

● HOSTEL LUNA

† CATHEDRAL

ARTESENIA LA ESQUINA ●▼

■ HOTEL LOS ARCOS ●▼

● CAFE BAR VUELA VUELA

Central Park

● PUNTO DE ENCUENTRO

■ LIBRERÍA RUBÉN DARÍO

■ ALCALDIA

■ INTUR

▼ CENTRO CULTURAL JUVENTUS

Rio Esteli

© AVALON TRAVEL

ESTELÍ AND THE SEGOVIAS

0 200 yds
0 200 m

To El Sauce

PAN-AMERICAN HIGHWAY

THE CAVE
PULLASO OLÉ
MOCHA NANA
CALLE TRANSVERSAL
PHONE OFFICE
ARTESENÍA NICARAGUENSE
DON PAN
LA CASA DE CULTURA
COMEDOR PINAREÑO
LA ESQUINA DE LOS BANCOS
BUFFET LAS DONAS
CAFE DON LUIS
GRAN VIA
CAFETÍN EL RECANTO
BANCENTRO
CASA VECHIA ITALIA
LECHE AGRIA
PALI
HOSPEDAJE FAMILIAR
PIZZA DOUGH
SUPER LAS SEGOVIAS
PETRONIC
POST OFFICE
AVENIDA PRINCIPAL
AVENIDA 1 SO
LA TAGE
Parque Infantil
REPOSTERIA GUTIÉRREZ
SPANISH SCHOOL HORIZONTE
SUPER EL HOGAR
SHELL ESQUIPULAS
COTRAN NORTE
COTRAN SUR
To Hospital and Managua
To Hospital
Market
To Baseball Stadium

1 SE
2 SE
3 SE
4 SE
5 SE
6 SE
7 SE
8 SE
9 SE
10 SE
11 SE

THE CHILDREN'S MURAL WORKSHOP

In 1987, in response to a request for help from community leaders in the struggling Barrio Batahola in Managua, three former art students began teaching mural workshops to children. The program was a success, and two years later, the three muralists passed their roles on to other youth in Managua and moved to Estelí to continue their program. The idea was to empower the people while at the same time reclaiming Nicaraguan culture and promoting the participation of children in society. They found that painting murals was an empowering achievement for the participants, and the creation of the murals was invariably tied to further community activities and social work (and lots of pretty pictures to look at).

Today, the mural project is known as the **Fundación de Apoyo al Arte Creador Infantíl** (FUNARTE), a nonprofit, nongovernmental organization run by a group of young adults who grew up through the original mural workshops. They offer weekly painting workshops to hundreds of Esteliáno children for free and give special workshops for impris-oned teenagers and children with disabilities. The murals depict their history, culture, and the daily reality in which they live.

There are well over 100 murals in Estelí, the majority of which were painted by participants of FUNARTE's workshops. The murals are best viewed and photographed in the late afternoon sun, as many of the best are on west-facing walls. The paintings are everywhere, but take special note of those on the Alcaldía (mayor's office), Casa de Cultura, and in and around the Parque Infantíl (nine blocks south of the main plaza). Also, be sure to get a good look at the long, horizontal mural on the wall of the army base along the Pan-American Highway, just south of the main bus station.

To visit FUNARTE's headquarters (tel. 505/2713-6100), walk four blocks south from the southwest corner of the plaza, then two west to reach the main workshop, itself covered in powerful paintings; continue another block west, turn right past the mural depicting the book *The Little Prince*, and make your next left to arrive at the offices and classroom.

Ixcoteli Bar and Restaurant, or Friday nights at **Mocha Nana Café**. To just sit back and catch up on conversation, go to **Habana Sports Bar**. Take a taxi to the south side of town and spend an evening just walking from one to the other.

For dancing, **The Cave Club** (adjacent to Whitehouse Pizza near the cathedral, tel. 505/2713-2116) has three levels, including a bar and a truly cavelike basement disco that really thumps. A newer, hipper place is **Cigarzone** (Barrio Justo Flores, from the Petronic station 75 meters south), Estelí's most stylish disco where a strict dress code is enforced. The arctic air-conditioning ensures that clubbers remain cool.

Karaoke is as popular as ever in Nicaragua and Estelí keeps pace. **La Confianza** (from Payless, 1.5 blocks north) is the place for beers, chatting, and interesting regulars. The atmosphere allows for conversation, but also boasts lots of space and karaoke. **Be Lounge** has karaoke during the week; weekends are usually crowded with the younger Esteliános. **Las Vegas** is often a late-night stop, open until 6 A.M. with a small dance floor that alternates from karaoke to disco music in a black-light room of Las Vegas kitsch.

SHOPPING

Provided you're not interested in fruits and vegetables (in which case you want the *mercado* on the south end of Estelí), the entire length of Avenida Principal is lined with boutiques.

Artesanías

Two shops—**Artesanía La Esquina** (one block north of the cathedral, tel. 505/2713-2229) and **Artesanía La Sorpresa** (one block south of the

SMOKIN' NICARAGUA

There is history in that cigar you're smoking—stories hidden among the tightly packed folds of tobacco and along the delicate veins of its wrapper leaf. As you light the *puro* in your hand and watch it turn into ash and smoke, take a sip of rum and ponder the unique legacy of the Estelí cigar industry.

It all began with the 1959 Cuban revolution, when capitalist Cuban cigar lords found their businesses liquidated into the new socialism. These artisans of the finest cigars in the world quickly gathered illicit caches of the precious tobacco seeds their families had been cultivating for centuries and fled to Miami. From there, it was only a couple of years before they discovered Nicaragua. One grower told *Cigar Aficionado* magazine that Cuba and Nicaragua "have the most fertile dirt in the world for tobacco. It's almost like God said, 'I'm going to pick these two countries and I'm going to use them for tobacco.'"

And so the core of the old Cuban cigar aristocracy moved to Estelí, and with their precious seeds from the homeland, began turning out world-renowned cigars once again. They endured another popular revolution in 1979, the ensuing civil war and land redistribution, and then survived the cigar boom and bust of the 1990s, followed by the waters of Hurricane Mitch that tore through their fields in 1998. But the business is sunk deep into the rich soil, and the handful of familial cigar dynasties that first came to Nicaragua 30 years ago are still here, and still rolling world-class cigars.

Most of the tobacco fields and giant wooden drying barns are found across the Estelí valley as it runs north away from the city, as well as in many upper reaches all the way to Jalapa. In Estelí there are about 10 serious cigar producers, a few of which will let travelers in their doors

for an informal tour and perhaps a taste test. Most businesses are *zona franca* (free-trade zone), however, which prohibits them from selling their product within Nicaragua. Don Orlando Padrón, head of Cubanica Cigars, keeps the doors to his Estelí factory shut for another reason: to protect the trade secrets that produce one of the most internationally acclaimed cigars in the world, El Padrón.

Some of the other heavy hitters are Latin Tobacco, Estelí Cigar, Tabacalera Perdomo (formerly Nick's Cigars), Plasencia, and Nicaraguan American Tobacco (NATSA). Don Francisco's Tabacalero Santiago is the newest company, one that grows and rolls organic tobacco. The factories are scattered across Estelí, and unless you've got pretty good Spanish, bring a translator. Although the main tourist office will tell you all the factories in Estelí offer tours, hospitality varies widely. Don Francisco's production manager can arrange a tour if arranged a day in advance, and Don Kiki, of Estelí Cigars, sometimes gives casual tours, maybe even a cup of Cuban coffee and a smoke.

Cigar making is a proud family tradition here and elsewhere in the world, and there's no denying the craftsmanship of a fine cigar. But as the blunt you're smoking burns lower, and the heat of the cherry seeps into the leaf between your fingers, consider the yang side. Organic tobacco is grown in Nicaragua, but barely; most production employs massive quantities of chemicals, which invariably find their way into the earth, the water, or the lungs, hands, and feet of the workers. Tobacco handlers often absorb the toxic elements of the leaf, and although at least several of Estelí's factories have impressive, airy environments for their workers, conditions for the rollers are often no better than the worst sweatshops. And the history burns on.

ESTELÍ AND THE SEGOVIAS

---

cathedral, tel. 505/2713-4456)—each have a huge selection of Nicaraguan arts and crafts from all over the country. In general, prices are cheaper in the Managua and Masaya markets, but for locally produced items, like soapstone carvings and Ducualí pottery, these are good places to shop. Artesanía La Sorpresa also has a small section with herbal medicines. **Café Luz,** the sister restaurant to Hostel Luna, the only *hostal* in Estelí, has a number of talented local artists selling their arts and crafts products. Casa Estelí near the Tip Top on the Pan-American

ESTELÍ AND THE SEGOVIAS

© AMBER DOBRZENSKY

Estelí is a great place to pick up handcrafted cowboy gear, including leather boots.

Highway is another interesting location for buying unique Nicaraguan souvenirs.

Books and Music

The tiny **Librería Leonel Rugama** (on Ave. Principal, across from the Kodak) is a bookshop run by the famous poet-martyr's parents. Rugama's dramatic death at the hands of Somoza's National Guard is legendary: Cornered in a building in Managua, the young soldier single-handedly held off a contingent of guardsmen while Carlos Fonseca escaped through the sewers. Ordered to his knees by the Guardia, he was commanded, *"¡Rindase, Sandinista!"* ("Surrender, Sandinista!"). Rugama retorted famously, *"¡Que se rinda tu madre!"* ("Let your mother surrender!") before he was shot. **Mocha Nana** has a small English-language bookstore, where no one has to surrender at all.

Guitarras y Requintas el Arte (from Camera de Commercio, two blocks west, tel. 505/2713-7555) sells handmade guitars,

mandolins, and *guitarrónes* (the bass guitar used by mariachis).

ℂ Custom Cowboy Boots

Estelí is the place to buy handmade leather goods like belts, saddles, and cowboy boots: Find them in stores all along the southern half of Avenida 1 SO. A pair of quality cowhide boots (or deerskin or snakeskin, the latter of which might get confiscated at your home customs office) go for $60–100 and take a week to make when custom fit to your foot. Order a pair on your way north and pick 'em up on the way back to Managua.

SPORTS AND RECREATION

If you want to study a traditional form of hatha yoga from a guru-trained Nicaraguan yogini, be at **Licuados Ananda**'s (one block south of the central park, next to the Casa de Cultura) 10 minutes before 6 A.M. or 6:40 P.M. (Mon.–Fri.) with a towel or mat. Classes have monthly and individual charges.

ACCOMMODATIONS

All of the Spanish schools have networks of families accustomed to housing foreigners for a weekly or monthly rate. Doña Edith at the **Hospedaje Familiar** offers extended room-and-board deals, starting at $150 a month. **Centro Cultural Juventus** (tel. 505/2713-3756) can offer housing for visiting students or those in language school. For house and apartment rentals, call **Bienes Raices Gomez** (tel. 505/2713-3835).

Under $25

(Hostel Luna (one block east and one block north of the cathedral, tel. 505/8441-8466, www.cafeluzyluna.com, dorm $8, private room $22) is run by British expat Jane Boyd. Jane is a valuable source of knowledge on activities in the area and can help arrange anything from a trip to Miraflor to a cigar factory tour, or a walking mural tour with a local guide. Breakfast is served at **Cafe Luz** across the street, where you can hang in the garden hammocks. Close by, **(Hotel Puro Estelí** (one block east of Luna's, tel. 505/2713-6404, $10–30) is the flash-packers choice, consisting of one dorm ($10 per person) and 10 spotless private rooms, all with private bath, hot water, cable TV, and Wi-Fi. There's also a full bar and restaurant and secure parking. Cigar tours and nearby excursions can be arranged and laundry service is provided ($3).

The eight rooms at **Hotel El Mesón** (one block north of the cathedral, tel. 505/2713-2655, www.hotelelmeson-esteli.com, $15–25) include private bath and fan (a few have a/c). The hotel is made up of a bar and restaurant, garden, car rental and travel agency, and can change travelers checks. **Hospedaje Familiar** (half a block north of Super Las Segovias, next to the Tip Top distributor, tel. 505/2713-3666, $10–13) is run by Edith Valenzuela Lopez, a tried-and-true Sandinista with more than 33 years of hosting *internacionalistas*. Rooms have private bath and TV.

$25-50

The gorgeous **Hotel Los Arcos/Café Vuela Vuela** (one block north of the cathedral, tel. 505/2713-3830 or 2712-6720 $45–75) is run by a Spanish development organization in a charming colonial edifice. All profits go toward development activities like schools, continuing education programs, and helping street children. If you're more interested in a relaxing evening than a night in town, **(Hotel Cualitlán** (from COTRAN Sur, two blocks south, four east, and one north, tel. 505/2713-2446, from $30) is a walled-in guesthouse compound unlike any other in Estelí. It has a verdant sitting area with a tree-canopy roof, soothing music, and a creative menu geared to the international traveler. Choose one of several delightfully appointed cabanas—something like Swiss chalets—set around the lush tropical courtyard, all with hot water and cable TV. They have two rooms that can house up to six for $20 per person, all with breakfast included.

FOOD

The Esteliano diet is hearty and satisfying. Local venues tend to mostly serve steaks, fried chicken, and bowls of soup big enough to drown in, though you'll find plenty of alternatives including vegetarian and health-conscious options. The nicest restaurants are found in the town's upscale hotels and on the blocks around the park.

Bakeries and Cafés

There is an excellent Spanish bakery, **Repostería España** (3.5 blocks north of the central park) and a German one, **Repostería Alemán** (behind the cathedral). **(Mocha Nana** (Casa de La Cultura 3.5 blocks east, tel. 505/2713-3164, mochanana@hotmail.com, 10 A.M.–8 P.M. Mon.–Sat.) is a perfect afternoon respite from the sun; in addition to fine cappuccinos, mochas, coffee, and espresso they have bagels, waffles, and a small English-language bookstore and trade library. Two blocks south of the central park on the Avenida Principal, you'll find **CaféDon Luis,** with good lattes and panini, and Wi-Fi access for customers.

Licuados Ananda (tel. 505/8844-1615, 8 A.M.–5 P.M. Mon.–Sat.) serves health food, yogurt, natural juices, and fruit smoothies in a green patio surrounding an empty swimming pool. Try the vegetarian *nacatamales,* veggie burgers, and sandwiches. They also offer educational opportunities on many facets of Eastern and natural medicine.

The menu is simple, healthy, and homegrown at ◖**La Casita** (across from La Barranca, south entrance, tel. 505/713-4917, casita@sdnnic.org.ni, 9 A.M.–6.30 P.M. Tues.–Sat.). Yogurt, home-baked breads, fresh cheese, vegetables, granola, juice, and coffee drinks are all served in a pleasant park along the shore of a babbling brook. La Casita is located on the Pan-American Highway, a few kilometers south of the city. Take an *urbano* bus to the hospital, then walk south around the bend in the road. Or hail a taxi for about $2—it's well worth the trip. In addition to wonderful food and mellow music, La Casita also sells local crafts and plants, including herbs, ornamentals, and much more.

Juventus Centro Cultural (two blocks west of the central park's southwest corner, tel. 505/2713-3756, 9 A.M.–6 P.M. Mon.–Sat.) is situated on top of the hill that drops down to the river. Enjoy great panoramas of the river and mountains to the west as you enjoy *licuados,* granola, open-face swiss and brie sandwiches, and hot drinks.

Fritanga and Comida Típica

For low cost and finger-lickin' goodness, the many *fritangas* and pizza trucks in the park and scattered around town are hard to beat. For excellent *empanadas,* step across the street from La Galería de Héroes y Mártires at night. Also easy on the wallet is **Don Pollo's** fried chicken, one block north and half a block east of the cathedral. **Cafe Luz,** one block east and one block

north of the church, serves a variety of international and *comida típica* fare that is particularly appealing to the *gallo pinto*–weary traveler.

Leche Agria (2.5 blocks south of *la esquina de los bancos*) serves excellent *quesillos* (cheese and tortilla snack), juices, and cheeses.

Pupusas are traditionally from El Salvador but have been adopted by the Nicaraguan culture. If you are in the mood for some great local food at an amazingly cheap price, try **Pupusas Nicaragua,** the little grill located near the Hospedaje Familiar; it's by far the best in the country. (There is no official sign, just look for the garage door painted with a Pepsi sign.) At $0.50 per *pupusa* it makes a great way to fill up on local flavor at hardly any expense.

Comedor Popular La Soya (Ave. Principal, 2.5 blocks south of the park, under $4), true to its name, serves soy-based meals and soymilk drinks. For an excellent local breakfast or quick lunch, try **Cafetín El Recanto** two blocks south of the park. For a quick and tasty lunch at the park, order a lunchtime plate ($2.50) at **Delicias Loco,** which includes a drink or hamburgers and tacos at night.

For a bit of a splurge, try ◖**El Pullazo Olé** (5–10 P.M. daily, $5–12) and join the fierce Nicaraguan competition for the best beef in the nation; they also serve fantastic sausages and desserts.

International

La Gran Vía (just south of *la esquina de los bancos,* open Mon.–Sat., $4) serves Chinese meals. The **Monkey House** (five blocks south and half a block west of Super El Hogar, open Wed.–Mon.) serves a variety of international dishes for brunch and dinner, but is most popular for its wings, which come in three secret-recipe flavors ($5–9).

For excellent Cuban cuisine try **El Rincón Pinareño** (tel. 505/2713-4309, tel. 505/2713-0248), located two blocks south of the cathedral. This family-run establishment serves authentic food in an impeccable atmosphere. For Italian-esque, try **Pizza Dough** (noon–9 P.M. daily), half a block west of the Super Las Segovias. A decent pie starts at $7 and the calzones aren't bad either. Pricier but not a great deal better is **Casa Vechia** (1.5 blocks west of the CaféDon Luis, $7–12), offering pastas and pizzas in a dark but cozy dining room.

INFORMATION AND SERVICES
Tourist Information
Casa Estelí (tel. 505/2713-4432 or 505/2713-2584, casaesteli@nortedenicaragua.com, www.nortedenicaragua.com) is a highly informative tourist office with maps, translators, Internet access, and an on-site café as well.

INTUR's Estelí office (on the second floor in Plaza Plator, half a block west of the central park, tel. 505/2713-6799, www.intur.gob.ni, 8 A.M.–1 P.M. Mon.–Fri.) is filled with brochures of all the northern regions and has helpful, trained staff to point you in the direction of reliable guides. The public **library** (four blocks north and one east of the central park, tel. 505/2713-7021, 8 A.M.–noon and 2–5 P.M. Mon.–Fri.) is in a huge building built with foreign donations.

Banks
There are three respectable banks at *la esquina de los bancos* (the corner of banks), one block west and one south of the park; Bancentro is 2.5 blocks south on Avenida Principal. All have ATMs, as does the Texaco station on the northern border of the city. The travel agency in Hotel Mesón changes travelers checks, as do most of the banks. The street money changers, a.k.a. *coyotes,* are safe to use and often give you a better exchange rate than the banks. You'll usually find bunches of *coyotes* at various corners of Estelí: near the old hospital, the Petronic gas station on the Avenida Principal, and the corner close to Quesillos y Leche. These will be the gentlemen usually sitting on the corner in mysterious dark sunglasses, holding or shaking loads of money. Don't let their appearance sway you; they will have certification to show they are legit.

Emergencies
El Hospital Regional de Estelí (tel. 505/2713-6300) is located just south of the city. For minor cuts and bruises, Avenida Principal's many private clinics are a better option. The **police station** (tel. 505/2713-2615) is located on the main highway, toward the northern exit.

Internet
There are several Internet cafés within two blocks of the park; most are open 8 A.M.–9 P.M. Monday–Saturday and 8 A.M.–6 P.M. Sunday. **Estelí@Net** (one block south of the park on Calle Transversal near Farmacia Estelí) is the most convenient and comfortable, and is air-conditioned. **Cyber Place** (one block north of the park from the traffic light) is also decent.

Mail and Phones
The **post office** (8 A.M.–4:30 P.M. Mon.–Fri.) closes for lunch noon–1:30 P.M. The **Farmacia Corea** (Petronic El Carmen, one block east, half a block south, tel. 505/2713-2085) offers mail and package service, as well as money transfers. **ENITEL** (tel. 505/2713-2222, 8 A.M.–8 P.M. Mon.–Fri., 8 A.M.–5 P.M. Sat.) is one block south of the church and half a block east.

GETTING THERE
Express and ordinary buses for Estelí leave from Managua's Mayoreo terminal. Seven *expresos* per day pass Estelí bound for Managua, making stops along the highway. If you're arriving from Honduras, buses leave daily from Somoto and Ocotal, the last one leaving at 5 P.M.

From Estelí, *ordinario* buses leave the COTRAN Norte at regular intervals (4 A.M.–5 P.M.) for Ocotal, Somoto, and points north; they leave COTRAN Sur for Managua, Matagalpa, León, and Yalí. Ocotal *expresos* stop off at the Shell Esquipulas approximately every hour on the half hour. From COTRAN Sur there are dozens of daily buses to both Managua and Mataglapa, leaving from the wee hours until 6 P.M.; three express buses to León depart before 7 A.M., plus a few daily microbuses to León (they leave when they fill up, and competition is fierce). Also departing from COTRAN Sur are two daily buses to La Garnacha and El Tisey, at 6:30 A.M. and 1:30 P.M.

GETTING AROUND
Estelí is a long city; you can cut short the walking by hopping a cab (about $0.30–0.70) anywhere in the city (except La Casita restaurant on the south side of town). *Urbano* buses ($0.25) are safe to ride and run a big loop around the city, including up and down the main avenues and nearby barrios.

Car Rental
Agencia de Viajes Tisey (in Hotel El Mesón, tel. 505/2713-3099, fax 505/2713-4029, barlan@ibw.com.ni) is a modern and professional agency that deals with airlines, international reservations, and Budget rental cars.

Casa Estelí (on the Pan-American Hwy., 20 meters south of the *monumento centenario*) has a Budget rental car office, with four-wheel drive trucks for about $60 per day. The **Dollar** car rental agency is located with the Toyota dealer on the highway; economy sedans run $35 a day and pickup trucks are $70 a day.

Near Estelí

◖ EL SALTO ESTANZUELA AND RESERVA EL-TISEY
Estelí's most famous swimming hole, this is a gorgeous, 15-meter, rainy season–only cascade you can swim behind, plunging into a cold, shady pool, all smothered in colorful native flora and fauna. It's just southwest of the city. You can hike to the waterfall from the highway. The road to Estanzuela leaves the Pan-American Highway just south of the hospital and is sandwiched between two *pulperías,* where you can stock up for the journey. This is the terminus of the *urbano* bus routes which start at the central park; or take a taxi from the city center for about $0.50. The five-kilometer walk should take 60–90 minutes each way. It's an easy hike, but with lots of ups and downs. Otherwise, hop a bus for the 20-minute ride (buses leave COTRAN Sur at 6:30 A.M. and 1:30 P.M.). Before you reach the hamlet of Estanzuela, look for a gated road on your right; the waterfall is at the bottom of a hill after the first two dilapidated wooden homes of the village. Villagers charge 30 *córdobas* ($1.50) to hike down to the falls. Head downward for

about 10 minutes until the track veers steeply down to the left. If you take one of the side trails to the left at this point it will lead you to the top of the falls. Before the road turns to the right again, take the path in front of you straight down to the falls; there is a large sign for the Ministerio del Ambiente. You should now be able to hear the falls.

Visiting Reserva El-Tisey
Down the same road to El Salto Estanzuela, the 9,344-hectare co-managed Reserva El-Tisey makes available a rustic ecolodge, fields of organic vegetables, a network of hiking trails, and trips on horseback, not to mention spectacular panoramas. From the top of Tisey on a clear day, you can make out the Pacific coastal plain and the entire chain of volcanic peaks from Cosigüina to Lake Managua and Momotombo, the Estelí valley, and north to the mountains of the Segovias on the horizon. The reserve is run by government body MARENA; contact their Estelí delegate (tel. 505/2713-2302) for more information.

Start by settling in at **Eco-Posada Tisey**

© AMBER DOBRZENSKY

Sunsets in Reserva El-Tisey are spectacular.

(tel. 505/2713-6213 or 505/8836-6021), which charges $7 per person for communal living, $15 for a double bed and some privacy, and $2–5 per meal. They will find you guides, rent horses, or show you around the organic farm that stocks most of Managua's super-markets with fresh veggies. There's more to see there than you'll likely have time for, so plan a few days at least. One trail climbs to a lookout (1,300 meters) where you'll enjoy the phenomenal view and the falls. The folks here can show you some of the reserve's other highlights, like the septuagenarian sculptor who picked up hammer and chisel to ab-sorb some of his nervous energy when he quit drinking, or the bat cave, local hangout for more than 10,000 winged friends (hint: bring a hat). Closer to the lodge, taste fresh cheese and vegetables, or spend a night in the farm-ing community of La Garnacha. To get there, catch a bus to El Jalacate.

La Garnacha is the heart of Reserva El-Tisey; the only way to get here is to hike or hire a truck from Eco-Posada Tisey. The biological station is the headquarters for the reserve where you can get maps, talk with the rangers, and arrange for guides. There are five-person cab-ins here with fantastic views of the surrounding forest and hills, but these were not opera-tional at the time of publication. Speak with community organizers Paulo Centeno (tel. 505/8658-1054) and Maria Elsa Gutierrez (tel. 505/8601-2151) to arrange a stay in the com-munity (rooms $15, cabins $15–20). Meals can be found at the **Pajaro Carpintero** *comedor* for under $5. There are many marked trails that leave from either the biological station or the guest quarters—one heads due west from the station and winds through rocky hillsides and pine forest to several highpoints with views of the volcanoes to the west. Winds stir the trees and the smell of pine needles is everywhere.

STONE MAN: A CHAT WITH ALBERTO GUTIERREZ

Self-taught sculptor Alberto Gutierrez, at nearly 70 years old, has done hundreds, if not thousands, of carvings and sculpting of the rocks on his family farm. He says he started his art based on a dream he had when he was nine years old on the night of his birthday. An angel visited him in his sleep and laid out the plan for all the sculptures he has created. Alberto says he didn't think much about the dream until many years later when he began having problems controlling his drinking. He visited a priest and asked for guidance on how to manage alcohol. The priest gave him the advice to find something to occupy his time. So, Alberto picked up a piece of metal and began carving. In a short while he had formed a perfectly proportioned elephant about three feet tall protruding out of the rock face. He kept going.

You can visit Alberto. He'll most likely offer you a tour. Being very spiritual, he has hundreds of interpretations of Jesus, and small versions of churches he has created. His inspiration also includes Nicaraguan poets, self-portraits, quetzal birds, and eagles. Although each one may seem the same to the uncommon visitor, Alberto will be sure to tell you each story and why that particular carving is unique.

Beyond his artistic abilities, Alberto lives in one of the areas with the best views of the mountains surrounding Estelí. As you walk, he will stop to point out the beauty and give you a sense that he himself is noticing it for the first time, although he has had over 9,000 visitors to his home since 2004 (you will be asked to sign his guest book so he can remember your visit).

Alberto Gutierrez also has hundreds of varieties of orchids, pineapples, bananas, and medicinal plants. He will rattle off the names of each one faster than Bubba in *Forrest Gump*. You will always leave with a gift of whatever he has in season: oranges, bananas, pineapples, or some other type of plant.

VISITING THE ROCK SCULPTURE GALLERY

Make sure to wear comfortable shoes, be in good enough shape for a decent hike, and carry a long-sleeved shirt, jacket, or something to keep warm and block the wind. It can get surprisingly chilly at the farm. About 1.5 kilometers down the road toward La Garnarcha from Eco-Posada Tisey, you will come across a sign that says "Ministerio del Ambiente Y Los Recursos Naturales Area Protegida Tisey-Estanzuela." Stop and admire the spectacular view for a moment, then pass through the gate just down the hill. Most likely it will feel like trespassing on private property, but it's okay. Follow the main trail and ask the local farmers along the way if necessary. Just keep walking down the hill.

After crossing a cow pasture and continuing on a well worn trail, you will see another state sign that says "Bienvenidos A Galeria Esculturas En Piedras." Cross over the wooden bar used as a gate and start calling out. Eventually someone will come, either at your voice or the sound of the barking dogs, which will have picked up on your presence way before anyone else. Alberto will never ask for any money for the visit, but the experience may move you to make a donation, which is welcome.

–Contributed by Rodney McDonald.

LA TRINIDAD

Just as the Pan-American Highway begins its curvy climb into higher altitudes, midsize La Trinidad, named for the three hills that surround it, is a festive village of bakers, bus drivers, musicians, and cowboys. Its unhurried and friendly populace can often be found hanging out in the well-tended central plaza—kept green even in the height of the dry season. The Catholic church, although decidedly ugly by Latin American standards, may be worth a visit during mass to hear the dueling mariachi choirs. La Trini's rip-roaring *fiestas patronales,* celebrating La Virgen de Candelaria and Jésus de Caridad, occur during the last week of January and roll raucously into the first week of February, with a famous *hípica* (horse parade) that attracts riders from all over Central America.

Take a walk up to the old **Spanish cross** or west up the river valley road to the **Rosario shrine**—allow about an hour each way. The hill to the east of the highway is the legendary Mocuana, with its caves of witches, gold, snakes, and a tunnel to Sébaco, if you believe everything you hear.

Hotel Tzolkin (tel. 505/2716-2124 or 505/8437-6067, winstonmairena@yahoo.com, $15–20), used to have the best restaurant in town, but it is now closed. Located just off the southwest corner of the park, the hotel's basic rooms have shared or private baths. Dine at **Don Juan's Las Sopas,** on the southern outskirts of town. This is a popular stopover for Pan-American commuters and truck drivers, with an open-air patio and a fantastic menu of soups—including *huevos de toro* (bull balls), ox tail, and chicken soup.

◖ MIRAFLOR NATURE RESERVE

More than a trip into Estelí's misty mountains, a visit to Miraflor is a trip back in time. Perhaps this is what Costa Rica's Monteverde was like 40 years ago before it was populated with four-star resorts and laced with splinter-free wooden walkways. Miraflor is unabashedly rustic, natural, and unpretentious. Declared a protected natural reserve in 1990, this rudimentary tourist infrastructure was developed by locals with their own sweat and labor and in the absence of any external help.

Miraflor as an entity is a little vague. There's no town, per se, or even a real center. Rather, the 5,000 Mirafloreños live dispersed throughout the 206 square kilometers of the reserve in a geographically dispersed but socially united community. The Miraflor Reserve is privately owned, cooperatively managed in many parts, and almost entirely self-funded by associations of small-scale producers. Most notable among these is the UCA Miraflor (or in full, the Union de Cooperativas Agropecuarias Héroes y Mártires de Miraflor)—not to be confused

with the University of Central America—an association of 14 small farmer cooperatives and 120 families living within the protected area. UCA Miraflor is primarily an agricultural credit and loan institution, but it has also tackled issues and begun programs, such as community health and education, organic agriculture and diversification of crops, cooperative coffee production, gender and youth groups, and conflict resolution. Tourism, Miraflor's greatest potential, was just an afterthought.

Visiting Miraflor

Start with a call or visit to the UCA Miraflor office in Estelí (from the cathedral three blocks east, half a block north, tel. 505/2713-2971, miraflor@ibw.com.ni, www.miraflor.org, 8 A.M.–12:30 P.M. and 2–5 P.M. Mon.–Fri.). They will present your options and help arrange lodging, tour guides, and horse rental—taking care to distribute guests fairly among the various families who have agreed to host guests. Expect to pay $15–25 per service requested.

At 1,400 meters above sea level, Miraflor is remote, cloud-covered, and sometimes downright chilly. Be prepared for inclement weather (buy a sweatshirt at one of Estelí's millions of used-clothing stores) and bring your own bottled water if you're concerned. A flashlight or candles will be helpful on that midnight walk to the latrine.

Sights

Miraflor has something for everyone—nature lovers, hikers, social-justice workers, organic farmers, artists, horse lovers, orchid fanatics, birders, and entomologists—each of whom will find their own personal heaven here. You can certainly visit parts of Miraflor in a day trip from Estelí, but read on and consider experiencing the unique accommodations.

Every attraction in Miraflor is privately owned, often by poor *campesinos.* Your financial support leads to the continued preservation of these magnificent forests, because, "Hey, this

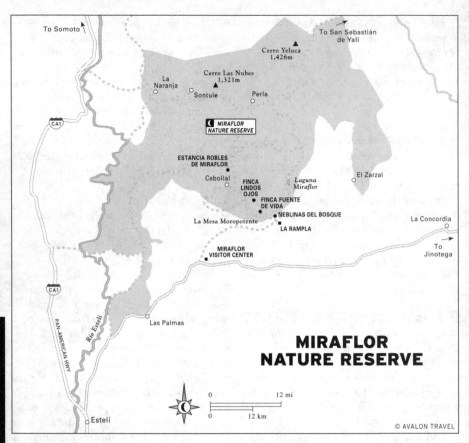

MIRAFLOR NATURE RESERVE

would be a great place to chop down the trees and plant some beans."

The community of La Fortuna has a small **museum** that they are trying hard to improve, which has indigenous relics from the area and articles from the war. It is a great place to get out of the weather in the rainy season.

If you enjoy inspired agriculture and alternative farming practices, the *campesinos* at Miraflor will gladly show you their cutting-edge lifestyle, including organic compost, natural pest management, watershed protection, live fences, crop diversification, soil management, reforestation, worm farming, and environmental education. In addition, Miraflor's small-scale, fair trade, organic coffee cooperatives and cupping lab (in Cebollál) are among the nation's finest.

FLORA AND FAUNA

The distinct bird species number 236, belonging to 46 different families which inhabit or fly through these mountains. That's nearly 40 percent of all bird species in the country, including four species of the elusive quetzal *(Pharomachrus mocinno),* toucans, the *ranchero (Procnias tricaruntulata),* with its three dangling chins, and the Nicaraguan national bird, the *guardabarranco.* Miraflor is also one of your best chances to spot coyotes, sloths, deer,

SWAMP THINGS: LEGENDS OF THE MIRAFLOR LAGOON

La Laguna de Miraflor is, compared to other *lagunas* (lakes) in the country, a mere puddle, whose marshy banks are crowded with vegetation and birdsong. Its fame lies not in its grandeur, but in its myth. There are at least five legends surrounding the lagoon, stories passed down over the years that have smothered the 10-hectare body of water in a shroud of mystery as thick as the white clouds sweeping over its surface.

The most famous of these legends is the **Ramo de Flores.** Every Thursday of Semana Santa (Holy Week), a cluster of beautiful flowers rises to the surface of the lagoon and circulates around and around. The flowers, say some, are bringing a message to the people that they should unite. The name Miraflor (flower view) comes from this legend, and variations tell of a tiny dancing prince in the middle of the flowers and dwarfs bearing the flowers to give to local girls.

Also well known is the story of the **Ciudad Perdida** (the Lost City). Only the oldest of Mirafloreños know of the hidden entrance, but everyone knows of the vast fields of exotic fruit-bearing trees in the city at the bottom of the lagoon (which, by the way, has been measured at 27 meters deep, plus three meters of sediment). One can eat all they want when in the city, but if they try bringing the fruit back to the surface world, they will not be allowed to pass.

Every now and then, the water of the lagoon turns jet black; evidence, say some, of the giant **black serpent** that lives in the water and occasionally stirs up the sediment on the bottom. The snake may or may not have something to do with the lagoon's vengeful nature, punishing anyone who speaks disrespectfully of it or disbelieves its power. One unfortunate young man did so while swimming in the middle—he had barely spoken his blasphemy when a whirlpool formed, sucked him under, and then spit him back up, whereupon he apologized profusely and pledged his eternal respect for the enchanted waters.

Just across the road, the **Laguna de Lodo,** or Lagoon of Mud, has its share of legends as well. The mud pond is half the size of its counterpart and lies above the subterranean river that feeds the main lagoon. One day, a local *leñador* (lumberjack) was working near the Laguna de Lodo and dropped his axe into the mud, which promptly swallowed it up. He cried and cried and cried, until his axe finally rose to the surface...with a head and blade of shining gold.

howler monkeys, or one of six different feline species, not to mention raccoons, skunks, armadillos, and exotic rodents.

Miraflor is one of the richest and most unexplored orchid-viewing regions anywhere. Among the more than 300 identified species is an enormous colony of *Cattleya skinniri* (the national flower of Costa Rica), not to mention scads of bromeliads and a museum of other orchids from throughout the reserve.

HIKING

Short hikes are possible through any of the hundreds of pockets of forest, but ask your guide to take you on one of the more adventurous trips. Although difficult to access, the 60-meter waterfall at **La Chorrera** is one of the wildest spots in the reserve. **The Caves of Apaguis** were dug in pre-Columbian times by gem seekers and have been occupied ever since by *duendes* (dwarves), as any local will inform you. The mature cloud forest of **Bosque Los Volcancitos** is Miraflor's highest point at 1,484 meters and is known habitat for howler monkeys and quetzals. If the monkeys don't snatch away your binoculars, expect fantastic views from El Tayacán, Cerro Yeluca, Cerro El Aguila, La Coyotera, and Ocote Calzado. Furthermore, the forests are replete with mysteries, such as the *casa antigua,* a 1,200-year-old foundation in the Tayacán area, surrounded by dozens of other unearthed *montículos*

© ESMIR CALDERON

The rugged landscape of Miraflor sharply contrasts that of nearby Estelí.

(mounds). Archaeologists haven't even begun to investigate the rest of them.

The lagoon in Miraflor is a great place to pass time, maybe stop for a great lunch. If you are lucky, you will get a chance to see monkeys in the area, but don't leave your food for long or it may become theirs.

Accommodations and Food

Most accommodations are well kept; some do not have electricity. To arrange lodging and other assistance, contact the UCA Miraflor office in Estelí (from the cathedral three blocks east, half a block north, tel. 505/2713-2971, miraflor@ibw.com.ni, www.miraflor.org, 8 A.M.–12:30 P.M. and 2–5 P.M. Mon.–Fri.). Overnight accommodations run $13–17 per person per night, with all meals included.

Of the variety of accommodation options, several stand out above the rest. For upscale ecolodging, visit [[Finca Neblinas del Bosque (www.visitamiraflor.com, $25 pp

including meals). Solar-powered bamboo cabins feature outdoor showers with hot water—much appreciated in this cloud forest. There are also economic dorm beds ($7) and the liveliest restaurant in the reserve, all set within a luscious patch of cloud forest with misty views. Ask about guided tours of the area and Spanish classes. **Finca Fuente de Vida** (tel. 505/8717-7315, www.fuentedevidamiraflor.com, $20 per person including meals) is a locally owned option, with basic concrete and wood rooms set in a wild garden.

Though the grounds are as woodsy and lush than elsewhere in these parts, the accommodations at **Finca Ojos Lindos** (tel. 505/2713-4041, www.finca-lindos-ojos.com, rooms $20 per person, cabins $35 per person, including meals) are sturdy but less inviting. The **Estancia Robles de Miraflor** (tel. 505/2713-9451, www.estanciaroblesmiraflor.com, $20–35 per person including meals) is ideal for larger groups, with five large private cabins as well as simpler rooms within a farmhouse. The Estancia is a working farm full of chickens, ducks, and a pond full of tilapia, and the grounds are home to more than 35 species of orchid.

Campesino homes is an option that features a network of families trained in the subtle art of entertaining picky travelers; their homes, while clean and well maintained, are usually quite rustic.

Getting There

Until the road from Estelí is finally paved, expect bumps, dust, and mud on the slow ride into the hills. There are four buses a day from Estelí: two leave for La Pita from Pulpería Miraflor by the Texaco Starmart at the north end of town (6 A.M. and 1 P.M.). The buses to Sontule and La Perla leave from COTRAN Norte at 2 P.M. and 3:40 P.M. The UCA Miraflor office may also be able to arrange transport.

Returning to Estelí, buses depart La Pita at 8:10 A.M. and 3 P.M., from Sontule at 8 A.M., and from La Perla at 7:30 A.M. The bus from Yalí passes by La Rampla at 7 A.M., 11 A.M., and 4 P.M. Hitching in this remote area of the Estelí countryside is very difficult, as there are not many rides.

CONDEGA

The 9,000 inhabitants of the Tierra de los Alfareros (Land of the Potters) eke out a living raising cattle, corn, and beans as did the Nahuatl centuries before. Truckloads of pre-Columbian pottery have been dug out of area cornfields, and the tradition lives on today with a women's pottery cooperative in Ducualí Grande. Before the revolution, only three *terretenientes* (landowners) owned all the land from Condega to Yalí. Condegans proudly supported the Sandinistas, which led to lots of harassment from Somoza's National Guard (Commandante Omar Cabezas once hid out for months with his troops in the mountains outside Condega, reportedly in a cave near El Naranjo). In 1979, the Sandinista government confiscated those properties and redistributed them to the locals.

Contra soldiers found easy pickings in the unprotected farms of the Canta Gallo Mountains east of Condega, where several major skirmishes took place during the 1980s. Most locals can tell you some of the horror stories. In 1998, Hurricane Mitch destroyed more than 200 homes and two of the three local industries (a cigar box factory and a tannery).

Sights

Toward the end of his grip on power, Somoza took to strafing the northern regions with his air force. When, on April 7, 1979, the Sandinistas downed one of his planes, it was considered a major victory and huge morale booster. Follow the dirt road behind the cemetery, then 100 meters to the top of the hill to the **downed airplane**—now a monument—complete with a simulated airport control tower viewing platform. In the course of a recent restoration, however, the original blue and red dot, symbol of the Somoza Air Force, was replaced by the stars and bars of the U.S. Air Force. Ignorance or revisionist history? You make the call.

The **Casa de Cultura** is a former command post of the National Guard. In its musical instrument workshop, you can order a custommade guitar, *guitarrón*, or violin. Among other attractions, the **Julio Cesár Salgado museum** (8 A.M.–4 P.M. Mon.–Fri., reading room open 1–5 P.M. Mon.–Fri., $0.50), named after the town's first archaeologist, has a collection of pre-Columbian ceramic work that local farmers have unearthed.

The **Taller de Cerámica Ducualí Grande** is an artisan's workshop founded in the 1980s with the help of a Spanish volunteer; the 13 workers continue to create charming ceramics using the simplest of wheels and firing the pieces in a woodstove. Pottery costs about $1–7. To get there, take a bus north about two kilometers and get off where a large concrete sign points west to the workshop. Follow that road one kilometer across the bridge and through the community of Ducualí Grande. Turn left when you see the small church, and look for the white sign on the right side.

Take in some baseball weekends at the ball field just north of town, or catch the **fiestas patronales** on May 15, traditionally the first day of the rainy season—a double cause to celebrate in this rain-starved region.

Accommodations and Food
Pensión Baldovinos (south side of the park, tel. 505/2715-2222, $10) has six simple double or triple rooms with shared bath and decent meals, set around a pretty courtyard with a shaded patio. Next door, **Hospedaje Framar** (tel. 505/2715-2393, $5) offers seven (mostly windowless) rooms with shared bath; doors close at 10 P.M.

Belgian-Nicaraguan **Rincón Criollo La Gualca** (tel. 505/2715-2431, $3–8) has cheap rooms rented by the hour as well as the night; you're better off eating here as the burgers ($3) aren't bad. **Hostal and Mirador La Granja** (half a block east of the park by the Catholic church, tel. 505/2715-2357, $10 pp) has clean rooms with private bathrooms and Wi-Fi access. Their balconies offer splendid views of the area.

◖ **Campestre La Granja Hospedaje** (from Instituto Marista on the Pan-American Highway, one km east, tel. 505/2715-2521, $7–35) is in a beautiful location with lots of greenery, a pool, and a restaurant that sees plenty of local business on the weekends.

To sample the best of local produce, head to ◖ **Lacteos Gualca** (on the Panamerican Highway, 7 A.M.–8.30 P.M. daily, $1–3), an open-air restaurant with a lactose-heavy menu of tropical-flavored yogurt, milkshakes, cacao, and *quesillos*.

Getting There
Any bus that travels between Ocotal, Somoto, or Jalapa and Managua or Estelí can drop you off on the highway in front of Condega, a two-block walk from the center of town. Or take the Yalí–La Rica buses from Estelí (5 A.M.–4:10 P.M.). Make sure to ask if the bus goes through Condega, as there are two routes to Yalí. Express buses will let you off on the highway by the cemetery; *ordinarios* will let you off in front of the park. From Condega, walk out to the Instituto on the highway to try to catch north- or south-bound *expresos*, or wait for slow buses at the park.

PALACAGÜINA AND COFFEE COOPERATIVE
The town of Palacagüina is best known as the pastoral setting for Carlos Mejía Godoy's revolutionary religious anthem, "Cristo de Palacagüina," in which Jesus is born *"en el cerro de la iguana, montaña dentro de la Segovia."* In the song, the Christ child's *campesino* parents, Jose and María, are dismayed when, instead of becoming a carpenter like his father, he wants to be a guerrilla fighter.

One of Nicaragua's largest fair trade coffee cooperatives, **PRODECOOP** is composed of 2,000 coffee-growing families; they export as many as 30,000 *quintales* (100-pound bags) a year. PRODECOOP can house and feed up to six guests in brand-new accommodations atop the cupping lab overlooking the drying beds, which bustle with activity during the harvest. There is also a swimming pool and a 360-degree view of the surrounding hills. For reservations, contact their office in Estelí (75 meters west of *la esquina de los bancos*, tel. 505/2713-3268 or 505/2722-1497 www.prodecoop.com). The coffee compound is between Palacagüina and the northern exit to the highway.

Most *ordinario* buses (not *expresos*) traveling between Estelí and Somoto or Ocotal pass through Palacagüina. If you take an *expreso*, the walk from the highway into town will be long and dusty, but there are usually taxis waiting for just a few *córdobas*.

PUEBLO NUEVO
First inhabited in 1652, Pueblo Nuevo is one of the few northern towns unaffected by the

Contra war. There are about 3,000 folks in town and another 19,000 living off the land in the surrounding countryside. Pueblo Nuevo honors San Rafael Arcángel during the week leading up to October 24.

Doña Selina will rent a room in her house, feed you, and can help you find a local guide to go hiking in the surrounding hills. One nice hike is to the community of Pencal, across the river and about 1.5 hours each way. You can also stay in the farmhouse/*hospedaje* Finca La Virgen. While in Pueblo Nuevo, take a look at the infrequently visited **Museo Arqueológico** (next to the phone office, tel. 505/2719-2512, 8 A.M.–noon and 2–5 P.M. Mon.–Fri.) in the Casa de Cultura. Exhibits include pottery, old farm implements, and archaeological pieces found in the area.

Twelve kilometers west of town on the road to Limay, you'll find **El Bosque,** an archaeological dig site where the bones of

San Juan de Limay is known for its soapstone carvings.

several mastodons, glyptodons (predecessors to modern armadillos), and early ancestors of the horse species have been uncovered. At 18,000–32,000 years old, the bones are considered one of the oldest archaeological sites in the Americas. Closer to the surface, remnants of Paleolithic weapons were discovered on an upper stratum of soil.

Buses leave Estelí twice a day at 11:45 A.M. and 3:10 P.M., leaving Pueblo Nuevo at 6:30 A.M. and 8:30 A.M.; ask in the park about transportation that continues farther west into the country.

◖ SAN JUAN DE LIMAY

Since 1972, Limay's claim to fame has been its *marmolina* (soapstone) sculptors, trained by a priest named Eduardo Mejía so they could improve their living conditions. Padre Mejía helped the new artists mine the soapstone from nearby Mount Tipiscayán (Ulúa-Matagalpa for "mountain of the toucan"), develop their talent, and market their beautifully polished long-necked birds, kissing swans, iguanas, and Rubenesque women. After the revolution, minister of culture Ernesto Cardenal, helped the sculptors organize a short-lived cooperative. A core of local carvers still lives and works in Limay, and you can watch them work and purchase some pieces with little effort. In town, just ask for the *artesanos de piedra*.

Nearby Río Los Quesos meanders outside the city limit. Ask a local kid to show you the Poza La Bruja swimming hole, ringed with pre-Columbian petroglyphs. Find a place to bed down for the night at **Pensión Guerrero** (a pink corner building located one block north of the Catholic church, $2.50 s). Limay is part of a sister-city program with Baltimore, Maryland.

San Juan de Limay is a 40-kilometer bus ride from Estelí that traverses a 1,000-meter mountain pass through coffee fields. Buses follow two routes to Limay (via La Shell and via El Pino) and leave Estelí's COTRAN Norte at 8:45 A.M., 9:15 A.M., 12:15 P.M., and 2 P.M.

Ocotal

Built on a thick bed of red sand and surrounded on all sides by mountains draped with green Ocote pines, Ocotal is the last major settlement before the Honduran border at Las Manos and the unbroken wilderness that stretches eastward to the Caribbean. Since 2000, it has seen a lot of development: Formerly sandy streets are now paved. There are two big supermarkets, San Judas and Palí, both located just north and west of the park. The feeling of Ocotal is one of progress. For most travelers, Ocotal may be nothing more than a place to sleep before hitting the border—but for many coffee growers and subsistence farmers, Ocotal is still "the big city" for supplies and business. And in many ways, Ocotal marvelously represents the kind of quiet, steady growth that goes unnoticed until you've been away for a while and then takes you by surprise. Steadily, Ocotal is reinventing itself as a great place to do business. Here you are indeed getting close to the frontier, and you only have to head a mile out of town in any direction before you are back to the rutted dirt roads, soporific cow towns, and sweeping valleys that make Nicaragua at once so charming and so challenging.

ORIENTATION

Buses will deposit you at the COTRAN bus station located within the "new market" to the south of the city, about one kilometer from the central park. Two main *entradas* (entrances) to the city, one from the south, and another from the highway to the west, lead straight into the town center. If you enter from the west, pause at the top of the monument to San Francisco to appreciate the layout of the city before continuing into town. Most of the commercial activity occurs between the park, the market, and around the Shell station on the highway. Ocotal is walkable but also has numerous taxis.

SIGHTS
Iglesia de Nuestra Señora de la Asunción

Start your introduction to Ocotal with this three-naved church in the center of town. Construction began in 1804, and the northern bell tower (the left one) wasn't completed until the 21st century! Two centuries of inhabitants have taken the liberty of scratching their names into its soft adobe walls, including U.S. Marines in the 1930s. The church looks out over Ocotal's **central plaza,** one of Nicaragua's most gorgeous. Shady and green, it fills up in the evenings with sparrows and gossiping *campesinos.*

Mirador la Fortaleza

South of town and across the river is a museum built to commemorate the battles of Sandino and his army against the "Yanquis." Completed in 2009, it is less inspiring than the view of Ocotal it commands, as it is perched on the top of a hill.

Half a block west of the park's southwest corner (across the street from Restaurante Llamaradas del Bosque), the **Casa de Cultura** boasts an impressive collection of photos of gringo military defeat and General Sandino's resistance. Yes, "boast" is the right word there. Ironically, the Marines lodged their troops in the Casa de Cultura as well as most buildings surrounding the park during their stay in Ocotal.

ENTERTAINMENT AND EVENTS

Centro Turistico El Krique (11 A.M.–7 P.M. Mon.–Tues. and Thurs.–Fri., 11 A.M.–10 P.M. Sat.–Sun.) is a bit out of the way—just after the bridge over the Río Coco walk one kilometer east on the dirt road. You will not be alone here; the two very well-maintained swimming pools, games, sporting equipment, trampoline, and soccer field are Ocotal's equivalent of the local country club. Eat here for about $8 after your swim.

Ocotal's two main discos compete for crowds

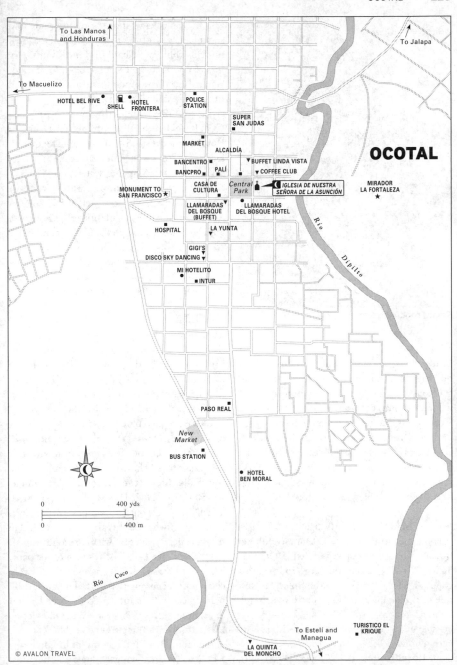

To Las Manos and Honduras

To Jalapa

To Macuelizo

HOTEL BEL RIVE
SHELL
HOTEL FRONTERA
POLICE STATION
SUPER SAN JUDAS
MARKET
ALCALDÍA
BANCENTRO
BANCPRO
PALÍ
BUFFET LINDA VISTA
COFFEE CLUB
CASA DE CULTURA
Central Park
IGLESIA DE NUESTRA SEÑORA DE LA ASUNCIÓN
MONUMENT TO SAN FRANCISCO
LLAMARADAS DEL BOSQUE (BUFFET)
LLAMARADAS DEL BOSQUE HOTEL
HOSPITAL
LA YUNTA
GIGI'S
DISCO SKY DANCING
MI HOTELITO
INTUR

OCOTAL

MIRADOR LA FORTALEZA

Río Dipilto

PASO REAL

New Market

BUS STATION

HOTEL BEN MORAL

0   400 yds
0   400 m

Río Coco

TURISTICO EL KRIQUE

To Estelí and Managua

LA QUINTA DEL MONCHO

© AVALON TRAVEL

© AMBER DOBRZENSKY

Saint Francis guards the northern city of Ocotal.

Friday–Sunday. **Disco Sky Dancing** (three blocks south and one block west of the central park) is popular with the younger crowd, while **La Quinta del Moncho** (on the road from Condega) is frequented by families during the day and a more mature crowd at night. Ocotal celebrates its *fiestas patronales* August 14–15, when you can expect to find Ocotaleños blowing their hard-earned cash on horse shows, live music, gaming tables, and the like.

ACCOMMODATIONS

The most central location is **Llamaradas del Bosque** (south side of the park, tel. 505/2732-3469, $20–40), where the large rooms are a good value for the money. **Hotel Bel Rive** (west side of the highway across from the Shell, tel. 505/732-2146 or 505/732-3249, $20–40) is a big step up in quality with doubles with private bath, phone, TV, fan, and parking.

Mi Hotelito (tel. 505/2732-3071, $7–20),

just a few blocks west of the main square and seven blocks east from the bus station, is a great no-frills (but very clean) option. Rooms vary in size and include TV, private bath, and hot water. Breakfast, lunch, or dinner are served upon request for just a few dollars.

Just about one kilometer from the COTRAN, on the first entrance to the city, is **Hotel Ben Moral** ($15–35), a favorite for quality and price. Rooms include private bath, phone, TV, air-conditioning, hot water, and Wi-Fi.

Ocotal's finest lodging is **Hotel Frontera** (just east of the Shell station, tel. 505/732-2668, $45), featuring rooms with private bath, phone, and TV, plus a slick poolside bar, conference room, parking, Internet access, a restaurant, and pleasant, airy porches overlooking the city and mountains. More expensive rooms are by the pool, while cheaper rooms are in the back.

FOOD

The menu in these parts is chicken, steak, and fish; avoid the fish this high in the mountains. **Llamaradas del Bosque** (on the south side of the park, 6:30 A.M.–8 P.M. Mon.–Sat., $2) is a favorite, serving three meals buffet-style; breakfasts are renowned for the city's best coffee.

La Yunta (two blocks north of the INTUR office, Tues.–Sun., $8–13) is a steakhouse, and one of the fanciest eateries in town, with live music most Thursdays and karaoke on the weekends. **Gigis** (a block south of La Yunta, tel. 505/2732-2967, 11 A.M.–10 P.M., Thurs.–Tues., $3–9) has burgers and pasta served by a Nicaraguan who spent years in New York. He makes a mean steak sandwich—recommended.

La Esquinita (five blocks south of the park, 7:30 A.M.–3 P.M. daily, $5) is immaculately clean with generous portions. The cheerfully painted **Coffe Club** (under $5), tucked behind the church, serves *fritanga* fare and sandwiches. **Restaurante Paso Real** (two blocks north of the Hotel Ben Moral, noon–midnight daily, $4–7) serves great wings, fajitas, and burritos, as well as cheap litres of beer, in a pretty ranchito with a verdant garden. Set to expand, the place really gets going on the weekends when it's karaoke on command.

For great food and an amazing view of Ocotal, head a few kilometers out of town toward Estelí to **Roca Dura** (tel. 505/8853-7696 or 505/8834-6949, 10 A.M.–11 P.M. Mon.–Thurs., 10 A.M.–12:30 A.M. Fri.–Sun., $6–12) for chicken, steak, burgers, and a truly impressive view. A taxi there will run you about $1, or $0.25 by bus in the daytime. This place is rapidly becoming the weekend party spot.

INFORMATION AND SERVICES

The Ocotal **INTUR** office (from the central park, four blocks south, one block west, tel. 505/2732-3429, 7:30 A.M.–4:30 P.M. Mon.–Fri., 8:30 A.M.–12:30 P.M. Sat.) is better than most regional branches. They train waiters and hoteliers, and organize cultural exchanges with other parts of Nicaragua. Bancentro and other banks are located one block west and one north of the park. The **post office** (8 A.M.–noon and 2–5 P.M. Mon.–Sat.) is one block south of the cathedral and one east. **ENITEL** (7 A.M.–5 P.M. Mon.–Sat.) is two blocks north of the park. Find a cybercafé across from the police station, or a half-block west of the northwest corner of the park; expect to pay about $0.50 per hour.

GETTING THERE

At least 11 express buses leave Managua's Mayoreo terminal for Ocotal, stopping along the highway in Estelí to pick up additional passengers. Sixteen buses ply the route between Somoto and Ocotal daily, 5:45 A.M.–6:30 P.M. If you miss the *expreso* buses, there are countless additional, painfully slow ordinary buses from Mayoreo.

Near Ocotal

ESTELÍ AND THE SEGOVIAS

MOZONTE

An easy 60-minute walk from Ocotal, Mozonte, of largely indigenous descent, is notable for its workshops of potters who produce ceramics from a particularly fine clay. You can spend the better part of a morning (start walking early to avoid the heat) in Mozonte admiring the craftsmanship of these potters. Both the **Centro de Artesanías** and the **Centro de Artesanía Ojos de Mujer** exhibit a variety of ceramic pieces for sale.

CIUDAD ANTIGUA

Ciudad Antigua was the second Spanish attempt to settle Nueva Segovia. (The remnants of the first settlement, built in 1543 at the bequest of then-governor Rodrigo de Contreras, are called Ciudad Vieja, and can still be seen near Quilalí at the junction of the Jícaro and Coco Rivers). The wooden church doors still bear the scorch marks of one attempted sacking of the city by pirates. You can pore over some well-loved religious pieces, a few historic documents, and other colonial structures that survived the onslaughts of the 19th century at the **Museo Religioso de Ciudad Antigua** (next to the Iglesia Señor de los Milagros, 8 A.M.–4 P.M. Mon.–Fri.). The only accommodation in town is at **Hospedaje La Esperanza** (tel. 505/8353-1457, $7), run by Nica Melvin Baldivia, who spent years living in the U.S. The simple but spotless rooms with shared bath are part of this newly built home. Baldivia will happily whip up some gringo-style food on request. Two daily buses head here from Ocotal at 7 A.M. and noon.

SAN FERNANDO AND PICO MOGOTÓN

San Fernando is a notably picturesque village of thick adobe-walled homes set around the town park and **Templo Parroquial.** Its 7,000 inhabitants live on more than 200 individual coffee farms and produce an estimated 25,000 *quintales* of coffee annually. More famous than its coffee, however, are its inhabitants, who since the colonial days have been a little lighter-skinned and a little more Spanish-looking. Many have blue or light brown eyes. How do they do it? Well, just don't ask about those last name combinations: Herrera-Herrera, Urbina-Urbina, and Ortez-Ortez, though many attribute the blue eyes to the town's occupation by the U.S. Marines 1927–1931. Life revolves around coffee in San Fernando, and many homes double as coffee-processing mills *(beneficios)*.

You can stage a hike to Pico Mogotón, Nicaragua's highest point (2,106 meters) from San Fernando, but even from there, Mogotón is 20 kilometers away. A better hike is to the **Salto San José,** where water rushing off the Dipilto mountain range cascades into a small pool. Take a bus to the community of Santa Clara and get off across from the ball field, turn left (north), and walk the 6–8 kilometers to the river. To be sure of the trail, hire a local kid for some food and a couple of *córdobas* to take you.

LAS MANOS BORDER CROSSING

The Honduran border is 24 kilometers north of Ocotal, and is open 24 hours. You will be charged $2 to leave Nicaragua and $7 to enter Honduras (or $4 exit, $9 entry after normal business hours or on weekends). There are several small eating booths, two places to change money, and not much else. Fill out the immigration form at the little grey building and walk 100 meters farther down the road to the immigration building to pay and get your exit stamp. Honduran buses to Danlí stop running after 4:30 P.M. To get to the border from Ocotal, buses leave 5 A.M.–4 P.M. ($0.50), or take a cab (around $4–6, depending on how hard you bargain). You should not need another visa for Honduras thanks to Nicaragua's participation in the CA-4 Border Control Agreement of 2006.

SAN NICOLAS TREE FARM

At Km 267 on the Pan-American Highway, you'll find a sea of pine at **Finca Forestal San Nicolas** (tel. 505/8856-5105 or 505/8858-2205), Nicaragua's first pine tree farm. A handy base for walkers and hikers, the farm offers meals (advance planning required), several basic wood cabins ($20–30), a dorm ($5), or a place to pitch a tent ($3). Friendly owners Pedro and Vilma are passionate about nature, know every sight in the area, and can arrange horse tours and guided hikes or point you in the right direction.

JALAPA

Tucked back in one of Nicaragua's farthest populated corners, Jalapa enjoys a cool, moist microclimate suitable for the production of tobacco and vegetables, which its drought-stricken neighbors could only hope for. Only four kilometers from the border, it is surrounded on three sides by Honduras and only surpassed in its remoteness by nearby border outpost Teotecacinte. That isolation made Jalapa prime stalking ground for Contra incursions from three nearby bases in Honduran territory—Pino-I, Ariel, and Yamales. The city of Jalapa was flooded with refugees from farming communities farther afield in response to Contra attacks like that of November 16, 1982, when a Contra unit kidnapped 60 *campesinos* at Río Arriba. Muddy and isolated, Jalapa is a peaceful and laid-back place these days, most concerned with good tobacco and coffee harvests. The whole town comes to life every year at the end of September for the **Festival de Maíz** (Corn Festival). Look for local *artesanía* of baskets made of coiled and lashed pine needles. **Grupo Pinar del Norte** has lots of fine examples of this unique craft.

There are a few hotels in town, but visitors will find the best accommodations at **Hotel Campestre El Pantano** (eight blocks west of the ProCredit bank, tel. 505/2737-2031, www.

hotelelpantano.com, $17.50–32.50), a *quinta* with a fresh climate and wonderful view. Pitch a tent in the garden ($3.50), but be prepared for chilly mornings! Or stay in comfortable private rooms equipped with Wi-Fi, which the on-site restaurant also shares.

TEOTECACINTE BORDER CROSSING

About half an hour north of Jalapa is the small border crossing at Teotecacinte (open 24 hours), which leads north to Trojes, Honduras. Travelers will be charged $2 to leave Nicaragua and $7 to enter (or $4 to exit, $9 entry after normal business hours or on weekends).

QUILALÍ

Starting in the 1930s when Sandino dug into the area of El Chipote and held off the U.S. Marines, Quilalí has been bloodied by decades of battle. But the town remains steadfastly anti-Sandinista to this day and is home to both El Chacál (José Angel Talavera) and El Chacalín (Alex Talavera), the leaders of the Resistance Party (made up of ex-Contras). Upon entering town, you'll notice Quilalí is surprisingly well developed, courtesy of international aid money destined to support the Sandinista government's opponents. Look for U.S. Army tin cups, knives, and mosquito nets in town, relics from the intense military training given to local Contras in the 1980s. The area is also well known for its marijuana production. A recommended read if you travel this area is *White Man's Burden* by William Easterly, who uses the town of Quilalí as a case study for the effectiveness of development assistance.

The road to Colina La Gloría offers beautiful views of surrounding mountains and passes at least two swimming holes, one each in the Río Jícaro and Río Coco. **Hospedaje Tere** (on the main street, $5) is the cleanest place in town. Several informal family establishments, including **Comedor Jackson and Sholla** ($4) serve typical food. Quilalí has a very good hospital supported by Médicos sin Fronteras (Doctors Without Borders), and standard services like ENITEL and Correos.

Four buses a day leave Ocotal via Santa Clara. The first bus is at 5 A.M. From Estelí, five buses depart (5:45 A.M.–1:40 P.M.) for a five-hour bone-cruncher through San Juan del Río Coco and onward to Wiwilí.

Somoto

Located on the south side of the Pan-American Highway as it veers westward toward the Honduran border at El Espino, Somoto is an average-size city of 15,000 and capital of the department of Madriz. Tucked into the Cordillera de Somoto at 700 meters above sea level (the highest point of this range is Cerro Tépec-Xomotl at 1,730 meters), Somoto enjoys a fresh climate most of the year. Originally named Tépec-Xomotl, or Valley of the Turkeys, Somoto is known today more for its donkeys, *rosquillas* (baked corn cookies), and blowout carnival each November. A tributary of the Río Coco traverses the city.

U.S. Marines built an airstrip here, three blocks south of the park (now lost forever under a modern development), to try out a military technique they'd just invented: the air strike. They used the base in Somoto to bomb Ocotal in the 1930s in a failed attempt to root out General Sandino. These days, the Ciudad de Burros has not much more to offer than a quiet evening in its quaint and friendly park and a pleasant village ambience.

ROSQUILLAS SOMOTEÑAS

© AMBER DOBRZENSKY

Although *rosquillas* are baked in adobe wood-burning ovens all over Nicaragua, Somoto is particularly renowned throughout the country for the quality of this baked treat. The *rosquilla* is a crunchy ring of salted corn dough baked with cheese. When they're not baked the traditional way, you'll find them as flat, molasses-topped *ojaldras* or thick nugget-pockets called *pupusas*. Serve them up with a cup of steaming hot black coffee, still fragrant with smoke from the wood fire, and enjoy: The two tastes naturally complement each other. The two main producers in town are **La Rosquilla Somoteña Betty Espinoza** and **Rosquilla Garcia,** both two blocks west of the COTRAN on either side of the street. *Somoteñas* are the most famous regional variety of *rosquillas*—if you're traveling anywhere else in the country, they make a cheap, simple gift, greatly appreciated by any Nicaraguan.

SIGHTS

La Parroquia Santiago de Somoto is one of Nicaragua's oldest churches. Construction began in 1661, some 86 years before León's great cathedral. If you're around Somoto on the eighth of any month, consider joining the religious masses on their pilgrimage to the tiny community of **Cacaulí,** all hoping for a glimpse of the Virgin Mary. Ever since she appeared to a young farmer named Francisco in the late 1980s, thousands of people have arrived to try to repeat the miracle. They each carry a clear bottle of holy water, which they hold up to the sun at exactly 4 P.M.; the Virgin should appear in the water. Whenever the eighth falls on a Sunday, the believers turn out in larger numbers.

Somoto's *fiestas patronales* fall on July 15–25, but the town is more famous for the **carnival of November 11** (or the second Saturday of the month), when it celebrates the creation of the department of Madriz in 1936. All of Nicaragua's best party bands make the trip north, each setting up on one of seven stages—plus mariachis, dance parties, and the standard bull- and cockfighting.

Pass through the **Mercado Municipal 19 de Julio** to rub shoulders with the locals, mostly farmers. Or check out the two scenic view overlooks: The first is just west of the city and offers a quick, easy walk and a rewarding view. The second, **Mirador de Canopy Castillo** (tel. 505/8648-1452), has a small café and a four-cable canopy tour that looks steeper than it should be—be cautious.

◖ Grand Canyon of Somoto

"Discovered" only in 2006, Somoto's best swimming hole permits you to float through limpid, cool pools penned between the lush vegetation of the canyon walls, home to cliff bats and rare birds. The deep pools are separated by shallow sections and so preclude boating. Rather, spend all day splashing and jumping from pool to pool. Bring some *rosquillas* for snacking and plastic bags to keep things dry.

This is possible as a day trip from Estelí, though it's nearly three hours each way to get there and the last express bus back to Estelí leaves at 3:30 P.M. Catch a bus to Somoto, then another to El Espino (every 45 minutes or so), getting off at *entrada para Cañon de Somoto* (25 minutes from Somoto). About 200 meters down the path is a gate and cabin, with guides who can offer you anything from a 5–6-hour guided hike ($20) to a rented inner tube for floating the canyon ($6). Local tour coordinator **Henry Soriano** (entrance to Somoto Canyon, tel. 505/8610-7642, henrysoriano@gmail.com) will fix you up with a guide or assist with any queries you might have. For rappelling and bouldering, as well as visits

to nearby communities, contact Gonzalo at **Namancambre Tours** (tel. 505/2722-0826 or 505/8821-8931, www.namancambretours.com).

ACCOMMODATIONS AND FOOD

The best inexpensive lodging in Somoto can be found at family-run **Hostal Oriental** (one block east and half a block west of the ENITEL, tel. 505/2722-2445, $9–20), which offers plain but tidy rooms with private bathroom. The **Hotel Panamericano** (on the north side of the park, tel. 505/722-2355, $10–15) has hot water and additional amenities in a variety of rooms; there are a few interesting animals in captivity here. **Reinel Mendoza Gradiz** (tel. 505/2722-2340 or 505/8817-1096, reymen2008@hotmail.com) gives tours, including of the canyon.

The ◖**Hotel Colonial** (half a block south of the church, tel. 505/722-2040, www.hotelcolonialsomoto.com, $20–40) has a restaurant and large patio, rooms with private bath, cable TV, and parking, with breakfast included. **Hotel El Portal del Angel** (one block west, one south of the police station, tel. 505/2722-0244, portalhotel@yahoo.com, www.hotelportaldelangel.com, $40–100) has sumptuous rooms, a restaurant, and an upstairs bar with a nice view of the mountains. The attached **Bukanas Disco** is the hippest nightspot in Somoto, so you may want to think twice about staying here on the weekend.

Comedor Soya (on the plaza) serves soy with a smile; all kinds of surprising and cheap meals are available. For juice drinks, snacks, and fries, check out **Café Santiaguito** (1.5 blocks south of the church). The market is full of other delicious treats, all of them fried.

Comedor Bamby (2.5 blocks west from the Enitel office, 8 A.M.–8 P.M. Mon.–Sat.) works for lunch on just a few dollars; a lunch buffet is served 11 A.M.–2 P.M., or until they run out of food.

The Almendro (across from the Colonial, 10 A.M.–9 P.M. daily, $5) was mentioned in a

Mejía Godoy song *("el almendro de donde la Tere")* and has decent meals.

If you're brave enough to venture past the obscure, cantina-style entrance, **Don Chu**'s ($7) bar and restaurant serves hearty plates of Nica food in a large hall.

INFORMATION AND SERVICES

There is a bank across the street from the Alcaldía. The post office is across from the Hotel Colonial, and ENITEL (open until 5 P.M.) is behind the church. A modern health clinic, Profamilia, is two blocks south of COTRAN and is open 24 hours a day.

GETTING THERE AND AROUND

Buses to Somoto from Estelí run every hour 5:30 A.M.–5:20 P.M. There are also regular express buses from Mayoreo in Managua.

EL ESPINO BORDER CROSSING

The least-used border crossing in Nicaragua, El Espino is open 24 hours. To get there from Somoto, take one of the regular buses ($0.50) that head toward El Espino, or chip in for a cab (about $5). It's a 15-minute ride from Somoto. At the crossing, you first receive and fill out an immigration form at the booth next to the steel railroad crossing–style gate, then proceed 100 meters up to the little building on the right, where you'll pay $2 to exit ($4 after hours) or $12 to enter. Continuing bus service into Honduras is just over the hill and runs until 4:30 P.M. You should not need another visa for Honduras thanks to Nicaragua's participation in the CA-4 Border Control Agreement of 2006.

THE MATAGALPA AND JINOTEGA HIGHLANDS

As you turn eastward from the Pan-American Highway and begin the gradual climb upwards, the character of the Matagalpan and Jinotegan highlands will attract your attention immediately. This rugged, determined region of blue-green hillsides, sometimes thickly forested mountains, and small farming villages of adobe homes and clay-tile roofs is unlike anywhere else in the country. As highlands go, Nicaragua's center is not that high, rising to barely 2,000 feet above sea level, but after visiting the torrid plains around Granada and Managua, the relatively cool air and the smell of pines will be a welcome surprise. The temperatures favor vegetable production, though many quiet valleys are still thick with corn and red beans. They also favor the production of coffee, and east of Matagalpa, the rumpled landscape of hardwoods and coffee plants dominates. Coffee's preference for shade has encouraged the preservation of much of this region's forests, and the mornings resonate with birdcall and the bellow of the howler monkeys.

Matagalpa is the more elegant and historical of the region's two big cities, with a large cathedral and several big, shady parks. A city draped over the curves of more than one hill, your legs will quickly notice the changes in altitude as you explore. Jinotega is farther north into the mountains, higher, and smaller. Emphasizing its sense of isolation are the green walls of the valley that cradles it; even the cathedral in the

HIGHLIGHTS

HONDURAS

Hotel de Montaña Selva Negra

La Sombra Ecolodge **(**

Jinotega ○

Matagalpa

Finca Esperanza Verde

Parque Darío

La Catedral de San Pedro de Matagalpa

Grupo Venancia

Lago Xolotlán

○ Boaco

0   20 mi

0   20 km

© AVALON TRAVEL

LOOK FOR (TO FIND RECOMMENDED SIGHTS, ACTIVITIES, DINING, AND LODGING.

(Parque Darío: End your self-guided walking tour of Matagalpa City here, in this shady plaza where you can watch the world go by and listen to the deafening calls of the birds in the treetops (page 239).

(La Catedral de San Pedro de Matagalpa: One of the north's finest structures, this gorgeous cathedral can be spotted from anywhere in town (page 239).

(Grupo Venancia: Rub shoulders with Matagalpa's enlightened citizens and visitors while you enjoy stimulating theater and great music (page 243).

(Finca Esperanza Verde: Call ahead to reserve space at this award-winning ecotourism effort in the hills above San Ramón, with hiking trails through area coffee farms and deep, fertile valleys (page 252).

(La Sombra Ecolodge: Hardwood forest and coffee intermingle at a lovely forest lodge perfectly situated for forest excursions to the remarkable Peñas Blancas (page 253).

(Hotel de Montaña Selva Negra: A hotel quite unlike any other, Selva Negra has enough farm tours, mountain hikes, good food, and quiet, peaceful relaxation to rest any weary soul (page 255).

town's center is dwarfed by the immensity of nature in its lush plaza. Jinotega remains somewhat of a cowboy town, the uncouth little brother of more cultured Matagalpa. Jinotega feels like the end of the road, the gateway to the hundreds of remote kilometers that separate the Atlantic coast from the rest of Nicaragua.

Both Jinotega and Matagalpa suffered mightily during the revolution and ensuing Contra war. But today's *norteños* work their farms without the fear of war, bending their backs instead in the struggle against rural poverty, drought, and the whims of the world coffee market.

In general, residents of Matagalpa and Jinotega are accustomed to adversity and live bright, intense lives. Spending time among them will give you a perspective you won't find in the more frequently visited corners of Nicaragua.

HISTORY

Periods of tremendous violence and warfare have racked the mountainous north for over a century. In the early 1930s, Augusto César Sandino fought U.S. Marines and the National Guard here; 40 years later, young revolutionary Sandinistas faced Somoza's National Guard in several bloody battles, particularly in the region of San José de Bocay, Matiguás,

MATAGALPA

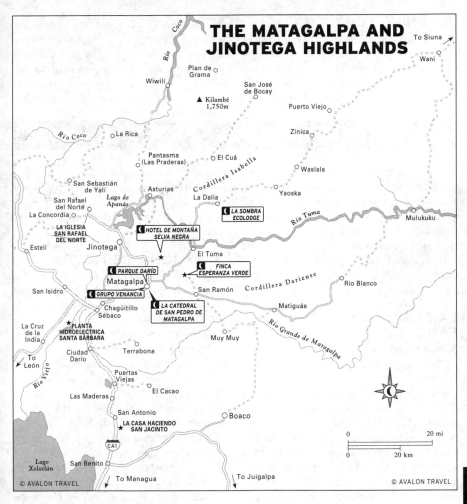

THE MATAGALPA AND JINOTEGA HIGHLANDS

To Siuna
Wani
Río Coco
Plan de Grama
Wiwilí
San José de Bocay
▲ Kilambé 1,750m
Puerto Viejo
Zinica
Río Coco
La Rica
Pantasma (Las Praderas)
El Cuá
Cordillera Isabella
Waslala
San Sebastián de Yalí
Asturias
La Dalia
Yaoska
San Rafael del Norte
Lago de Apanás
LA SOMBRA ECOLODGE
Río Tuma
Mulukuku
La Concordia
LA IGLESIA SAN RAFAEL DEL NORTE
HOTEL DE MONTAÑA SELVA NEGRA
Estelí
Jinotega
El Tuma
PARQUE DARÍO
FINCA ESPERANZA VERDE
Matagalpa
Cordillera Dariense
Río Blanco
San Isidro
GRUPO VENANCIA
San Ramón
Chagüitillo
Sébaco
LA CATEDRAL DE SAN PEDRO DE MATAGALPA
Matiguás
La Cruz de la India
PLANTA HIDROELECTRICA SANTA BÁRBARA
Río Grande de Matagalpa
To León
Río Viejo
Ciudad Darío
Terrabona
Muy Muy
Puertas Viejas
Las Maderas
El Cacao
San Antonio
Boaco
LA CASA HACIENDO SAN JACINTO
CA1
0   20 mi
0   20 km
Lago Xolotlán
San Benito
To Managua
To Juigalpa
© AVALON TRAVEL
© AVALON TRAVEL

MATAGALPA

and Bilampi. Far more devastating than either of those conflicts, however, were the 1980s, when Matagalpa and Jinotega (along with the RAAN, or North Atlantic Autonomous Region) experienced the worst of the war between the Sandinista military and Contras. Travelers along the region's few roads were frequently ambushed and soldiers from both sides raided villages as a matter of course. Farmers learned to tend their crops with rifles slung over their shoulders.

Peace swept the region at the start of the 1990s and the past decade has transformed Matagalpa and Jinotega into an agricultural powerhouse. Gone are the thousands of cold, wet, and hungry guerrilla soldiers that muddily marched through these hills. Some of the same rugged trails are now popular with campesinos and foreign travelers intent on visiting coffee cooperatives, climbing mountains, and swimming in waterfalls.

PLANNING YOUR TIME

Two or three nights is sufficient for seeing Matagalpa and Jinotega, but allow an extra day or two if you plan to explore any of the surrounding countryside. Those looking for a peaceful mountain retreat often spend 2–3 nights at either Hotel de Montaña Selva Negra, La Sombra Ecolodge, Finca Esperanza Verde, or with a homestay program run by a coffee cooperative. Combining such a trip with a night or two in the city can easily consume five or six days—more if you visit the more remote communities.

The Road to Matagalpa

The highway from Managua climbs from the verdant plains of sugarcane and rice up through a series of plateaus with long horizons and broad panoramas before reaching the long mountain valleys that characterize the north. Most travelers take an express bus straight through most of the landscape and beeline for the mountains, but Matagalpa's dry lowlands hide a few interesting places if you have your own vehicle.

LA CASA-HACIENDA SAN JACINTO

A must-see on the high school curriculum of all Nicaraguan history students, the Casa-Hacienda San Jacinto, located about 35 kilometers north of Managua along the Pan-American Highway, merits its own roadside statue. The monument guards the turnoff to the battlefield of San Jacinto and depicts a defiant Andrés Castro standing atop a pile of rocks. This is the site where, in 1856, the Liberals—supported by William Walker and his band of filibusters—and Conservatives battled fiercely. Conservative Andrés Castro, out of ammunition, picked up a rock and hurled it at the enemy, killing a Yankee with a blow to the head and becoming a symbol of the Nicaraguan fighting spirit that refuses to bow to foreign authorities.

Three kilometers east of the highway (a flat, 30-minute walk), the museum at the restored San Jacinto ranch house is run-down and little visited except by occasional hordes of high school students. For $1 admission, you can explore the period relics and admire the displays.

If no one's manning the ticket window, just shout until the caretaker rides her bike down from the main building. Bring water: There are no facilities at the site itself, and just one mediocre restaurant at the highway turnoff.

LA LAGUNA DE MOYOÁ AND LAS PLAYITAS

After conquering the first big ascent on the highway from Managua (known as Cuesta del Coyól), you'll be greeted by the Laguna Moyoá (Nahuatl for "place of the small mosquitoes") on the west side of the highway and the swampy Laguna Tecomapa to the east (unless it is a dry year, when both disappear). Geologists believe they are the remnants of the ancient Lake of Sébaco, a giant reservoir that formed the heavy clay soils of today's Sébaco Valley. A tectonic shift ages ago sent the Río Grande de Matagalpa flowing eastward toward the Atlantic instead of into Lake Xolotlán through Moyoá, and the lake gradually disappeared. It experienced a brief revival during Hurricane Mitch, when Lake Moyoá rose to the edge of the highway and Tecomapa became a legitimate lake through which wading cattle grazed.

Moyoá was once home to the Chontaleña people, and it is possible that they had a fixed settlement on the island in the lake. Some clay pottery has been uncovered from the A.D. 500–1500 period, which would indicate they at least frequented the site, probably to fish and hunt.

The locals do a good business catching fish out of Moyoá—mostly *mojarra* and *guapote*—both very good for eating, and both of which you'll see held up on strings along the side of the road. To visit the lake, stop in at Comedor Treminio and ask for Anita Vega or Humberto Treminio, the owners of the land that borders the lake. You can eat your meals at their establishment, and strike a deal with them for the right to camp out on their land. Try the shady grove down at the end of the road that leads to the lake. Birds you might see at Moyoá include *playeritos, piches, zambullidores,* and several types of heron.

CIUDAD DARÍO

Named after the prized poet of Castilian literature, Ciudad Darío was known by the indigenous name of Metapa until 1867 when Rubén Darío was born. Today, a battered but handsome brass statue of the author stands at the southern approach to the city.

Darío's primary attraction is the unassuming **Casa Natal Rubén Darío** (along the main street in front of the ENITEL building, 8 A.M.–12:30 P.M. and 2–5 P.M. Mon.–Fri.). Darío was born here and then moved to the city of León shortly afterward to live with relatives. The eastern part of the house has been converted into a small amphitheater for the presentation of cultural shows.

For a plate of *gallo pinto,* hit the **Comedor Clementina** (from the mayor's office, two blocks north and half a block west) for a hearty beef soup or her famous chicken and *ayote* (a type of squash). There are plenty of fresh fruit juices to sip while you wait for your meal and try to talk with her pet parrot, who speaks Italian (so she claims!). A half a block east from Clementina's is a big *fritanga* ($1–2 a plate) that opens up around 6 P.M.

Restaurante El Coctél (from the Pulpería Masaya, go west one block and north a half block) likes to serve crowds coming out of the

Matagalpa is nestled in the highlands.

museum, and specializes in *carne a la plancha;* a bit pricier than the other options in town—you can pay more than $7.50 for some things—but it's one of the few restaurants with a real ceiling overhead. The favorite restaurant among the NGO and businessperson crowd is **Doña Conchi's** (a block north of the Shell station toward the north end of town, tel. 505/2252-7376), a relatively upscale place with a full menu ranging $3–10 per dish.

Express buses between Managua and points north save an hour off the trip by not entering Ciudad Darío. So, if you're headed there by bus (from Managua's Mayoreo terminal), make sure to take an *ordinario*. Any local bus leaving Matagalpa or Estelí headed to Managua will go by way of Darío.

Near Ciudad Darío

Anyone between the ages of 7 and 15 will know exactly how to help you find the following historical and geological destinations in the Darío neighborhood of Santa Clara, located about one kilometer east from the town's park (not far from the Carlos Santí baseball stadium).

To get to the **petroglyphs,** start at Darío's mayor's office in the park and head east toward the stadium at the top of a hill (0.5 km). On the other side of the stadium is a school for deaf children. Beyond that, the paved road will turn to dirt as you enter Barrio España. There is a *pulpería* on the corner where you can get directions to the petroglyphs, less than a 30-minute walk.

La Posa de Las Yeguas (The Mare's Pool) is a deep spot in the creek where, supposedly, women who weren't faithful to their husbands were turned into mares and went to live. Several rocks there bear petroglyphs and more modern graffiti. It is said the friars of old would go to meditate at **La Cueva del Fraile** (The Friar's Cave), not far from La Posa de Las Yeguas.

SÉBACO

The name Sébaco comes from the Nahuatl name Cihuacoatl (the "snake-woman"). In

THE LEGEND OF CIHUACOATL

At the edge of the Río Viejo, there was once a powerful community ruled by a mighty cacique. His wife was considered the most beautiful woman in the country, but she made regular suspicious trips down to the river with great quantities of carefully prepared foods: beverages of seeds and berries, and birds prepared with spices and grains. One day, one of the cacique's men decided to follow the woman down to the river to see what she did. There, he watched as the woman sat calmly on a rock at the river's edge and struck the palm of her hand against the water's surface several times with a sharp smacking sound. From out of the ripples on the water's surface emerged a giant snake, which rose halfway out of the water and placed its head on the woman's beautiful, smooth thighs. She fed the snake, its head resting on her lap, and afterwards the two made love at the water's edge. Then the serpent slithered back into the river, down to its underwater cave, and the woman gathered her things to leave.

The cacique's servant ran quickly back to tell the story, trembling as he related the infidelity to the cacique. When the woman returned home, her husband, in a jealous rage, killed the woman with a single stroke of his knife. The snake, upon realizing his lover had been slain, agitated the river with its tail, causing it to rise up violently and destroy the entire community. The goddess Cihuacoatl (Snake Woman) has been worshipped ever since by the Nahuatl people in the area.

1527, the Spanish founded the city they called Santiago de Cihuacoatl on the banks of the Río Viejo alongside the indigenous settlement of Cihuacoatl, capital of the Chontales people. But when a major flood put the town under water in 1833, Sébaco was moved to the hill east of town, where the remnants of Sébaco

Viejo can still be found. The **Templo Viejo** houses a simple collection of archaeological artifacts, including pieces of pottery and ceramics, some small statues, and a wooden carving of the deity Cihuacoatl.

When they moved, the residents of Sébaco packed up their buildings piece by piece and transported the materials to the new location, where they reconstructed the buildings to approximately their original form. Since then, the houses slowly crept down the hill and back to the water's edge, waiting for history to repeat itself. And that's exactly what happened. In 1998, Sébaco was hit so hard by Hurricane Mitch it became one of the primary obstacles separating Managua from the north. The large bridge at the south end of town resisted the floods of the Río Grande de Matagalpa, but the river overflowed its banks just south of the bridge and sliced a new channel through the road hundreds of meters wide. The combined torrent swelled into a deadly wall of water that ripped through Ciudad Darío.

No matter where you travel in the north of Nicaragua, at some point you'll pass through Sébaco. Located right where the highway splits to take travelers to either Estelí and the Segovias (fork left) or Matagalpa, Jinotega, and the northeast (fork right), Sébaco, a.k.a. La Ciudad de Cebollas (City of Onions), is known throughout the region for its lively roadside commerce. If you're traveling at night, Sébaco is a sudden blast of streetlights, traffic, and bustle after two hours of darkness since Managua.

While travelers are more typically interested in the Texaco station's restrooms, most Nicas pick up fresh produce—carrots, beets, and of course, onions at one of the many identical stands on the true roadside market. Sébaco's aggressive road vendors will scale the side of your bus and display their goods through your window (hope you don't mind a faceful of carrot tops). If you have a long bus ride ahead of you, this is a good place to pick up bags of fruit

juice, snacks, or veggies, which make good gifts for your Nicaraguan hosts.

Accommodations and Food

Although there are a few cheap but unimpressive places to crash in town, you'd be much wiser to continue to Matagalpa or Estelí, either about a 45 minute drive away. The dozens of decent roadside restaurants offer similar menus of chicken, tacos, beef, and sandwiches. ◖ **El Sesteo** (a few blocks west of the BDF bank) is the best sit-down spot, with uniformed waiters, an air-conditioned *sala,* and an array of steak, chicken, and seafood dishes. On the east side of the intersection across from the triangle, the cheaper **Sorbetería Mac-et** serves sandwiches, hot dogs, light lunches, fruit juices, and ice cream. Sébaco also has several banks, a telephone office, and a private health clinic.

CHAGÜITILLO

About two kilometers north of Sébaco along the highway to Matagalpa, Chagüitillo is a small community with access to several dozen pre-Columbian petroglyphs scratched into the stone walls of a canyon just outside the village. The site **Apamico** is named in the Nahuatl for "place of the monkeys." Relics depicting monkeys, shamans carrying human heads, and hunting scenes line the banks of the Aranca Burba stream. The locals can easily help you find the two streambeds and show you the petroglyphs; both sites are an easy walk from the center of town. Particularly good guides are Orlando Dávila and Melvin Rizo, who speaks some English. Dávila lives in front of the school whose tall green wall is painted with representations of the petroglyphs; Rizo lives a block or two closer to the highway.

In town, find the *pulpería* run by Bernabe Rayo (located on a side street off the main road through town). Chagüitillo is the source of a water project for the city of Matagalpa, and engineers digging the trenches for the pipelines

MATAGALPA

have unearthed many additional artifacts. Some are scattered amongst the many houses of the community, but Rayo has done an admirable job of collecting some of them and trying to form a small community museum out of the pieces. You can support him by purchasing something from his store. He's got an interesting collection of old ceramic pots, cups, and small statues, plus some larger pieces he's reconstructed from the shards.

Matagalpa City

The department of Matagalpa is the most mountainous in Nicaragua, and its capital city remains true to form. As you walk up and down the steep streets, you'll realize the city is draped like a blanket over the rolling valley floor beneath it. Nicknamed La Perla del Septentrión (The Pearl of the North), Matagalpa's true precious stone is a ripe, red coffee bean, the production and harvest of which is essential to the region's—and the nation's—economy. Matagalpa enjoys clean mountain air, but water is another story. Radically depleted by deforestation and human contamination, clean water is in dreadfully short supply here. During the driest times, city officials cope with the problem by implementing draconian rationing schemes. The surrounding mountains have been mostly scraped clean of trees, but during the wet season, they turn emerald green and remain so throughout the Christmas season, when the coffee harvest turns the city of Matagalpa into a lively center of coffee pickers, prospectors, packers, and processors.

Nahuatl influence is more prominent in Matagalpa than elsewhere, particularly in regional vocabulary, which retains much pre-Columbian vocabulary. The Nahuatl word *chüisle,* for example, is used instead of the Castilian *quebrada* for stream. The city's central office for the region's indigenous community settles land disputes and other issues. Modern-day Nicaraguan politicians prize Matagalpa because its high population can often swing the vote, but tourists will prize Matagalpa as a welcome respite from the heat of the lowlands, plus a chance to sip the best coffee in the world while plotting forays deeper into the mountains. Ignore the inflated population sign as you enter the valley—the latest figures put Matagalpa's urban population at just over 100,000.

HISTORY

The beautiful valley where the city of Matagalpa now sits was already a cluster of Nahuatl communities—including Solingalpa and Molagüina, which still exist today—when the Spanish first set eyes on it. Nahuatl traditional histories don't include any stories of their people having arrived in this valley—as if they have always been here. Long before it was called the Pearl of the North, Matagalpa was known as the City of Ten in Nahuatl, in reference to the 10 small settlements within the valley. The name is also attributed to the powerful cacique Atahualpa, who governed the area during the time of colonization (Solingalpa was his wife).

The Spanish established a camp alongside the Nahuatls around 1680. Some powerful Spanish families made up the first settlers; their last names are still common in the region: Alvarado, Castañeda, Reyes, Rizo, Escoto. They set up extensive cattle ranches and planted fields before coffee was even a dream. In 1838, the area was named Departamento del Septentrión, and in 1862, Matagalpa was elevated to the status of city. Even with that status, the city of Matagalpa was of far less economic importance to the nation than Sébaco.

That changed in the second half of the 19th century, when Matagalpa saw a flow of German immigrants. They had not arrived in Nicaragua to plant coffee, as is commonly believed, but to develop the gold mines in the east. Once established in Nicaragua, however, they quickly realized how perfect the climate was for the cultivation of coffee and their interest switched to the crop that would define Nicaragua's economy for the next 150 years. Matagalpa had developed a new reason for being, and coffee has been the focus of Matagalpa ever since.

Today, several problems constrain Matagalpa from the prosperity it enjoyed in the 19th century. Most critical is the lack of potable water—even the Chagüitillo water project may provide water for no more than 10 years—but both developing rural roads and dealing with the growing solid waste problem will be necessary before Matagalpa returns to its status as a pearl.

SIGHTS
◖ Parque Darío
Grab a bench in Parque Darío and buy a crushed ice *raspado* to enjoy while people-watching. There are probably more trees jammed into the park's tiny confines than any other in Nicaragua, and come sunset the branches fill with thousands of birds. A permanent fixture in the park is a vendor with rows and rows of handmade ceramic piggy banks for sale, none of which costs more than $1.

El Templo de San José de Laborío
El Templo de San José de Laborío sits at the edge of the Parque Darío at the south end of town. It's probably as old as the colonial presence in Matagalpa, but no one is quite sure exactly when it was built. It was rebuilt in 1917 on top of its old foundation, but underneath that foundation are the ruins of another that date to at least 1751, and possibly a bit earlier. In 1881, an indigenous uprising used the church as its garrison.

La Casa Cuna Carlos Fonseca
Matagalpa was the birthplace of the founder of the FSLN, Carlos Fonseca. The house he was born in has been converted into a museum. Known as La Casa Cuna Carlos Fonseca (one block east of Parque Darío's south side, tel. 505/2772-3665 or 505/2772-2932, 8 A.M.–noon and 2–5 P.M. Mon.–Fri., small donation), the tiny corner building has the original brick floors, mud walls, and tile roof, as well as an interesting assortment of documents, photos, and memorabilia, including Carlos's typewriter and his gear from military training in Korea.

La Iglesia de Molagüina
The history of La Iglesia de Molagüina, found in the center of the city, has been forgotten. It was probably constructed between 1751 and 1873, though those dates have been questioned by historians. Simple and monastic, it is a well-used and well-loved church: Molagüina is home to a Catholic order of nuns and the College of San José.

Museo de Café
Museo de Café (located on the main street 1.5 blocks north of the mayor's office, 8 A.M.–5 P.M. Mon.–Fri., closed for lunch, open Sat. mornings) displays some interesting murals and photographs from Matagalpa's history, plus a small collection of indigenous artifacts.

◖ La Catedral de San Pedro de Matagalpa
At the northeastern end of town, La Catedral de San Pedro de Matagalpa was a disproportionately large cathedral—the third largest in the nation—when it was built in 1874, reflecting the opulence of Matagalpa at the time. The cathedral is built in the baroque style, with heavy bell towers set at both sides and an airy, spacious interior. It's the most prominent building in town and is easily visible from the hillsides north of town on the road to Jinotega. The cathedral's interior is crisp and cool, tastefully adorned with bas- and medium-relief sculpture, carved wood, and paintings. Mass is held nightly at 6 P.M.

MATAGALPA

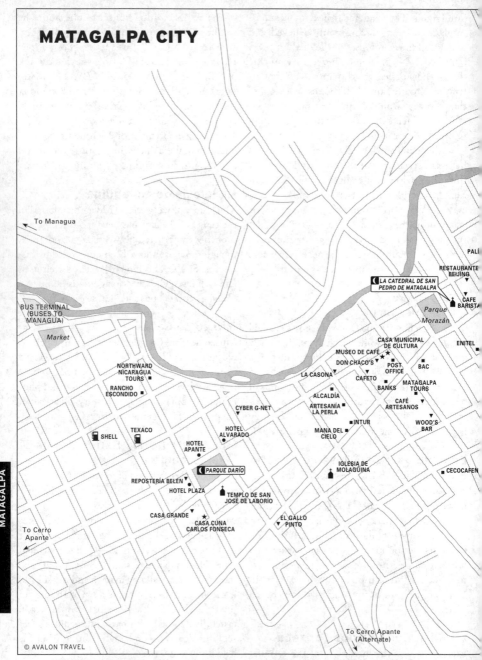

MATAGALPA CITY

To Managua

PALÍ

RESTAURANTE BEIJING

LA CATEDRAL DE SAN PEDRO DE MATAGALPA

CAFÉ BARISTA

BUS TERMINAL (BUSES TO MANAGUA)

Parque Morazán

Market

ENITEL

CASA MUNICIPAL DE CULTURA

MUSEO DE CAFÉ

NORTHWARD NICARAGUA TOURS

DON CHACO'S

POST OFFICE

BAC

LA CASONA

CAFETO

RANCHO ESCONDIDO

BANKS

MATAGALPA TOURS

ALCALDÍA

ARTESANÍA LA PERLA

CAFÉ ARTESANOS

CYBER G-NET

HOTEL ALVARADO

INTUR

WOOD'S BAR

MANA DEL CIELO

TEXACO

SHELL

HOTEL APANTE

IGLESIA DE MOLAGÜINA

CECOCAFEN

PARQUE DARÍO

REPOSTERÍA BELEN

HOTEL PLAZA

TEMPLO DE SAN JOSÉ DE LABORÍO

CASA GRANDE

CASA CUNA CARLOS FONSECA

EL GALLO PINTO

To Cerro Apante

MATAGALPA

To Cerro Apante (Alternate)

© AVALON TRAVEL

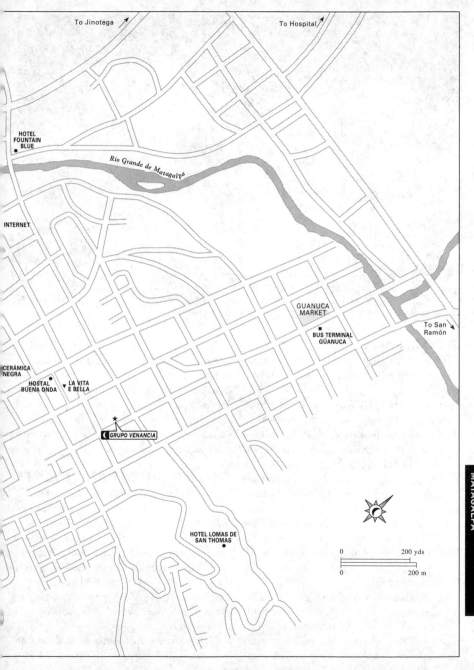

To Jinotega

To Hospital

HOTEL
FOUNTAIN
BLUE

Río Grande de Matagalpa

INTERNET

GUANUCA
MARKET

BUS TERMINAL
GÜANUCA

To San
Ramón

CERÁMICA
NEGRA

HOSTAL   LA VITA
BUENA ONDA   E BELLA

GRUPO VENANCIA

MATAGALPA

HOTEL LOMAS DE
SAN THOMAS

0   200 yds
0   200 m

La Cathedral de San Pedro de Matagalpa towers over the city.

© AMBER DOBRZENSKY

MATAGALPA

El Castillo del Cacao

The Castle of Chocolate (tel. 505/2772-2002, www.elcastillodelcacao.com) is the Willie Wonka factory of Nicaragua, located 500 meters north of the Las Marias Esso station, about a five-minute cab ride from the city center. Here you can tour the factory, visit a chocolate museum, and learn about the production of organic chocolate in Nicaragua. Nicaraguan cacao is known as a *landrace,* or a traditional variety almost identical to pre-Columbian cacao. It has a rich, complex, nuttier flavor than the heavily cultivated and hybridized strains grown elsewhere in the world. For tours of the factory, call 505/722-0108 and plan to go in the afternoon.

Cemeteries

There are two adjacent cemeteries on the hillside east of the city, about a 30-minute walk from town. One is for locals and one is for foreigners, a rare arrangement in Nicaragua. Both contain headstones hand carved from

dark rock, something seen only in Matagalpa. Buried in the cemetery higher up on the hill in the local section is one of the most famous casualties of the 1980s war: Benjamin Linder. An American, Linder was an avid juggler and unicyclist, and his headstone reflects those passions, along with some doves, the symbol of the peace he never lived to see.

ENTERTAINMENT AND EVENTS

Matagalpans celebrate their *fiestas patronales* on September 24, and the anniversary of their becoming a city on February 14. Every September there is a rowdy country fair that brings in crowds from the north and east, and cattle traders from all over the country. This is the best time of year to catch Matagalpa's traditional music of polkas, mazurkas, and *jamaquelos,* performed by the roving street bands that play at restaurants.

The **Arabesco Academía de la Danza de Matagalpa,** under the able direction of Marcos

MATAGALPA, WATER, AND THE LEGEND OF THE SERPENT

Matagalpa is a water-stressed city. In some neighborhoods, the water pressure is only turned on once a day; in others, Matagalpinos are forced to walk to distribution points to fill up containers from tanker trucks. You may see these trucks along the city streets in the early mornings, when everyone comes out with buckets and pans to get what water they can.

At the same time, there's more water in Matagalpa than some people know what to do with. Time and time again, shallow excavations in the city for routine projects have turned up a moist layer of earth just several meters below the surface. When a well-loved priest died in the 1990s, his tomb was dug underneath the floor of the cathedral. Before they had finished digging, the hole had begun to flood. Studies have determined the water under the city of Matagalpa isn't exploitable in quantities great enough to supply the city, and so other alternatives are being developed.

Much of Matagalpa's limited water supply comes from the forested hillsides that surround the city, hillsides that are rapidly being stripped of their timber. Matagalpinos speak of an old legend: The hill known as Apante, just southeast of the city, was said to be an enormous upwelling of water trapped within a pocket of soil and rock. Within the water lived a great snake. One day the snake began to shake, and the hillside began to crumble, threatening to unleash a massive landslide upon the residents of the city. In despair, they turned to the Virgin Mary for protection. Mary fought the snake and subdued it by planting its tail underneath the foundation of the church of Molagüina in the center of the city.

But the snake grows stronger each day... when it finally has enough strength to break free, it will shake its tail again, causing the hills to crumble and collapse upon the city. If the deforestation of the hillsides surrounding Matagalpa continue, this prophecy may very well come true.

Valle, who studied modern dance in Spain, puts on dance presentations several times a year. If there's going to be a show, it will be advertised at the Casa Municipal de Cultura, next to the fire station.

Local radio stations include Radio Norteña, FM 94.1; Radio Stereo Apante, FM 94.9; and Radio Yes, FM 90.1. The latter has several programs for a rural audience, including impersonations, jokes, and news commentary. Their morning news program is worth a listen in the early hours of the day while you're taking a cold-water mountain shower. A women's cooperative runs the show at FM 101.7.

◖ Grupo Venancia

Grupo Venancia (1.5 blocks south of La Iglesia de Guadalupe, tel. 505/2772-3562, www.grupovenancia.org, open Thurs.–Sat.) is a convivial open-air bar surrounding a stage and sometimes dance floor. They host music, dance, theater, artsy international films, and both local and global activism. The place is renowned for its free shows every Saturday night. Grupo Venancia is also a nonprofit women's group that can probably be called ground zero of Nicaragua's feminist movement. It was founded in 1990 and in addition to the gathering space, runs urban and rural workshops on women's rights and domestic violence. Ask about their published materials, ways to volunteer, and try to catch their Saturday morning radio show, "La Hora Lila," on Radio Yes (FM 90.1) at 8:30 A.M.

Nightlife

There's no doubt that the Matagalpinos like to shake their boots as much as other Nicaraguans, though they prefer *ranchera,* merengue, and Reggaeton over salsa. Matagalpa's

LA RUTA DE CAFÉ: COFFEE TOURISM IN THE NORTH

Today, both international coffee merchants and *café-turistas* can travel a circuit of coffee cooperatives scattered through the mountains of Jinotega, Matagalpa, and the Segovias. As a participant in this Ruta de Café, not only will you sample coffee in special cupping labs, you'll also visit coffee-growing families and their farms, which are often magical cloud forests shrouded in cool mists; you can stay for a couple of hours or a couple of days, living with the families, eating meals with them, picking coffee, and learning about all stages of the process. As a *café-turista*, you'll experience the communities of real people who have been behind every sip of coffee you've ever taken. What's more, you will learn why the quality of a coffee is inextricably tied to the quality of life of those that produce it, as well as the quality of the environment in which they live. Finally, you will learn what organic, bird friendly, and fair trade-certified coffees are (visit www.transfairusa.org and www.globalexchange.org for details).

To experience the most activity, be sure to arrange your visit during the peak of the harvest, usually mid-December–February. Make your arrangements in advance with the ecotourism project of **CECOCAFEN** (Center of Northern Coffee Cooperatives, tel. 505/2772-6353, turismo@cecocafen.com), whose main office in Matagalpa city is located two blocks east of Banco Uno. They can arrange anything from an afternoon coffee cupping at their Sol Café *beneficio* (coffee-processing mill) to a day trip, visiting some of their farmers, to a multi-night excursion, staying in *campesino* homes and touring their farms (or even putting some work in during the harvest). Trips include transportation and food, and hikes (with pickups) can be arranged between towns. Prices fully depend on the trip. Or consider a stay at **Finca Esperanza Verde** (www.fincaesperanzaverde.org), an acclaimed accommodation and working organic coffee farm located outside San Ramón.

In Jinotega, **SOPPEXCA** (Society of Small Coffee Producers, Exporters, and Buyers, tel. 505/2782-2617, soppexcc@tmx.com.ni) is eager to serve as your tour guide of the region, arranging any number of hikes, trips, and homestays among its growers in the surrounding hills. Their office and cupping lab is located in Jinotega, one block west of the Ferretería Blandón.

There are also several welcoming coffee cooperatives in the hills north of Estelí with similar tours available.

various *discotecas* may be open Thursday–Sunday nights, in general, but the only consistently happening night—with guaranteed crowded and electric dance floors—is Saturday. For dancing, **Las Tequilas,** on the road heading out of town toward Managua ($2 or less taxi ride from downtown), is popular. More mature revelers and couples enjoy the hassle-free dance floor at **Rincón Paraíso.**

Open all week for mediocre lunch and dinner, **La Casona** comes alive as Matagalpa's premier Friday night fiesta, with live music in a crowded, open-air back patio.

The bohemian hang-out of choice is **Cafe Artesanos** (a half-block up from BAC next to Matagalpa Tours, tel. 505/2772-2444), sometimes with live music from around the country. Next door, the noisy **Wood's Bar** has become a favorite with young Matagalpinos on the weekends.

SHOPPING

The north's famous black pottery—darkened by a particular firing technique—is unique in Nicaragua, where pottery is typically a natural reddish-orange color. Find it for sale throughout the city. Multiple shops bearing the name **Cerámica Negra** are spread throughout the city, offering similar selections, but if you are looking for a specific location, a kiosk is located in Parque Darío. Even La Vita e Bella restaurant offers an excellent variety of ceramics and jewelry.

You'll find a great selection of local crafts at **Centro Girasol** (a bright yellow corner building right across the first bridge as you enter Matagalpa from Managua, tel. 505/2772-6030). They've also got local jams, honey, coffee, and yogurt.

SPORTS AND RECREATION
Hiking
Immediately recognizable by the cluster of antennas on its peak, **Cerro Apante** (1,442 meters) towers above Matagalpa. Officially, it is a nature reserve, though most of its steep flanks are privately owned, covered by thick vegetation and a handful of small farms. Apante is a well-preserved piece of tropical humid forest that contains decent stands of oak and pine, as well as several hundred types of wildflowers. It is protecting an important source of water for the city (*apante* is Nahuatl for "running water"). It is crisscrossed with many small trails that lead to its streams and lagoons, all of which are easily accessed by foot from the city. In an effort to provide more funding to protect the natural resources of Nicaragua, the county has implemented a fee of 30 *córdobas* ($1.50) to enter the park.

The two routes to the top both begin by standing at the northwest corner of Parque Darío (in front of Hotel Alvarado). Walking south on the *calle principal* will take you up to the Apante neighborhood on the edge of town (also serviced by the Chispa–Apante Rapibuses). Continue up the road, keeping the summit to your left and continually asking if you're on the right track, to *el cerro*. From the same corner in town, travel due east up a road that climbs steeply, eventually deteriorating into a rutted road. The road switches back a few times, ending at a hacienda atop a saddle in the Apante ridgeline. From there, find a footpath to the top. The actual summit is off limits, and is guarded by a caretaker and his dog, but the nearby ridge enjoys a breathtaking view

of its own. You can link the two hikes into a three-hour loop; bring lots of water for the trail.

Tours
Start by picking up a map at the **Centro Girasol** (a bright yellow corner building right across the first bridge as you enter Matagalpa from Managua or two blocks south and one west from the COTRAN Sur, tel. 505/2772-6030). The *Treasures of Matagalpa* map costs less than $2, benefits local children with disabilities, and outlines a number of walks, offering guide service as well.

Matagalpa Tours (a half-block east of BAC, tel. 505/2772-0108 or 505/2647-4680, www.nicaraguatravels.net) is a guide service, travel agent, and backcountry outfitter run by a Dutch expat and his Nicaraguan wife, who manage the on-site Spanish language school. Let them arrange a variety of packages, shuttle service from Granada ($25 per person), homestays, Bosawás treks, coffee plantation tours, and community tourism for anywhere from $15–60 per day depending on the extent. Arien has explored, hiked, and camped throughout the Matagalpan countryside and has even drawn a number of trail maps. The Bosawás tours are major wilderness excursions that need to be arranged far in advance. Inside the office is a great local crafts shop run by a local women's organization called Zona Franja.

Northward Nicaragua Tours (2.5 blocks west of the Dario Park street light, tel. 505/2772-0605, www.adventure-nicaragua.com) is a younger company with an adventurous staff who will organize off-the-beaten-path tours of the country, as well as adrenaline activities in the vicinity. Rappelling, bouldering, and mountain biking tours are just a few of the ways in which you can explore this region. Contact the office for packages and prices.

Nativos Tours, currently operating out of the Buena Onda hostel (tel. 505/8493-0932), is the best bet for budget-conscious travelers. Run by young bilingual guide Guillermo Gonzalez, the 12 tours are all under $20, a great way for those with budget and time constraints to explore the area.

ACCOMMODATIONS
Under $25

Hotel Plaza (on the south side of Parque Darío, tel. 505/2772-2380) has been a stalwart in the Matagalpa lodging scene for decades. The 18 rooms range from $5 cubbyholes with shared bath to $15 doubles with private bath, TV, and fan. On the west side of Parque Darío, **Hotel Apante** (tel. 505/2772-6890) charges $10 per person for shared bath, fan, and TV in its bright, clean rooms (no Internet access).

One of the best, safest budget options is **Hotel Alvarado** (across from the Parque Darío's northwest corner, tel. 505/2772-2830 or 505/2772-3534, $9–20), run by a friendly Christian doctor couple who also run a pharmacy downstairs. Ask for one of the top-floor rooms, which boast private bathrooms, a breeze, and views of the city and mountains from the small balconies. If their eight rooms are full, ask about their other location across town.

❰ Hotel Fountain Blue, a.k.a. Fuente Azul (third entrance to Matagalpa just west of the bridge, or from Salomón López 1.5 blocks west, tel. 505 /2772-2733), has a dozen practical rooms. Choose a double with private bath, hot water, TV, and fan for $25, or pay $15 per person for a smaller room with a shared bath. This place is quiet and comfortable, with a pay phone, Internet access, free coffee, and guarded parking.

For larger groups, **Hotel Mana del Cielo** (2.5 blocks south of Banpro, tel. 505/2772-5686, www.hotelmanadelcielo.com, $15–40) has 30 rooms all equipped with TV, fan, hot water showers, and Wi-Fi access. The rooms are a good deal unless you need a/c (for which you'll pay double). Head to the fourth floor, where the rooftop terrace offers fantastic city views.

A peaceful respite in the heart of Matagalpa, **❰ Hostal La Buena Onda** (tel. 505/2772-2135, www.hostelmatagalpa.com, $7–30) is located 2.5 blocks east of Union Fenosa, walking distance from the best attractions and food in the city. The name roughly means "good vibes" and travelers flock to the large, revamped two-story house to lounge in the garden patio hammocks and take in the surrounding mountains from the upper balcony. There are communal rooms, each with bathroom, hot shower, lockers, and handcrafted wooden bunk beds, as well as private rooms that can sleep up to four. They also have all-day breakfast at the adjacent **Restaurante Buena Onda,** free Wi-Fi, book and DVD library, laundry service, and a handy luggage storage. *Buena onda,* indeed.

$25-50

Hotel Lomas de San Thomas (350 meters east of Escuela Guanuca, tel. 505/2772-4189, www.hotellomassnthomas.com, $35–75), a mustard-colored, three-story establishment on a breezy hill just east of town, lords over the city. The 25 rooms have private bath, hot water, TV, and telephone, many with an excellent balcony. There is also a bar and restaurant on-site. It gears itself for business conventions and the NGO crew, offering secretarial services, conference rooms, fax, Internet, and a tennis court. To get there, leave the highway at the third entrance to Matagalpa and pass straight through town following the signs. At the eastern edge of Matagalpa, turn left and climb the hill on a cobblestone road to the hotel.

FOOD
Bakeries and Cafés

There is no shortage of coffee up here where it's produced: **❰ Cafeto** (half a block west of Citibank, 7 A.M.–8 P.M. daily $2–5) never fails to impress, with hot and cold sandwiches, panini, salads, waffles, smoothies, and ice cream.

Sniff around just east of Bancentro and you will surely catch a whiff of warm, fresh breads and pastries wafting out from the

Panadería Belén (8 A.M.–6 P.M. Mon.–Sat.). **Repostería Gutierrez** (one block east and half a block south of the southeast corner of Parque Morazán, 7 A.M.–8 P.M. daily) is a favorite among locals, with savory, cheap Nica dishes. **Coffee Shop Barista** (right behind the cathedral, 8 A.M.–9 P.M.) offers the full barista experience plus pastries and sweets.

(**Cafe Artesanos** (a half-block up from BAC next to Matagalpa Tours, tel. 505/2772-2444, 8 A.M.–noon and 3 P.M.–midnight daily) is one *norteño's* cathedral to coffee. Proprietor Noel Montoya offers a close look—and taste— of Nica beans at their best, and is happy to introduce you to the art of roasting and brewing. Mix the black liquor with Flor de Caña. In addition to coffee, Artesano's is one of the most relaxing hangouts in the city. It's open for breakfast and dinner and is especially soothing in the morning. The place features local artists' paintings and murals on the walls of an old colonial building.

Comida Típica

Local snacks and simple dishes are Matagalpa's specialty. As always, there's tasty street food in both parks, and also as always, it's *vigorón* or *chancho con yucca* (both include pork and yucca served on banana leaves). However, during the lunch hour, several *fritangas* at Parque Morazán serve a more robust menu.

One of the friendliest *comedores* is **Don Chaco's** (1.5 blocks east of the Alcaldía, 7:30 A.M.–9 P.M. Sun.–Thurs., 7:30 A.M.–5 P.M. Fri., $3–7), where in addition to heaping plates of *comida típica* (with great veggie options), you'll find a delicious *batido* (smoothie) menu of fruits, vegetables, and even soy milk. If you prefer buffet, lunch-line style, with a smorgasbord of Nica food lined up in front of you, the hugely popular (**Mana del Cielo** (below the hotel, located 2.5 blocks south of the banks, $4–8) will surely satisfy; it's owned by a retired baseball player who played in Nica's pro leagues for a number of years.

To taste the sweet goodness of Matagalpa's best *güiríla* (a sweet-corn pancake wrapped around a hunk of salty *cuajada* cheese, about $0.35), you'll have to brave the chaos of the crowds that cluster around the smoky stands across the street from Palí.

Everbody loves Don Tano's **Picoteo Café** (located just east of the post office, 7:30 A.M.– 10 P.M. daily, $2), serving chicken, burgers, pizza, and lots of beer. The walls are covered with platitudes painted on wooden plaques.

Pique's (not far from the Parque Morazán, $2–4) is a stylish Mexican joint. Their *chalupas* and mole are especially good, and the atmosphere is relaxing.

La Casona (on the main drag, across from the mayor's office, 9 A.M.–11 P.M. daily, $3–4) offers a lunch buffet and a variety of bar-type foods. It's open later on the weekend, when it turns into a popular bar. Look for the big 7-Up sign outside.

For passable Chinese, follow locals to **Restaurante Beijing** (tel. 505/2772-2893, 10 A.M.–10 P.M. daily, $4–5), next to the cathedral, for heaped plates of fried rice or noodles.

Upscale

One of the cornerstones of Matagalpa's dining scene, (**La Vita e Bella** (tel. 505/2772-5476, vitabell@ibw.com.ni, 12:30–10:30 P.M. Tues.– Sun., $4–6) is tucked into an alley in the Colonia Lainez. La Vita e Bella serves Italian and vegetarian dishes, and desserts that will make you glad you found the place. This is possibly the best restaurant in the city for nonchicken and nonbeef dishes. There's also an excellent wine selection.

The **Sacuanjoche Restaurant and Bar** ($5–15) at the Hotel Lomas de San Thomas offers standard fare at stiff prices—steaks, fajitas, shrimp dishes, and salads—as well as a ceramic shop and taxi service ($1.50 to or from the town center).

INFORMATION AND SERVICES
Tourist Information

The Museo de Café houses the **CIPTURMAT office** (8 A.M.–12:30 P.M. and 2–5:30 P.M.

BLACK GOLD: NICARAGUAN COFFEE

In 1852, Germans Ludwig Elster and his wife Katherina Braun were passing through Nicaragua on their way to the California gold rush. They never made it to California, but they did find gold. Rather, Katherina did.

While crossing Nicaragua, Ludwig met many disheartened travelers returning home from failure in California. He and Katherina decided to cut their journey short and look for gold in the mines of San Ramón, Matagalpa. While Ludwig worked the taxed gold deposits of Matagalpa, Katherina Braun established a home garden and planted some of the coffee beans they'd picked up in Managua. Her discovery—that Matagalpa's climate and soils were just right for the cultivation of the bitter but full-bodied arabica coffee bean—dwarfed the importance of San Ramón's gold mines and changed the course of Nicaragua's history.

Coffee fever gripped Matagalpa in the 1880s, and the Nicaraguan government, eager to capitalize on the crop, threw its weight behind the Germans. Laws were passed encouraging young Germans to immigrate to Nicaragua. One such law gave them free land to work; many of these family farms are still operating today.

At first, coffee was shipped in bean form through the port of Corinto, around Cape Horn to European importers in Bremen and Hamburg. By 1912, though, the Nicaraguan German community had established their own processing plants where they milled and processed the coffee beans. They used a new "wet" method that stripped the beans of their pulp over grated steel cylinders. Today, more than 40 wet coffee mills, plus thousands of micromills on individual farms process coffee throughout the nation.

One of the truly unique aspects of Nicaraguan coffee, besides its exceptional quality, is how much of the process is performed on the farm, before the product is shipped elsewhere.

This is a significant difference from the routine adopted by Costa Rican coffee growers, most of whom send off their harvest immediately after picking. As much as 80 percent of Nicaraguan cooperative-produced coffee can be considered "quality coffee" because it fills the following internationally recognized requirements:

- They are arabica beans (not robusta) grown at an altitude of 900 meters or higher.

- Consisting of big beans, the lots are aromatic, well sorted, and free from broken or burned beans and small stones.

- Beans are given one month to sit during processing and are not dehulled until just before shipping.

- Beans are transported in sealed containers.

- Beans are adequately stored by the purchaser.

- Upon roasting, the beans are sealed immediately in special one-pound vacuum-packed bags that prevent the introduction of light, air, and moisture, but permit carbon dioxide to escape.

- The consumer can buy the coffee in whole-bean form, not ground.

An increasing number of small-scale Nicaraguan coffee farmers are learning to recognize and judge the quality of their product and eliminate the middlemen, or *coyotes*, who have traditionally taken the lion's share of coffee profits. One tool that allows them to do this is the cupping lab—a specially equipped kitchen where Nicaraguan cooperative members are trained to grind, brew, and rate their own coffee using internationally recognized criteria. One of the key figures in the cupping lab project was Paul Katzeff, CEO and roastmaster of Thanksgiving Coffee Company (www.thanksgivingcoffee.com).

Mon.–Fri.), which has brochures and current contact information for hostels, homestays, farms, and tours in the area. The main **ENITEL** building (7 A.M.–9 P.M.) is located to the east of Parque Morazán (look for the big antenna jutting out from the city skyline).

Banks

There are a half-dozen banks in Matagalpa— BAC, Banpro, Banexpo, Banco Caley Dagnall, Bancentro, and Banco Mercantíl—and a fistful of money changers that hang out around the southeast corner of Parque Morazán. The banks are mostly clustered in a three-block strip, starting at the southeast corner of Parque Morazán. Nearly all have ATMs.

Emergencies

All emergency services are covered in Matagalpa—fire (tel. 505/2772-3167), police (tel. 505/2772-3870), and hospital (tel. 505/2772-2081). The hospital is located at the north end of town on the highway to San Ramón. But you'll get better medical treatment at the Clínica Maya Flores.

Media and Communication

Correos de Nicaragua Matagalpa (tel. 505/2772-4317, 8 A.M.–12:30 P.M. and 2–5:30 P.M. Mon.–Fri., 8 A.M.–1 P.M. Sat.) is located one block west of Parque Morazán, tucked into a side street that runs south from the main drag. Fax, phone, and mailbox services are available.

There are a number of card-based public phones and BellSouth posts all over town, especially along the main *calle principal.*

The fastest, most advanced cybercafé in town is **Matt's Cyber** (located two blocks north of Parque Darío, 8 A.M.–10 P.M.). **CyberCafe Downtown** (a half-block west of the southwest corner of the Parque Darío, 8:30 A.M.–8 P.M. Mon.–Sat., 10 A.M.–7 P.M. Sun.) is popular and fast. Walking north on

the *calle principal,* about halfway to Parque Morazán, you'll find **NetCom** (8 A.M.–9 P.M. Mon.–Fri., 8 A.M.–8 P.M. Sat., 8 A.M.–7 P.M. Sun.) just past La Casona; it provides decent service. One of the fastest servers in town is at **Cybercafe Matagalpa** (9 A.M.–9 P.M. Mon.–Sat., 9 A.M.–7 P.M. Sun., about $2 an hour); it is located a half-block north and one block west from the Palí supermarket, across the street from Mi Favorita store. Cheap membership deals are also available.

Cheap, web-based international call service is available at all three Internet cafés.

GETTING THERE

Matagalpa has two bus terminals—which one you head to depends on your destination. At the south end of town, the **COTRAN Sur** (tel. 505/2772-4659 or 505/2603-0909) services Managua, Estelí, León, Masaya, and Jinotega.

OPPORTUNITIES TO VOLUNTEER

At least 16 Matagalpan organizations accept volunteer help from time to time if you'd like to make this your home for a few months or more. The **Movimiento Comunal** (tel. 505/2772-3200) deals with indigenous rights issues and fights against water privatization. **La Casa de la Mujer Nora Hawkins** (tel. 505/2772-3047) promotes social programs that benefit women. The **Comunidad Indígena** (tel. 505/2772-2692) is rather disorganized but well intentioned and could certainly use your assistance if you can find a way to be useful. **Habitat for Humanity** (located two blocks east and half a block north of the Deportiva Brigadista, tel. 505/2772-6121) has built several housing settlements in the area and continues to be active. Ask about volunteer opportunities at **Matagalpa Tours** or **Centro Girasol.**

There's a public bathroom there ($0.15) and several small eateries.

Express buses to Managua depart every hour 5:15 A.M.–5:15 P.M. Nonexpress Managua-bound buses leave every half hour 3:30 A.M.–6 P.M. Direct buses to Masaya leave at 2 P.M. (daily except Thursday and Sunday).

To León via San Isidro and Telíca, there are two daily expresses, leaving at 6 A.M. and 3 P.M. There are also *interlocales* minivans that leave whenever they fill up; or take any bus bound for Estelí, get off at the Empalme León, and catch a bus to León (departing just about every 20–30 minutes).

There is a constant flow of buses to Estelí and Jinotega, leaving every half hour 5 A.M.–5:40 P.M. (Estelí) and till 6 P.M. (Jinotega). One daily direct bus to Chinandega leaves Matagalpa at 2 P.M.

At the north end of town, the **COTRAN de Guanuca** services the interior of Matagalpa, including El Tuma–La Dália, San Ramón, Río Blanco, Muy Muy, and Bocana de Paíwas. The ride to San Ramón takes about 45 minutes. Road conditions in these areas are bad in the dry season, and horrible in the rainy season when bus service sometimes slackens. Buses to points east depart approximately every 15 minutes to an hour until around 4:30 P.M.

From Managua
Express buses from Managua leave the Mayoreo bus terminal every hour 5:30 A.M.–5:30 P.M. The ride takes two hours and costs about $2.50.

If heading north from Granada or Masaya, you can bypass Managua by grabbing one of two direct buses from the Masaya bus terminal, leaving at 5 A.M. and 6 A.M. and taking less than three hours; these are full-size buses and run every day except Thursday and Sunday.

From Other Cities
From León, there are two daily expresses, leaving at 4:30 A.M. and 2:45 P.M.; this ride takes less than three hours and costs about $2.50 per person. Matagalpa-bound buses leave every half hour, starting about 5 A.M. from both Estelí (last bus leaves at 5:45 P.M.) and Jinotega (last bus leaves at 7 P.M.). There is one direct bus from Chinandega to Matagalpa, leaving at 5 A.M.

GETTING AROUND
Matagalpa is a perfectly good city for walking, except for all those hills, where you'll sweat out all that *fritanga* grease; the taxi fare within town is under $1. City buses ply three different routes back and forth across town, and cost about $0.25. Particularly useful is the bus route called El Chispa.

If you plan on navigating the winding roads around Matagalpa and Jinotega yourself, both **Budget** (Km 126 on the Managua-Matagalpa road, tel. 505/2772-3041, matagalpa@budget.com.ni) and **Dollar** (Casa Pellas Matagalpa, one block south of ENITEL, tel. 505/2772-4640) offer local car rentals.

East of Matagalpa

Segmented by dozens of rivers—some of which are impassible in the wet season—and bereft of roads throughout much of the area, the lands east of Matagalpa made good training grounds for the guerrillas who followed Fonseca into battle against Somoza's troops in the 1970s. More than 40 years later, the population has grown, but the wild and rugged landscape is as impenetrable as ever. The mostly undeveloped hillsides that stretch from Matagalpa to the Honduran border vary from dense tropical jungle to pine forest to shallow, bushy hillsides.

Heading into the geographic heart of the nation, the traveler encounters broad hillsides of shiny coffee bushes beneath shady canopies, plots of corn and beans, and small communities of tile-roofed adobe houses sitting among the rugged mountains that are the eastern reaches of the Cordillera Dariense. The *campesinos* in the folds of these mountains live much the way they have for centuries, even as governments, revolutions, and natural disasters have swirled violently around them.

The major communities of the east, Río Blanco, Matiguás, and Muy Muy, serve as commercial and transportation centers for the region, and they offer rudimentary accommodations for the traveler. But don't expect any luxury rides here: The roads east of Matagalpa are some of the most neglected in the country, notably the stretch between Siuna and Mulukuku, which is practically impassable during the wettest months of the year. That said, you will be traveling through some of the most beautiful—and least visited—parts of Nicaragua.

SAN RAMÓN

Only 12 kilometers from Matagalpa, the village of San Ramón is nestled in a lovely valley at the base of several steep hills. Founded in the late 1800s, San Ramón got its start around the La Leonesa and La Reina gold mines, and today is a peaceful, friendly hamlet, about five blocks square and surrounded on all sides by green farms and forests penetrated by a number of roads and trails. San Ramón has two parks, a health clinic, a gas station, and a number of nonprofit and coffee-related administrative offices. Because of sister-city relationships with Catalan (Spain), Henniker (New Hampshire), and Durham (North Carolina), small groups of wandering foreigners are not uncommon and San Ramón adeptly hosts both foreign groups and individuals in one of several guesthouse and homestay programs.

Use San Ramón as a more rural alternative to Matagalpa (travel to and from the city is a cinch), or sample one of the short local excursions, such as the walk to the La Pita coffee cooperative. On the way, you'll pass the 100-year-old ruins of the Leonesa mine, overtaken by moss, ferns, and giant ceiba trees. **Cesar Davila** (work tel. 505/2772-9734 or cell 505/2478-3519) has a privately owned nature preserve that he has reforested practically right in San Ramón. Cesar, an ex-soldier, is full of stories of the war, and has knowledge about forestry, birds, and herbs. He has built a trail across his lands for a half-hour hike to the point of the cross above San Ramón, with beautiful views of surrounding hills.

El Sueño de la Campana (tel. 505/2772-9729, fundacionlacampana@gmail.com, www.fundacionlacampana.es, $25–30)—located just down from the gas station, across the creek at the bridge and on the left—is not only a hostel but a Spanish NGO that supports work with children with disabilities in San Ramón, as well as a Casa de Cultura. Rooms are clean and cozy, and the wooden cabins are nice and private if more rustic. There's also a restaurant with *comida típica,* laundry service, library,

MATAGALPA

Internet, 24-hour reception, and trails on the property. Stay as a guest or get involved in some of the projects.

Find the office of Finca Esperanza Verde (an ecoresort outside town) by walking east from the Shell station past the police station, and through a small gate at the dead end. This is the place to inquire about the **Club de Guías** (trained young guides, $10/day, some with English) and the local **Casa de Huespedes** or guesthouse system (tel. 505/2772-5003, fincaesperanza@gmail.com), which offers a secure room, private bath, and three meals for $15 a day.

There are no true restaurants in San Ramón, but plenty of more casual eateries, including tasty *comedores* along the sidewalk across the highway from the Shell station. **Doña Nelys Arauz** serves heaping plates of originally styled Nica food for under $4.

Buses to and from San Ramón are frequent, leaving the Guanuca terminal every hour or more 6 A.M.–7 P.M., in addition to the many other eastbound buses that pass through San Ramón on their way elsewhere. A cab from Matagalpa costs about $5 per person, if you're interested in day- or night-tripping into the city of Matagalpa.

◖ FINCA ESPERANZA VERDE

Although its office and many of the community programs it supports are in the village of San Ramón, Finca Esperanza Verde (tel. 505/2772-5003, www.fincaesperanzaverde.org) is its own destination. A cool, green getaway 18 kilometers east of San Ramón and 1,180 meters above sea level, travelers will find a range of peaceful accommodations, as well as beautiful sunsets, delicious food, and a menu of educational and recreational activities. FEV is closely associated with the Durham, North Carolina–San Ramón Sister City Project.

The open-air lodge and cabanas have wide, west-facing vistas, surrounded by shade-grown, organic coffee plantations and second-generation cloud forest, through which winds an impressive and varied trail system; hike it on your own or, to see more of the 150 species of birds, howler monkeys, numerous orchids, and medicinal plants, hire one of the farm's guides.

FEV's property features several waterfalls, a butterfly house and breeding project, and a delicious spring-fed, potable water supply. From November through February, pick, process, and sort the coffee beans, then follow the coffee to Matagalpa where it is sun dried, sorted, graded, cupped, and exported. The farm's all-Nicaraguan staff enjoy teaching visitors about coffee and are proud that their care of the farm makes it a home to hundreds of species of birds, butterflies, mammals, trees, and orchids. Other possible activities include a cooking demonstration and class, and a folk music concert. Or just relax on the hammock terrace watching the jungle and the sunset.

The lodge and cabins, built of handmade brick and other local materials, can accommodate up to 26 people and are equipped with solar electricity, flush toilets, sinks, and warm sun showers. There is a range of accommodations—bunks cost $20 per person, and a private cabin for two with a view, $25–45 including meals (the bigger your group, the better the deal). Meals include fresh juices, fruits, vegetables, and eggs from neighboring farms, and of course, homegrown organic coffee. A gorgeous camping area features tent sites ($7 pp, bring your own gear) and a roofed picnic table in the middle of a coffee and banana grove. You can book a variety of package tours, and get a detailed breakdown of pricing at their website.

If you have a vehicle with moderate clearance (and four-wheel drive for the rainy season), FEV is a 40-minute drive from San Ramón. Follow the road to Yucúl, then turn left and follow the signs to the *finca*. By bus, take the Pancasan–El Jobo bus from the COTRAN Guanuca terminal in Matagalpa, and get off in Yucúl past San Ramón; then follow the signs to FEV, a beautiful 3.5-kilometer uphill walk that should take under an hour. Don't forget a long-sleeved shirt and a rain jacket.

RÍO BLANCO AND CERRO MUSÚN

Cerro Musún, one of Nicaragua's youngest and least visited parks, encompasses the 1,460-meter peak of the same name and is still the haunt of some of Central America's more elusive mammals, like the puma. In 2004, however, Musín ("water mountain" in Nahuatl) lived up to its name when heavy rains caused several of its lower slopes to collapse, destroying several hillside communities in a massive mudslide.

The town of Río Blanco is your jumping-off point for hikes in this tremendous reserve area. Rest and feed up at **Hotel y Restaurante Bosawas** (tel. 505/2778-0914 or 505/8856-9884, $15 with fan, $20 with a/c), or at the rudimentary **Hospedaje Blanco** ($5), before tackling hikes up to the seven waterfalls or the peak itself. Your hikes start at the FUNDENIC guide station (about one km out of town), where you can hire a guide to lead you through the reserve (from $10/day).

While you're in town, check out the statues in the Catholic church, artifacts from the pre-Columbian civilizations that occupied these lands. They left behind some petroglyphs at the river's edge (visible only during the dry season). Start searching near the red hanging bridge on the exit to Barrio Martin Centeno.

Two express buses leave for Río Blanco from Managua's Mayoreo terminal around noon; additional service is available from the COTRAN Guanuca in Matagalpa.

BOCANA DE PAÍWAS AND MULUKUKU

Bocana de Paíwas has a *hospedaje* and several restaurants, including the well-liked **Restaurante Mirador,** located on a long peninsula overlooking the Río Grande de Matagalpa. This is also the site of some pre-Columbian petroglyphs, tucked into the rocks alongside the Río Grande de Matagalpa.

Mulukuku was founded primarily to support a Sandinista military base in the 1980s, but quickly became a refugee center for those fleeing battles farther north; today's descendants of that time live in a humble but vivacious village on the edge of the mighty Río Tuma.

Mulukuku is well known for one of its expat residents, Doña Dorotea, a nurse born in 1930 who's lived and worked in the community for decades. Because of her work with Sandinista charities, she became a target for former president Alemán's political mischief and blind personal vengeance—he even ordered her deported after falsely accusing her of performing abortions. Over a period of several weeks in 2001, Dorotea's fellow townspeople rallied behind her as Alemán continued threatening to throw her out of Nicaragua and she pleaded that she had nowhere else to go. Though she was never deported, she spent several frustrating years hassling with her residency permit and is finally back in Mulukuku and continuing her work; Alemán was never asked to explain.

◪ LA SOMBRA ECOLODGE

Intimately connected to the Contra war of years past, El Tuma–La Dália are local commercial centers serving the local farming region. Both host resettlement camps where Contras gave up their weapons in exchange for a piece of land to farm. The La Sombra Ecolodge (tel. 505/8455-3732 or 505/8468-6281, sombra_ecolodge@yahoo.es, www.lasombraecolodge.com, $40–50) is an ecotourist facility set in a private forest reserve on about 200 hectares of shade-grown coffee and hardwoods. Stay in their enormous, wooden lodge house, with spacious balconies overlooking the greenery, where the price includes three meals and coffee, tours, and a guided trip to Peñas Blancas—well worth it, and the guides do a commendable job of interpreting the local ecosystem for you. They also lead guided trips on horseback, and more.

About 10 kilometers (15 minutes) southwest of La Dália, Piedra Luna is a rainy season—only swimming hole formed by the waters of the Río Tuma swirling around a several-ton rock sitting midstream. The swimming hole is easily seven meters deep, and local kids come from all over to dive off the rock into the pool. How did the rock get there? Ask the locals, who will relate the fantastic legend of the spirits that carried it there from someplace far away.

SANTA EMILIA AND EL CEBOLLÁL WATERFALL

The farming community of Santa Emilia is marked by a left turn at about Km 145; a bit farther, you'll find a 15-meter waterfall spilling impressively into a wide hole flanked by thick vegetation and a dark, alluring rock overhang. The falls are known alternately as Salto de Santa Emilia and Salto el Cebollál. Access is

just beyond the Puente Yasica, a bridge at about Km 149; look for a small house and parking area on the right, where a soft-drink sign reads "Balneario El Salto de Santa Emilia." You'll be asked to pay a $1 parking fee unless you're just jumping off the Tuma–Dália bus.

PEÑAS BLANCAS

Located on the road that leads between El Tuma–La Dália and El Cuá, the cliffs of Peñas Blancas (1,445 meters) are several hundred meters high and carved out of the top of a massive hillside. This is unquestionably one of the most stunning natural sights in northern Nicaragua and the widely respected Gateway to Bosawás. At the top of the cliff is a waterfall, gorgeous and little known, even by Nicaraguans who live outside of the immediate area. The cliffs and waterfall are easily visible from the highway, next to property owned by Alan Ball. He's currently developing hikes and tours to

Balneario El Salto de Santa Emilia

© JOSHUA BERMAN

the waterfall, but you can be proactive and get there yourself by asking around.

Getting there by yourself requires some effort—it's much easier to rely on a local provider like La Sombra Ecolodge in Tuma–La Dalia. Take the El Cuá–Bocay bus from Matagalpa (leaves Guanuca station at 7 A.M.), and about an hour after La Dália, get off at the entrance to the reserve and Centro de Entendimiento con la Naturaleza. From there, ask for the best route to the falls. The hike is only possible in the dry season, and there is no well-established trail to the falls. The walk is worth it, as you'll pass through a series of humid forest ecosystems of orchids and mossy trees. Near the falls, the wind is full of spray. The hike up and down can be done in two hours, but expect to get extremely muddy and wet. A Matagalpa-bound bus will pass the entrance to the reserve at 2 P.M. Peñas Blancas is run by a *cooperativa* and costs about $5 to go up with a guide. There are screened-in cabins for hikers that want to stay the night.

OLD MATAGALPA-JINOTEGA HIGHWAY

The sinuous mountain road between Matagalpa and Jinotega is considered one of the most scenic roads in all of Nicaragua. The road was first opened around 1920 by the English immigrant and coffee farmer Charles Potter for use by mules and wagons taking coffee from his farm to Matagalpa. No small feat of engineering, the road had to negotiate over 100 curves, the worst of which was the Disparate de Potter (still legendary). A stubborn old man, Potter built his road in spite of the naysayers, and it's said he used the road to carry a piano—strung atop two mules—all the way to his farm.

The long valley panoramas are often breathtaking: Momotombo and the Maribio volcanoes are visible when the sky is clear. You'll pass neatly arranged coffee plantations shaded by windrows of cedar and pine, banana trees, and canopies of precious hardwoods. There is also an endless succession of vegetable and flower fields, and roadside stands that sell farm-fresh goods. Should you take the express bus, you'll miss the opportunity to stop and take photographs, buy fresh vegetables, and hike into the coffee plantations. But if you drive, you may need to concentrate on the road so much that you'll miss the scenery. Jinotega and Matagalpa are the two most copious producers of vegetables in Nicaragua, and a set of small farm stands along the road are evidence of the rich harvests of this area. Whether you want to eat them or just photograph them, the stacks of fresh cabbage, carrots, broccoli, radishes, beets, lettuce, squash, and greens are a culinary feast for the eyes. The stands are typically run by the family's older children, who might just sweet-talk you into making a purchase.

◖ HOTEL DE MONTAÑA SELVA NEGRA

Hotel de Montaña Selva Negra (tel. 505/2772-3883/5713, reservaciones@selvanegra.com, www.selvanegra.com) has been an anchor in Nicaragua's tourism scene since well before there ever *was* a tourism scene. With a name meaning Black Forest, it remains popular for people looking to hike, dine, and monkey-watch, though San Ramón and La Sombra now provide some healthy competition.

The resort is, at its heart, a coffee farm by the name of La Hammonia, owned and run by Eddy Kühl and Mausi Hayn, third- and fourth-generation German immigrants and members of the founding families of the country's coffee industry. The farm—considered one of the most diversified in Central America, and winner of the 2007 Sustainability Award from the Specialty Coffee Association of America—is based on the German tradition of chalets set around a peaceful pond with access to short hiking trails up the adjoining 120-hectare hillside and along its ridge. Rooms run from $10 for a spot in the youth hostel to $45 for a

MATAGALPA

© GRACE GONZALEZ

Vast stretches of woodlands line the old Matgalpa-Jinotega Highway.

in the United States). The entrance to Selva Negra is marked by an old military tank on the side of the road, a relic from the revolution and painted over with the rainbows of Doña Violeta's UNO coalition in the early 1990s.

Selva Negra is a birder's paradise with some 200 species of birds that have been identified. You can see a list of identified bird species on their website, and try to spot them with one of the professionally trained bird guides. Tours of the coffee farm, flower plantations, the cattle, and livestock start at 9 A.M. and 3 P.M.— in Spanish, English, and German when Mausi is available. Almost everything on the farm is recycled, even down to using plastic bottles as pest control. The tour is an amazing education in permaculture and innovative organic methods. Or you can easily rent a horse for the day and ride the many roads that crisscross the plantation on your own. In 2000, the Kühls built a gorgeous, orchid-adorned stone chapel for the wedding of their daughter, and they now rent out the facilities—chapel, horse-drawn carriage, and fresh-cut flowers—for guests who come to get hitched.

double overlooking the lake, or from $85 for a private bungalow. There are larger bungalows for groups and families. The restaurant serves hearty, home-cooked meals using organic ingredients produced entirely on the farm; you'll dine on a gorgeous outdoor patio overlooking the water. Needless to say, the coffee is superb and fresh (and sold at Whole Foods Market

Expect to have a chat with the owners while you're there—Eddy is a wealth of knowledge, a prolific writer, and a well-loved amateur anthropologist; many of the family's ideas have come from the suggestions and talent of the guests who visit them.

Jinotega City

When walking the cobbled streets of Jinotega, you can't help but feel you're at the edge of the world, with all kinds of unknowns in the hills to the north and east. In fact, hundreds of kilometers of wild, lush mountain country beckon to the east. East of the city the pavement stops, the roads turn rutted and bumpy, bus service is less frequent, and the accommodations dwindle—at least the kind where they

leave a mint on your pillow and fold the edge of the toilet paper into a little triangle. But the immense department of Jinotega is made up of hundreds of small communities and thousands of farmers who make their livelihood in the hills around them—including many who have barely ever traveled beyond this land in their lives. Jinotega is replete with fragrant valleys of orange groves, white corn, plantains,

MATAGALPA

sweet vegetables, and a whole lot of cattle. But in between the small farms, Jinotega is open space—virgin forest, small freshwater lagoons, stately mountain ranges, and some of the loveliest rivers in Nicaragua, including the mighty Río Coco (which forms the northern border of the Jinotega department) and the Río Bocay, one of the Coco's most important tributaries.

Jinotega, or La Ciudad de las Brumas (the City of Mists), is the watering hole and commercial center for the department of the same name. Farmers from the north and east inevitably find their way here to do their business and trading, and Jinotega City has built itself into a clean, prosperous community around the business needs of those farmers. It's a working town whose streets are lined with cobblers, tailors, barbers, blacksmiths, watch repairers, and merchants who deal in housewares, veterinary supplies, saddles, cowboy hats, firearms, auto parts, and an endless stock of farming tools. It's a town very much in tune with the rugged and self-sufficient life of the Nicaraguan *campesino,* and you will learn much just by wandering its streets among such hardy characters. Jinotega, your gateway to the wide-open expanses of the east, is at once charming and thrilling. As late as the mid-1960s, it wasn't uncommon to find wild monkeys in the old-growth park canopy of *lechito* trees.

Travelers enjoy Jinotega because its high elevation (a full kilometer above sea level) gives it a pleasant climate, especially nice in the picturesque setting. Jinoteganos themselves are at once friendly and aloof—they might leave you to your own, but if you make the effort to talk to them, you'll find them warm, open, and full of country hospitality.

HISTORY

The name Jinotega is said to come from the Nahuatl name Xilotl-Tecatl ("place of the jiñocuabo trees"; also translated as "the place of the eternal men and women"). Indeed, the natives who lived in this peaceful valley enjoyed healthy and prosperous existences and were known to live to more than 100 years of age. Today's department of Jinotega was in those days the border between two diverse indigenous peoples: to the north, in the Bocay region, lived the Chontales (Kiribie) people, and near the present-day city of Jinotega, the Chorotega. They were an agricultural people who lived off small plots of corn, beans, cacao, roots, tubers, and fruit orchards. They wove their own clothing from wood and cotton fiber, as well as animal skins tinted with plant extracts. In the late 18th century, the Spanish chose to inhabit the southern part of Jinotega, forcing the indigenous peoples to move north. The community was officially recategorized as the Valley of Jinotega in 1851, and as a city in 1883.

For better or for worse, nearly every major armed uprising in recent Nicaraguan history began in the Jinotega department. The young Sandinistas first took to the hills here to battle squadrons of the National Guard in the 1960s, and when the Sandinistas took power, the first groups of Contras took to the hills, again in Jinotega. At the end of the Contra war, the two groups that refused to lay down their weapons and accept the peace treaty (the Recompas and Recontras) fled back into the mountains of Jinotega to keep up their fight.

For most of the 1990s, remnants of fighting groups, like FUAC, plagued certain wilder areas of northeastern Jinotega, hassling the peace-loving Jinotegan farmers trying to raise crops and their families at the same time. Jinotega was possibly the worst-affected department in Nicaragua during the 1980s, as Contras and Sandinistas fought each other on the mountain roads and the deep valleys. In those days, there was only one bus per day between the city of Jinotega and Managua (as compared to one every hour now), and travelers intent on driving their own vehicles ran the daily risk of being ambushed, robbed, raped,

MATAGALPA

MATAGALPA

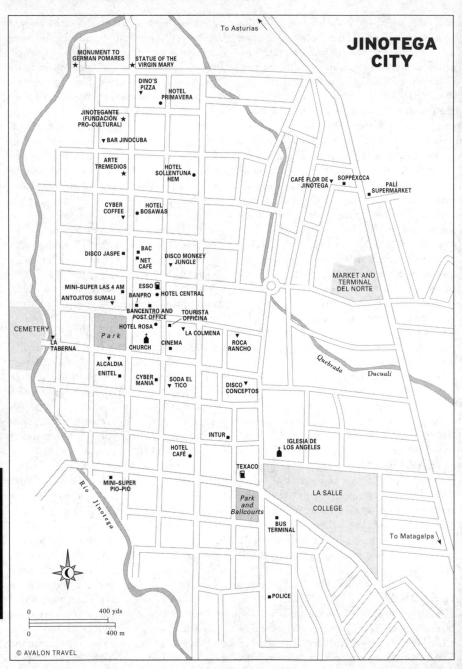

JINOTEGA
CITY

To Asturias

MONUMENT TO GERMAN POMARES ★
STATUE OF THE VIRGIN MARY ★
DINO'S PIZZA ▼
HOTEL PRIMAVERA ●
JINOTEGANTE (FUNDACIÓN PRO-CULTURAL) ★
▼ BAR JINOCUBA
ARTE TREMEDIOS ★
HOTEL SOLLENTUNA HEM ●
CAFÉ FLOR DE JINOTEGA
SOPPEXCCA ■
PALÍ SUPERMARKET ■
CYBER COFFEE ▼
HOTEL BOSAWAS ●
DISCO JASPE ■
BAC ■
NET CAFÉ ■
DISCO MONKEY JUNGLE ▼
MARKET AND TERMINAL DEL NORTE
MINI–SUPER LAS 4 AM ■
ANTOJITOS SUMALI ■
ESSO 🏪
HOTEL CENTRAL ●
BANPRO ●
BANCENTRO AND POST OFFICE
TOURISTA OFFICINA ▼
HOTEL ROSA ■
LA COLMENA ▼
CEMETERY
LA TABERNA ▼
Park
CHURCH ✝
CINEMA ■
ROCA RANCHO ▼
Quebrada Ducualí
ALCALDIA ■
ENITEL ■
CYBER MANIA ▼
SODA EL TICO ▼
DISCO CONCEPTOS ▼
INTUR ■
HOTEL CAFÉ ●
IGLESIA DE LOS ANGELES ✝
TEXACO ⛽
MINI–SUPER PIO–PIO ■
Río Jinotega
Park and Ballcourts
LA SALLE COLLEGE
BUS TERMINAL ■
To Matagalpa
POLICE ■

0   400 yds
0   400 m

© AVALON TRAVEL

or killed. Since the 1980s, Jinotega has voted steadfastly against the Sandinistas, who they claim are responsible for 10 years of devastation. The survivors of the generation that was marched off to the mountains as machine-gun fodder are resentful and frustrated now, robbed of their adolescence, and desperately trying to make a decent, honest living off the land.

ORIENTATION AND GETTING AROUND

Jinotega occupies the bottom of the steep-walled bowl formed by the mountains that surround it on all sides. The highway passes along its east side, and the cemetery is at the western edge. It's a city with a pleasant, cool climate and not too much vehicular traffic, both of which make it a pleasurable city for walking. There are no city buses, nor is there need for them.

There are several taxi cooperatives that circulate the city streets and that will take you across town for $0.50. But Jinotega isn't a big place, and the temperature never gets hot enough to be unpleasant. You should be able to walk anywhere you need to go.

SIGHTS

There are few traditional tourist sights in Jinotega, but lots to see and do. Jinotega was the scene of a few ferocious battles during the revolution years, and it was down by the riverside in Jinotega where much-loved Sandinista commander **German Pomares** (a.k.a. El Danto) was killed in battle. Pomares and his troops had fought many battles against Somoza's National Guard and had been instrumental in the operation that led to political prisoner Daniel Ortega's release from jail. His sacrifice has not been forgotten, and a very carefully maintained red-and-black memorial marks the spot where he was killed.

Don Pilo is a second-generation medicine man who lives in an unknown location in the mountains west of Jinotega city. Twice weekly, he climbs down out of the mountains with his bags of herbs and potions and sets up camp at the cemetery to sell them. He's a well-loved town character who some put off as a charlatan, and others consider a true magician and physician. Regardless, both rich and poor wait for him Tuesday and Friday to see if he can cure their ills, from intestinal parasites and coughs to bad marriages, naughty children, and spurned lovers. And you don't need a prescription, just a strong stomach. The cures are all natural and brewed out of the stronger medicinal plants of the region, plus bark, moss, and sometimes even soil.

Artes Treminio (two blocks south of the BAC bank, tel. 505/8619-3493, 8 A.M.–6 P.M. daily) is a gallery-cum-cultural center, where you can appreciate (or purchase) canvases and sculptures by a variety of local artists. On the last Saturday of each month, the venue hosts a *Noche Cultural Tertulia,* uniting local creatives with an evening of music, poetry and dance.

ENTERTAINMENT AND EVENTS

The best bar in town is the biker hangout **La Taberna** (on the right just before the cemetery gate, open Tues.–Sun.), serving food, booze, and a list of unique cocktails. This place takes the cowboy motif to an extreme with a woven bamboo roof and barstools with saddles. However, the carefully partitioned and cozy feel lends a romantic air. Also a friendly bar, **Roca Rancho** (a couple blocks east of the park across from the Beneficio Ducalí, tel. 505/2782-3730, noon–midnight daily) is a unique space where the beer flows smoothly and you sit in a kingly, high-backed bar stool.

There are two small discos in town. Start with the tried-and-true **Conceptos,** not far from the center of town, formerly a house but was converted into a dance hall with a house-party feel. Newer and more modern **Monkeys Jungle** is a half-block north of the downtown Esso in an old theater.

Jinotega's *fiestas patronales* begin on May

BEN LINDER (1959-1987)

As the only reported incident in which a United States citizen was killed by Contra soldiers, Benjamin Linder's death had enormous repercussions, stemming primarily from the fact that he was shot with weaponry purchased by his own government, and by soldiers carrying out a hotly contested policy of violence supported by the same government. Linder's death was elevated to the status of martyrdom by those who shared his values. He was one individual in a huge wave of international supporters of the Sandinista revolution, leftists from Europe and North America who saw a chance to take part in the real-world political laboratory of Nicaragua. Some came to make a stand against the policies of the Reagan administration; some to physically help as development workers, teachers, and coffee pickers; and some came simply to experience the new world order at ground level.

Oregon native Ben Linder graduated from the University of Washington in 1983 with a degree in mechanical engineering, and because he believed in the ideals of the revolution, came to Nicaragua like thousands of other *internacionalistas* to help the revolution reach the poor. He moved to Nicaragua shortly after graduation, where he shared a small apartment in the capital and worked for the electric company. In his free time he would delight the Nicaraguan children by dressing up in a clown suit and rubber nose and pedaling around on a unicycle.

In mid-1985 Linder moved to Jinotega to help install a minihydroelectric plant in the town of El Cuá. This was an area overrun with raiding Contras, and the danger in the region was real. But rather than avoid the danger, his engineer's passion for solving problems led Ben farther into the bush, to San José de Bocay, to repeat the success he'd had at El Cuá. Bocay was even farther out of Sandinista control than El Cuá, and the Contras were everywhere. On April 28, 1987, Linder and a crew of Nicaraguans went into the field to build a small concrete weir that would measure the flow in a stream Linder thought would be a good site for a hydroelectric plant. His crew crossed paths with a squadron of Contras that had been stalking Sandinista supporters. He, and several others with him, were assassinated at point blank range.

The political repercussions were enormous and the Sandinistas, the Contras, and the U.S. government all angrily accused each other. Though the Contras claimed that Linder had been dressed in combat uniform, was carrying a weapon, and that Linder's team had fired the first shots, the evidence did not support it. That an American had been killed in Nicaragua, with a bullet also paid for by the American people, resonated deeply.

Linder was buried in a small, neat grave in the Malagalpa cemetery. Today, his legend and inspiration live on; if you wander through the peaceful community of San José de Bocay, you'll notice the town has been electrified, courtesy of the Benjamin Linder Mini-Hydroelectric Power Plant, constructed after his death. The Benjamin Linder School is down the road, and one of Bocay's more newly settled neighborhoods was christened Barrio Benjamin Linder.

Today, the Asociación de Trabajadores de Desarrollo Rural Benjamin Linder (The Benjamin Linder Association of Development Workers) continues to do what Linder was doing the day he was killed: build small-scale hydroelectric plants to promote rural development. The association is located 25 meters south of the Hotel Bermúdez (tel. 505/2612-2030) in Matagalpa and is managed by Linder's coworker Rebecca Leaf. To learn more about Ben, visit the Quaker House in Managua, the Ben Linder Café in León, or read the book *The Death of Ben Linder: The Story of a North American in Sandinista Nicaragua* by Joan Kruckewitt (Seven Stories Press, 2001).

The streets of Jinotega don't see a lot of traffic.

1 and continue through May 15. You can expect to see folks from all over the north of Nicaragua showing up for the occasion. The *fiestas patronales* of San Juan de Jinotega are June 24. In addition (perhaps just to round out the year with parties), the Aniversario de la Creación del Departamento de Jinotega is celebrated on October 15.

SPORTS AND RECREATION

Basketball is the game of choice in Jinotega, and there are pickup games most evenings on the *cancha* (town court). Jinotega has an active youth league and both women's and men's teams; the players are better than you'd expect, if you're thinking about getting in a game.

Hiking

The western wall of the Jinotega valley makes a popular climb for a Saturday morning. Start at the cemetery and work your way upward to **Peña de la Cruz,** where the cross is planted.

Depending on how ambitious you are, the hike is 30–90 minutes, and you'll be rewarded with an impressive view of the city and the verdant valley of Jinotega. The cross isn't the original—locals say its predecessor was bigger and "better"—but the modern cross is illuminated, thanks to an electric cable that climbs the same steep hillside you just did. Look for the shining beacon of Christianity at night from the city. During misty nights, it's particularly eerie, emitting a diffuse white glow through the mists.

The eastern wall of the valley is steeper and longer, and there are no trails. That doesn't stop many locals from making their way to the top for a look around. Plan on two hours for this one. The easiest way to do it is via the steep, winding dirt road that climbs abruptly out of the city and snakes its way to the top of the ridge. By road, it's around an hour on foot, but it's still not an easy walk, as the road is exceptionally steep. Watch your step on the loose gravel.

ACCOMMODATIONS

Keep in mind that until recently, Jinotega's chief clientele were the small-scale farmers of the east who come in for weekends at a time to see a dentist, sell some corn, and have their boots fixed. They don't require many luxuries and don't want to waste too many *córdobas* while they're in town, as evidenced by all the under-$3 *hospedajes* that spot the neighborhood around the market. The following are some more "upscale" options. As you choose your lodging, remember to ask about hot water: this is one of the few areas in Nicaragua where you'll want it.

Under $10

Hotel Rosa (one block south of the Esso gas station, no tel.) is the oldest gig in town, and more than a hundred years ago, when it first opened its doors, it was the only gig in town. Its 19th-century feel remains in massive wooden beams and simple rustic rooms. Somewhat dark and dingy, the 30 rooms cost $4–10 per person.

Toward the north end of town, but still in a quiet residential area, **Hotel Primavera** (tel. 505/2782-2400, $7 per person) is run by a family that expects you to behave; the 28 small rooms set around a courtyard are nothing special, but they're clean, simple, and cheap. There are also rooms with private bath for a relatively steep $12–15. Inside the family's living room, there's a pay phone available. The doors close at 10 P.M. and don't open until morning—make sure you're on the right side of the door and mind the sign "No Women of Bad or Dubious Conduct."

$10-25

Hotel Sollentuna Hem (two blocks east of Artes Treminio, tel. 505/2782-2334, $18–25) is owned by a Swedish-Nica woman—the name is Swedish for "home of the green valley." In business since 1988, the hotel has 17 different rooms that are Scandinavian clean, with a quirky, mismatched style and with private baths, hot water, and Wi-Fi access. Breakfast ($4) is available, and

meals can accommodate vegetarians. Complete laundry service is also offered, as are tours of the farm on the outskirts of town.

Four kilometers outside of town, on the old road to Matagalpa, is a truly unique escape. **Biosfera Hospedaje Montañero Lodge** (tel. 505/8698-1439, info@hijuela.com, www.hijuela.com, $12/s dorm beds, $6/s with work exchange) is an educational eco-adventure retreat. The lodge here offers rustic, environmentally friendly (but comfortable) accommodation, home-cooked exotic meals (Indonesian, Mediterranean, etc., under $5), motorcycle tours, camping, and hiking. Expect to roll up your sleeves and work, but you'll get a discount and maybe have some fun. Reiki and herbal cleansings are also available (email owner Suzanne for more details).

$25-50

Hotel Campestre La Quinta (two blocks north of the Virgin Mary statue, tel. 505/2782-2522, $20–45) offers nine dark but tidy rooms in a ramshackle house. The onsite restaurant doubles as a disco on Saturday evenings, while the garden pool proves popular with families during the weekend's daylight hours.

Jinotega's classiest accommodation, the ◖**Hotel Café** (one block west, a half-block north of the Texaco station, tel. 505/2782-2710, www.cafe-hoteljinotega.com, $60) stands head and shoulders above the rest with its 16 tidy, comfortable, and tastefully decorated rooms. The hotel takes up two stories, surrounding a lush garden and spiral staircase. The rooms feature private baths, hot water, cable TV, telephones, desks, and air-conditioning; minisuites are a few bucks more, continental breakfast included. You'll also find valet parking and laundry service. Hotel Café accommodates groups and has a conference room, business center, and some great views of the surrounding city and countryside, as well as Jinotega's nicest restaurant and bar.

FOOD

Meals are simple but hearty in this neck of the woods. There are few fine dining options; after dark the streets fill with *fritangas,* while families open their front doors to create cheap eateries in their living rooms and front parlors. Start at the southeast corner of the park and troll the two main streets through a sea of enchiladas, *papas rellenas* (stuffed and fried potatoes), and *gallo pinto* (the national dish of rice and beans).

Soda El Tico, just east of the park, is a local lunch favorite and has a clean and inexpensive lunch buffet and simple menu ($3–6).

Look for **Dino's Pizza** (half a block south of the Virgin Mary statue, 8 A.M.–10 P.M. daily), serving a variety of thin-crust pies ($7–11), as well as pasta, lasagna, and quesadillas that could feed a small army. You'll find excellent, reasonably priced meals and a friendly open-air atmosphere at **Roca Rancho** (tel. 505/2782-3730, noon–midnight daily); local volunteers rave about the jalapeño steak.

Restaurante La Colmena (The Beehive) is one of the nicest restaurants in town with a menu of beef, chicken, and fish ($5–12), good service, and a pleasant atmosphere. A close rival is the **Restaurante Borbón** at the Hotel Café (tel. 505/2782-2710, www.cafehoteljinotega. com), with sandwiches and meals ($7–15), and a full wine and foreign drink list at the bar. The chicken cordon bleu is spectacular.

For baked goods hit **Repostería Silvia** next to the BAC. Be sure not to miss C **Cafe Flor de Jinotega,** a small-scale coffee producers' cooperative located next to the SOPPEXCCA coffee exchange. Here you can have a cappuccino as good as any in Nicaragua, peruse educational displays on coffee and coffee economics, and check out packages as they're sold in the U.S. Hit it before or after you get on the bus for the hinterlands at COTRAN Norte.

INFORMATION AND SERVICES
One locally produced online portal is **www. jinotegalife.com.** Also check out the **Alianza Turística,** one block east and one block south of the church.

Not only does **Luis Lautaro Ruiz** (tel. 505/2782-4460, goyomiel@yahoo.com) seemingly know all there is to know about his native Jinotega and the surrounding mountains, he speaks some English and is a professional writer, film producer, musician, and clown. As a flexible freelance tour guide, he charges comparable prices to guides in Managua ($15–20 a day). He also claims his house, located a half-block north of the Escuela Mistral, is a museum.

Banks
There's a bank on practically every corner in Jinotega. All the major players are present— Banpro, Bancentro, BAC, and more. Bank hours are standard; check your firearm at the door, please. The most reliable ATM is found at BAC, 1.5 blocks north of the central park.

Media and Communications
Internet access rates are standard at about $0.25 per hour. **Cybermania,** across from Soda El Tico has plenty of computers with a fast connection. **Cyber Coffee** (one block north of the BAC bank, 8 A.M.–9 P.M. daily) doesn't actually sell coffee but the computers are new and the connection is speedy.

The **ENITEL** office (7 A.M.–5 P.M. daily) is located just north of the park along the main street. The **post office** (8 A.M.–4 P.M.) is a bit hard to find: It's tucked into a business complex behind Bancentro. As you're facing the front door of the bank, look for a sidewalk that leads behind the building to the offices that are part of the same complex. A fax machine is available.

GETTING THERE
Buses at the Terminal del Sur head south to Matagalpa and Managua, including several express buses that make one stop along the highway at Matagalpa without entering the city itself, then continuing straight on to Managua. Express buses to Managua ($4) leave every hour, and more express buses are being put into

service every day, so ask ahead of time to find out what your options are. These buses may or may not make a brief stop along the highway at Matagalpa before continuing straight on to Managua (3–4 hours).

To Points South

The bus terminal (actually, just a parking lot) is located across from La Salle (a Catholic high school). Several eateries line the road behind the station, where you can relax and wait for the bus to leave, as the terminal doesn't have any facilities for passengers. Buses to Matagalpa leave every half hour 5 A.M.–6 P.M. (the trip takes one hour). Buses leave for Estelí from the COTRAN Norte on a long, roundabout overland route that may require making a connection in La Concordia or San Rafael del Norte. It is much easier to get to Estelí by simply taking any Managua bus to Sébaco, and transferring to a northbound bus heading to Estelí, Ocotal, Somoto, or Jalapa.

To Points North and East

Buses at the Terminal del Norte go to points inland in Jinotega and beyond, including El Cuá, San José de Bocay, San Rafael del Norte, and Wiwilí. This is where the adventure starts, and the rugged conditions at the terminal should prepare you mentally for what awaits you inland: mud, livestock, and a lot of friendly people moving sacks of produce, selling grains and cheap merchandise, and laughing. There are five express buses for Estelí, 5:15 A.M.–3:30 P.M. There are 10 regular buses for San Rafael del Norte, starting at 6 A.M. with the last bus at 6 P.M. Regular buses for Wiwilí leave between 4 A.M. and 1:15 P.M. (seven hours). Regular service to El Cuá–Bocay begins daily at 4 A.M. for the four-hour trip. There is regular service to Pantasma about once per hour (two hours) until 4:40 P.M. Pantasma buses go past Asturias and the dam at Lago Apanás.

The northern terminal also has regular bus service to San Sebastián de Yalí and La Rica, via San Rafael del Norte and La Concordia, from where you can get back-road bus service to Estelí—a fun way to make a loop through some really beautiful country.

The Frontier: Beyond Jinotega

LA BASTILLA ECOLODGE

La Bastilla Ecolodge (tel. 505/2782-4335, www.bastillaecolodge.com, $15–40) boasts some of the oldest forest in the country. The lodge is situated high on a jungle hilltop inhabited by howler monkeys, fireflies, and a wealth of interesting mammals you're unlikely to see elsewhere. Birders will delight in the wealth of feathered visitors—if you get lucky, you may even spot the elusive resplendent Quetzal. Hikers enjoy access to seemingly endless trails of fairly dense jungle.

Cozy dorms (with private bathrooms and hot water) are a good deal at $15 per person, while the private cabins ($60 d) offer a greater feeling of seclusion. An open-air restaurant offers good meals of upscale *comida típica* ($5–10) made almost entirely from ingredients cultivated within the reserve. The staff consists of students from the attached farming/ecoschool; some of the proceeds from your stay goes toward their education.

The lodge is 15 kilometers from Jinotega, a 40-minute drive on an unpaved road that definitely requires four-wheel drive. Bring a flashlight, a thick sweater, and any food or supplies you might need—there's no shop within a 30-minute drive. Be sure to reserve your stay in advance, as the restaurant only operates when guests are expected.

EL VALLE DE TOMATOYA

Located just north of the city of Jinotega on the road to San Rafael del Norte, El Valle de Tomatoya is the home of a women's cooperative that produces the region's famous black pottery. The production of black pottery is a little more intricate than other types of ceramic arts, and these women have produced some very beautiful pieces of art, including faithful replicas of some pre-Columbian designs. **Grupo de Mujeres de Las Cureñas** has some fine pieces for sale.

Along the highway is **El Centro Recreativo de Tomatoya,** a bathing area created by damming up the San Gabriel stream. Your host, Blanca Dalla Torre, regularly empties out the pool and lets it refill with fresh water. Drinks and snacks are available, as well as a complete selection of beer.

LAGO DE APANÁS AND THE MANCOTAL DAM

Lake Apanás is the largest artificially constructed body of water in Nicaragua. Luís Somoza Debayle's administration created it in 1964 by damming the Río El Tuma, flooding the broad valley just north of Jinotega, which until that time was pasture, small farms, and an airstrip that serviced the north of Nicaragua. Today, Lake Apanás is a long, irregularly shaped lake. It feeds the twin turbines at the Planta Hidroelectrica Centroamérica, which produces 15 percent of the nation's hydropower (downstream along the Río Viejo, the same water passes through the turbines at Santa Bárbara and Lago La Virgen, which produce an additional 15 percent). Apanás is not a typical reservoir; unlike many hydropower plants that are located at the dam itself, the Planta Centroamérica is located at the upstream end of the lake, so keeping the lake full is essential.

Hurricane Mitch nearly sent the whole works downstream in 1998, when waters overtopping the "morning glory" spillway (the concrete structure that looks like a flying saucer on its head in the middle of the lake), flowed through the secondary spillway under the bridge, and down a long stair-step energy dissipater. The volume of water rushing through the channel quickly eroded it away along with all of its concrete, nearly destroying the dam itself and nearly causing a wall of water that would have raged for hundreds of kilometers downstream. The government has been negotiating since 1999 to find a way to repair the spillway and return the dam's safety structures to normal, while the IMF and World Bank have been trying to privatize the whole system.

To get to the dam, take any bus headed toward Pantasma and get off at Asturias (60–90 minutes from Jinotega). The highway crosses the dam, so you'll know when you've arrived. The lake itself is picturesque, but equally impressive are the remains of the damaged spillway. On the lake side of the road are the remains of an old military base built in the 1980s to prevent Contra troops from destroying the dam. (The Planta Centroamérica was a highly sought Contra target in the 1980s and was similarly tightly guarded to prevent its destruction. Some land mines still litter the hills around the hydropower plant.)

You can fish here, for giant tilapia and guapote, or take a dip. There are several grassy areas at the lake's edge where you can jump in the surprisingly cold water of Apanás. From the dam, walk along the highway in either direction and choose your place. The lake is safe—there are no underwater structures or water intakes to be afraid of, and the water is quite deep and refreshing. Obviously, stay away from the spillover drain.

LAGO ASTURIAS AND THE EL DORADO DAM

The El Dorado dam was completed in 1984 and filled in in 1985 as a supplement to the Mancotal Dam. Water is captured in Asturias and pumped up to Apanás, where it flows

MATAGALPA

through the turbines for energy production. Anglers in the know realize that Asturias is home to some monster freshwater fish. To get there from the Mancotal Dam, walk back toward the city of Jinotega about one kilometer to the first major intersection. That road descends quickly past a few coffee farms and small farming communities to the El Dorado Dam.

El Dorado also experienced severe damage during Hurricane Mitch. As you look at the lake, imagine that the same massive deluge that destroyed Mancotal's spillway also flowed through that placid little lake and out the other side—then appreciate how fortunate it is to have withstood the hurricane.

There's a little grassy hill on the upstream side of the dam where you can pitch a tent and do some fishing. If you'd like to try to hitch a ride with all your catch, occasional vehicles transit this road—mostly old IFAs and pickup trucks—bound for the communities east of El Dorado.

SAN RAFAEL DEL NORTE

This remote, cloud-shrouded town has a cool climate and is surrounded by green hills year-round. To know San Rafael is to know history. A visit to the **General Augusto César Sandino Museum** (right off the park) gives you a sample of the small town's pride at having served as the proving grounds for the general's legendary battles with the U.S. Marines in the 1930s. Sandino's wife was a San Rafaelina, and Nicaraguan folk musician Carlos Mejía Godoy wrote moving lyrics about love and war in Sandino's hills there.

There are some precious swimming holes around San Rafael, the easiest of which to access are in the two creeks that meet at **Los Encuentros** restaurant, a 10-minute walk on the road to Yalí. You can also hike into the gorge that runs on the north edge of town; descend from the Hospedaje Rolinmar, and then start upstream to where cold water rushes out of a narrow canyon.

La Iglesia San Rafael del Norte is more impressive than you'd expect for such an out-of-the-way town; some call it the most beautiful church in all of Nicaragua. Pastel-colored windows admit a calming light in which to view the many bright murals, reliefs, and shrines. Many locals distinguish between Sandino the man and Sandinismo as practiced by Daniel Ortega. Look closely at the inside left wall of the church, where a painting of the devil implies that Daniel has betrayed the ideals of Sandino.

The church was a project of Italian priest Odorico d'Andrea who gave much more than that to this town. From his arrival in 1953 to his death in 1996, Father Odorico achieved virtual sainthood among the people of San Rafael and surrounding communities. His image, a smiling man in plain brown robes, can be seen in nearly every home, business, and vehicle in the town. Among his achievements are a health clinic, library, several neighborhoods for the poor, and the renovation of the church. Odorico's soul has multiplied posthumously; many believe he performed miracles and that his body has not decomposed. You can check for yourself at its resting place, the **Tepeyac** church, on the hill overlooking the town. Ascending the stairs, you'll pass the 12 stations of the cross until you reach the shrine on top where the tomb lies—as well as gorgeous views. An impressive stand of old trees shades the hilltop. Virgin pine forests carpet the countryside.

There are great eats at **Doña Chepita's,** and there are two places to stay. ◖ **Hotel Casita San Payo** (2.5 blocks north of the park, tel. 505/2784-2327) is a cute family-run place that doubles as a local watering hole. A room will run you $15–25, and you can get good meals here as well for $4–6. **Comedor y Hospedaje Aura** (on the main street east of church) is a typical Nicaraguan *hospedaje* catering more to the traveling *campesino* than foreign traveler. Just four kilometers north of town is the pine

boat traffic on the Río Bocay

canopy adventure **La Brellera** (tel. 505/2782-4335 or 8654-6235, $15 pp); look for the sign and kiosk on the right-hand side when entering from San Rafael. Zip across 1,500 meters of cable and 12 platforms through enormous pine trees, and across a pretty mountain valley. Those on a tight budget can try shorter versions of the tour just for $7–13.

Buses pass through San Rafael del Norte regularly en route between Jinotega and San Sebastián de Yalí/La Rica. There is also one express bus to Managua that leaves at 4:30 A.M., passes through Jinotega at 5:30 A.M., and continues south through Matagalpa to Managua. The same bus leaves Managua at 3 P.M. and retraces the route to San Rafael del Norte, arriving sometime after 7 P.M.

EL CUÁ, SAN JOSÉ DE BOCAY, AND AYAPAL

Two-and-a-half hours outside of Matagalpa, El Cuá is best known for Benjamin Linder, the only known American casualty of the Contra war. El Cuá and San José de Bocay are illuminated by minihydroelectric power plants he helped design and implement. Both towns were completely enveloped in conflict during the 1980s, overrun first by Contras and then by the FSLN. Today it's a logical place from which to hike, or just visit, the Peñas Blancas.

Of El Cuá's three *hospedajes,* travelers prefer **Hotel Chepita** (tel. 505/2784-5158 or 505/8437-1531, reservaciones@hotelchepita.com, www.hotelchepita.com), run by an affable, anglophone Nicaraguan woman by the name of Josefa. She has 16 rooms ($11 s, $22 d) with fan, TV, and Internet access.

There's one *hospedaje* in Bocay, a few small eateries, and a gas station.

Ayapal is a small community on the banks of the Río Bocay. From here, you can hire boats to take you downstream to several Miskito communities (not cheap), or visit the surprisingly expansive **Cuevas de Tunowalam,** a sandstone cave

MATAGALPA

© RANDALL WOOD

structure north of San José de Bocay. Guides are available through Hotel Chepita in El Cuá.

WIWILÍ

The upstream capital of the Río Coco region lies snug near the Honduran border and a long, bumpy, five-hour slog north of Jinotega. Wiwilí is a mestizo town, meaning it's of Spanish, not indigenous origin. Waspám, 550 kilometers downstream, is the other anchor at river's end, and is mostly indigenous.

Wiwilí is split by the Río Coco, which runs through the middle of town. Several hundred inhabitants of Wiwilí lost their lives to the river during Hurricane Mitch, and political fallout outlasted the storm. Post-Mitch, the two sides of the community went their own separate ways to find international aid, and subsequently decided to become independent. While they retained the same name, Wiwilí on the north side of the river is now part of the department of Madriz, while Wiwilí on the south bank remains part of Jinotega. Both are important port towns with access to the deep waters of the Río Coco.

Local coffee cooperative members can lead individuals or groups on community-led tours to nearby Kilambé National Park and other surrounding treasures. This is some truly wild country and few souls have attempted the epic six-day trip downstream to Waspám, braving crocodiles, bandits, and drug smugglers; there are reportedly guides that will take you on rafts, camping along the river, and hanging out with wandering dugout canoe–paddling fishermen, known as *nomados* by locals.

On the edge of the reserve, you'll find **Hospedaje Kilambé** (tel. 505/8410-9068 or 505/8410-9064, $25) offering a bed with private bathroom and meals ($3). There are a few decent *comedores* and a couple of crash pads in Wiwilí: **Hotel Central** ($6 bed with shared bath, $20 double with private bath) and **El Hotelito** ($7 standard singles with shared bath).

CHONTALES AND THE NICARAGUAN CATTLE COUNTRY

East of Lake Cocibolca lie hundreds of thousands of hectares of rolling hillside in a broad ecological transition zone where undulating, scrubby pastureland gradually unfolds into the pine savannas and wetlands of the Caribbean coast. Less populated than the Pacific region, in Chontales and Boaco residents are easily outnumbered by their cattle, and in reality it's the cattle that make this area famous. Chontales ranches produce more than 60 percent of Nicaragua's dairy products, including dozens of varieties of cheese and millions of gallons of milk.

This entire regions is firmly off the beaten path, so expect to be the only tourist for miles in most of the towns and sights in this region.

Overall, Boaco is less well-to-do and less enticing than relatively upscale Juigalpa, which dwarfs it in every sense. Boaco makes a reasonable base for treks or drives into the hills between Boaco and Matagalpa Departments. Juigalpa is a much bigger and much more important urban center that remains an overgrown cowboy village. Here you'll rub shoulders with cowboys and *campesinos* sporting their cleanest boots on their twice-a-month trip to the city to pick up supplies, strike a few deals, and do their errands.

Juigalpa's patron saint celebrations in mid-August are among the best in Nicaragua and draw a crowd from as far away as Managua to enjoy the elaborate bull-riding competitions,

© AMBER DOBRZENSKY

CHONTALES

HIGHLIGHTS

(Boaca *Fiestas Patronales*: Boaco's monthlong festival celebrates the town's patron saint with horse parades and colorful folk dances (page 275).

(Museo Arqueológico Gregorio Aguilar Barea: This warehouse of statuary is filled with treasures the Chontales carved long before Columbus (page 283).

(Juigalpa *Fiestas Patronales*: Juigalpa throws a cowboy party unsurpassed in the nation. Join Juigalpans for rodeo, mechanical bull-riding contests, and down-on-the-farm good times (page 285).

(Punta Mayales Nature Reserve: This isolated peninsula jutting into Lake Cocibolca is a fine example of rural tourism (page 287).

LOOK FOR (TO FIND RECOMMENDED SIGHTS, ACTIVITIES, DINING, AND LODGING.

horsemanship contests, and traditional dances, all under the magnificent backdrop of the Amerrisque mountain range. These mountains remain little explored, and the continual discovery of ancient Chontal statues and sculpture imply the grandeur of the mysteries this area still retains.

HISTORY

The lands now known as Boaco and Chontales were first settled by the Chontal people (not their own name for themselves—the word is Nahuatl for the "mountain people," implying "savages" or "foreigners"). Less is known about them than the Nahuatl, but we know

the Chontals were responsible for much of the statuary and stone monuments unearthed over the past decades in the Amerrisque mountain range north of the highway.

The first Spanish settlements of El Corregimiento de Chontales suffered often at the hands of aggressive Miskitos and Zambos (and the British who armed them), whose frequent attacks devastated 7 out of 12 Spanish settlements. In 1749, Camoapa, Boaco (today Boaco Viejo), and Juigalpa were attacked; the towns were nearly destroyed and the churches burned to the ground. Boaco's then-governor, Alonso Fernández de Heredia, returned the aggression, leading an excursion that returned with

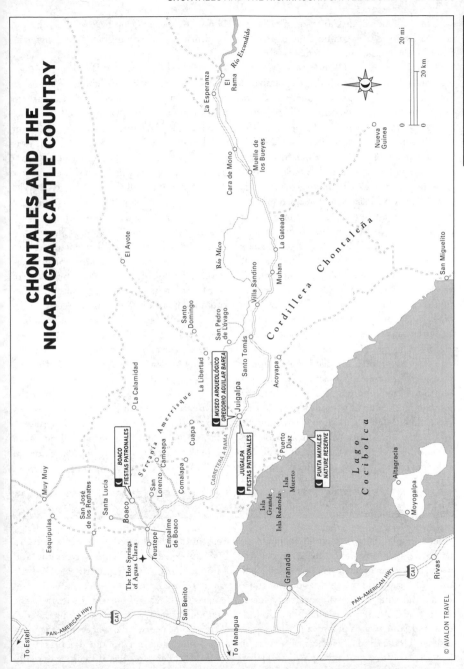

CHONTALES AND THE
NICARAGUAN CATTLE COUNTRY

© AVALON TRAVEL

more than a hundred Miskito prisoners. The settlers reestablished their communities eight kilometers to the south. Nothing remains of Boaco Viejo today. From 1750–1760, these same indigenous groups attacked Juigalpa, Camoapa, Lóvago, Lovigüisca, Yasica, Guabale, Santa Rosa, and nine other communities. In 1762, Boaco was reestablished by Father Cáceres, who was killed shortly thereafter by yet another Miskito attack. In 1782, the church in Juigalpa was—you guessed it—burned to the ground.

As the threat of attack diminished, the lands east of Lake Cocibolca were developed into extensive cattle ranches. Coffee was introduced around the Boaco area, but before long its production had been pushed up into the better lands in northern Boaco and southern Matagalpa. Cattle quickly became the economic mainstay, followed by the extraction of gold from the mines at La Libertad and Santo Domingo.

The social and economic reorganization of the Sandinista years earned the unbridled antipathy of the people of Chontales and Boaco, who were generally frontier-minded people uninterested in government regulation. As their lands were confiscated and reorganized, they naturally had more sympathy for the Contra forces, whom they clandestinely supported throughout much of the 1980s. Much of the violence of the 1980s occurred in the towns that border both sides of the highway and inland. Since the

1990s, both departments have voted against the Sandinista party with overwhelming margins.

PLANNING YOUR TIME

Many travelers treat this whole region as an uninteresting and unavoidable expanse to pass through as quickly as possible en route to Nicaragua's Atlantic coast, but the flavor of Chontales and Boaco play no small part in the flavor of Nicaragua as a whole—from the cowboys, to the wide open sky, to the pre-Columbian relics and the small-town lifestyle. Travelers who tire of the Granada hype and the overwhelming presence of other foreigners will be amply rewarded with a trip to Chontales.

How much time you'll need in this region depends on your inclination for adventure and ability to forgo some creature comforts. You could easily spend a day and a night in one of many quiet agrarian towns like Boaco, Camoapa, and Cuapa. The attraction is simply a bucolic, rural lifestyle. Most towns in the area have some sort of basic accommodation and small local sites of historical, cultural, or geologic interest. Add an additional day if the bouldering and hiking opportunities at Cuisaltepe or Cuapa whet your appetite, and another day on horseback in San José de los Remates (you can even continue on the high road to Matagalpa).

Boaco

Tucked snugly in a 379-meter-high notch in the Amerrisque Mountains, Boaco is a departmental capital, an agriculture center whose soil struggles to support both cattle and corn, and a commercial center beset with poverty. Modern Boaco (the city's name is a combination of Aztec and Sumu words that mean "land of the sorcerers") is the third city to bear the name: In the 18th and 19th century, two previous Boacos

were built and destroyed in the same place. In 1749, an expedition of Zumos, Miskitos, and Zambos armed with English rifles sacked the original Boaco, killed the priest, took several females hostage, and burned the town to the ground. The settlers started over along the edge of the Río Malacatoya in what's now the town of Boaquito, and in 1763, due to a brutal outbreak of cholera and the difficulties the land

© ESMIR CALDERON

Boaco was built on several levels of rolling hills.

presented for agriculture, moved to the present site of Boaco. By the 19th century, Boaco was a cow town, though residents raised several crops, including *cabuya,* for making rope, to sell in the markets of Masaya, a four-day mule-drawn wagon trip.

The modern city of Boaco began on a hilltop and crept down the hillside into a valley, earning the nickname The City of Two Floors. During the Contra war, Boaco was spared from direct battles, but in the hillsides that surrounded the city, Contras and Sandinistas fought skirmishes in Muy Muy, San José de los Remates, and San Francisco. The violence dislodged countless *campesinos,* all of whom eventually found their way to the city of Boaco seeking refuge. Many decided to stay, and Boaco has swelled over the past 20 years, faster than it can provide for its new inhabitants, most of whom occupy neighborhoods of small concrete homes around the outskirts of the city.

Boaco was an inspiration to several

notable Nicaraguan authors and scholars, four of whom—Diego Sequeira, Antonio Barquero, Hernan Robleto, and Julian N. Guerrero—won the Nicaraguan Rubén Darío prize for literature. A monument in their honor, just east and north of the park, overlooks the city from a sort of balcony.

Boaco's best mayor was a man of the cloth, Father Niebrowski of Poland, who arrived in 1916. While preaching to an underserved community, Niebrowski took it upon himself to better their lot in life and used his determination and practical know-how to bring Boaco into the modern world. Niebrowski built a cinema, a brick factory whose bricks he used to rebuild the church, and a small hydropower plant on the Río Fonseca, which provided electric light to the city for the first time. Niebrowski also established the first hospital, the first community music band, and countless other things that contributed to Boaco's social welfare. To this day, the Niebrowski Foundation is active

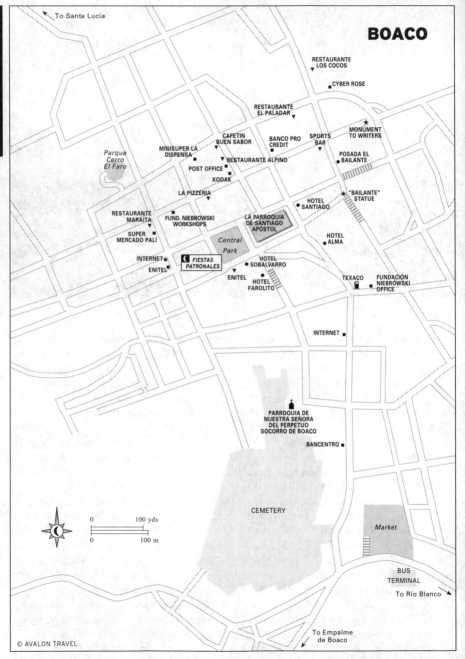

BOACO

To Santa Lucía

RESTAURANTE LOS COCOS

CYBER ROSE

RESTAURANTE EL PALADAR

Parque Cerro El Faro

MINISUPER LA DISPENSA

CAFETIN BUEN SABOR

BANCO PRO CREDIT

SPORTS BAR

MONUMENT TO WRITERS

POSADA EL BAILANTE

POST OFFICE

RESTAURANTE ALPINO

KODAK

LA PIZZERIA

"BAILANTE" STATUE

HOTEL SANTIAGO

RESTAURANTE MARAITA

FUND. NIEBROWSKI WORKSHOPS

LA PARROQUIA DE SANTIAGO APÓSTOL

SUPER MERCADO PALÍ

Central Park

HOTEL ALMA

INTERNET

FIESTAS PATRONALES

ENITEL

HOTEL SOBALVARRO

ENITEL

HOTEL FAROLITO

TEXACO

FUNDACIÓN NIEBROWSKI OFFICE

INTERNET

PARROQUIA DE NUESTRA SEÑORA DEL PERPETUO SOCORRO DE BOACO

BANCENTRO

0   100 yds
0   100 m

CEMETERY

Market

BUS TERMINAL

To Río Blanco

To Empalme de Boaco

© AVALON TRAVEL

in the city and provides for small programs in the Boaco area, while the church, factory, and hydropower plant have all faded into memory.

SIGHTS

Boaco's churches neatly serve the residents of Boaco's two levels without their having to traipse up and down the hill. In the lower half, the **Parroquia de Nuestra Señora del Perpetuo Socorro de Boaco** is an elaborate nontraditional church whose architecture is nearly Greek orthodox. A statue of the Virgin Mary keeps watch over the earth from its starched white rooftop. Inside, statues of Jesus and the Virgin Mary line up side by side with the carved stone statuary of Boaco's Chontal and Sumu ancestors, an intriguing compromise between the religions of new and old. A statue located one block east of the church represents a dancer, complete with snake stick in one hand and brass knuckles in the other.

© AMBER DOBRZENSKY

This cowboy town is a good place to pick up a saddle.

The freshly painted **Parroquia de Santiago Apóstol,** located at the top of the hill, has been a Boaco landmark since the mid-1800s. Mass is held every day, with several masses held on the weekends, when the ringing of the church bells fills the town square and scatters the pigeons. The square, also known as the **Niebrowski** central park, is a small tree-lined plaza next to the church. Find an empty bench here and soak up local activity, or observe the hustle and bustle from Hotel Sobalvarro's terrace just across from the park.

Boaco's highest point is **Cerro El Faro,** the lighthouse without a sea. A concrete pedestal and tower, the Faro offers a good view of the city and the valley of the Río Mayales. Technically, the tower is open all week, but the caretaker closes it when he pleases. Underneath is the town convention center and a popular gymnasium. Evenings, the Faro is one of Boaco's more popular places to steal a few kisses.

ENTERTAINMENT AND EVENTS

Boaco's sole disco is **Mangos Ranch,** a kilometer or two out of town along the highway to Muy Muy. Its low-key atmosphere is perfect for a drink and some traditional Latin music: salsa, *cumbia,* and merengue are popular, as is the occasional Mexican *ranchera* cowboy song. By 10 P.M. on the weekends the dance floor is packed, especially when there's live music. Take a taxi for $1. There are many bars in town offering cheap beer and a relaxed atmosphere until about 11 P.M., or visit the **Star City Casino** for 24-hour drinking and gambling action.

◖ Boaco *Fiestas Patronales*

Boaco's patron saint is Santiago Apóstol, and the *fiestas patronales* in his honor are particularly interesting and historic. The festival lasts the entire month of July, during which time the saint's statue is paraded daily from one neighborhood to the next. During the week of festival build-up, you can expect some of

CHONTALES

EMPALME DE BOACO'S FIELD OF DREAMS

In 1990, a North American traveler named Jake Scheideman fell ill during an ambitious bicycle tour of Central America and was taken in by a family at Empalme de Boaco. They befriended this complete stranger and helped him until he was healthy and ready to continue his travels. In 1998, after Hurricane Mitch, Scheideman returned to Nicaragua after many years of having been away, wanting to do something for the community that had taken care of him when he was ill. He asked what they would like, and all they wanted was a place to play baseball.

The ballpark, constructed in Empalme de Boaco (the intersection of the road to Boaco) took more than two years to complete, but is now the best of its kind east of Lake Cocibolca; games are Saturday and Sunday afternoons in season.

The project has expanded past baseball fields, building 65 homes, a high school, and a community center, and they're still going, pushing for higher education and economic development in the area. They are always looking for volunteer Spanish-speaking teachers and computer experts. Contact Jake and friends to participate, donate, or learn more through the website of his bike shop in Northern California: www.sthelenacyclery.com or www.casanica.net.

the wildest cowboy exhibitions in the country, including a booze-soaked horse parade, the *Bailantes de Boaco,* two independent parades of music, folkloric costumes and dance, all of which navigate the city's hilly streets in a riot of noise and color. The crux of the ceremony is July 23–25 when the procession is accompanied by dancers whose performance tells an elaborate tale of the expulsion of the Moors from Spain.

ACCOMMODATIONS

Many of the *pensiónes* near the bus terminal and along the main road of Boaco's lower level do a brisk trade in prostitution and romantic getaways for young couples and should be avoided. Because of Boaco's constant water problems, ask about reserves and be prepared to grin and bear it with a manual (i.e., bucket) shower if need be. At the south edge of the park, **Hotel Sobalvarro** (tel. 505/2542-2515, $10–25) has been lodging travelers and passers-through since before the revolution, and the facade still retains the faded charm of yesteryear. Tiny, bare-bones rooms with fan or air-conditioning are set around an unkempt courtyard; the terrace overlooking the lower half of town and the grand front porch overlooking the park are the hotel's finest assets.

Hotel Alma (tel. 505/2542-2620, $30), near the stoplight where the steep road turns nearly vertical, has the most expensive lodgings in town. Clean rooms have either a private or shared bathroom, plus a good view.

Posada El Bailante (tel. 505/2542-4909, www.posadaelbailante.com, $15–30) is a popular central accommodation, although several travelers have reported poor management services. It's located down the block from the dancer's statue, and offers cable TV, Wi-Fi, and air-conditioning in all 22 rooms, as well as an on-site bar that gets rowdy on the weekends.

Hotel Farolito (tel. 505/2542-1938, $12–27) is just south of the steep hill stoplight. This friendly and safe little hotel offers six well-attended rooms with cable TV, private bathroom, and a fan (a/c is an extra $5).

FOOD

Pastries and snacks are for sale in the park; they go well with a shake from the ice cream parlor at **Hotel Sobalvarro** (south edge of the park, tel. 505/2542-2515). Several restaurants on the hillside of Boaco serve traditional Nicaraguan dishes, of which the least expensive is **Restaurante Maraíta,** also a popular drinking hole.

American-owned **La Pizzeria** (75 meters west of BanPro, tel. 505/8885-6636, 4–10 P.M. Wed.–Fri., $5–10) serves hearty pies, including a "big meat pizza" with ham, pepperoni, bacon, and hamburger. Pricier than most in town, but still reasonable, **Restaurante Alpino** hits the spot with great beef *churrasco* (around $10). Next door, **Cafetin El Buen Sabor** (8 A.M.–5 P.M., $5) has a tiny interior, making it more of a pit stop and less of a dining experience. You'll find great fruit juice, coffee, and breakfast in the morning, and a varied afternoon menu of *comida típica mixed*, chop suey, and lasagna. Get your food to go and eat al fresco in the park. The **Sports Bar** (a block and a half north of the Posada Bailante, 10 A.M.– close Tues.–Sun., $2–7) serves up tasty pupusas and a selection of grilled meats, as well as cheap litres of beer. Tasty **Restaurante Los Cocos** ($6–10), a block farther north on the same street, has a nice back patio lined with trees and plants.

SERVICES

ENITEL (8 A.M.–9 P.M. Mon.–Fri.) is located across from the cathedral's northeast corner. There are several banks in Boaco. In the lower valley, **Banpro** is located on the main street. In the hillside part, **ProCredit** is a block north of the back side of the church. **Western Union** (8 A.M.–4:30 P.M. Mon.–Sat.) is near the market. One of the better Internet joints is **Cyber Rose** (near the writer's monument), which has six computers and a nice smoke-break balcony. The **post office** (8 A.M.–5 P.M. Mon.–Fri., 8 A.M.– noon Sat.) is 1.5 blocks north of the church on the left side and there's a pay phone out front.

GETTING THERE

Buses to Boaco leave every 30 minutes or so from the Mayoreo terminal in Managua. From Boaco, the most comfortable way to travel to Managua is by microbus. Two microbuses leave each day from the terminal, at 6:30 A.M. and 12:30 P.M. ($2). Regular buses leave every 30 minutes for Managua until 5:40 P.M.

Five buses leave each day for Santa Lucía (10:30 A.M.–5 P.M., one hour). Buses bound for Río Blanco (three hours) and Muy Muy leave 5:50 A.M.–5 P.M.

NEAR BOACO
Eco Albergue La Estrella

Situated on a large *finca*, **Eco Albergue La Estrella** (tel. 505/2549-5703 or 505/8937-0211, $15–45) lies 38 kilometers from Boaco on a bone-crunching road. La Estrella, a private park and floriculture center, offers visitors the chance to stay in relative isolation in the depths of a jungle. While the grounds are teeming with ancient trees and a myriad of flora and fauna, the lodge and restaurant accommodate visitors in relative luxury. Rooms (though not strictly eco) are comfortable, spotless, and equipped with private bathrooms. Reservations are necessary eight days in advance, and transportation from Boaco or Managua can also be arranged.

Aguas Claras Hot Springs

Locals say the *aguas termales* at Aguas Claras are heated by an underground volcano— probably not too far from the truth, given Nicaragua's seismicity. In 2000, an entrepreneur channeled the geothermal waters into pipes and through a series of concrete pools protected by palm-thatch roofs. The resulting **Aguas Claras Hot Springs and Hotel** resort complex (tel. 505/8856-7306) has six pools available to the public and another two pools reserved for hotel guests. All pools are clean and professionally maintained. The water isn't boiling hot, but it is extraordinarily warm, and therefore more enjoyable at night. While lounging in the pool, you can order from an extensive menu of traditional Nicaraguan food and drinks. The hotel features 17 private rooms with air-conditioning ($23–46); just coming in for the day costs about $1. Credit cards are

© RANDALL WOOD

leisure time in Chontales

accepted for hotel and restaurant expenses, but not for the entrance fee.

During Semana Santa and weekends in the dry season, the hotel can fill quickly, so make reservations. The *aguas termales* are located seven kilometers west of Empalme de Boaco and are tough to reach by public transportation.

La Cebadilla

Around the turn of the 20th century, a farmer from the mountain town of Cebadilla was surprised to see the Virgin Mary appear before him amongst the rocks where he was tending his cattle. The site has been treasured by the locals ever since.

La Cebadilla is no easier to get to than it ever was, and if you're interested in a hike through an out-of-the-way corner, try walking up the mountain to La Cebadilla. At one time a small chapel was erected in honor of the Virgin, and there was a small well where it was said the water was blessed. Today, the chapel has mostly fallen to bits.

This hike starts 1.6 kilometers east of Empalme de Boaco; on the south side of the highway there's a dirt road leading south to the community of Asedades and a steel sign with a picture of the Virgin Mary and the words La Cebadilla. The road leads south one kilometer to Asedades, a poor community of adobe houses, flower gardens, and rocky fields. It's imperative that you find a guide in Asedades to take you up the mountain to La Cebadilla. There are many small footpaths that lead up the hill, but they intertwine and none is more obvious than the others. The walk up the hill will take 3–4 hours—take water and food and make sure you have something to share with your guide. The walk back to Asedades can take 2–3 hours. Your guide will recommend that you stay at the top of the hill through midday and do your walking in the cool of the afternoon.

At La Cebadilla, you may or may not have visions of the Virgin Mary, but you will certainly

HIKES IN THE BOACO AREA

MOMBACHO

Camoapa's Mombacho is a forested mountain with a rocky protuberance jutting out of the top. It is lined with several coffee plantations and a handful of radio towers and makes a pleasant day hike from Camoapa. Long ago, Mombacho was the site of a moonshine distillery, the products of which were sold under the name Mombachito.

Hiking the hill is significantly easier than hiking Cuisaltepe and offers a beautiful view of Camoapa's open ranges. From Camoapa, the road to Mombacho can be accessed by the Salida de Sangre de Cristo (Sangre de Cristo is the name of a church found along the first part of that road). From ENITEL in the center of Camoapa, walk six blocks west, crossing over a small bridge and arriving at the public school. Turn right at the school and head north until you see the Iglesia de Sangre de Cristo. Continue on that road until you reach Mombacho. The hike from town takes 3-4 hours. There's a dirt road that leads up Mombacho from Camoapa to the radio towers. In Nahuatl, *mombacho* means "steep," so be prepared.

PEÑA LA JARQUÍNA

At the entrance to Camoapa on the southeast side of the highway (to your right as you head toward Camoapa) is a broad, rocky cliff face at whose base is a hardwood forest. This is Peña la Jarquína, named after a prominent local family. It's an easy 90-minute hike from the entrance to Camoapa, around the back side of the hill to the top. Skilled climbers might find it makes a suitable technical ascent; the rock is solid and has plenty of cracks—and is almost assuredly unclimbed.

CUISALTEPE

Cuisaltepe inevitably catches your eye: a massive, rocky promontory that juts out of the hillside between San Lorenzo and the entrance to Camoapa. In Nahuatl, Cuisaltepe means "place of the grinding stone"; it was a good source of the volcanic rock the indigenous peoples used for making long, round stone implements with which to grind corn into dough. Cuisaltepe was also the home of the last cacique of the region, Taisigüe.

Hiking Cuisaltepe is no casual endeavor. More than 300 meters high, much of the south side of the rock is a series of vertical crevasses and overhangs, and much of the rest of it is prohibitively steep. However, there is one summit approach—from the north side of the rock—which you can reach from Camoapa. Hike with caution. The climb takes around six hours round-trip, but adjust that estimate according to your own hiking ability. You should have good shoes, as much of the route is loose, slippery gravel.

Your point of entrance is the road to Camoapa. Any bus traveling between Managua or Boaco and the east will take you there, leaving you at Empalme de Camoapa (also called San Francisco) along the highway. A better option is to take a direct bus to Camoapa, 10 of which leave per day from Managua (5 on Sundays). From the highway, the road that leads to Camoapa climbs 25 kilometers. Get off the bus before you reach Camoapa at Km 99, where a small turnoff to the west leads to the community of Barrio Cebollín with a little red bus stop at the entrance. Access to the summit is neither obvious nor easy, and involves climbing partway up, crossing the small forest in a notch in the hillside, then climbing the ridge to the summit. You can find guides in Barrio Cebollín in the first house on the left after you pass the school (the house nearest the utility pole).

The rugged terrain of Chontales is great for hiking.

have a fantastic view of the valley below and the hills of Boaco to the east, sometimes all the way to Lake Nicaragua.

San José de los Remates and Esquipulas

The picturesque cowboy towns of San José de los Remates and Esquipulas can be the backdrop to guided horse tours and hikes to local waterfalls. Catch a ride to **Cerro Cumaica Natural Reserve** from either town; Cumaica's peak is closer to Esquipulas while Alegre is best accessed from San José. The weather here is usually a perfect 20°C (70°F) with a slight breeze almost year-round. Consider visiting both of these towns on the back road to Matagalpa. The bus trip is bumpy, but the views are grand.

One of the main attractions is the "original

black Jesus." In fact, thousands of national and international pilgrims descend each year on Esquipulas during the *fiestas patronales* (Jan. 14–15) to catch a glimpse of their saint icon, **El Señor de Esquipulas,** housed in one of the best-kept churches in Nicaragua. Locals believe that only due to the power of their patron saint was the town spared from all the wars that over the centuries had engulfed the surrounding hills.

In San José de los Remates, visit the **Cruz del Milenio,** worthy of the long walk—on a clear evening, you can see the lights of Granada and Cerro Negro in León in the distance.

Technically situated within the Matagalpa department, nearby Esquipulas also offers access to Cerro Cumaica and other hiking opportunities. The friendly local tourism committee is headed by **Doña Berena** (tel. 505/8426-8238, berenatellez@gmail.com) who can arrange visits to Salto de Limon in the nearby Cumaica Nature Reserve, petroglyph walks, and all-inclusive tourism packages with rural, cultural, and historic elements in and near Esquipulas. Ask about Cerro El Padre (a giant granite rock on top of a large hill) and the *miradores* (viewing points) that some of the locals are putting up in their backyards. Don't ask about the *cususa* (corn mash moonshine as clear as water and as strong as gasoline) the area is famous for.

For food, try **El Quelite** or **El Campero,** both on the main street. For accommodations, **El Hotelito** (near the park, tel. 505/2772-9132, $11–14) has seven cozy rooms.

There are daily north-bound buses from Managua and Boaco, which pass through San José and then Esquipulas on the way to Muy Muy and beyond. When moving on, hop a south-bound bus to the Boaco turnoff and visit Boaco and Chontales, or head north-east on the long and winding road to San Ramón and Matagalpa; those not interested in this scenic route should head west to rejoin the Pan-American Highway, from which Managua and Matagalpa are both easily accessed.

Santa Lucía

The town of Santa Lucía was created in 1904 by decree of President José Santos Zelaya in an effort to concentrate the dispersed and poorly administered farming communities of the hillsides north of Boaco. Its well-planned and organized beginning boded well for Santa Lucía, which, more than a century later, remains a picturesque and enchanting mountain village in a valley ringed by green mountains.

Santa Lucía itself doesn't have hotel rooms or fancy restaurants, but travelers sometimes come for the scenery around Cerro Santo Domingo, the long rocky precipice of Peña La Brada, and **Las Máscaras** petroglyphs in the valley of the Río Fonseca.

Nearby **Salto de los Americas** is a seven-meter waterfall with a deep pool, located a short walk up the river off the road to Boaco. There are several families of monkeys that live in the area. **Peña La Brada** is a cliff edge outside town, with an amazing panoramic view of Boaco and beyond.

There are no official accommodations in Santa Lucía, but the **Comedor Santa Lucía** will put you up and feed you in a pinch. More good food can be found in the *comedor* in the park, which specializes in grilled meat. A direct bus leaves from Managua for Santa Lucía at 10:30 A.M. ($1.50), bypassing Boaco entirely. The same bus leaves Santa Lucía for Managua early in the morning.

Camoapa

A cowboy town of 13,000 set in the mountains east of Boaco, Camoapa got its name from a Nahuatl phrase that can be translated as either "place of the parrots, place of the dark rocks," or "place of the yams." (How's that for precision?) Once an indigenous community ruled by the cacique Taisiwa, it was later absorbed by

© AMBER DOBRZENSKY

Camoapa's finely woven hats and baskets are reputed across the nation.

the Spanish settlers and incorporated under the name San Francisco de Camoapán.

To this day, the town has remained an off-the-beaten-path cowboy post with a fine reputation for dairy production; you'll see more four-wheel drive "tractors" here than anywhere else in the country.

In the 1960s, a school for promoting the art of weaving was formed, and the art passed through several generations. There are still many weavers in Camoapa, so it's a great place to pick up a custom-made straw hat. The hats they are known best for are created from intricately and tightly woven strips of fibrous white *pita* and are sold all over Nicaragua's craft markets. The supply is erratic, as the materials grow naturally and are not cultivated. Visit the home of **Elsa Guerrera Arroliga** (one block east of the Alcaldia and central park, tel. 505/2549-2338), where you'll find three generations of weavers. Peruse the available selection of finely woven pita hats, baskets, and bags, or order a customized item.

Camoapa's economy is largely dependent on three dairy cooperatives, whose employees like to party and relax on the weekends when they return from their farms and ranches outside of town. Camoapa's *fiestas patronales* begin on October 2 in honor of San Francisco de Asís, with bull riding, cattle contests, and the like. Camoapans boast that they have the toughest bulls and best horses around. Other weekends, the disco at **Atenas** is the place to be, unless you're a true cowboy, in which case the party is at **La Asociación** (Asogacam) out by the ballfield. Beer, mariachi music, and the occasional brawl—what did you expect?

Stay at **⟨ Hotel Las Estrellas** (seven blocks east of the church's north side, tel. 505/2549-2240, $10–15), a former auto-hotel turned honest business, which offers the best value rooms in this price range. Smaller but closer to town along the main road, **Hotel Taisiwa** has 11 extremely basic rooms with private bath ($2–4). In addition to Atenas, solid meals are found at **Camfel** (one block west of the church's north side), a clean place run by seven women.

Buses from Managua to Camoapa depart Mayoreo Monday–Saturday, starting at 4:30 A.M. and running through 4:10 P.M. The Sunday schedule provides fewer buses. Buses to Managua depart from the shady side of the church (whichever side that is as the day progresses) Monday–Saturday beginning at 6:25 A.M. and running through 5 P.M. There is a minibus that shuttles between the Empalme del Camoapa (San Francisco) and Camoapa, but it's irregular. A ride between the two points will cost you $1.

Comalapa

In 1752, Friar Morel de Santa Cruz visited Comalapa and said, "This is a town of Indians located in a land that's stony, mountainous, and fenced in by hills. Its church is of straw, reduced and indecent, lacking a vestry, but possessing an altar...100 families and 484 persons both Indian and Ladino." Comalapa is largely the same 250 years later, though the church is now a quaint stone structure. Access to Comalapa is through Camoapa, 20 kilometers down the road. There is one bus per day, leaving Camoapa at 6:30 A.M. The same bus leaves Comalapa at 4 P.M. At other times of the day, hitch a ride with pickups traveling between the communities, or try hiking a piece of the road.

Juigalpa

The last big settlement on the road southeast to El Rama (or south to San Carlos and the Río San Juan), Juigalpa is a prosperous city of some 70,000 cattle ranchers and farmers. Juigalpa bears the traces of its indigenous roots in elaborate statuary and other archaeological pieces still being discovered in the mountains east of town. Juigalpa in Aztec means "great city" or "spawning grounds of the black snails." Its first inhabitants were likely the Chontal, displaced from the Rivas area by the stronger Nicaraos. They resisted the Spanish occupation fiercely in the 16th century, rising up no fewer than 14 times to attack the installations of the colonial government.

Upon Nicaragua's independence, the land that comprised Chontales and Boaco was controlled by Granada. In 1858, the Department of Chontales was formed. In the 18th and 19th centuries, travelers bound for the gold mines of Santo Domingo and La Libertad crossed Lake Cocibolca, landed in Puerto Díaz, and spent a night in Juigalpa before proceeding.

SIGHTS

◖ Museo Arqueológico Gregorio Aguilar Barea

Juigalpa's most interesting attraction is the Museo Arqueológico Gregorio Aguilar Barea, a museum housed in an airplane hangar–like building stuffed with a collection of more than a hundred examples of pre-Columbian statuary, uncovered in the folds of the Amerrisque mountain range. Ranging 1–7 meters tall, the pieces are reminiscent of totem poles, elaborately carved in high- and low-relief, with representations of zoomorphic figures and humans (the latter often clutching knives or axes in their hands, or presenting their arms folded across their chests). The statues, thought to be 1,000 years old, were the work of the Chontal people, driven to the east side of Lake Cocibolca by the more powerful Nicaraos some 1,500 years ago.

Unlike the Nahuatl and Nicarao, relatively little is known about the Chontal culture and its statues, more of which are continually being discovered in the Amerrisque range.

The museum was built in 1952 by the well-loved former mayor of Juigalpa, Gregorio Aguilar Barea. It also exhibits a bizarre mix of taxidermy (creatures with genetic malformations), Nicaraguan coins, gold figurines, original paintings by the museum's namesake, and several historical paintings and photographs. The museum is open 8 A.M.–noon and 2–4 P.M. Monday–Friday, and only in the morning on Saturday; it is closed Sunday. The entrance fee is less than a dollar. The building has an open front, so even if the gate to the museum is locked, all the statues can be seen from the street.

Parque Palo Solo

The view from the park at the north end of town, Parque Palo Solo, is elevated above the surrounding streets, giving the impression of looking over the bulwark of a fortress. The fortress feeling isn't entirely accidental: Juigalpa was built at the top of the hill to offer it some means of defense from the Miskito and Zambo peoples who once raided it from those same mountains 200 years ago. The park was built by Mayor Aguilar Barea in the 1960s and named after the one tall tree that dominated its center. The tree has since been replaced by a fountain adorned with images of the mainstays of the Chontales economy: corn and cattle. The park's on-site restaurant is one of the best dining spots in town.

Juigalpa's other park, in the center of town, is an orderly and clean place, whose statue of a boy shining shoes was made by a former mayor who spent his early years earning money as a shoe-shine boy. The statue bears the inscription: "Hard work dignifies a man."

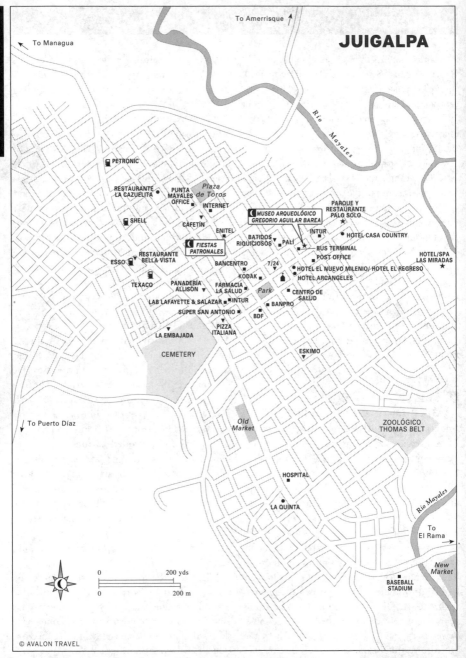

To Amerrisque ↑

To Managua

JUIGALPA

Río Mayales

PETRONIC

RESTAURANTE
LA CAZUELITA

PUNTA
MAYALES
OFFICE

Plaza
de Toros

INTERNET

PARQUE Y
RESTAURANTE
PALO SOLO

SHELL

CAFETÍN

MUSEO ARQUEOLÓGICO
GREGORIO AGUILAR BAREA

HOTEL CASA COUNTRY

ENITEL

BATIDOS
RIQUICIOSOS

PALI

INTUR

FIESTAS
PATRONALES

POST OFFICE

BUS TERMINAL

HOTEL/SPA
LAS MIRADAS

ESSO

RESTAURANTE
BELLA VISTA

BANCENTRO

7/24

HOTEL EL NUEVO MILENIO / HOTEL EL REGRESO

KODAK

HOTEL ARCANGELES

TEXACO

PANADERÍA
ALLISON

FARMACIA
LA SALUD

Park

CENTRO DE
SALUD

LAB LAFAYETTE & SALAZAR

INTUR

BANPRO

SUPER SAN ANTONIO

BDF

PIZZA
ITALIANA

LA EMBAJADA

CEMETERY

ESKIMO

To Puerto Díaz

Old
Market

ZOOLÓGICO
THOMAS BELT

HOSPITAL

LA QUINTA

Río Mayales

To
El Rama →

New
Market

0   200 yds

0   200 m

BASEBALL
STADIUM

© AVALON TRAVEL

⚈ Juigalpa *Fiestas Patronales*

Juigalpa's *fiestas patronales* (Aug.11–18) attract visitors from the entire nation and even Honduras and Costa Rica. Much of the festivities take place on the north side of town in the Plaza de Toros, but you'll find parties, bull riding, rodeos, and horseback games all over the place at all times. In one of these, called the *carrera de cinta,* mounted riders gallop underneath a wire from which is suspended a small ring. If a rider successfully puts a pencil through the ring at full gallop, he can present it—and a kiss—to the woman of his choice among the contestants vying to be queen of the festival. The woman who receives the most rings is crowned the queen.

ENTERTAINMENT AND EVENTS

The best disco in town is **La Quinta** (out on the highway, Sat. night only). Second best is **Caracoles Negras** (a half-block south of the Petronic station along the highway), which picks up the slack on Sunday night and appeals to the cowboy crowd more than La Quinta.

Toward the center of town, **Casa Bravo Club** is an upscale pool hall behind tinted glass and in the comfort of an air-conditioned hall. Near the park, **7/24** is brash and nonstop, with a giant projector screen and a menu based on local cheeses for snacking. The **baseball** field is located by the river at the south end of town in Barrio Paimuca; games are on Sunday.

ACCOMMODATIONS

Many of Juigalpa's cheapest *hospedajes* are meant to be occupied one hour at a time, and travelers should avoid these. Rather, stay to the east (rear) side of the church. **Hotel El Regreso** (the one-story establishment, tel. 505/2512-2068, $10–15 with shared or private bath) has 18 clean rooms and a friendly owner. Opt for an upstairs room, as those below are mostly windowless. **Hotel La Quinta** (tel. 505/2512-2574, hotellaquinta@hotmail.com, $15–20) east

along the highway and across from the hospital, is the best option for groups as there are 38 rooms. Avoid staying here on weekends if you're in need of rest as the on-site disco (Thur.–Sun.) draws a full crowd with pumping music.

⚈ **Hotel Casa Country** (opposite Parque Palo Solo at the north end of town, tel. 505/2512-2546, $20–25) has nine large rooms on the second story of a new colonial-style house. All rooms have private bath, air-conditioning, wireless Internet access, and TV.

The fanciest place in town, with the best view bar none, is ⚈**Las Miradas Hotel & Spa** (in Barrio Tamanes west of the town center, tel. 505/2512-4525, hotellasmiradas@hotmail. com, $60 includes breakfast). In addition to the most stunning view in the city, you'll find luxury accommodations (hot water, a/c, Wi-Fi), a hair salon, massage studio, private barbecue lounge, small gym, and a glass-wall sauna with that same five-star view. Las Miradas only has four rooms, so make reservations. Ask Doña Edelmira about the *guardabarrancos* that nest in the hotel wall. Another higher-end option is the **Hotel Los Arcangeles** (tel. 505/2512-0847, $40), conveniently located directly behind the church. The 13 impeccable rooms with king-size beds are set around a leafy courtyard.

FOOD

Juigalpa has a variety of food—often at reasonable prices—and naturally, massive quantities of beef and dairy on the menu. Case in point: **La Embajada** (difficult to find, but everyone knows it; just ask around). The only thing on the menu at this hole in the wall is meat, ordered by the pound (about $4). The "Meat Lady" has a secret marinade recipe she learned from her grandmother and is currently passing down to her granddaughter. The meat is served with salty *cuajada* cheese and tortillas. Native Chontaleño Daniel Ortega has been known to make an appearance here, and it is also frequented by the bigwigs of Chontales.

La Cazuelita (three blocks east and two blocks north from the Esso, closed Mon.) sells a remarkable barbecue chicken sandwich (less than $4 with fries). This air-conditioned restaurant is popular with Peace Corps volunteers and well-off Juigalpans for its excellent Nicaraguan food, all of which you can sample via a *surtido* ($15, serves 2–3).

Right across from the cathedral is **7/24,** offering burgers ($3) and *comida típica;* several large TVs mark this as the spot for watching games and fights. For good fresh bread and pastries, stop by **Panadería Allison** (5 A.M.–7 P.M. daily), two blocks west and two blocks north of the park. **Batidos Riquiciosos,** next to the Palí, is a rapidly expanding smoothie-and-shake shack, where you can try one of many tropical fruit flavors or go for a gringo-style coffee shake ($2–4).

On the highway in front of the Esso station, **Restaurante Tacho** has great chicken and steak at moderate prices ($3–5) in a pleasant atmosphere. Roving bands of mariachis frequent the place, which has a mostly male crowd. Across the street, and next door to the Esso, is **Bella Vista,** serving up a large choice of meat ($5–7) with a dance floor open till 2 A.M. on the weekends. For more upscale dining, try the restaurant ❲**Palo Solo** at the edge of Park Palo Solo. Soak up fantastic views of the surrounding hills in the breezy courtyard setting, and choose from a large, beef-oriented menu ($5–15). The house specialty is bull balls, or *huevos de toro* (prepared in every imaginable way).

INFORMATION AND SERVICES
ENITEL (8 A.M.–noon and 1:30–5:30 P.M. Mon.–Sat.) is four blocks north of the park. The INTUR tourist office (tel.505/2512-2445), located one block west and half a block north of the park, can provide you with brochures and recommendations on where to stay and what to do. For Internet access, check behind the Texaco station or just walk around town.

There is an ATM located off of the central park outside the Banpro. The post office is located down the street from the church.

One of the better pharmacies in town is **Farmacia La Salud** (at the northwest corner of the park, tel. 505/2512-0932). Hospital La Asunción (on the southeast side of town along the highway) doesn't have very good facilities. A better option for travelers is the **Lab Lafayette & Salazar** (two blocks west of the park, tel. 505/2512-2292), a private clinic and doctor's office. There is a **Centro de Salud** (8 A.M.–9 P.M. Mon.–Fri., 8 A.M.–1 P.M. Sat.–Sun.) across the street from the church.

The old movie theater is now a Palí grocery store; Supermercado San Antonio has a better selection and is locally owned.

GETTING THERE
Microbuses to Managua depart from the north or east side of the church at 6 A.M. and 1:40 P.M. (2.5 hours). The larger buses depart Juigalpa from the cramped bus terminal in the market. Ask around to be sure where your bus departs. Buses leave hourly for El Rama (4:30 A.M.–1:30 P.M.) and every half hour to Managua (4 A.M.–5 P.M.). You'll also find daily service to Nueva Guinea until 3:20 P.M., to Boaco (via Camoapa and Comalapa), and other local destinations.

NEAR JUIGALPA
Puerto Díaz
It's a short but uncomfortable ride from Juigalpa down to the village of Puerto Díaz, a sleepy lakeside town of fishing families that pretty much live off what they catch. Puerto Díaz doesn't have any facilities for travelers but is worth a day trip on a lazy Saturday to see how the "far" side of the lake (i.e., the world across the lake from Granada) lives. Buses leave from Juigalpa three times a day at 5 A.M., 2 P.M., and 5 P.M. From the bus terminal, they cross the highway at the Esso station before working their way slowly down to the shoreline.

© RANDALL WOOD

Balneario El Salto

◖ Punta Mayales Nature Reserve

Located an hour from Juigalpa, Punta Mayales is home to 250 species of birds including owls and hawks; mammals like porcupines, anteaters, sloths, and monkeys; and an incredible assortment of flora with a backdrop of Lake Cocibolca and the Isla de Ometepe and Zapatera volcanoes. There are three cabins of various sizes and tents for camping, plus five trails, ranging from 1–3 kilometers, and each offering a unique view of the peninsula.

Stop in the Juigalpa office (near ENITEL, tel. 505/2512-2322, arbagar@yahoo.com) to arrange a day trip or an overnight stay. Camping is $15 with breakfast; cabins cost $60 per person a night, which includes three meals, guided walks, and an aquatic tour down the Mayales River and out into the lake. If you'd just like to visit for the day, entrance is $3, a land tour is $8 with the option to take horses, and the river tour is $7. Snake shows and caiman-watching trips are easily arranged.

Balneario El Salto

Somewhat neglected and a bit dirty these days, Juigalpa's favorite swimming hole is located an easy two kilometers out of town on the highway to Managua. Look for the big blue sign on the northeast side of the highway; the falls are located a scant 100 meters from the highway. El Salto is formed by a concrete dam that causes water to pool up in a natural reservoir. In the dry season, there's no waterfall at all, though the swimming hole remains quite deep. In the rainy season, the water from the Río Mayales tumbles first over the concrete dam and then through a gorge of enormous boulders carved into fantastic shapes by the flowing water.

The near shore gets littered with the remains of old picnics after major holidays (like Semana Santa, when the place is packed), but the far shore is tree-lined and grassy. Consider swimming across to the far side and watching the local kids turn somersaults off the wooden-plank diving boards. There is supposedly a $1 fee to get

HIKES NEAR JUIGALPA

EL MONOLITO DE CUAPA

The Cuapa Monolith is a 75-meter-high chunk of granite that projects like a giant needle out of a field, as though it dropped from the sky and pierced the ground; it's first visible on the bus ride to Cuapa.

Climbing El Monolito isn't easy, but it isn't impossible either. It's a hike, not a technical rock climb. The locals in Cuapa know all the trails that lead there, and any young campesino will be glad to show you the way to the top to see the cross. From the town of Cuapa, it's a 2.5-hour hike to the top, including several extremely steep sections. Hike with good shoes; locals recommend not climbing it on particularly windy days. Ask around for Nicolas, an English-speaking resident of Cuapa (originally from Bluefields), who can be a guide. He runs a tire repair shop next to Parque Zapera.

SERRANÍA AMERRISQUE

A powerful backdrop to Juigalpa, the Amerrisque mountain range forms a rocky backbone to the history of the city. Most of the archaeological pieces in the Juigalpa museum were unearthed in the Amerrisques, and countless other sites have yet to be explored. Although the area is undeveloped for tourists, the rocky peaks make a tempting hike and the locals claim the east side of the range contains several caves.

Your starting point is the road called the Camino de la Vaticana, built by Rome and Holland in the late 1990s. It will lead you nine kilometers east toward the range and the tiny farming community of Piedra Grande. From there, you can strike into the hills to explore. You can try hitching a ride out there to trim down the flat, boring part of the hike, but it won't be easy, as traffic along the road is sparse at best. There are few communities along its length. Consider hiring a pickup truck in town; a group of five travelers offering $15-20 might be able to convince someone to drive them out there. Try to swing a deal for the ride back while you're at it.

Daniel Molina can serve as a guide (tel. 505/2512-2940). He is a young man who speaks English and can arrange a trip out to the mountains, where he'll help you find a local guide to show you the trails.

---

in, but the locals have skirted the fee for so long by entering downstream and walking up the streambed that, with the exception of Semana Santa, no one seems to try to charge any more.

Cuapa

Tiny, isolated Cuapa, once just another anonymous farming town in the foothills of the Amerrisque mountain range, gained an awful sort of notoriety during the 1980s, when it came to represent the worst of what the Contra war had become. In 1985, Contras attacked and took control of Cuapa, holding it for several hours. They captured the Sandinista mayor Hollman Martínez, but later released him when the townspeople pled for his life. Twelve other Sandinista activists, sent from the capital to work in Cuapa, weren't so fortunate: The Contras marched them out of town and executed them at the roadside. When the Sandinista military got wind that Contras occupied the town, they dispatched a truckload of 40 soldiers to defend the town. Contras ambushed the vehicle along the road to Cuapa, killing nearly all of them. A small roadside monument bearing the Sandinista flag commemorates both the civil servants and the soldiers killed during the war.

Cuapa is famous among devout Catholics. In late 1980 and early 1981, the Virgin Mary appeared several times—bathed in radiant light and dressed in pure white—to local farmer Bernardo Martínez. She told Martínez she had a message for the world and for Nicaragua: "Don't preach the kingdom of God unless you are building it on earth. The world is threatened by great danger." She later asked for prayers for unbelievers and for peace on earth. Devout Catholics were overjoyed at the appearance of the Virgin, but even that moment became rapidly politicized in the toxic climate of the 1980s. Some claimed her message was a coded recrimination of the Sandinista government, and the Sandinistas responded by clamping down on all press coverage of miracles not previously accepted by the Vatican. An elaborate and well-maintained statue and sign greet you at the entrance to **Cuapa with Bienvenido a la Tierra de María** (Welcome to Mary's Land). Believers from all over eastern Nicaragua flock to Cuapa on May 8, the anniversary of the day the Virgin first appeared. (Read a fascinating fictionalized account of the events surrounding the apparition in Silvio Sirias's novel *Bernardo and the Virgin*.)

Whether you've come to see the shrine or to climb the impressive, needlelike **monolith** outside of town, Cuapa isn't a bad place to spend the night. One option for the climb is to arrive in the evening, spend the night at Cuapa, and set off to climb the monolith the following morning. You can find accommodations and meals at **Restaurante Hospedaje La Maravilla** (tel.505/2519-4019) with rooms in the $6–15 range and dishes served in a dingy dining hall for about $5. The hotel fills up the week of June 19–27, when Cuapa celebrates its patron saint, San José. The only other restaurant in town is the **Comedor Oluma** in front of the central park, worth a visit for delicious tacos ($1) and good fritanga fare ($5).

Six buses leave Juigalpa for Cuapa every day, the first starting at 6 A.M. and the last departing at 6 P.M. Buses from Cuapa to Juigalpa leave from the town center every day, 6 A.M.–4:30 P.M.

Agua Caliente

While eastern Nicaragua lacks the volcanoes of the Pacific horizon, it too was formed volcanically and these hot springs are evidence that under the surface, even quiet old Chontales is bubbling and tectonically active. When they're hot they're hot, but when they're not, a trip out to the hot springs at Agua Caliente yields nothing more than a trickle of water seeping out of the side of the creekbed. When they're active, however, expect torrents of bubbles gushing out of the creekbed in water too hot to touch.

To get there, take the Camino de la Vaticana as though you were going to the Amerrisque Mountains, but take the first major left-hand turn instead; Agua Caliente is 4.8 kilometers down the road. You'll know you've reached the site when you get to a relatively new school building followed immediately by a streambed. The hot springs are located about 100 meters upstream from where the road crosses the stream.

La Libertad and Santo Domingo

These two pueblos have been the site of small-scale gold mining for well over a hundred years. British mining engineer Thomas Belt was surveying in the Santo Domingo area when he wrote his book *A Naturalist in Nicaragua* in 1874. The mines were run by a Canadian organization that ceased activities around 2000. The curious may be interested in poking around either town, both of which, though run-down and slightly decrepit, still very distinctly bear the traces of a small boomtown atmosphere. La Libertad is the birthplace of president Daniel Ortega as well as Nicaragua's outspoken and politicized Catholic archbishop Miguel Obando y Bravo.

Nueva Guinea

This region is nearly as off the beaten path as you can get in Nicaragua. Technically, the town of Nueva Guinea is part of the RAAS (Southern Atlantic Autonomous Region), but it is more easily accessed from the Rama Highway and Juigalpa than Bluefields and the Río Escondido. A full 293 kilometers southeast of Managua, Nueva Guinea lies in the tropical, humid, rolling lowlands that stretch toward the Caribbean. It's one of the rainiest corners of Nicaragua, receiving an average of 8,000 millimeters (yes, that's eight meters) of rainfall each year, but that varies from town to town, based on the forest cover of the area. In terms of population, it is the second-largest municipality in Nicaragua, with a de facto population of 120,000 people, many of whom technically live in the municipality of Bluefields, but whose transport and public services are provided via Nueva Guinea.

In the 1960s, Nueva Guinea was a rich, dense, tropical rainforest with a wide variety of animal life, but since then, due to poor public policy, misguided development projects, and inadequate agricultural practices, much of the territory has been transformed into barren, useless pasture. Forested areas include the land that borders the Reserva Indio-Maíz and the Reserva Natural Punta Gorda. Even that land is in the process of being slowly and illegally colonized and exploited, and poor farmers in desperate need of land overwhelm the capacity of the Nicaraguan government to prevent their homesteading.

Nueva Guinea was founded as part of U.S. President John F. Kennedy's Alliance for Progress, a program meant to defuse demands for land reform across Latin America in the wake of the Cuban revolution and the postcolonial struggles in the rest of the world. Original settlers were given 1 *manzana* of land (about one hectare) in the urban center, and 60 in the countryside. The same program was applied

to help victims of natural disasters—victims of both the Managua earthquake of 1972 and the eruption of Cerro Negro near León in 1973 were shipped out to Nueva Guinea. In the 1980s, the area was a hot spot of Contra activity under the command of Edén Pastora's group, ARDE, based across the Costa Rica border.

These days, farmers in the area of Nueva Guinea live in some 140 neighborhoods and produce an uninspiring variety of the same thing everyone else does—corn, beans, and rice—plus ginger. Nueva Guinea is a wild place, with horses parked outside of bars and people walking their pigs or herding cattle down the main street. The town of Nueva Guinea has few facilities, but the curious traveler may appreciate visiting a place so out of the way.

SIGHTS

For the extreme wilderness adventurer, Nueva Guinea is also your base for exploration of two of Nicaragua's most pristine nature reserves—**Punta Gorda** and **Indio-Maíz.** Retrace the steps of colonial Spanish captains, Calero and Machuca, who sought the best route to the Caribbean coast through the communities of Puerto Prinicipe, Atlanta, and others, concluding in the coastal community of Punta Gorda. Arrange for a guide at the mayor's office. Less demanding is the one-hour hike to the falls at **Salto Esperanza:** Take the bus to the community of Esperanza and ask around.

At **Finca La Esperanzita** (tel. 505/8843-5010), you can glimpse an organic agriculture project where small farmers are growing cacao, vanilla, pepper, and several species of tropical hardwoods. They'll gladly provide you with a tour of the facilities, including a coffee-, cacao-, and cinnamon-processing plant run by World Relief (one block south and one block east of the hospital), and will also put you up in a pinch ($3).

ACCOMMODATIONS AND FOOD

There are few options in Nueva Guinea, excluding *hospedajes* with rooms-by-the-hour.

Hotel Nueva Guinea (on the main drag, tel. 505/2575-0090, $10–25) has a variety of rooms, some with air-conditioning, cable TV, and bath. Newer, quiet **Hotel Miraflores** (300 meters south of URACCAN, from $15) has good mattresses. **Hotel La Colina** (a block south and 400 meters west of the Municipal Stadium, tel. 505/2575-0828, $10–25) offers the best lodging in town. Set within a green *quinta,* the comfortable rooms are equipped with either fan or a/c, and allow for easy access to the on-site restaurant.

Llamas del Bosque (next to the Esso station) serves the best food in town for about $6. Sit poolside at **Ranchón Kristofer** (three blocks north of the park) or join the crowd on the dance floor. **Comedoría Dalili** (across from the mayor's office) is the least expensive *comedor* in town—less than $3 for a meal.

GETTING THERE

Buses leave for Nueva Guinea from Managua's Mayoreo terminal approximately every hour for the six-hour trip on an entirely paved road. In your own vehicle, it takes as little as four hours.

SOLENTINAME AND THE RÍO SAN JUAN

The Río San Juan carries the waters of Lake Cocibolca to the Caribbean through a lush landscape of extensive nature reserves and broad cattle ranches. Five hundred years ago, the Spanish, intent on piercing the Central American isthmus, focused their efforts on the Río San Juan, which nearly connects the two sides of Central America, save for a thin strip of land. In 1524, Hernán Cortés wrote King Carlos I of Spain, "He who possesses the Río San Juan could be considered the owner of the World." The strategic and economic importance of this region has not diminished since.

The principal settlement in the area, San Carlos, is transforming from edgy port town to quaint destination, and you'll inevitably pass through it on the way to various adventures. The town is thick with itinerants, rowdies, farmers, fishers, swindlers, and you. Offshore, the Solentiname Archipelago is a quiet group of islets as pertinent to the revolution years as to Nicaragua's prehistoric past, and a center of production for some of the country's most gorgeous paintings.

Or you can take a wooden boat down the river towards the Atlantic on a sun-baked ride back through time. El Castillo, one of Spain's most permanent colonial legacies, remains little changed from the 17th century and the days of marauding pirates. From there, downstream fishing village follows pasture follows rapids until you reach San Juan de Nicaragua, the

© GRACE GONZALEZ

HIGHLIGHTS

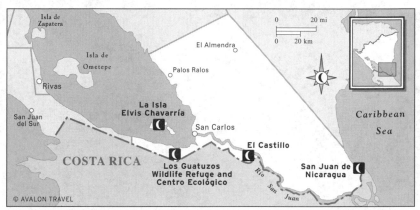

© AVALON TRAVEL

LOOK FOR ◖ TO FIND RECOMMENDED SIGHTS, ACTIVITIES, DINING, AND LODGING.

◖ **La Isla Elvis Chavarría:** One of the Solentiname archipelago's jewels, La Elvis features a museum, a hiking trail, an arboretum, and a wonderful host community of farmers, fishers, and artists (page 305).

◖ **Los Guatuzos Wildlife Refuge and Centro Ecológico:** This is one of the best places in the south to get down and dirty with nature. Start by identifying a few of the 389 species of tropical birds (page 306).

◖ **El Castillo:** The mighty embattlements of this historic mud-river fortress have watched over the river since the days pirates prowled the Spanish mainland (page 311).

◖ **San Juan de Nicaragua:** Remote and thick with history, San Juan de Nicaragua is an adventure in itself. The local blue lagoon swimming hole is dramatic and an easy dugout-canoe ride away (page 313).

SOLENTINAME

little town where it all began and where it all ends, remote and untamed.

It's not easy to get to the Río San Juan, and tougher still to get around, but everyone agrees that things are rapidly changing for the better, due in large part to a $14 million tourism development plan called La Ruta del Agua, the effects of which you'll see as soon as you step onto the refurbished dock or recently paved airstrip at San Carlos. This region isn't part of the casual traveler's itinerary, but if you can invest a little more time than usual, the dramatic landscapes and remoteness of this region will impress you, and the tourism potential here is enormous.

HISTORY
Colonial Times to Independence

The mouth of the Río San Juan, choked with labyrinthine estuaries, had eluded explorers for years, including Christopher Columbus, who failed to find it in 1502. The Spanish founded Granada in 1524. In 1539 Spanish explorers finally reached the Atlantic by sailing downstream from Granada. This made Granada Spain's first quasi-Atlantic port in Central America. To consolidate their hold on the river, the Spaniards began persecuting the indigenous people living along its banks and on the Solentiname Islands.

SOLENTINAME

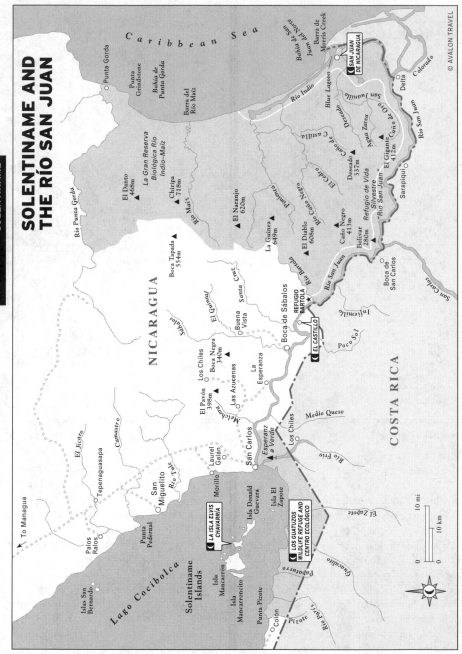

SOLENTINAME AND THE RÍO SAN JUAN

© AVALON TRAVEL

In 1567, the first Spanish trade expedition set sail from Granada: three ships laden with agricultural products for Panamá. They made it as far as the Caribbean, where English pirates plundered the vessels and fed the surviving sailors to the sharks. Tension and conflict between European nations over the next 300 years led to a virtual state of war between Spain's colonial holdings in Nicaragua and English, Dutch, and French pirates, whose respective governments encouraged them to give the Spanish hell. Until the Spanish improved their fortifications along the Río San Juan, the pirates were disastrously successful at sacking and burning Granada, which suffered repeatedly. By 1724, however, a dozen fortresses guarded the river and the pirates' pillaging came to an end.

Throughout the 19th century, the Río San Juan grew in importance for commerce and for its value as a shortcut through the isthmus for foreigners traveling between New York and California, the most famous of whom was Mark Twain, who passed in 1866 on Cornelius Vanderbilt's steamship route. After dreams of a cross-isthmus canal petered out and Vanderbilt's steamship business came to a halt, the river slipped back into bucolic obscurity for a century.

The Contra War

As a sensitive border area during the 1980s, the Río San Juan was a southern front for Contra forces, particularly for the Alianza Revolucionaria Democrática (ARDE), under the leadership of Edén Pastora, a.k.a. Comandante Cero, who fought on the southern front years after the CIA stopped supporting him. Troops from both sides planted fields of antipersonnel mines, and entire communities evacuated the war zone, fleeing south to Costa Rica or west to other points in Nicaragua. The population of the region dropped to fewer than 40,000, then nearly doubled in the 1990s as

people returned with new families, stressing already environmentally sensitive land.

The Río San Juan Today

In spite of relentless "El Río San Juan is ours!" chest-thumping up in Managua, the Nicaraguan government has traditionally ignored the people of this region, spurring tens of thousands of Nicaraguans to emigrate to Costa Rica, legally and illegally, in search of work and better living conditions. For those Nicaraguans living along the river, most television and radio stations come from Costa Rica, as do some schools and health services. Many towns—especially San Juan del Norte—use the Costa Rican *colón* as well as the *córdoba*. Increased government attention has begun to improve the area, helped in part by wealthy Managua legislators purchasing land along the river for their own use and development. But the greater force has been private development of tarpon fishing lodges, ecoresorts, and similar, providing needed jobs and economic stimulus in a region otherwise limited to cattle raising.

PLANNING YOUR TIME

Allow a full week for exploration of this region. Make your plane reservation from Managua to San Carlos early, as seats fill up fast. Expect about 25 percent higher costs for most goods in this isolated region (35 percent more on Solentiname). In San Carlos, find updated boat schedules, make contact with downstream river lodges, and stock up on snacks and supplies. Public transportation is both slow and capricious, but inexpensive. You're better off hiring a boat and driver or making arrangements with a tour company, which will affect your budget. You could make it to Solentiname and back in two days if the stars align, but boat schedules will make it more like three or four. It's only a day more to see El Castillo, which you should not miss.

San Carlos

SOLENTINAME

Surrounded on three sides by a watery horizon, San Carlos's sky is frequently pierced by bright rainbows sparked by afternoon showers. San Carlos, a town of about 13,000 people, is one of the oldest towns on the continent, and has served as a raucous and spirited way station for many travelers over the centuries. San Carleños are a lively bunch. Many were born elsewhere in the country and ended up here on their way to somewhere else—field hands on their way to Costa Rican harvests, border soldiers on leave from remote posts, and lake and river merchants trading with Chontales cattlemen.

All foreign travelers in the Río San Juan region are obliged to pass through San Carlos, the departmental, economic, and transport hub of the region. The city has cleaned up its act and greatly improved in the last few years, with a new waterfront park, new bus station, improved airstrip, and an increasing number of services (the region's first ATM was installed in 2009). In the words of one reader: "It's a bustling, cheerful place, and in spite of the odd rough spot, it may be the cleanest city in Nicaragua." Indeed, there are garbage cans on every corner, street sweepers, and newly painted homes, giving San Carlos a whole new look and feel.

ORIENTATION AND GETTING AROUND

The main center of San Carlos is only about a dozen city blocks, all south of the central park on the flank of a hill looking south over the water. The waterfront can be a little confusing, but all in all, there's not much actual "town" in which to get lost. Main Street runs along the waterfront, from which the city sprawls northward along the highway to the hospital and airport. If you are landing at the airstrip, grab one of the rickety taxis to take you the couple of kilometers into San Carlos—the five-minute ride costs less than $1. The bus station is more or less in the town center, across from the gas station and docks. Arriving by boat dumps you right in the middle of the *malecón*.

SIGHTS AND ENTERTAINMENT

The old **Spanish fort,** aggressively restored in recent years, enjoys a nice view overlooking the town and lake. Its cultural center and library were founded with Cuban support—to wit, countless volumes of communist propaganda—and has since been supported by the Netherlands. At the *mirador,* you'll find old cannons, a romantic sunset setting, and one of the nicest restaurants in town.

For nightlife, locals make their way to **La Champa,** a bar so popular, its name has become a verb among locals (as in, "Let's go *champear!*"). **El Bocano** is newer and located just north of the water tower. Bars line most streets throughout town, with the rowdiest ones down by the waterfront; try the **Granadino** or the **Kaoma** for a mellower vibe. The annual **sportfishing competition** in September is a big deal for Nicaraguan anglers and attracts crowds from across the nation for prizes like outboard motors and more. Enjoy the *fiestas patronales* on November 4. Most radio stations in the area are Costa Rican and feature Spanglish reggae and *soca.*

ACCOMMODATIONS

San Carlos's half-dozen greasy *hospedajes* on the main drag charge as little as $3 per person, but you get what you pay for. If you're short on cash, or just into slumming, try **Hospedaje Peña** (a block back from the water, tel. 505/2583-0298, $4 pp), a cheap but relatively secure dump with 10 rooms and streetside balcony.

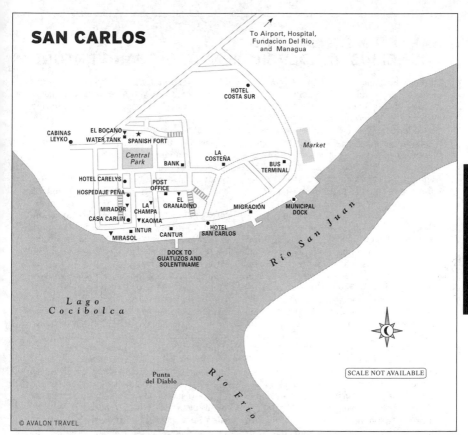

SAN CARLOS

To Airport, Hospital,
Fundacion Del Rio,
and Managua

HOTEL
COSTA SUR

CABINAS
LEYKO

EL BOCAÑO
WATER TANK   SPANISH FORT

*Central
Park*

Market

BANK   LA
COSTEÑA

BUS
TERMINAL

HOTEL CARELYS
HOSPEDAJE PEÑA

POST
OFFICE

EL
GRANADINO

LA
CHAMPA

MIGRACIÓN   MUNICIPAL
DOCK

MIRADOR
CASA CARLIN   KAOMA

INTUR
MIRASOL   CANTUR   HOTEL
SAN CARLOS

DOCK TO
GUATUZOS AND
SOLENTINAME

Rio San Juan

*Lago
Cocibolca*

SCALE NOT AVAILABLE

Punta
del Diablo   *Rio Frio*

© AVALON TRAVEL

A better bet is to walk 200 meters north of the bus station to **Hotel Costa Sur** (tel. 505/2583-0224, orlando104@hotmail.com, $7–14); rooms are clean and far quieter than the budget options in town. The owners can arrange day trips to Solentiname and other sites; they are part of a local tour guide effort and can recommend unique tours throughout the area.

◖**Hotel Carelhys** (a half-block south of the park, tel. 505/2583-0389, $15) is also known as Aquiles or Doña Coco. The 14 well-kept and pleasant rooms are the cleanest in the city and include private bath, fan, and complimentary drinking water, and old magazines in Spanish.

Having served many a traveler over the years, **Cabinas Leyko** (two blocks west of the park, tel. 505/2583-0354, $18–40) is a safe bet; somewhat damp rooms have private baths, fan or a/c, and Wi-Fi access. Find the plushest rooms in town at **Casa Carlin** (opposite Kaoma restaurant, tel. 505/2583-0290, $25–50); the more expensive doubles have a/c and a balcony with a fine view.

FOOD

The row of *comedores* alongside the bus station offers the best cheap meals in town ($3 for a big plate). Otherwise, dockside ◖ **El Granadino** serves chicken plates from $4, fish from $5. Its

SOLENTINAME

SAN JUAN'S STEAMERS: CORNELIUS VANDERBILT'S NICARAGUAN VENTURE

Entrepreneurs and fortune-hunters heading to California in the famed 1849 gold rush found it easier to traverse Central America than to brave the long, perilous overland trek across the United States. American businessman Cornelius Vanderbilt formed the first company that provided passage between New York and San Francisco via Nicaragua. The 45-day trip from New York to California cost $145. Vanderbilt made the first successful voyage himself in 1851. Upon reaching the Nicaraguan shore at Greytown in great, square-rigged clipper ships, passengers boarded side-wheeled *vapores* (riverboats), including the 120-ton iron-hulled *Director* and the smaller *Bulwer*, which worked different stretches of the river (to get around unnavigable rapids, passengers disembarked and transferred to the next upstream ship). The second leg sailed past San Carlos, then traversed the lake to the town of Virgen; there, passengers boarded horse carriages and traveled overland to San Juan del Sur where another clipper ship took them to California.

The route was an immediate success, and by 1853, Vanderbilt's company could scarcely provide enough ships to meet the demand. Vanderbilt's company remained uncontested and by 1854, had transported more than 23,000 passengers between New York and California. Business was booming along the route, which now included a short railway to avoid the rapids at

El Castillo. San Juan del Norte became a rip-roaring port town with 127 foreign consulates and embassies, and a stream of adventuring gringos, foreign investors, and New Orleans prostitutes, prompting U.S. envoy E. G. Squier to remark on the town's "general drunkenness and indiscriminate licentiousness."

The most famous of Vanderbilt's passengers was also one his biggest critics: After Mark Twain made the voyage in 1867, he took Cornelius to task in "An Open Letter to Commodore Vanderbilt." In it, he complained about the wretched quality of the steamship line. More of Twain's comments on Nicaragua are found in a posthumously assembled collection called *Travels with Mr. Brown*.

The boom lasted another half century, fueled after the end of the gold rush by the prospect of an interoceanic canal. The dream all but died when the bid went to Panamá in 1902, and communities up and down the Río San Juan began to wither. Outside San Juan del Norte, the remains of an old iron steam-dredge stand in the shallows of the river where it foundered, testament to the boldest of dreams and the still-unwritten future of transoceanic shipping in Nicaragua.

To learn more about this fascinating chapter of Río San Juan history, read *Tycoon's War: How Cornelius Vanderbilt Invaded a Country to Overthrow America's Most Famous Military Adventurer,* by Stephen Dando-Collins (Da Capo Press, 2008).

---

food is the best in town, though slow to get to your table. Down the block, popular **Kaoma** has a similar menu but better service, with prices starting at $7; it's open late on weekends when the downstairs disco gets going. **The Mirador,** aptly named for the landmark on which it sits, has good food for under $5, and pleasant lake views from the outside seating area. Try the jalapeño steak and imagine shooting cannonballs at pirates. Just below the cannons in the same area is the less impressive **Mirasol,** with similar fare.

INFORMATION AND SERVICES

INTUR (one block south of the park, tel. 505/2583-0301, riosanjuan@intur.gob.ni) may be able to help you arrange for special transport and can provide a brochure or two about the region. Directly in front of the same dock is the office for CANTUR, which when staffed can provide information on public boat schedules, contacts for private services, and a list of tours offered on Solentiname. The kiosk selling tickets near the entrance to the municipal dock can provide the balance of the updated boat schedules.

SOLENTINAME

San Carlos sits on Lago Cocibolca, at the mouth of Río San Juan.

Banks

You still need lots of cash down here. San Carlos got its first ATM from Banpro in 2009—one of two in the region—but it's heavily used and out of order when the power goes out, so arrive prepared. The other ATM is at Bancentro. Some of the main area lodges take credit cards: always confirm. Both banks will exchange dollars, but will not deal with travelers checks, Costa Rican *colónes,* or credit-card cash advances. There are plenty of *coyote* money changers down by the Migración office, trading *córdobas,* dollars, and *colónes.* Otherwise, head for the Western Union just southwest of the church.

Communication

There are cheap Internet cafés all over town; start near the park. You can make phone calls from most Internet places, and both Nicaraguan cell phone companies offer service around San Carlos.

The San Carlos **post office** (located a block south of the park, tel. 505/2583-0276, tel./fax 505/2583-0000, 8 A.M.–5 P.M. Mon.–Fri., 8 A.M.–1 P.M. Sat., closed for lunch) receives and sends mail via the daily La Costeña flights.

Emergency Services

The **police station** (tel. 505/2583-0350) is located three kilometers from the center of San Carlos on the road to Managua. **Hospital Luis Felipe Moncada** (tel. 505/2583-0238 or tel. 505/2583-0244) is north of town on the highway; or try the **Centro de Salud** (505/2583-0361). San Carlos's medical services may be okay for minor problems, but for any real emergencies, you're better off chartering a boat south to the hospital in Los Chiles, Costa Rica (one hour or less by boat) or trying to get a flight back to Managua.

Tour Guides

Most river lodges and hotels can arrange daily trips and activities, or hire a local guide in San

Carlos. Ronny Zambrana of **Ryo Tours** (tel. 505/2252-8595 or 505/8828-8558, ryobigtours@hotmail.com, www.turismo-ruralriosanjuan.com.ni) is part of a growing group of professionally trained young Nicaraguan guides. Many national tour operators based in Granada and Managua offer package trips to the Río San Juan region.

To paddle the Río San Juan and camp along its banks, contact **Green Pathways** (in León tel. 505/2315-0964, www.greenpathways.com) and ask about their 12-day Río San Juan kayak expedition (minimum of three people and two weeks advance notice).

GETTING THERE
By Air
This is the recommended way. There are two daily 50-minute flights from Managua on weekdays, one at 8 A.M. and one at 1:30 P.M. The view as you arc over the lake and volcanoes is stunning. Only the morning plane leaves on Saturdays and just the afternoon plane makes the flight on Sundays. The return flight departs San Carlos immediately after landing and unloading. The round-trip costs $120. Contact **La Costeña** in Managua (tel. 505/2263-2142), or in San Carlos, find the La Costeña office (tel. 505/2583-0048) in front of the cemetery. Always reserve your spot as far in advance as you can, as flights fill up fast. Getting on the waiting list for stand-by works more often than you would think for a 12-person plane.

By Land
A long-term highway project connecting Managua and San Carlos was finally completed in 2011, and has cut the journey time in half; the trip now takes about six hours by public transport. Buses leave Managua's Mayoreo market, starting at 5 A.M. with the last night bus leaving at 6:30 P.M. The first of the seven buses to Managua is at 6:30 A.M., the last at 10 P.M. The 300-kilometer trip costs about $10.

In San Carlos, buses for all destinations leave from the terminal near the municipal dock.

By Boat
TO GRANADA AND OMETEPE
There's currently only one boat that runs this route. An older ferry leaves Monday and Thursday at 2 P.M., making stops at Altagracia, at Ometepe at 6 P.M., and at Morito and San Miguelito before arriving in San Carlos around 6 A.M. ($10 for padded first-class seats w/a-c, $55 VIP suite). The same boat departs San Carlos bound for Granada on Tuesday and Friday at 2 P.M.; be there at least an hour in advance to get your ticket. This boat passes Ometepe around 1 or 2 A.M., where you can get off at Altagracia. The boat gets crowded at times, especially around Semana Santa, when the hot easterly winds chop the lake into steep swells, and the voyage degenerates—if you're prone to seasickness, brace yourself. Get there early and be aggressive to stake your territory topside. At other times of the year, the ride is long but generally pleasant, and sailing west is always easier than sailing east. For more information, contact **Empersario Portuario** (tel. 505/2583-0256, 7:30 A.M.–5 P.M. Mon.–Sat.).

DOWN THE RÍO SAN JUAN
All boat tickets are sold at the **Empresario Portuario** (tel. 505/2583-0256, 7:30 A.M.–5 P.M. Mon.–Sat., hours vary to match boat schedules) on the main drag toward the gas station. Inside the building you'll find up-to-date schedules and advance ticket sales for its fleet of *lanchas*. All boats for El Castillo also stop in Boca de Sábalos. The first boat leaves San Carlos at 6:30 A.M., the last one at 4:30 P.M. Four slow (2–3 hours) boat trips to El Castillo depart daily (slow boats $4, faster boats $6).

Boats to San Juan de Nicaragua (San Juan del Norte) are less frequent. A few boats make the trip, both fast and slow. These leave on

© AMBER DOBRZENSKY

Boat ferries connect the Río San Juan, Solentiname, and Lago Cocibolca.

Western Union, viajesturisticosortiz@hotmail. es, tel. 505/2583-0039 or 505/8828-8550) specializes in private tours and transfers. Rising gas prices make chartered trips cost hundreds of dollars. As the demand for transportation continues to grow and shift, so do boat schedules. Always check departure times at the docks well in advance, and be sure to get a second (and third) opinion.

RÍO FRÍO BORDER CROSSING

Boating south into Costa Rica begins with a visit to the *migración* office, located on the *calle principal* in San Carlos, on the waterfront near the park with a line that forms before 7 A.M. The office is open 8:30 A.M.–6 P.M. daily. There are usually three or four boats to Los Chiles, starting at 10:30 A.M. The hour-long chug up the Rio Frío to Los Chiles, Costa Rica costs about $12 each way. To enter Nicaragua costs $12.

Once in Los Chiles, Costa Rica Migración is located 200 meters up the road from the dock, where you *must* get stamped. Daily direct buses depart for the five-hour trip to San José ($10). Boats leave Los Chiles to San Carlos throughout the day (or, when there aren't enough people, not at all, forcing you to spend the night in Costa Rica). Note: Be aware that a second town by the name of Los Chiles is about two hours northeast of San Carlos, in Nicaragua. Be sure to distinguish between the two when asking for directions.

Tuesday and Friday (ask about Wednesday and Sunday departures) and come back on Thursday and Sunday. The slow boat ($13, 12 hours) leaves San Carlos at 6 A.M. and San Juan del Norte at 5 A.M. The fast boat ($25, 6 hours) leaves an hour after the slow boat.

Arrange private boat trips through the INTUR or CANATUR offices, or directly with a *panguero* (private boat owner). Armando Ortiz's **Viajes Turisticos** (one block from the

SOLENTINAME

The Solentiname Islands

The 36 volcanic islands in southern Lake Cocibolca have a long history of habitation; signs of its original residents are abundant in the form of petroglyphs, cave paintings, and artifacts. The name Solentiname comes from Celentinametl, Nahuatl for "place of many guests."

The islands are of volcanic origin with rocky, hard-to-farm soils. More effort is going into avocados these days. Somoza's logging companies deforested most of the archipelago, and Boaco cattlemen cut the rest to make pasture. In the last three decades, however, much of the forest has been allowed to regenerate, and the rebirth has attracted artists and biologists from all over the world. Fishing, of course, remains a mainstay of the islanders' diet.

Today, 129 families (about 750 people) share the archipelago with an amazing diversity of vegetation, birds, and other wildlife. Solentiname's most unique and well-known attraction is the creativity of its inhabitants, a talent Padre Ernesto Cardenal discovered in 1966 when he gave brushes and paint to some of the local *jícaro* fruit carvers. Cardenal, recently returned from a Trappist monastery in Kentucky in the late 1960s, formed a Christian community in Solentiname and stayed on Isla Mancarrón to work and write for the next 10 years (he is locally referred to as "El Poeta"). Under his guidance, the simple church at Solentiname became the heart of Nicaragua's liberation theology movement, which represents Christ as the revolutionary savior of the poor. It inspired Carlos Mejía Godoy to write "La Misa Campesina" in 1972. Masses were communal, participatory events, and Cardenal's book, *The Gospels of Solentiname,* is a written record of the phenomenon, with transcriptions of a series of *campesino*-led services throughout the 1970s.

On October 13, 1977, a group of anti-Somoza Solentiname islanders staged a daring and successful assault on the National Guard post in San Carlos. Somoza retaliated by torching the islands. In 1979, Ernesto Cardenal, now the Sandinista minister of culture, formed the Asociación Para el Desarollo de Solentiname (Solentiname Development Association, or APDS). Under APDS, much of what had been destroyed was rebuilt, and the arts continued to flourish and receive much attention from the rest of the world. Today, there are no fewer than 50 families who continue to produce balsawood carvings and bright "primitivist" paintings of the landscape and community.

ORIENTATION AND GETTING AROUND

Essentially only the four largest of the nearly three dozen islands are inhabited: Isla Mancarrón, Isla Elvis Chavarría (a.k.a. Isla San Fernando), Isla Donald Guevara (a.k.a. Isla la Venada), and Isla Mancarroncito. Only the first two have services for tourists. If you are on a budget, getting around the islands will be your biggest challenge, especially considering that the *colectivo* water taxis run only twice a week, ensuring a minimum stay of three days. To get around, you can either catch a free or discounted ride in someone's *panga,* or you can rent a dugout canoe or rowboat and do some paddling.

Fundación MUSAS (in Managua, tel. 505/2277-0424 or 505/2265-4679), the same foundation that runs the museum on Isla Elvis Chavarría, also arranges a fully guided, four-day exploration of the entire Solentiname archipelago and the Río Papaturro in Los Guatuzos, including all of its natural, archaeological, and cultural attractions.

MANCARRÓN

The biggest (20 square kilometers) and tallest (at 257-meter Cerro las Cuevas) island, Mancarrón is populated by 34 families—about

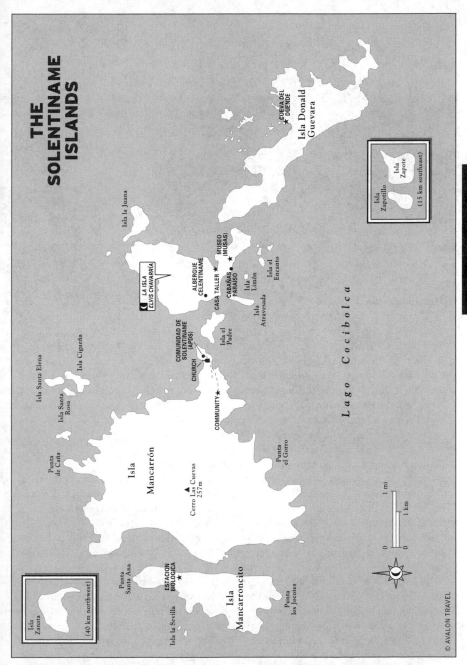

THE
SOLENTINAME
ISLANDS

Isla
Zanata
(40 km northwest)

Isla Santa Elena

Isla Santa
Rosa

Isla Cigueña

Isla la Juana

LA ISLA
ELVIS CHAVARRÍA

ALBERGUE
CELENTINAME

CASA TALLER ★

MUSEO
(MUSAS)

CABAÑAS
PARAISO ●

CUEVA DEL
DUENDE
★

Isla Donald
Guevara

Isla
Zapotillo

Isla
Zapote

(15 km southeast)

COMUNIDAD DE
SOLENTINAME
(APDS)

CHURCH

COMMUNITY ★

Isla el
Padre

Isla
Limón

Isla
Atravesada

Isla el
Encanto

Lago Cocibolca

Punta
de Caña

Punta
Santa Ana

Isla
Mancarrón

Cerro Las Cuevas
257m ▲

Punta
el Gorro

ESTACION
BIOLOGICA
★

Isla la Sevilla

Isla
Mancarroncito

Punta
los Jocotes

0   1 mi

0   1 km

© AVALON TRAVEL

SOLENTINAME

The Solentiname archipelago is a nature-lovers' utopia.

© AMBER DOBRZENSKY

200 people. The "town" of Mancarrón, built up in the 1980s, is simply a cluster of houses, a health center, school, and *pulpería,* five minutes up the muddy path from the dock. **Casa Taller de la Cooperativa** has a large collection of works by artists from different islands. The cooperative shares the profits from the individual sales. Much of the rest of the island is off-limits and has supposedly been purchased by cattle ranchers from Boaco, though conspiracy and corruption theories abound.

Ernesto Cardenal's project began in the 1960s in the church, which he reconstructed and designed. It is unlike any house of worship you've ever seen, featuring children's paintings on the whitewashed adobe walls, a unique crucifix sculpted by Cardenal, and an altar decorated in pre-Columbian style. The nearby APDS compound includes a library, a museum, an art gallery, a display of indigenous artifacts, and an eclectic collection of books in a variety of languages, including the complete works of

Ernesto Cardenal, who still maintains a residence in the APDS compound. There are other works on liberation theology, plus the original primitivism painting by local resident Eduardo Arana that helped start the whole project. Ask if they can show you the 1970s BBC video documentary about the Solentiname Islands.

Accommodations

A local collective of families offer homestay accommodations; go to the community center and inquire at **Hostal Familiar El Buen Amigo** (tel. 505/8869-6619, $8 pp). One of their rooms has a private bath, and meals run $2–3. Nearby, **Los Pesecitos Castillo** (tel. 505/2277-3495 or 505/8976-7056, $8) is a small hostel with basic rooms. **Hotel Catalanica** (tel. 505/8764-6804 or 505/8375-3363, www.catalanica.com, $35 pp with three basic meals) offers the most comfortable lodging on the island, with clean rooms set around a green courtyard, and lush grounds with a little *ranchito* for chilling.

☪ LA ISLA ELVIS CHAVARRÍA

"La Elvis" owes its name to a young martyr who participated in the 1977 raid on San Carlos and was subsequently captured and killed by the National Guard. The island has a health center, a school (Escuela Mateo Wooten, named after the Peace Corps volunteer who led its construction in the mid-1990s), a museum, and a hiking trail.

El Museo Archipiélago de Solentiname (MUSAS) (at the top of the steep path out of town, 7 A.M.–noon and 2–5 P.M. Mon.–Sat., $3) was built in September 2000 to preserve and display the natural and cultural heritage of the Solentiname Islands and its people. The flowers along the path on your way up were planted to attract butterflies and hummingbirds. Inside, local artists have painted scenes of the islands' early history. Also find interesting maps of the area, archaeological information, and a display of traditional fishing techniques and the balsa-wood carving process. Behind the museum are a natural medicine garden, arboretum of 42 tree species, a model organic avocado and balsa-wood plantation, and a weather station.

The Fundación MUSAS (made up of six community leaders, the Italian nongovernmental organization [NGO] ACRA, and several other organizations) also organizes environmental education workshops in the island's school and supports a number of research projects in the area. The museum is open daily, but if you find it closed, ask around for Socorro, the local curator, caretaker, and key master. For more information, contact the Managua office (tel. 505/2277-0424).

At the peak of the dry season (Mar.–Apr.), **La Cueva del Duende** becomes accessible. It is usually underwater, and is an important archaeological site that the islands' past inhabitants believed to be the entrance to the underworld. They painted faces to represent their ancestors, believed to reside there, and left other markings including a female fertility figure. The cave is located on the nearby Isla Donald Guevara, but you can arrange the tour with CANTUR here.

Accommodations

Doña María Guevara has been running the ☪ **Albergue Celentiname** (tel. 505/8893-1977, celentiname7@yahoo.es, from $35 for a double room, rate includes three meals, cash only) since 1984 on a beautiful point at the western edge of the island. She and many of her family members are painters, participating in Cardenal's project since its earliest days. All of the electricity in the hotel is solar generated. The eight cabanas have capacity for up to 25 people, all with private bath (cold showers). There is a picturesque porch, a bar, and a *comedor*. The flower-framed views are priceless. Kayaks and fishing gear are available for rent. Try to make reservations in advance if possible. They can help arrange for transportation when it's available, but expect round-trip transportation from the island to run upwards of $120.

Several hundred meters east at **Mire Estrellas** ($8, $10, and $15 per person), Don Julio rents three rooms in his rustic and comfortable lakefront homestead with its own dock on the southern shore of the island. Don Julio's brother, Chepe, runs transport to and from San Carlos and can arrange custom trips. Their sister Doña Maria Magdalena Pineda has her own hotel another couple of minutes east along the shore: **Cabañas Paraíso** (tel. 505/8827-5627, 505/2278-3998 Managua office, or 505/8614-1440, hcpsolentime@yahoo.es, $40 d w/private bath, $45 pp all inclusive) has a dining room (meals under $7), rents kayaks, and offers tours around the island and beyond. These are the only places on the island that accept credit cards; they also have an office in San Carlos and a gallery in Managua, plus excellent local guides.

ISLA DONALD GUEVARA

Also known as Isla la Venada, or "La Donald," Isla Donald Guevara's namesake was martyred alongside his *compañero* Elvis Chavarría. La Venada is home to Rudolfo Arellano, one of the original artists from the islands. His family has a total of seven artists now who exhibit their work at the gallery and family house on the south side of the island.

MANCARRONCITO

Mancarroncito is the most well preserved, wild, and least inhabited of the main islands. Its steep, thickly vegetated hills rise to a 100-meter peak. The Estación Biológica is run by a local NGO, Fundación del Río, and offers lodging for up to 10 people at $11 per person (meals $5). Make reservations in advance by contacting Fundación del Río in San Carlos (tel. 505/2583-0035).

ZAPOTE AND ZAPOTILLO

Zapote and Zapotillo are the two closest islands to the mainland and are both owned by APDS, which has essentially decided to leave them alone. Zapote is a key nesting area for a variety of birds and turns into a whitewashed, foul-smelling squawk-fest in March and April, when some 10,000 breeding pairs build nests there. Observe the reproductive mayhem from your boat only, as landing there disturbs the birds.

Smaller Zapotillo has less bird activity and a more sordid history, involving a fruit farm, an orphanage for boys, and a pedophile Evangelist priest who was eventually chased into Costa Rica, barely escaping with his life.

ISLAS EL PADRE AND LA ATRAVESADA

Located just off the western tip of La Elvis, El Padre island became a howler monkey sanctuary when a single breeding pair introduced in the 1980s subsequently reproduced into a family of some 50 members. Isla la Atravesada, just off La Elvis and to the east of Isla el Padre, is owned by a North American, but inhabited by Solentiname's densest crocodile populations.

GETTING THERE

From San Carlos, boats depart on Tuesday and Friday at 1 P.M. for the two-hour trip to the archipelago (about $2 pp). The return trip leaves Solentiname on Tuesday and Friday at 5 A.M., arriving in San Carlos in time to catch the boat to Managua. Should you want to leave the islands at any other time, a private boat starts at about $100. CANATUR (tel. 505/2583-0251, www.riosanjuancanatur.org) can also arrange transportation to Los Guatuzos or San Carlos.

Near San Carlos

🄲 LOS GUATUZOS WILDLIFE REFUGE AND CENTRO ECOLÓGICO

The 438-square-kilometer strip between Nicaragua's southern border and Lake Cocibolca is a protected wetlands and wildlife reserve replete with myriad species of animals and inhabited by some 1,700 anglers and subsistence farmers in 11 small communities. The locals are descendants of the Zapote and Guatuzo (or Maleku) peoples as well as the mestizos who arrived in the late 19th century

to cultivate rubber. These same *huleros* reverted to the slave trade when the world rubber market crashed, selling Guatuzos for 50 pesos a head to the gold mines of Chontales. Today, there are only a handful of full-blooded Malekus, mostly over the border in Costa Rica.

In the 1930s, settlers introduced cacao to the region, which, because of the crop's need for shade, preserved much of the area's original forest canopy. When plummeting cacao prices and a deadly fungus wiped out the industry in the 1970s, hardwood logging ensued. Only military conflict in the 1980s stopped the logging, but it also drove nearly the entire population of Los Guatuzos into Costa Rica. When families returned in the early 1990s, the area's ecosystem was still largely intact, and the new government quickly acted to protect it from destruction.

Today, residents count on the richness of their natural surroundings to attract visitors and scientists. No fewer than 389 species of birds have been observed here, and between February and April, flocks of migratory species fly through in spectacular concentrations. Los Guatuzos contains dense populations of crocodiles; caimans; feral pigs; jaguars; and howler, white-faced, and spider monkeys. This is also home to a rare, ancient species of fish called the gaspar (*Actractoseus tropicus*), a living, armored relic of the Jurassic age that uses its snout and fangs to eat other fish, crabs, and even small turtles.

The research center and guest facilities are located 40 kilometers from San Carlos, up the Río Papaturro, which drains the slopes of Costa Rica's northern volcanoes. The narrow river's fauna-rich jungle gradually swallows you as you approach the community of Papaturro.

Accommodations

Research station, nature center, and isolated backpacker's hideaway, the **Centro Ecólogico** has two eight-bed dorms at $11 a night, plus campgrounds (tents and sleeping pads for rent). Arrange your meals in advance in the nearby village for about $5.

Arrange birding safaris, fishing trips, kayak excursions, nighttime wildlife safaris, boat trips in the wetlands and lake, and tours of local villages (the most expensive tour costs $11 pp). A multiplatform suspension canopy bridge allows for incredible bird and wildlife viewing in the upper reaches of the rainforest. There is also an orchid display of over 100 species, including the tiniest one in the world; a butterfly farm; a turtle nursery for export to the pet industry;

and a caiman nursery for scientific research, export, and tourist adrenaline production. The center also has a conference room, workshop facilities, and support for anyone coming to do field research (GPS equipment, bird nets/traps, and field assistants). They will gladly work out deals for researchers and students. Bring quick-drying clothes and adequate protection from the sun, rain, and especially bugs.

For more information or reservations contact **Amigos de la Tierra** in Managua (tel. 505/2270-3561 or 505/8762-9630, reservacion@losguatuzos.com, www.losguatuzos.com).

Another excellent option is only a five-minute boat ride from San Carlos but in a world of its own. **Hotel La Esquina del Lago** (tel. 505/8849-0600 or 505/8842-7673, www.riosanjuan.info, $50 d includes San Carlos shuttle and breakfast) is a jungle lodge that evolved from a French expat's world-class sportfishing trips and area nature tours. Despite cold water, bugs, and broken fixtures, the rooms are homey and charming. Access is only by boat, and the spot feels incredibly remote, with views of surrounding volcanoes and the lake. They offer all kinds of tours and water activities, specializing in birding, kayaking, and fishing adventures, as well as transfer services, boats for personal use, 24-hour electricity, Internet access, and package deals with meals included.

Getting There

From the west dock near the CANTUR kiosk in San Carlos, *colectivos* leave for Papaturro at 7 A.M. Monday, Tuesday, and Thursday; the four-hour trip costs $3.50 a person and stops at the small island of Chichicaste where fried fish and soup are available for about $1. The same boat returns to San Carlos the day after arriving, leaving Papaturro at 7 A.M. Or you can rent a private *panga*—which costs $120, but can take up to 10 people to Los Guatuzos in only 1.5 hours.

SOLENTINAME

SOLENTINAME

ESPERANZA VERDE

Part of the Guatuzos Reserve, this 5,000-hectare protected area is part of an effort to reforest and protect the overgrazed watershed of the Río Frío and the Río San Juan. From the dock of Esperanza Verde and the military post, walk 500 meters downstream to the **Centro de Interpretación Ambiental Konrad Lorenz,** and a row of six guest rooms with 20 beds ($45 pp with tours, transportation, and food); inquire about special rates for NGOs, students, and Nicas. The barren area immediately surrounding the guest facilities is uninteresting, but a 40-minute walk up the road brings you straight into the heart of the rainforest—monkeys, 200 species of birds, giant spiders, and potentially even pumas. There are a total of three trails and numerous aquatic trips. Contact Leonel Ubau with **FUNDEVERDE** in Hotel Cabinas Leyko in San Carlos (tel. 505/2583-0459 or 505/2583-0354, fundeverde@yahoo.es). Located 15 minutes from San Carlos, take any *colectivo* heading up the Río Frío toward Los Chiles.

NORTH OF SAN CARLOS
San Miguelito

A peaceful, lakeside community, San Miguelito has an interesting Casa de Cultura and access to the island of El Boquete. You can also venture up various rivers, into local wetlands, or over to Solentiname. In town, stay at **Hotel Cocibolca** (tel. 505/2552-8803, $15), a tranquil hardwood building of 16 rooms, all with shared bath, and incredible sunset views of Ometepe's silhouette. Just outside of town, the **Finca el Cacao** (tel. 505/8414-9927) offers a more bucolic stay, with cow-milking, crocodile-searching, monkey-watching, and similar, plus three meals a day for $40 per person. One daily direct bus leaves Managua's Mayoreo at 7 A.M.; in San Carlos, ask at the bus station. You can also take the slow boat from Granada and get off in San Miguelito before it reaches San Carlos.

Down the Río San Juan

The 190-odd-kilometer journey to the sea takes you down the broad, lethargic Río San Juan through forests and isolated cattle farms. You'll have the opportunity to stop in several villages, isolated clusters of stilted homes, or in one of several river resorts and research stations. There are a few minor *raudales* (rapids) where the channel suddenly narrows, including the infamous **Raudal el Diablo** in front of El Castillo. Enormous silver *sábalos reales* (tarpon) are often seen rising just upstream from these fast waters. Downstream of El Castillo, things become decidedly wilder, especially on the Nicaraguan side, where the enormous Gran Reserva Río Indio-Maíz spills over the left bank. Finally, you'll reach San Juan del Norte, with all its ghosts, and a long sandbar, beyond which lies the Caribbean. (Note: The terms

"river right" and "river left" refer to a boater traveling downstream).

BOCA DE SÁBALOS

A two-hour *lancha* ride from San Carlos brings you to this town, six kilometers upstream of El Castillo. Boca de Sábalos is a working town of about 1,200 souls, located at the mouth of one of Río San Juan's nearly 1,000 tributaries. Boca de Sábalos has more bars, *hospedajes,* and places to eat than El Castillo, and is actually the de facto seat of the El Castillo municipality (it was transferred here from El Castillo temporarily during the war, and then never moved back).

Sights

Don Julio Murillo (across from the big bar on the walkway leading north from the dock)

NICARAGUA'S FAMOUS FRESHWATER SHARK

How *Carcharhinus leucas* became the only shark in the world able to pass between saltwater and freshwater is a fascinating story. After thousands of years of hunting in the brackish outflow of the Río San Juan, Nicaragua's freshwater sharks made their way up the river and formed a healthy population in Lago de Nicaragua. The tale continues with the arrival of humans and their role as both victims and hunters of Nicaragua's bull shark, told in full in Edward Marriott's 2001 book *Savage Shore*.

Indigenous tribes on Ometepe worshipped the shark, sometimes feeding their dead to it. This fear and reverence only faded when the Asian market for shark-fin soup helped to create an industry around harvesting the famous fish, culminating in the late 1960s, when Somoza's processing plant in Granada butchered up to 20,000 sharks a year. Today, the only freshwater shark in the world is seldom seen, although it is still inadvisable to swim in the waters near San Juan del Norte.

SOLENTINAME

speaks English, organizes tours on Río Sábalos, and rents canoes and kayaks for $5 per hour without a guide and $10 per hour with a guide. He can also arrange an all-inclusive adventure kayaking trip to San Juan del Norte ($300 pp) or take you on one of the 10 tours designed by the Sábalos tourism collective.

El Quebracho Wildlife Reserve has two trails (one of which is self-guided) through a wildlife-rich setting. The reserve can accommodate up to 25 people for $20 per person including three meals, and guides can be hired from $10 per day (discounts for groups larger than 10). Count on spending the night, as its isolation makes day trips challenging. Make arrangements at the office of **Fundación del Río** (a block south of the *alcaldía* in Sábalos, tel. 505/8419-0675 or 2583-0035), which owns and operates the reserve, or contact the main office near the hospital in San Carlos.

Hire a vehicle to take you to the shady, pleasant 2,000-hectare **African palm plantation,** about a half hour outside of town, one of only two such operations in Nicaragua. Before being purchased by the Chamorro family, it employed hundreds of locals.

You can also hike down the Río San Juan to the 100-year-old, half-buried hulk of the **steamship wreck.** To go tarpon fishing, get a permit from the town MARENA office (hook only, no spears), and then hire a guide and boat to take you to just above the Toro Rapids, less than five minutes down the Río San Juan.

Accommodations
IN BOCA DE SÁBALOS
Walking up from the dock, you'll see the pretty hardwood **Hospedaje Katiana** (from $12 pp), offering a variety of 14 rooms, some with private bath, all in a nice homey setting. Next door, **Hospedaje Clarissa** (from $16 pp including breakfast) has 11 rooms with mosquito net, fan, some with shared bath, and one of the most popular eateries in town. Across the street, the **Hotel Central** ($5 s with fan) is inexpensive and seedy, described by one reader as "a dump on top of a bar."

◼ **Hotel Sábalos** (tel. 505/8659-0252 or 505/2271-7424, www.hotelsabalos.com.ni, $25–40 includes breakfast) is located down the river at the confluence of the Río Sábalos and the Río San Juan, built on a big dock over the water. The view from the deck might be the best in the entire Río San Juan area. Also enjoy hot water, private bathrooms, classy accommodations, and a *panga* that can take you on tours around the area. Arrange a ride to the hotel at their family's store next to Hospedaje Katiana on the main street.

SOLENTINAME

© GRACE GONZALEZ

Water-transport is the best way to navigate the Río San Juan.

VICINITY OF BOCA DE SÁBALOS

A one-time amphibian farm, growing everything from poison dart frogs to snakes for export to the U.S., **🌑 Sabalos Lodge** (tel. 505/8823-5514 or 505/2278-1405, sales@sabaloslodge.com, www.sabaloslodge.com, $35–75, includes breakfast) now focuses on tourism, with 10 riverside bamboo and wood cabins with thatched roofs, hammock lounge, and a dining area. The meals and the service are excellent, $5 for breakfast and $10 for lunch and dinner (huge portions). Hiking trails and inner tube floats are available, plus three *pangas* for pickups from San Carlos and tours to the sunken ship, nighttime caiman-watching, and more; also tours to Indio-Maíz biological reserve, kayaks, and horses. The lodge is a five-minute boat trip (or 15-minute walk) downstream from Boca de Sábalos.

The lodge is associated with the private nonprofit, nonpartisan San Juan Rio Relief (sanjuanriorelief@cox.net, www.sanjuanriorelief.

org), a team of dedicated people from the U.S. and Nicaragua who came together in 2003 with the goal of bringing free medical healthcare to the people of the Río San Juan.

Located downstream from Boca de Sábalos on river right (before reaching El Castillo), **Montecristo River Resort** (tel. 505/8649-9012 or 505/2583-0197 in San Carlos, montecristoriver@yahoo.com, www.montecristoriverlodge.com, $75 all-inclusive) is a calm, riverside resort offering sportfishing, birding, hiking trails, horseback riding, and tours of local cacao farms and reforestation projects; a variety of rooms on a neatly kept compound and private nature reserve of 120 acres. They can also get you to area reserves and Solentiname. Your all-inclusive package includes three meals, horses, boats, and other activities; ask about discounts.

Getting There

Seven boats make the trip to El Castillo from San Carlos and back every day (reduced service

© GRACE GONZALEZ

The fort at El Castillo is where the Spanish kept watch over river traffic.

on Sunday), stopping at Boca de Sábalos and the lodges upon request.

◖ EL CASTILLO

The fortress of El Castillo de la Inmaculada Concepción de María was strategically placed with a long view downriver, right in front of the shark- and crocodile-infested Raudal el Diablo (still a navigational hazard). Now dark, moss-covered ruins, the Fortress of the Immaculate Conception is the one place in this region you should not miss.

The town (pop. 1,500) has neither roads nor cars—reason enough to visit. Its residents work on farms in the surrounding hills, fish the river, commute to the sawmill in Sábalos, the palm oil factory up the Río San Juan, or one of the new resorts up and down the river. In between harvests, a lot of folks cross illegally into Costa Rica—an easy 45-minute walk. El Castillo celebrates its *fiestas patronales* on March 19.

History

Ruy Díaz, following the first Spanish exploration of the river in 1525, built the first fortification in 1602, on a section of the river he called "The House of the Devil." In 1673, Spain commissioned the building of a new fort, which, when completed two years later, was the largest fortress of its kind in Central America, with 32 cannons and 11,000 weapons. Granada, at long last, felt safe.

But in 1762 Spain and Britain began the Seven Years War, prompting the governor of Jamaica to order an invasion of Nicaragua. An expedition of 2,000 soldiers took all the fortifications until they reached El Castillo, where a massive battle commenced on July 29. Rafaela Herrera, the 19-year-old daughter of the fort's fallen commander, Jose Herrera, seized command of her father's troops and succeeded in driving off the British, who retreated to San Juan del Norte on August 3.

Eighteen years later, 22-year-old Horatio

SOLENTINAME

Nelson entered the Río San Juan with a force of 3,500 men. He captured the fortification at Bartola on April 9, and then, two days later, El Castillo via a surprise landside assault. Nine months later, sans reinforcement, the soon-to-be Lord Admiral Horatio Nelson and his handful of surviving soldiers—all rotting from sickness—pulled out and went home.

Visiting the Fort

Celebrating 500 years in the Americas, the government of Spain restored the fortress at great cost, building both a historical museum and lending library, plus the nearby school and Hotel Albergue. The **museum** (8 A.M.–noon and 1–5 P.M., $3) is pertinent and interesting, showing the history of the fortress and a collection of arms and other items dating as far back as the 1500s, including a pile of cannonballs and early rum bottles. A nearby *mariposario* (butterfly farm) was also built by the Spanish, although much more recently.

Recreation

Asociación Municipal Ecoturismo El Castillo (AMEC) can help with boat rental ($15 per hour for two people) and fishing (rods and lures for $10 per day, $20 to replace a lost lure), or charter fishing (from $150 per day). These prices keep rising as El Castillo becomes more popular, so be sure to check them beforehand.

The AMEC *casita* can also help you arrange full- or half-day river and tributary tours and hikes, jungle tours (popular, $75–100 for up to six people), canoe trips ($15 pp for two people), horseback tours, or a nighttime caiman-watching tour ($55 for a group of four). Unfortunately smaller groups pay the same minimum price.

Accommodations

Most *hospedajes* are downstream from the dock. On a side street there's **Nena Lodge and Tours** (tel. 505/2583-3010 or 505/8419-8158, nenalodgeandtours@yahoo.es, www.nenalodge.

com, $7–26), with 10 rooms and a streetside balcony, and **Hotel Richarson** (tel. 505/8652-6020, $12 pp). The most comfortable of the budget options is **Casa de Huespedes y Restaurante El Chinandegano** (tel. 505/2583-3011, $6 pp shared bath, $2 extra private bath).

The two-story, wooden **☾ Hotel Albergue El Castillo** (tel. 505/2583-3007 or 505/8924-5608, minar.calero@yahoo.com, $15 pp with breakfast) was built in 1992 with the help of the Spanish government. Its comfortable double balcony overlooks the town, the river, and rapids beyond. The hotel sleeps up to 35 people, with shared bath, free bottomless cup of coffee (legitimate coffee, not instant—a rarity in these parts), and Internet access. The bar and restaurant are roomy and classy.

Hotel Victoria (tel. 505/2583-0188, $40–47 including breakfast) is newer and cleaner than some of the cheaper hotels, and has hot water. Many of the rooms have bunk beds, however, and most have shared baths. Victoria is at the very end of the road leading downstream from the dock.

Travelers on a larger budget will want to treat themselves to **Posada del Rio** (on the left side of the walkway down from the dock, tel. 505/8616-3528, $75, includes breakfast). Hotel Colonial in Granada is owned by the same family, and the luxury is similar. The rooms are well decorated and all have private balconies overlooking the water, private state-of-the-art bathrooms, hot water, and air-conditioning. Laundry service is available.

Food

There are delicious and frighteningly large river shrimp beside the dock at **El Cofalito,** and steaming bowls of soup at **Soda Conchita,** served on a nice second-story deck. **El Chinandegano** is a great value ($5) for basic meals, but there is lots of similar fare down by the dock. **La Orquidea,** next to the Nazareno Church, serves coffee and cheap meals. **Border's Coffee,** just up from Nena's Lodge, has a real espresso machine and serves the good stuff. Their meals are also tasty.

Information and Services

The tourist *caseta* in front of the dock is actually a group operation known as the Asociación Municipal Ecoturismo El Castillo (AMEC) and headed up by a guy named Cofal. AMEC is constantly working on an updated list of local guides and boat services, and has compiled a series of hikes and other things to do while in town; contact them via the phone at the Albergue.

Getting There

Lanchas colectivas (to El Castillo 3–4 hours, $4–6) depart San Carlos daily at 6 A.M. (fast boat), 8 A.M., 10:30 A.M., 1:30 P.M., and 4:30 P.M. (fast boat). The last fast boat makes part of the journey after dark, which is more dangerous. Returning boats leave for San Carlos 5 A.M.–3:30 P.M., with two fast boats at 5:30 A.M. and 11:30 A.M.

To go downstream, ask around the dock or at the Albergue. Boats for San Juan del Norte pass through on Tuesday and Friday around 9 A.M. They head upstream on Thursday and Sunday, passing El Castillo in the early afternoon. It costs $13 to get to San Juan del Norte from El Castillo, or $24 on the fast boat, which is more than worth it for the six hours it saves you.

REFUGIO DE VIDA SILVESTRE RÍO SAN JUAN

This two-kilometer-wide belt that follows the north side of the river is part of the **Río Indio-Maíz Biosphere Reserve,** a 3,618-square-kilometer virgin rainforest, inaccessible to all but the most persistent scientists armed with a permit from the MARENA office in Managua. The first access point to the Refugio is just six kilometers downstream of El Castillo (or about three hours by boat from San Carlos). The western border of the reserve is made up by the Río Bartola at its confluence with the

Río San Juan. Arrange a hike through the local MARENA post, with AMEC in El Castillo, or at the ecolodge and research station, **Refugio Bartola** (tel. 505/8401-0341, refugiobartola@ yahoo.com, $55 pp with breakfast). There are 11 rooms here on the corner of the protected area with wonderful views of the river. The compound and natural history museum is surrounded by rainforest and fueled by solar energy but is difficult to contact: You may need to wait until you're in El Castillo.

Farther down the river you can access the Refugio de Vida Silvestre Río San Juan through any of the army posts including Boca San Carlos, Sarapiqui, and Delta. Do not expect much more than a place to pitch your tent and friendly, if camouflaged, company.

◀ SAN JUAN DE NICARAGUA

Still commonly referred to by its previous names of Greytown and San Juan del Norte, this settlement near the mouth of the river is located 100 winding kilometers beyond El Castillo. San Juan de Nicaragua is a remote jungle village in Nicaragua's extreme southeast corner, inhabited by some 2000 residents and visited by the odd intrepid traveler. Sir Charles Grey, governor of Jamaica, first seized the land for the English in 1848 and built the rowdy port of Greytown, which lasted about 150 years. When the British pulled out, it melted into a forgotten backwater, and these days nothing but a historic cemetery of segregated plots with both British and American headstones.

Present-day San Juan lies hidden in the brackish swamps at the confluence of Río Indio with the Río San Juan. San Juan del Norte suffered during the Contra war in the 1980s, during which time Hurricane Joan also flattened it. During this time, the residents all but deserted the area; some moved further up the river, others went south to Costa Rica. Postwar, returning residents permanently resettled in San Juan de Nicaragua some 10 minutes

SAN JUAN DEL WHAT?

Sometimes knowing a place's name is all you need to understand its history. San Juan del Sur is an elegant example. The story begins in the 16th century. Spanish explorer Diego de Machuca first reached the mouth of the winding river the Spanish called *el desaguadero* (the outlet or the drain) on June 24, 1538, feast day of Saint John the Baptist. They added "del Norte" to denote the North Sea (the Atlantic), as it was known at the time (the Pacific was the South Sea).

Rodrigo de Contreras, Nicaragua's first Spanish governor, renamed it San Juan de la Cruz in 1541, upon establishing the area's first military garrison. And so it ostensibly remained for the next 300 years, except that owing to the proliferation of Spanish San Juans around the Caribbean, traders began calling it San Juan de Nicaragua. In 1796, the Spanish declared San Juan de Nicaragua a Free Port, which the British, slowly expanding their Atlantic Coast protectorate, must have found amusing: Soon it would be theirs alone.

In 1821 Central America declared its independence from the Spanish crown, and in the ensuing power vacuum, the British took possession of the Atlantic coast with the assistance of their well-armed allies, the local Miskito Indians. At first the British helped the Miskitos take control in 1841 in return for the right to explore. In gratitude, the Miskito King Mosco renamed the town in honor of the Jamaican Governor, Sir Charles Edward Grey, who became the de facto governor of the British protectorate.

Greytown, as it was now called, grew to be the eastern terminus of one of the most popular interoceanic trading routes, and the English sent in the army to occupy the settlement in 1848, now far too important for indigenous control. Cornelius Vanderbilt's steamships made Greytown into a booming port town that received thousands of interoceanic visitors each year. During this period, Greytown was destroyed twice, once by the American Navy and once by flooding in the Río San Juan. But before it could fully recover, the steamship line closed down, gold rush traffic trickled off, and the world forgot about the little town at the end of the river and end of the world.

San Juan del Norte has essentially remained in that condition ever since, but its name continues to change. During the jingoistic war of words with Costa Rica over ownership of the river, President Arnoldo Alemán renamed the town San Juan de Nicaragua in 2002, a name often ignored by many people and mapmakers.

—Contributed by Roman Yavich, former Fulbright scholar and Nicaragua tourism expert.

north of the original site. Today, this isolated, sleepy town occasionally accommodates a few tourists, although the remote location means this area is still firmly off the beaten path.

Sights

The most popular attraction in the area are the **colonial cemeteries** which line the runway of the airport. History buffs should enjoy this area, but most will find the few remaining tombstones of little interest. This strip is a 10-minute *panga* ride from town, and a slightly shorter distance to the Caribbean ocean (often rough and unsuitable for swimming). Aside from the guides at the Rio Indio Lodge,

Cabinas Escondite (tel. 505/8414-9761) offers the only bilingual tours of the area and also runs the local turtle conservation watch; they can arrange trips to see hawksbill and green turtles come ashore to lay their eggs (Mar.–Nov.). **Don Enrique** (of Hotelito Evo) also offers several tours around the area including the largest coconut farm in Central America, sportfishing trips, and visits to the indigenous Rama Kay community. His son Raul (tel. 505/8624-6401, n.gutierrez16@yahoo.com) is an INTUR-certified guide, and has full access to the Río Indio-Maíz reserve; be aware that these tours are led in Spanish only. A two-day trip for four to six people, including hiking to hot springs, sleeping in hammocks, food, transportation, and a visit to an indigenous village, costs $400.

Across the river from San Juan del Norte, **La Laguna Azul** is a small pool of clean, blue water surrounded by coconut palms and lush vegetation. Guides Rasta and Raul can both arrange visits to this and other nearby lagoons.

Accommodations and Food

There are several decent options. Long-running **Hotelito Evo** (located on the fourth walkway parallel to the river, tel. 505/2583-9019, evohotel@yahoo.es, $15 pp) has seven clean rooms, three with a private bath. For more rustic lodgings, head to the thatched-roof cabins at **Cabinas Escondite** (tel. 505/8414-9761, $12 pp), known locally as Rasta's Place. Owner Edgar is a Caribbean-Cajun Rastafarian who's also a trained chef and guide; he serves some of the best grub in town. To get here, ask around near the military post at the north end of town, or walk down the third walkway until it ends and turn left.

Cabinas Monky (about 300m left of the dock, $20) is almost waterfront and set in a well-maintained garden. The five private cabins were undergoing renovation at the time of research, but should provide comfortable accommodation for up to three people. Tours to local sights can also be arranged by the owners.

Bar y Restaurante Tropical, located at the very southern end of the first walkway, is the town's biggest dancehall and throbs with Caribbean beats on the weekends; they also serve meals, but it's one of the priciest spots in town. For quieter dining, **Restaurante y Hospedaje Familiar** is located on the waterfront and specializes in seafood, with plates of jumbo river shrimp for about $12. They also offer seven clean and fairly spacious rooms ($14–20); two rooms jut right out over the river and share a breezy balcony. Find simple dishes at **El Ranchón** (under $5) at the southern end of town. Freshly baked breads and cookies can be picked up at Doña Berta's on the main boulevard.

Services

Services are limited, and so is the water and power supply. There is public Internet access in the library and mayor's office (*la alcaldía,* tel. 505/2583-9018). The area outside the building is a Wi-Fi hotspot for anyone in town with a laptop.

Getting There

The easiest way to get to San Juan del Norte is to fly from Managua into the newly built airport, a well-built airstrip surrounded by tropical rain forest. At the time of research there were no boats waiting to pick up passengers and move them downstream; advance hotel reservations are the best option, as your transport will then be arranged. **La Costeña**'s (tel. 505/2263-2142) biweekly flights make the run in about an hour ($110 or $165 round-trip). If flights don't suit your budget, you'll have to take the long boat ride downriver from San Carlos. A variety of *pangas* make the trip nearly every day of the week, but the schedule is in flux. The slow boat takes at least 11 hours, and costs $13 each way. The fast boat costs $25, and takes half the time. Buy your downstream ticket at the San Carlos municipal dock the day before your trip.

Rumors about scheduled weekly boat service between San Juan del Norte and Bluefields have yet to be established as true. **Captain Pastor García** (tel. 505/8513-3440 or 505/8828-9964) is set to make this weekly run for $40 per person; the trip takes about five hours. There are also weekly commercial boats that make the trip; you just may have to wait around for the departure.

THE RÍO INDIO LODGE

Since 2002, the multimillion-dollar, five-star ◖ **Río Indio Lodge** (Costa Rica tel. 506/2231-4299, U.S. tel. 866/593-3168, reservations@bluwing.com, www.bluwing.com), an ecotourism and sportfishing resort, has welcomed guests on the outskirts of the Indio Maíz Natural Reserve. The Lodge is geared to the luxury adventure traveler—one night costs about $135 per person for three fantastic meals, a night tour, and all the rum you can drink. Activities include guided fishing trips, bird-watching, kayaking, hiking, and visits to nearby Laguna Silico.

The Lodge's extensive grounds include a natural-water swimming pool (watch out for basking crocs!) and a spa and yoga pavilion were under contruction at the time of research. You can also sign up for the Bushmaster Survival School course (seven days, $1,950) based out of the lodge. Led by a vastly experienced team with extensive jungle wilderness training, you'll learn basic survival skills in the heart of the jungle.

A biological research station is currently being set up with the help of the Smithsonian Institute. The completed station will eventually include research of the abundant flora and fauna, as well as work with an enormous wildlife rescue center (also under construction) to provide homes for previously captured animals that cannot be set free into the wild.

The Lodge is situated across from the old dredge, a rusty 150-year old remnant of Nicaragua's canal aspirations, and a five-minute *panga* ride from both the airport and town of San Juan de Nicaragua; guests should make advance reservations which will include an airport pickup.

BLUEFIELDS AND THE CORN ISLANDS

The Atlantic coast of Nicaragua is a land unto itself. It extends eastward from the Amerrisque mountains, down the rivers Coco and San Juan, descending through pine savannahs to mangroves and estuaries, and finally the Caribbean. Culturally, Nicaragua's vast semi-autonomous Atlantic regions are influenced more by the English than the Spanish and ethnically, more by indigenous and African blood than by mestizos (though the "Spanish," as western Nicaraguans are known, are quickly moving in and catching up).

The vast majority of Nicaragua's 450 kilometers of Atlantic coastline are unexplored, undeveloped, and unapproachable. Writer Edward Marriot called it "Nicaragua's jungle coast.

Not the 'Caribbean'—despite cartographers' insistences—but, deliberately, the 'Atlantic'.... This was the Atlantic coast, with its mangrove swamps and alligators, hurricanes and stiff westers that washed up bales of high-grade cocaine, shrink-wrapped for export."

The Atlantic coast is languid and lazy, but it's got an edge too—in the form of bitter poverty and drug-related danger. It also has sultry mangrove estuaries, white, sandy beaches, and a relaxed lifestyle. The warm, humid breezes smelling of coconut palms and vegetation is a nice break from the dry, dusty highlands. Bluefields is an ever-expanding Caribbean port city, with enough fresh seafood to wear you out, an oppressive afternoon sun, and

HIGHLIGHTS

Puerto
Cabezas

0   40 mi

0   40 km

Wawachang and
Khaka Creek Reserve

Tasbapauni

Diving Little
Corn Island

Pearl
Lagoon

Corn
Islands

Bluefields

Diving Big
Corn Island

Palo de
Mayo
Festival

Caribbean

Sea

San Juan
del Norte

**COSTA
RICA**

© AVALON TRAVEL

LOOK FOR ◖ TO FIND RECOMMENDED
SIGHTS, ACTIVITIES, DINING, AND
LODGING.

◖ **Palo de Mayo Festival:** Sensual and rhythmic, Bluefields' joyous May Day celebration is one of the flashiest shows in the country (page 321).

◖ **Pearl Lagoon:** The quiet lanes of this waterside village beg to be explored. Follow them all the way out to the beach (page 332).

◖ **Wawachang and Khaka Creek Reserve:** Few foreigners have yet ventured up the Wawachang River to this guesthouse and forest reserve, one of Nicaragua's newest community-based ecotourism ventures (page 335).

◖ **Diving the Corn Islands:** Snorkel, swim, or scuba to visit the reefs and marine life just offshore (pages 341 and 344).

a no-hurry attitude. Corn Island and Little Corn Island are another scene altogether: the soft sand beaches and rustling palm fronds of your most primitive Caribbean fantasy, plus an isolated feeling that's hard to find elsewhere.

HISTORY

The Atlantic coast of Nicaragua was originally populated by native Miskito, Mayangna (Sumu), and Rama people, who settled along the rivers and coastline and lived on fishing and small-scale agriculture. Columbus mentioned the area when he cruised by in 1502, but throughout the 16th century, its general inhospitality kept it free of foreign influence.

Spanish friars hoping to Christianize the Mayangna, Tawaka, and Miskito were killed immediately, and Spain subsequently lost interest in this part of Central America. That made it attractive to English and Dutch pirates like Abraham Blauveldt in the 1630s, whose name in English, Bluefields, came to represent the bay and later the coastal city that emerged.

In the 1700s, the English organized the Atlantic coast into a British protectorate, establishing "Miskito Kings," whom the British educated and maintained in power. Throughout the 1700s, England armed the Miskito and Sambo people, and encouraged them to raid nearby lands, including Spanish territories in

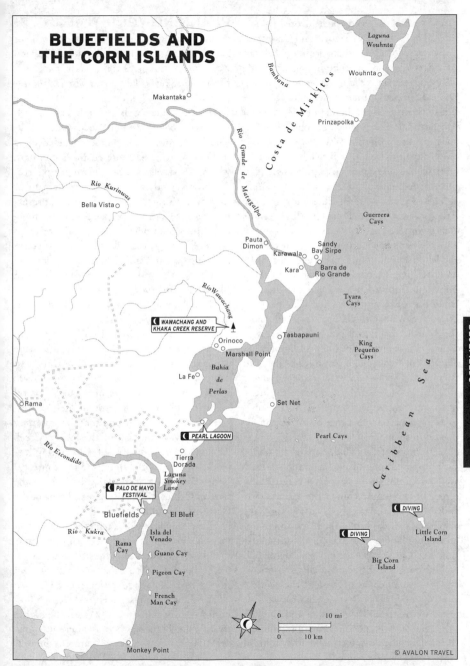

BLUEFIELDS AND THE CORN ISLANDS

Laguna Wouhnta

Wouhnta

Bambana

Costa de Miskitos

Makantaka

Río Grande de Matagalpa

Prinzapolka

Río Kurinwas

Bella Vista

Guerrera Cays

Pauta Dimon

Sandy Bay Sirpe

Karawala

Kara

Barra de Río Grande

Río Wawashang

Tyara Cays

WAWACHANG AND KHAKA CREEK RESERVE

Orinoco

Marshall Point

Tasbapauni

King Pequeño Cays

La Fe

Bahía de Perlas

Rama

Set Net

Caribbean Sea

Río Escondido

PEARL LAGOON

Pearl Cays

Tierra Dorada

Laguna Smokey Lane

PALO DE MAYO FESTIVAL

Bluefields

El Bluff

DIVING

Río Kukra

Isla del Venado

DIVING

Little Corn Island

Rama Cay

Guano Cay

Pigeon Cay

Big Corn Island

French Man Cay

0   10 mi

0   10 km

Monkey Point

© AVALON TRAVEL

BLUEFIELDS

inland Nicaragua, where the bellicose Miskitos reached as far as Nueva Segovia and Chontales.

German Moravian missionaries integrated with Atlantic coast communities beginning in the early 1800s; their legacy is a largely protestant population and distinct, Spartan churches. In 1860, the British departure was followed by the advent of American businesses, which established timber and banana company camps all along the Atlantic coast. Bluefields became a thriving commercial center with regular steamship connections to New Orleans, Baltimore, Philadelphia, and New York.

Such was the state of Bluefields and the Atlantic coast when President José Santos Zelaya ordered its military occupation in 1894. General Rigoberto Cabezas sailed down the Río Escondido in February, deposed the Miskito government, and officially united Nicaragua from Atlantic to Pacific for the first time. But once united to Spanish-speaking Nicaragua, Managua felt free to tax and ignore the Atlantic coast, and Zelaya and successors roundly abused indigenous rights for centuries. The foreign companies began to withdraw, and Sandino and his anti-imperialist troops brutally attacked those tempted to linger. In the aftermath and right up to the present, the Atlantic coast has decayed into a state of corruption, financial mismanagement, and poverty.

Costeños were decidedly apathetic about their supposed Sandinista "liberation" in 1979 and many were hostile to it after major FSLN errors in the region. Since the Contra war ended, Spanish-speaking Nicaraguans have arrived en masse, putting the black and indigenous populations in the minority for the first time ever. Considering their long-held isolation and resistance to the Managuan government, this is no small change. Tensions rise as these new "Spaniards" (as Costeños have always referred to mestizos) seek housing and employment, and at the same time, attempt to import their language, music, food, and other cultural aspects to their new home.

PLANNING YOUR TIME

If you pack a good stack of books, a bottle or two, and a jug of sunscreen, you could spend weeks on Nicaragua's right coast, exploring the islands, reefs, bays, and broad pine savannahs and villages along the coastline. Big Corn Island caters well to families and travelers seeking comfort and basic luxuries. Those who really crave remoteness should beeline to Little Corn, the more rustic of the pair, where 2–4 days will provide ample opportunity to dive and explore the reefs. Remember that everything except seafood is more expensive here—expect to pay 2–3 times more than you would on the Pacific side for lodging, beef, beer, rum, and soft drinks. If you're traveling overland from Managua, schedule in one day for the trip and another to recover in Bluefields. Otherwise, take an afternoon flight to Bluefields and spend the rest of the day poking around the city.

A night or two in both Bluefields and Pearl Lagoon is enough to get a basic taste of Creole culture, but if you have time, you can take a cooking class, sign up for Creole and Garífuna dance lessons, meet natural medicine doctors, poke around the two universities. Or head north on the early morning *panga* to Wawachang and the Khaka Creek Reserve. Spend a couple of days hiking, exploring the fauna and flora, and meeting local farmers. Then catch the *panga* back down the river to Orinoco, the Nicaraguan home of the Garífuna. Spend a day trying local foods and listening to village elders tell their unique history on a front-porch step. See if anyone wants to walk up to Marshall Point with you. A couple of days later, hop back on the *panga* and stop in Pearl Lagoon for as long as you desire.

The Atlantic coast receives 3,000–6,000 millimeters of rain annually (with the higher levels falling in the southern Región Autónoma del Atlántico Sur), making it among the wettest places on the planet. The rainy season is punctuated by hurricanes in September and October and can extend well into December, sometimes longer. The end of December is marked by cool "Christmas" winds. Most visitors come during the period between late January and April when things are generally dry and sunny. The biggest crowds arrive for Christmas, Semana Santa (the Holy Week before Easter), and during various regional fiestas, when making reservations is a good idea.

Safety

A note on safety: International drug trafficking continues to impact the Atlantic Coast of Nicaragua, including Bluefields and the Corn Islands, which have, at times, seen incidents of both petty crime and more serious assault against tourists. It is not recommend to explore too far off the beaten track in this region; stay in groups, especially on beaches, do not explore the cities alone at night, and keep your wits about you.

Bluefields

Bluefields is a waterfront melting pot of nearly 50,000 souls, many of whom make a living in the fishing and timber industries, or working on cruise ships, where their bilingual skills are prized. The city has never been connected to western Nicaragua's highway system and can be reached only by water or air. Bluefields Bay remains an important Atlantic port, and the city itself is the capital of the RAAS and home to several universities. Despite all the activity, unemployment is acute and drugs and crime are prevalent. Bluefields's primary attraction is its Creole culture. Do not miss the Palo de Mayo celebrations, an exuberant and erotic calypso-inspired dance and music event, unique to the city and celebrated fervently throughout the month of May.

ORIENTATION AND GETTING AROUND

From the Bluefields airport take a taxi for the several-kilometer approach to town for $1. Overlanders traveling from El Rama will arrive by *panga* at the municipal wharf downtown. Parque Reyes is located three blocks west of the waterfront road. Bluefields is small enough that you should need a taxi only to go to the extremes of town—the URACCAN campus at the north and the airport at the south, or when you feel unsafe. Two nearly identical bus routes run 6 A.M.–7:30 P.M. Get on and off where you like for $0.50.

SIGHTS

Bluefields does not offer much in the way of sightseeing, but if you're up for a stroll, there are a few places to visit. Start at the red-roofed **Moravian church,** built in 1848 with English, French, and Caribbean influence, the first of its kind on the Central American coast. About a block and a half west, the whitewashed wood and stained glass **Catholic cathedral** is captivating, airy, and modern.

The **Historical Museum** (located in the CIDCA building, half a block from the police station, 8 A.M.–noon and 2–5 P.M. Mon.–Fri.) is worth a visit if you'd like to learn more about Bluefields. The museum has a collection of historical objects and fascinating photos of Bluefields before Huricane Joan, the last Miskito King, and many more.

◖ Palo de Mayo Festival

Also known as the *¡Mayo Ya!* festival, Bluefields's May Day celebration is unique in Central America. In North America, this pagan-rooted party is about springtime, fertility, and the reawakening of the earth after a long winter. In Bluefields, May falls on the cusp of the rainy season, and the entire month is a bright burst of colors, parades, costumes, feasting, and most importantly, dancing around the maypole. Every night is a party, and the festival comes to

BLUEFIELDS

To Uraccan, Lunas Ranch, Playa Bonita, and Casa Rosa

MIDNIGHT DREAM
HOTEL BLUEFIELDS BAY
TIA IRENE

OASIS HOTEL & CASINO

MORAVIAN CHURCH
MUNICIPAL DOCK

Parque Reyes

CATHEDRAL
HOSTAL DOÑA VERO
CAFETIN DOMINGUEZ
BLUE CITY
BANPRO
SOUTH ATLANTIC II
PALADOR COSTENO
ALCALDÍA
BANCENTRO
COPICENTRO
MERCADITO MAS Y MENOS
ENTITEL
MINI-HOTEL
MARKET
CHEZ MARCEL
CIMA CLUB & CIMA KARAOKE
LA OLA
PIZZA MARTINUZZI AND DOS PISOS
RESTAURANTE TIP TOP
TAURO'S
MARDA MAUS
HOTEL HOLLYWOOD
THE LOBSTER POT
HOTEL CARIBBEAN DREAM
CIDCA/ HISTORICAL MUSEUM
CLINICA DE MEDICINE NATURAL
TWINS BAR & RESTAURANT
CASINO TEXAS
MR SELSO (NATURAL MEDICINE)
POLICE
CEMETERY
HOTEL EL DORADO

HOSPEDAJE CAMPELL

HOSPITAL

FOUR BROTHERS

0   200 yds
0   200 m

Bahía de Bluefields

RESTAURANT LOMA RANCHO
BICU UNIVERSITY

LA LOMA

To Airport

© AVALON TRAVEL

a rip-roaring peak at the end of the month with the celebration of the tululu dance, starting in Old Bank and parading through the Beholden, Pointeen, Central, and Cotton Tree neigborhoods.

In English and Nordic tradition of the 19th century, on the first of May young men and women would collect freshly cut flowers. This was known as "going-a-maying." A long, straight pole was set in the center of town and decorated with the fresh flowers and colored ribbons anchored to the top of the pole. The celebration ushered in the spring and expressed hopes for happiness and a good harvest.

How the Palo de Mayo got to the Atlantic coast of Nicaragua remains a mystery, though it very probably passed directly from England during the years the Atlantic coast was an English protectorate, possibly by way of Jamaica, where it evolved into something more Caribbean and erotic. To date, the Palo de Mayo is celebrated in such disparate locales as Austria, Spain, and among the Wenda and Galla people of Africa.

A FEW CREOLE EXPRESSIONS

Put your Spanish dictionary away in Bluefields—you're in Creole country! Creole is a complete language system, currently being documented by the Institute of Linguistic Promotion, Investigation, and Rescue of the Culture (IPILC) at the University of the Autonomous Regions of the Atlantic coast of Nicaragua (URACCAN). Popular books are being written to teach Creole students to read and write in their first language. The campaign slogan is: *Kriol iz wi langwij, mek wi rait it!* (Creole is our language, let's write it). At times, the rhythms of the Costeño tongue are difficult to understand, but not so tough to speak. And of course, coastal communication slides easily in and out of English and Spanish. For instance, *"Dem aprovecharing beca dem mama no de"* means "That person is taking advantage of the fact that his mother is not home." Listen for the following expressions—and try them out, if you're feeling up for it.

"She done reach Raitipura." (She arrived at Raitipura.)
"How you mean?" (Explain that please.)
"No feel, no way." (Don't worry, it's okay.)
"I no vex." (I'm not angry.)
"Dat nasty." (That's awesome!)
"That ain't nothing." (Thank you.)
"Check you then." (Goodbye.)
"Make I get tree o dem." (Give me three of those.)
"She feel fa eat some." (She's in the mood to eat.)
"He own" (His.)
"It molest we." (It bothers us.)
"Nice." ("It's all good," or goodbye.)
"Uno jus keep walking." (You all just keep walking.)
Wabool (Cassava pounder, or penis)
Coco (Coconut, or vagina)

—Thanks to "Dr. G.," a.k.a. Georgie Cayasso, Bluefields native and distinguished Creole linguist.

In Bluefields, the Palo de Mayo refers to the monthlong celebration in Bluefields, Pearl Lagoon, and the Corn Islands, and also the name of a dance and style of music. The dance has gotten progressively more sensual in recent decades—sometimes appearing as simulated sex on the dance floor (more conservative Costeños have started a movement to return the dance to its more respectable origins).

ENTERTAINMENT AND EVENTS
Nightlife

You'll hear the reggae bumping wherever you go, from dance hall, roots, *soca, punta,* and Palo de Mayo to reggae *romantica,* and of course, long sets of Bob Marley. Interestingly, the Atlantic coast's second favorite is American country music, which locals proudly call their "coastal music."

To safely sample the nightlife of Bluefields, it's recommended to move around only in groups and to arrive at clubs before 10 P.M. and leave by midnight, before the crowd gets rowdy and dangerous. For dancing, **4 Brothers** (six blocks south of the park, 9 P.M.–4 A.M. Thurs.–Sun.) has been the heart of the Creole social scene since the 1990s. Expect a small, cramped juke joint with a wooden-plank dance floor and ice-cold beer. You'll need that beer to help you master the sensual Caribbean "hug-up" grind.

Cima Club (half a block up from Bancentro on the left, 2nd floor) draws a lively Creole crowd with its intimate dance floor; upstairs, **Cima Karaoke** offers louder music, a spacious dance floor, a longer bar, and a more diverse crowd (both are open seven days a week). **Midnight Dream** (Barrio Pointeen, two long blocks from the Moravian church, open daily), known locally as Lala's (a.k.a. Lawrence Omeir, owner, former mayor, and town celebrity) is a prominent drinking and dancing social center with a dark, open-air bar and dance floor with a view of the bay. They also serve food; both the *rondon* and the soup here come highly recommended.

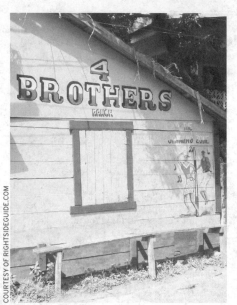

COURTESY OF RIGHTSIDEGUIDE.COM

4 Brothers is the heart of Bluefields nightlife.

BLUEFIELDS

Live Music and Radio

Soak in the culture with programs like *Roots Rap Reggae* (9 A.M. on Radio Zinica, 95.9 FM), *Energía Volumen* (4–6 P.M. on Radio La Morenita, 102.1 FM), and *Caribbean Breeze* (1 P.M. on Radio Punto Tres, 90.7 FM). Radio La Costeñísima plays regular sets of Miskito music (101.1 FM). Hear the Voice of America daily at 6 A.M. on Radio Bluefields Estereo (96.5 FM), followed by a country music show. On 97.7 FM, Radio Riddim hosts Creole talk radio programs about local politics and autonomy, as well as good reggae and dance hall music.

To hear local artists in the process of making music, and to pick up CDs of their recordings, stop by the **Bluefields Sound System** studio, found kitty-corner to the Oasis Hotel and casino. This multimedia learning and cultural center also hosts occasional live music shows, and is a great place to tap into popular Bluefields culture.

Festivals and Events

The biggest show in town is Palo de Mayo,

but since the 1950s, when Bluefields adopted the patron saint of the city of Masaya, **San Jerónimo** is honored each September 30 with fireworks and celebration. These festivities roll right into the city's birthday celebrations which last throughout the month of October. October 30 is the anniversary of the 1987 passage of the Autonomy Law; its commemoration features cuisine competitions between all the ethnic groups. This is a great time of year to sample the foods of the coast, learn about the autonomy process (and its history), and meet community leaders and politicians.

SHOPPING

Visiting the town market on the municipal dock is a dark, damp experience, with cramped stalls in an ugly metal building, but it's interesting nevertheless, especially if you need to stock up on homemade cheese and buns. **Joyería y Artesanía Gutierrez** (Barrio Central in front of the SOS Farmacia) sells Caribbean-inspired wood carvings, which you'll also find at some hotel shops. **Julio Lopez,** a Garífuna originally from Orinoco (Barrio 19 de Julio, in front of INAFOR) and **Leo Bolanos Padilla** (Barrio 19 de Julio, *"contiguo donde fue la cocotera,"* or "next to where the coconut trees used to be," tel. 505/2572-0070) are renowned local artisans. **Mr. Rene Hodgson** (tel. 505/2572-1658) is a talented, self-taught Creole painter and local Adventist pastor whose work is frequently displayed at the Bluefields Bay Hotel.

SPORTS AND RECREATION

For professional catch-and-release river and deep-sea fishing (and wildlife tours), contact Randy and Rosa at the **Casa Rosa Lodge** (local cell 505/8832-4269 or 505/8853-4080, toll-free 912/275-5485, randyrosa97@hotmail.com, www.rumbleinthejungle.net, $45 d). For $325 a day per person, you get a large room, all meals, guide, boat, and gear; bar drinks and tip are not included. Ask about discounts for stays of more than one night.

CRAB SOUP!

Be here at the end of August (27-28) for the **Crab Soup Festival,** a commemoration of the islanders' emancipation from British slavery in 1841. The governor of this then-British protectorate, sitting miles away in Kingston, Jamaica, was authorized to pay slave owners compensation for the loss of their "assets," while the newly freed slaves scrambled to put together a meal out of what was most handy—crabs. Be sure to catch the crowning of Miss Corn Island, Miss Coconut, and Miss Photogenic.

ACCOMMODATIONS

Bluefields is more dangerous than other Nicaraguan cities, and the city is grimy and less sanitary in general—just get an eyeful of all the dirty water and mangy mutts slithering down the roads. So this is one place where "roughing it" in the cheapest flophouses (there are a few obvious ones near the dock) is asking for trouble. If you do decide to go for one of the budget hotels, assess both its security measures and the kind of people hanging around. Insist on a window with screens and a mosquito net. Avoid the Pension Lopez, famous for drunk men and hourly room rentals.

Under $25

Hospedaje El Dorado (Barrio Punta Fría, across from the Cruz Lorena, tel. 505/2572-1435, $6–10) is a good option if you are determined to stick to a strict budget. The hotel offers relatively clean, well-maintained rooms with private bath and cable TV. **Lobster Pot** (on the main drag in Barrio Central, no phone, $6–8 pp) is owned by a Creole-speaking Cayman Islander who runs a large establishment that rents many of its rooms to permanent guests. The clean (if dingy) rooms with a shared bath are better than some other run-down places but that's about it. ◖ **Hostal Doña Vero** (half a block

west and half a block south of the cathedral, tel. 505/2572-2166, $10–15) is the best budget option, where safe and clean rooms come with fan, private bathroom and wireless Internet access. **Hospedaje Campbell** (tel. 505/8827-2221, $11 w/fan, $20 with a/c), on the road from the airport, competes for best budget lodgings with basic rooms, all en-suite with cable TV.

Mini-Hotel Central (Barrio Central, across from Bancentro, tel. 505/2572-2362, $15 with fan, $20 with a/c) has been a mainstay of Bluefields since 1983 and its 10 rooms are nearly always booked. It has a popular restaurant and outside veranda, and small but well-maintained rooms that include private bath and cable TV.

$25-50

Bluefields Bay Hotel (tel. 505/2572-2143, www.bluefieldsbayhotel.com, $35 d includes tax and breakfast) is on the water, away from the hustle and bustle of the central barrio, yet still within walking distance of town. It's a uniquely Costeño establishment that helps fund university programs and has clean, comfortable rooms with hot water and air-conditioning. It's also home to the Tía Irene Bar and Restaurant.

Hotel Caribbean Dream (Barrio Punta Fría, 30 meters south of the main market, tel. 505/2572-0107, $27 d) offers spacious, well-appointed rooms with private bathroom, closets, cable TV, new air-conditioning units, hot water, Wi-Fi, an on-site restaurant, a bright atmosphere, and an upstairs veranda. **Hotel South Atlantic II** (Barrio Central, half a block south of the Moravian church, tel. 505/2572-1022, $20–32) is a friendly, centrally located Creole establishment, popular with Nicaraguan business travelers. They offer a safe environment and well-maintained rooms with air-conditioning, cable TV, hot water, and an on-site restaurant and travel agency.

Over $50

Oasis Hotel (on the corner near the municipal

wharf, tel. 505/2572-2812, reservations@oasis-casinohotel.com, www.oasiscasinohotel.com, $75–90 pp plus tax, includes breakfast) was opened in 2005 by a North American business-man who also owns the two casinos in town (one of which is on-site). This is the classiest hotel in town, with both carpeted and hard-wood floors, Wi-Fi, and good views. The hand-ful of spacious rooms have lovely bathrooms, minibars, safe, TV, and air-conditioning. There are a few larger suites, and the top floor is a ri-diculously huge presidential apartment with a hot tub overlooking the bay; it used to belong to a foreign playboy.

FOOD
Breakfast and Cafés

Some of the best coconut bread in town can be picked up at **Mission House** in front of the central park, or at "Brother Ray's" bakery at the Marinatha Church. For a true coast snack, try the moist Coco Cake: grated taro with coconut milk, cinnamon, nutmeg, and sugar. For savory small loaves of coconut bread, bun, soda cake (coco-nut bread with ginger and sugar), and *pico* (bread with sugar and cheese), go to the woman in front of Mercadito Mas y Menos in Barrio Central.

You won't find pancakes or gringo breakfast in Bluefields, but the **Cafetin Dominguez** next door to Hostal Doña Vero does a mean coco-gallo pinto plate with eggs for under $3.

Nica and International

Mini-Hotel Central Café (a few doors down from the Enitel office) offers a wide range of well-prepared Nicaraguan and Costeño dishes at reasonable prices. **Tía Irene Bar and Restaurant** (below the Bluefields Bay Hotel, www.bluefieldsbayhotel.com, under $9) serves simple plates on a waterfront *rancho* with good views of town.

Try **Segundo Piso** (upstairs from Pizza Martinuzzi, next to Parque Reyes, from $6)

Creole dishes such as *rondon* feature plenty of seafood.

SEA TO SOUP: ATLANTIC COAST COOKIN'

Atlantic coast cuisine is marked by its simplicity and freshness. That lobster on your plate was probably picked off the ocean floor this morning; the fish were swimming hours ago. The only way you'll get fresher fish is by cooking it on the ship—or eating it raw: **ceviche** with lime juice, tomato, and onion. Seafood on the Nicaraguan Atlantic is cheap by international standards, delicious by anyone's standards, and well worth the wait (most Bluefields restaurants are slow, even by Nicaraguan standards). If your travel complaints don't evaporate in the garlicky steam of lobster under your nose, then you obviously are going to need to spend another couple of days.

Start off with **yellowfin, snapper,** or **sea bass,** grilled or fried. **Conch,** when tenderized correctly, is soft and delicate, less briny than other seafood but with a soft texture. Or enjoy a lobster *al vapor,* bulging with delicate, white meat you can pull from the shell with your fingers, drenched in butter and lime.

Mixed soup is served in a helmet-sized bowl choked with crab, lobster, conch, and fish. Not hearty enough? Then reach for **rondon,** or rundown, a thick stew of fish (or endangered turtle), vegetables, and coconut milk thickened with starchy tubers and plantains. In August, don't miss the Corn Island **Crab Soup Festival,** when Costeños cook tons of soft crabmeat into a festival you won't forget. Atlantic coast crabmeat is particularly soft, with a delicate flavor unique to the tropics.

You don't have to stick to seafood to eat well on the Atlantic coast. Even the *gallo pinto* tastes better here: That's because it's cooked in sweet coconut oil. Between meals, fill up with **coco bread**—football-sized loaves of soft, rich wheat flour cooked up with coconut and served hot out of the oven. Another treat is kind of like cinnamon rolls but without the cinnamon: hot coconut **bun** is sweet and sticky.

whose pies are pretty close to the real thing. Both joints are under the same ownership, but locals prefer the taste of the second-floor pizzas. A step above the street *comedores* is **La Ola,** with *comida típica* and a few Chinese-style dishes ($3–7). The upstairs balcony is a great spot for people-watching and offers some respite from the baking heat of the street.

Street Food and *Frito*

In Bluefields, Creole *fritanga* (usually just $1) features stewed chicken with a savory brown and salty sauce, served in a small, plastic bag with *tajadas* and Creole cabbage salad. The mestizo version of *frito* consists of fried or slow-roasted chicken plus all your favorites from Spanish-speaking Nicaragua. Try Doña Arlen's un-named *comedor*—known locally as **Berjas Blancas**—in Barrio Central, right across the street from the well-known Galileo store; or right across the road from the *comedor* known as **Plata.** Enchiladas ($0.25) and cheap beef tacos are on the menu at **Pulpería El Guayabo.**

Upscale

Twins Seafood and More (Barrio Central, next to Texas Casino) is the hip restaurant in town, specializing in seafood, vegetarian, and salads. After 4 P.M., the bar and dance floor upstairs are popular with the moneyed Creole crowd. **Loma** (near BICU) is another semi-elegant option with a view from your table, a longer menu, and steeper prices. Feel free to drink the ice (they have a water purification system for ice and fresh drinks), in a delicious piña colada or a fresh fruit punch.

Tía Irene Bar and Restaurant is located over the water at Bluefields Bay Hotel; service is slow and the menu is small, with dishes under $9, but the location does offer a nice view of the bay. ◖ **Lunas Ranch** (Barrio Loma Fresca, almost across from URACCAN) is a well-known restaurant in the newer part of town. Decorated with the traditional thatched-roof design, the restaurant offers great food, midrange prices, and a very professional staff. **Chez Marcel** (a few doors down from Pizza Martinuzzi, $5–10) is another long-time standby, especially if you're craving steak.

Playa Bonita (jeanlouis.vigo@gmail.com) opened in 2007 by a French–Bluefields couple, offers a varied menu in an open-air, waterfront setting in Barrio Loma Fresca; take a taxi. **Casa Rosa Lodge** (www.rumbleinthejungle.net, $6–12) is a small, family-run restaurant specializing in seafood. It is located next to Playa Bonita and on the waterfront.

INFORMATION AND SERVICES
Tourist Information
The **INTUR** office (tel. 505/2572-0221) can't hold a candle to CIDCA, the Research and Documentation center for the Atlantic coast (affiliated with the UCA, 50 meters north of the police station, 8 A.M.–5:30 P.M. Mon.–Fri., with a break for lunch). CIDCA makes available to the public a wide selection of materials about Caribbean cultures and languages, including several Miskito-only publications.

The most up-to-date information on Bluefields and travel to surrounding areas can be found online (http://therightsideguide.com), with a handy transport schedule and useful phone numbers.

The only tour company in town is **Atlantic Travel** (tel. 505/2572-2259 or 505/8693-6554, atlantictour.caribe@hotmail.com), run by local Cesar Patterson; ask for guided tours of Bluefields and elsewhere on this stretch of coast. Another great source of information on Bluefields is **Kenny Siu** (tel. 505/8837-2861, ksiu2000@yahoo.com), a Corn Island native who teaches tourism at the university. Kenny is a wealth of information; he worked with a Travel Channel film crew when *Bizarre Foods with Andrew Zimmern* came to film in Bluefields.

Services
The fire department (tel. 505/2572-2298) is just north of the Moravian church; the **police** (tel. 505/2572-2448) are located on the same side of the street, three blocks south; and the **Red Cross** (tel. 505/2572-2582) can be found in Barrio Fatima. **Hospital Ernesto Sequeira** (tel. 505/2572-2391 main switchboard or 505/2822-2621 emergency) is located about five, long blocks south and west of the park.

The **Claro phone office** (8 A.M.–5 P.M. Mon.–Fri., 8 A.M.–noon Sat.) is located next to Mini-Hotel Central. The **post office** is half a block west of the Texas Casino building, and the two **Western Union** offices are located one and two blocks east of the park.

Banpro is the older of the two banks on the Atlantic coast and is located in front of the Moravian church. **Bancentro** is located just around the corner on Calle Cabezas. Both are open 8 A.M.–5 P.M. Monday–Friday and 8 A.M.–noon Saturday. Money changers are on the corner between the two banks and are both safe and useful. Both banks feature 24-hour ATM service, though the one at Banpro dispenses the money in much more reasonable denominations (100 *córdoba* vs. 500 *córdoba* bills, which can be hard to change in Bluefields). The town hall (or Palacio) also has a 24-hour ATM booth, located just east of the park, across the street.

Bluefields has faster Internet access than much of western Nicaragua. For the best chance of securing a decent computer without a long wait, check out the original Bluefields cybercafé, **Copicentro.** Another good option is **Blue City;** it offers a nice atmosphere, many computers, air-conditioning, beverages, CD burning, printing, and a music studio. All offer Internet access for about $0.75 per hour.

GETTING THERE
By Land
The overland route is no longer the heroic journey it once was before they repaved the highway to El Rama in 2002–2003, but you'll still need some stamina and patience. Most people leave Managua for El Rama at night, then board a predawn *panga* and soak up two hours

BLUEFIELDS

Commercial boats, or "chicken boats," are also used to transport passengers.

of fresh air during a sunrise trip down the Río Escondido to Bluefields (bring a sweater for both parts of the trip). This route is cheaper than flying, and also offers you a true appreciation for Nicaragua's sheer girth—and the Atlantic coast's geographical isolation.

Six daily buses to El Rama leave from Managua's Mayoreo terminal (tel. 505/2248-3005, 6 A.M.–9 P.M.) and from Mercado Ivan Montenegro (tel. 505/2280-4561) daily at 9 P.M. Call ahead for seats. Express buses don't linger in Juigalpa or stop along the road, shaving two hours off the trip. All boat transportation to Bluefields is found at the Rama municipal wharf: *pangas* cast off from the dock as they fill up, 6 A.M.–4 P.M. (1.5-hour trip to Bluefields, $11 pp). There are several larger ships that carry freight and passengers between El Rama, Bluff, Corn Island, and Puerto Cabezas, but they are slow. They leave El Rama every Tuesday and Saturday at 11 A.M. (call the *Captain D* at 505/8690-9719 or 8850-2767).

By Air

La Costeña (tel. 505/2263-2142 or Bluefields Airport branch, tel. 505/2572-2750) offers regular, daily flights between Bluefields, Managua, and Big Corn Island. The trip from Managua to Bluefields takes about one hour and costs $83 for a one-way ticket ($127 round-trip). To fly directly from Managua to Corn Island will cost $107 ($165 round-trip). The flight from Bluefields to Corn Island costs $65 ($99 round-trip). It is easy to buy a Managua–Corn Island round-trip ticket with a stopover in Bluefields on the way to Corn Island for $197. Buying an "open" ticket means no dates are fixed, so you can arrange your onward flight by calling or visiting the airport, or by dealing with a ticket broker in town (South Atlantic II hotel is a good one, or look for the Costeña and Atlantic signs elsewhere).

By Boat

Passenger-boat traffic to El Rama, Pearl

Lagoon, Orinoco, and Pueblo Nuevo (up the Wawachang River) originates from the main municipal dock. Pay the $0.10 entrance fee at the first window (pays for their cable TV connection). Trips to El Bluff ($2.50 each way) originate at a much smaller MINSA dock next to the municipal market (inquire at the market). Old cargo-passenger boats leave three times a week for Corn Island. If you choose this route instead of flying, take lots of water, sun protection, a barf bag, and a sense of humor. The *Captain D* (tel. 505/8690-9719 or 8850-2767, about $35, 12 hours) reportedly makes monthly runs to Puerto Cabezas around the middle of the month, but I've never heard of anyone making this trip.

There is no scheduled boat service between Bluefields and San Juan del Norte, but this may change. Ask around at the dock, or check online (http://rightsideguide.com) for current information.

Near Bluefields

EL BLUFF

Once connected to the mainland before 1988 when Hurricane Joan breached the bar, El Bluff is an industrial platform that happens to be adjacent to a gorgeous little Caribbean white sand beach. Reconnected in 2006 by pedestrian walkway, El Bluff makes an exotic day trip for Bluefielders tired of the "big city," but only attracts the most adventurous foreigners. El Bluff remains an important port, deepened in the 1980s by Bulgarian cooperation and currently in search of private investment to build out Nicaragua's ties with the eastern U.S. and Europe.

Hire a Bluefields *panga* to get to El Bluff (from the MINSA dock next to the municipal market in Bluefields for $1.50, 30-minute ride, embarking as soon as they fill up with 12 passengers. The last boat returns to Bluefields around 4 P.M.). From Hotelito El Bluff, walk out the main entrance of the hotel, take your first left onto a paved path and follow it through a residential area until it ends (about 10–15 minutes). Keep going straight for about 200 meters, at which point you will be able to see the beach.

There's no reason to stay here, as Bluefields has better options. But for the determined, **Hotelito El Bluff** (tel. 505/2577-0059, $5) is located right next to the park, with basic rooms with cable TV and fan. Skip the hotel restaurant in lieu of **La Casona Bar and Restaurant** (open Tues.–Sun. nights), located along the paved path towards the beach.

RAMA CAY

Fifteen kilometers south of Bluefields is Rama Cay, ancestral home of the Rama people. About 800 souls live on this small island. According to historians, the Rama people are originally descended from the Chibchas and Aruac Rama from the Amazon basin; several oral histories explain how the Rama came to occupy this isolated island at the end of the 17th century. Rama culture is now disappearing: Only a small handful of elders still speak the language.

A tour of the island is sometimes available to visitors for $3 ($6 if you want lunch). Getting to Rama Cay is an easy $6 *panga* ride from Bluefields; it takes about an hour to cross the bay.

RESERVA SILVESTRE GREENFIELDS

On the outskirts of Kukra Hill, Reserva Silvestre Greenfields (tel. 505/2279-0589 or 505/8428-8403, info@greenfields.com.ni, www.greenfields.com.ni) is a protected reserve, characterized by scenic beauty, silence, and its proximity to nature. Privately managed as an ecotourism business, the reserve offers more than 25 kilometers of hiking trails; canoe through jungle watercourses, or rest and enjoy the silence

AFRICAN-DERIVED SPIRITUAL PRACTICES OF THE ATLANTIC COAST

A distant cousin to the voudoun ("voodoo") of Haiti and Benin, **Obeah** refers to sorcery, folk magic, and other religious practices brought by Central and West African slaves to the Americas. Using herbal teas and baths, charms, amulets, and prayer, Obeah is best described as a method of communication with the supernatural world, and a means of calling on metaphysical powers through shamanistic rituals.

Obeah was frowned upon by Christian missionaries and slave masters, resulting in the awkward Christianization of modern Obeah: Many African deities now bear the names of Catholic saints. Obeah is most commonly used in the West Indies, but is widely practiced in Caribbean and Latin American nations whose African descendants have maintained a connection to this aspect of their ancestry, including the Creole, Garífuna, and Miskito people on Nicaragua's Atlantic coast.

Contrary to popular belief, Obeah is not always used for negative purposes. In fact, often times Costeños pay a practitioner to heal a medical, emotional, or spiritual problem; to influence events in a person's favor; to achieve success in a particular endeavor; or to find out the answer to an important question (such as "Who is my husband sleeping with?" "Who stole my cows?" etc.).

However, among the Miskito and Afro-Caribbean peoples, negative Obeah is not unheard of: Locals will even resort to Obeah revenge rather than the police department. Whether you personally believe in Obeah or not, on the Atlantic coast you are entering a world where the practice and the belief of Obeah are a large part of the culture, and every Costeño believes, just a little, in its power.

When visiting the Caribbean coast of Nicaragua, there is no need to fear Obeah (unless you take away another's lover!). Moreover, the way that most Costeños approach Obeah is indicative of their overall spiritual perspective on life. For example, in Creole culture, there is a strong nine-day ritual that follows a person's death: As soon as the person is pronounced dead, word begins to spread among the Creole community. The family's closest friends and family quickly arrive at the house to clean, cook, and receive the multitudes that will soon come to accompany the family during their grief. This setup occurs 24 hours a day (though most people come at night) and appears to be like a party without the music—crowds of people eating, drinking rum, and talking. On the ninth night, the night before the person is finally buried, a very specific ritual occurs: The same close friends and family of the deceased go through the house and remove all bed linens, tablecloths, and curtains. At midnight, all present sing to the spirit of the deceased to signal that it is now time to ascend to heaven. It is widely believed that failure to perform this ritual will cause the spirit of the dead person to wander the earth as a miserable ghost, causing trouble, harm, and sometimes death to the living.

For more information, check out the novels and memoirs of Jamaica Kincaid, or *Vampire the Masquerade, Unburnable,* and *Brown Girl in the Ring* by Nalo Hopkinson.

In Bluefields, Mr. Selso (tel. 505/8845-4137 or 505/2572-2176) is a traditional and fascinating Miskito **"Bush Docta"** and Obeah practitioner who is highly sought after for spiritual, emotional, and medical issues that doctors trained in western medicine have been unable to resolve.

The small **Clinica de Medicina Natural en Terapias Alternative** (Barrio Teodoro Martinez, Avenida Cabeza, in front of Escondite bar, 5:30-8 P.M.) is a natural medicine clinic offering beach flower therapy, healing massage, and medicinal plants.

—Contributed by Phoebe Haupt-Cayasso, trip leader and experiential learning consultant with a decade of experience working with students in Bluefields and Atlantic coast communities.

surrounded by lush vegetation. There are two cabins ($50 double, $100 two-bedroom, rate includes lodging and equipment use) for overnight use. Or rough it and camp ($50 per group up to six people) in very basic conditions—bring a mosquito net. Meals can be cooked in the two-room cabin, or served at the *rancho* for an additional $15 pp per day. All trips must be previously arranged and reservations need to be received at least four days in advance.

KARAWALA AND SANDY BAY

Sandy Bay, located three hours north along the Caribbean coast, is one of the only Miskito communities accessible from Bluefields, and nearby Karawala is the last indigenous Ulwa site in the world (the Ulwa are related to the Mayangna but have distinct cultural characteristics and language). The boat ($17 one-way) to both places leaves the *muelle* (dock) in Bluefields on Mondays and Fridays at 10 A.M.—or whenever they fill up; it returns on Wednesdays and Fridays. There's not much to do in Sandy Bay for nonanthropologists, although the beach is nice. Karawala, however, is situated between pine forest and mangrove swamps and offers world-class tarpon fly-fishing. In town, you'll find basic accommodations and simple meals. Sand flies in both places can get pretty bad, so be prepared with long pants and baby oil.

◖ PEARL LAGOON

Tucked away one lagoon north of Bluefields, Pearl Lagoon (Laguna de Perlas) is a small community whose natural splendor is a welcome respite from Bluefields, where sandy streets are easily explored on foot. This little village gives access to local Miskito communities and the enchanting Pearl Cays. The locals earn their living from the water—you'll see boats of the five companies that deal in fishing

Traffic is slow-to-none in this quiet Caribbean town.

and fish processing tied up along the docks or moored in the lagoon. Denmark and Norway have been active in the economic development of the region, constructing municipal piers in Pearl Lagoon, Haulover, Tasbapauni, Kakabila, Brown Bank, and Marshall Point to assist local fishermen in getting their catch to market.

Sights and Entertainment

It's hard to miss the **"the great gun,"** as the locals lovingly call the iron cannon mounted in front of the municipal dock and surrounded by a tiny garden. Embossed with the seal of the British empire and the year 1803, it dates back to the protectorate. The clean architectural style of the most eye-catching building in town, the whitewashed **Moravian church**, was typical of the period. Attending an evening service there is memorable (dress appropriately).

Catch a night of reggae at one of Pearl Lagoon's several small *ranchos*, or clubs, the most popular of which is **Bar Relax.**

Pearl Lagooners love baseball, and compete on teams with names like the Buffalos, Mariners, Young Stars, Hurricanes, Sweet Pearly, First Stop, Young Braves, and the Haulover Tigers—watch them battle it out at the stadium on Saturdays and Sundays September–January.

Accommodations

Pearl Lagoon has several guesthouses and hotels, all within several blocks of one another. The best of the family-run guesthouses is **Ⅽ Green Lodge Guesthouse** (tel. 505/2572-0507, $15), a pleasant place on the main drag. **Hospedaje Slilma** (one block south and half a block east of the Claro center, tel. 505/2572-0523, $7–20) has two floors of well-maintained rooms in a large, pastel-colored house. Downstairs rooms with shared bathrooms are cheaper, while those upstairs catch a better breeze and are all en-suite. (*Slilma* is the Miskito word for star, so locals refer to this

hotel as La Estrella.) Right on the main drag in front of the dock, **Sweet Pearly's** (tel. 505/2572-0520, $10–13) is another standby with 11 small, clean rooms with fans, plus a bar, restaurant, and ice-cream parlor downstairs.

Casa Blanca Hotelito y Restaurante (about two blocks northwest of the baseball stadium, tel. 505/2572-0508, $10–30) is clean, well liked, and run by a Danish-Creole couple intent on making your trip pleasurable. **Hotel Casa Ulrich** (400 meters north of the dock, tel. 505/2572-5009, casaulrich@hotmail.com, $15 w/fan and shared bath, $30 en-suite bath and a/c) is a higher-end choice on the waterfront with comfortable rooms and easy access to the dining *rancho* (easily one of the best restaurants on the Atlantic coast).

Food

Miss Betty's Bread Shop is the place to go for coffee, pastries, juices, and sweets, specializing in all things coco-based. The **Green Lodge** serves fresh, well-prepared food; their plate of the day costs $3–5, though breakfast is cheaper. **Warner's Place** (tel. 505/8426-7565), across from the school, serves upscale local food with international influences, such as jerk chicken and BBQ shrimp. Warner's is open for dinner only, when the pleasant garden seating affords a fine view of the starry sky. Guests staying in the on-site rooms ($25) can order breakfast if desired.

Ⅽ Queen Lobster (100 meters north of the municipal dock, 10 A.M.–11 P.M. daily, $7–15) has a tranquil setting on the lagoon and serves mostly seafood, with plenty of its namesake lobster. The two stilted waterfront cabins (from $35) here also provide the most romantic lodgings in the Pearl Lagoon.

The **Casa Blanca Restaurante** has a varied menu served in a pleasant ambience, though a few readers have complained about poor service. Shrimp dishes start at $6; lobster at $8.

The restaurant **Ⅽ Casa Ulrich** ($6–14) is owned and run by a multilingual chef who garnered some of his culinary skills in France and Switzerland. The atmospheric *rancho* overlooks the water and is a great place to sample Pearl Lagoon's famous fruits of the sea.

Services

The ENITEL office and a police post are in the center of "town" by the wharf. The health clinic is a few blocks south, to the right of the Moravian church. Four pharmacies can take care of basic medical needs. For more serious medical emergencies, you will be strapped into a *panga* and rocketed off to Bluefields. With that in mind, stay safe.

Getting There

The *panga* trip up the Río Escondido and then north through a complex network of waterways to Pearl Lagoon is a beautiful ride that takes under an hour and costs $7 each way. On the way, you'll pass several shipwrecks, and the active dock at Kukra Hill, named after a long-assimilated cannibalistic tribe. Go to the municipal dock in Bluefields around 7 A.M. to sign up for the Pearl Lagoon *panga*. Boats leave as soon as they have 20 passengers, all day until 3 P.M. The last *panga* back from Pearl Lagoon leaves between noon and 3 P.M. but won't leave if the boat isn't full.

Traveling to and from El Rama by land is also possible. A daily bus departs from the wharf in El Rama for Pearl Lagoon at 4 P.M. ($6); be prepared for a bumpy 4.5-hour ride. A daily bus returns to El Rama, departing from Pearl Lagoon at 6 A.M.

THE PEARL CAYS

Most of the 18 specks of land that make up the Pearl Cays archipelago remain untouched and relatively accessible, though a few cays are being built up by wealthy foreigners, and controversy over their ownership and development is building. The cays (pronounced "keys") are six kilometers east of a small Miskito coastal village called Set Net. Hire a boat from Pearl Lagoon and enjoy the ride through the harbor, into the open Caribbean, then up the empty coastline to the cays.

So far, the Pearl Cays have zero tourist facilities (though islands may be rented privately; one resort has come and gone, and more may follow), so bring water and your *Gilligan's Island* survival kit to be safe. Arrange a trip through La Casa Blanca or the Queen Lobster (www.queenlobster.com) in Pearl Lagoon. A round-trip *panga* ride to the Pearl Cays can cost $150–300, and gas prices continue to rise, so the more people chipping in the better. If you find yourself sharing one of the islets with local anglers cutting down coconuts and telling fishing stories over a fire on the beach, feel free to strike up a deal for some fresh seafood for the grill.

VILLAGES NEAR PEARL LAGOON
Awas

The town of Pearl Lagoon sits on the southeast side of a small prominence jutting out into the bay. Walk west from the town (to the left of the dock) to get to the broad, shallow lagoon-beach community of Awas. This half-hour walk down a flat, sandy road will cross a saltwater estuary and a small footbridge. When you get to the Miskito community of Raitipura (Miskito for "on top of the cemetery"), turn left and follow the road to Awas. Rent a small palm-thatch hut from one of the locals for $2–4, kick back, and relax. Take advantage of the **Bar and Restaurant Tropical View,** built out over the water.

Tasbapauni

Farther up the coast, on the Caribbean side of the land, is the community of Tasbapauni (two hours from Pearl Lagoon), set on a thin strip of land right between the Caribbean and the lagoon, close to the Man of War Cays. There is one place to stay: **Mini Hotel, Bar & Restaurant Yadosh** (tel. 505/2572-9080, $10) with seven rooms with private bathrooms; the restaurant offers a wide variety of seafood. Beware of the sand flies when the breeze is not blowing (same with visiting Set Net). From Bluefields, you can go directly here via *panga* for $13 each way.

Pueblo Nuevo

To hear the Bluefielders tell it, Pueblo Nuevo, 45 minutes up the Wawachang River just to the west of Orinoco, is home to farming families that began slashing and burning back in the Pacific, and mowed their way east until they hit the Atlantic. FADCANIC is here teaching organic farming and forest management in order to save the only remaining tropical forest in the region. Catch the Pueblo Nuevo *panga,* departing Bluefields on Sundays and Wednesdays ($12 pp each way), and returning on Mondays and Thursdays. He passes Wawachang and the Khaka Creek Reserve on his way to Pueblo Nuevo. It's harder to catch *at* Pueblo Nuevo, when it might already be full. Either way, reserve your return seat in the boat on your way upstream.

◖ Wawachang Center and Khaka Creek Reserve

The Wawachang region is serviced by the Foundation for the Autonomy and Development of the Atlantic Coast of Nicaragua (FADCANIC, www.fadcanic.org.ni). Founded by a small group of passionate Creole leaders in the early 1990s, FADCANIC manages a number of successful development programs, financed largely by the Norwegian government and various nongovernmental organizations (NGOs). The **Wawachang Center for Sustainable Agro-Forestry Development** is FADCANIC's largest microcredit program. Stop by to visit the Agro-Forestry high school and walk the fields, seedling nursery, and model farm.

The Wawachang Center (tel. 505/2572-2386, email geovasandoval@yahoo.com) is ideal for ecological research and is equipped

with solar energy, Internet access, screened windows, and purified water. A guesthouse offers seven rooms (one with a double bed and private bath) that can accommodate 25 people; the cost is $5 per person per night for lodging, $3.50 per meal, and about $10 for the services of a local trail guide. To arrange your stay and horseback pickup service, stop by the FADCANIC office located just up from Mini-Hotel. You'll have to make your own way out here on one of two weekly *pangas* from the dock in Bluefields (departing for Khaka on Wed. and Sun.; returning to Bluefields on Thur. and Mon., $11 each way).

Located about a kilometer up the river from Wawachang, Khaka Creek Reserve is the epitome of the local, grass-roots ecotourism movement which is providing alternate means of subsistence in a delicate ecosystem. Run by FADCANIC, modern tourist facilities allow visitors to take advantage of this wilderness area, with hiking trails, eight cabins, and trained guides knowledgeable in local flora and fauna.

ORINOCO AND MARSHALL POINT

Orinoco is the southernmost home of the Garífuna people, a distinct ethnic group with strong West African roots unique to Central America. On May 18, 2001, UNESCO proclaimed the Garífuna language, music, and dance a "Masterpiece of the Oral and Intangible Heritage of Humanity." Their dancing, drumming, and singing manifests strongly African roots. Try to visit on November 19, the Garífuna Arrival Day in Nicaragua and National Day for the Garífuna People, featuring talented Garífuna singers, drummers, and dancers from the coast, as well as from Belize, Honduras, and Guatemala.

Marshall Point is a typical small Creole community. You can reach Marshall Point by going to Orinoco and then walking or hiring a *panga* to take you around the corner. Do not walk alone.

The Garífuna capital of Orinoco was declared part of UNESCO's Intangible "Heritage of Humanity."

Tip: Grease the edge of your shoes with a thick line of petroleum jelly as you arrive in Orinoco and Marshall Point, as grass lice can be abundant.

Try to sample some *fufu,* a cassava dish common throughout West Africa, or the Garífuna *ereba* or *bami,* flat bread also made from cassava. Invite community leaders Frank Lopez, Ramon Martinez, and Fermin Gonzalez to lunch to hear about the history and culture of the Garífuna and Orinoco. You may extraordinarily witness a *walagallo,* or *dugu,* ceremony, a healing ritual that has been known to bring people back from the brink of death. The spirit of an ancestor appears to someone in a dream, giving the specific recipe for that particular *walagallo.* Dancing, singing, and sacrificing of chickens then continues until the dying person gets up from the sickbed to start dancing, signifying to the crowd that he or she has been cured.

Accommodations and Food

The only lodging option in Orinoco is the **Hostal Garífuna** (tel. 505/8927-0123 or 505/8648-4985, www.hostalgarifuna.net, $13–20), a nice guesthouse with seven large rooms and a pleasant area for relaxing. Arrange to eat your meals ($4–7) at the hostel to experience authentic Garífuna cooking. The owners can help direct all your activities and transport in the area.

Getting There

From the municipal dock in Bluefields, take a *panga* ride up into the Laguna de Perlas (the water body, not the town) to Orinoco and Marshall Point. The famous "hardway *panga*" ($11 one-way) leaves Bluefields on Mondays, Thursdays, and Saturdays, and returns to Bluefields on Mondays, Tuesdays, Thursdays, and Fridays. You can sometimes catch this boat from Pearl Lagoon, depending on whether or not they filled up with passengers in Bluefields. You can also rarely catch the Pueblo Nuevo boat.

EL RAMA

At the eastern terminus of the highway from Managua, El Rama straddles the frontier between Atlantic and Pacific more perceptibly than any other Nicaraguan town. A long-time riverine port and trader town, El Rama is a melting pot of some 50,000 people, where mestizo cattle traders meet Caribbean steamer captains, and dark-skinned Creoles mix with "Spaniards" from the Pacific.

The name Rama is a tribute to the Rama people who once inhabited the shores of the Siquia, Rama, Escondido, and Mico Rivers. The inhabitants of today's El Rama, however, are the progeny of immigrants from Chontales, Boaco, and Granada, all of whom swarmed here in the late 18th century to take advantage of the boom in the wood, rubber, and banana trade. Before 1880, the original port of El Rama was located on the southwest shore of the Río Siquia but was relocated to the present location due to the unbearable mud, floods, and swamps that plagued the original location.

While Nicaraguans from all over the country resented the stringent rationing of food and basic goods during the war years of the 1980s, no one was more indignant than the people of El Rama, whose international port was where the millions of metric tons of military hardware were brought onshore from Eastern-bloc freighters to be shipped up the Rama Highway to military bases around the nation. In the 1980s, while locals were forming lines to receive a half bar of soap and one pound of rice, they watched steel-armored convoys of tanks, fighter planes, and trucks full of rifles, grenades, and antipersonnel land mines pass through their town bound for the battle lines. Short of the trenches of the front line, nowhere was the military buildup—and the irony of the shortage of basic goods—more obvious.

El Rama, though wholly dependent on the river, is also at the mercy of it. El Rama has been under water several times, including during Hurricane Joan, when for three days the only thing seen above the surface of the boiling, muddy waters of the swollen Río Escondido was the church steeple. Deforestation upstream means the river floods more and more frequently these days, and with less advance warning. An electronic system of flood warning devices was installed along the river in 2000 to give residents a chance to evacuate.

Sights

The typical traveler spends no more than 15 minutes in El Rama between the time he or she gets off the bus and on to a boat to Bluefields. But should you find yourself stuck here, you may find El Rama to be worth a second look, and even useful as the base for an expedition or two. The folks at El Rama are interested in developing a tourism infrastructure; they just don't know how to do it yet (the first step should be to pick up all the garbage).

Any adventuring you do in the region will require ingenuity and patience. Divided by rivers and swamps, the lands around El Rama are teeming with places to explore and look for wildlife. **Los Humedales de Mahogany** is a wetlands reserve important for the reproduction of local species. It's a 4–5-hour trip by boat downstream in the direction of Bluefields along the Mahogany River near the entrance to the Caño Negro (Black Creek). **Cerro Silva** was declared protected in 1997; it's located 2.5 hours along the Río Rama in the direction of San Jerónimo. Once you disembark from your boat, it's a 2.5-hour hike from the river's edge to the park; find a guide in San Jerónimo to lead you there.

The falls of **Salto Mataka** are found along the Río Siquia, 2.5 hours from La Esperanza (the town with the big bridge, just west of El Rama). Also located near La Esperanza is **El Recreo,** a popular swimming hole three kilometers north of town.

THE ROAD TO EL RAMA

If you've got a few extra days to spare, consider the overland route to Bluefields from Managua. The road is in better condition than it ever has been and takes you through some out-of-the-way corners of the country.

During the 1980s, the highway from San Benito (Managua) to Rama, known as the Rama Highway, was a hotly contested military prize. At stake was control of the port at Rama, through which Managua received much of its oil and supplies from the Baltic states and the Soviet Union. The Contras finally succeeded in capturing the highway in 1987 with a massive offensive of 2,500 troops, who laid waste to government buildings in La Gateada, Santo Tomás, and San Pedro de Lóvago and demolished five bridges, all but the crown jewel—the bridge at Muelle de los Bueyes, which, standing 150 meters high over the Río Mico, remains the highest and most irreplaceable bridge in Nicaragua. The highway, a pothole-ridden disaster by the end of the war, was completely resurfaced during 2002–2005.

Between Villa Sandino and La Campana are hundreds of pre-Columbian petroglyphs in situ, around which the **Parque Arqueológico Piedras Pintadas** (tel. 505/8850-2121, $3 entrance fee) was developed in 2008 with help from Finland. From Villa Sandino it's 20 minutes by bus, but you can easily walk it. Stay in Villa Sandino at **Hotel Santa Clara** (tel. 505/2516-0055, maisalar@hotmail.com) where you'll find rooms for $20 with air-conditioning and hot water, $15 with fan; or the more economical **Hospedaje Chavarria** across from the Medical Center.

Accommodations and Food

It's slim pickings for lodging in these parts; **Hospedaje García** (tel. 505/2517-0318, $3.50 s, $7 d) is the best of the flop-houses around here; fancier rooms on the second floor ($15) have air-conditioning and a view of the river. Another budget favorite is the **Hospedaje Solidaridad Tres Rios** (a few hundred meters up from the dock, on the left along the main drag, tel. 505/2517-0152, $5–7) with very basic rooms run by a nice family.

The smartest rooms in town are at **Casa Huesped Rio Escondido** (tel. 505/2517-0287, next to Restaurante el Expreso, $15–20), where en-suite private rooms are safe and clean. **Nuevo Oasis del Caribe** (one block south of the bus station, tel. 505/2517-0264 $8–15) has clean rooms with TV, fan, and private bathroom, and is your next best choice.

◖ Eco Hotel El Vivero (Km 291 on the highway from Managua, tel. 505/8617-6001, ecohotelvivero@hotmail.com, $10–20) is a quiet, peaceful place located within a private reserve about two short kilometers from the city of El Rama. The wooden cabins and decent meals (under $5) have been recommended by several readers.

Restaurante El Expreso is slow, but serves good seafood, soups, chicken, and steak. The **Eskimo** sells sandwiches in addition to ice cream. A good *fritanga* sets up shop evenings near the market.

Services

The **ENITEL** (7 A.M.–9 P.M. Mon.–Sat.) and post office are located across the street from each other. For late-night phone calls, try the Pepsi booth on the street that leads to the municipal pier (i.e., the pier with boats for Bluefields); there's a phone there that the owner will let you use. **Farmacia El Carmen** (8 A.M.–1 P.M. and 2–6:30 P.M. Mon.–Sat.) is well stocked with medicines, sanitary supplies, and more.

Getting There

Buses to El Rama leave five times daily from Managua's Mayoreo terminal (tel.

505/2248-3005) and an express bus leaves from Mercado Ivan Montenego (tel. 505/2280-4561) daily at 9 P.M. Call ahead for seats. (Choose the express bus, since they don't linger in Juigalpa or stop along the road, shaving several hours off the trip.) All boat transportation to Bluefields is found at the municipal wharf: *pangas* cast off from the dock as they fill up, 6 A.M.–4 P.M. (1.5-hour trip to Bluefields, approximately $10 pp). There are several larger ships that carry freight and passengers between El Rama, Bluff, Corn Island, and Puerto Cabezas, but they are slow. These boats leave El Rama every Tuesday and Saturday at 11 A.M. (call the *Captain D* at 505/8690-9719 or 505/8850-2767).

Big Corn Island

Eighty-three kilometers due east of Bluefields Bay's brackish brown water, the Corn Islands are a pair of Tertiary-period volcanic basalt bumps in the Caribbean. Formerly home base for lobster fishermen and their families, the islanders are increasingly turning to tourism for their future. How well the fragile island ecosystem will support it will determine the fate of the islands.

Big Corn Island is 10 square kilometers of forested hills, mangrove swamps, and stretches of white coral beaches. The mangrove swamps and estuaries that line several stretches of coastline are crucial to the island's water supply, and the islanders have fiercely resisted attempts by foreign investors to drain or fill them. The highest points are Quinn Hill, Little Hill (55 and 57 meters above sea level, respectively), and Mount Pleasant (97 meters).

Of the six sea turtle species swimming off Nicaragua's shores, four live in Caribbean waters. On land, Corn Island boasts three endemic species of reptiles and amphibians, all threatened by the continued swamp draining.

Like many Caribbean islands, time is measured "since the last hurricane," which at press time, was Hurricane Ida on November 5, 2009. It toppled power lines, coconut trees, houses, churches, and schools; the waves and wind smashed boats as well. Reconstruction began immediately.

HISTORY

Pirates on their way to maraud the coast of Central America and Nicaragua's Río San Juan first visited here in the 16th century, sometimes by accident after the reefs tore the bottom of their ships open. But Corn Island was inhabited long before that by the Kukras, a subtribe of the Mayangnas whose penchant for consuming the bodies of their enemies inspired the first English visitors to call them the Skeleton Islands. The Kukra were eventually assimilated into the Miskitos. Nowadays, the native Creole population shares the island with an increasing number of menial laborers from the mainland, who have overtaken the Creoles in number and have increased the island's total population to nearly 12,000 people.

Native islanders are direct descendants from several of the more infamous European pirates, as well as English royalty and plantation owners—don't be surprised if you meet people with names like Kennington, Quinn, Dixon, or Downs.

SIGHTS

The incongruous **Golden Pyramid** on the top of Quinn Hill was built in 2006 by the Soul of the World society, a group whose members believe Quinn Hill is one of eight spots in the world where the vertices of a cube—with a diameter the same as the earth itself, and placed inside the Earth's orb—intercepts the land surface of the globe. Got that? The other vertices are found in the Cocos

BLUEFIELDS

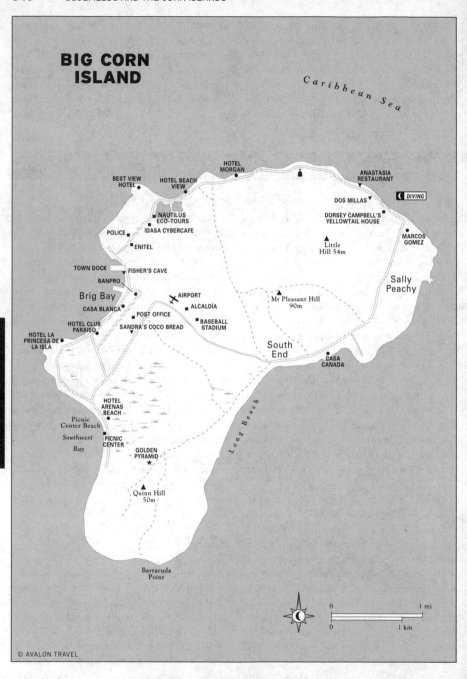

BIG CORN ISLAND

Caribbean Sea

BEST VIEW HOTEL

HOTEL MORGAN

HOTEL BEACH VIEW

ANASTASIA RESTAURANT

DIVING

NAUTILUS ECO-TOURS

DOS MILLAS

DORSEY CAMPBELL'S YELLOWTAIL HOUSE

POLICE

IDASA CYBERCAFE

MARCOS GOMEZ

ENITEL

Little Hill 54m

TOWN DOCK

FISHER'S CAVE

Sally Peachy

BANPRO

Brig Bay

AIRPORT

CASA BLANCA

ALCALDÍA

Mt Pleasant Hill 90m

POST OFFICE

HOTEL CLUB PARAISO

SANDRA'S COCO BREAD

BASEBALL STADIUM

HOTEL LA PRINCESA DE LA ISLA

South End

CASA CANADA

HOTEL ARENAS BEACH

Picnic Center Beach

Southwest Bay

PICNIC CENTER

Long Beach

GOLDEN PYRAMID

Quinn Hill 50m

Barracuda Point

0   1 mi

0   1 km

© AVALON TRAVEL

Islands (Indian Ocean), Hawaii, Santiago de Compostela (Spain), South Island (New Zealand), Buryat (Siberia), Tierra del Fuego (Argentina/Chile), and the Kalahari desert (Namibia).

Picnic Center Beach is the most popular swimming beach; **South West Bay** is a long, golden crescent of soft sand and turquoise water, with a smattering of cheap restaurants and not-so-cheap hotels. Or go to **Long Beach,** just as pretty, but a bit rougher and with fewer services.

SPORTS AND RECREATION

For a walking adventure, tackle the shore between Marcos Gomez's hotel and the South End Cemetery in Sally Peaches, or break a sweat on the hike up Mount Pleasant where the view from the top of the old lighthouse tower is well worth the effort. A path leads up to Mount Pleasant opposite the **Casa Canada.** When you reach the local school, take the path that winds up behind the school to the left.

🄲 Diving

Three distinct layers of reef, composed of more than 40 species of coral, protect the north side of the island. Though the diving and snorkeling are impressive (divers regularly see nurse sharks, eagle rays, and lots of colorful fish), the reefs closest to shore have deteriorated over the past decades, victims of overfishing, predatory algae (which grow as a result of increased nutrient levels in the water from sewage runoff), sedimentation, storm damage, and global warming.

Out at sea, **Blowing Rock** is a rock formation with lots of color and dozens of varieties of tropical fish, worthy of a day trip. The island's only dive shop, **Dive Nautilus** (tel. 505/2575-5077, divechema@yahoo.com, www.divebig-corn.com) offers scuba gear and the dive-master services of "Chema" Ruiz, a jolly Guatemalan with a wall full of framed scuba diplomas and a full-service, modern dive shop: $75 for an introductory course, $60 for a two-tank dive, $250 for open-water certification, or $90 for two dives at Blowing Rock.

A few sandy stretches of beach along the north shore allow you to get into the water. One good one is in front of Dorsey Campbell's Yellowtail House.

ENTERTAINMENT AND EVENTS

Weekends, the islanders dance to island rhythms at **Reggae Palace,** just south of the docks in Brig Bay, and at **Nico's** in the South End. Corn Islanders are serious about their **baseball:** A league of eight teams (including two from the Little Island) play in the quite-nice stadium east of the airport.

ACCOMMODATIONS

Traditionally more expensive than elsewhere in Nicaragua, Corn Island's stiff lodging competition has kept prices reasonable. There are now at least two dozen hotels and guesthouses on Big Corn Island; many small ones come and go. Following is the cream of the crop.

Under $10

Practically the only place on the island with a room for less than $10 is **Hospedaje Angela** (across from the bank, tel. 505/2575-5134, $7–20 with shard or private bathroom).

$10-25

Stay with the impressive family of **Marcos and Jeanette Gomez** (tel. 505/2575-5187, $10), who rent two clean, safe rooms out of their house or additional outbuildings. Nearby **Dorsey Campbell's Yellowtail House** offers two self-catering private cabins ($15; ask for Dorsey at the *Pulperia Victoria* in Sally Peachy), plus boat or accompanied snorkel trips from the shore out to the reefs ($15 per hour). Dorsey knows the reefs better than anybody. No meals, but Seva's Dos Millas is conveniently right around the corner.

$25-50

🄲 **Hotel Morgan** (north end, near the brewery,

tel. 505/2575-5052, kerrygean.morgan@gmail.com, $15–40) on the north side has six cabins ($40) and simple rooms, some with air-conditioning, fridge, TV, and private bath. The hotel serves three meals a day in the restaurant, or climb the stairs to the open-air balcony for drinks and a top-notch ocean vista. **Hotel Best View** (tel. 505/2575-5082, $25) is less polished, but has a nice second-story balcony overlooking the water.

$50-100

◖ **Paraíso Beach Hotel** (tel. 505/2575-5111, info@paraisoclub.com, www.paraisoclub.com, $45–70), tucked away on its own grounds in Barrio Brig Bay, has 14 modern cabana-style rooms with private baths, and fan or air-conditioning, including a honeymoon suite. Laundry service, plus food and drink service to guests on the nearby beach; snorkeling trips on their boats are also available, and Swedish massage (starting at $20). Under Dutch management since 2005, the hotel offers excellent service and the restaurant, though expensive, has the best menu on the island (breakfasts from $4 and $5 burgers, all the way up to the $17 surf and turf) and is open till 10 P.M.

Locally owned, wonderfully clean **Hotel Sunrise** (three minutes from the airport, tel. 505/8828-7835, www.southendsunrise.com, $35–55) has 15 double rooms with air-conditioning, TV, and hot shower; nice beach area nearby.

The **Picnic Center Hotel & Restaurant** (tel. 505/8420-6186, $50) enjoys the best uninterrupted crescent of white sand on the island; rooms are a little overpriced for quality of the services, though they are well equipped with air-conditioning, TV, queen-size beds, and private baths and superb hot showers. The restaurant is an enormous, palm-thatched open-air patio.

Arenas Beach (tel. 505/2575-5223, info@arenasbeachhotel.com, www.arenasbeachhotel.com, $90) has 26 rooms and large, clean, and well-equipped bungalows with deck verandas, all finished in tropical timber, on the same South West Bay. It has a bar on the beach, and next door you can rent golf carts to tour the island.

La Princesa de La Isla (tel. 505/8854-2403, info@laprincesadelaisla.com, www.laprincesadelaisla.com, $55–70) is a secluded, immaculately designed beachfront hotel at Waula Point, run by a very amiable Italian and his family. Meals here (arranged in advance) are the real Italia deal. The hotel is at the south end of Brig Bay and accessed by a beach road that passes by the shrimp processing plant.

Over $100

◖ **Casa Canada** (tel. 505/8644-0925, Canada and U.S. tel. 306/861-9224, casacanada@canada.com, www.casa-canada.com, $140 d) has a superb location at South End overlooking a turquoise bay and reef. The resort is luxurious, from sumptuous towels and hot showers to the minibar, cable TV, air-conditioning, fridge, and coffee machine. Each cabin features king-size beds and overstuffed sofa and chairs. Dip in the infinity pool, or explore the beach and rocks. The restaurant serves excellent seafood and strong coffee at breakfast.

FOOD

Aside from the hotels, there are very few restaurants. One exception is **Fisher's Cave**, adjacent to the docks, with a breezy deck. ◖**Seva's Dos Millas** (Two Miles) on the north side of the island has seen better times, but still serves reliably tasty seafood and ice-cold beer. **Anastasia's by the Sea** will convince you lobster tastes best by the water. Meals are served in a building on stilts directly over the water. A couple of hundred meters south of Brig Bay town, **Comedor La Rotonda** makes a mean *gallo pinto* with toasted coco bread for $2.

Fill up on **coconut bread,** which usually comes out around midday. Ms. Sandra, 50 meters south of the Banpro building (look for a small roadside sign), bakes the best coco bread on the island, as did her mother.

© AMBER DOBRZENSKY

The main dock on Big Corn Island welcomes commerical boats, as well as the *pangas* to Little Corn.

INFORMATION AND SERVICES

Before you go, check for updates and announcements online (www.bigcornisland.com) for updated listings of all the island's businesses. Cell phone services are available from the two main local carriers, Movistar and Claro, or roaming from your own phone. Internet is available at most of the hotels on the island or **Idasa Ciber Café** (100 meters down the road from Nautilus Dive Shop, tel. 505/2575-5082, 8 A.M.–noon and 1:30–6 P.M. Mon.–Fri.) offers Internet services, as well as national and international phone calls. ENITEL (the phone office) is north of the docks and around the corner. Big Corn has no post office.

Banpro is the only bank on the island, occupying a building in Brig Bay, at the corner where the road turns parallel to the runway; they have the only ATM on the island. Dive shops and larger hotels take credit cards, but some only take Visa; check before you go.

There is a small and improving hospital with limited ability.

GETTING THERE
By Air

La Costeña offers several daily flights to Corn Island from Managua (which stop in Bluefields). Round-trip flights from Managua to Corn Island are about $165 round-trip. Call the following numbers for an updated schedule:
Managua: 505/2263-2143 or 505/2263-2142, fax 505/2263-1281
Bluefields: 505/2572-2500
Corn Island: 505/2575-5121

By Boat

The quickest ride is the Rio Escondido boat, which leaves the municipal dock in Bluefields to Corn Island on Wenesdays and returns on Thursdays from Corn Island's municipal dock to Bluefields, $12 one-way. The *Captain*

D, a larger, smaller craft, leaves Bluefields (El Bluff, actually) bound for Corn Island on Wednesdays and returns Sundays. It's a 4–6-hour, sun-baked trip. Contact the **Emusepci** office (7 A.M.–5:30 P.M. daily), just inside the gates of the municipal dock for current ship schedules, or call their office in El Rama (tel. 505/2572-1467). The same ship can take you upriver to El Rama—or, if the stars align in your favor, to Puerto Cabezas.

GETTING AROUND

From the airport building, it's a five-minute taxi ride ($0.75 by day, $1.50 by night) to almost anywhere on the island, though buses circulate about twice per hour ($0.50). A walk to Brig Bay, which is the "downtown" area, is around 2.5 kilometers or 20 minutes. A paved road circumnavigates the island and bicycles can be hired at some hotels, including Hotel Morgan. The municipal docks are in Brig Bay with *panga* service to Little Corn.

Corn Island Car Rentals (next to Arenas Hotel, tel. 505/8643-9881 or 505/8413-9553, nestort0110@hotmail.com) offers golf carts, scooters, bicycles, and boat rides; they also rent diving and fishing gear.

Little Corn Island

A humble, wilder version of Big Corn, "La Islita" is a mere three square kilometers of sand and trees, laced with footpaths and encircled by nine kilometers of coral reef. Little Corn is a delicate destination, visited by an increasing number of travelers each year. There are clever accommodations for several budgets here to meet the demand, but rough boat transport from Big Corn—an experience one traveler likened to pursuing a *narco-panga* across 15 kilometers of open swell—will help hold the masses at bay. Bring a flashlight, your snorkel gear, and a good book.

Note that Little Corn Island is irregularly policed by volunteers and has experienced a handful of violent attacks on tourists in recent years. The security situation is sometimes better, sometimes worse, so be sure to ask your hotel for the latest news—and advice on staying safe. Above all, don't walk alone on the beaches, or at night.

SPORTS AND RECREATION

Beach hikes, snorkel excursions, and lots of time reading and swinging in your hammock will fill your day. **Casa Iguana** (casaiguana@mindspring.com, www.casaiguana.net) offers fishing, snorkeling, and picnic trips, and most of the beachfront hotels have snorkel gear for rent. For a rewarding hike, walk to the school, turn right, and follow the sidewalk to its end; then follow the footpath up and to the left to reach the **lighthouse** (about 20 minutes from the waterfront), perched on Little Corn's highest peak. You can climb up to get a view of the entire island.

◖ Diving

Little Corn's delicate reef system is unique for its abundance of wildlife and coral formations—these include overhangs, swim-throughs, and the infamous shark cave. Most dives around the island are shallow (less than 60 feet), but a few deeper dives exist as well.

The island's largest scuba shop, **Dive Little Corn** (www.divelittlecorn.com, $65 for a two-tank dive), operates out of a wooden building just south of the newer pier on Pelican Beach. They offer morning and afternoon dives for novices through advanced divers, night dives by appointment, hourly and all-day snorkel trips, PADI certification, and kayak rentals. Hotel Delfines also has **Dolphin Dive** (www.dolphindivelittlecorn.com), with competitive prices and equally competent staff.

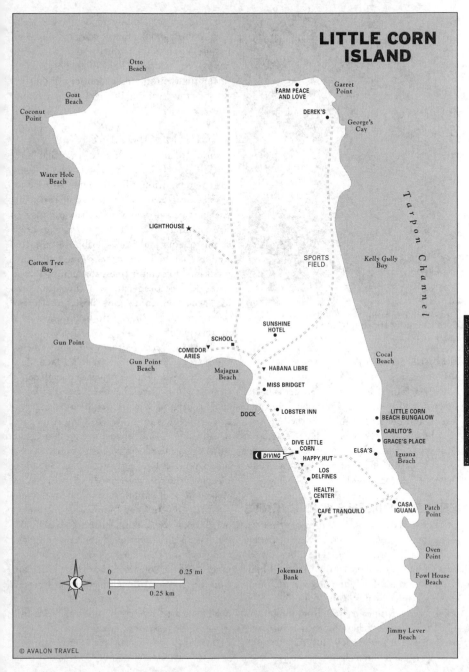

LITTLE CORN
ISLAND

Otto
Beach

Goat
Beach

Coconut
Point

Water Hole
Beach

Cotton Tree
Bay

Gun Point

Gun Point
Beach

Majagua
Beach

DOCK

FARM PEACE
AND LOVE

Garret
Point

DEREK'S

George's
Cay

Tarpon Channel

LIGHTHOUSE ★

SPORTS
FIELD

Kelly Gully
Bay

SUNSHINE
HOTEL

SCHOOL
COMEDOR
ARIES

HABANA LIBRE

Cocal
Beach

MISS BRIDGET

LITTLE CORN
BEACH BUNGALOW

LOBSTER INN

CARLITO'S
GRACE'S PLACE

DIVE LITTLE
CORN

ELSA'S

Iguana
Beach

DIVING

HAPPY HUT

LOS
DELFINES

HEALTH
CENTER

CASA
IGUANA

Patch
Point

CAFÉ TRANQUILO

Oven
Point

Jokeman
Bank

Fowl House
Beach

0   0.25 mi

0   0.25 km

Jimmy Lever
Beach

BLUEFIELDS

© AVALON TRAVEL

© AMBER DOBRZENSKY

You can almost fully circumnavigate Little Corn Island by sticking to the beach.

Fishing

Within a couple kilometers of shore, you'll find schools of kingfish, dolphin, amberjack, red snapper, and barracuda. Fly fishers can catch tarpon and bonefish right from the beach, or Casa Iguana will take you out for $59 a person. Boat trips can also be arranged with a number of locals, or at Hotel Delfines—ask around on the front side for a good deal.

ENTERTAINMENT AND EVENTS

The best place on the island to sip a drink and enjoy the gorgeous waterfront view of the big island on the horizon is **Habana Libre,** owned by a Cuban transplant to the island ("I married an islander. Everyone here has the same story," laughs owner Ronaldo). They offer good *mojitos,* with mint fresh from the garden. The bar is also homebase for the Island Braves baseball team. The **Happy Hut** is another option, a reggae-colored building on the front side, which is a grinding good time on weekends. **Cafe Tranquilo** (www.cafetranquilo.com) has quickly become a tourist home base with happy-hour specials. They often host parties (including their infamous bonfire nights) that see the crowd spilling off the front porch and onto the street.

ACCOMMODATIONS

A variety of accommodations are available on Little Corn, from palm-thatch huts to cabins to conventional hotel rooms with color TVs. Cocal beach on the east side has the cheapest accommodation on the island; native Islanders Elsa, Grace, and Carlito offer cabins oozing laid-back Caribbean vibes, as well as thatched dining *ranchitos,* and hammock-lined coconut trees, for about $15 pp. The rasta-colored camp in the middle is **⬛ Grace's Place,** the only hostel to offer an open kitchen, while Carlito next door does a mean fried chicken.

Get back to nature (that's why you came to Little Corn, after all) at **Derek's Place** (dereksplace@gmail.com, www.dereksplacelittlecorn.com). Derek has been here for years and his original backpacker desert island getaway continues to evolve. You can still camp if you want ($4), or shack up in a thatch hut ($14) or in raised cabins with electricity and breezy porches looking over the reef ($45–85). Delicious international meals are available, as are snorkel trips and transfers.

Hotel Los Delfines (hotellosdelfines@hotmail.com, www.hotellosdelfines.com.ni, $20–60) has 18 air-conditioned concrete and glass bungalows on the water. They'll be glad to arrange trips for you and private boat transport from Big Corn. A bit simpler but still breezy and clean, **Hotel Lobster Inn** ($25) has basic rooms with private bath and fan, and a full menu in the restaurant downstairs.

Casa Iguana (casaiguana@mindspring.com, www.casaiguana.net, $35–75) is easy to recommend: Located on the cliffs of the southeast, breezy side of the island, Casa Iguana consists of raised wooden cabins clustered around a communal hilltop lodge where guests gather to eat, drink, and listen to the waves. The 15 cabins are a nice compromise between rustic simplicity and comfort, and include soft mattresses, outdoor showers, private, breezy porches with hammocks, and shelves full of books. Join the other guests each morning for breakfast, lunch, and each evening for happy hour and family-style dinner, frequently the day's catch.

Little Corn Beach & Bungalows (tel. 505/8333-0956 or 505/8662-7033, info@littlecornbb.com, www.littlecornbb.com, $48–85) is impressive: Their eight bungalows have private bathrooms and small kitchens, just steps from the water. Co-owner/architect Scot Smyth (winner of an Innovative Builder of the Year Award from the Northern Colorado home builders association) has ensured his ecofriendly design includes shower water from rooftop rain barrels, and coming soon, wind and solar power. The owners have sponsored several veterinary clinics on the island, resulting in the spaying and neutering of hundreds of pets; ask how you can help.

Hard to find but worth the effort, **Farm Peace Love** (paola@farmpeacelove.com, www.farmpeacelove.com) offers rich, fresh Italian and Caribbean dinners from local ingredients ($18 prix fixe) and also a classy guest suite for $70 per couple (or three people), including breakfast. They also have a fully equipped cottage with bedroom, living room with futon, and full kitchen; it costs $85 a night for up to three people (five-night minimum). Get your boat to drop you off to avoid the 45-minute overland trek. Ask about weekly and monthly rates, or low-season discounts May–October. Reservations are required; snorkeling and horseback riding available.

FOOD

Nearly every accommodation offers meals. **Elsa's Great Food and Drinks** offers just that, but slowly, in a beachside barbecue setting on the east side of the island. On the front side, **Bridgett's First Stop Comedor** is a good choice for home cooking. For loaves of coconut bread, head to **Esther's** house opposite the school; Esther supplies most of the island with her homemade delicacy.

Cafe Tranquilo (www.cafetranquilo.com) is hugely popular with foreigners, serving great coffee and a varied menu which includes mean fish tacos and enormous cheeseburgers. The wireless Internet, outdoor movie theater, and onsite gift shop are three more reasons to stop and rest a while.

Located on the trail that divides the island, Rosa's Restaurant and Store, serves tasty made-to-order meals all day. Breakfast is around $4, and lunch and dinner are $6. Good menu options for vegetarians and vegans, including delicious curry.

Little Corn B&B (about $10 a plate) serves good seafood, as well as the best baby-back ribs in the country; wash these down with a real piña colada made from freshly toasted coconuts.

Italian native Paola Carminiani will cook a legitimate three-course Italian (or Caribbean) meal with fresh ingredients, $18 a person at her place, **Farm Peace Love** (paola@farmpeacelove.com, www.farmpeacelove.com). Contact her at least one day in advance.

SERVICES

The **ENITEL** office (8 A.M.–5 P.M. Mon.–Fri.) is the yellow building with the satellite dish, across from the big blue *acopio*. You can find a wimpy health clinic just south of the Hotel Delfines. Anything more complicated requires a *panga* ride back to the big island, or even Bluefields. You'll find the **Idasa Ciber Café** (11 A.M.–7 P.M. Mon.–Sat.) in the Delfines Hotel, with Internet and telephone service.

GETTING THERE

Two scheduled *pangas* ply the route between Corn Island and Little Corn Island ($8 each way, 40 minutes) and are coordinated with the departure and arrival of the two rounds of daily flights. Boats depart from Big Corn Island (pay a $0.20 harbor tax) at about 9 A.M. and 4 P.M.; boats depart Little Corn Island at 7 A.M. and 2 P.M.

The trip to Little Corn is often choppy and rough, especially when the seas are up. During the windiest time of year (December–April), if it gets too rough, the port authority can stop shuttle service until conditions are safer. You can expect to get wet regardless of the weather. Also, the *panga* drivers sometimes enjoy racing their friends, tipping a cold one before getting behind the wheel and gunning it on waves to catch mad air. Seats in the front afford a more violent bashing; seats in the back are prone to more frequent splashes of spray. The *pulperías* across from the dock on Big Corn sell heavy, blue plastic bags that fit over a backpack for less than $1—an essential investment for keeping your gear dry. Alternatively, rent your own boat and driver, which runs $70–90 each way. Smooth-drivin' Charlie, on Little Corn, provides this service; he can be contacted through any of the hotels there.

A number of larger fishing boats travel between the islands, and these may agree to take on a paying passenger. See Miss Bridgett for the day's schedule.

GETTING AROUND

Unless you make special arrangements with your *panga* driver to take you elsewhere, you will be let off at the southwestern-facing beach, where you'll find a cement sidewalk that runs the length of the village. This is called the "front side" by islanders and is the center of most social activity.

Walk north along that sidewalk to the school, baseball field, and phone office before the road deposits you in the unsavory barrios where migrant workers camp out in huts of black plastic and corrugated steel. Turn right at the school for the walk up to the lighthouse and the north side of the island, or follow the red muddy track from Miss Bridget's place through forests and swamps to the north beach and Derek's place. Just south of the dive shop is another muddy track that leads across to the "breezy side" of the island and the Casa Iguana.

Circumnavigating the island on the beach is ill-advised, as the sandy shoreline is interrupted by long, rocky, impassible sections, both at Goat Beach and the southern tip of the island. Elsewhere, there are long sandy stretches of beach to enjoy and explore.

PUERTO CABEZAS AND THE RÍO COCO

Isolated from the rest of Nicaragua by vast tracts of inaccessible forest and coastline, Puerto Cabezas (Bilwi) and the Río Coco watershed are remote, wild, and unique. Spanish-speaking Nicaragua has always felt nationalistic about its right to alternately claim and ignore this far-off corner of the country. Managua has incited neighboring Honduras over the subtleties of the border, yet the only road to Puerto Cabezas degenerated into bumpy oblivion decades ago, making Puerto somewhat of an island in itself. Tourism is undeveloped throughout this region, which for some travelers makes it all the more enticing.

This is far and away the most indigenous region of Nicaragua, where Miskito is heard more than Spanish. At first glance, Puerto Cabezas and the Río Coco might have the air of a drowsy backwater unchanged through the centuries, but to the contrary, the area is affected by many modern issues, including drug trafficking, global lobster prices, and international development projects.

The Río Coco is Central America's longest river and the cultural and spiritual heart of the Miskito people, who live a rather traditional lifestyle on both banks of the waterway. The whole region burned white-hot during the revolution years, and the scars run deep, but these days the rhythm of the days revolves around fishing and farming, as it has for centuries.

Inland, the "mining triangle" is composed

HIGHLIGHTS

◖ Moravian Churches: The Moravian religion took root early in Nicaragua's Atlantic coast and remains an important influence. Join a Sunday church service given in the Miskito language: only here! (page 353)

◖ Tours to the Miskito Communities: Nicaragua's indigenous fishing communities are practically a country unto themselves, and AMICA, an association of indigenous women, will take you there (page 359).

◖ Waspám: This is the spiritual home of the Miskito people and gateway to Central America's longest river, the Río Coco. It's about as rough and remote as you can get in Central America (page 361).

◖ Bosawás Biosphere Reserve: No corner of Central America is wilder or less explored than this unbroken stretch of cloud forest (page 365).

LOOK FOR ◖ TO FIND RECOMMENDED SIGHTS, ACTIVITIES, DINING, AND LODGING.

of the three pueblos of Siuna, Bonanza, and La Rosita. The area no longer produces the quantity of gold or guerilla warriors it once did, but there is yet a pioneering feel to the area, which is still host to a Canadian gold-mining company and a few casinos in the town of Bonanza. This area is also the jumping-off point for the country's most rugged adventure, an expedition into the sprawling and untamed Bosawás Reserve.

HISTORY

The Mayangna inhabitants that settled in Puerto Cabezas gave it the name Bilwi, in reference to the great quantity of leaves and the equally great number of snakes hidden in the foliage.

Renamed in the early 1900s after the general who President Zelaya sent out to the Atlantic coast to unify the nation, Puerto Cabezas—like much of Nicaragua's Atlantic coast—has seen more glorious days. Its zenith was probably at the start of the 20th century, when Puerto was the center for exportation of Atlantic coast lumber and mineral products, including gold from the mining triangle. Its airstrip was, in 1964, the longest in Central America. Testimony to the wealth of Puerto Cabezas during the lumber boom is the enormous wooden dock that juts into the Atlantic, built in the mid-1940s out of locally cut hardwoods.

Somoza was well liked in Puerto and the

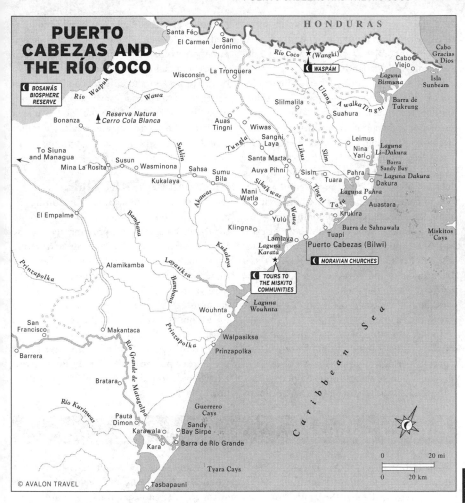

PUERTO CABEZAS AND THE RÍO COCO

HONDURAS

Santa Féo
El Carmen   San
Jerónimo   Río Coco   ★ (Wangki)   Cabo   Cabo
La Tronquera   ■ WASPÁM   Viejo   Gracias
a Dios
Wisconsino   Laguna   Isla
Bismuna   Sunbeam
◄ BOSAWÁS
BIOSPHERE   Río Wasp uk   Wawa   Barra de
RESERVE   Slilmalila   Tukrung
Reserva Natura
Bonanza   ▲ Cerro Cola Blanca   Auas   Suahura
Tingni   Wiwas
Sangni   Leimus
Laya   Nina   Laguna
Li-Dakura
To Siuna   Susun   Wasminona   Sahsa   Santa Marta   Yarī   Barra
and Managua   Auya Pihni   Sisin   Pahra   Sandy Bay
◄   Mina La Rosita   Sumu   Tuara   Laguna Dakura
Kukalaya   Bila   Mani   Dakura
Watla   Laguna Pahra
El Empalme   Sikikwas   Krukira   Auastara
Yulú   Barra de Sahnawala   Miskitos
Klingna   Tuapí   Cays
Lamlaya   Puerto Cabezas (Bilwi)
Alamikamba   Laguna
Karatá ★   ◄ MORAVIAN CHURCHES
♥ TOURS TO
THE MISKITO
COMMUNITIES
Wouhnta   Laguna
Wouhnta
San
Francisco   Makantaca   Walpasiksa
Barrera   Prinzapolka

Caribbean Sea

Bratara

Río Kurinwas   Guerrero
Cays
Pauta   Sandy
Dimon   Karawala   Bay Sirpe
Kara   Barra de Río Grande   0   20 mi
© AVALON TRAVEL   Tyara Cays   0   20 km
Tasbapauni

northeast. Puerto locals fondly recall the times Tacho would arrive on the Atlantic coast in his private plane, barbecuing with the locals and telling jokes. Somoza had largely left the Atlantic coast to its own devices and Costeños generally viewed the goings-on in Managua as news from a foreign country. When the Sandinistas arrived to unite the country after taking power in 1979, the revolution collided with a growing sense of Native American autonomy worldwide. Originally intending to

work with the Sandinistas, indigenous leaders soon disputed Sandinista authority to rule the Atlantic coast. The Sandinistas retaliated by forcing the relocation of entire Miskito communities and razing the villages, ostensibly to deny support to Contras. Ten thousand Miskito villagers resettled in refugee camps, while another 40,000 Miskito and Mayangna escaped over the Río Coco to Honduras, some of whom returned as Contras themselves. In 1985, Minister of the Interior Tomás Borge conciliated, and the Río Coco communities have slowly rebuilt their original villages in the delicate autonomy now granted to the two departments of the Atlantic coast.

While a significant number of Puerteños work in government jobs—Puerto is not only the departmental capital, but also the center of the indigenous community's government—several thousand workers were laid off when the Chamorro government replaced the FSLN, and the city has never quite recovered. Puerto Cabezas is largely a coastal backwater and commercial hub for the northeast. Its small economy is based on commerce—particularly of lobsters, wood, fish, and transport. The Nicaraguan military maintains a naval base here, from which it patrols the northern Atlantic coast and Miskito Cays. There are scattered jobs in the timber and fishing industries, and many people looking for a legitimate way to earn a living.

Today, life struggles on, with a wary eye on the future. Tankers from Venezuela and Curaçao periodically pull up at the dock to replenish the town's supply of petroleum, and a Louisiana-based engineering company continues to fuss with plans to build a modernized port complex complete with grain silos, a power plant, container storage, industrial cargo cranes, and facilities for deepwater tankers. In the meantime, Puerto Cabezas continues to experience a two-headed wave of immigration: poor Miskito families from the Río Coco area in search of a better life, and wealthy families from Managua who are starting businesses and buying beachfront properties.

PLANNING YOUR TIME

It's safe to say Puerto Cabezas, the mining triangle, and the indigenous communities along the Río Coco don't figure prominently into the travel itineraries of many, so if you're traveling here, chances are you are an aid worker, gold miner, or documentary filmmaker and already have your itinerary planned. Though it's easy enough to hop a puddle jumper in Managua for an hour-long flight to Puerto, Siuna, or Waspám, you should always plan more time than you think you'll need when traveling in these areas: perhaps a few days in Puerto with a few days allowed to head up the coast or to nearby villages.

Puerto Cabezas

Far away from everything, Puerto Cabezas (usually referred to as just "Puerto" or "Port") is connected to Pacific Nicaragua only by semipassable, seasonal roads. Most travelers fly to this outpost city from Managua.

It is entirely possible that you'll be the only traveler in this town of about 50,000 inhabitants, but enough foreign volunteers and missionaries have passed through that you won't draw too much attention. In Puerto, most streets are nothing more than streaks of bare red earth connecting neighborhoods of humble wooden homes set on stilts. It's a glimpse of many worlds, with Miskitos tying wooden canoes alongside steel fishing boats at the pier. It's an easy walk from anywhere in town to the water's edge, but there are no real recreational beaches, and the water is shallow and rocky. The Mayangna inhabitants named it Bilwi, because the leaves *(wi)* were full of snakes *(Bil)*. These days you should worry less about serpents than the increasing drug traffic slowly impacting the social norms of the region: You are closer to trouble here than elsewhere, because of that same remoteness.

To Airport, Famahl,
and Estiliano II

PAULINA'S
KITCHEN

BARRIO
EL COCAL

HOSPEDAJE
WANGKI

INTERNET

MINI-SUPER

HOTEL CASA
MUSEO

HOSPEDAJE
BRITON   HEALTH CLINIC
INTERNET   ALCALDÍA/
            POST OFFICE

MORAVIAN CHURCHES

RED CROSS   HOTEL PÉREZ

LA ESQUINITA   HOTEL EL
DEL SABOR   CORTIJO 2

INTUR

MARKET   MIRAMAR

            HOTEL EL
            CORTIJO

INTERNET
COMEDOR AQUÍ   Central   DISCO ZAIRE
ME QUEDO   Park

ASADOS   ENITEL
EL PATIO

                 BANPRO

HOTEL AND
SUPERMERCADO
MONTER

To Bus Terminal, Airport,   ESTADIO MUNICIPAL
road to **WASPÁM**,   ERNESTO HOOKER
Siuna, and Managua

                    EL MALECÓN   To Kabu Yula

                    AMICA

To Kabu Waína   KABU   La Bocana
                    PAYASKA

**PUERTO
CABEZAS
(BILWI)**

Caribbean Sea

0   200 yds

0   200 m

© AVALON TRAVEL

SIGHTS

Near the center of town is an interesting house/
museum/hotel, the **Casa Museo** (entrance $1),
commemorating the life and work of Judith
Kain Cunningham, a local painter who passed
away in 2001. A prolific artist, her subject matter was the Río Coco and the Miskito communities of the Waspám. Also on display are
works of macramé, sculpture, artifacts celebrating local indigenous movements, and more.

At the north end of town just past Kabu

Payaska restaurant is **La Bocana,** a sandy
Atlantic coast beach that is unfortunately
getting a bit dangerous, so enjoy its tranquil
beauty from afar.

The **URACCAN** campus is located a few kilometers down the road out of town. There's
a good library there, as well as people with a
wealth of information about the area.

◖ Moravian Churches

Puerto is more Moravian than Catholic, and

YATAMA AND THE STRUGGLE FOR INDIGENOUS SELF-DETERMINATION

Fraught with frequent reversals and setbacks, the struggle of Nicaragua's indigenous Miskito people for human rights, electoral privileges, and autonomy has never been easy. The FSLN (Sandinista National Liberation Front) came to power just when a sense of unity and independence was growing among the Miskito people. The new government gave the native peoples a unique opportunity to press for their own interests and historic demands. The Sandinistas moved quickly to attempt to incorporate the indigenous movement into their own organizational structure, but soon learned the Miskito people were not interested in being a part of any group led from Managua. The indigenous peoples of the Atlantic coast instead organized themselves into the political group MISURASATA and renewed their fight for self-determination.

The Sandinistas met the growing resistance of the Miskito with violence and repression. Organized disruptions led to a massive increase in government military presence; in 1981, more than 30 Miskito leaders were rounded up and arrested. The arrests cemented the Miskito's hatred of the new government, and many communities packed up and moved to Honduras, where the Contras tried to win them over. The Sandinista government broke ties with MISURASATA, forcefully relocated the remaining Miskito villages to refugee camps outside of Puerto Cabezas.

MISURASATA leaders hoped to convert the entire Atlantic region into an autonomous, self-governing reserve for indigenous peoples. Sandinista minister of state Tomás Borge offered them instead a few concessions that, when accepted, eventually helped to restabilize the region. In 1987, after just over two years of consulting with the Atlantic coast communities, the government went a step further in reaching out to the indigenous peoples of the coast: they signed into law an autonomy statute.

The statute guaranteed self-rule and first-class citizenship for all minority groups without sacrificing their cultural roots or identities; permitted them to use their own languages and common land; to have a say in the development of natural resources; and it called for two 45-member coastal governments to govern trade, the distribution of goods, and the administration of health and education. The statute's one weakness was its flexibility, which opened the door for internecine feuds and leadership rivalries.

The Miskitos organized themselves into a group called Yatama (Yapti Tasba Masraka Nanih Aslatakanka, or Sons of the Mother Earth). With the advent of the Chamorro government, the Yatama made the conversion from armed movement to political party. Chamorro's effort to stabilize the region, plus her government's respect for the newly created autonomous regions, earned her the respect of the indigenous peoples. In contrast, the government of Arnoldo Alemán apparently tried to set the indigenous movement back a hundred years, causing the political climate to become more tense as a result.

During the departmental elections of 2000, violence erupted when Yatama was completely excluded from the ballot and elections. Representatives of Yatama vowed that unless they were permitted to participate in the municipal elections, there would be no elections. The military was sent to Puerto Cabezas and bullets flew in armed confrontations with protesters. Several people were killed. During the elections, there was significant Miskito abstention, resulting in the election of a Sandinista mayor.

Yatama supporters accused Alemán of trying to politically eradicate the indigenous community, abandoning the Miskito, Mayangna, and Rama peoples to poverty and exploitation. The Bolaños government (2002-2007) largely ignored Yatama, whose leaders were subsequently wooed into an alliance with the Sandinistas. Sandinista cadres now complain that Yatama has effectively displaced them in regional governments.

© AMBER DOBRZENSKY

The old wooden pier, once a major attraction in the city, was badly damaged in 2007's Hurricane Felix.

its quaint churches betray the region's separate history. In Barrio El Cocal, in the northern part of town, the Moravian church is the only place on earth you can hear services given in Miskito (Sunday mornings only). You may also visit the Moravian church and school in the center of town, and the Catholic church, replete with stained glass; the remnants of the former Catholic church stand behind it.

ENTERTAINMENT AND EVENTS

Karaoke Payito is a small, low-key bar with a proclivity for '80s and '90s music and cold beer without the booming sound systems that prevail in most of Puerto's discos and bars. Climb to the second floor of **Mirador Kabu Yula,** a friendly bar with views of the bustling dock.

For dancing, the **Malecón** is Puerto's overall most happening nightlife venue, with inside and outside tables overlooking the beach and two dance floors that start throbbing on the weekends. **Disco Maria** (two blocks west of the park) rules the disco scene, but there's *reggaetón* at **El Rincón** (north of town just past the Petronic gas station). *Soca* and salsa beats throb at **Disco Zaire,** and a group of other discos that surround the park.

Semana Santa in Puerto Cabezas is an unforgettable event during which many overseas Puerteños try to return home. The town sets up dozens of thatch *ranchos* at La Bocana beach, and the 24/7 party lasts at least a week: food, drink, music, and nonstop Caribbean grinding.

ACCOMMODATIONS
Under $10

Family-run **C Hospedaje Britton** (Calle Central, across from the Moravian church, tel. 505/8450-8504, elvinkind@yahoo.com, $5 per person) has 10 rooms with shared bath and fan, plus two cabins for $15 (ask about monthly rates), all set on a couple acres of tropical fruit

PUERTO CABEZAS

trees. Norton the owner can arrange everything from day trips to swimming holes on the Rio Tuapi to sailboat tours and lobster dives; he loves to talk about Nicaragua, knows where absolutely everything is, and speaks English, Spanish, Miskito, and Creole.

Hospedaje Wangki (Calle del Aeropuerto, next to CSE, tel. 505/2792-1545, $8–25) has 15 decent rooms, your choice of shared or private bath with or without air-conditioning. Breakfast is available.

$10-25

Hotel Casa Museo (tel. 505/2792-2225, casa-museojudithkain@hotmail.com, $14–27) was built in and around the Judith Kain Cunningham museum; a handful of accommodations on wooden stilts with bright, well-appointed rooms surrounds a central garden with sprawling comfy sofas, tables, benches, and other sitting areas. The on-site café serves breakfast and lunch as well as coffee and sodas throughout the day.

Hotel Triple H (tel. 505/2792-1615, $15–20 includes breakfast) is a newer hotel in Barrio Cocal, across from Kabu Payaska. Six bright and clean rooms have Wi-Fi, air-conditioning, cable TV, and private bath. **Hotel Pérez** (tel. 505/2792-2362, $12–25) has eight rooms set in an old wooden house on the main drag, some with air-conditioning, all with private bath and use of the kitchen.

$25-50

El Cortijo (tel. 505/2792-2340, $25) is on the main drag, a block south of the mayor's office with air-conditioning, private bath, and cable TV. ◖ **El Cortijo 2** (tel. 505/2792-2223, $25) is classier and more elegant, two blocks away and sitting atop a bluff over breaking surf. Guests here enjoy stained hardwood interiors, a wonderful ocean-facing deck, garden, and a semiprivate beach at the bottom of the stairs.

Over $50

◖ **Hotel Monter** (tel. 505/2792-2669,

hotelmonter@gmail.com, www.hotelmonter-nicaragua.blogspot.com, $28–63) is a class act, centrally located above the Supermercado Monter and across the street from the baseball stadium. It's the only hotel that offers airport transfers. Breakfast and Internet access are included and the rooms with balconies are the nicest; all have private bath, air-conditioning, and fans.

FOOD

Puerto has a good selection of simple *comedors,* typically offering barbecue beef and chicken. **Asados Corner** is only open on weekends and is run out of the family's home. **Asados El Patio** is open noon–midnight Wednesday–Sunday. There is always a line in front of the grill at **Comedor Aqui Me Quedo,** kitty-corner from the central park. Nearby, you can order one-dollar tacos and a milkshake at **La Esquinita del Sabor** (across from the *alcaldía*), a favorite *comedor* serving three square meals a day. If for some reason you find yourself out, about, and hungry between the hours of 9 P.M.–3 A.M., stop by **Karen's Fried Chicken.** Karen, a Miskito woman, has been frying chicken at her street stand half a block up from the northeast corner of the park for ages, and whatever hour of the night, you'll wait in line behind a crowd of locals.

At the **MiniSuper,** grab a stool at the counter or out on the patio for a cheeseburger and fruit drink ($3 for a meal). The owner, a nice guy with impeccable English, retired in 2009 from working cruise ships out of the southern United States. For traditional local food, **Paulina's Kitchen** ($3–5) is only open for lunch 11 A.M.–2 P.M.; try the *gallo pinto* with coconut, *rondon,* and other regional meals.

There are a handful of nicer restaurants throughout town, all offering essentially the same menu of shellfish, fresh fish, soups, beef, and chicken. At the north end of town, the best meal in the city is at ◖ **Restaurante Kabu Payaska** (Sea Breeze), serving seafood on a beautiful grassy lawn overlooking the ocean; $6–8 for lobster, shrimp, or fresh fish. **Miramar** is a little cheaper and closer to the center of town, with a nice view as well (dancing here on weekends makes some people think of it only as a disco).

There are two good restaurants near the airport: **Famahi** ($6–10) is open for three hearty meals a day; their breakfast and house *mondongo* (tripe soup) is their specialty; **El Esteliano II** ($6–10) is a local favorite which blasts country and *ranchero* music all day long; they have excellent *carne a la plancha,* fish, shrimp, lobster, pork, and beef dishes.

INFORMATION AND SERVICES

For a taste of life in Puerto and Nicaragua's northeast, tune in to one of the local radio stations for news and commentary—even more interesting if you speak Miskito. Radio Miskut (104.1 FM) has lots of Miskito music and other programming. Radio Van (90.3 FM) presents itself as "The Voice of the North Atlantic," but throws in a cheesy *ranchera* song now and again just for good measure.

Supermercado Monter has a surprisingly full repertoire of canned and dry goods, fresh foods, and basic housewares. The **post office** (8 A.M.–noon and 1:30–5 P.M. Mon.–Fri., (8 A.M.–noon Sat.) is located two blocks northeast of the park. The phone company, **ENITEL** (7 A.M.–9:30 P.M. Mon.–Fri.), is located a block southeast of the park.

Both banks in town have ATMs. **Bancentro** (a block south of the *alcaldía*) and **BanPro** (across from ENITEL, tel. 505/2792-2211, 8 A.M.–4:30 P.M. Mon.–Fri., 8 A.M.–noon Sat.) sometimes have long lines—bring a good book.

For Internet, the café two buildings down from the **MiniSuper** has the best connection, newest computers, and air-conditioning. Also check email at **Bilwinet** (behind the Pegatel), the place with air-conditioning right across from the mayor's office and next door to Casa Museo. Bilwi Internet is down the block from

Cifra. The run-down municipal hospital is a block from the bus terminal.

GETTING THERE AND AROUND
By Air

The **La Costeña** (tel. 505/2263-2142) flight from Managua takes about 90 minutes and costs about $150 round-trip. From Bluefields, it's about one hour and costs about $75. There are three or four scheduled flights a day to and from Managua, and one daily from Bluefields. Always confirm flights beforehand; reservations or advanced ticket purchases are recommended. If you need to make changes to flight reservations it is best to do this at the local office.

By Land

Oh, you are a brave soul indeed! Two daily buses (9 A.M. and 1 P.M.) make the arduous 24-hour journey from Managua, through Nicaragua's muddy interior. The municipal bus terminal in Puerto Cabezas is located on the western edge of town. Puerto buses leave Managua's Mayoreo terminal, or you can piece the trip together from Jinotega's north terminal on a bus bound for Waslala; from there, you board a second bus to Siuna, and then another to Puerto Cabezas. There's an alternate road from Matagalpa to Siuna by way of Río Blanco and Mulukuku. Both roads are largely impassable during the wet season. One reader found his own route: "I've just come by bus from León to Puerto Cabezas. At each stop I took the next bus that was going in the right direction [east]. From León to Matagalpa, then Río Blanco, then Santa Rita (overnight), then Siuna, Rosita, Sahsa (overnight), and finally to Puerto Cabezas.... It's not for everyone, but I'm thrilled with the close look I've gotten at the heart of Nicaragua."

By Boat

When asked about ship service to points south, one official said, "There used to be two [boats

HEALTH AND SAFETY CONCERNS IN THE RÍO COCO REGION

Due to its low, wet geography, the Río Coco area is particularly prone to malaria and dengue fever outbreaks. All travelers here should ensure they're taking a prophylaxis to prevent malaria, as well as standard precautions to prevent being bitten by mosquitoes: keep your skin covered, try to stay indoors around 5 P.M., and use repellent and a mosquito net. A major issue is the availability (or lack) of medical facilities and supplies in the region.

At the same time the Río Coco is venerated by local communities, it is also the public toilet for most of the communities that line its shores. Don't be surprised to see someone scooping a bucket of river water out for cooking just downstream of someone defecating. Although the water is usually treated with chlorine, you should pay extra attention to the food and beverages you ingest, and especially all water and water-based drinks. Treat all water with iodine pills or a portable water filter before drinking. That goes double any time you are downstream of Waspám. If you are not carrying bottled water from Managua, it is recommended that you use a good water filter. While it is possible to purchase bottled water in Waspám, the supply is not always guaranteed, so don't rely on it.

This health warning must be taken even more seriously since Hurricane Felix devastated the northeast part of the country in August 2007. Flooded latrines have contaminated wells, and various disease vectors have multiplied alarmingly.

In addition, the Río Coco was a heavily land-mined area in the 1980s. Though the land mines have largely been cleared away, known mined areas still exist and have been cordoned off with ribbon or wire. Ask the locals before you go wandering too far from the road or riverbank. Additionally, the locals took care of some land-mine clearing operations themselves to speed the process of returning to their homes by scooping up the mines and throwing them into the river. Some of them probably settled down into the mud, and others were carried downstream. Be wary at all times.

Finally, the entire Atlantic coast is experiencing the effect of drug trafficking from Colombia, and the Río Coco area provides particularly good hiding spots. The delta at Cabo Gracias a Dios is a known point of entry for small smugglers who take advantage of the almost total lack of police vigilance there.

making the run] but the other boat sank." The one left is the **Captain D** (tel. 505/8690-9719 or 8850-2767), which does a quasimonthly run to Big Corn Island (12 hours overnight, about $40), continuing to El Bluff and El Rama (another six hours, after a layover in Big Corn to unload freight). Ask at the municipal dock; boats usually leave around the middle of the month.

GETTING AROUND

Puerto Cabezas has no bus system, though the mayor's office is trying to put a couple of local city buses in place. In the meantime, Puerto has an astounding number of taxis (many of which are pirate cabs without plates, but you can use them too). The price is fixed at about $0.75 per

person to go anywhere in town, a bit more to go from the airport to the pier or bus terminal.

NEAR PUERTO CABEZAS

Tuapí, just 10 kilometers north of Puerto, has a popular swimming hole on the banks of the eponymous river. Buses leave for Tuapí several times a day from the terminal in Puerto. It's also possible to travel by boat north or south along the Atlantic coast to visit Miskito communities.

Traveling Along the Coast

For points north, make arrangements with a boat owner at the old dock in Puerto Cabezas. You'll have better luck in the early mornings when the boats are setting out for a day's

You can catch boats heading north from Puerto Cabezasa.

fishing. Someday, travelers will have interesting adventures in the gorgeous beachfront community of **Sandy Bay** (two hours from Puerto Cabezas) and the **Miskito Cays** (two hours across the open sea from Sandy Bay), but as of press time, both locations are known rendezvous points for drug runners and other dangerous types.

For points south, take a bus or taxi ($5 per person) to the community of **Lamlaya**; or hop a bus or truck in front of Hotel El Cortijo. From there, boats leave daily for **Wawa** and **Karata** between noon and 1 P.M., charging $4 one-way for a *panga,* and $2 for a "punkin" local boat (which takes twice as long). Or hire a boat to **Prinzapolka**, quite possibly the single hardest destination to reach in Nicaragua and the statistically poorest community in the nation. You should have a basic command of Miskito to visit these communities on your own, both to avoid suspicion and to be able to communicate.

◖ Tours to the Miskito Communities

Hurricane Felix pummeled many Miskito communities in 2007 and recovery has been slow. Most people are friendly, living in very rustic circumstances. **Norton Perilla** (tel. 505/8630-9906 or 505/8450-8504, elvinkind@yahoo.com), an American expat, can arrange day trips to the mainland Miskito communities of Tuapí and Boom Serpi.

The best way to visit local indigenous communities is with **AMICA** (Asociación de Mujeres Indígenas de la Costa Atlántica, one block south of the baseball stadium, tel. 505/2792-2219, asociacionamica@yahoo.es), an organization making an effort to promote the empowerment and development of women along the northern Atlantic coast. AMICA gives training in gender development, reproductive health, leadership, and AIDS, plus the laws that affect indigenous women. AMICA offers trips to the Miskito communities of Haulover, Wawa Bar, and Karata, with homestays, nature tours, and dance or cultural presentations.

© RANDALL WOOD

PUERTO CABEZAS

THE ATLANTIC COAST DRUG TRADE

Long the territory of pirates plying the waves in tall ships, the hidden and sparsely populated rivers, cays, and lagoons of Nicaragua's Atlantic coastline are a favorite haunt of South American cocaine merchants and their local cronies. During the 1980s, each Atlantic coast community had a Sandinista police force and a boat to patrol the coastal waters and estuaries. Succeeding governments pulled the police out to save money, and in the vacuum of power, the Atlantic coast became a lawless and virtually unpatrolled haven. Colombian drug runners would land onshore to refuel their boats and consolidate, divide, and distribute their merchandise. The Nicaraguan military's meager resources have been a poor match for the well-equipped drug boats sporting 250–500 horsepower engines with the latest in GPS, radar, and weaponry.

It's a well-known fact that many drug boats pass through the wilds of the Miskito Cays, an archipelago of islets, mangrove swamps, and trackless lagoons where the police have found stashes of gasoline. Other points of entry to Nicaragua include Cabo Gracias a Dios and the Río Coco, the city of El Rama, the Río Escondido, the northern half of the Pearl Lagoon, Corn Island, and the community of Sandy Bay. Some traffickers purchase gasoline from willing locals, paying with bales of high-grade, uncut product; this devastating introduction of cocaine and crack has threatened to unravel the social fabric of many coastal communities.

Sometimes drugs come to shore when Colombian traffickers transiting Nicaraguan waters jettison their cargo into the sea when threatened with boarding or capture, either abandoning it entirely, or circling back later, using their ample knowledge of the Atlantic currents to predict where the packages will turn up on the beach.

In early 2001, three Colombians turned up dead in the coastal community of Sandy Bay with no explanation; supposedly, they were assassinated by Yatama (an indigenous political party) for trying to hook the locals on their product, which they were offering at ridiculously low prices. In 2004, hired gunmen burst into the police station at Bluefields, blowing away six officers in a carefully planned hit. And in 2009, a plane full of coke dropped from the sky, crashing near Waspám in the north. By the time the authorities arrived, the plane was empty, and nobody knew a thing.

When Nicaraguan police chief, Aminta Granera, a one-time trainee to become a nun, was appointed at the end of 2006, the war against the drug barons turned serious. The police and military presence on the Atlantic coast increased dramatically and major busts became a weekly occurrence.

In 2009, Nicaraguan soldiers occupied several villages in the area in search of Colombian drug traffickers, with whom they eventually engaged in deadly firefights. Rioting subsequently broke out in Puerto Cabezas after indigenous leaders accused Nicaraguan soldiers of using drug searches as a pretext to destroy property, steal, and even kill local Miskito citizens (charges the government denies).

Travelers should expect police to thoroughly inspect bags at every dock and airport in the area.

Accommodations aren't as rustic as you'd think—including box spring mattresses and towels. Prices depend on recent transport costs; renting a boat adds considerably to the cost (about $85 pp per night, meals around $3, all negotiable depending on the number of people and number of nights). In all cases, it's crucial to call at least three days ahead.

A FEW MISKITO PHRASES

The Miskito language doesn't use the vowel sounds *e* (as in bread) or *o* (as in boat), which makes it a flowing, rhythmic language of *a, i,* and *u,* as in the following sentence, which exhorts the locals not to let the Yellow Coconut Virus infect the coconut plantations: *Coco lalahni taki pruiba sikniska alki takaskayasa.*

Here are a couple of words you might come across during your travels in the northeast.

English	Miskito
Hello	*Naksa*
Goodbye	*Aisabi*
What is your name?	*Ninam dia?*
How are you?	*Nahki sma?*
Fine	*Pain*
Bad	*Saura*
Sick	*Siknis*
Thank you	*Tingki pali*
Toilet	*Tailit*
Water	*Li*
Dirty	*Taski*
Clean	*Klin*
Food	*Plun*
Meat	*Wina*
Chicken	*Kalila*
Rice and beans	*Rais n bins*
Fish	*Inska*
Small boat	*Duri*
Lagoon	*Kabu*
River	*Awala*
Birds	*Natnawira nani*
Parrot	*Rahwaa*

Waspám and the Río Coco

◖ WASPÁM

Waspám, in the far northern reaches of the Miskito pine savanna and at the edge of the mightiest river in Nicaragua, is the gateway, principal port, and economic heart of the Miskito communities that line the banks of the Río Coco. It is, in itself, a difficult place to get to, yet it is really the first step of the voyage to places even farther away still. The communities here would prefer to be left to their own ways, but this has not been the case, and the Miskito peoples of the Río Coco suffered more than most during the 1980s, including a massive relocation that is still cause for resentment.

Waspám is not expecting travelers. You will find no package tours here, no one hawking T-shirts, real estate, or their new bed-and-breakfast. Rather, you will be immersed in a community that lives in a very traditional way, that retains a strong cultural identity despite growing mestizo influence, and that is prepared to show you exactly what it is, not what it expects you are expecting.

The Miskito people live largely off the river, fishing for small freshwater species, and off their small, neatly tended fields of corn, beans, and even upland rice. Their version of the ubiquitous tortilla is a thick, wheat-flour cake, which is fried in coconut oil. Starch makes up the rest of the diet along the Río Coco, including tubers like *quiquisque* (taro) and yucca. *Rondon* is a fish stew (and along the Río Coco it will be made of fish, not turtle, like on the coast), and the *gallo pinto* is cooked in coconut milk. Wild game also finds its way on to the menu; don't be surprised to find boar, deer, and armadillo.

Waspám proper has a few paved streets but little traffic to speak of, a point in its favor. It also has a growing solid waste problem (the bane of every rural community's early development). Once you have gotten a feel for town, a trip up the Río Coco is the natural way to glimpse the communities—usually just a couple of families living together—that make up the Miskito landscape. This endeavor is neither cheap nor easy, but you will find it rewarding,

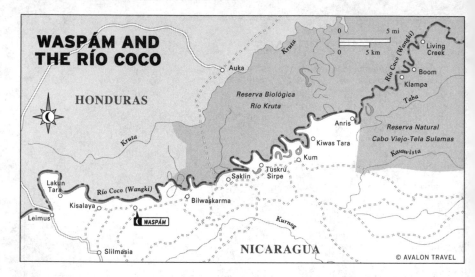

more so if you can speak enough Miskito to speak with the locals. In fact, some basic Miskito is nearly obligatory throughout your exploration of this region.

Accommodations and travelers' facilities in the traditional sense of the word are practically non-existent. The chance to visit this frontier—and it is truly frontier—to live and travel amongst the Miskito people, and to feel the spiritual power of the mighty Río Coco should not be missed.

The Miskito people are reserved but friendly—once you've broken the ice, you'll find them helpful and inquisitive. They're also more conservative than other Nicaraguans, so leave the short-shorts and bikini tops back home. Most Miskito people speak Spanish as a second language and practically no English at all. Foreigners who speak languages other than Spanish or Miskito will inevitably be called Miriki (American). Even Nicaraguans from the Pacific region are considered foreigners and are referred to as mestizos.

Accommodations and Food

Accomodations are pretty basic, but reasonable. **Las Cabañas** (no phone) has rooms from

$4–14 depending on how much comfort you'd like, but at the top end even have cable TV.

Hotelito El Piloto (tel. 505/8642-4405, from $25) is located at the north end of the main street, about two minutes from Wangki. They have 11 air-conditioned rooms with private bathrooms, and a kitchen area with meals available. Right across from the airport is **La Estancia de Rose** (tel.505/8944-2335, $11 d with fan, from $20 with a/c). In the main house, all the rooms have private bathrooms and 24-hour electricity; three meals are available, as well as Internet and satellite TV. Rose also has a small movie theater, and the town's only Internet connection is hers as well, adjacent to the hotel.

There are several small eateries in town, most serving rice and beans accompanied by a hunk of meat, sometimes fish. You can ensure fish—or shrimp—for dinner by arranging beforehand with the restaurant where you intend to eat later that day. Vegetables are scarce and any salad usually consists of cabbage and some tomatoes in vinegar; eggs are usually available as well. Ask to try some *wabul*, a thick, warm, green banana drink, which has many

traveling by canoe on the Río Coco

variations. Coconut bread can be found street-side, or at the market during the evening when it's still warm from the oven. The best restaurant in town is **Papta Watla,** situated between the dock and the church. Popular with foreign aid workers, it serves hearty meals for under $6.

Information and Services

The **ENITEL** phone office (8 A.M.–noon and 1–5 P.M. most weekdays, 8 A.M.–noon Sat.) is located just west of the Rotonda Centroamerica. The post office—a private home with a "Correos de Nicaragua" sign posted out front—is along the airstrip.

There is a local, underequipped police station in town and a health clinic with very basic services. The Catholic church has a private clinic with slightly better service and more supplies; in case of an emergency go to the convent and tell the nuns. One of the attending doctors speaks good English.

Getting There

La Costeña (tel. 505/2263-2814) pilots radio ahead to have someone shoo the cattle away. Daily morning flights leave Managua most of the week; the flight is about 90 minutes long over some of the most exotic scenery in Nicaragua; $103 one-way ($159 round-trip).

Land transportation to Waspám can be arranged in Puerto Cabezas. The grueling bus trip takes 5 hours when the road is in good condition and it isn't raining; in the rainy season the trip can take as long as 12 hours. Two or three daily Waspám-bound buses leave Puerto at the crack of dawn and cost $10; get there early for the 6 A.M. bus. The following day, the same buses leave Waspám at the crack of dawn bound for Puerto Cabezas. Because all the buses leave their respective starting points in the morning, day trips are impossible.

Additionally, there's a truck that leaves Puerto Cabezas every morning between 5 and 6 A.M.—a lumbering, diesel-belching IFA—and many opt to travel with El Chino Kung Fu, a local character with a decent pickup truck

PUERTO CABEZAS

who makes regular trips between Waspám and Puerto Cabezas. Ask around and try to form a group to share the costs. Bear in mind that hitchhiking runs the danger of being an unknowing accomplice to transporting narcotics.

RIVER TRIPS FROM WASPÁM

Waspám is your gateway to the Río Coco, and small boats—fiberglass *pangas* and dugout *batu* canoes—are your means of transport. One local volunteer recommends the *panga* trip to San Carlos, which has a simple *hospedaje*. In the upriver villages located between Waspám and Leimus, visitors are not common and facilities are somewhere between limited and nonexistent. Don't plan on staying overnight or finding food for sale.

Nothing is easy or cheap, by the standards of travelers accustomed to the prices of the Pacific side. In general, expect to pay $45–100 per person per day for boat transportation along the Río Coco, which includes the boat, the gasoline, and the boatman. The dream adventure is a trip all the way up to Wiwilí, the upstream port town. El Bailarín makes the trip from time to time, but charges $1,000 round-trip per person for the extended 550-kilometer voyage one-way.

Two tributaries to the Río Coco, the Yahuk and the Waspuk, are both home to waterfalls the locals say are beautiful places to visit, but make for long trips. To visit the Yahuk, for example, you'd have to hire a boat for two days. The first day, you can motor up the Río Coco to the Yahuk and continue upstream to the falls, then spend the night in San Carlos, and return the following day. The Waspuk falls are reportedly a site of religious significance to the Miskito people. The trip is just upwards of 130 kilometers in each direction.

TRIPS BY LAND FROM WASPÁM

Travel is difficult, transportation infrequent, and food and lodging service nonexistent. If necessary, you can try arranging a meal with a local family, for which you'll pay. There are two local villages that are close to Waspám: **Kisalaya** (five kilometers) and **Ulwas** (three kilometers, a 30-minute walk through pleasant country). Locals will point you in the right direction. **Bilwaskarma** (10 kilometers, approximately a 90-minute walk from Waspám) is a pleasant village with a small health center that was a world-famous nursing school before the conflict of the 1980s.

Siuna and the Mining Triangle

In the heart of the mining triangle is Siuna, a town of about 12,000 people and the best point of entry for the Bosawás nature reserve. It is also home to a growing number of Mayangna Indians who have gradually migrated from the Atlantic coast and the Río Coco. Throughout the mining triangle (the term refers to the towns of Siuna, Bonanza, and Rosita), roads, power supply, and water systems are unreliable, and the towns are filled with drunks and cowboys. Sound like a good time? There are cheap places to stay and eat in all three towns, and Bonanza has a working Canadian-owned

gold mine and a dozen depressing casinos. Each town also has a handful of natural attractions nearby and local guides to get you there. The Bosawás reserve, to the north, is one of the largest expanses of wilderness in Central America.

HISTORY

In the early 20th century, Siuna was a bustling mining town that drew workers from as far away as Jamaica. But in 1968 the foreign companies closed the mines (Yamana Gold out of Toronto, Canada has recently taken a renewed interest). Distant and poorly patrolled, the whole triangle made an easy target for Contra operations during the 1980s, and indeed several serious skirmishes took place in the region. When the war ended, an uneasy peace ensued, for the entire area was peppered with land mines, now lost or abandoned, and many well armed but still unemployed men gave up guerilla warfare for a life of petty banditry.

Regaining a sense of civility took more than a decade. There have been no attacks on foreigners, with the 1999 exception of Manley Guarducci, a Canadian mining engineer who was kidnapped and held for ransom for five weeks before being released unharmed.

ACCOMMODATIONS AND FOOD

Hotel Siu (Barrio Sol de Libertad, from the police station, one block west and one south, tel. 505/2794-2028, $20 with fan, $25 with a/c) has nice rooms and tasty meals; **Los Chinitos** (tel. 505/2794-2038, $7–20) is also clean and well recommended with a nice wooden deck and lounging area and a range of 15 rooms, some with private bathrooms and a/c.

Las Praderas (Barrio Campo Viejo, near URACCAN, $6–10) is the top spot in town for dining; or rub elbows with the cowboys over steaks at **El Machin.**

Not surprisingly, beer joints are everywhere. Locals prefer **El Secreto** (right on the landing strip in the center of town), a gritty disco that seems to be full all weekend; eat at the *fritanga* right outside.

◖ BOSAWÁS BIOSPHERE RESERVE

Located 350 kilometers north of Managua, the 730,000 hectares of forest, mountains, and rivers collectively known as Bosawás are located within the municipalities of Waspám, Bonanza, Siuna, El Cuá–Bocay, Wiwilí, and Waslala. Although inhabited by some 40,000 widely dispersed people (more than half of whom are

© GRACE GONZALEZ

the church in Rosita

PUERTO CABEZAS

Mayangna and Miskito), most of Bosawás remains unexplored, unmapped, and untamed. Its name is derived from the region's three most salient features: the Río Bocay (BO), Cerro Saslaya (SA), and the Río Waspuk (WAS).

It's the largest uninterrupted tract of primary rainforest north of the Amazon, and besides unparalleled stretches of cloud forest, Bosawás contains tropical humid forest, rainforest, and a wealth of disparate ecosystems that vary in altitude from 30 meters above sea level at the mouth of the Waspuk River to the 1,650-meter peak of Cerro Saslaya. Bosawás is a Central American treasure, an immense genetic reserve of species that have vanished elsewhere in Mesoamerica, including jaguars, rare small mammals, 12 kinds of poisonous snakes, and many bird species, including the gorgeous scarlet macaw and 34 boreal migratory species.

Bosawás was designated a protected reserve in 1997, but where there is no money, there is little enforcement and few rangers—there are many more desperately poor who continue to make a living from this ancient land. In many cases, this translates into slash-and-burn clearing of the forests and the continual push of the agricultural frontier, mostly for subsistence. The 1.8 million acres of protected area was declared a part of the Nature Conservancy's international Parks in Peril program in 2001.

Visiting the Reserve

To do anything in Bosawás, you *must* receive permission (at time of printing, free). Talk to the **Bosawás Office** (at central park near the stadium, not far from Hotelito Los Chinitos, tel. 505/2794-2036) who will help arrange a guide. The **MARENA office** in Managua can also help (tel. 505/2233-1594). Guides are both obligatory and absolutely necessary and cost about $10–20 per day plus food. You may be convinced to hire two guides for your trip, a recommended safety and comfort precaution.

There is also a park office in Bonanza (tel. 505/2794-0109), located a mile or so out of town, that can help you find local trails and guides.

Unless you have months to explore the reserve, you'll have to pick and choose from various possible destinations. Get off the bus at Casa Roja (1.5 hours from Siuna) to stage an ascent of Cerro Saslaya (4–5 days); or continue to Santa Rosita (2.5-hour bus ride) for a two-hour hike to the river or trailhead to Cerro El Torro (4–5 days). Waslala is a 4–5 hour ride from Siuna and home to the original tomb of Carlos Fonseca (his remains were moved to Managua after the revolution's victory).

Be advised: Any trip in Bosawás is a serious backcountry undertaking and should not be attempted without proper supplies, some wilderness experience, a tolerance for dampness and discomfort, and a basic survival instinct. You should already have supplies like water bottles, a mosquito net, and some kind of pump or purifying tablets for water (start your hike with at least three liters in your bag; a fresh source is available in the park), a brimmed hat, sunscreen, sturdy shoes, and a medical kit. Additional supplies that can be purchased in Siuna include rubber boots (for snakes and knee-level mud), four yards of heavy black plastic for a roof in the jungle, a piece of plastic or waterproof cover for your backpack, a machete, a hammock, extra rope, and food.

Take a local bus to Rosa Grande, then walk or rent a horse ($5 per day) to Rancho Alegre. From there the journey is a challenging one-hour hike through the community of Rancho Alegre to a series of waterfalls at Salto Labu. Another hour hike up a steep path leads you to Mirador, a lookout and an incredible view of an absolutely stunning waterfall before you reach the primary forest on the path into Bosawás.

BACKGROUND

The Land

The largest and lowest Central American country, Nicaragua is a nation of geographical superlatives. Located at the elbow where the Central American isthmus bends and then plummets southward to Panamá, Nicaragua is almost dead center between North and South America. Part of a biological corridor that for millions of years has allowed plant and animal species from two continents to mingle, it boasts an extraordinary blend of flora and fauna.

In the 16th century, Nicaragua's geographical beauty enchanted the conquistadores, who reported, "The Nicaraguan plains are some of the most beautiful and pleasant lands that can be found in the Indies because they are very fertile with *mahicales* and vegetables, *fesoles* of diverse types, fruits of many kinds and much cacao."

Nicaragua is roughly triangular in shape and dominated by two large lakes in the southwest. Its 530-kilometer-long northern border with Honduras is the longest transect across the Central American isthmus. To the south, the southern shore of the Río San Juan defines the better part of the Nicaraguan–Costa Rican border. Wholly within Nicaragua, the San Juan has been a continual source of conflict to this

© JOSHUA BERMAN

day with Costa Rica, whose attempts to navigate and patrol the river have been met aggressively by the Nicaraguan government. To the east and west lie the Caribbean Sea and the Pacific Ocean, respectively. With 127,849 square kilometers of land area, Nicaragua is approximately the size of Greece or the state of New York. But Nicaragua has lost some 50,000 square kilometers to her neighbors over the past several centuries: the eastern third of what is now Honduras, as well as the now–Costa Rican territories of Nicoya and Guanacaste, plus the Caribbean island of San Andrés.

Administratively, the nation is divided into 15 units called *departamentos,* and two vast autonomous regions on the Atlantic coast known as the North and South Atlantic Autonomous Regions (RAAN and RAAS). The departments, in turn, consist of 145 municipalities. The two autonomous regions elect their own officials on a separate electoral calendar.

Nicaragua's three largest cities are Managua, León, and Granada, followed by Estelí, Masaya, and the remaining department capitals.

GEOGRAPHY

Nicaragua's favorite nickname, "The Land of Lakes and Volcanoes," evokes its primary geographical features: two great lakes and a chain of impressive and active volcanoes. Nicaragua's water and volcanic resources have had an enormous effect on its human history, from the day the first Nahuatl people concluded their migration south and settled on the forested shores of Lake Cocibolca (Lake Nicaragua) to the first Spanish settlements along the lakes to the many as yet unrealized plans to build a trans-isthmus canal.

Geologic History and Formation

The isthmus now known as Central America took shape 60 million years ago (MYA); Nicaragua's northern third is geologically the most ancient.

Nicaragua is known as "the land of lakes and volcanoes."

© JOSHUA BERMAN

In the area of Telpaneca and Quilalí, rocks dated at 200 million years old are thought to have once been part of a small Jurassic-Cretaceous continent that included the modern-day Yucatán Peninsula in Mexico and the Antilles Islands. To the south, what are now Costa Rica's Talamanca Mountains formed an archipelago of isolated volcanoes. During the Tertiary period (65–1.7 MYA), intense volcanic activity and erosion produced large amounts of sediment and volcanic flows that accumulated underwater.

At least two periods of intense volcanic activity, one in the Eocenic-Oligocenic epoch (55–25 MYA) formed the lesser features of Nicaragua's central highlands, and a second in the Miocene (25–13 MYA) produced the larger mountains in Matagalpa and Jinotega. Eleven million years later, shifting tectonic plates in the Pacific and Caribbean lifted the seabed, forming the Pacific region.

When the Cocos plate slid under the Caribbean plate, the main volcanic mountain range running northwest–southeast across the Pacific plains blistered to the surface. Ocean water from the Atlantic rushed in along a broad sunken valley of the Pacific plate now known as the Nicaraguan Depression and pooled, forming the lakes. Some geologists believe the Atlantic and Pacific actually connected at this point in time and were later cut off by volcanic sedimentation. Erosion began pulling material from the landmass outward to the sea, building up Nicaragua's Pacific region and gradually forming the Atlantic coast.

Plate tectonics theory, in spite of being widely accepted since the 1960s, is most frequently criticized for its failure to adequately explain the geology and geography of several regions of the world, including Central America. It is highly probable that our concept of the geological events that formed Central America will change as geologic science progresses. Regardless of the mechanism, however, convergence of the plates ensures crustal instability, which manifests itself in frequent volcanic and earthquake activity in all of Central America, and especially in Nicaragua.

Volcanoes and Mountain Ranges

Nicaragua has about 40 volcanoes, a half dozen of which are usually active at any time, whether venting light clouds of gas or actually erupting. Running parallel to the Pacific shore, Nicaragua's volcanoes are a part of the Ring of Fire that encompasses most of the western coast of the Americas, the Aleutian Islands of Alaska, Japan, and Indonesia. The Maribio (Nahuatl for the "giant men") and Dirian volcano ranges stretch nearly 300 kilometers from the Concepción and Maderas in the middle of Lake Nicaragua to Cosigüina, which juts into the Gulf of Fonseca.

The first volcanic event in recorded history was a major eruption of Volcán Masaya in the early 1500s. The lava formed the present-day lagoon at the base of the mountain. Another great lava flow occurred in 1772, leaving a black, barren path still visible today where the Carretera Masaya highway crosses it. In 1609, Spanish settlers abandoned the city of León when Momotombo erupted. And in January of 1835, Volcán Cosigüina violently blew its top, hurling ash as far away as Jamaica and Mexico, covering the area for 250 kilometers around the volcano in ash and burning pumice and forcing the entire peninsula into three days of darkness. All this volcanic activity is responsible for the exceptional fertility of Nicaragua's soils, most notably the agricultural plains around Chinandega and León.

Volcán Masaya is the most easily accessed of Nicaragua's volcanoes and boasts a paved road leading right to the lip of the crater. Volcán Masaya is actually formed of three craters, the largest of which, Santiago, is the only crater in the Americas that contains a visible pool of incandescent liquid lava in its center. The visibility of this lava fluctuates on a 30-year cycle and was best seen 1965–1979.

Climbing a few Nicaraguan giants is a great way to experience Central America. San Cristóbal is the highest peak, at 1,745 meters. A smaller peak adjacent to San Cristóbal, Volcán Casitas still bears the immense scar of the landslide that buried thousands in an avalanche of rock and mud during Hurricane Mitch—and trembled briefly again in January of 2002. Isla de Ometepe's twin cones are popular for hiking and easily accessible. No matter where you hike, always hire a guide, as several foreigners have gotten lost and perished while peak bagging.

Momotombo, San Cristóbal, and Telíca are the most active peaks and are prone to emit plumes of poisonous gases, smoke, and occasionally lava. La Isla de Ometepe's Volcán Concepción (1,610 meters) last blew its top in 2005 and 2007. The other half of Ometepe (Nahuatl for "two peaks") is Volcán Maderas (1,394 meters) which sleeps, its crater drowned in a deep lagoon that feeds a thriving jungle.

Volcán Telíca, just north of León, erupts approximately every five years, while gas vents at its base churn out boiling mud and sulfur. Neighboring Cerro Negro is one of the youngest volcanoes on the planet: It protruded through a farmer's field in the middle of the 1800s and has since grown in size, steadily and violently, to a height of 400 meters. Cerro Negro's last three eruptions have been increasingly powerful, culminating in 1992 when it belched up a cloud of burning gases and ash seven kilometers high, burying León under 15 centimeters of ash and dust. Eight thousand inhabitants were evacuated as the weight of the ash caused several homes to collapse. Volcán Momotombo's (Nahuatl for "great burning peak") perfect conical peak is visible from great distances across the Pacific plains, as far away as Matagalpa. Momotombo is responsible for approximately 10 percent of Nicaragua's electricity via a geothermal plant located at its base. It hasn't erupted since 1905, but Momotombo remains a monster whose menace is taken quite seriously. In April

2000 it rumbled long enough to get Managua's attention, then quieted back down (for now).

A popular day trip from Granada is the cloud forest park and coffee plantations of Volcán Mombacho (1,345 meters), a dormant volcano whose explosion and self-destruction formed the archipelago of *isletas* in Lake Cocibolca. Mombacho took its modern shape in 1570 when a major avalanche on the south slope opened and exposed the crater, burying an indigenous village of 400 inhabitants in the process.

Three lesser mountain ranges dominate Nicaragua's center and north: the Cordilleras Isabelia, Huapi, and Chontaleña. These three ranges radiate northeast, east, and southeast, respectively, from the center of the country, gradually melting into the lowland jungle and swamps of the Atlantic coast. Their half-dozen prominent peaks were the scene of intense fighting during several conflicts in Nicaraguan history. Nicaragua's highest point, Cerro Mogotón, at 2,107 meters, is located along the Honduran border in Nueva Segovia.

Lakes and Lagoons

Two lakes, Cocibolca (Lake Nicaragua) and Xolotlán (Lake Managua), dominate Nicaragua's geography, occupying together nearly 10 percent of the country's surface area.

Lake Xolotlán, although broad (1,025 square kilometers), is shallow with an average depth of only seven meters. It reaches its deepest—26 meters—near the island of Momotombito. Lake Managua is, for the most part, biologically dead, after a century of untreated human waste and extensive dumping of industrial wastes during the 1970s, including lead, cyanide, benzene, mercury, and arsenic. The tremendous opportunities for tourism, recreation, and potable water for human consumption that a clean lake would facilitate have led to an ambitious plan to detoxify Xolotlán. Backed by loans from Japan and the World Bank, the project has already begun collecting and treating

Managua's sewage and, gradually, cleansing the lake itself in water treatment plants on the lakeshore. See the result for yourself on a booze cruise from Managua's Malecón.

Lake Cocibolca is the larger of Nicaragua's two lakes and one of Nicaragua's greatest natural treasures. At 8,264 square kilometers and 160 kilometers long along its axis, Lake Cocibolca is nearly as big as the island of Puerto Rico and lies 31 meters above sea level. It's also deep—up to 60 meters in some places, and relatively clean. The prevailing winds, which blow from the east across the farmlands of Chontales, make the eastern part of Cocibolca calm and the western half choppy and rough. A massive pipe system is presently being designed which, if built, will carry drinking water from Cocibolca to Managua to help meet the needs of the capital's rapidly growing population.

Nearly a dozen stunning lagoons mark the maws of ancient volcanic craters. Around Managua are the Nejapa, Tiscapa, and Asososca Lagoons. West of Managua, the picturesque twin craters of Xiloá and Apoyeque form the Chiltepe Peninsula. Near Masaya, the 200-meter-deep Laguna de Apoyo was formed sometime in the Quaternary period (1.6 MYA) by what is thought to be the most violent volcanic event in Nicaragua's prehistory. Not far away is Laguna de Masaya, at the base of the volcano of the same name. Other gorgeous lagoons flank Volcán Momotombo in the craters of the Maderas and Consigüina Volcanoes.

Rivers

To the original Spanish settlers in Granada, the Río San Juan was the elusive "drain" of Lake Cocibolca; since then, the possibility of traveling up the Río San Juan, across Lake Cocibolca, and then by land to the Pacific Ocean has made the San Juan the most historically important river in Nicaragua. In the years of the gold rush, thousands of prospectors navigated up the Río San Juan en route to California; some made the return trip laden with riches, others with nothing. These days, several sets of rapids and decades of sedimentation reduce its navigability, exacerbated by shifts in the riverbed from occasional earthquakes. Cattle ranches and small farms primarily producing basic grains line both shores (farmers on the southern shore identify more closely with Costa Rica and even use its currency).

Formed by the confluence of three major rivers—the Siquia, Mico, and Rama—the Río Escondido is the principal link in the transportation corridor from Managua to Bluefields and the Atlantic coast. Produce and merchandise (and busloads of travelers) reach El Rama and then proceed down the Escondido. The Escondido and its tributaries are important to the cattle industry in Chontales, but massive deforestation along its banks have unleashed dangerous floods that frequently put the river port of El Rama under water.

The 680-kilometer-long Río Coco is the longest river in Central America, fed by headwaters in both Nicaragua and Honduras. Also known as the Río Segovia or its indigenous name Wanki, the Coco traverses terrain that varies from several minor canyons to vast stretches of virgin forest. The indigenous Miskito people, for whom the river bears great spiritual significance, live in small communities along its shores.

The Estero Real (Royal Estuary), at 137 kilometers in length, is the most consequential body of water on the Pacific coast and is one of Nicaragua's best places to spot waterfowl. It drains most of northwestern Nicaragua through extensive mangroves and wetlands to the Gulf of Fonseca and is the nucleus of extensive shrimp-farming operations.

Soils

In the Pacific region, the volcanic soils are highly fertile and mineral rich. The mountainous north and central regions of Nicaragua are

© AMBER DOBRZENSKY

A visit to the *campo*, or countryside, gives travelers a taste of rural Nicaragua.

less fertile basalt, andesite, and granite-based soils, and their steeper slopes are prone to erosion and soil degradation. The better soils are usually found alongside rivers where deforestation and fierce storms such as Hurricane Mitch (1998) haven't carried it away, stripped it of its nutrient value, or buried it under thick layers of sand. In the north and northeast towards the Caribbean, the weak, quartz-based soils can bear little more than thin stands of white pine. The Sébaco Valley, thought to have once been the bed of an immense lake, has thick, black clay soils that impede the production of corn or beans but greatly facilitate wet rice farming.

CLIMATE

Located between 11 and 15 degrees north latitude, Nicaragua's tropical climate ranges from 27–32°C (81–90°F) during the rainy season, and 30–35°C (86–95°F) in the dry season, but varies remarkably by region: In the mountains of Matagalpa and Jinotega, the temperature can

be 10°C cooler, while in León and Managua, they can be 10°C warmer, making ordinary travelers feel like glazed chickens roasting over the coals. Nicaragua's *invierno* (winter, or rainy season) lasts approximately May–October, and *verano* (summer, or dry season) lasts November–April—rain during these months may mean just a quick shower each afternoon, or a deluge that goes on for days. As you travel east toward the Atlantic coast or down the Río San Juan, the rainy season grows longer and wetter until the dry season lasts for only the month of April.

ENVIRONMENTAL ISSUES

Nicaragua's environmental issues betray a rat's nest of bigger problems, from politics, land rights, and population pressure to war and natural disasters. The remedies are anything but simple.

The primordial environmental concern is the rapid loss of forests—at the rate of 150,000 hectares per year. Some analyses indicate Nicaragua's timber reserves will be completely

HURRICANE MITCH

It was late October 1998, and the rainy season had been reduced to sporadic drizzle, just right for the red beans that were slowly gathering strength in the fields. The newspapers mentioned a hurricane forming in the Atlantic, but Nicaragua seemed spared when the storm, called Mitch, shifted to the north instead of making landfall on the Caribbean coast.

Instead, on October 28, rain began to fall steadily from a leaden sky over most of Nicaragua. Mitch had come to a near complete stop off the north coast of Honduras, and thick gray arms of clouds swept in long spirals across the entire Central American isthmus, greedily gathering strength from both the Caribbean and Pacific Ocean, while winds around the eye of the hurricane reached 290 kilometers per hour. The rains fell day and night for seven days. The country roads of red earth turned muddy, then became dangerous rivers of coffee-colored water coursing through the centers of towns, while cattle that had been left in the fields found high ground or were drowned and swept away. Swollen to 10 times their normal size, Nicaraguan rivers flared over their banks, tearing out trees, snatching away homes, and breaking apart (or just tearing around) every bridge in their path. On October 29, the electricity failed in most of the north as power lines fell and poles were swept away. In Sébaco, the Río Viejo and the Río Grande de Matagalpa, which normally pass within a kilometer of each other, rose and combined before tearing through Ciudad Darío.

The waters of Lake Xolotlán rose three meters over the course of three days. Overtopping the basin, the waters barreled through the old, dry channel of the once-intermittent Río Tipitapa, raising the level of Lake Cocibolca and the Río San Juan; the town of Tipitapa, built in the low saddle between the two lakes, was completely inundated. On the Pan-American Highway, the enormous bridge that crossed over the Tipitapa River was damaged, then destroyed, and finally carried away completely. By October 30, the entire northern half of the country was isolated: Major bridges had been demolished in Sébaco and Tipitapa, and every bridge without exception between León and Managua had been destroyed.

But Mitch was cruelest in Posoltega, Chinandega, where the equivalent of a full year's rainfall came down in under four days. The intense rains filled the crater of Volcán Casita with rainwater, and at 2 P.M. on October 30, the southwest edge of the crater lip tore away, unleashing a deadly avalanche of mud, water, and rock 1.5 kilometers wide and three meters high upon the three small communities below. Thousands died immediately, as the mudflow poured southwest more than four kilometers to the highway, crossed it, and continued southwest into the town of Posoltega. In the aftermath, there was no hope of recovering or even identifying victims.

By the time the rains finally stopped, Hurricane Mitch had reduced Nicaragua's GDP by half and destroyed more than 70 percent of the country's physical infrastructure. Hundreds of health clinics and more than 20,000 homes were carried away, and arable farmland was reduced by 11,550 hectares. Overall, economic losses sustained by this already poor nation were around $1.5 billion. Mitch also opened up political and social scars less obvious than deforested hillsides. Under duress, political divisions reopened as relief money poured in and politicians—particularly President Alemán—struggled to divert it for their own interests.

Though the press called Mitch "the storm of the century," scientists estimate it was much more severe even than that and declared it the most deadly storm event in at least 200 years. However, the hundreds of millions of dollars of aid money that poured into Nicaragua in the aftermath have provided Nicaragua with a much-needed opportunity to strengthen and rebuild, and much effort has gone into ensuring that the Nicaraguan government and people are more capable of dealing with future disasters through training programs, flood-warning detection systems, computer models, and more. These are crucial to Nicaragua's future well-being, because Hurricane Mitch will surely not be the last storm to wreak havoc in Nicaragua.

depleted by 2015, but the extent of the risk is disputable, as the calculations rely on figures collected in the 1970s.

The great majority of country dwellers cook on *leña* (firewood), so increasing population expansion into previously unsettled lands has boded poorly for forests. Population pressure and the swelling cattle industry have pushed the agricultural frontier inward from both the Atlantic and Pacific sides of the country, reducing Nicaragua's forests by 4.6 million hectares from 1950–1995. On the Atlantic coast, much of the hardwood logging is happening at the hands of U.S., Canadian, and Asian companies that have negotiated lucrative timber concessions with Nicaragua's successive cash-strapped governments.

Nueva Segovian pine forests are under further ecological pressure from pine bark beetles, a major outbreak of which decimated 6,000 hectares across the north from 1999–2001, particularly the area around Jalapa. The beetle attacks both young and mature pines weakened by fires, resin harvesting, and poor management, boring into the tree to feed on the resin between the wood and the bark. At the start of each rainy season, young beetles disperse and fly longer distances. The infestation can spread up to 20 meters per day—that is a full kilometer in just under two months.

Deforestation exposes fragile tropical soils to rainfall, leading to erosion, contamination and elimination of water sources, and outright microclimate changes. This is the case in much of Nicaragua, where within one human generation, rivers and streams that were once perennial now flow only sporadically, if at all. As any *viejito* will tell you, "It doesn't rain as much as it used to." On the Pacific coast, decades of chemical-intensive agriculture and wind erosion have caused the loss of once-rich volcanic soils as well. In general, the entire Pacific, central, and northern regions of the country are at immediate risk of sustained soil erosion.

Sustained efforts are underway to attack the problem from all sides, from environmental education of children to active replanting of hillsides, to the introduction of less-destructive agricultural techniques.

Flora and Fauna

FLORA

Nicaragua's variety of ecosystems, and its position at the biological crossroads between North and South America and between the Atlantic and Pacific Oceans have blessed it with an astonishingly broad assortment of vegetation and wildlife. Of the world's known 250,000 species of flowering plants, an estimated 15,000–17,000 are found in Central America. Nicaragua is home to some 9,000 species of vascular plants, many of medicinal value. But outside a few protected areas, conservation efforts are half-hearted or underfunded, and even protected areas are under intense pressure from the agricultural frontier and the scattered human settlements grandfathered within the confines of the reserves.

Trees

The *madroño (Calycophyllum candidissimum)* is Nicaragua's national tree. The hills south of Sébaco form the southern limit of the pine family found on the continent; south of Nicaragua, the pines are out-competed by other species. At the turn of the 21st century, Nicaragua's forest area measured 5.5 million hectares, the majority of which is broadleaf forest, followed by pine *(Pinus caribea* and *P. oocarpa)*. At altitudes greater than 1,200 meters, the forests also include the conifers *P. maximinoi* and *P. tecunumanii*. A full 2.5 million hectares of forest are classified as commercial timber forest. Though often privately owned, the Nicaraguan government regulates exploitation of forest products (and not infrequently simply sells the forests for its own profit).

Principal Ecosystems

Nicaragua's varied topography and uneven rainfall distribution, not to mention the presence of tropical reefs, volcanoes, and volcanic crater lakes, result in a phenomenal diversity of terrain and ecosystems. On any trip, watch prairie grasslands melt into rolling hills into near-desert into craggy mountain ranges whose peaks are draped in cloud forest. You can burn your feet on an active volcano's peak and cool your heels in ocean surf the same day. Nicaragua's higher peaks are isolated ecosystems in their own right and home to several endangered as well as endemic species, and the streams, rivers, and two very different coastlines furnish myriad other distinct ecosystems. In general, the land is composed of the following ecological zones:

Pacific Dry Forest: The lowlands of the Pacific coast, specifically the broad, flat strip that borders the Pacific Ocean from sea level to approximately 800 meters in altitude, are a rain-stressed region dominated by thorny, rubbery species. The region typically receives less than 2,000 millimeters of rain per year. Both trees and noncactuslike plants in this ecosystem shed their leaves in the middle of the dry season in preparation for the rain, and burst into flower in April or May.

Upland Pine Forest: With the exception of the slopes of several Pacific mountains, namely San Cristóbal and Las Casitas in Chinandega and Güisisíl in Matagalpa, the majority of Nicaragua's pine forests are found in the north near Jalapa and Ocotal. Pines particularly thrive on poor, acidic soils, which erode easily if the area is logged.

Lower Mountainous Broadleaf Forest: Nicaragua's higher peaks are cloud covered for most of the year and home to a cool, moist biosphere, rich in flora and fauna. Most of these areas are the more remote peaks of Matagalpa and Jinotega, like Kilambé, Peñas Blancas, Saslaya, and Musún. It's easier to enjoy this ecosystem on the beautiful and easily visited peaks of Volcán Mombacho near Granada, and Volcán Maderas on Ometepe.

Caribbean Rainy Zone: The Atlantic coast receives rain throughout nearly 10 months of the year and the humidity hovers around 90 percent year-round. Most of the Atlantic coast is covered with tropical forest or even lowland rainforest, with trees that often reach 30 or 40 meters in height. In the north along the Río Coco are the remains of Nicaragua's last extensive pine forests *(Pinus caribaea),* presently subject to intensive logging by national and international concessions.

FAUNA

Nicaragua is home to a great deal of exotic wildlife, much of which—unfortunately—you'll only see for sale on the sides of the highways and at intersections in Managua, where barefoot merchants peddle toucans, reptiles, ocelots, parrots, and macaws. This is a considerable, largely unchecked problem, more so because, of the animals that are captured for sale or export in Nicaragua, 80 percent die before reaching their final destination. To view fauna in their natural habitat involves getting out there, being very, very quiet, and looking and listening. Most critters are shy and many are nocturnal, but they're out there. To date, 1,804 vertebrate species, including 21 species endemic to Nicaragua, and approximately 14,000 invertebrate species have been defined. However, Nicaragua remains the least-studied country in the region. Excursions into the relatively unexplored reserves of the north and northeast will surely uncover previously undiscovered species.

Mammals

One-hundred seventy-six mammal species (including sea life) are known to exist in

© GRACE GONZALEZ

The howler monkey is one of the three primate species found in Nicaragua.

Nicaragua, more than half of which are bats or small mammals, including rodents. Of the at least three endemic mammal species, two are associated with the Caribbean town of El Rama—the Rama squirrel *(Sciurus richmondi)*, considered the tropical world's most endangered squirrel due to reduced habitat, and the Rama rice mouse *(Oryzomis dimidiatus)*.

Nicaragua is also home to six big cat species, but there's no guarantee they'll be around for long. All six are listed as endangered, most seriously of all the jaguar and puma. Once common, both require vast amounts of wild hunting territory. In the Pacific region, isolated communities on the higher slopes of some forested volcanoes like Mombacho may remain, but they have not been seen. In the Atlantic region, small communities of cats eke out their survival in the dense forests of the southeast side of the Bosawás reserve. These species are unstudied and untracked, and are presumably preyed upon by local communities. The smaller feline species like ocelots and *tigrillos* have fared better. Though they are largely trapped in the central forests, the latter at least makes a decent living preying on farming community chickens.

There are three kinds of monkeys in Nicaragua: the mantled howler monkey *(Alouata palliata)*, known popularly as the *mono congo;* the Central American spider monkey *(Ateles geoffroyii);* and the white-faced capuchin *(Cebus capucinus).* Of the monkeys, the congo is the most common: 1,000 individuals roam the slopes of Mombacho alone. You can also find them on Ometepe and the mountains of Matagalpa, particularly Selva Negra. Howler monkeys are able to project their throaty, haunting cries to distances as great as several kilometers. They eat fruits and leaves and spend most of their time in high tree branches. The threatened white-faced capuchin lives in the forests in southeastern Nicaragua and parts of the Atlantic coast. But the spider monkey has nearly been eliminated and is the most threatened of the three.

The Baird's tapir is present in very small

numbers in eastern Nicaragua; several communities of this three-toed ungulate inhabit Bosawás, but this species is threatened with extinction. The agouti paca (a large, forest-dwelling rodent known in Nicaragua as the painted rabbit), the white-tailed deer *(Odocoileus virginianus)*, and the collared peccary *(Tayassu tajacu)*, a stocky, piglike creature with coarse, spiky fur, though abundant, are under much pressure from hunters throughout northeastern Nicaragua. You may still see an agouti or peccary east of Jinotega if you're lucky.

Aquatic Life

A wide variety of both saltwater and freshwater species of fish take advantage of the two large lakes, two ocean coastlines, and numerous isolated crater lakes. Among Nicaragua's many saltwater species are flat needlefish *(Ablennes hians)*, wahoo *(Acanthocybium solandri)*, three kinds of sole, spotted eagle rays *(Aetobatus narinari)*, the Gill's sand lance *(Ammodytoides gilli)*, two kinds of moray *(Anarchias sp.)*, croakers *(Bairdiella sp.)*, triggerfish *(Balistes sp.)*, hogfish *(Bodianus sp.)*, eight kinds of perch *(Diplectrum sp.)*, sea bass *(Diplectrum sp.)*, and a dozen kinds of shark, including blacktip *(Carcharias limbatus)*, great white *(C. carcharias)*, silky *(C. falciformis)*, and spinner *(C. brevipinna)*.

Among the freshwater species are needlefish *(Strongylura sp.)*, grunts *(Pomadasys sp.)*, introduced tilapia *(Oreochromis aureus)*, catfish *(Hexanematichthys sp.)*, mojarra *(Eucinostomus sp.)*, and snook *(Centropomus sp.)*. Some species of cichlid *(Amphilophus sp.)* found nowhere else in the world swim in Nicaragua's varied crater lakes.

At least 58 different types of marine corals have been identified in the Atlantic, specifically in the Miskito Cays, Corn Island, and the Pearl Cays. Nicaragua's most common coral species include *Acropora pamata, A. cervicornis,* and *Montastrea anularis.* Brain coral *(Colypophylia natans)* and black coral *(Antipathes pennacea)* are common. Studied for the first time in 1977 and 1978, the shallow reefs of the Pearl Cays contain the best coral formations in the nation, but are now threatened by the enormous sediment load discharged by the Río Grande de Matagalpa.

The manatee *(Trichechus manatus)* is an important species currently protected by international statutes. You may see it at the mouth of the Río San Juan and in the coastal lagoons, notably in Bluefields Bay. In 1993, the freshwater dolphin *(Sotalia fluviatilis)* was first spotted in Nicaragua and since then has been occasionally sighted in Laguna de Wounta, despite conjecture that this species' northern range was Panamá.

Birds

Many thousands of bird species migrate through the Central American biosphere corridor. To date, 676 species of birds in 56 families have been observed here, the more exotic of which you'll find in the mountains of the north and east, and along the Atlantic shore. Nicaragua has no endemic bird species of its own, but hosts 87 percent of all bird species known. The most exotic species known to reside in Nicaragua is also its most elusive, the quetzal *(Pharomacrus mocinno)*, known to inhabit highlands in Bosawás, Jinotega, and Matagalpa, especially along the slopes of Mount Kilambé, and in Miraflor in Estelí.

Nicaragua's elegant and colorful national bird, the *guardabarranco (Momotus momota)*, is more easily found than you'd think. The Guardian of the Stream (as its Spanish name translates) can be found catching small insects in urban gardens in the capital. It is distinguished by its long, odd-shaped, iridescent tail, which it carefully preens to catch the eye of the opposite sex. The *urraca* is a bigger, meaner version of the North American blue jay, with a dangly black crest on the top of its head. It's one of the larger of the common birds in Nicaragua and scolds humans from the treetops. Though the *urraca* are everywhere, a particularly sizeable population patrols the slopes of Ometepe's twin volcanoes and Las Isletas by Granada. Also in Las Isletas, look for the brightly colored oropendolas *(Psarocolius wagleri)* that hang their elaborate, suspended bag-nests from the treetops around the lakeshore.

Reptiles

Of the 172 reptile species in Nicaragua, nearly half are North American, found in Nicaragua at the southern limit of their habitat. Fifteen species are found only in Central America and another five are endemic to Nicaragua.

Nicaragua's several species of marine turtles are all in danger of extinction. The Paslama turtle *(Lepidochelys olivacea)* in the Pacific and the Carey turtle *(Eretmochelys imbricata)* and green turtle *(Chelonia mydas)* in the Atlantic are protected, and much effort has gone into setting aside habitat for them, particularly nesting beaches. However, the struggle is fierce between those who aim to conserve the turtles and those who'd like to harvest their eggs, meat, and shells. There are approximately 20 beaches in the Pacific whose conditions permit the nesting of these turtle species, most of which play host to only occasional nesting events. But two beaches, Chacocente and La Flor on the Pacific coast, are the nesting grounds of the Paslama turtle and experience massive annual egg-laying events between July and January (primarily during the first and third quarters of the moon). In them, 57,000 and 100,000 turtles crawl up on the moist sand at night to lay eggs. It's a safety-in-numbers survival strategy—only 1 out of 100 hatchlings makes it to adulthood. Armed guards on these beaches do their part to make sure the youngsters make it to the sea instead of the soup.

Alligators, crocodiles *(Crocodilus acutus)*, caimans *(Caiman crocodilus)*, and the Ñoca turtle *(Trachemys scripta)* are frequently seen along the Río San Juan and some larger rivers of Jinotega. The *garrobo* is a bush lizard the size of a small house cat you're more likely to see suspended by its tail on the side of the road than in the wild. Poor *campesino* children hunt and sell them to passing motorists who take it home to make soup. Similarly, the *cusuco (Dasypus novemincinctus)* is a type of armadillo with plated sides and sharp-clawed feet commonly found in drier areas of the countryside.

Amphibians

Sixty-four known species of amphibians, four of which are endemic, live in Nicaragua's humid forests and riversides. They include the Mombacho salamander *(Bolitoglossa mombachoensis)*, the miadis frog, the Cerro Saslaya frog *(Plectrohyla sp.)*, and the Saslaya salamander *(Nolitron sp.)*.

Insects

Each of Nicaragua's different ecosystems has a distinct insect population. Estimates of the total number of species reach as high as 250,000, only 1 percent of which have been identified. Notable species to seek out are several gigantic beetles, including *Dynastes hercules* (found in cloud forests); several species of brilliant green and golden Plusiotis (found in Cerro Saslaya and Cerro Kilambé); the iridescent blue butterfly *Morpho peleides,* common all over the country; and its less common cousin, *M. amathonte,* found at altitudes of 300–700 meters, especially in the forests of Bosawás. Nocturnal moths like the Rothschildia, Eacles, and others are common. For more information about bug hunting in Nicaragua, you'll want to contact Belgian entomologist Jean-Michel Maes (www.bio-nica.info, jmmaes@ibw.com.ni), who, with nearly 20 years of research experience in Nicaragua, knows his stuff. He runs the entomological museum in León (normally closed to the public), and sells a CD-ROM entitled *Butterflies of Nicaragua* ($30). There is an increasing number of *mariposarios* (butterfly farms) in Nicaragua, notably in Los Guatuzos, Papaturro, El Castillo (Río San Juan), and San Ramón (Matagalpa).

National Parks and Reserves

Nicaragua's complex system of parks and reserves encompasses more than two million hectares. The Sistema Nacional de Areas Protegidas (SINAP) is made up of 76 parks, reserves, and refuges classified as "protected" by the Ministerio del Ambiente y los Recursos Naturales (Ministry of the Environment and Natural Resources, or MARENA). Of these, many are privately owned land, which strains enforcement of their protected status. That, combined with MARENA's paltry resource base and budget, has led to the decentralization of park management. Since 2001, MARENA has been experimenting with the co-management model in six natural reserves, handing natural-resource management responsibilities over to local nongovernmental organizations (NGOs) who work with the communities within the areas to create sustainable alternatives to natural resource use and ecotourism infrastructure. Co-management is a novel, ongoing experiment, and while it has been surprisingly successful in some areas, the great majority of protected lands in Nicaragua remain unmanaged, unguarded, and completely undeveloped for tourism. They are sometimes referred to as "paper parks," existing only in legislation and studies, not in reality. The Río Estero Real, a wetlands preserve in the northwest corner of the country, is one of those, where half of the "protected" territory has been granted to private shrimp farmers who have eliminated most of the mangrove swamps and lagoons where shrimp once bred naturally, replacing them with artificial breeding pools.

Remoteness and neglect provide meager protection to some regions, but more frequently Nicaragua's richest treasures succumb to foreign and national cattle, logging, and mining interests. *Campesino* populations given little incentive or education to better manage the land are equally destructive. Worst of all are the cases where the government "protects" a territory where people have been living traditionally for generations. They are suddenly expected to drastically alter their fishing, hunting, and planting patterns to protect a "park" that is and always has been their homeland. That has been the experience in the Bosawás Biosphere Reserve, where Mayangna and Miskito people were not consulted during the planning of the reserve and have consequently fought against new regulations that interfere with their traditional lifestyle.

Conversely, Fundación Cocibolca, managing La Flor, has both staffed the reserve with local residents and turned to them for input on how to run it. Tourism can go a long way toward bolstering local incentive to protect—rather than consume—the natural world.

The following is a selection of some of the more accessible (or just spectacular) of Nicaragua's protected areas.

NATIONAL PARKS
Volcán Masaya
Nicaragua's best-organized and most easily accessed park features a paved road to the crater, a museum, interpretive center, and paid guides to lead you through more than 20 kilometers of nature trails. Declaring the 5,100 hectares that surround Volcán Masaya a national park was one of President Anastasio Somoza García's last moves before he was deposed in 1979. The park's extensive lava fields are home to coyotes, *garrobo* lizards, white-tailed deer, and *cusucos*. A rare variety of sulfur-tolerant parakeets inhabits the inside of the crater's walls.

Zapatera Archipelago
Thirty-four kilometers southeast of Granada on the western side of Lake Nicaragua is an

archipelago formed by Zapatera Volcano (629 meters) and the eight islets that surround it. Although owned by private landholders, the islands gained national park status in the 1980s in recognition of their immense natural, cultural, and historical value, and the government subsequently took control over much of the land. The islands still contain virgin forests and lovely shorelines, but are perhaps most famous for their pre-Columbian statuary, many of which are displayed in the Convento San Francisco in Granada. Isla Zapatera and surrounding islets, like Isla de la Muerte, were at least used for ceremonies and rites, though they may have also been burial sites. In addition to the statues are extensive petroglyphs that date from contact with the first Spaniards.

BIOLOGICAL RESERVES
Miraflor

Draped with Spanish moss and carpeted with orchids and lush vegetation, the more than 5,600 hectares of the Reserva Natural Miraflor are one of the most important natural cloud forest reserves in Nicaragua. The area is entirely privately owned and managed by several farmer associations and *campesino* cooperatives. This is one of few places in Nicaragua to spot the exotic, elusive quetzal, but up to a third of Nicaragua's bird species can be observed here as well.

Río Indio-Maíz

Close to 4,000 square kilometers of jungle pressed between the Indio and Maíz Rivers make up La Gran Reserva, which abuts two additional protected areas, the Punta Gorda Nature Reserve to the north, and the Río San Juan Wildlife Reserve to the south. Together, the reserves are part of the Biósfera del Sureste de Nicaragua, an immense territory dedicated to the preservation of animal and plant species along with their natural ecosystems in the Río San Juan watershed. The reserve is one of the few remaining areas in the Americas where you can experience virgin tropical humid forest as it was 200 years ago. It is one of the last refuges in Nicaragua for ocelots and other big cat species, but its remoteness has made inventorying the wildlife challenging, and little is known about its interior.

Cayos Miskitos

Defined as all the cays and small islands found in a 40-kilometer radius from the center of Isla Grande in the Atlantic Ocean off Puerto Cabezas, plus a 20-kilometer swath of shoreline from Cabo Gracias a Dios to the south, the Reserva Biológica Cayos Miskitos has important economic and cultural significance to the Miskito people, who depend on it for fish and shellfish. The Cayos Miskitos are an ecological treasure whose impenetrable lagoons, reefs, mangrove forests, and swamps are home to marine turtles, manatees, dolphins, and several types of endangered coral species. The mangrove forests give shelter to bird species, such as *pancho galán, garza rosada,* and the brown pelican. Substantial petroleum deposits lie below the continental shelf in the Cayos Miskitos area, so the management of the region will warrant much caution and a careful balance. In the meantime, the cays' most immediate threat is drug traffickers, who use the area as a lair.

WILDLIFE RESERVES
Río Escalante-Chacocente

Named for the peculiar smell of *choco* (rotting turtle egg shells after a hatching), the Refugio de Vida Silvestre Río Escalante-Chacocente encompasses 4,800 hectares of dry tropical forest along the edge of the Pacific Ocean. The area was declared a reserve primarily because of its importance as the nesting ground of the endangered tora and Paslama turtles, incredible multitudes of which crawl up on the beach each year to lay eggs in the sand. Exotic orchids, like the *flor de niño* and *huele noche* fill the nocturnal air with a sweet, romantic fragrance. But Chacocente is also home to important forest species, mangrove systems, and the "salt tree." Check the treetops for howler and white-faced monkeys, and keep an eye peeled for the many reptiles, pelicans, white-tailed deer, and *guardabarrancos* that are watching you from the forest edges.

La Flor

This southern Pacific beach, a gorgeous white sandy crescent at the edge of an 800-hectare broad strip of tropical dry forest, is one of the most beautiful beaches in Nicaragua. Thousands of Paslama turtles beach themselves here annually to nest and lay eggs, one of just a handful of beaches in the world that witness such a spectacle. Many *garrobo negro, iguana verde, lagartijas,* monkeys, coyotes, raccoons, and skunks (some of which prey on the turtle eggs) also make their home in the reserve. The skies at La Flor are full of bird species that make their homes in the relatively intact dry forest: *urracas, gavilanes caracoleros, chocoyos, querques, garzas,* and *sonchiches.*

Los Guatuzos Wildlife Refuge

The 43,000 hectares of protected wetlands that separate the southern shore of Lake Cocibolca from the Costa Rican border are a remnant of a Sandinista-era wildlife reserve called Sía-Paz (a play on words meaning yes to peace). Los Guatuzos preserves both the spirit and the wildlife of the reserve and offers valuable habitat to hundreds of different species, plus several small border settlements of people.

NATURAL RESERVES

There are many more nature reserves that those listed here; many are small and designated as such in an attempt to protect a very specific resource. In addition to those mentioned, there are 11 reserves that protect volcanic or coastal lagoons, 16 that protect specific peaks, such as Kilambé and Pancasán, 6 that protect volcanic complexes, such as San Cristóbal or Pilas–El Hoyo, plus dozens of others.

Volcán Cosigüina

In the farthest northwestern corner of Nicaragua, more than 12,000 hectares of the Cosigüina peninsula have been declared a natural reserve. The area has been quietly revegetating itself since the volcano's massive eruption in 1835, predominantly as dry tropical forests of *genícero, tempisque,* and *guanacaste* trees. Its nearly inaccessible crater has become the home to spider monkeys, coyotes, black iguanas, white-tailed deer, and coatis, but more obvious to the naked eye are the hundreds of bird species, notably the scarlet macaw. Climbing the volcano—no easy feat—offers a phenomenal view of the crater lake (which began filling after the eruption 150 years ago), the Gulf of Fonseca, and beyond.

Isla Juan Venado

Much more than a sandy barrier beach island, Isla Juan Venado contains 4,600 hectares of estuary and coastline along the Pacific coast west of León. Its vegetation is successional, going from mangroves at the water's edge to inland dry tropical forest. Isla Juan Venado is rife with bird species due to the estuary system—its mangroves are home to the nests of thousands of parrots and herons—as well as crabs, mollusks, and more than 50 species of mammals and reptiles.

Volcán Mombacho

A scant 41 kilometers from the lowland heat of Managua is an otherworldly island of cloud forest atop an ancient and dormant volcano. Volcán Mombacho's lower slopes are devoted to agriculture, cattle raising, and coffee production, but its upper third—above 800 meters—is a spectacular, misty wildlife and cloud-forest reserve. Mombacho is managed by the Fundación Cocibolca, which has done an admirable job of constructing trails and low-impact guest and research facilities. Mombacho is home both to several endemic species of butterflies and the endemic Mombacho salamander.

Chocoyero–El Brujo

The closest natural reserve to Managua, Chocoyero–El Brujo makes up for its small size with the sheer quantity of *chocoyos* (parakeets) that inhabit its cliff caves. There's no excuse for not exploring Chocoyero–El Brujo some lazy afternoon at sundown when the skies fill with the ruckus of thousands of squawking green *chocoyos*. Chocoyero is set in a semihumid forest of stately *pochote, tigüilote,* and cedar trees, and in addition to its famous birds, provides habitat for several types of owls, monkeys, and squirrels.

Estero Padre Ramos

In the northwest corner of the department of Chinandega, Estero Padre Ramos is a mangrove forest reserve with more than 150 bird species, and untouched, pristine beaches as far as the eye can see. The fingers of the estuary are a sea kayaker's dream, or you can try the local *botes.*

BIOSPHERE RESERVES

Nicaragua's two biosphere reserves were indirectly based on a model proposed for protecting several vast areas in the southeast United States. The strategy is to create a central "nucleus zone," with wilderness status totally preventing human activity. The nucleus is then surrounded by various levels of buffer zones with increasing, but still regulated, resource exploitation permitted as the distance increases from the center. That's the intention, anyway. The virgin lands of Bosawás and the Río San Juan areas have long served as "safety valves" for Nicaragua's expanding population, accommodating *campesinos* as they look for new forestland to clear and farm. Several hundred *campesino* families currently inhabit the Bosawás reserve, and in the absence of regulation, more will surely follow.

Located in the remote north-central wilds of Nicaragua, Bosawás is the largest continuous expanse of virgin cloud forest in Central America. In the extreme southeast of Nicaragua, the Refugio de Vida Silvestre Río San Juan stretches from El Castillo southeast to the Atlantic Ocean along the north edge of the Río San Juan. In addition to the river itself, an important part of the reserve are the four interconnected lagoons at the river's mouth and their related pools, all of which are crucial habitat for manatees and several other mammals.

PRIVATE RESERVES

A handful of protected areas are privately owned. Reservas Silvestres Privadas (Private Wilderness Reserves) are entirely private landholdings granted protected status through the SINAP project. Interested landowners must meet a number of criteria and present an approved management plan. Such reserves are usually near other parks or reserves, contain substantial vegetation and wildlife, and are often a part of some biological corridor. At this early point in the game, they are in varying stages of developing their tourism infrastructures. The original six private reserves are Montibelli near Chocoyero, Domitila outside Nandaime, La Maquina on the road to the coast from Diriamba, Toromixcal in San Juan del Sur, César Augusto in Jinotega, and Greenfields near Pearl Lagoon. Look for them in the appropriate regional chapters.

History

PRE-COLONIAL YEARS

A Caribbean coastal people known as Los Concheros (the shell collectors) are the first evidence of human settlement on Nicaraguan soil 8,000 years ago. Two thousand years later humans living on the southern shores of Lake Managua left their footprints in drying mud in an archeological site called Las Huellas de Acahualinca. Agriculture began around 5,000 years ago with the cultivation of corn, and pottery-making followed 2,000 years later.

Sometime in the 13th century, the Chorotega and Nicarao people, under pressure from the aggressive Aztecs in Mexico, fled south through the Central American isthmus, led by a vision of a land dominated by a great lake. The Chorotegas settled on the shores of Lake Cocibolca and around the volcanic craters of Masaya and Apoyo, and the Nicaraos farther south.

COLONIALISM (1519-1821)

In July of 1502, on his fourth and final voyage, Christopher Columbus (Cristóbal Colón in Spanish) skirted Nicaragua's Mosquito Coast, then continued on to South America. Seventeen years later, the conquistador Pedro Arias Dávila returned under orders from the Spanish crown to explore the land bridge of Nicaragua. Indigenous leaders Nicarao and Diriangén engaged them in a brief battle. Regardless, Francisco Hernández de Córdoba arrived soon after to establish Spain's first settlements in the new land. Córdoba settled Granada alongside the Chorotega communities on the banks of Lake Cocibolca, and forging farther inland and up the Tipitapa River, the settlement of León on the western shores of Lake Xolotlán. Nicaragua remained a part of Spain's overseas possessions for the next 300 years under the governance of the colonial capital in Guatemala.

INDEPENDENCE, WILLIAM WALKER, AND THE U.S. MARINES (1821-1937)

Central America won its independence from Spain in 1821, and for a short time remained united as the five provinces of the Central American Federation. The belief that Europe would act militarily to return the former colonies to Spain forced the United States to issue the Monroe Doctrine in 1823, declaring the New World off limits to further European colonization and interference, paving the way for two centuries of political domination in Latin America. The Central American Federation was short-lived, however: When Nicaragua withdrew from the federation in 1838, the remaining states opted to become individual republics as well and the federation dissolved.

Newly independent Nicaragua was anarchic for years, dominated by the independent, feuding city-states of León and Granada until 1845, when a national government was finally agreed upon (the political rivalries that endure to this day). In the early 19th century, export of cacao, indigo, and cattle allowed the landed and merchant classes to accumulate considerable wealth at the expense of the Native Americans and landless class. A nascent liberal class grew in León, inspired by the French and American revolutions that sought for more equal distribution of wealth.

Nicaragua's unique geography has inspired multiple plans for a transcontinental canal, even today. During the California gold rush (1849–1856), prospectors transited Nicaragua courtesy of steamship baron and businessman Cornelius Vanderbilt's Pacific Steamship Company, then operating in Panamá. Travelers bound for California sailed up the Río San Juan and across Lake Nicaragua to the small port at San Jorge. There, they were taken by horse

U.S. INTERVENTION IN NICARAGUA

In President Teddy Roosevelt's addition to the Monroe Doctrine of regional dominance, he proclaimed that the United States, by virtue of its status as a "civilized nation," had the right to stop "chronic wrongdoing" throughout the Western Hemisphere. Subsequently, the so-called Roosevelt Corollary was used to justify troop deployment to Latin America 32 times between the end of the Spanish-American War and the years of the Great Depression. President William Howard Taft provided further rationalization for aggressively dominating Latin America with his Dollar Diplomacy, an unabashed strategy to advance and protect U.S. businesses in other countries. Nicaragua, which had been host to U.S. fruit, mining, and transportation interests since the 1850s, was a frequent recipient of such foreign policy.

U.S. Marines landed at least seven times during the aforementioned period, and spent a total of 21 years occupying Nicaragua. Official reasons for these visits included "pacification of Nicaragua," "prevention of rebellion," and, of course, "protection of U.S. interests and property." It would be unfair to call these visits uninvited, since nearly all were ostensibly serving the purpose of one or more Nicaraguan parties, usually the Conservatives.

The following is a more detailed list of gringo interventions.

1853-1856: U.S. citizen William Walker usurps power and declares himself president of Nicaragua; he is briefly recognized by Washington before the other Central American nations unite, drive him out, and eventually execute him by firing squad.

1894: The U.S. Marines under Lieutenant Franklin J. Moses have a monthlong occupation of Bluefields.

1896: From May 2-4, when fighting near Corinto "endangers American holdings," 15 Marines, under First Sergeant Frederick W. M. Poppe, and 19 seamen land in Corinto and stand guard in a "show of force."

1898: As President Zelaya extends his tenure for still another term, the local U.S. consular agent requests the U.S.S. *Alert*, at anchor in the harbor of Bluefields, to stand by in case of an attack on the city. On the morning of February 7, the U.S. flag on shore rises "union downward" over the consulate, signaling a force of 14 Marines and 19 seamen to land; they withdraw the following day.

1899: Another display of force lands, this time with a Colt automatic gun "to prevent both rebels and government troops from destroying American property."

1910: Marines and Navy vessels concentrate in Nicaraguan waters and land in Bluefields and Corinto on May 19 "to guard American property."

1912: Nicaraguan president Adolfo Díaz requests the support of U.S. forces. The United States complies when the U.S.S. *Annapolis* arrives in Corinto, deploying a contingent of naval officers to Managua on August 4. Three companies of marine infantry also land and are transported to Managua by train.

1927-1933: President Coolidge sends Marines to find Sandino and "gun the bandit down." They fail.

1981-1990: The CIA runs a secret command operation directing and financing Contra forces in their attempt to topple the Sandinista government. U.S operatives carry out supply and intelligence activities, train commanders and soldiers, plant harbor mines, and sabotage Sandinista holdings.

—All citations from Marine Corps Historical Reference Series, The United States Marines in Nicaragua, *by Bernard C. Nalty.*

cart 18 kilometers across the narrow isthmus through Rivas to the bay of San Juan del Sur. Ships waiting in the harbor then carried the travelers north along the Pacific coastline to California. Vanderbilt dredged the channel of the Río San Juan and built roads, railroads, and docks on both coasts to accommodate the traffic. At about that time, the Leóneses, embroiled in a bitter battle with the Conservatives of Granada, enlisted the help of William Walker, an American filibuster who eventually installed himself as president of Nicaragua, razed the city of Granada, and caused a whole lot of trouble.

Though the relative peace of the 30-year Conservative period fostered many advances in infrastructure and technology, including the Granada–Corinto train and the telegraph, Nicaragua remained several decades behind its neighbors in coffee exportation and the economy mostly stagnated. The bourgeoisie became restless and rebelled, installing Liberal General José Santos Zelaya as president. Zelaya was a fierce nationalist who, among other things, reclaimed the Atlantic region at gunpoint from its British occupants (the two administrative units of the Atlantic coast bore Zelaya's name until the 1990s). Zelaya furthermore rejected Washington's proposals to build a cross-isthmus canal through Nicaraguan territory while courting Great Britain to finance the construction of a transcontinental railway.

The United States, which since 1904 had been building the Panama canal, was unimpressed by the nationalist leader and his railway proposal, and in 1909, sent the U.S. Marines to secure Zelaya's ouster. The U.S. intervention reestablished the Conservatives in power until 1912, when Liberal and nationalist Benjamin Zeledón led another rebellion. This time the U.S. Marine occupation happened on a much larger scale: 2,700 marines landed at Corinto and took immediate control of the railways, ports, and major cities.

Nicaragua became subject to the United States financially at about this time, as U.S. financial institutions began to quietly acquire coffee-export businesses and railway and steamship companies, easing Nicaragua into a credit noose. Under the watchful eye of the U.S. Marines, governmental control was handed over to the Conservatives, whom Washington thought would more faithfully represent U.S. business interests. But the Liberals staged 10 uprisings between 1913 and 1924, all of which the U.S. military quelled.

In 1924, Conservative President Bartolomé Martínez instituted a novel form of government—a power-sharing arrangement between the Liberals and the Conservatives at the local level. The United States withdrew Marines in 1925 but they were back within the year. No sooner had power sharing begun than ambitious Conservative Emilio Chamorro staged a coup d'état, seized power, and sparked the Constitutional War. The United States stepped in to prevent the imminent takeover by the Liberals, but because the Conservatives had discredited themselves, the United States was unable to simply hand the power back to them. The deal they worked out was known as the Espino Negro Pact (named after the town where it was signed; Spanish for Black Thorn). It was a crucial moment for the Liberals. One of their generals, Augusto C. Sandino, was opposed to the pact, and fled with his men to the northern mountains to start a guerrilla war in opposition to the continued presence of the United States in Nicaragua. The leader of the Constitutional Army was forced to declare, "All my men surrender except one."

The U.S. military tried unsuccessfully to flush Sandino from the mountains despite drastic measures like the aerial bombing of Ocotal, so in 1933, Washington tried a new approach. Withdrawing U.S. troops from Nicaragua, the United States formed a new military unit called the National Guard and placed young Anastasio Somoza García at its head.

During the presidency of Juan Bautista Sacasa, Sandino enjoyed overwhelming support in Nicaragua's northern mountains as he was perceived to have successfully accomplished the repatriation of both U.S. armed forces and the removal of Conservative oligarchy from power. But he represented a major threat to Somoza's political and military ambitions. In February of 1934, President Sacasa invited him to Managua to negotiate an agreement. When Sandino left the presidential palace that night, several

National Guard members ambushed and assassinated him on the streets of Managua. The National Guard immediately swept the northern countryside, destroying cooperatives, returning lands to their previous owners, and hunting down, exiling, imprisoning, or killing Sandino's supporters.

THE SOMOZA ERA (1937-1979)

General Anastasio Somoza García overpowered Sacasa in 1937; his enormously wealthy and powerful family dynasty would permanently reorient and dominate Nicaraguan politics for the following 42 years. Nicaraguans and foreigners to this day refer to the nearly continuous succession of three Somoza presidents as one all-powerful "Somoza." The Somozas were wily politicians with a near-genius for using existing political conflicts to their personal advantage; they were also expert practitioners of a favorite trick of Latin American dictators, *continuismo,* in which a puppet leader would be elected but resign shortly afterward, handing the power back to the Somozas. Five such "presidents" were elected during the 42-year reign of the Somozas, not one of which lasted longer than three years. The Somozas maintained a strong foothold in the national economy as well by manipulating government licensing requirements and importing duty-free goods with the complicity of the National Guard. If there was money to be made in any economic sector, the Somoza family quickly came to control it. They extracted personal income from public utilities and the financial sector, monopolized the cotton industry when it surged in the 1950s and, later, meat, shrimp, and lobster export in the 1960s and 1970s. They owned the nation's prime food-processing industries; sugar refining; cement production; the cardboard, tobacco, and recording industries; and sea and air transport. In fact, by the late 1970s, the Somoza family owned just about everything in Nicaragua worth owning.

Born in San Marcos, Carazo, and educated in Philadelphia, Anastasio Somoza García ascended rapidly through the military. The Roosevelt administration overlooked his rapacious greed, questionable politics, and strong-handed military tactics in exchange for a Central American ally. World War II was an economic windfall for Nicaragua—and Somoza's industries, which exported raw material—but just in case, Somoza declared war on Germany and Japan as a pretext for confiscating the valuable German-owned coffee land. Somoza García's administration oversaw construction of the Chinandega–Puerto Morazán railway, Managua's city water system and International Airport, and the Pan-American Highway. Popular frustration at his heavy-handedness grew until 1956 when, at a celebratory ball in the Social Club of León, poet, political idealist, and frustrated nationalist Rigoberto López Pérez shot him.

Anastasio's son Luís Somoza Debayle took the reins, overseeing the construction of the hydropower plant and reservoir of Lake Apanás in Jinotega; the improved port facilities at Corinto; the highway from San Benito to El Rama, which helped unite the Atlantic and Pacific coasts; and the nation's first social security system (INSS). In 1963, Tacho lost in popular elections to the Liberal Renée Schick, and died of a heart attack four years later.

The third of the Somozas was the most avaricious and cruel. As "Tachito," a 1964 graduate of the West Point Military Academy, rose to power, the nascent Sandinista (FSLN) movement was gaining attention in the north through attacks and kidnappings; over the next decade, they would goad Tachito into becoming the most bloodthirsty president the nation had ever seen. The earthquake of December 1972 provided Tachito a unique opportunity: Appointing himself head of the Emergency Committee, he did little more to rebuild the country than funnel aid money into his own

AUGUSTO CÉSAR SANDINO (1893-1934)

Augusto C. Sandino was born in Niquinohomo (Nahuatl for "valley of warriors"), the illegitimate son of a wealthy, landed judge and one of his servant women. But while the judge lived well in town, Sandino's family was so poor they often resorted to stealing crops to eat. Sandino grew disgusted at Nicaraguan society, which engendered such inequity, and questioned both civil society and the Catholic Church, which he believed was guilty of propping up the aristocracy. At the age of 17, Sandino witnessed the U.S. Marines' invasion of Nicaragua to prop up Adolfo Díaz's failing Conservative presidency. When they crushed a rebellion led by General Benjamin Zeledón, their parading of Zeledón's dead body through the streets of Masaya affected Sandino deeply. Nine years later, Sandino fled to Mexico, where he was inspired by Tampico laborers struggling to unionize in spite of resistance from the U.S.-owned oil companies. Sandino returned to Nicaragua with a new sense of purpose and a strong self-identity shaped by anarchy, socialism, and armed conflict.

Sandino became a renegade general from the Liberals and set up his camp in the mountains outside San Rafael del Norte, Jinotega. He became one of the first to practice guerrilla warfare, staging effective hit-and-run raids against U.S. Marine installations in Ocotal and the north. Sandino's men grew to number nearly 1,800 by 1933 and his troops were brutal. The U.S. military struggled fruitlessly for seven years to flush Sandino out of the hills. But he was slippery: Sandino's advantage was a profound knowledge of the land, vast popular support, the willingness to live poor, and an uncanny ability to vanish into thin air.

While Sandino's struggle was ostensibly to force the U.S. military and business interests out of Nicaragua, he represented much more than brute nationalism. In the Segovias, where Sandino enjoyed massive popular support, he formed agricultural cooperatives of landless peasants, imposing taxes on wealthy ranchers and businessmen to support them. He also fought in support of the exploited timber, banana plantation, and mine workers.

During the Great Depression, the Marines eventually left Nicaragua, and the new president of Nicaragua, Anastasio Somoza García, had Sandino assassinated in February 1934. Sandino's body was never found.

Thirty years after Sandino's death, a young idealistic student named Carlos Fonseca Amador resurrected Sandino's image and ideals as the basis of a new political and guerrilla movement, which he called the Frente Sandinista de Liberación Nacional (FSLN)—the Sandinista National Liberation Front. The FSLN greatly exaggerated Sandino's reputation as a peasant who fought righteously against the imperialistic designs of the United States, because it suited their ideology. Rather, Sandino's crusade was often against the bourgeois Nicaraguan Conservatives. His ideology was a mix of his own peculiar leftism with a curious indigenous mysticism; he changed his middle name from Calderón to César in honor of the Roman emperor, claimed he could give orders to his troops using silent mental communication, and predicted Nicaragua would be the site of Armageddon, where "armies of angels would do battle alongside more temporal troops."

To this day, Sandino remains a hero to Nicaraguans and the world's leftist community. He spearheaded a movement that fought for drastic social and political change and sought to make up for centuries of class discontent that continues even today.

bank accounts. He was reelected in 1974, but Tachito's increasingly flagrant human rights violations, including the assassination of journalist Pedro Joaquín Chamorro, and his increasingly violent responses to FSLN attacks earned him international opprobrium. When the FSLN finally ousted him on July 16, 1979, he fled to Miami, and then to Paraguay, where on September 17, 1980, he was assassinated with an antitank rocket.

THE SANDINISTA REVOLUTION (1977–1979)

Guerrilla groups opposed to the Somoza dynasty and inspired by Fidel Castro began training in clandestine camps in the northern mountains of Nicaragua in the early 1950s and coalesced a decade later when Carlos Fonseca Amador, Silvio Mayorga, and Tomás Borge formed the **Frente Sandinista de Liberación Nacional (FSLN)**. Carlos Fonseca's ideas, an inspired combination of Marxism (which he'd experienced firsthand in a trip to Moscow) and the nationalist, anti-imperialist beliefs of Augusto Sandino formed their ideological framework: Sandinismo.

Early Sandinista insurrections in Río Coco and Bocay (1963) and Pancasán (1967) were easily crushed, but legitimized the FSLN. As trade unions, student organizations, and private and religious organizations all threw their weight behind the Sandinista insurgency, Tachito grew more brutal and outraged. In January 1978, Pedro Joaquín Chamorro, editor of *La Prensa* and a relentless critic of Somoza, was gunned down in Managua. His death fooled no one. One month later, the largely indigenous population of the Masaya neighborhood of Monimbó protested for five days until the National Guard responded by massacring hundreds. By May 1979, the guerrillas were ready for the final insurrection, which would last 52 days.

Combat erupted simultaneously around Chinandega, León, and Chichigalpa in the Pacific, and in the mining triangle in the northeast. At the same time, Sandinista troops began pressing north from the border with Costa Rica. They entered León, capturing the city after a two-day battle. The rest of the nation began a massive general labor strike. On June 8, 1979, Sandinista soldiers and supporters began marching from Carazo, just south of Managua, into the capital itself. The National Guard responded by shelling Managua. Most of the fighting in Managua took place in the lower-middle-class neighborhoods of Bello Horizonte and El Dorado, where extensive networks of concrete drainage ditches made easy battle trenches. The people tore up the concrete *adoquines* (paving stones) of the streets and erected barricades with them. The world watched, appalled, as Somoza's aircraft indiscriminately strafed the capital.

The FSLN captured Matagalpa on July 2, 1979, and the strategic town of Sébaco the day after. The Estelí military barracks—the last and most important one after Managua—fell on July 16. Finally, with complete control of the north, FSLN forces surrounded the capital. Trapped by the Sandinistas and abandoned by the United States, Somoza fled Nicaragua in the predawn hours of July 17.

THE FSLN GOVERNMENT (1979–1991)

The exuberance of military victory quickly faded as the new leaders struggled to convert revolutionary fervor into support for the new nation they wanted to build. They were starting from scratch: Somoza had run Nicaragua as his own personal farm, and overthrowing him had implied dismantling the national economy. The sweeping economic, political, and social reforms of the Sandinista revolution therefore made Nicaragua a real-time social experiment, and the entire world looked on with anticipation and anxiety.

The new Nicaraguan government was a battleground of competing interests exacerbated by the dire need to reactivate the economy. The "Group of Nine" fatigue-clad FSLN *comandantes* elbowed a supporting conservative alliance aside and revealed their legendary **Plan 80,** which revealed the FSLN as Marxist-Leninist and their planned economy as a delicate balance between private ownership ceding to increasing state control. Appalled, betrayed, and frequently victimized as "supporters of the dictator," the upper class abandoned ship and fled to Miami, where they stayed for a decade. Their personal boycott of the revolution hastened its demise.

Land reform proceeded immediately. The Sandinistas confiscated two million acres of Somoza's holdings and distributed it to the poor for farming. Though this was true social revolution, the environmental impact of previously unexploited and delicate hillsides being cleared and planted was massive deforestation and erosion. Worse, the Sandinista elite kept most profitable lands for themselves, a hypocrisy that did not go unnoticed.

A massive and world-acclaimed literacy campaign saw thousands of volunteers—typically zealous university students—teaching reading, writing, and basic math skills to the illiterate majority. The literacy rate soared to nearly 90 percent, but the Cuban-inspired mix of education and revolutionary propaganda meant many *campesinos'* first reading lessons taught revolutionary dogma, and the math exercises frequently involved counting items like rifles and tanks. Nonetheless, the literacy campaign encouraged young idealists to explore and take pride in their own country and culture, and has reinforced Nicaragua's nationalism and self-identity to the present.

THE CONTRA WAR (1980-1991)

In their zeal to "defend the revolution at all costs," Sandinista leaders ran into opposition from all sides—from the business community (headed by the business organization COSEP and future president Enrique Bolaños); from Somoza's former cronies who missed their days of wealth and privilege and were enraged by the policy of confiscation; from the former members of the National Guard, many of whom regrouped outside of Nicaragua and became the nucleus of the military *contra-revolucionarios* (Contras); and lastly, from the United States government under President Reagan, which remained deeply distrustful of the Sandinistan Communist tendencies.

The Sandinistas openly collaborated with Cuba and the Soviet Union and supported El Salvador's FMLN, a similar revolutionary group, three policies that led the United States to impose an economic embargo in 1985. Many moderate Nicaraguans supported the U.S. government intervention. They had supported overthrowing the dictator, not the establishment of a repressive Marxist-Leninist economy. Furthermore, land confiscation didn't end with Somoza's reign; the Sandinistas confiscated the land of any Nicaraguan that opposed them. To moderate Nicaraguans, the FSLN had simply imposed themselves as a new elite.

Negligent Sandinista economic mismanagement and the embargo hastened economic collapse. By 1985, export earnings were half the prerevolution figures, and much of the confiscated agricultural land remained unproductive in cooperatives. The business class recoiled in fear of further expropriation, and skilled laborers fled the country in search of profitable employment elsewhere. In order to combat the Contras, the Sandinistas increased military spending and sent much of the country's productive labor force into battle. Austerity measures didn't earn the Sandinista government many friends either, as previously common goods, like toothpaste and rice, were parsimoniously rationed and shoddy Eastern-bloc goods replaced imports of better quality. Finally, to counter the increasingly violent Contra attacks in Matagalpa, Jinotega, and much of the east, the Sandinistas instituted a much-despised obligatory draft, forcing Nicaraguans to defend—with their sons' lives—a revolution in which they were rapidly losing faith. *Servicio militar patriotico* (patriotic military service), or SMP, was parodied by young men as *Seremos muertos pronto* (soon we will be dead).

Regardless, in 1984 the Sandinistas easily won an election international observers declared fair and transparent while the economy spiraled and the military conflict grew

WHO WERE THE CONTRAS?

The Contras remain one of the most powerful, divisive, and enigmatic elements of Nicaragua's recent history. They owe their name to the Sandinista leaders who christened them *contra-revolucionarios*. The Contras preferred to call themselves La Resistencia, and others called them "freedom fighters," "bandits," "heroes," and "outlaws."

Not long after the Sandinistas took power in 1979, discontent was already swelling among some groups of *campesinos*, who sensed that the Sandinista revolution had gone wrong: Small farmers were being forced to join collectives or were jailed; political meetings were frequent; government propaganda smacked of atheism (or dubious support for the Catholic Church); the government was full of Cuban advisors; price controls were making it hard to turn a profit in agriculture; and a lot of people were incarcerated, including many indigenous Miskito people, who had never wanted much more than to be left alone. The revolution was supposed to have made the lives of the poor farmers easier, not harder.

Though the first *campesinos* received some early training and help from Argentine military advisers, the Contras weren't an organized force per se until late in the game. Even then, they were composed of numerous factions rife with internal divisions, petty grudges, and ambition among and within their units. The Contras survived on limited supplies, donations from sympathizers in Miami, and whatever they could take at gunpoint. The only thing that united the various Contra groups was the feeling that the Sandinista revolution had been a step in the wrong direction. That group included U.S. President Ronald Reagan. At various points in the 1980s, the U.S. government played a critical part in the financing and arming of the Contras, in violation of its own laws and without the knowledge of the public.

Based out of camps along the Honduran border, the Fuerza Democrática Nicaragüense (FDN) was led primarily by ex-National Guard officers and groups of farmers who called themselves Milicia Popular Anti-Somoza (MILPA). Fighting a completely separate battle along the Río San Juan from camps over the Costa Rican border was the Alianza Revolucionaria Democrática (ARDE), led by the infamous Edén Pastora, a.k.a. Comandante Cero (Zero), former Sandinista militant turned Contra. ARDE was a military disaster from the start, so thoroughly riddled with Sandinista spies it never had any hope of victory. Pastora was a would-be *caudillo* (chief) who hated organization, refused to delegate authority, and kept his own men divided to prevent any claims to his throne. His macho posturing and reputation for womanizing made him an easy target for female Sandinista spies. Pastora's own men feared he was really a Sandinista sympathizer sent to lead them into military devastation.

Though the Sandinista military committed its share of mistakes and atrocities, the Contras' propensity for brutality and terror is well documented and undeniable. They seeded terror in the hillsides with their barbaric tactics. Contra troops took at gunpoint anything they needed from local *campesinos*. Along the way, many young women and girls were raped and killed; young boys and men were routinely mutilated before being killed.

The Contras never had the satisfaction of a military victory. Rather, when the Sandinistas lost public elections and handed power over to the Chamorro government, the incentive to be a Contra vanished. Though some Contras rejected the peace accords and slipped back into the mountains to continue fighting, most disarmed and went back to farming. In the end, though foreign powers had helped the Nicaraguans to nearly destroy themselves over ideology and geopolitics.

bloodier. Washington continued to fund the Contras, and Cuba and the Soviet Union continued to fund the Sandinistas, in a proxy war that made Nicaragua a geopolitical pawn.

At the close of the 1980s, both the Contras and the Sandinista government were physically and economically exhausted. The collapse of the Soviet Union left the Sandinistas without a sponsor, while the Contras had little real hope of a military victory. The Iran-Contra scandal in the United States exposed the illegal mechanisms President Reagan's team were employing to fund their Contra "Freedom Fighters" and torpedoed the Contras' funding source. The moment was propitious for Costa Rican president Óscar Arías to propose a peace initiative. In 1987, five Central American presidents attended talks at Esquipulas, Guatemala, and emerged with a radical peace accord. The Sandinistas organized elections in 1990 to show the world that their government was committed to democratic principles and to give Nicaraguans the chance to reaffirm their support for the FSLN. To their surprise, the Nicaraguan people overwhelmingly voted them out of office. The revolution had ended.

If Nicaragua was going to revert to capitalism, the Sandinista elite wanted to ensure they got their share, so on their way out the door, the Sandinistas signed over hundreds of millions of dollars of state property to themselves in a hypocritical disgrace now known as the Piñata. FSLN party heads privatized many state companies under anonymous cooperatives and passed a series of decrees ensuring they would retain some power—and the new bourgeoisie of former bourgeoisie-haters was born.

THE NEW DEMOCRACY (1991-2006)

Violeta Barrios de Chamorro, widow of the slain journalist Pedro Joaquín Chamorro, became president with a coalition of Sandinista opposition groups called the Unión Nacional Opositora (UNO). Her charisma and leadership led the nation through a period of reconciliation and rebuilding. She reestablished diplomatic and economic ties with the rest of the world, ended the draft, reestablished the army and the police under civil control, and disarmed the Contras. To help them reassimilate into the agrarian workforce, they were offered 1,600 square kilometers of land, including much of the Río San Juan area and some parts of Jinotega and Matagalpa. Failure to live up to some of these land promises set the stage for further unrest in the 21st century. The international donor community pardoned much of Nicaragua's debt, but did little else to help: Once the proxy war ended, it seemed as though the world had lost interest in Nicaragua.

The elections of 1996, run without the massive international funding that characterized previous elections, were rife with abnormalities, near-riots, and chronic disorder: Polling places opened hours late, bags of discarded ballots were found afterward in the houses of officials, and the communication network failed. Not surprisingly, in the aftermath, all sides had reason to accuse the others of vote-rigging and fraud. Even so, Nicaraguans turned out in record numbers and elected Managua's slippery mayor, Arnoldo Alemán.

Arnoldo Alemán was a political conservative and hard-core capitalist lawyer with a sworn aversion to all things Sandinista and a professed admiration for the Somozas. Alemán oversaw the continued growth of the economy, boosted the development of *zonas francas* (free trade zones) and the construction of *maquiladoras* (export clothing assembly plants). Politics returned to the back room, where endless scandals of kickbacks, insider deals, and frenzied pocket-filling embarrassed and infuriated the nation. His personal fortune soared from $20,000 when he took office as mayor of Managua to $250 million when he was voted out in 2001. But as he came under increased political and popular pressure for corruption, he and Ortega (accused of allegedly molesting his stepdaughter Zoilamerica Narvaez) engineered the infamous *El Pacto*. The agreement provided them both diplomatic immunity and a lifetime seat in the Assembly, and divided up the government's most important roles between the FSLN and PLC, including the Supreme Court and the Consejo Supremo Electoral (which runs elections). Other political parties were excluded from the power sharing arrangement. Together, Nicaragua's top two *caudillos* (political strongmen) had eviscerated Nicaraguan democracy and divided the spoils.

Enrique Geyer Bolaños, Arnoldo Alemán's nondescript vice-president and former head of COSEP (the Nicaraguan private industry association) won the 2001 election for the PLC party on an anticorruption platform that resonated with Nicaraguans appalled with Alemán's avarice and duplicity. Upon entering office, Bolaños moved quickly to bring indictments against high-ranking PLC officials, including Alemán himself. Alemán, under other conditions, might have been able to muster the support to resist the charges, but, as his allies slipped away, he was found guilty of corruption and money laundering, and sentenced in December 2003 to 20 years in prison. This was the first time in recent Latin American history that an overtly corrupt leader had been convicted and punished. But Alemán continued to wield considerable political influence even from house arrest, and the majority of the PLC turned against Bolaños in retribution for biting the hand that fed him. Congress, evenly divided between PLC and FSLN members, mostly opposed Bolaños's legislation, and the PLC mounted a vindictive effort to convict him of corruption himself. Ironically, Enrique Bolaños had better political support from the outside world than he did from his own political party, and relinquished his mandate in 2006 having accomplished very little of value despite the best of intentions.

THE RETURN OF ORTEGA (2006-PRESENT)

The Pact strengthened Ortega's hand, and through the Sandinistas in the National Assembly he methodically weakened and divided the political opposition. Mayoral elections in 2004 went overwhelmingly to the Sandinista party, while Bolaños's new coalition, APRE, suffered significant defeats in most departments. Alemán, under house arrest, could do little to counter him, and in late 2004 Ortega's and Alemán's people again conspired to change the criteria under which one could become president: the threshold for victory was lowered from 45 percent to 35 percent and the mandatory margin over the second candidate was set at 5 percent, both criteria skillfully tailored to Ortega's proven electoral capacity. The FSLN party was by then largely only Daniel supporters or "Danielistas," the old guard of the Revolution having been blocked in an FSLN primary, while breakaway Sandinistas' new party, the Movimiento Renovador Sandinista (MRS) lost its chance when its popular candidate, Herty Lewites, was felled by a mysterious heart attack while campaigning. Ortega, ever the opportunist, embraced the Catholic church by supporting a total abortion ban, assured the private sector and Brettons Woods institutions that he had no intention of returning to a policy of land confiscation, and that he would support free enterprise and a capitalist economy. He married his longtime partner, Rosario Murillo, and "atoned for the sins committed during the FSLN in the 1980s." Said Álvaro Vargas Llosa, "What this farcical saga tells us is that Daniel Ortega was much more interested in being president than in being principled." In November 2006, Nicaraguans turned out in record numbers to vote; Daniel Ortega had won the presidency with only 38 percent of the vote.

Ortega kept his promise to respect private enterprise, but he worked vigorously to ensure his return to power would be permanent. Despite

© GRACE GONZALEZ

Hand-painted propaganda was part of Ortega's victorious 2011 re-election campaign.

rhetoric about the continuation of the 1979 Revolution, there was nothing revolutionary about Ortega's mandate. His administration relentlessly pursued political foes and solidified FSLN control of the courts, the National Assembly, and attempted the same with the police and military to lesser effect. State agents ransacked the offices of a leading investigative journalist, Carlos Fernando Chamorro (son of the former president and slain newspaper man), and a women's NGO, and sent agents to confiscate the computers of 15 other organizations including Oxfam, under suspicion of money laundering and "subversion," a provocative accusation of supporting opposition political parties. Masked gangs attacked both major newspapers in November 2009, launching mortars and rockets at the building. Meanwhile, youth spray-painted "Viva Daniel" from one end of Managua to the other.

Under the new administration, Sandinista "supporters" were required to register with their local Consejo Popular Ciudadano (Community Citizen Committee, CPC) and receive a membership card. Non-cardholders found life close to impossible, as suddenly doors were closed to them. Cardholders were permitted to skip certain college exams, non-cardholders could not; cardholders got chosen for scholarships, non-cardholders did not; cardholders got discounted food at the markets, non-cardholders did not. Government workers have also been subjected to intimidating and illegal workplace recruitment campaigns by the Sandinista party, facing the threat of dismissal if they refuse to accept the party card. Once signed up, one of their new political obligations is to turn up at party rallies, and stand at key intersections in the capital waving party flags in their spare time.

Within the same strategy, the CPCs aligned themselves with criminal gangs and disaffected youth to ensure opposition protestors were unable to assemble in public places. With thinly veiled threats of "the Sandinistas control the streets," popular protests were quickly put down over 30 times in 2008 alone by stone-throwing Sandinista "supporters"—little more than paid mobs—and dissent of any form was stifled. An opposition march organized by civil society groups brought more than 50,000 people to the streets to protest at the 2008 electoral fraud and Ortega's reelection plans. Thanks to a massive police turnout—70 percent of the 10,000-strong national police force—the march was protected from threatened attacks by flag-waving thugs.

Ortega strengthened diplomatic ties with Libya's Mohammar Qhadaffi, Iran's Mahmoud Ahmadinejad, Venezuela's Hugo Chávez, and of course Cuba's Fidel Castro. Nicaragua was the only nation to recognize the two republics Russia liberated from Georgia (South Ossetia and Abkhazia), and the abortion ban claimed its first female victims, starting with an 18-year-old who was denied the right to terminate a pregnancy that had developed life-threatening medical complications. Both she and the five-month-old fetus perished.

In 2008, municipal elections for regional officials were overtly sabotaged to engineer a victory for the Sandinistas. It drew the immediate ire of the international community, who withdrew financial support for development projects. Between the United States, which suspended its Millennium Challenge program, and the member states of the European Union, over $300 million in funding was suspended. Ortega responded by threatening to send a trillion-dollar bill to the European Union to compensate for the ravages of colonialism, and Hugo Chávez offered to substitute the $300 million, which he never did. In 2009, the Supreme Court justices (loyal to Daniel) met over a weekend and ruled that the presidential term limits were a violation of Daniel Ortega's constitutional rights. Despite blustering by the opposition members of the National Assembly, Ortega declared, "This decision is stone; it cannot be altered."

In November of 2011, the presidential elections allowed no international observers or peacekeeping organizations to oversee the voting. Amidst international controversy of voting scams and polling spikes, Daniel Ortega retained leadership for a third term. The ever-growing Sandinista Youth movement, which organizes large events carting busloads of young Nicaraguans to join and celebrate the country and government, is a testament to the continuing strength of the party. Some of the increasingly skeptical populace is gauging whether they are ready to accept Ortega as their newest leader-for-life, while supporters shed tears of joy for the continued leadership of their beloved *presidente*.

Government and Economy

With the exception of perhaps Violeta Chamorro and Enrique Bolaños, it seems Nicaraguan politicians' sole purpose for governing is to manipulate the boundaries of the system sufficiently to ensure their indefinite power and/or enrichment. But it's more complicated than just that: Talk to any Nicaraguan and you will find Nicaraguan politics are infinitely subtle and the battlefield is constantly being redrawn.

ORGANIZATION

The Republic of Nicaragua is a constitutional democracy; Nicaragua gained its independence from Spain in 1821. The two autonomous regions of the Atlantic coast are governed somewhat separately, and choose their leaders through elections independent of the national government.

Branches of Government

Nicaragua's government is divided into four branches. The executive branch consists of the president and vice president. The judicial branch includes the Supreme Court, subordinate appeals courts, district courts, and local courts, plus separate labor and administrative tribunals. The Supreme Court oversees the entire judicial system and consists of 12 justices elected by the National Assembly for seven-year terms. Though the judicial system is relatively ineffective and plagued by party interests and manipulation by the wealthy elite, it does have some points in its favor, including an approach that attempts to reduce crowding in jails by having the aggressor and the aggrieved meet to strike a deal. For minor offenses, this is effective. There is no capital punishment in Nicaragua, the maximum sentence being 30 years (though the abominable conditions of Nicaraguan prisons makes one wonder if the sentence isn't equally harsh).

The legislative branch consists of the Asamblea Nacional (National Assembly), a chamber in which 90 *diputados* (deputies) representing Nicaragua's different geographical regions vote on policy. The *diputados* are elected from party lists provided by the major political parties, though defeated presidential candidates who earn a minimum requirement of votes automatically become lifetime members, and by law, former presidents are also guaranteed a seat.

The fourth branch of Nicaraguan government is unique to Nicaragua: The Consejo Supremo Nacional runs the elections and oversees the campaign period. Politicized since the Pact of 2000, the body is rampantly abused to further the interests of Arnoldo Alemán and Daniel Ortega.

Prior to his election in 2006, Ortega attempted repeatedly to implement a parliamentary system that would weaken the executive and permit a sort of power sharing favorable to the Sandinistas, without success. Upon regaining the presidency, he immediately instituted direct or participatory governance through Chávez-esque **Consejos Populares Ciudadanos (CPCs).** Though they ostensibly reach down to permit the poor a more direct engagement with the government, in practice they undermine the other layers of government and facilitate rabble-rousing by Nicaragua's populist and billigerent president.

Elections

The president and *diputados* are elected every five years. The president could not run for consecutive terms until 2009, when Ortega had a Supreme Court justice overrule that decision (to the dismay of many). The Consejo Supremo Electoral (Supreme Electoral Council, or CSE) consists of seven magistrates elected by the National Assembly for five-year terms. The CSE has the responsibility of organizing, running, and declaring the winners of elections, referendums, and plebiscites. However, electoral reforms put in place in 2000 allowed the FSLN and the PLC the new ability to name political appointees to the Council, politicizing the CSE to the extreme. The international community decried the fact that the entire process of recognizing new political parties, declaring candidates, and managing the mechanics of holding elections could be so easily subverted to ensure the two strongest parties—the PLC and the FSLN—divide the spoils of government between themselves. These "reforms" have led to a perceived reduction in the transparency of the Nicaraguan government as a whole.

Note another trend as well: Nearly every Nicaraguan presidential candidate (with the exception of Doña Violeta), has been, at one time or another, jailed by a previous administration. Tachito jailed Ortega, and Ortega in turn jailed at one point or another both Arnoldo Alemán and Enrique Bolaños.

THE CONSTITUTION

The present constitution, written in 1987 by the FSLN administration, was amended

THE PACT

Seldom have two bitter enemies been such good friends. In January 2000, outgoing president Arnoldo Alemán was struggling to find a way to avoid charges of embezzling over $100 million during his presidency, and sideliner Daniel Ortega was looking for a way to avoid facing charges of sexual abuse of his stepdaughter Zoilamerica Narvaez. The gentlemen's (may we use that word?) agreement now known as El Pacto suited them both politically.

The Pact is essentially a power-sharing agreement between the two men's respective political parties. It granted political impunity to ex-presidents (which, when later revoked, landed Alemán in jail), and guaranteed seats on the Assembly to outgoing presidents. It also ensured all government bodies were enlarged and filled with an equal number of PLC and FSLN party representatives.

To ensure no additional parties arose to challenge either exisiting party's power, the Pact enacted more stringent requirements for the formation of new parties as well as the requirements for individual candidates for mayor. This worked marvelously for its intended effect: the political abandonment of potential political menace Pedro Solorzano.

The Pact has single-handedly eviscerated the democratic apparatus of post-revolutionary Nicaragua and ensured that the ongoing political shenanigans of both Ortega and Alemán are not only tolerated, but inevitably lead to their personal political benefit. It is universally criticized as the single most important factor in Nicaragua's future political and economic development. And an entire generation of Nicaraguans suddenly looks back on the Somoza years with a bit of nostalgia, wondering, with a sense of horror, if things were actually better back then.

---

in 1995 to balance the distribution of power more evenly between the legislative and executive branches. The National Assembly's ability to veto was bolstered and the president's ability to veto reduced. It was revised in 2000 to increase the power of the Supreme Court and the comptroller-general's office, and in 2008 to do away with mandated term limits.

Civil Liberties

Prior to Ortega's return in 2006, Nicaraguans enjoyed far greater freedoms than most other Latin American nations, including unparalleled freedom of speech, freedom of religion, freedom of movement, and the right to assembly and to form unions. In practice, these freedoms have slipped dramatically under the new Ortega administration. While officially there is no government censorship of journalists, in practice, journalists and photographers report unsubtle harassment, interference, and threats of violence, and Ortega has not hesitated to

send the police through offices of newspapers and NGOs that don't fully toe the party line. The Nicaraguan constitution prohibits discrimination by birth, nationality, political belief, race, gender, language, religion, opinion, national origin, or economic or social condition. And Nicaraguans are permitted to form labor unions. Nearly half of the workforce, including much of the agricultural labor, is unionized.

POLITICAL PARTIES

You'd think the political party in Nicaragua is more for organizational convenience than for conviction of principles. Nicaraguan politicians change from one political party to another as necessary to suit their own ambitions while smaller parties coalesce into alliances that later fracture into new arrangements. Infighting and division have been an integral part of the Nicaraguan political scene since the 1800s' Liberal-Conservative split. No other major political party came onto the scene until the FSLN took power in the 1980s. By 1990, no fewer than 20 political parties had risen in opposition to the FSLN; Doña Violeta's UNO coalition was formed from 14 of them. In the 1996 election, 35 different parties participated either on their own or as one of five coalitions. In 2000, new legislation made more stringent the requirements for a political party to participate in elections. While the exclusionary tactics diminished the previous election's free-for-all, skeptics believe the purpose of the law was to deny newcomers a piece of the pie.

Four parties participated in the presidential election of 2001: the FSLN; the PLC; the Partido Conservador Nicaragüense (PCN), the moderate-right representatives of the Conservative party; and the PLC-dominated Alianza Liberal (Liberal Alliance) under Enrique Bolaños, who ultimately won the election. Five competed in the 2006 election: the FSLN; the PLC; and three new ones—a liberal alliance by the name of ALN-PC, a Sandinista splinter party called the MRS (Movimiento Renovador Sandinista) headed by Managua's well-loved mayor Herte Lewites, and the tiny AC party (Alternativa para Cambio) under ex-Contra rebel Eden Pastora. The 2011 elections saw only four major parties participate: the FSLN, the ALN, the PLC, and PLC splinter party PLI-UNE (the Partido Liberal Independiente and the Unidad Nacional por la Esperanza).

THE ECONOMY

Two successive governments have had to jumpstart the Nicaraguan economy from a standstill: the Sandinistas, who picked up the shattered remains upon ousting Tachito, and Doña Violeta, who had to recover from the war and a decade of socialism. Her administration made dramatic progress, reducing the foreign debt by more than half, slashing inflation from 13,500 percent to 12 percent, and privatizing several hundred state-run businesses. The new economy began to expand in 1994 and grew at 4 percent

until 2006, weathering several major catastrophes, including Hurricane Mitch in 1998.

Nevertheless, Nicaragua remains the second-poorest nation in the Western hemisphere with a per capita gross domestic product of $780 and its external debt ratio—nearly twice the gross national product. Unemployment is pervasive: More than half of the adult urban population scrapes by in the informal sector (selling water at the roadside, for example), and population growth is probably going to keep it that way. High demand for jobs means employers can essentially ignore the minimum-wage requirement, especially in the countryside, where agricultural laborers typically earn as little as $1 a day, insufficient for survival even by Nicaraguan standards. Nearly 600,000 people face severe malnutrition.

Nicaragua's economy is based almost entirely on agricultural export of primary material, plus recently tourism and several nontraditional exports like sesame, onions, melons, and fruit. Export earnings are $700 million and rising: Agricultural programs in 2000 and 2001 that helped increase Nicaragua's ability to export beef and milk give hope that exports will rise in the latter part of the decade. Traditional export products include coffee, beef, and sugar, followed by bananas, shellfish (especially lobster tails and shrimp), and tobacco.

The upward trajectory of Nicaragua's economy has slowed radically under President Ortega, and rolling blackouts left much of Nicaragua without energy in 2006 and 2007. This was the combined result of Hugo Chávez's failure to deliver the cheap petroleum he'd promised and ostracism by foreign energy suppliers. Ortega's long-term economic plans remain muddled.

Debt, the HIPC, and Foreign Aid

For years, Nicaragua has been one of the most highly indebted nations of the world. When Somoza fled the country, he took the capital reserves of the banks with him, leaving behind $1.6 billion of debt. The Sandinistas, through a combination of gross economic mismanagement, extensive borrowing (primarily from Eastern bloc nations), the U.S. economic embargo, and high defense expenditures augmented the national debt by a factor of 10, nearly half of which was in arrears. By 1994, Nicaragua had the highest ratio of debt to GDP in the world, a challenge every successive administration has had to deal with. Germany, Russia, and Mexico were the first nations to forgive Nicaraguan debt entirely.

Propitious to Nicaragua's future economic growth was its inclusion in the Highly Indebted Poor Countries (HIPC) debt relief initiative in 2000. Inclusion in the initiative means Nicaragua will be exonerated from the majority of its international debt upon compliance with an International Monetary Fund (IMF) and World Bank program, but that program mandates several austerity measures, debt restructuring, and the opening of its economy to foreign markets. More hotly contested is the mandated privatization of public utilities, including the telephone system (privatized in 2002) and municipal water distribution. City water systems have not yet been privatized and the issue is extremely controversial with those who consider water a human right rather than a commodity. Central to the HIPC initiative is Nicaragua's continued effort toward macroeconomic adjustment and structural and social policy reforms, particularly basic health and education.

Agriculture

Nicaragua is, above all, an agricultural nation—a third of its gross domestic product is agriculture-based, and agriculture represents the fastest-growing economic sector, at 8 percent growth per year. However, much of the new land put into agricultural production is opened at the expense of the forests, the

Agriculture is the strongest sector of the Nicaraguan economy.

© GRACE GONZALEZ

CORN CULTURE

The planting cycle of *maíz* (corn) has governed the life of Nicaraguans and their Mesoamerican descendants ever since the first yellow kernels were laid in the dark volcanic soil. *Maíz* is as central to the Nicaraguan diet as white rice is to the people of Southeast Asia. Beans are just as critical a staple (and a nutritionally critical complement), but in Nicaragua, corn is prepared with more variety, taste, and frequency.

Corn is prepared and consumed in more than a hundred different ways: hot, cold, cooked, ground, and liquefied, in both food and in beverages. Tortillas are, of course, flat cakes of corn dough softened with water and cooked on a slightly rounded clay pan known as a *comal*. The only place you'll find a flour tortilla is in a Mexican restaurant in Managua; Nica corn tortillas are thick, heavy, and (hopefully) hot off the wood stove and slightly toasted. When the same dough is fortified with sugar and lard, then rolled into small lumps and boiled while wrapped in yellow corn husks, the result is a *tamal*, steaming heavy bowls of which market women balance on their heads and loudly vend in the streets. *Nacatamales*, a Nicaraguan classic, are similar but with meat—often spiced pork—in the middle. *Atol* is corn pudding, and *güiríla* is a sweet tortilla of young corn, always served with a hunk of *cuajada* (salty white cheese).

Elote is corn on the cob, especially tasty when roasted directly over open coals until the kernels are dry, hot, and a little chewy. When harvested young, the ears of corn are called *chilotes* and are served in soup or with fresh cream. Corn is also oven-baked into hard, molasses-sweetened cookie rings called *rosquillas,* flat cookies called *ojaldras,* and many other shapes. The same dough is also combined with cheese, lard, and spices to produce dozens more items, including *perrerreques, cosas de horno,* and *gofios.*

What do you wash it down with? More corn, of course. *Pinol,* drunk so frequently in Nicaragua the Nicaraguans proudly call themselves *pinoleros,* is toasted and ground corn meal mixed with water. *Pinolillo* is *pinol* mixed with cacao, pepper, and cloves; *tiste* is similar. *Pozol* is a ground cornmeal drink prepared from a variety of corn with a pinkish hue. The ultrasweet pink baggies of *chicha* are made from slightly fermented cornmeal (especially strong batches are called *chicha brava*). Then, of course, there is crystal clear Nicaraguan corn tequila, or *la cususa.*

Corn: It's what's for breakfast, lunch, and dinner.

indiscriminate harvesting of which has a negative overall effect on the environment and water supply. Agriculture employs 45 percent of the workforce. Outside of the small, upscale producers who export to international markets, the majority of Nicaraguan agriculture is for domestic consumption, and much of that is subsistence farming. Drought years often require importing of basic grains.

Subsistence farmers typically grow yellow corn and red beans. The choice of red beans over black beans and yellow corn over white corn is cultural and presents additional challenges to farmers, as red beans are more susceptible to drought (and less nutritious) than black or soybeans.

The Sébaco Valley is an agriculturally productive area and the primary source of wet rice for local consumption; it's also widely planted with onions. Extensive irrigation of rice plantations caused the water table in the Sébaco Valley to drop more than three meters in the 1990s. Jinotega's cool climate is a major source of fruit and vegetable production, including cabbage, peppers, onions, melons, watermelons, squash, and tomatoes.

The Coffee Economy

There's no underestimating the importance of coffee to the Nicaraguan economy. Coffee is produced on more than 100,000 hectares of Nicaraguan land, contributes an average of $140 million per year to the economy, includes more than 30,000 farms, and employs more than 200,000 people, about 10–20 percent of the agricultural workforce. Nicaragua exports its beans primarily to North America, Europe, and Japan—to the tune of one million 100-pound burlap sacks every year. These beans are roasted and ground (usually abroad) to produce 11 billion pounds of java.

Because most Nicaragua growers produce full-bodied arabica beans under the shade of diverse trees at altitudes of 900 meters and higher, the quality of its crop is recognized the world over. The June 2004 issue of *Smithsonian* magazine reported Nicaragua as "the 'hot origin' for gourmet coffee, with its beans winning taste awards and its decent wages for many small farmers a hopeful beacon for a global coffee market under siege." It also declared Nicaragua a country where "the goals of a better cup of joe, social justice and a healthier environment are nowhere more tightly entwined." This is important as Nicaragua struggles to emerge from the worst crash in the global coffee economy in a century.

THE COFFEE CRISIS

Producing and selling Nicaraguan coffee, challenging even in good times, was dealt a staggering blow in 1999, when low-quality Vietnamese and Brazilian robusta beans drove world prices to their lowest rates in 30 years (discounting for inflation, they were the lowest prices in a century). This was compounded by corporate consolidation in the trading and roasting industries, which dealt coffee farmers a blow while well-off overseas consumers were spared the extra costs. With market prices well below the cost of production, the effect on rural Nicaraguan coffee workers has been devastating.

Conditions bottomed out when hacienda owners could no longer afford to even feed their workers, let alone pay them wages, and thousands of families (called *plantónes*) migrated to the cities, marched and camped along the highways, and demanded assistance from the government, including land, food, education, and temporary work. With the help of the cooperatives and some of the hacienda owners, the farmworkers union finally negotiated most of their demands and now more than 2,000 families are getting the title to their own land. The next step will be to see, if the crisis continues, whether they will be able to keep their small allotments in the face of neoliberal national governmental policies.

THE FUTURE OF COFFEE

Discerning North American and European java swillers have created an enormous demand for a superior cup of coffee—and they are willing to pay extra for it, as we all well know. If the Nicaraguan coffee industry is to continue to gain ground, it must maintain its reputation for quality coffee. This requires a government-level effort to address environmental issues like soil fertility and water contamination, the modernization of processing methods, and the resolution of severe microcredit and marketing issues. The industry will also need to pay higher prices for top-quality coffee, and even fair trade and organic coffee price premiums have failed to keep up with the costs of sustainable production. Addressing the coffee crisis may provide the framework for dealing with the social ills inherent in modern coffee production, such as the feudal system of ownership and labor that still exists at many of the larger hacienda-style plantations; on these farms, seasonal pickers and their families are paid the barest survival wages and are sucked into a never-ending debt cycle that keeps them desperate and working.

The future of sustainable coffee production, many agree, is in family-run cooperatives in which small-scale farmers, rather than a single, rich hacienda owner, possess the power to control their product. At present, nearly 20 percent of Nicaraguan coffee is grown by 8,000 small-scale *campesino* producers working as members of nine cooperatives in the country's northlands (that's an increase of 10 percent and 2,000 farms since the last edition). As much as 80 percent of their coffee can be marketed as specialty coffee for the specialty, fair trade, and organic markets, making these growers less vulnerable to the extreme price oscillations of conventional coffee.

Nicaragua has a number of other advantages over other similarly struggling coffee-producing nations in the region. First of all, nearly 95 percent of Nicaraguan coffee is grown under a forest canopy that provides shade for coffee bushes and, at the same time, habitat for migratory birds. This can earn a grower a "Bird Friendly" sticker, which, like organic certification (not using chemicals and properly disposing of waste products), gains a significantly higher market price.

Coffee families and their communities also benefit enormously from the fair trade–certification program (www.transfairusa.org), in which participating companies must comply with strict economic, social, and environmental criteria, guaranteeing producers a fair price. The small-scale farmers who represent most of the certified-organic producers and those linked to fair trade markets recently organized to represent their interests at the national and international level by forming an association of small-scale coffee farming co-ops called **Cafenica.**

Finally, a number of coffee growers, especially those who own their own land, have diversified their income with various noncoffee crops and activities, including several awesome ecotourism projects.

Industry

Industrial production in Nicaragua reached its zenith in 1978 under Anastasio Somoza, who encouraged industrial expansion in Managua at the expense of the environment, especially Lake Xolotlán. Investment policies of the time exonerated industries from the need to worry about environmental protection. Industry—even agro-industry—has been underdeveloped in the years following the revolution. There is a small amount of production for domestic and regional markets, including cement processing, petroleum refining, and some production of plastic goods. Another aspect of Nicaragua's export industry is the steadily increasing number of *zonas francas* (free trade zones) near Managua, Sébaco, Masaya, and Granada, where tens of thousands of Nicaraguans are employed in foreign-owned sweatshops.

Tourism

The so-called "industry without smokestacks" is widely hoped to be a panacea to Nicaragua's economic ills. The government agency in charge of tourism development and marketing is El Instituto Nicaragüense de Turismo, better known as **INTUR** (www.intur.gob.ni). At present, tourism represents the third largest source of foreign exchange. Public Law 306 provides a 10-year tax break to newly constructed tourist facilities that meet certain criteria. More beneficial still are travelers like you, who spend a little money and hopefully take home a good impression of Nicaragua. Since the mid-1990s, investment in tourism has skyrocketed, notably in Managua, Granada, and San Juan del Sur. The total number of visitors to Nicaragua has increased from under 600,000 visitors in 2001 to more than 800,000 in 2005, the majority arriving from Central and South America. Most foreign visitors come from North America and Europe. In 2007, nearly half a million people arrived by international flight to Nicaragua.

ECOTOURISM

The word "ecotourism" was coined in the 1980s with the best of intentions. The idea is to prevent tourism from spoiling the environment, or to use it to provide an alternative to spoiling the environment. The success of the concept and its marketing value led to a worldwide boom in the usage of that prefix that we know so well, even when its actual practice has sometimes fallen short of original intentions. Indeed, the warm and fuzzy "eco" has been used, abused, prostituted, and bastardized all over the world, and Nicaragua is no exception. Alternative tourism goes by many other names as well: "sustainable," "responsible," "ethical," "rural," or "fair trade" tourism, to name a few.

The concept of protected areas and national parks is relatively new in Nicaragua and is, in some places, viewed with skepticism—especially by poor *campesinos* who live near (or sometimes within) these areas and have always used the forests to supplement their paltry incomes. They need wood for fuel, land for farmland, and game for protein. MARENA, the government ministry charged with protecting Nicaragua's vast system of parks and refuges, has scant resources to prevent such activities. If money comes from nature-loving visitors, an alternative use for the forest has been created. Foreigners come to see the local waterfall or coffee cooperative and need to eat breakfast, hire a guide, rent a horse, and witness how people in this particular corner of the continent live. Community-sponsored tourism efforts are there, namely in Granada, Isla de Ometepe, Matagalpa, and the Miraflor region of Estelí. Here, existing cooperatives have arranged homestay opportunities that involve volunteer work, Spanish language class, alternative agriculture, and trips to local sites.

The People

POPULATION

Nicaragua's population is fast approaching six million, about a full third of whom live in Managua. Nicaragua is both the least populous Central American nation and the fastest growing, at just over 3 percent annually. At this rate, the country's strained resources will have to support between 9 and 12 million people by the year 2030. In addition, well over a million Nicaraguans live outside of the country, particularly in Costa Rica (679,000) and the United States (500,000), not to mention thousands more living in Mexico and other Central American nations.

ETHNIC GROUPS

While Nicaraguans can trace their ancestry back to many sources, most of the population is a blend of Spanish, Native American, and sometimes other European stock. Indigenous blood runs most strongly in the northeast, where the Spanish had less influence, and on the mid-Atlantic coast, where English and African influences were dominant.

In the Pacific region, the indigenous population thinned from 800,000 when the Spanish arrived to less than 60,000 after a couple centuries of conquistador policy (i.e., war, slavery, genocide, and disease). The native peoples of the northeast, including Matagalpa and Jinotega, were less affected, and thus retain larger indigenous populations today.

Mestizos

The term mestizo refers to any mixture of Spanish and indigenous blood and describes the majority of Nicaraguan citizens, whose Spanish colonial ancestors began intermingling with the locals about as soon as they got off the boat. A second wave of *mestizaje* (mixing) occurred from the 1860s through the 1890s, during the wave of rubber and banana production along the Atlantic coast, and again in the 1950s as Pacific farmers moved eastward in search of new agricultural lands at the expense of the Sumu-Ulúa and Miskito peoples. Note: Mestizo Nicaraguans sometimes use the term "indio" as a derogatory label for anyone with Native American features (high cheekbones, straight black hair, short eyelashes, and dark brown skin).

Creoles

After decimating the indigenous peoples of the New World, the Spanish realized they lacked laborers, so they imported African slaves to their colonies in the Americas. Beginning in 1562, English slave traders, and later Dutch, Spanish, and others, supplied the colonies with human cargo. Along the Atlantic coast of Nicaragua, African slaves intermingled with Miskitos, giving birth to the Zambo (or Sambo) people. They also bred with the Spanish and English, forming the Creoles, primarily found today in Bluefields and San Juan del Norte. Creoles speak a form of English that still bears traces of 19th-century Queen's English, as well as Caribbean and Spanish traits. Their culture includes distinct African elements, including the belief in a form of African witchcraft called *obeah* or *sontín,* the latter a corruption of the English "something," or "something special."

Miskitos

Modern-day Miskitos are really a mixture of several races, and include traces of English and African blood. The Native American Bawihka people, whose territory extended from the Río Coco (Wangki) at Cabo Gracias a Dios south to Prinzapolka, mixed with the African-slave refugees of a Portuguese ship that wrecked on the Miskito Cays in 1642. They later mixed with the English during their long occupation of the Atlantic coast. Over the centuries, the word "Miskito" has been written many other ways, including "Mosquito," "Mosca," "Mískitu," and others. The name derives not from the insect but from the Spanish word *mosquete* (musket), a firearm the British provided the locals to ensure a tactical advantage over their neighbors.

The Miskitos' warlike nature and superior firepower helped them subdue 20 other Native American tribes along the Atlantic coast of Central America. They were valuable allies to the English, who used them in raids against inland Spanish settlements, and crowned their "kings" in an Anglican church in Belize City. The Miskitos also absorbed the Prinsu tribe (located along the Bambana and Prinzapolka Rivers) and the Kukra tribe.

Today the Miskitos inhabit much of the Atlantic coast of Nicaragua, from Bluefields northward and all along the Río Coco, which they consider their spiritual home. There are additional Miskito settlements on both Corn Islands, but their two principal centers are Bilwi (Puerto Cabezas) and Waspám. Their language, Miskito, is the old indigenous Tawira language enriched with English and African vocabulary.

The Kukra

The Kukra people were assimilated by the Miskitos over the last two centuries and no longer exist as a tribe. Of unknown but reportedly cannibalistic Caribbean origin, they once inhabited Bluefields, the Corn Islands, and the area around Pearl Lagoon. Today, the only trace of them is the name of the small Pearl Lagoon community of Kukra Hill.

The Garífuna

The Garífuna, as a distinct culture, are relative newcomers to the world. Their history began on the Lesser Antillean island of San Vicente (Saint Vincent), which in the 1700s had become a refuge for escaped slaves from the sugar plantations of the Caribbean, including Jamaica. These displaced Africans were accepted by the native Carib (Arawak) islanders, with whom they freely intermingled. As the French and English settled the island, the Garífunas (as they had become known), established a worldwide reputation as expert canoe navigators and fierce warriors, resisting the newcomers. The English finally got the upper hand in the conflict after tricking and killing

© GRACE GONZALEZ

Garífuna culture in Nicaragua is kept alive with the practice of traditional music and dance.

the Garífuna leader, and in 1797, they forcefully evacuated the Garífunas from San Vicente to the Honduran Bay Island of Roatán. From there, many of the Garífunas migrated to the mainland communities of Trujillo, Honduras and Dangriga, Belize. Today, they exist up and down most of the Central American Caribbean coast, with a small but distinct presence in Nicaragua, primarily around Pearl Lagoon. Orinoco (originally Urunugu) is the largest settlement of Garífunas in Nicaragua, established in 1912 by the Garífuna John Sambola. The communities of San Vicente and Justo Point are both Garífuna as well. During the 1980s, the Contra war forced many Garífunas out of their communities and into Bluefields, Puerto Limón (Costa Rica), and Honduras.

The Mayangna

"Sumu" is a derogatory word the Miskito used for all other peoples of Ulúa descent (it means stupid; conversely, the Mayangna name for the Miskito was *wayas,* which means "stinky"). The Mayangna, as they prefer to be called, are a combination of several Ulúa tribes, including the Twahka, Panamka, and Ulwa, who once settled the Kurinwas, Siquia, Mico, Rama, and Grande Rivers of the Atlantic coast. Mayangna tradition has it that in the 9th and 10th centuries they were the inhabitants of a territory that extended from the Atlantic coast and Río Coco to the Pacific, but they were forced off the Atlantic coastal lands by the more aggressive and warring Miskito and out of the Pacific by the Nahuatls, Maribios, and Chorotegas. The Mayangna are now centered around the mining triangle and the massive forest reserve of Bosawás.

The Rama

The Rama are the least-numerous indigenous people in Nicaragua, numbering only several hundred. Their language is distinct from Miskito and Mayangna and is closely related to the ancient tribal languages of Native American tribes of Panamá and Colombia. Today, only several dozen people can still speak Rama and anthropologists are scrambling to document what they can of the language before it disappears entirely. The Rama people inhabit the pleasant bay island of Rama Cay in the Bay of Bluefields, where they fish and collect oysters. They also grow grains and traditional crops on small plots of land on the mainland of Bluefields Bay and along the Kukra River. The Rama people are reserved and keep mostly to their traditional ways, even using traditional tools and implements. They are excellent navigators and fishers.

The Arts

Nicaraguans are by nature a creative people, and the many countries and cultures that have taken part in their country's history have each left an unmistakable mark on dance, sculpture, painting, writing, and music. There are many opportunities to experience traditional dance and song, but equally vibrant are the artisans, writers, and performers who are creating in the present, helping to form an artistic environment that's very much Nicaragua's own.

The city of Masaya and its surrounding pueblos present the nation's best opportunity to admire—and acquire—elaborate pottery, intricately woven hammocks, wood carvings, ceramic miniatures, leatherwork, and embroidered *guayaberas.* Here's a brief guide to some of the items you'll find in Nicaragua.

ARTS AND CRAFTS
Basketwork
The basketwork you'll find around the country is an extension of the bamboo baskets you see stacked up with produce in countryside markets. Nueva Segovia and the northeast Miskito regions of Nicaragua, in contrast, produce curious baskets and urns from bundles of wrapped pine needles that have been bound into long coils, then wound in concentric coils. Look for them in Ocotal and the markets in Managua.

Hammocks
Nicaraguan hammocks are well made and reasonably priced: around $30–60, depending on size and quantity. Though you can also find good-quality hammocks at the Roberto Huembes market in Managua, the heart of Nicaragua's home-crafted hammock industry is Masaya, and visiting the many family "factories" is as easy as walking up to the porch and saying *"Buenos días."* Check the weave and the quality of the cord—stiffer cord tends to last longer and tighter weaves tend to be more comfortable.

Pottery
Nicaraguan pottery designs have continued uninterrupted from pre-Columbian times to the present. Today's potters produce all manner of vases, bowls, urns, pots, and other forms in rich earthy hues, some delicately etched, some left crude. You'll find fantastic mobiles and wind chimes of clay birds, bells, or ornamental shapes, like stars and planets. Get gorgeous, export-quality pieces in Masaya or San Juan del Oriente (Catarina and increasingly the other pueblos are getting into the act now, too). Or find earthy, rustic pieces not too different from what the Nahuatls must have used up north: Jinotega's black pottery or red clay pieces in Estelí and Matagalpa.

Primitivist Paintings
The first primitivist paintings from the Solentiname archipelago came into the world spotlight in the 1960s as an offshoot of Padre Ernesto Cardenal's liberation theology movement on the islands. Instantly recognized the

world over as an art form unique to Nicaragua, the vibrant paintings typically portray romanticized scenes of tropical Latin America: markets, oxen, trees laden with fruit, and skies full of toucans and parrots. You'll have a better story to tell if you buy them from the source on the Solentiname islands, but if your schedule doesn't permit, you can do just as well at the Galería Solentiname in Managua. Lower-priced pieces are available in Huembes market, but you'll have to look harder to find the better works.

Soapstone

The soapstone *(marmolina)* sculptors of San Juan de Limay (a small village north of Estelí) produce polished figurines inspired by animals, Rubenesque (and pregnant) women, and pre-Columbian designs. Smaller pieces are simple to transport, but in Masaya, you can have larger pieces packed and shipped home. You'll see iguanas, parrots, frogs, oxen, wagons, and more, plus ornately carved nativity scenes and chess sets, all carefully rendered in the salmon and ivory hues natural to the Limay soapstone. Wooden Furniture

The carpenters and craftspeople of the small towns around Masaya turn out gorgeous wooden furniture, which you'll see lining the roadside during your drive-by browsing. Rocking chairs called *abuelitas* ("little grandmothers") or *mecedoras* are sturdy and comfortable, and if you ask, they'll gladly disassemble them and condense their products into well-wrapped airline-suitable packages.

LITERATURE

"Nicaragua," wrote the poet Pablo Neruda, "where the highest song of the tongue is raised." José Miguel Oviedo called the writing of Nicaragua "the richest and most tragic national literary tradition on the continent." Most start the story of Nicaraguan literature with the groundbreaking words of Rubén Darío. It continues with the vanguardists of the 1950s and 1960s, the subsequent generation of revolutionary poets and novelists, and the current wave of soul-searchers.

Though poverty has placed books out of the economic reach of most Nicaraguans, the Casa de los Tres Mundos art gallery in Managua doubles as ground zero for the Society of Nicaraguan Writers, and is a good place to start if you have questions about readings, book releases, or other events. There are a few bookstores in Managua that carry Nicaraguan and Latin American selections, as well as Spanish translations of foreign works; Estelí and León also boast interesting bookstores to explore.

Poet and author Gioconda Belli was called one of the 100 most important poets of the 20th century. Her work deals with the themes of feminism, mystical realism, and history, all mixed with a breath of sensuality. Her books *Wiwilí, Sofía de los Presagios,* and *El País Bajo Mi Piel* (The Country Under My Skin) are widely acclaimed.

The writing of Ricardo Pasos Marciacq reflects not only his appreciation for the long and tumultuous history of Nicaragua but for the richness of its society. His books *Maria Manuela Piel de Luna* and *El Burdel de las Pedrarias* are modern classics; the former evokes the years when British-armed Miskitos were wreaking havoc on the Spanish settlements of the Pacific.

Rubén Darío is loved throughout the world of Latin American literature and is considered the father of modernism in Spanish literature. A few of the many other books by Nicaraguan writers worth reading if you have the time and the facility of the language include *El Nicaragüense* by Pablo Antonio Cuadra, *Nicaragua, Teatro de lo Grandioso* by Carlos A. Bravo, and *El Estrecho Dudoso* by Ernesto Cardenal.

DANCE AND THEATER

Nicaragua's traditional folk dances are often mixed with a form of theater, like a play in a parade. There are several dance institutions

THE POET IS THE HIGH PRIEST

In *Risking a Somersault in the Air,* Margaret Randall wrote, "Throughout Nicaraguan culture, the poet is the high priest. The prophet. The maker of visions. The singer of songs. The one who knows and can say it for others the way others feel it but cannot say it for themselves." Salman Rushdie was equally impressed when, during his tour of Nicaragua and the Sandinista government in the mid-1980s, he found himself surrounded by young warrior-poets at all levels of society.

Indeed, an inordinate number of the revolution's leaders were published writers—including Minister of the Interior and Head of State Security Tomás Borge, and President Daniel Ortega, both of whom published poems from Somoza's prisons in the 1970s (Somoza's forces found and destroyed the only manuscript of the book Ortega wrote during the same time period). Ortega once told Rushdie, "In Nicaragua, everybody is considered to be a poet until he proves to the contrary."

Literature (and painting, pottery, theater, music, and crafts) was strongly supported by the Sandinista government, whose minister of culture, Father Ernesto Cardenal, stayed busy instituting poetry workshops and publishing magazines and books. Cardenal's poetry is internationally acclaimed and widely translated. Another revolutionary, Gioconda Belli, whose work evokes the sensuality of her country's land and people, was named one of the 100 most important poets of the 20th century. But Nicaraguan poetry, no matter how entwined with the revolution, goes way back, before the life of Sandino.

Invariably, one must turn to Nicaragua's literary giant, Rubén Darío, who 100 years ago set the stage for his nation's love affair with poetry by producing a style unprecedented in Spanish literature. Darío is called the father of the modernist movement in Spanish poetry, a literary style that shed long, grammatically intricate Spanish phrases for simplicity and directness. His experimentation with verse and rhythm made him one of the most acclaimed Latin American writers of all time. Darío's legacy stands firm, and stories about his drinking bouts and international exploits still abound. Poet, journalist, diplomat, and favorite son of Nicaragua, Rubén Darío has become the icon for all that is artistic or cultural in Nicaragua. Today, his portrait graces the front of the 100 *córdoba* bill, his name is on most of the nation's libraries and bookstores, and his sculpted likeness presides throughout the land. His legacy is incredible, and Randall asks if today's poets owe everything to him or to the fact that they, like their hero, glean their inspiration "from that violent expanse of volcanic strength called Nicaragua."

A hundred years later, the Sandinistas pointed to Darío's anti-imperialist references, including a passage written at the time of the Spanish-American War in which he denounces the North Americans as "buffaloes with silver teeth."

The muse still reigns in today's generation. *Rubén's Orphans* is an anthology of contemporary Nicaraguan poets, with English translations by Marco Morelli, published in 2001 by Painted Rooster Press. Also, seek out Steven F. White's book *Poets of Nicaragua, a Bilingual Anthology,* which covers the poets following Darío up to the revolution (1983, Unicorn Press).

in Managua that teach folk classics alongside modern dance and ballet, and sponsor frequent performances. The presence of dance schools outside the capital is on the rise, which means fortunate travelers have a good chance of seeing a presentation outside of Managua, especially in Masaya, Diriamba, Matagalpa, León, and Granada. "El Güegüense," for example, is a 19th-century dance of costumed dancers in wooden masks that satirically represents the impression Nicaragua's indigenous people first had of the Spanish and their horses. This dance and others are often featured at *fiestas patronales* (patron saint celebrations), notably in the Masaya and Carazo regions. "El Viejo y La Vieja" ("The Old Man and Woman") pokes ribald fun at old age and sexuality. One dancer, dressed up as an old gentleman with cane and top hat, and the other, dressed up as a buxom old woman, perform a dance that usually involves the old man trying to dance with young female members of the audience while his wife chases him, beating him with her cane. "Aquella Indita" is a celebration of the Nicaraguan woman and her reputation for being graceful and hardworking. "El Solar de Monimbó" ("Monimbó's Backyard") is a traditional dance from the indigenous neighborhood of Masaya, which captures the spirit of community and celebration.

Besides the traditional folk pieces, Nicaraguans love to dance. Period. And there is no occasion (except maybe a funeral) at which it is inappropriate to pump up the music and take to your feet. The ultrasuave, loose-hipped movements associated with merengue, salsa, *cumbia,* and reggae are most commonly seen at discos, street parties, or in living rooms around the nation. The Palo de Mayo is a popular, modern Caribbean dance form featuring flamboyant costumes, vibrating chests, and not-so-subtle sexual simulations. When you see mothers rocking their babies to loud Latin rhythms, and two-year-old girls receiving hip-gyrating lessons, you'll understand why Nicaraguans are able to move so much more fluidly on the dance floor than you are.

VISUAL ARTS

There are a number of Nicaraguan sculptors and painters whose work is displayed at galleries in Managua, Granada, León, and other places. Though the primitivist painters of Solentiname have gotten the lion's share of the press, there is much more in Nicaragua to be seen. In Managua, there are frequent expos of art, often accompanied by buffets or musical performances.

MUSIC

Music, in an infinite variety of forms, is essential to Nicaraguan society. Expect to find loud, blaring radios in most restaurants, bars, vehicles, and homes. It may seem strange at first to find yourself listening to fast, pulsing merengue beats at six in the morning on a rural chicken bus (or in your hotel lobby at midnight for that matter) when the only people listening are sitting calmly in their seats or rocking chairs. Realize, however, that this behavior is seen as a way to inject *alegría* (happiness) into the environment, or alternately, to get rid of the sadness that some Nicaraguans associate with silence.

Radio mixes are eclectic, featuring the latest reggaetón hits, Mexican and Miami pop, cheesy *romanticas,* plus a bizarre U.S. mélange of dated tunes, while hipster radio shows for the country's youth have begun to play more electronic music. Another wildly popular genre is the *ranchera,* which comes in the form of either polka beats or slow, drippy, lost-love, mariachi tearjerkers, performed by one of a handful of super-celebrity Mexican crooners. Old, rootsy, U.S. country music is extremely popular on the Atlantic coast, and in northern Nicaragua, Kenny Rogers (pronounced "Royers") is recognized as the undisputed king of "La Musica Country."

Managua is host to a small, exciting scene of young local bands and solo musicians, most of whom are direct descendants—children, nephews, cousins—of the generation of musicians that brought Nicaraguan folk music to the world. Their acts range from quiet acoustic solo sets to the head-banging throaty screams of a couple of angry, politically minded metal bands. You can hear a lot of them at El Caramanchel.

Live music is also found at most *fiestas patronales,* performed by one of several Nicaraguan commercial party bands whose sets imitate the radio mixes of the day. Among the most popular bands is Los Mokuanes (named after the enchanted mountain and its resident witch in La Trinidad, Estelí),

NICARAGUAN BASEBALL FEVER

A hundred years of North American and Cuban influence has engendered a nation of baseball fanatics unrivalled in Latin America. Soccer (*fútbol*) has a few fans in Nicaragua—especially in the Carazo region—but it's *el béisbol* that gets most Nicas' blood boiling.

Throughout Nicaragua, very few pueblos lack a ball field of some sort, even if the kids put together games with homemade bats and balls of wound twine and tape. The casual traveler is more often than not welcome to join. A plethora of municipal leagues, town leagues, little leagues, competitions between universities, and even between government ministries, make up the bulk of the national sport. Nicaragua's pro league seems to be constantly in flux, often due to funding problems. At last check, only four teams were competing in the top division—Managua (El Boer), Masaya (San Fernando), the León Lions, and Chinandega Tigers. These teams play with professional ringers from the United States who come to Nicaragua to stay in shape during their off-season. The other division consists of ballclubs from Estelí, Granada (Los Tiburones, or the Sharks), Matagalpa, and Rivas. **The Federación Nicaragüense de Beisból Asociado** (tel. 505/222-2021) has an office in the national stadium in Managua.

There are several concurrent seasons, with the pros playing November–February, and the minors starting around January. Playoff games and a seven-game championship series are played in the spring. The games are serious—as are the fans—but the series' charm is its humility: Unlike elsewhere, baseball is a sport and a pastime, not a mega-marketed seven-figure-salary circus. Not that Nicaraguan players don't dream of one day making it big in "the Show" like their colleagues, Vicente Padilla and Marvin Bernard. Padilla is a star pitcher who, at the age of 26, signed a $2.6-million contract with the Philadelphia Phillies in 2004. Bernard

took $4.2 million from the San Francisco Giants in 2003. Like all Nicas who make it to the big leagues, their every move is followed passionately in the Nicaraguan sports pages.

Going back a few years, one of Nicaragua's most admired national heroes is **Dennis "El Presidente" Martínez,** the kid from Granada who left home in 1976 to make it to the big leagues, where he pitched more winning games than any other Latino. In 1991, he pitched the 13th perfect game in major league history against the first-place Dodgers. Nicaraguans followed every detail of his career with avid determination, as he pitched for the Baltimore Orioles (1976-1986), Montreal Expos (1986-1993), Cleveland Indians (1994-1996), Seattle Mariners (1997), and finally the Atlanta Braves (1998). Martínez was a breath of fresh air and a source of much-needed relief throughout the 1980s, when his pitching and hitting stats were the only good news associated with this war-torn nation; talking baseball was a popular respite from the tragedy and destruction. Martínez retired in 1998, and today his name graces the stadium in Managua, as well as several charitable foundations, like the **Dennis Martínez Foundation** (www.dennismartinezfoundation.org).

Also respected is Puerto Rican-born Pittsburgh Pirate, **Roberto Clemente.** Clemente was so moved by the distress in Nicaragua's capital after the 1972 earthquake that he rounded up a planeload of clothes, blankets, and food, and flew to Managua to personally distribute it. He never arrived. Immediately after taking off from San Juan, Puerto Rico, his DL-7 plane faltered and plunged into the Caribbean. Investigators suggested the unrestrained cargo shifted during flight and threw the plane off balance; five additional people perished trying to rescue him.

who have been around in one form or another for more than three decades. During the war, they were conscripted by the government to don fatigues and perform at army

bases throughout the country. Other favorite bands are Macolla and, representing the Palo de Mayo side of things, Sir Anthony and his Dimensión Costeño.

ESSENTIALS

Getting There

BY AIR

All international flights arrive and depart from the **Augusto C. Sandino** airport (www.eaai.com.ni) on Carretera Norte in Managua. From here, La Costeña (tel. 505/2263-2142, www.lacostena.com.ni) operates daily flights to and from Bluefields, Corn Island, Puerto Cabezas, Las Minas (Siuna, Bonanza, and Rosita), Waspán and San Carlos. American Airlines (www.aa.com) has daily flights via Miami, Continental Airlines via Houston, and Delta Airlines (www.delta.com) via Atlanta. The Salvadoran airline TACA (www.taca.com) also has daily flights from Miami with a brief stopover in San Salvador; this is typically a less expensive flight, but the cheapest possible flight is from Fort Lauderdale, Florida, on Spirit Airlines (www.spirit.com). For travel within Central America, Copa Airlines (www.copaair.com) offers three daily flights to Panama City; Nature Air (www.natureair.com) has introduced four high-season flights a week between Managua and San José.

Augusto C. Sandino airport is surprisingly decent. From the airport you can arrange rental cars, stop by the INTUR desk for hotel

© JOSHUA BERMAN

recommendations, and even buy or rent a cell phone. Skycaps will help you with your luggage for about $2; don't use the services of anyone not sporting a skycap uniform.

BORDER CROSSINGS

The three northern border posts are (from west to east): Guasale, Chinandega; El Espino, Somoto; and Las Manos, Somoto. Travelers who entered the region via Guatemala, Honduras, or El Salvador can enter Nicaragua without getting additional visas thanks to Nicaragua's participation in the CA-4 Border Control Agreement of 2006. Under the agreement, your initial entry visa is valid for the whole region for up to 90 days and can be extended once without too much hassle.

On the southern border, Peñas Blancas is the principal corridor on the Pan-American Highway leading to Costa Rica, and no such agreement exists, so you'll need a stamp if arriving from Costa Rica. You can also enter Nicaragua in the south from Los Chiles, Costa Rica, a trip that involves a lovely boat ride to San Carlos at the head of the Río San Juan.

Note that every overland crossing involves two steps: exiting the first country and entering the second. If you forget to get the second stamp in your passport you will regret it.

By Car

If you are driving your own vehicle, the process to enter Nicaragua is lengthier, but usually not difficult. You must present the vehicle's title, as well as your own driver's license and passport. You will be given a temporary (30-day) permit to drive in Nicaragua, which will cost $10—should you lose the permit, you will be fined $100. Alamo Rent A Car shares cars among Costa Rica and Nicaragua, permitting you to pick up in one country and drop off in another.

By International Bus

A half-dozen long-haul bus companies run between Managua and other Central American capitals, and most are based out of Barrio Martha Quezada in Managua. They each offer competing schedules and prices. Several have affiliate offices in other Nicaraguan cities, like Rivas and León. From Managua to San José, Costa Rica takes about 10 hours and costs about $30 each way. To Tegucigalpa, Honduras, is also up to 10 hours (depending on the line at immigration), from $25 each way. Many departures are before dawn, leaving Managua at 3:30–6 A.M., so plan accordingly.

TicaBus (two blocks east of the Antiguo Cine Dorado, tel. 505/2222-6094 or 505/2222-3031, ticabus@ticabus.com, www.ticabus.com) is the oldest and best-established Central American international bus company, with three daily departures to San José, as well as service to the rest of Central America with connections all the way to Mexico. The other companies with stations in Managua (all within a few blocks of each other) are **King Quality** (tel. 505/2222-3065, www.king–qualityca.com), **Del Sol Bus** (tel. 505/2222-4420, www.busesdelsol.com), **Central Line** (tel. 505/2254-5431), and **Transnica** (tel. 505/2270-3133, nuevo.transnica.com).

Nicaragua's sole domestic air carrier, La Costeña, has a small fleet of planes to get you to remote corners of the country.

Getting Around

BY AIR

La Costeña (tel. 505/2263-2142, 505/2263-2143, or 505/2263-2144, reservacion@lacostena.com.ni, www.lacostena.com.ni) is Nicaragua's sole domestic airline, whose humble fleet of small planes fly between Managua and the Atlantic coast, Mining Triangle, Puerto Cabezas, Waspám, Bluefields, Corn Island, and San Carlos. Seats are limited on the 12-passenger twin-prop Cessna Grand Caravans (they have one 40-passenger Short 360 aircraft as well), and cost about $80 one-way, $120–160 round-trip. It is almost imperative that you reserve your flight before arriving in Nicaragua; this has been difficult in the past, but La Costeña's new online booking system will help matters.

BY BUS

Nicaragua intercity bus system is made up primarily of retired American yellow school buses, each one lovingly customized with stickers and plastic streamers. Modern, air conditioned coaches are increasingly joining the line-up for popular express routes. Bus coverage is excellent, though the ride is bumpy and often slow. Each major population center has one or two bus hubs, with regular and express service to nearby cities and to Managua, plus rural routes to the surrounding communities. If you've got the time in your travels, riding the Nicaraguan bus network will provide endless memories and probably make you a couple of friends, as there's little else to do on the ride but chat.

Local buses are called *ordinarios* or *ruteados*

and they stop for anyone standing by the roadside and flapping their hand. *Expresos* are more expensive and make fewer stops; they are also often better-quality vehicles as well, and are well worth the extra 25 percent you will pay for a ticket. In addition, *expresos* usually work on a reserved/numbered seat basis. Before you settle into town it's worth spending a couple more minutes at the bus station to make your onward reservations, if possible.

To points west and south from Managua, there is an especially large number of express microbuses (minivans or *interlocales*) that leave every 20 minutes—or whenever they fill up.

On the *ruteados,* you'll board the bus, find a seat, and then wait for the *ayudante* (driver's helper) to come around and collect your *pasaje* (fare). Ask a fellow traveler how much the ride should cost just to be sure, though our experience is that the *ayudantes* are typically honest. The *ayudante* will write the amount owed to you on your ticket if he doesn't have exact change, returning later in the trip to pay you. Most buses have overhead racks inside where you can stow your bags. Less desirable, but common, is for the *ayudante* to insist you put your backpack on the roof or in some cargo space in the back of the bus. It is safer to keep your stuff on your lap or at least within sight, if possible.

Do not use the Managua bus system unless you are with a Nicaraguan; the routes are long and confusing and the money you save—a couple of dollars, usually—is not worth the dramatically increased risk of robbery. Even Nicaraguans lose their belongings at knifepoint on these crowded, dilapidated buses. In other Nicaraguan cities *urbanos* are usually much safer and have shorter routes.

BY TAXI

The old Russian Ladas that plied the city streets in the 1980s and '90s are fast giving way to newer Japanese and Korean imports. Taxis are a great way to get around and are well worth the extra money if you want to save time; in Managua, they're essential for security reasons.

In every city except Managua, urban taxis operate on a fixed zone rate, usually under $1 within the central city area. In the capital, however, it's a different story, and you are expected to bargain out a rate before sitting down. In all cases, avoid taxis where the driver is traveling with a friend, and pay attention to where you're going.

SHUTTLE SERVICES

This is a relatively new option in Nicaragua, a direct response to travelers in Granada and León who would rather not negotiate taxi fees or muck around with the chicken buses. You'll board a new minivan filled with other tourists willing to spend $15–20 to be whisked between the pueblos, beach towns, and ferry docks. Most offer airport service as well.

Start with **Nica Express** (tel. 505/2552-8461, info@nica-adventures.com, www.nica-adventures.com); they maintain a set schedule of departures throughout the country. **Paxeos** (tel. 505/2552-8291 or 505/8465-1090, www.paxeos.com) is another reliable shuttle service, based in Granada, specializing in personal airport pickups at any time of night (and they have an online booking service). **Adelante Express** (tel. 505/8850-6070, www.adelante-express.com) is based in San Juan del Sur and also offers full service shuttles and transport; 24-hour advance reservation required.

You can also check tour operators, especially **Vapues Tours** and **Tierra Tours,** who offer shuttles and airport transfers.

BY CAR
Renting a Car

While it seems convenient to zip out of the airport in a rented car, the hassle of driving and the risk of making sure the car doesn't get stolen or damaged are not to be underestimated. If you are traveling with a lot of luggage, children, or surfboards, it's a no-brainer, but be aware that if you have just a little bit more time, you

TOUR OPERATORS

Nicaragua's independent tour companies offer a variety of trips—from afternoon city tours to weeklong expeditions to the farthest reaches of the country, the logistics of which would be nearly impossible for the solo traveler. You can pay for exclusive personal guides and drivers, or visit Nicaragua as part of a group. Doing so decreases your independence, but provides added security and freedom from planning. In general, all-inclusive nine-day tours cost $1,000-2,000, but companies vary. Following are some of the most reliable outfitters.

- **Explore Nicaragua Tours** (U.S. tel. 800/800-1132, www.explorenicaragua. com) has 15 years of experience leading both individual and group tours in Nicaragua and staying at top properties.

- **Green Pathways** (www.greenpathways. com) is a León-based outfit with trips to far-flung locations with a focus is on environmentally conscious travel.

- **Global Exchange** (www.globalexchange. org) offers Reality Tours in Nicaragua. These educational trips explore various social-justice issues, including the fair-trade coffee economy, monitoring elections, and learning about labor rights in free trade zones.

- **Nicaragua Adventures** (tel. 505/2552-8461, info@nica-adventures. com, www.nica-adventures.com) is a full-service, Granada-based outfit with a wide range of services.

- **Oro Travel** (Calle Corral, tel. 505/2552-4568, www.orotravel.com) is another expert outfit based in Granada with excellent packages and experienced guides.

- **Roadmonkey Adventure Philanthropy** (www.roadmonkey.net) expeditions combine physically challenging adventures with sustainable, custom-designed volunteer projects that team members finish on site, working with Nicaraguan communities in need.

- **Solentiname Tours** (tel. 505/8421-5689 or 505/2270-9981, info@solentinametours.com, www. solentinametours.com) has offices in Managua and San Carlos, and specializes in bird-watching, nature tours, and the Río San Juan region.

- **Tierra Tours** (tel. 505/2311-0599, tierratour@gmail.com, http://tierratour. com) has offices in Granada and León, and has a long menu of volcano or history tours, countrywide all-inclusive packages, international bus tickets, and domestic flight booking.

- **Tours Nicaragua** (tel. 505/2265-3095, info@ toursnicaragua.com, www. ToursNicaragua.com) offers private, fully guided trips using the best hotels in each locale. Their expert guides include working biologists, national museum archaeologists, historians, etc.

- **¡Un Buen Viaje!** (U.S. tel. 612/386-0839, info@ToursToNicaragua.com, www. ToursToNicaragua.com) is a unique grassroots tour company started by former Peace Corps volunteer Jessica Schugel. "You'll meet people who live, work, and play in the places we visit. We'll visit their homes and communities. You'll learn about Nicaragua from the inside out, through the voices of its people, its complex history, and rich culture."

- **Vapues Tours** (tel. 505/2315-4999, info@vapues.com, www.vapues.com) has offices around the country and offers a huge range of reasonably priced trips, plus shuttle services between cities.

- **Wildland Adventures** (tel. 800/345-4453, www.wildland.com) has a number of both family-oriented and experiential trip offerings, with many knowledgeable Nica guides on their staff.

- **Witness for Peace** (www.witnessforpeace. org) is a grassroots organization based in Managua. Witness for Peace has maintained a permanent presence in this Central American country since 1983; they offer a huge range of delegations to "combine international travel and education with the struggle for peace, economic justice, and sustainable development."

can get around extremely easily in taxis, shuttles, and public buses.

That said, all the major car rental agencies have set up shop at the Managua airport, and you can also arrange a car through most hotels costing $50 or higher. Be sure to reserve in advance: **Alamo Rent A Car** (tel. 505/2233-3718, www.alamonicaragua.com), **Avis** (www.avis.com.ni), **Budget** (tel. 505/2255-9000, U.S. tel. 305/433-7708, www.budget.com.ni), **Hertz** (tel. 505/2233-1237, www.hertz.com.ni), **National** (tel. 505/2270-8492 or 505/2233-3718, www.nationalnicaragua.com), **Thrifty** (tel. 505/2233-2192, www.thrifty.com.ni); several other chains are listed at www.nicaraguarentalcars.com. In addition to the airport, Thrifty has an office at Plaza España, and National has an office adjacent to the Hotel Hilton Princess and in the Hotel Colonial Granada.

Plan on spending about $30 per day, $175 a week during the high season for the smallest four-seater "econobox," or $75 a day, $450 a week for a pickup truck, plus insurance costs and gasoline, which is well over $4 per gallon.

Vehicular Safety

The most dangerous thing you will do in Nicaragua, without a doubt, is travel on its highways. Outside the cities, roads are poorly lit, narrow, lacking shoulders, and are often full of axle-breaking potholes, unannounced speed bumps, fallen rocks, and countless other obstacles. Even in Managua, you can expect to find ox carts and abandoned vehicles in the lanes, and hungry dogs and grazing horses wandering the streets. Because there are no shoulders for taxis to use when boarding passengers, they stop in the right lane and let traffic swerve around them. There are also macho, testosterone-crazed bus drivers trying to pass everything they can on blind, uphill curves. The fact that beer and rum are sold at most gas stations should give you an idea of how many drivers are intoxicated, especially late at night.

When possible, avoid traveling during peak rush hours in the cities, and after dark anywhere. New highway projects since 2000 have improved the roads in many parts of the country, but many drivers take advantage of the improved straightaways to speed like bats out of hell. Take time before entering a city to plan your route, as you will not have the luxury of reading the map while you navigate traffic. That goes double for Managua, where choosing the wrong lane can be disastrous!

Traffic Accidents

So how's that Spanish coming along, amigo? Nicaragua's police force is poorly paid and not averse to a little pocket money (if you catch my drift). Foreign drivers without diplomatic plates are frequent targets for document checks, but if you commit a *mala maniobra* (moving violation, literally "bad move") in their presence, you'd better have your papers ready. (Here's a really bad move: calling your interlocutor *"compañero"* is likely to double the bribe.) Crooked cops will demand to confiscate your license and threaten to hold it hostage until you come in the following week to pay the fine—unless, of course, you'd rather take care of the issue right then, hint hint, wink wink.

If you are involved in a vehicular accident, *do not* move your vehicle from the scene of the crime until authorized by a police officer, even if it is blocking traffic. Lacking high-tech crime-scene equipment, Nicaraguan police will try to understand how the accident occurred based on what they see at the site. Drivers who move their vehicle at the scene of the accident (thus altering the crime scene) are legally liable for the incident. Any driver in Nicaragua that causes injuries to another person will be taken into immediate custody, regardless of insurance and circumstances, and remain there until the courts reach a decision—sometimes

© GRACE GONZALEZ

There are many hazards on the road in Nicaragua.

weeks later—or until the injured party signs a waiver releasing the driver of liability. To avoid a lengthy court proceeding and horrifying jail stay, it may be worth your while to plead guilty and pay a fine (which historically does not exceed $1,000, even in the case of a death). But call your embassy and get a lawyer immediately, nevertheless; this is what they do best.

MOTORCYCLES AND BICYCLES

If you intend to ride a motorcycle or bicycle in Nicaragua, be sure to bring a helmet, an item largely ignored by Nicaraguans, many of whom manage to fit a family of four on one bike. Good quality helmets are not easy to purchase in Nicaragua. If biking, keep your eyes on the road; the entrances to Matagalpa and Granada have unmarked speed bumps which serve as invisible bike-launchers-of-death.

Biking Central America is a breathtaking experience (not just because of the heat!), but puts you at risk in a couple of new ways. Dozens of thru-bikers have reported that Nicaragua is no better nor worse than the rest of Central America. Small shoulders at roadside are par for the course, as is the occasional bottle-throwing idiot careening by in a fast car. Travelers have reported some harassment and even robbery of bikers in the stretch between San Juan del Sur and the Costa Rican border.

BOATS

In several regions of Nicaragua—notably Solentiname, Río San Juan, Río Coco, and the entire Atlantic coast—a boat will be your only means of transportation. Here, rising gasoline prices determine the fare, which will be more expensive than you expect. Locals get around in public water taxis called *colectivos* that help cut costs. Any water-bordering community will likely have small boats the owners use for fishing or transport. Ask for a *canoa, panga,* or *botecita,* and see what shows up. Dugout canoes are common throughout the country, and you can ask to rent one along the Río San Juan and other areas. For recreation, there are a handful of sailboats that can take you out in San Juan del Sur, and some boat-based tour companies out of Granada and León. **Ibis Exchange** (www.ibiskayaking.com) offers paddle trips in the Estero Padre Ramos in expedition ocean kayaks.

Visas and Officialdom

PASSPORT AND VISA REQUIREMENTS

Every traveler to Nicaragua must have a passport valid for at least six months following the date of entry. A visa is required only for citizens of the following countries: Afghanistan, Albania, Angola, Bangladesh, Bosnia and Herzegovina, Cameroon, Colombia, Cuba, Dominican Republic, Ecuador, Egypt, Ghana, Haiti, India, Iran, Iraq, Jordan, Kenya, Lebanon, Libya, Mozambique, Nepal, Nigeria, Pakistan, People's Republic of China, People's Republic of Korea, Peru, Romania, Somalia, Sri Lanka, Sudan, Syria, Ukraine, Vietnam, and Yemen. Everyone else is automatically given a tourist visa at the airport or land border, good for three months, in the form of a $10 tourist card. Don't lose the card, as you may need to return it when you leave the country. Technically, you must have an onward/return ticket, and evidence of sufficient funds; in practice, this is never checked.

Renewing a visa has gotten easier in the new tourist-friendly Nicaragua. In Managua at the Metrocentro shopping mall, there's an Immigration branch office (no phone, 10 A.M.–6 P.M. Mon.–Fri., 10 A.M.–1 P.M. Sat.–Sun.) that will process your request for an extension. You'll pay $0.25 for the form, and must present photocopies of your passport's information page as well as the page with your visa. A 30-day tourist visa extension is $22, and if you've overstayed your current visa you will pay an additional $2 for each day over the limit. Many travelers in San Juan del Sur prefer to just take a bus over the Costa Rican border, and return the same day on a fresh, new tourist visa. Furthermore, Nicaragua entered into the CA-4 Border Control Agreement permitting travelers to travel among Nicaragua, Guatemala, Honduras, and El Salvador without getting additional visas: Your initial entry visa is valid for the whole region for up to 90 days and can be extended once with little hassle.

Anything more serious than a basic tourist visa extension requires a trip to the main **Office of Immigration** (Dirección General de Migración y Extranjería, 1.5 blocks north of the *semáforos* Tenderí, tel. 505/2244-0741, 505/2244-1320, or 505/2244-3960, 8:30 A.M.–noon and 2–4:30 P.M. Mon.–Fri.); show up at least four days before it expires with your passport, current visa, and cash.

CUSTOMS

Tourists are invariably ignored by customs officials, who have their eyes peeled for wealthy Nicas returning from shopping binges in Miami. Should they go through your luggage, you can expect to be taxed for carrying items you obviously don't intend to use yourself, including electronics, jewelry, and perfume. To save trouble for yourself, avoid carrying more of anything valuable (such as a laptop) than a traveler would typically need. Surfers, that goes for your boards, too: If it looks like you're importing sales stock, you will be stopped and hassled.

FOREIGN EMBASSIES AND CONSULATES IN NICARAGUA

All diplomatic missions in Nicaragua are located in Managua, mostly along Carretera

NICARAGUAN CONSULATES AND EMBASSIES

IN THE UNITED STATES

Washington, D.C. (Embassy and Consulate)
1627 New Hampshire Ave. NW
Washington, DC 20009
U.S. tel. 202/939-6531 or 202/939-6532
fax 202/939-6574

Houston, TX
8989 Westheimer Rd., Suite 103
Houston, TX 77063
U.S. tel. 713/789-2762 or 276/789-2781

Los Angeles, CA
3550 Wilshire Blvd., Ste. 200
Los Angeles, CA 90010
U.S. tel. 213/252-1171 or 213/252-1174
fax 213/252-1177

Miami, FL
8532 SW 8th St., Suite 270
Miami, FL 33144
U.S. tel. 305/265-1415
fax 305/265-1780

New York, NY
820 2nd Ave., 8th Floor, Suite 802
New York, NY 10017
U.S. tel. 212/986-6562
fax 212/983-2646

San Francisco, CA
870 Market, Suite 1050
San Francisco, CA 94102
U.S. tel. 415/765-6821, 415/765-6823, or
415/765-6825

fax 415/765-6826

IN CENTRAL AMERICA

Costa Rica
Avenida Central No. 2440, Barrio La California
San José, Costa Rica
tel. 506/222-2373
fax 506/221-5481

El Salvador
71 Avenida Norte y Primera Calle Poniente No. 164
Colonia Escalon, San Salvador
tel. 503/298-6549
fax 506/223-7201

Guatemala
10 Avenida, 14-72, Zona 10
Guatemala
tel. 502/268-0785
fax 502/337-4264

Honduras
Colonia Tepeyac, Bloque M-1, No. 1130
Tegucigalpa, Honduras
tel. 504/232-7224
fax 504/239-5225

Panama
Intersección de Avenida Federico Boyd y Calle 50
Apartado 772, Zona 1
Corregimiento Bella Vista
Ciudad de Panamá, Panamá
tel. 507/223-0981
fax 507/211-2080

Masaya and Carretera Sur. The city of Chinandega hosts consulates from El Salvador, Honduras, and Costa Rica, and the city of Rivas has a consulate from Costa Rica.

United States and Canada

Americans living or traveling in Nicaragua can register with the **U.S. Embassy** in Nicaragua (Km 5.5, Carretera Sur, Managua, tel. 505/2252-7100, nicaragua.usembassy.gov) at the main international travel page of the U.S. State Department (www.travel.state.gov). Registering is not a legal requirement but is encouraged by the embassy so that they can send you updated travel and security advisories regarding Nicaragua. These advisories—and the warden messages on the embassy website—are invariably on the conservative side, as far as risk assessment. Other contacts: Information Resource Center (tel. 505/2252-7237) or

American Citizens Services (ACS.Managua@ state.gov).

The **Canadian Embassy** in Managua is actually an outpost of their main embassy in San José, Costa Rica. The address in the Bolonia neighborhood is on Calle El Nogal, one block east from the Casa Nazareth (tel. 505/2268-0433 or 505/2268-3323, fax 505/2268-0437, mngua@ international.gc.ca). For emergencies involving Canadian citizens, call the emergency consular service in Ottawa collect at 613/996-6885.

Central America

- **Costa Rica:** half a block east of Estatua Montoya along Calle 27 de Mayo, tel. 505/2268-7460. There is also a consulate in Rivas and Chinandega.
- **Cuba:** Carretera Masaya from the third entrance to Las Colinas, two blocks east, 75 meters to the south, tel. 505/2276-2285
- **El Salvador:** Las Colinas, Ave. El Campo Pasaje Los Cerros no. 142, tel. 505/2276-0160
- **Guatemala:** Carretera Masaya Km 11, tel. 505/2279-9834
- **Honduras:** Carretera Masaya Km 12, 100 meters toward Cainsa, tel. 505/2279-8231
- **Panamá:** third entrance to Las Colinas, then two blocks east and 75 meters south, tel. 505/2276-0212

Europe and Asia

- **Austria:** from the Rotonda El Güegüense, one block north, tel. 505/2266-0171 or 505/2268-3756
- **Belgium:** Consulado de Bélica, Reparto El Carmen across from the Esso station, Calle 27 de Mayo, tel. 505/2228-2068
- **China:** Planes de Altamira, from the Copa office 200 meters south across from the tennis courts, tel. 505/2267-4024
- **Denmark:** Plaza España one block west, two blocks north, half a block west, tel. 505/2268-0253

- **Finland:** Bolonia, one block north, 1.5 blocks west of the Hospital Militar, tel. 505/2266-3415
- **France:** Reparto El Carmen, 1.5 blocks west of the church, tel. 505/2222-6210
- **Germany:** 1.5 blocks north of the Rotonda El Güegüense, tel. 505/2266-3917
- **Great Britain:** Los Robles, from the old Sandy's on Carretera Masaya, one block south, a half-block west, tel. 505/2278-0014 or 2278-0887
- **Italy:** one block north and half a block west of the Rotonda El Güegüense, tel. 505/2266-6486
- **Japan:** Bolonia, from the Rotonda El Güegüense one block west, one block north, tel. 505/2266-1773
- **The Netherlands (Holland):** Bolonia canal 2, half a block north, one block west, tel. 505/2266-4392
- **Norway:** one block west of Plaza España, tel. 505/2266-4199
- **Russia:** Las Colinas, Calle Vista Alegre No. 214, tel. 505/2276-0131
- **Spain:** Las Colinas, Avenida Central No. 13, tel. 505/2276-0968
- **Sweden:** one block west, two blocks north, and half a block west of the Rotonda Plaza España, tel. 505/2266-8097
- **Switzerland:** Consulado de Suiza, one block west of the Las Palmas Clinic, tel. 505/2266-5719

OFFICIAL HOLIDAYS

Expect all public offices to be closed on the following days. Also remember that Nicaraguan holidays are subject to decree, shutting the banks down without warning to suit some politician's inclination.

- January 1: New Year's Day
- Late March/early April: Semana Santa, including Holy Thursday, Good Friday, and Easter
- May 1: Labor Day
- May 30: Mother's Day
- July 19: National Liberation Day
- August 1: Fiesta Day
- September 14: Battle of San Jacinto

- September 15: Independence Day
- November 2: Día de los Muertes (All Souls' Day)
- December 8: La Purísima (Immaculate Conception)
- December 25: Christmas Day

Like the rest of Latin America, every single town and city has its own patron saint whom the residents honor each year with a prolonged party that lasts 1–3 weeks. These *fiestas patronales* combine holy religious fervor with the consumption of alcohol in biblical proportions. Most celebrations include Virgin and Saint parades, special masses, fireworks, cockfighting, rodeos, concerts, gambling, dances, and show-horse parades (hípicos). Many towns have additional celebrations of specific events in their history.

Semana Santa (or Holy Week) is the biggest celebration of the year, occurring during the week leading up to Easter Sunday. The weeklong vacation sends most city folk to the beach for sun and debauchery (and usually a couple of drownings, too) while shops close their doors and everyone takes a breather. In popular beach areas like San Juan del Sur, expect hiked prices and few vacancies. In other areas, you may also encounter altered bus schedules and other travel annoyances.

Conduct and Customs

Nicaraguans are generally open, talkative, and hospitable. In most areas of the country, Nicaraguans are accustomed to seeing foreigners, but they are still curious—and not very discreet about it. Expect blunt questions right off the bat about your age, marital status, and your opinions about Nicaragua. The reaction is nearly always one of curiosity, hospitality, and friendliness.

Despite their directness, Nicaraguans are prone to circuitous, indirect behavior associated with the cultural concept of "saving face." When asked something they don't know, people often invent an answer so that neither party is embarrassed (this is especially true about directions and distances; as Allan Weisbecker observed, "No one, *no one,* south of the Mexican border has any idea how long it takes to go from anywhere to anywhere else"). Business contracts are rife with implied obligations neither party wants to discuss openly, even simple payment details and the work to be done.

Many Nicaraguan city dwellers are, in fact, recently immigrated *campesinos,* and they often bring their country ways—and livestock—with them to the city.

Anti-Americanism, in my experience, is rare, Nicaraguans being particularly adept at distinguishing between a nation's people and its government's policy. In addition, because most Nicaraguan families adore cable TV and have at least one relative sending money back from Miami, Houston, or Los Angeles, many are quite fond of the United States and maintain the dream of traveling there one day. The word "gringo" is used more often as a descriptive, casual term for anyone who comes from north of the Mexican border. In rare cases, it is meant as an insult (in which case, it will likely be preceded by *"pinche"*). Likewise for *chele, chela,* and their diminutives, *chelito* and *chelita,* all of which simply mean pale or light-skinned, and are in no way disrespectful. In fact, many cries of, *"¡Oye, chele!"* ("Hey, whitey!") are used as much for light-skinned Nicaraguans as for foreigners.

FAMILY

The Nicaraguan family is the most basic and strongest support structure of society, and, like in most developing world nations, it is usually large—rural women have an average of 4–6 children, and families of a dozen or more aren't uncommon. Urban couples, particularly in Managua, typically have

A GUIDE TO NICARAGUA'S FIESTAS

Every Nicaraguan city has its own patron saint, with annual *fiestas patronales* that revolve around the local saint's birthday. The most elaborate festivals involve bands, parades, and food throughout the night. Semana Santa (Easter Week) is a particularly big deal—everyone parties like rock stars and prices skyrocket across the board. In addition, city-specific festivals happen throughout the year with great amounts of local pride and revelry. Participating in these events can be a memorable experience.

JANUARY

1: New Year's Day
18: Fiestas Patronales, El Sauce
Third Sunday: Señor de Esquipulas, El Sauce (León)
Third weekend: Viva León Festival, León; San Sebastían, Acoyapa (Chontales), Diriamba, Carazo (San Sebastián)
Last weekend: La Virgen de Candelaria, La Trinidad (Estelí)

FEBRUARY

Second weekend: Music and Youth Festival, Managua
mid-Feb.: International poetry festival, Granada

MARCH

Third weekend: Folklore, Gastronomy, and Handicraft Festival, Granada

APRIL

Semana Santa (Holy Week), the week that precedes Easter Sunday
First week: Religious Ash Paintings in León
19-21: Fiestas Patronales, San Jorge (Rivas)

MAY

1: Labor Day; Fiestas Patronales, Jinotega
15: San Isidro Labrador, Condega (Estelí)
30: Mother's Day
Third weekend: Palo de Mayo Festival, Bluefields

JUNE

16: Virgen del Carmen, San Juan del Sur (Rivas)
24: St. John the Baptist, San Juan de Oriente (Carazo), San Juan del Sur (Rivas), San Juan de Jinotega (Jinotega)
29: St. Peter the Apostle, Diriá (Masaya)
Last Friday: El Repliegue Sandinista (Managua)

JULY

Second Saturday: Carnaval, Somoto
15-25: Fiestas Patronales, Somoto
19: National Liberation Day
25: Santiago, Boaco, Jinotepe (Carazo)
26: St. Ana, Nandaime (Granada), Chinandega Ometepe

AUGUST

1-10: Santo Domingo (Noches Agostinas), Managua
10: St. Lorenzo, Somotillo (Chinandega)
14: Gritería Chiquita, León
14-15: Fiestas Patronales, Ocotal
15: The Assumption of Mary, Granada; The Assumption and Fiesta del Hijo Ausente, Juigalpa
Third weekend: Mariachis and Mazurcas Festival, Estelí

SEPTEMBER

10: San Nicolás de Tolentino, La Paz Centro (León)
14: The Battle of San Jacinto
14-15: Fishing Fair, San Carlos (Río San Juan)
15: Independence Day; Patron Saint Festival of Villa Nueva, Chinandega
20: San Jerónimo, Masaya
24: La Merced, León, and Matagalpa
Fourth weekend: Polkas, Mazurcas, and Jamaquellos, Matagalpa; Festival of Corn, Jalapa

OCTOBER

12: San Diego (Estelí)
Second weekend: Norteño Music Festival in Jinotega
24: San Rafael Arcángel, Pueblo Nuevo
Penultimate Sunday: Fiesta de los Agüisotes, Masaya
Last Sunday: Toro Venado, Masaya

NOVEMBER

2: All Souls' Day
3-5: Equestrian Rally in Ometepe
4: San Carlos Borromeo, San Carlos (Río San Juan)
12-18: San Diego de Alcalá, Altagracia (Ometepe)
Fourth Sunday: Folkloric Festival, Masaya

DECEMBER

First Sunday: Procesión de San Jerónimo, Masaya
6: Lavado de La Plata, Virgen del Trono, El Viejo (Chinandega)
7: Purísimas (Immaculate Conception Celebrations) in Managua, Granada, Masaya, and León
18-25: La Navidad (Christmas) throughout Nicaragua.

no more than three or four children. In addition, extended families-cousins, in-laws, aunts, and un-cles—are all kept in close contact and relied upon during hard times (which, for many, is their whole lives). Families live close together, often in small quarters, and the North American and European concepts of independence and solitude are not well understood.

CLOTHING AND APPEARANCE

Nicaraguans place a great deal of importance on cleanliness. Even the poorest *campesino* with threadbare and patched clothing takes great care to tuck his shirt in and keep his clothes clean and wrinkle-free. Managuans are just as conscientious about looking good and smell-ing clean. Nicaraguans only wear shorts for playing sports or lounging around the house. Nicaraguan women dress the spectrum from long, conservative dresses to bright, tight, and revealing outfits.

Unshaven *internationalistas* wearing cargo shorts, ripped T-shirts, and flip-flops stand out like sore, malodorous thumbs, even with-out their trademark bulky backpacks. If you plan on being taken seriously in any kind of day-to-day business activities, a little effort in your wardrobe and hygiene will go a long way... and will help do away with the question, "Is it true that people in your country don't bathe because it's too cold?" If, however, you prefer to remain true to your filth, seek out the bohe-mian population of tattooed Managuans who take well to carefully unkempt foreigners with Che T-shirts and creative facial hair.

CONCEPT OF TIME

Hay más tiempo que vida. (There is more time than life.) So why hurry? The day-to-day ap-proach to living life in Nicaragua may come from the necessity of survival, or it may just be an effect of the hot sun. Probably both. Nicaraguan life, in general, goes according to *La Hora Nica* (Nica Time), which means a meeting scheduled in Managua for 2:30 P.M. might not start until 3 P.M., or an hour later in the countryside. Foreign travelers accus-tomed to La Hora Gringa, in which every-thing starts and stops exactly when planned, will spend their days in Nicaragua endlessly frustrated (and consistently early for meet-ings). Appointments and meetings are loose, and excuses are easy to come by and univer-sally accepted. Gradually, as you experience Nicaragua, this concept of time will win you over; just be careful when you go home.

ALCOHOL
Rum

It goes largely undisputed that Nicaragua makes the best rum in all of Central America. Flor de Caña is the highest caliber, of which the caramel-colored, 7-year Gran Reserva is only surpassed by the 12-year Centenario (which is twice as expensive). Flor de Caña produces a half-dozen varieties of rum, which increase in price and quality as they age. A *media* (half liter) of seven-year, bucket of ice, bottle of Coke, and plate of limes (called a *servicio completo*) will set you back only $5 or so. Rum on the rocks with a squirt of Coca-Cola and a spurt of lime is called a Nica Libre. A national competition in search of Nicaragua's new "official drink" awarded the prize to a pediatrician from Granada, the creator of the Macuá. The drink is a refresh-ing combination of one part guava juice, one part white rum, a half part lemon juice, and some sugar and ice, and was chosen not only for its suitability to Nicaragua's agriculture but its suitability for the tropical climate.

Reach for a clear plastic bottle of Caballito or Ron Plata, and take a giant step down in price, quality, and class. Enormously popular in the *campo,* "Rrrrron Plata!" is the proud spon-sor of most baseball games—and not a few bar brawls. Bottles are $1 or less.

But wait—you can get drunk for even less! Most street corners and town parks are the

© JOSHUA BERMAN

Toña is one of the country's national beers.

backdrop for many a grimace-inducing shot of Tayacán, or its homemade, corn-mash equivalent, often served in clear plastic baggies. West Virginians call this stuff "that good 'ole mountain dew"; Nicaraguans call it *la cususa, el guaro,* or *la lija,* brought down from the hills by the moonshine man on his mule. *La cususa* is gasoline-clear, potent in smell (including when you sweat it out the next day), and will bore a hole through your liver quicker than a 9-millimeter. It's sold by the gallon for about $4, often in a stained, sloshing, plastic container that used to contain some automobile product, and then resold in baggie-size portions that look like they should have a goldfish swimming in them.

Beer

The national beers—Victoria and Toña—are both light-tasting pilsners and, well, you can't really say anything bad about an ice-cold beer in the tropics. Expect to pay anywhere from $0.80 to $2 a beer, depending on your environs. Recent additions to the beer selection are Premium, Bufalo, and Brahva, largely indistinguishable, and the Victoria Frost, an ice-filtered beverage with slightly higher alcohol content. Brahva is the only alcoholic beverage whose production or distribution isn't controlled by the Pellas family, which produces every other beverage mentioned in this book. Together, Victoria, Toña, and Flor de Caña are known affectionately as "Vickie, Toni, and Flo."

Alcoholism

Alcohol abuse is rampant in Nicaragua and increasingly acknowledged as a problem. Most towns have an Alcoholics Anonymous chapter, and many churches forbid their members to drink. Nevertheless, most otherwise religious holidays (including Sundays)—in addition to all nonreligious events—serve as excuses to get falling-down drunk. Just about all men drink and are firm believers in the expression *"una es ninguna"* ("one is none"). Their benders often

Individual homes often host makeshift altars.

start before breakfast and end when the liquor does. In small towns, women are socially discouraged from drinking, though they sometimes do so in the privacy of their own homes or with close friends. Bigger towns and cities, of course, are more modern in this regard.

Should you decide to partake in this part of the culture and find yourself drunk *(borracho, bolo, picado, hasta el culo)*, be sure you have a decent understanding of your environment and feel good about your company. Remember that most travelers' disaster stories begin with, "Man, I was so wasted...." Always take it slow when drinking in a new place, and remember that your hydration level has an enormous impact on how drunk you get.

And oh, by the way, rum does *not* make you a better dancer, but it may improve your Spanish.

RELIGION

Officially, the Republic of Nicaragua endorses no religion. In practice, the overwhelming majority of Nicaraguans call themselves Catholic, with over a hundred evangelical Protestant sects comprising about 9–15 percent and increasing annually. Beginning in the early 1970s and continuing through the revolution, Nicaragua created its own version of liberation theology, a school of Christianity and bourgeois thought that equated Jesus's teachings with Marxism. The degree to which biblical parables were equated to the Marxist struggle varied, and the most radical versions placed Sandino as Jesus or Moses, Somoza as the Pharaoh, and the Nicaraguan masses as the Israelites searching for their promised land through revolutionary struggle.

A tiny percentage of Nicaraguans are descendents of one of the several Jewish families that found refuge here during World War II. Some of them still identify themselves as Jewish, but there is no real practicing community. The only synagogue was dismantled and sold in 1980. A Torah did not return to Nicaragua until 2008. Most Nicaraguans, especially in the countryside, have little concept of Judaism as a modern religion, relating the word *judío* only to the ancient race of *hebreos* they read about in the Old Testament. In 2008, the construction of a mosque in Managua raised eyebrows in the diplomatic community, who feared increasing Iranian influence. It was instead the work of the growing Lebanese community, present in Nicaragua for a century but only now numerous enough to consider building their own place of worship.

LANGUAGE

Spanish is, according to the Nicaraguan constitution, the official language of the republic, though indigenous languages are respected and even used officially in certain areas of the Atlantic coast. Ninety-six percent of

OLD WIVES' TALES: NICARAGUAN *CREENCIAS*

Like any society with a tradition of rural folk culture, Nicaraguans have hundreds of unique beliefs, or *creencias*, which explain mysteries, offer advice, and dictate practices that prevent or cure common health ailments. In general, most behaviors are associated with causing harm to oneself, and Nicaraguan mothers can be heard admonishing their children, *"¡Te va a hacer daño!"* ("It will cause you harm!").

Nicaraguans are sensitive to subtle differences in temperature, and many of the *creencias* involve avoiding hot things when you are cold, or vice versa. Conventional wisdom dictates that intense bodily harm can come from drinking a cold beverage after eating something hot, bathing in the evening after a hot day in the sun (or bathing with a fever), and ironing with wet hair. If you come in from the fields on a hot day and you're sweaty, drinking a cold glass of fruit juice or water can make you sick, especially your kidneys. Better is a cup of hot coffee. If you want to walk outside at night after drinking coffee, however, you should protect yourself by draping a cloth over the top of your head, being careful to cover the ears. Dietary rules tie into the same theme and other worries as well: no fish, eggs, or beans while menstruating, no citrus when sick, and no fish soup when *agitado* (worked up or sweaty).

The belief in the *mal de ojo* (evil eye) is not unique to Nicaragua, although the local version states that a drunkard who looks directly into an infant's eye can kill the child or make it evil. A person well versed in the art of applying the evil eye can cause birth defects in newborn babies, stroke, paralysis among the living, and other woes like the loss of a job or bad luck. You'll frequently see children wearing a red bracelet with two small gray beads–this is to protect the child from *mal de ojo*. Similarly, if a sweaty man looks at a baby, the only cure is to wrap the baby up in the man's sweaty clothes. To guard against the risk, many babies are kept well covered when out of the house. Allowing dew to fall on a baby's brow will stunt its growth (look for women holding umbrellas over their children on a clear night), and letting a baby look in a mirror will cause his or her eyes to cross permanently.

If you have trouble with bats, you can keep them away by hanging a red cloth from the rafters. To keep flies off your food, suspend a bag of water over the table. To avoid family fights, don't cook with a knife in the pan.

Some Nica *creencias* coincide with North American and European practices even if the reasoning is different. For example, Nicaraguans recommend you don't walk around barefoot, but not because you run the risk of contracting ringworm; rather, walking barefoot, they claim, is an unhealthy temperature combination (hot feet on cold floor). Foreigners tempted to make fun of the "crazy" Nicaraguan beliefs will do well to remember our own societies' *creencias*. Whether scientifically grounded or not, Nicaraguan beliefs are popular because they have been passed from generation to generation, and should be given proper regard.

Nicaraguans speak Spanish as their first language, 3 percent speak indigenous languages (Miskito, Mayangna, and Rama), and 1 percent speak languages of African origin (Criollo and Garífuna). To hear pure Miskito, travel north from Bluefields or visit Puerto Cabezas or any village along the Río Coco; in some of these villages, Spanish is completely unknown.

Nicaraguan Spanish is probably unlike any Spanish you've ever come across. The chameleonlike ability of the Spanish language to adapt to new areas of the world is strong in Nicaragua, where it is spoken rapidly and liquidly, the words flowing smoothly together and eating each other's tails. Central Americans enjoy making fun of how their Latin neighbors talk, and the Honduran nickname for Nicaraguans, *mucos* (bulls whose horns have been chopped off), is a reference to the Nicaraguans' habit of chopping the "s" off the ends of spoken words. Backcountry *campesino* Nicaraguan Spanish is inevitably less intelligible to the untrained

A FEW *NICARAGUANISMOS*

The textbook Spanish you learned back home will be understood without trouble, but Nicaraguans take pride in the fact that their version of the old-country Castilian is decidedly unique. When you try to look up some of the new words you're hearing and realize they're not in the dictionary, you'll see what we mean.

Blame it on *campesino* creativity and the Nicas' propensity for inventing words they need; blame the centuries of educational starvation, during which language evolved on its own; blame the linguistic mishmash of pre-Columbian Central America and the words left behind. Or just get out your pencil and paper and try to write down some of the unique vocabulary and phrases you hear, because you won't hear it anywhere else. Nicaraguan Spanish uses some old, proper Spanish no longer used in the Old World, and has assimilated pre-Columbian words from Nahuatl and Chorotega tongues as well (especially local plant and animal names). Still other words are pure onomatopoeia. Those interested in pursuing the topic should seek out Joaquim Rabella and Chantal Pallais's *Vocabulario Popular Nicaragüense*, available in some bookstores in Managua. Here's an incomplete sampling (with the Castilian in parentheses when possible).

ia la puchica!: Wow!
arrecho: extremely angry *(enfurecido)*
bochinche: a fistfight among several people
boludo: lazy, unmotivated *(haragán)*
bullaranga: loud noises, ruckus *(tumulto, alboroto)*
ichocho!: Holy cow! Dude!

curutaca: diarrhea *(diarrea)*
cususa: country moonshine *(aguardiente)*
chapa: earring *(arete)*
chigüin: little kid *(bebé)*
chinela: sandal *(sandalia)*
chingaste: the granular residue of a drink like coffee *(poso, resíduo)*
chunche: any small, nameless object *(cosita)*
chusmón: mediocre
dalepué: OK, I agree, let's do that.
¿ideay? (eedee-EYE?): What was that all about? What do you mean?
guaro: general term for booze or alcoholic beverages
hamaquear: to rock something rhythmically *(mecer rítmicamente)*
hijueputa: extremely common, from the vulgarity *hijo de puta* (son of a whore), pronounced hway-POO-tah and used liberally.
moclín: perverted old man
ñaña: excrement *(excremento)*
panzona: big-bellied, implies pregnant *(embarazada)*
pinche: cheap *(tacaño)*
pipilacha: small airplane *(avioneta)*
* iqué barbaridad!:* What a barbarity! How rude! What a shame!
salvaje: awesome; literally, "savage;" fun response to *"¿Como estás?"*
isí hombre!: Yeah man!
timba: big belly *(barriga)*
tranquilo como camilo: Chillin' like Dylan; fun response to *"¿Como estás?"*
va pué: OK then; see you; I agree; or whatever (short for *va pués*)

ear than its urban counterpart, but it is also distinctly more melodic, with a cadence and rhythm distinct to the countryside and celebrated in many of Carlos Mejía Godoy's songs.

And then, of course, there are the vulgarities. Ernest Hemingway wrote, "There is no language so filthy as Spanish. There are words for all the vile words in English and there are other words and expressions that are used only in countries where blasphemy keeps pace with the austerity of religion."

In Nicaragua, even a simple fruit or vegetable name can cause a room to break out in wild laughter if said in the right tone and context (and if accompanied by the appropriate hand gesture). After you've learned a few dirty words, be careful—the degree to which most *vulgaridades* are considered offensive varies depending on the gender of your company, their age, your relationship with them, and a variety of other factors. Cussing can be a fun, complex, and subtle game if you have the patience to learn—*y los huevos?*

Body Language

Limber up your wrist and stretch out those lips. You'll need 'em both if you want to communicate like a true native. Watch people interact on the buses, in the markets, and on the streets, and see if you can spot any of the following gestures in action—then try some out yourself.

Probably the single most practical gesture is a rapid side-to-side wagging of the index finger. It means "no," and increases in strength as you increase the intensity of the wagging and the amount of hand and arm you use in the motion. In some cases, a verbal "no" in the absence of the **Finger Wag** is disregarded as not serious enough. Use this one liberally with pushy vendors, beggars, and would-be Romeos.

To pull off the **Nicaraguan Wrist Snap,** simply join the tips of your thumb and middle finger and let your index finger dangle loosely. Then with a series of rapid wrist flicks, repeatedly let your index finger slap against the middle one, exactly as you would do with a round tin of tobacco dip. The resulting snapping noise serves to either emphasize whatever it is you're saying, refer to how hard you've been working, or, when combined with a nod and a smile, infer something like, "Damn, that's good!"

You can ask, "What?" (or "What do you want?") with a quick **Cheek Scrunch,** occasionally performed with a subtle upward chin tilt. Use the **Lip Point** rather than your finger to indicate something by puckering up as if for a kiss and aiming where you want. Or if you are listening to a friend's dumb story, point to the speaker with your lips while looking at everyone else to imply, "This guy's crazy or drunk."

The gesture North Americans would normally use to shoo something away—the outstretched, waving, down-turned hand—means just the opposite in Nicaragua, where the **Downward Wave** (occasionally combined with the whole arm for emphasis) means "Come here." This one is a favorite with drunks in the park who love to talk at foreigners for as long as they are tolerated. The North American

"come here," i.e., the upturned and beckoning index finger, is a vulgar, possibly offensive gesture. Speaking of vulgar, a closed fist atop a rigid forearm indicates the male sex organ, and an upturned, slightly cupped hand with the fingertips pressed together into a point is its female counterpart. Here's one more for the road: Make a fist, lock your elbow into the side of your body, and move your hand up and down; combined with a dramatic grimace, the **Plunger Pump** tells the whole world you have diarrhea.

ETIQUETTE AND TERMS OF ADDRESS

Latin America is not homogenous across state borders when it comes to addressing each other: While Costa Ricans tend to gravitate toward the formal *usted* form of address among themselves, Nicaraguans prefer the friendly *vos* (second person) form with each other, although *tú* is widely understood. For travelers, it's best to use *usted* until you've really gotten to know someone (or mastered the tricky *vos* form), particularly after a night out or a long drinking session (you'll be surprised how quickly alcohol lubricates friendships at this latitude).

The term *don* for men and *doña* for women is a colonial term of respect usually related to aristocracy or landownership, but in Nicaragua it's far more commonly used than elsewhere in Latin America, and indicates a higher level of respect or affection, particularly for the elderly, the important, or the wealthy. Practitioners of certain careers sometimes drop their names entirely and go by their profession. That is, it's not uncommon to be presented to someone everyone calls simply *"la doctora," "el ingeniero,"* or *"la abogada."* Just go with it and smile.

It's customary to kiss women on the cheek when greeting, but women will provide the signal whether that's appropriate or not by turning their cheek toward you. Men will offer you their hands for a stiff handshake. When

POPULAR NICARAGUAN SAYINGS

Nicaraguans in general, and *campesinos* in particular, love to speak using *refranes* (sayings or refrains). They're an easy way to make a point, and both the way they are phrased and the points they make say much about the country folks' way of thinking. If you learn a refrain or two and throw one out once in a while in casual conversation, you will be sure to earn broad smiles.

Hay más tiempo que vida. There is more time than life. (There's no need to rush things.)

Él que a buen árbol se arrima, buena sombra le cobija. He who gets close to a good tree will be covered by good shade. (He who seeks protection will find it.)

Perro que ladra no muerde. Dogs who bark don't bite.

No hay peor sordo que él que no quiere escuchar. There's no deaf person worse than he who doesn't want to hear.

A cada chancho le llega su sábado. Every pig gets his Saturday. (Everyone eventually gets what he deserves.)

Indio comido, puesto al camino. An Indian who has eaten gets up immediately from the table. (A way of pointing out someone ready to leave as soon as he/she gets what he/she wants.)

Quien da pan a un perro ajeno, pierde el pan y pierde el perro. If you give bread to someone else's dog, you'll lose the bread and lose the dog.

Él que madruga come pechuga, él que tarda, come albarda. He who gets up early eats the best piece of chicken, he who gets up late eats the saddle.

Él que no llora no mama. He who does not cry does not suckle. (If you don't complain, you'll never get any attention.)

Él que anda con lobos, aullar aprende. He who walks with wolves learns to howl. (A warning about the company you keep.)

Barriga llena, corazón contento. Full belly, happy heart. (Lean back and use this one after a big meal.)

Él que tiene más galillo, traga más pinol. He who has a bigger throat, drinks more *pinol*. (Being aggressive will get you farther.)

---

someone new enters the room, rise from your seat to greet them, and when you're ready to end a conversation or leave the room, a friendly *"con permiso"* will pave the way to the door.

TABLE MANNERS

Dig in! Grab that fried chicken between two hands and gnaw at it, shovel down *vigorón* from its banana-leaf wrapper as best as you can without letting all the shaved cabbage and *chile* spill down your shirt. Chase it with long swigs of a cold drink. Nicaraguans enjoy good food and good times, and if you're too dainty, the signal is all too clear you're not pleased with the meal. There are limits, of course, so keep an eye on your dining companions for what's appropriate and what's not, but while you're picking away at your fried cheese and sweet plantains, the guy next to you has finished his meal, pulled his shirt up with one hand, and is happily rubbing his belly with the other. Don't be afraid to enjoy what's on your plate. If you'd like to get a laugh out of your Nicaraguan hosts or waiters, after you've finished your plate, tell them, *"Barriga llena, corazón contenta"* ("Belly full, happy heart").

Tips for Travelers

WHAT TO TAKE

Everything you bring to Nicaragua should be sturdy and ideally water-resistant, especially if you intend to visit the Atlantic coast or Río San Juan, where you'll inevitably find yourself in a boat. Also be prepared for rain during any part of the wet season. Choose a small, strong bag not so large you'll be uncomfortable carrying it for long distances or riding with it on your lap in the bus—and secure its zippers with small padlocks. If you're planning to stay in a midrange or upscale hotel for the duration of your trip, your bag is of less concern, but be sure to take a small daypack or shoulder bag for your daily walkabouts.

Make a photocopy of the pages in your passport that have your photo and information. When you get the passport stamped in the airport, it's a good idea to make a photocopy of that page as well after you get situated in your first hotel, and store the copies somewhere other than with your passport. This will facilitate things greatly if your passport ever gets lost or stolen. Also consider taking a copy of your health and medical evacuation insurance policy.

Clothing

Pick clothes that are light and breathable in the heat, and if your plans include Matagalpa, Jinotega, or Estelí, you may appreciate something a bit warmer, like a flannel shirt. For sun protection, don't forget a shade hat that covers the back of your neck.

No matter what your style, it is very important to look clean. Having a neat personal appearance is important to all Latin Americans, and you'll find being well groomed will open a lot more doors. In the countryside, Nicaraguan men typically don't wear shorts, unless they are at the beach or at home. Jeans travel well, but you will probably find them hot in places like León and Chinandega; khakis are lighter and dry faster.

Roads are rough, even in cities, so good walking shoes will ease your trip considerably; lightweight hiking boots or just sturdy sneakers are sufficient. You'll be hard-pressed to find shoes larger than a men's 10.5 (European 42) for sale in Nicaragua. Take a pair of shower sandals with you, or better yet, buy a pair of rubber *chinelas* anywhere in Nicaragua for about $1.

SINFUL SOUVENIRS: RUM AND CIGARS

Looking for a gift that keeps on giving? Nicaragua offers a selection of ephemeral pleasures, including fine cigars and rum.

Nicaragua's hand-rolled cigars start with Cuban seed and the good earth around Estelí. Find them for sale in the Huembes market in Managua, El Mercado Viejo in Masaya, or the cigar shops around Granada's central plaza (or at the source at cigar factories in Estelí). Gringos: Just because you can buy Cuban Cohibas in Nicaragua (which may or may not be genuine), U.S. customs may still enforce their anti-Cuban embargo—whether your cigars are real or counterfeit! Remove the labels to be sure.

The cheapest place to pick up souvenir bottles of Flor de Caña, widely accepted as one of the smoothest rums in all Latin America, is in a supermarket or corner *pulpería*; hotel gift shops and airport kiosks often charge double what you should be paying. Nicaragua customs limits you to six liter-sized bottles of rum at the airport, and if you're catching a connecting flight in the U.S., you'll have to transfer your liquids to your checked luggage, so plan ahead and make sure you have space to do so.

Personal Items

Bring a small first-aid kit, plastic bags and zip-locking bags for protection from both rain and boat travel, and a cheap set of ear plugs for the occasional early-morning rooster or *chichera* band. A lightweight, breathable raincoat and/or small umbrella are a good idea. A small flashlight or headlamp is indispensable for walking at night on uneven streets and for those late-night potty runs in your *hospedaje,* and an alarm clock will facilitate catching early-morning buses. If you wear glasses, bring along a little repair kit. Bring a pocket Spanish dictionary and phrasebook. Photos of home and your family are a great way to connect with your Nica hosts and friends. A simple compass is helpful for finding your way around, as directions in this book typically refer to compass directions (finding the hotel three blocks north of the park is a lot easier if you know which direction north is).

There are very few places left in the country for developing film. For digital, always come equipped with a large memory card or your own laptop to store and edit your photos; otherwise, find a reliable cybercafé, where most provide the service of burning your shots onto a CD at minimal cost. For extra safety, burn two copies of the disk and mail one to yourself, in case your camera and/or bag are stolen.

Tampons can be difficult to find, as almost all Nicaraguan women use pads *(toallas sanitarias)* due to custom and social stigma, as tampons are often associated with sexually uninhibited women. Try the bigger supermarkets if you're in a pinch; most pharmacies and *pulperías* carry pads, usually called "Kotex," regardless of the actual brand name.

PHOTO ETIQUETTE

Cameras are by no means foreign objects in Nicaragua, but in many towns and neighborhoods, they are owned only by a few local entrepreneurs who take pictures at weddings, baptisms, graduations, etc. and then sell the print to the subject. Because of this, some rural Nicaraguans may expect that the photo you are taking is for them, and that you will either charge them for the photo or that you are going to send them a free copy. In general, people love getting their pictures taken, but often insist on dressing up, stiffening their bodies, and wiping all traces of emotion from their faces. The only way to avoid this (apart from making monkey noises to get them to laugh) is to take candid, unsolicited photos, something adults may perceive as bizarre and possibly rude. A solution is to ask first, concede to a few serious poses, and then snap away later when they are more unsuspecting but accustomed to your happy trigger finger. If you promise to send someone a copy, take down their address and actually do it.

OPPORTUNITIES FOR STUDY AND EMPLOYMENT

In light of Nicaragua's exceeding poverty and sky-high unemployment rate, you'll have a tough time finding paying work. Immigration laws force you to prove your job couldn't have otherwise gone to a Nicaraguan. Still, there are plenty of foreigners who've pulled it off. They work for international corporations with services and products in Nicaragua, they start businesses of their own, and they work for international nongovernmental organizations (NGOs) like CARE, Save the Children, ADRA, Project Concern International, and Catholic Relief Services. If you are a licensed English teacher you might also try the universities in Managua, though your salary will be the same as a Nicaraguan's (i.e., you'll be able to sustain yourself from day to day but you'll wish you had a cousin in Miami sending you checks). Universidad Centroamericana (UCA), Universidad Nacional Autónoma (UNAN), and Universidad Americana (UAM) all have English departments that may be looking for staff. For more ideas, check out the book *Work*

U.S. SISTER CITIES WITH NICARAGUA

Amherst, MA	La Paz Centro	Montclair, NJ	Pearl Lagoon
Ann Arbor, MI	Juigalpa	Moscow, ID	Villa Carlos Fonseca
Bainbridge Island, WA	Ometepe	Newark, DE	San Francisco Libre
Baltimore, MD	San Juan de Limay	New Haven, CT	León
Beckley, WV	Mina El Limon	Newton, MA	San Juan del Sur
Bend, OR	Condega	New York, NY	Tipitapa
Bennington, VT	Somotillo	North Plainfield, NJ	Masaya
Berkeley, CA	León	Norwalk, CT	Nagarote
Bloomington, IN	Posoltega	Pittsburgh, PA	San Isidro
Boulder, CO	Jalapa	Pittsfield, MA	Malpaisillo
Brookline, MA	Quezalguaque	Platteville, WI	Mateare
Burlington, VT	Puerto Cabezas	Portland, OR	Corinto
Concord, MA	San Marcos (RAAN)	Racine, WI	Bluefields
Fresno, CA	Telpaneca	Richland Center, WI	Santa Teresa
Gainesville, FL	Matagalpa	Rochester, NY	El Sauce
Gettysburg, PA	León	Sacramento, CA	San Juan de Oriente
Hartford, CT	Ocotal	Santa Cruz, CA	Jinotepe
Holyoke, CO	Las Mangas	South Haven, MI	Quilalí
Hudson Valley, NY	Larreynaga	Stevens Point, WI	Estelí
Lansing, SC	Tipitapa	Tampa, FL	Granada
Madison, WI	Managua	Tucson, AZ	Santo Domingo
Merced, CA	Somoto	Waukesha, WI	Granada
Milwaukee, WI	Ticuantepe	Yellow Springs, OH	Jicaro

Abroad, edited by Clay Hubbs, available at www.transitionsabroad.com.

Volunteering

Nicaragua's poverty and history of social experimentation have always attracted altruistic groups and individual volunteers. Shortly after 1979, hordes of *"Sandalistas"* poured in from around the world to participate in the Sandinista revolution. They picked coffee, taught in schools, wrote poetry and editorials of solidarity, put themselves in the line of fire, and protested in front of the U.S. Embassy. Today, *internacionalistas* come as part of service brigades, government programs, religious missions, academic trips, or independently. Organizations (both faith-based and secular) work throughout the country to assist with construction, education, translation, agriculture, and general solidarity.

Check www.volunteerabroad.com for the most updated listing of available assignments, or inquire about opportunities with the following organizations:

Habitat for Humanity (www.habitat.org) is active building homes throughout Nicaragua. **American Jewish World Service** (www.ajws. com) runs the Jewish Volunteer Corps, providing support for professionals looking to volunteer in Nicaragua and other countries—to practice the Hebrew commandment "to heal the world." And if your social circle wants to participate in a Nicaraguan work trip, **Bridges to Community** (U.S. tel. 914/923-2200, www. bridgestocommunity.org) will help plan a trip, find a project, and facilitate logistics to connect you with small Nicaraguan communities where your communication, construction, and environmental skills will be put to good use.

Seeds of Learning (www.seedsoflearning.

org) is a group based in El Salvador, Ciudad Dario, Nicaragua, and northern California; they accept groups of 13 or more to volunteer with a community, help construct a school, and share in Nicaraguan culture; your fee covers living expenses and building materials.

The **Integral Program Educating with Love and Tenderness** (PIEAT, tel. 505/8638-4080, eddycard@yahoo.com or dyoung_pieat@yahoo.com) is associated with the Americas Association for the Care of Children and is based in Jalapa, Nicaragua. PIEAT is a volunteer association which brings education to primary caregivers (parents, teachers, nurses, therapists) about health, hygiene, education, child development, alternatives to domestic violence, along with 44 other themes. The association hosts delegations or individual travelers in Nicaragua and offers service-learning and Spanish-language opportunities.

Studying Abroad

There are a few possibilities for spending a summer, semester, or extended internship in Nicaragua. Programs range from biological fieldwork at remote research stations to language training and social justice programs. You'll find additional listings at **www.studyabroad.com.**

School for International Training (U.S. tel. 888/272-7881, www.sit.edu) has been running a semester program in Managua for years, titled "Revolution, Transformation, and Civil Society."

World Leadership School (www.worldleadershipschool.org) based in Denver, Colorado, has extensive experience with international travel, leadership training, and managing student groups overseas, and sometimes offers trips for teens in Nicaragua. On La Isla de Ometepe, near the village of San Ramón **Estación Biológica de Ometepe** (www.lasuerte.org) is a biological field station frequented by student groups and researchers from all over the world. At the **Mariposa Eco-Hotel and Spanish School** (www.spanishschoolnica.com), the owner Paulette Goudge, PhD, offers a three-month course in the "Politics of Development."

Spanish Language Schools

Nicaragua has a growing network of independent Spanish schools, and an increasing number of visitors to the country choose to combine their travels with a few days, weeks, or even months of language study. With new "schools" (from teenagers in a living room to full-fledged language institutes) popping up all the time, it is increasingly difficult to keep track of them all; listed below are the schools that stand out for their reputation and experience. Most schools follow the same basic structure, mixing language instruction with cultural immersion: 2–4 hours of class in the morning, community service activities or field trips in the afternoon, and optional homestays with Nicaraguan families.

To a certain extent, choosing a school is as much a question of your geographical preference as anything else, since there are quality schools across the country. If possible, it's a good idea to come down and personally look into a few options before making a long-term commitment. Get a feel for the teachers (ask about their experience and credentials), the professionalism of the business, and the lesson plan. Do not trust everything you see on the websites.

Also, please note that keeping up with prices is difficult in the competitive world of Spanish schools, so always confirm prices. In general, expect to pay around $150–300 per week, depending on the quality of services offered. This usually includes room, board, instruction, and sometimes tours. Schools in the northern regions are generally cheaper. You can create your own language tour by studying at several schools, using your class schedule and family homestays as a way to travel throughout Nicaragua.

Once in the classroom, remember that gaining a language takes time—you must learn one word at a time until they start flowing together in sentences and you stop translating everything in your head. Be patient, do your homework, and be ready to laugh at yourself (along with everyone else) as you make mistakes. *¡Suerte!*

MANAGUA

Viva Spanish School (tel. 505/8877-7179 or 505/2270-2339, vivaspanish@btinternet.com, www.vivaspanishschool.com) offers intensive classes to students of all ages and backgrounds, catering mainly to NGO members, embassy employees, and missionary workers. The school is located in the heart of Managua, just a couple of blocks from Plaza Metrocentro. Class costs are $90 semi-intensive (10 hrs/week) and $175 intensive program (20 hrs/week). Homestays and other lodging options available. Advanced and specialized classes are available as well as online classes and home-office classes.

GRANADA

Granada's status as ground zero for the Nicaragua tourism scene (from backpackers to upscale) makes it a natural choice for many students who love the city's aesthetic as much as its bar scene. **Casa Xalteva** (across from the church by the same name, tel. 505/2552-2436, www.casaxalteva.com) offers a similar package, $150 per week, with a stress on volunteer activities; it's highly recommended by former students, has a quiet location, and is part of a small group home for boys, which is supported by your tuition.

Roger Ramirez's **One-on-One Spanish Tutoring Academy** (on the Calle Calzada, four blocks west of the central park, tel. 505/2552-6771, oneononetutoring.granada@yahoo.com, www.1on1tutoring.net) offers 20 hours of instruction per week ($110, or hourly for $6), which includes various instructors and five afternoon activities (city tour, salsa lesson, field trips, etc.), plus an end-of-week dinner

celebration. Homestays are an additional $85 paid directly to the family.

You'll also find Spanish classes in the patio of **Maverick Reading & Smoothie Lounge,** and in the beautiful **Palacio de Cultura** (tel. 505/2552-7114), in a grand building on the west side of Granada's main plaza.

LOS PUEBLOS BLANCOS AND CARAZO

Tucked into the forest off the road to the village of San Juan de la Concepción (also known as La Concha, 12 kilometers west of Ticuantepe, under an hour from Managua), **Mariposa Eco-Hotel and Spanish School** (tel. 505/2418-4638, www.spanishschoolnica.com) offers language classes in an isolated-feeling setting which is only an hour from Managua or Granada; there are views of Volcán Masaya, riding horses, hiking trails, and a library. Mariposa's all-inclusive Spanish school packages ($300/week) receive rave reviews.

Just outside Jinotepe, **Futuro Mejor** (tel. 505/8871-4705, info@futuromejor.org, www.futuromejor.org) offers room and board, 20 hours of Spanish instruction for $200 a week, and an English-teaching exchange where you can volunteer in associated communities. It's part of a larger project led by a Danish traveler Brian Wolter, who is helping to start a soccer academy.

LAGUNA DE APOYO

If you prefer to avoid the bustle and nightlife of the city, **Proyecto Ecologico Spanish School and Hostel** (tel. 505/8882-3992, eco-nic@guegue.com, www.gaianicaragua.org) is the only Spanish school in Nicaragua in a purely natural setting—the lakeside lodge is in the crater of an ancient volcano. The spot is incredible, only an hour from Managua, less to Granada, yet still tucked away in its own green world. Lodging and food are excellent (homestays are possible too), and the organization is not-for-profit. One week costs $190 and includes classes, activities, and room and board in their lodge.

SAN JUAN DEL SUR AND ISLA DE OMETEPE

One of the best deals in the country is **Doña Rosa Silva's Spanish School** (located 30 meters west of the Mercado Municipal, tel. 505/8682-2938 or 505/8958-5262, spanish_silva@yahoo.com, www.spanishsilva.com), offering four hours of daily instruction ($100 a week for just lessons, $200 includes homestay and meals). Classes are small (or private, costs a bit more), mix conversation with grammar, and include readings by Nicaragua's best authors and poets. Rosa also has a school on La Isla de Ometepe (in the center of Altagracia, 50 meters east of the mayor's office).

Latin American Spanish School (tel. 505/8820-2252, info@nicaspanish.org, www.nicaspanish.org) is a good option, run by a half dozen entrepreneurial and professional Nicaraguan Spanish instructors with significant experience teaching foreigners. They offer a basic 20-hour instruction and activity package for $120, plus $90 a week for lodging with private bath and three meals a day, plus homestay and volunteer activities.

Across from the BDF bank, in the Lago Azul restaurant (right on the beach!), the **San Juan del Sur Spanish School** (tel. 505/8372-4666, sjdsspanish@yahoo.com, www.sjdsspanish.com) has all-inclusive packages for $200 per week; the teachers are experienced and very friendly. Homestays include private bathroom. They also have opened a sister school in Ometepe.

LEÓN

Vapues Tours (tel. 505/2606-2276, www.vapues.com) recently began offering an intensive, full-immersion Spanish course: $195 for 20 hours of one-on-one class (over five days), includes room and board. There are new schools all the time in León. Check the **Casa de Cultura** class schedule, or the bulletin board at the **Vía Vía Hospedaje** for private tutors and lessons.

La Isla Foundation (from Movistar, half a block south, tel. 505/2311-3101, laislafoundation@gmail.com, www.laislafoundation.org) is a nonprofit organization which offers both English classes to local residents and Spanish immersion courses to international travelers and students in León. There are beginner, intermediate, and advanced classes plus opportunities for tours and work exchanges.

ESTELÍ

You'll find a cool climate and a number of natural excursions available at these schools in Estelí, all of which have been around since the early 1990s. **Spanish School Horizonte Nica** (located two blocks east and half a block north of INISER, tel. 505/2713-4117, horizont@ibw.com.ni, www.escuelahorizonte.edu.ni) has one of the longest track records in town and proffers the lofty vision of "promoting peace and social justice for those living in poverty, those struggling against class, race, and gender prejudices, and those fighting for political freedom." It donates part of your $220 weekly fee to local organizations and has an afternoon activity program that includes visits to local cooperatives and community-development programs. Price includes 20 hours of intensive study, afternoon activities, and homestay; service projects sometimes available.

Centro Cultural Juventus (from the southwest corner of the central plaza, two blocks west, tel. 505/2713-3756, walter_delgado_2007@yahoo.com, www.vianica.com/juventus) is a super-*tranquilo* little compound with dorm facilities, nicer rooms, a shared kitchen, and a breezy café with cappuccino and fruit shakes. Various language professors are on hand to tailor your Spanish curriculum; $100 for 20 hours, lodging $35 per week in the dorm or $60 a night for lovely, modern private rooms.

Spanish School Güegüense (six blocks east of the Autolote car lot, tel. 505/2713-7580) offers afternoon activities, including trips to Jinotega, Quilalí, San Juan del Río Coco, and local Estelí attractions. Class and homestay cost $150 per week.

BUYING REAL ESTATE IN NICARAGUA

For better or worse, Nicaragua is the latest tropical country chosen by international speculators with hopes of carefree retirement and lucrative appreciation on their new plot of Central American soil. A steady stream of aging baby boomers, aspiring financial managers, and alcoholic ne'er-do-wells on the run from ex-spouses and the tax man continue to find their way to southwestern Nicaragua. Healthy foreign investment? Or the new face of Yankee imperialism? You decide.

Potential real estate moguls typically wind up in Granada (and its nearby *isletas*), Rivas, and San Juan del Sur, all of which buzz with both independent and corporate real estate agents of mostly U.S. and Canadian origin. Before signing that check, however, take a breath, open your eyes, and ask a lot of questions. Start by visiting your embassy. The U.S. Embassy (www.usembassy.state.gov) has made land reform a priority for its relations with the Nicaraguan government; experienced buyers also seek out Pro-Nicaragua (www.pronicaragua.org), an "Investment Promotion Agency" that can help with information and contacts.

Good deals are still found, but not without some risk. Much of the valued property that is up for grabs has two distinct and viable chains of title ownership: one that dates back to the Somoza period, and one that dates to the Sandinista government's failed agrarian reforms in which they confiscated land, Robin Hood-style, and redistributed it to the masses.

Some of this land is still owned by cooperatives and *campesino* families, and some was given to powerful supporters (and leaders) of the Sandinistas. In the aftermath of the revolution, many of these seizures have been contested, many still stand, and very frequently two or three people present legitimate claims to the same lot. Make sure you–and your lawyer–know the history of the property back to 1978, and consider buying title insurance. More than one new landowner has been surprised to have a stranger confront him with an obviously falsified property title. The Nicaraguan court system may or may not back you up. In the case of contested property, your policy may cover fraud and forgery.

Don't completely entrust the job to others–do your own research on the region, the lot, the original paperwork, community relations, year-round road conditions, etc. Was an environmental-impact statement done, as is required by law? If so, what did it conclude? Does your new piece of paradise have a freshwater supply? Lastly, watch out for the word "beachfront". Under Nicaraguan law, land 30–80 meters from the high-tide line (depending on who you ask) cannot be bought or sold, but only leased from either the national government or the local municipality as a "concession." Newly elected municipal governments (i.e., small-town mayors with grudges) often change policies on concessions, frustrating many a would-be gringo beach bum.

MATAGALPA

This is a remarkable, off-the-beaten-path city in which to spend a few weeks, attending **Spanish School Matagalpa** (tel. 505/2772-0108 or 505/8647-4680, escuela@matagalpa.info, www.matagalpatours.com). As a part of Matagalpa Tours, you'll have immediate access to a range of day trips and backcountry hiking expeditions in the surrounding mountains. The school is conveniently located next door to one of the country's most *suave* cafés, El Artesano.

ACCESS FOR TRAVELERS WITH DISABILITIES

Travelers with disabilities should contact **AccessibleNicaragua** (accessiblenicaragua@gmail.com, www.accessiblenicaragua.com) before visiting. Founder Craig Grimes, a disabled traveler himself, is somewhat of the authority on the matter. Wheelchair-bound travelers to Nicaragua have reported the two most important things to consider bringing are toilet seat extenders and suction cups, and point out

© AMBER DOBRZENSKY

There are plenty of solo women travelers in Nicaragua.

Nicaraguans will quite helpfully offer to help you up and down curbs as necessary.

Nicaragua's *descapacitados* (disabled) get around with much difficulty because of ruined sidewalks, dirt roads, aggressive crowds, and open manholes. While Nicaraguans agree people with disabilities have equal rights, no attempt is made to accommodate them, and the foreign traveler with limited mobility will certainly struggle, but will no doubt find ways to get by. The **Los Pipitos** organization, based in Managua with 24 chapters around the country, is devoted to providing support, materials, and physical therapy to Nicaraguan children with disabilities and their families. Los Pipitos is always looking for volunteers and support. The Managua office is located half a block east of the Bolonia Agfa (tel. 505/2266-8033).

TRAVELING WITH CHILDREN

Nicaraguans love children and dote on them. You may find that traveling with children opens doors and forms new connections. That said, your children will have to endure the same lack of creature comforts, change in diet, and long bumpy bus rides you do. Disposable diapers are expensive but readily available in supermarkets, as are powdered milk/formula, pacifiers *(pacificadores* or *chupetas),* and bottles *(pachas).* Ask your doctor and consult the CDC about malaria prophylaxis for your child.

Perhaps the most important thing to pack is strong sun protection for delicate skin and disinfectant hand soap or foam. Travel with a stroller is half useful and half annoying, as Nicaragua's sandy and cobbled streets frequently require bigger-wheeled strollers that are thus harder to pack and carry around. Make sure your rental car company can provide a car seat for you, or you will be required to bring one (highly recommended, considering the danger of Nicaraguan road travel).

WOMEN TRAVELING ALONE

In Nicaragua, as in all of Latin America, women are both adored and harassed to their wits' end by "gentlemen" hoping for attention. Catcalls and whistles are rife, often accompanied with an *"Adios, amorrrr,"* or a sleazy *"Tsstss!"* More often than not, the perpetrators are harmless, immature young men with struggling moustaches. It will either comfort or disgust you to know that Nicaraguan women are forced to endure the same treatment every day and you should note how they react—most ignore the comments and blown kisses entirely, and some are flattered and smile confidently as they walk by. Angrily losing your cool is ill-advised, as it will only feed the fire. Be prepared for this part of the culture, and decide ahead of time how you plan to react.

Physical harassment, assault, and rape are less common in Nicaragua than elsewhere in Central America, but they have all happened, especially when alcohol is involved. Take the same precautions you would anywhere else to avoid dangerous situations. For more, download a copy of "Her Own Way: Advice for the Woman Traveller" at the Canadian Consular Affairs website (www.voyage.gc.ca); also find good advice and tips at www.journeywoman.com.

GAY AND LESBIAN TRAVELERS

As of March 2008, consensual gay sex is no longer a criminal act in Nicaragua, though the Catholic church still forbids it and homophobia is rampant throughout Latin America. Even so, Nica society is generally tolerant of homosexuality. The gay or lesbian traveler should feel neither threatened nor endangered in Nicaragua provided they maintain a modicum of discretion and choose their situations wisely. Managua and Granada have a few openly gay clubs and gay-friendly hotels. Elsewhere same-sex couples may find local gay communities that will help orient them to tolerant clubs and bars.

Health and Safety

Dirk G. Schroeder's *Staying Healthy in Asia, Africa, and Latin America* is an excellent and concise guide to preventive medicine in the developing world and is small enough to fit in your pocket. Consult the "Mexico and Central America" page of the U.S. Centers for Disease Control (CDC, tel. 404/332-4559 or 877/394-8747, www.cdc.gov).

VACCINATIONS

Required: A certificate of vaccination against yellow fever is required for all travelers over one year of age and arriving from affected areas.
Recommended: Before traveling to Nicaragua, be sure your tetanus, diphtheria, measles, mumps, rubella, and polio vaccines are up-to-date. Protection against hepatitis A and typhoid fever is also recommended for all travelers.

MEDICAL SERVICES

Medical care is in short supply outside of Managua, and even in the capital city, doctors in public hospitals are underpaid (earning about $200 a month) and brutally overworked. Though there are many qualified medical professionals in Nicaragua who studied abroad in Mexico, Cuba, or the United States, there are also many practicing doctors and medical staff who have less-than-adequate credentials. Use your best judgment. Private hospitals and clinics typically expect immediate payment for services rendered, but their rates are ridiculously cheaper than they are back home. Larger facilities accept credit cards and everyone else demands cash.

Government-run health clinics, called **Centros de Salud,** exist in most towns throughout the country, usually near the central plaza. They are free—even to you—but poorly supplied and inadequately staffed.

The most modern hospital in the country is **Hospital Vivian Pellas,** a $23-million private institution seven kilometers south of Managua on the Carretera Masaya. For **dental emergencies,** or even just a check-up, seek out the bilingual services of Dr. Esteban Bendaña McEwan (300 meters south of the ENITEL Villa Fontana, tel. 505/2270-5021 or 505/8850-8981, estebanbm@hotmail.com); Dr. Bendaña is accustomed to dealing with foreign patients and his prices are reasonable.

Natural Medicine

Many *campesinos* have excellent practical knowledge of herbal remedies that involve teas, tree barks, herbs, and fruits. The first medicines came from the earth, and the Nicaraguans haven't lost that connection. Try crushed and boiled papaya seeds, oil of *apazote* (a small shrub whose seed is crushed for medicinal use), or coconut water to fend off intestinal parasites, *manzanilla* (chamomile) for stress or menstrual discomfort, or *tamarindo* or papaya for constipation. A popular cold remedy involves hot tea mixed with two squeezed limes, *miel de jicote* (honey from the *jicote* bee), and a large shot of cheap rum, drunk right before you go to bed so you sweat out the fever as you sleep.

Medications and Prescriptions

Many modern medicines, produced in Mexico or El Salvador, are sold in Nicaragua. Because of a struggling economy and plenty of competition, some pharmacies may sell you medicine without a prescription. For simple travelers' ailments, like stomach upsets, diarrhea, or analgesics, it's worth going to the local pharmacy and asking what they recommend. Even relatively strong medications like codeine can be purchased over the counter (in fizzy tablet form).

For birth control needs, condoms are cheap and easy to find. Any corner pharmacy will have them, even in small towns of just a few thousand people; a three-pack of prophylactics costs less than $2. Female travelers taking contraceptives should know the chemical name for what they use. *Pastillas anticonceptivas* (birth control pills) are easily obtained without prescription in pharmacies in Managua and in larger cities like León, Granada, and Estelí. Other forms of birth control and sexual protection devices, such as IUDs and diaphragms, are neither used nor sold.

STAYING HEALTHY

Ultimately, your health is dependent on the choices you make, and chief among these is what you put in your mouth. One longtime resident says staying healthy in the tropics is more than just possible—it is an "art form." As you master the art, expect your digestive system to take some time getting accustomed to the new food and microorganisms in the Nicaraguan diet. During this time (and after), use common sense: wash or sanitize your hands often. Eat food that is well cooked and still hot when served. Avoid dairy products if you're not sure whether they are pasteurized. Be wary of uncooked foods, including ceviche and salads. Use the finger wag to turn down food from street vendors and be aware that pork carries the extra danger of trichinosis, not to mention a diet of garbage (and worse) on which most country pigs are raised.

Also, be aware of flies as transmitters of food-borne illness. Prevent flies from landing on your food, glass, or table setting. You'll notice Nicaraguans are meticulous about this, and you should be too. If you have to leave the table, cover your food with a napkin or have someone else wave their hand over it slowly. You can fold your drinking straw over and put the mouth

GETTING IN HOT WATER

In the cooler parts of the country, namely Matagalpa and Jinotega, some hotels and *hospedajes* offer hot water by means of electric water-heating canisters attached to the end of the shower head. Cold water passing through the coils is warmed before falling through the spout. The seemingly obvious drawback to the system is the presence of electric wires in and around a wet (i.e., conductive) environment. While not necessarily the electric death traps they appear to be, they should be approached with caution. Before you step into the shower, check for frayed or exposed wires (or the burned carcasses of former hotel occupants on the shower floor). Set the control knob to II and, very carefully, turn the water on. Once you're wet and water is flowing through the apparatus, it's in your best interest not to mess with the heater again.

To save you many cold showers trying to figure out how the darned thing works, here's the secret: If the water pressure is too low, the heater isn't triggered on, and the water will not be heated; but if the water pressure is too high, it will be forced through the nozzle before it's had sufficient contact with the coils, and the water will not be heated. Open the faucet to a moderate setting, and rub-a-dub-dub, you're taking a hot shower. When you've finished, turn the water off first and dry off, then turn the little knob back to Off.

---

end into the neck of the bottle to prevent flies from landing on it, and put napkins on top of the bottle neck and your glass, too. Have the waiter clear the table when you've finished with a dish—and beware the waiter who, in response to your complaints about the flies, comes back and douses you and your dinner in an aerosol cloud of Baygon pesticide.

Sun Exposure

Nicaragua is located a scant 12 degrees of latitude north of the equator, so the sun's rays strike the Earth's surface at a more direct angle than in northern countries. The result is that you will burn faster and sweat up to twice as much as you are used to.

Ideally, do like the majority of the locals do, and stay out of the sun between 10 A.M. and 2 P.M. It's a great time to take a nap anyway. Use sunscreen of at least SPF 30, and wear a hat and pants. Should you overdo it in the sun, make sure to drink lots of fluids—that means water, not beer. Treat sunburns with aloe gel, or better yet—find a fresh *sábila* (aloe) plant to break open and rub over your skin.

Drinking Water

While most Nicaraguan municipal water systems are well treated and safe (sometimes over-chlorinated), there is not much reason to take the chance, especially when purified, bottled water is widely available. But rather than contribute to the growing solid waste problem in Nicaragua, why not bring a single reusable plastic water bottle and refill it in your hotel lobby's five-gallon purified water dispensers? If you are diligent about refilling, it is entirely possible to spend a week or more in Nicaragua drinking purified water without using a single plastic throwaway bottle.

If you'll be spending time in rural Nicaragua, consider a small water filter, or, alternately, use six drops of iodine (or three of bleach) in a liter of water; this will kill every organism that needs to be killed; good if you're in a pinch, but not something you'll find yourself practicing on a daily basis. Bringing water to a boil is also an effective means of purification.

Standard precautions include avoiding ice cubes unless you're confident they were made with boiled or purified water (which they are in many restaurants). Canned and bottled drinks without ice, including beer, are safe, but should never be used as a substitute for water when trying to stay hydrated.

Oral Rehydration Salts

Probably the single most effective item you can carry in your medical kit are the packets of powdered salt and sugar known in Spanish as *suero orál*. One packet of *suero* mixed with a liter of water, drunk in small sips, is the best immediate treatment for all of the following: diarrhea, sun exposure, fever, infection, or hangovers. Rehydration salts are essential to your recovery as they replace the salts and minerals your body loses from sweating, vomiting, or urinating, thus aiding your body's most basic cellular transfer functions. Whether or not you like the taste (odds are you won't), consuming enough *suero* and water is very often the difference between being just a little sick and feeling really, really awful.

Sport drinks like Gatorade are super-concentrated *suero* mixtures and should be diluted at a ratio of three to one with water to make the most of the active ingredients. If you don't, you'll urinate out the majority of the electrolytes. Gatorade is common in most gas stations and supermarkets, but *suero* packets are more widely available and much cheaper, found at any drugstore or health clinic for about $0.50 a packet. It can be improvised even more cheaply, according to the following recipe: Mix one-half teaspoon of salt, one-half teaspoon baking soda, and four tablespoons of sugar in one quart of boiled or carbonated water. Drink a full glass of the stuff after each time you use the bathroom. Add a few drops of lemon to make it more palatable.

DISEASES AND COMMON AILMENTS
Cholera

Cholera is present in Nicaragua, with occasional outbreaks, especially in rural areas with contaminated water supplies. Vaccines are not required because they offer incomplete protection. You are better off watching what you put in your mouth. In case you contract cholera (the symptoms are profuse diarrhea the color of rice water accompanied by sharp intestinal cramps, vomiting, and body weakness), see a doctor immediately and drink your *suero:* Cholera kills by dehydrating you.

Dengue Fever

Dengue ("bone-breaking") fever is the only thing that's worse than malaria. You know you have it if you truly believe you will die, and you feel relief that death will make the pain stop. You probably are *not* going to die, of course (unless you contract the rare hemorrhagic strain of dengue), but you're going to suffer royally. The symptoms may include any or all of the following: sudden high fever, severe headache (think of nails in the back of your eyes), muscle and back pain, nausea or vomiting, and a full-bodied skin rash, which may appear 3–4 days after the onset of the fever. Although the initial pain and fever may last only a few days, you may be out of commission for up to several weeks, possibly bedridden, depressed, and too weak to move. There is no vaccine, but dengue's effects can be successfully minimized with plenty of rest, Tylenol (for the fever and aches), and as much water and *suero* as you can manage. Dengue itself is undetectable in a blood test, but a low platelet *(plaquetas)* count indicates its presence. If you believe you have dengue, you should get a blood test as soon as possible to make sure it's not the rare hemorrhagic variety, which can be fatal if untreated.

Diarrhea and Dysentery

Everyone's body reacts differently to the changes in diet, schedule, and stress that go along with traveling, and many visitors to Nicaragua stay entirely regular throughout their trip. Some don't. Diarrhea is one symptom

A GUIDE TO NICARAGUA'S TOILETS

Nicaragua boasts an enormous diversity of bathrooms, from various forms of the common *inodoro* (modern toilet, a.k.a. *el trono*) to the full range of dark, infested *letrinas* (outhouses). Despite so many options, many regions of Nicaragua suffer a shortage of actual toilet seats, so having to squat over a bare bowl is common. Because water supplies are sometimes sporadic, even in cities, you may occasionally be forced to take a bucket bath and or employ a manual toilet flush. Mastering this move is important. Use the plastic bucket that should be sitting beside the toilet and dump the water into the bowl, all at once, forcefully and from high up to ensure maximum turd swirlage.

Unless you are staying in the most expensive hotels, you should probably be throwing your toilet paper in the waste basket next to the toilet, *not* in the bowl, so as not to clog up the weak plumbing; this is the norm in Nicaragua. Sure, it seems gross, but you'll get used to it. It's never a bad idea to travel with a roll or two of store-bought toilet paper *(papel higiénico)* protected in a plastic bag and easily accessible. Otherwise, try the following phrase with your host: *"Señor, fijase que no hay papel en el baño."*

of amoebic (parasitic) and bacillic (bacterial) dysentery, both caused by some form of fecal-oral contamination. Often accompanied by nausea, vomiting, and a mild fever, dysentery is easily confused with other diseases, so don't try to self-diagnose. *Examenes de heces* (stool-sample examinations) can be performed at most clinics and hospitals and are your first step to getting better (cost is $2–8). Bacillic dysentery is treatable with antibiotics; amoebic is treated with one of a variety of drugs that kill off all the flora in your intestinal tract. Of these, Flagyl is the best known, but other non–FDA approved treatments like Tinedazol are commonly available, cheap, and effective. Do not drink alcohol with these drugs, but do eat something like yogurt or acidophilus pills to refoliate your tummy.

Generally, simple cases of diarrhea in the absence of other symptoms are nothing more serious than "traveler's diarrhea." If you do get a case of Diriangén's Revenge, your best bet is to let it pass naturally. Diarrhea is your body's way of flushing out the bad stuff, so constipating medicines like Imodium-AD are not recommended, as they keep the bacteria (or whatever is causing your intestinal distress) within your system. Save the Imodium (or any other liquid glue) for emergency situations like long bus rides or a date with Miss Nicaragua. Most importantly, drink water! Not replacing the fluids and electrolytes you are losing will make you feel much worse than you need to. If the diarrhea persists for more than 48 hours, is bloody, or is accompanied by a fever, see a health professional immediately.

HIV and AIDS

Although to date Nicaragua has been spared a major HIV outbreak, health professionals estimate that geography, cultural, political, and social factors mean an outbreak isn't far off. Currently, there are about 1,500 HIV-positive cases registered with MINSA (the Government Health Ministry), but one World Bank official estimated actual cases at 8,000. Exacerbating the spread of AIDS (SIDA in Spanish) is the promiscuous behavior of many married males, an active sex-worker trade, poor use of condoms, and growing drug trouble. AIDS is most prevalent in urban populations, mainly Managua and Chinandega, and is primarily transmitted sexually, rather than through needles or contaminated blood.

Travelers should avoid sexual contact with persons whose HIV status is unknown. If you intend to be sexually active, use a fresh latex condom for every sexual act and every orifice. Condoms are inexpensive and readily available in just about any local pharmacy; in Spanish, a condom is called *condón* or *preservativo*.

Hepatitis B also lurks in Nicaragua. Avoid contact with bodily fluids or bodily waste. Get vaccinated if you anticipate close contact with the local population or plan to reside in Nicaragua for an extended period of time.

Leptospirosis

Leptospirosis is caused by a bacteria found in water contaminated with the urine of infected animals, especially rodents. Symptoms include high fever and headache, chills, muscle aches, vomiting, and possibly jaundice. Humans become infected through contact with infected food, water, or soil. It is not known to spread from person to person and can be treated with antibiotics in its early stages.

Malaria

Risk of malaria is higher in rural areas, especially those alongside rivers or marshes, but malaria-infected mosquitoes breed anywhere stagnant pools of water (of any size, even in an empty bottle cap) are found, including urban settings. At times, western Nicaragua is declared malaria-free, at other times, the U.S. CDC recommends weekly prophylaxis of chloroquine, specifically Aralen-brand pills (500 mg for adults). Begin taking the pills two weeks before you arrive and continue taking them four weeks after leaving the country. A small percentage of people have negative reactions to chloroquine, including nightmares, rashes, or hair loss. Alternative treatments are available, but the best method of all is to not get bitten.

The malaria bacterium (there are four different kinds) settle in your liver and begin replicating; the bacteria invades your red blood cells and causes them to burst, producing the telltale symptoms of fever followed by chills, fever,

and even nausea and vomiting on a 24 hours good/24 hours bad cycle. If you observe this pattern, seek medical attention immediately, as failure to treat malaria promptly is the primary cause for the disease becoming dangerous. They'll most likely take a blood test and if it tests positive, prescribe you a huge dose of chloroquine. Allow time to recover your strength.

Tuberculosis

Tuberculosis is spread by sneezing or coughing, and the infected person may not know he or she is a carrier. If you plan to spend more than four weeks in Nicaragua (or plan on spending time in a Nicaraguan jail), consider having a tuberculin skin test performed before and after visiting. Tuberculosis is a serious and possibly fatal disease but can be treated with several medications.

BITES AND STINGS

Most towns in Nicaragua, even rural ones, conduct a yearly **rabies**-vaccination campaign for dogs, but you should still be careful. Get a rabies vaccination if you intend to spend a long time in Nicaragua. Should you be bitten, immediately cleanse the wound with lots of soap, and get prompt medical attention.

Chagas Disease

The Chagas bug *(Trypanosoma cruzi)* is a large, recognizable insect, also called the kissing bug, assassin bug, and cone-nose. In Spanish it's known as *chinche,* but this word is also used for many other types of beetlelike creatures. The Chagas bug bites its victim (usually on the face, close to the lips), sucks its fill of blood, and, for the coup de grâce, defecates on the newly created wound. Chagas bugs are present in Nicaragua, found mostly in poor *campesino* structures of crumbling adobe. Besides the downright insult of being bitten, sucked, and pooped on, the Chagas bug's biggest menace is the disease it carries of the same name, which manifests itself in 2 percent of its victims. The first symptoms include swollen glands and a fever that appear 1–2 weeks after the bite. The disease then goes into a 5- to 30-year remission phase. If and when it reappears, Chagas disease causes the lining of the heart to swell, sometimes resulting in death. There is no cure.

Mosquitoes

Mosquitoes (Nicas refer to them as *zancudos*) are most active during the rainy season (June–November) and in areas near stagnant water, like marshes, puddles, or rice fields. They are much more common in the lower, flatter regions of Nicaragua than they are in mountains, though even in the highlands and major urban areas, old tires, cans, and roadside puddles can provide the habitat necessary to produce swarms of them. The mosquito that carries malaria bites during the night and evening hours, and the dengue fever carrier is active during the day, from dawn to dusk. They are both relatively simple to combat, and ensuring you don't get bitten is the best prophylaxis for preventing disease.

First and foremost, limit the amount of skin you expose: long sleeves, pants, and socks will do more to prevent bites than the strongest chemical repellent. Choose lodging accommodations with good screens, but if this is not possible, use a fan to blow airborne insects away from your body as you sleep. Avoid being outside or unprotected in the hour before sunset, when mosquito activity is heaviest, and use a *mosquitero* (mosquito net) tucked underneath your mattress when you sleep. Hanging-type mosquito nets are available in Nicaragua, or you can purchase *tela de mosquitero* anywhere they sell fabric and have a mosquito net made by a seamstress. Also, many *pulperías* sell *espirales* (mosquito coils), which burn slowly, releasing a mosquito-repelling smoke; they're cheap and convenient, but full of chemicals, so don't breathe in too much smoke.

Spiders, Scorpions, and Snakes

Arachnophobes, beware! The spiders of Nicaragua are dark, hairy, and occasionally capable of devouring small birds. Of note is the *pica-caballo,* a kind of tarantula whose name (meaning horse-biter) refers to the alleged power of its flesh-rotting venom to destroy a horse's hoof. Don't worry, though; spiders do not aggressively seek out people, and do way more good than harm by eating things like Chagas bugs. If you'd rather the spiders didn't share your personal space, shake out your bedclothes before going to sleep and check your shoes before putting your feet in them.

Scorpions *(alacránes)* are common in Nicaragua, especially in dark corners, beaches, and piles of wood. Nicaraguan scorpions look nasty—black and big—but their sting is no more harmful than that of a bee and is described by some as what a cigarette burn feels like. Your lips and tongue may feel a little numb, but the venom is nothing compared to their smaller, translucent cousins in Mexico. For people who are prone to anaphylactic shock, it can be a more serious or life-threatening experience. Be aware, in Nicaragua the Spanish word *escorpión* usually refers not to scorpions but to the harmless little geckos (also called *perros zompopos*) that scurry around walls eating small insects. And in spite of what your *campesino* friends might insist, those little geckos are neither malevolent nor deadly and would never, as you will often hear, intentionally try to kill you by urinating on you.

There are 15 species of poisonous snakes in Nicaragua, but your chance of seeing one is extremely rare, unless you're going deep into the bush. In that case, walk softly and carry a big machete. Keep an eye out for 1 of 11 pit viper species (family *Viperidae*), especially the infamous fer-de-lance *(Bothrops asper)*, or *Barba amarilla;* the most aggressive and dangerous snake in Central America, the fer-de-lance is mostly confined to the humid central highlands and the Caribbean coast. Less common pit vipers, but occasionally seen in western parts of the country, are the Central American rattlesnake *(Crotalus durissus)*, known in Spanish as *cascabel*, and a relative of the copperhead, the cantil, or castellana, *(Agkistrodon bilineatus)*. In addition, there are four rarely seen species of the *Elapidae* family (three coral snakes and the pelagic sea snake). Remember, there are many coral mimics out there with various versions of the famous colored markings; the true coral (only one species of which is found on the west side of the country) has ring markings in only this order: red, yellow, black, yellow.

CRIME

Believe it or not, Nicaragua was considered one of the safer countries in all of Latin America for a few years, though tourism-related crime like petty theft and scam artists (and the occasional robbery and assault) sometimes occur, usually at night and involving alcohol. There have also been some problems with carjackings by criminals posing as police. For the moment, Nicaragua has *mostly* escaped the gang violence that has plagued the cities of Guatemala, El Salvador, and Honduras.

The single biggest area of concern when it comes to security in Nicaragua is the country's place in the Colombia–U.S. drug route. Smugglers, mafiosos, dealers, and crackheads are found along the Atlantic coast, where rising drug-related crimes threaten the very fabric of some communities. The Corn Islands have experienced several rapes, including violent ones, and San Juan del Sur experienced a wave of violence in 2008 that was excessive by any standards, including a kidnapping. The Tipitapa–Masaya highway, formerly a convenient shortcut for going from the airport to Granada while avoiding Managua, is increasingly dangerous at night as it is the scene of fake "police inspections" that end up with

foreign tourists being forced to go from ATM to ATM, withdrawing cash.

Before traveling, check official reports, including the U.S. State Department's warnings at www.travel.state.gov and the travel forums at www.gotonicaragua.com. Managua is clearly the city with the most crime, but bigger cities, like Estelí and Chinandega, have neighborhoods you should skip as well (ask at your hotel to get the most updated local info). Avoid traveling alone, especially in remote areas including beaches, at night or while intoxicated, and pay the extra dollar or two for a cab. No one should take a cab when the driver has a friend riding up front—complain loudly if he tries—and pay attention to your surroundings and where you are going. You are most at risk of pickpocketing (or hat/watch/bag snatching) in crowds and on public transport: avoid urban buses in Managua. Keep a low profile and leave your flashy jewelry, watches, and expensive sunglasses at home. Keep your cash divided up and hidden in a money belt, sock, or your undergarments (take a cue from the many Nica women pulling soggy *córdoba* bills out of their cleavage).

If you are the victim of a crime, report it immediately to the local police department (dial 118), at minimum because your insurance company back home will require an official police report before reimbursing you. Nicaraguan police have good intentions but few resources, lacking even gasoline for the few patrol cars or motorcycles they have—don't be surprised if you are asked to help fill up a vehicle with gas. This is annoying but not uncommon, and chipping in for $20 of gas will help them get the job done, which they often do! While police corruption does exist—Nicaraguan police earn a pitiful $55–60 per month—the Nicaraguan police force is notably more honest and helpful than in some Central American nations, and has gotten more professional during the Ortega administration.

Illegal Drugs

Nicaragua is part of the underground highway that transports cocaine and heroin from South America to North America, and as such is under a lot of pressure from the United States to crack down on drug traffickers passing through in vehicles or in boats off the Atlantic coast. Drug-related crime is rapidly increasing on the Atlantic coast, particularly in Bluefields and Puerto Cabezas. All travelers in Nicaragua are subject to local drug-possession and use laws, which include stiff fines and prison sentences of up to 30 years.

Marijuana thrives in Nicaragua's climate and conditions. It is known locally as *la mota, el monte,* or in one remote Matagalpa valley, *pim-pirim-pím.* It is officially prohibited despite popular usage, and the current laws allow harsh penalties for possession of even tiny quantities of *cannabis sativa,* for both nationals and tourists alike. Canine and bag searches at airports, docks along the Atlantic coast, and at the Honduran and Costa Rican border crossings are the norm, not the exception.

As a foreign, hip-looking tourist, you may be offered pot at some point during your trip, especially on the Atlantic coast and in San Juan del Sur. The proposal may be a harmless invitation to get high on the beach, or it may be from a hustler or stool pigeon who is about to rip you off and/or get you arrested. Use the same common sense you would anywhere in the world.

Prostitution

The world's oldest profession nearly tripled in practitioners from 2000–2005, especially in Managua, Granada, Corinto, and border/trucking towns like Somotillo. Since then, flagrant roadside prostitution has been curbed, forcing the trade underground again. Though illegal, *puterías* (whorehouses), thinly disguised as "beauty salons" or "massage parlors," operate with virtual impunity, and every strip club in Managua has a bank of rooms behind the stage, some with an actual cashier stationed at the door. Then there are the commercial sex workers on Carretera Masaya, and the nation's numerous auto-hotels, which rent rooms by the hour.

The situation is nowhere near as developed as the sex tourism industries of places like Thailand and Costa Rica, but it is undeniable that foreigners have contributed in no small way to Nicaragua's sex economy. Travelers considering indulging should think seriously about the social impacts that result from perpetuating this institution, and should start by reading the section on AIDS in this chapter.

BEGGING

It is generally assumed that foreigners with the leisure time to travel to Nicaragua have lots and lots of money, no matter the actual size of your bank account or how much you scraped and saved for your trip. Poor children and adults will occasionally ask you for spare change wherever you travel, usually by either a single outstretched index finger or a cupped, empty hand, both accompanied with *"Chele, deme un peso"* ("Whitey, give me a coin," though in Granada, this has evolved into *"deme un dolar"*). It's low-key, so don't be worried or afraid.

Another poignant sight, encountered at sidewalk restaurants and market eateries, are hungry children watching you as you finish your meal. If you care to share your leftovers, they will not go to waste—a small concession. In many cities, including Granada, many children and adolescents asking for money are *huele-pegas* (glue sniffers) and your money will only go to buy them more of H. B. Fuller's finest. *Huele-pegas* are identified by glazed eyes, unkempt appearances, and sometimes a jar of glue tucked under a dirty shirt. Instead of giving money, give them some time, attention, and maybe a little food.

In general, giving money to beggars, especially in tourist centers, is a bad idea that perpetuates dependency, bad habits, and children plying tourists for coins and dollars. There are many other ways to direct your good intentions.

Information and Services

MONEY

Nicaragua remains a budget travel destination, with generally cheaper prices across the board than nearby Costa Rica and Belize. You can comfortably exist in Nicaragua on $50 per day, or half of that by eating the way the locals do and forgoing the jalapeño steak and beer. Budget travelers interested in stretching their money to the maximum should eat at *fritangas* and market stalls, take the slow bus, and stay at the simplest *hospedajes*. In Granada, León, and Managua, you can now choose to pay $50–150 for a room, so budget accordingly if you prefer extra comforts (like air-conditioning, security, and cleanliness).

Currency

Since 1912, Nicaragua's currency has been the *córdoba*, named after Francisco Hernández de Córdoba, the Spanish founder of the colony of Nicaragua. It is divided into 100 *centavos* or 10 *reales*. In common usage, the *córdoba* is also referred to as a *peso*. The U.S. dollar is also an official currency in Nicaragua and the only foreign currency you can hope to exchange (although many communities along the Río San Juan also use Costa Rican *colones*).

Under the Sandinistas, inflation ran to 30,000 percent. These days the córdoba is better managed and essentially stable, but to offset inflation, it is being steadily devalued at the rate of approximately US$0.37 every six months. You can do the arithmetic yourself before arriving in Nicaragua (the exchange rate is currently hovering around 20 *córdobas* to 1 dollar, making for simple calculations), or find the

It is generally fine to use licensed money changers on the street, often located near banks.

© JOSHUA BERMAN

actual rates at the Central Bank of Nicaragua's website (www.bcn.gob.ni).

In 2003, a new C$500 bill was introduced, and in 2007 the ratty old paper bills were phased out in lieu of crisp, newly designed currency that feels a bit like there's some plastic wrap mixed in with the paper. Be careful about confusing the C$20 and C$200 bills.

U.S. Dollars and ATMs

Since this book was first published in 2002, two things have made money management a lot easier: widespread use of U.S. dollars, and dramatically increased prevalance of ATMs. Travelers should bring U.S. dollars, preferably, or euros otherwise, as hardly any other currencies can be exchanged in Nicaragua, including those of the neighboring countries (exchange your Costa Rican or Honduran currency on the border before entering). Make sure your greenbacks are good quality, as ripped, tattered bills may be refused.

While it's easier to change money and travel using *córdobas,* virtually any merchant will take dollars these days, and give you the bank rate (which means you too need to know what the bank rate is, just to be sure) as change; they usually have trouble breaking anything bigger than a 20-dollar bill. ATMs, known in Spanish as *cajeros automáticos,* litter all major cities and bigger gas stations; you won't find them outside of the cities though, so plan accordingly. They dispense both *córdoba* (unfortunately, often in the larger, C$500 denominations) and U.S. dollars, and take cards from the Cirrus and Star networks, plus most Visa and MasterCards. Of course, you will pay a bank fee for each withdrawal, but it's worth it. You cannot rely on just one card, as some establishments will accept Visa but not MasterCard, or the opposite. And make sure you have photocopied the front and back of your cards and stashed the page somewhere safe, in case they are stolen; likewise, inform your credit card companies you will be traveling in Nicaragua so they don't balk and block your card, thinking the sudden spate of charges in Nicaragua indicate theft.

Travelers Checks

Travelers checks are nearly impossible to change in banks, and at exceedingly bad rates. Travelers checks for currencies other than U.S. dollars will not be cashed. You will need to show your passport to cash travelers checks, and be sure that your signature matches your previous one or you'll convert your precious dollars into a worthless piece of paper. Some banks actually demand to see your original receipts (the ones you are supposed to keep physically separate from the checks!). If you truly get stuck, every Nicaraguan city has a branch of Western Union, permitting family back home can wire you money, for a steep fee (up to 25 percent).

Bank Hours

Unless noted otherwise in this book, all bank hours are 8:30 A.M.–4 P.M. Monday–Friday and 8:30 A.M.–noon Saturday. Nicaraguans receive their pay on the 15th and 30th or 31st of every month (*días de pago* are the best nights to go out dancing in Managua and beyond). Should you need to go to a bank on those days, you can expect the lines to be extra long. Bide your time by watching businesspeople carry away large sums of cash in brown paper lunch bags.

Sales Tax

Nicaragua's sales tax (IGV or Impuesto General de Valor) is a whopping 15 percent—the highest in Central America. You'll find it automatically applied to the bill at nicer restaurants, fancy hotels, and upscale shops in major cities: check on your receipt, where it should be clearly indicated. Elsewhere, sales tax is casually dismissed. Should you decide to splurge on a fancy dinner (places where you'd expect to spend more than $6–10 a meal), expect to pay 25 percent of your bill for tax and tip. Prices in this book usually do not include the IGV. If a hotel does not charge you this tax, they (and you) are breaking the law.

Tipping

In better restaurants, a 10–15 percent *propina* (tip) will be graciously added on to your bill, even if the food was undercooked, the beer flat, and the service atrocious. You are under no obligation to pay it if it is unmerited. You might want to give a little something after getting your hair cut: 10 percent is appropriate. Skycaps at the International Airport in Managua will jostle to carry your luggage out to a waiting taxi for about $2. Taxi drivers and bartenders are rarely tipped and don't expect to be unless they are exceptionally friendly or go out of their way for you. If you accept the offer of children trying to carry your bags, find you a hotel, or anything else, you have entered into an unspoken agreement to give them a few *córdobas:* (5–20 *córdobas* or $1 or less).

Bargaining

Looking for a good deal is a sport in Nicaragua—half social, half business, and is expected with most outdoor market vendors and taxi drivers. But be warned: Bargaining in Nicaragua is *al suave!* Aggressive, prolonged haggling is not cool, won't affect the price, and may leave ill feelings. To start off the process, after you are given the initial price, act surprised and use one of the following phrases: *"¿Cuánto es lo menos?"* ("What is your lowest price?") or *"¿Nada menos?"* ("Nothing less?"). Remember these guidelines:

- Bargaining is social and friendly, or at least courteous. Keep your temper under wraps and always smile.
- Go back and forth a maximum of two or three times, and then either agree or walk away. Remember that some Nicaraguans, to save face, may lose a profit.
- Once you make a deal, it's done. If you think you've been ripped off, remember the $2 you

got overcharged is still less than you'd pay for a double-tall mocha latte back home. Keep it in perspective and be a good sport.

- When bargaining with taxi drivers in Managua, bargain hard, but agree on a price *before* you enter the cab—once the vehicle is moving, your leverage has vanished in a puff of acrid, black exhaust.

COMMUNICATIONS AND MEDIA
Mail

The national postal system is called **Correos de Nicaragua,** and is surprisingly effective and reliable. Every city has at least one post office, often near the central plaza and adjacent to the telephone service (but not always). Legal-size letters and postcards cost about $0.70 to the United States, and a little more to Europe. Post offices in many cities have a gorgeous selection of stamps. *Correos* are open standard business hours (with some variations), almost always closed during lunch, and are open until noon on Saturday.

To receive packages, have the sender use a padded envelope instead of a box, even if the shipment must be split into several pieces; keep the package as unassuming as possible, and try writing *Dios Te Ama* (God Loves You) on the envelope for a little help from above. In general, mail service to Nicaragua is reliable, even to remote areas. Boxes, on the other hand, of whatever size, are routed through the *aduana* (customs). This means traipsing to their office at the airport in Managua and enduring a horrific and uncaring bureaucracy intent on *not* giving you your goods. Most major international courier services have offices all over Nicaragua, including DHL and Federal Express, but they too are subject to the *aduana*.

Telephone and Fax

The national phone company **ENITEL** (Empresa Nicaragüense de Telecomunicaciones, tel. 505/2278-3131, fax 505/2278-4012, www.

enitel.com.ni) was privatized in 2003 and is modernizing quickly under private ownership. Note that it is sometimes called TELCOR, its old name. A 24-hour ENITEL customer service operator is available by dialing 121. Every major city has an ENITEL office, as do many small towns, and elsewhere you'll find families offering their phones for pay instead. But these offices are quickly becoming obsolete in the age of cell phones, which have permeated into even the poorest villages. You can also purchase phone cards that work in ENITEL and Publitel pay phones, located in any town bigger than Estelí. Most ENITEL offices have fax machines. A two-page international fax may cost you $4–5; a local fax will cost about $1. Also check in copy shops, Internet providers, and post offices. Many local cybercafés offer VOIP calls as well; of note is the **Llamadas Heladas** chain, present in at least 29 locations.

In 2009, Nicaragua switched from a 7-digit to an 8-digit phone number system. All land lines earned an additional "2" at the beginning, and all cell phones took on an additional "8." If you see a number with only seven digits, follow this standard.

Cell Phones

Nicaragua's two networks are Claro and Movistar (formerly Bell South). Claro has better coverage nationwide (even in Waspám!) but calls are more expensive; Movistar works best in city centers but drops out while you're on the road, and has more attractive pricing. Calls between networks are a bit more expensive than calls within networks, hardly enough to worry about, but enough for many Nicas to carry two cell phones.

Getting your own cell phone for travel is easy and inexpensive. Rent a cell phone from a booth in the airport in the luggage pickup area (open during daylight business hours only), but it may make more sense to purchase a nearly disposable cell phone *(chiclero)*, available in Claro and Movistar outlets and at most gas stations for less than $20.

You can also put a local SIM card in your own dual-band cell phone (Nicaragua operates on the 800 and 900 MHz frequencies); it's easy to get a chip for either of Nicaragua's two competing cell phone networks.

As you travel, you'll notice there are little booths all over the nation that offer *"recarga"* of minutes, and many other stores can recharge your phone as well. Just give them your money and your cell number and they'll dial it in; you'll get an SMS within 60 seconds confirming the added time. C$250 is probably enough for a week's worth of travel, depending on how long you chat or how often you phone home.

Important Numbers:

- Information: 113
- To place a collect call within Nicaragua: 110
- International operator: 116
- Police: 118
- Firefighters: 115 and 120
- Red Cross: 128

International Calls

Cybercafés throughout the nation offer Internet calling, and **Llamadas Heladas** specializes in VOIP-based, cheap international calls. Connection quality can be dodgy, but with rates as low as $6 per hour to call the United States, Canada, or Europe, this is a great way to quickly get in touch back home. Of course you can also call home on Skype or other broadband services, especially if you have a laptop, since many hotels now offer Wi-Fi in your room.

Internet Access

Internet cafés exist throughout the nation, and even in smaller towns you'll find several *cybers* (pronounced SEE-bear), run off a wimpy ADSL connection and a pirated copy of Windows XP (this author has yet to find a computer whose keyboard is configured properly in any of these village *cybers*). Prices start at about $1 per hour and go as high as $15 an hour

Cyber (or *ciber*) cafés are found in most towns and cities across Nicaragua.

in some hotel business centers. Furthermore, free Wi-Fi connections are spreading like the plague across Nicaraguan restaurants, hotels, and cafés. Note that these free networks are often riddled with security threats, so use them to check your email, not your bank account.

If you are staying a significant time in Nicaragua and need a connection in your home or business, visit a Claro or Movistar kiosk to inquire about cell phone dongles that let you access the Internet the way you'd make a cell phone call, with the same coverage. For landlines, **IBW Communications** (from Hospital Monte España, one block north, one block east, tel. 505/2278-6328, www.ibw.com.ni) offers dial-up access starting at about $10 per month.

Most Nicaraguans work with PCs, but if you have a Mac you can get repair services at **Mac Center** (located near the UCA, from the Metrocentro rotunda, 2 blocks west, 1.5 south, tel. 505/2270-5918, raguilar@mac.com). They are a certified dealer and service provider, with all kinds of Apple-related services, repairs, and products; also free Nica coffee and Wi-Fi.

Newspapers

Street vendors are out before 6 A.M. every day hawking the various daily papers, but you can often pick one up in most corner stores. *La Prensa* (www.laprensa.com.ni) was so aggressively anti-Somoza in the 1970s the dictator allegedly had the editor, Pedro Joaquín Chamorro, assassinated. Not long after the revolution, *La Prensa* turned anti-Sandinista and remains anti-Danielista to this day. In the days before an election, *La Prensa* typically runs a regular series of "flashback" articles recalling the atrocities of the Contra war in the 1980s and dredging up every unresolved Sandinista scandal available. *El Nuevo Diario* (www.elnuevodiario.com.ni) offers competing coverage of local news and events, sometimes with a *New York Post*–ish tabloidy spin.

International papers and magazines are sold

in Managua at the Casa de Café, a kiosk on the first floor of the Plaza Metrocentro, and in the lobbies of the major hotels.

Magazines

Created in 1981 to spread the news about the revolution to the English-speaking world, **Envío** (www.envio.org.ni) remains an interesting print and online magazine, providing "information and analysis of Nicaragua from Nicaragua."

MAPS AND TOURIST INFORMATION

Maps

The longtime champion map of Nicaragua is published by **International Travel Map** (ITM, www.itmb.com), scaled at 1:750,000, colored to show relief, and with good road and river detail. They also offer an excellent Central America regional map. It's found in many bookstores and travel shops, but not in Nicaragua.

A new favorite is produced by German cartographers **Mapas NaTurismo** (salsa_klaus@yahoo.de, www.mapas-naturismo.com). Their gorgeous 1:500,000 country map is water resistant and features detailed tourist attractions and natural reserves better than any other; it also has a few handy inserts, including Isla de Ometepe at 1:200,000; samples are available on their site, and they are currently producing city maps of Masaya and Granada and a regional map of Managua to Rivas. They go for about $7 at www.omnimap.com or www.gotrekkers.com.

The **Nelles Central America** map (1:1,750,000) offers a quality overview of the region (plus more detail on Costa Rica) and is good if you are traveling the whole area and don't intend to venture too far off the beaten track.

INETER, the Nicaraguan Institute of Territorial Studies, produces the only complete series of 1:50,000 maps (or topo quads) of Nicaragua, now available online at www.ineter.gob.ni. Produced in the 1960s and photorevised in the 1980s with Soviet help, these are the most detailed topographical maps of Nicaragua that exist. They can be purchased from the INETER office in Managua (and occasionally at regional offices) for $3 each. The Managua office is located across from Policlinica Oriental and Immigration (tel. 505/2249-2768, 8 a.m.–4:30 p.m. Mon.–Fri.).

Tactical Pilotage Charts (TPC K-25B and TPC K-25C) cover northern and southern Nicaragua, respectively, with some coverage of Costa Rica, Panamá, and Honduras at 1:500,000 scale. Designed for pilots, these maps have good representation of topography and are useful if you do any adventuring in the eastern parts of the country (far easier than carrying a stack of topo maps). Many smaller towns are shown, but only major roads.

Tourism Information

The **Instituto Nicaragüense de Turismo** (INTUR, one block west and one north of the Crowne Plaza Hotel, tel. 505/2222-3333, www.intur.gob.ni, 8:30 a.m.–2 p.m. Mon.–Fri.) has a sometimes-useful kiosk in the airport arrival area (just before you claim your baggage). The regional offices can give you a list of the year's upcoming festivals, a fistful of brochures, and can sometimes help arrange tours with local operators. Also visit their tourist-directed site www.visitanicaragua.com.

Other online resources include www.vianica.com and www.nicaragualiving.info. *Anda Ya!* (www.andayanicaragua.com) is a free Spanish language booklet packed with helpful contacts and listings in Granada, San Juan del Sur, León, Managua, and Estelí. Tourist-targeted, real estate–funded glossy publications are always on hand in hotel lobbies across the country.

WEIGHTS AND MEASURES

Time

Nicaragua is in standard time zone GMT-6, i.e., six hours earlier than London. Daylight saving time is not observed. During standard time, when it's 8 P.M. in New York it's 7 P.M. in Managua, and during daylight saving time, when it's 8 P.M. in New York it's 6 P.M. in Nicaragua. But no matter what your watch says, you're always on Nica time—everything starts a little late and meeting times are considered approximate.

Electricity

Nicaragua uses the same electrical standards as the United States and Canada: 110V, 60 Hz. The shape of the electrical socket is the same as well. Laptop users should bring a portable surge protector with them, as the electrical current in Nicaragua is highly variable, and spikes, brownouts, and outages are commonplace.

Measurements

Distances are almost exclusively in kilometers, although for smaller lengths, you'll occasionally hear feet, inches, yards, and the colonial Spanish *vara* (about a meter). The most commonly used land-area term is the *manzana,* another old measure, equal to 1.74 acres. Weights and volumes are a mix of metric and nonmetric: Buy your gasoline in gallons, your chicken in pounds, and so on.

RESOURCES

Glossary

alcaldía: mayor's office

arroyo: stream or gully

artesanía: crafts

ayudante: "helper"–the guy on the bus who collects your fee after you find a seat

barrio: neighborhood

beneficio: coffee mill

bombero: firefighter

bravo: rough, strong, wild

cabo: cape

cafetín: light-food eatery

calle: street

cama matrimonial: "marriage bed;" motels and hotels use this term to refer to a double, queen, or king-size bed; a bed meant for two people.

camión: truck

campesino: country folk

campo: countryside

carretera: highway, road

cayo: cay

centro de salud: public MINSA-run health clinic; there is one in most towns

centro recreativo: public recreation center

cerro: hill or mountain

cerveza, cervecita: beer

chele, chela: gringo, whitey

chinelas: rubber flip-flops

ciudad: city

colectivo: a shared taxi or passenger boat

colonía: neighborhood

comedor: cheap lunch counter

comida corriente: plate of the day

complejo: complex (of buildings)

cooperativa: cooperative

cordillera: mountain range

córdoba: Nicaraguan currency

corriente: standard, base

coyote: illegal-immigrant smuggler; or profit-cutting middleman

cuajada: white, homemade, salty cheese

departamentos: subsection of Nicaragua, akin to states or counties

empalme: intersection of two roads

entrada: entrance

estero: estuary or marsh

expreso: express bus

farmacia: pharmacy, drugstore

fiestas patronales: Saint's Day parties held annually in every town and city

fresco: natural fruit drink

fritanga: street-side barbecue and fry-fest

gallo pinto: national mix of rice 'n beans

gancho: gap in a fence

gaseosa: carbonated beverage

gringo: North American, or any foreigner

guaro: booze

guitarra: guitar

guitarrón: mariachi bass guitar

hospedaje: hostel, budget hotel

iglesia: church

isla: island

laguna: lake

lancha: small passenger boat

lanchero: *lancha* driver

malecón: waterfront

manzana: besides an apple, this is also a measure of land equal to 100 square *varas,* or 1.74 acres

mar: sea or ocean

mariachi: Mexican country/polka music

mercado: market

mesa/meseta: geographical plateau

mosquitero: mosquito net

muelle: dock, wharf

museo: museum

ordinario: local bus (also *ruteado*)

panga: small passenger boat

panguero: panga driver

pinche: stingy, cheap

playa: beach

pueblo: small town or village

pulpería: corner store

puro: cigar

quintal: 100-pound sack

rancheras: Mexican drinking songs

rancho: thatch-roofed restaurant or hut

rato: a short period of time

reserva: reserve or preserve

río: river

sala: living room

salida: exit, road out of town

salon: large living room, gallery

salto: waterfall

sierra: mountain range

suave: soft, easy, quiet

tope: a dead-end, or T intersection

tranquilo: mellow

urbano: public urban bus

vara: colonial unit of distance equal to roughly one meter

volcán: volcano

NICARAGUAN DINING
Desayuno (Breakfast)

huevos: eggs

enteros: hardboiled

revueltos: scrambled

volteados: over easy

Bocadillas (Appetizers)

ensalada: shredded cabbage, tomatoes, and a toasted white corn

maduro: ripe, sweet plantains fried in their own sugar

tajadas: crunchy, thin strips of green plantain

tostones: thick, fried, green plantain chips

Almuerzo y Cena (Lunch and Dinner)

carne/res: beef

desmenuzada: shredded and stewed

a la plancha: served on a hot plate

churrasco: grilled steak

filete jalapeño: steak in a creamy pepper sauce

puerco/cerdo: pork

chuleta: pork chop

pollo: chicken

empanizado: breaded

frito: fried

al vino: wine sauce

rostizado: rotisserie

valencian: a chicken and rice dish

mariscos: seafood

pescado entero: the whole fish

langosta al ajillo: lobster in garlic sauce

camarones al vapor: steamed shrimp

sopa de conchas: conch soup

huevos de paslama: endangered turtle eggs (Illegal)

Platos Tradicionales (Traditional Dishes)

baho: plantain and beef stew

caballo bayo: a sampler plate of traditional dishes

cuajada: white, farmer's cheese

gallo pinto: red beans and rice, generously doused in oil and salt

indio viejo: beef, veggie, and cornmeal mush

leche agria: a sour cream-yogurt combo

nacatamales: meat-filled corn tamal, wrapped and boiled in banana leaves

vigorón: pork rinds with yucca and coleslaw, served on a banana leaf

Bebidas y (Re)Frescos (Drinks and Fruit Juices)

chichi: rough-milled corn with vanilla and banana flavors, sometimes fermented

horchata: toasted and milled rice with spices

pinol: toasted, milled corn

pinolillo: pinol with pepper, cloves, and cacao

tiste: toasted cooked corn with cacao, pepper, and cloves

Postres (Dessert)

flan: flan

helado: ice cream

sorbete: sherbet

ABBREVIATIONS

ENEL: Empresa Nicaragüense de Electricidad (electric company)

ENITEL: Empresa Nicaragüense de Telecomunicaciónes (telephone company)

FSLN: Frente Sandinista de Liberación Nacional (Sandinista party)

IFA: (EEH-fa) East German troop transport, used commonly in Nicaraguan public transportation system; it probably stands for something in German, but in Nicaragua, it means *imposible frenar a tiempo* (impossible to brake on time).

INETER: Instituto Nicaragüense de Estudios Territoriales (government geography/geology institute)

MARENA: Ministerio del Ambiente y los Recursos Naturales (Ministry of Natural Resources and the Environment), administers Nicaragua's protected areas

MYA: Million Years Ago

NGO: Nongovernmental Organization

PCV: Peace Corps Volunteer

PLC: Partido Liberal Constitucionalista, the conservative anti-Sandinista party

SINAP: Sistema Nacional de Areas Protegidas (National System of Protected Areas)

UCA: Universidad de Centroamerica

UN: United Nations

UNAN: Universidad Nacional Autónoma de Nicaragua

USAID: United States Agency for International Development, channels congressionally approved foreign aid

Spanish Phrasebook

PRONUNCIATION GUIDE

Spanish pronunciation is much more regular than that of English, but there are still occasional variations.

Vowels

a   as in "father," but shorter

e   as in "hen"

i   as in "machine"

o   as in "phone"

u   usually as in "rule"; when it follows a "q," the "u" is silent; when it follows an "h" or "g," it's pronounced like "w," except when it comes between "g" and "e" or "i," when it's also silent (unless it has an umlaut, when it is again pronounced as English "w")

Consonants

c   as "c" in "cat," before "a," "o," or "u"; like "s" before "e" or "i"

d   as "d" in "dog," except between vowels, then like "th" in "that"

g   before "e" or "i," like the "ch" in Scottish "loch"; elsewhere like "g" in "get"

h   always silent

j   like the English "h" in "hotel," but stronger

ll   like the "y" in "yellow"

ñ   like the "ni" in "onion"

r   always pronounced as strong "r"

rr   trilled "r"

v   similar to the "b" in "boy" (not as English "v")

y   similar to English, but with a slight "j" sound. When standing alone, it's pronounced like the "e" in "me."

z   like "s" in "same"
b, f, k, l, m, n, p, q, s, t, w, x   as in English

Stress

Native English speakers frequently make errors of pronunciation by ignoring stress. All Spanish vowels—**a, e, i, o,** and **u**—may carry accents that determine which syllable of a word gets emphasis. Often, stress seems unnatural to nonnative speakers—the surname Chávez, for instance, is stressed on the first syllable—but failure to observe this rule may mean that native speakers may not understand you.

USEFUL WORDS AND PHRASES

Nicaraguans and other Spanish-speaking people consider formalities important. Whenever approaching anyone for information or some other reason, do not forget the appropriate salutation—good morning, good evening, etc. Standing alone, the greeting *hola* (hello) can sound brusque.

Hello. *Hola.*
Good morning. *Buenos días.*
Good afternoon. *Buenas tardes.*
Good evening. *Buenas noches.*
How are you? *¿Cómo está?*
Fine. *Muy bien.*
And you? *¿Y usted?*
Awesome! *De acachimba!*
So-so. *Más o menos.*
Thank you. *Gracias.*
Thank you very much. *Muchas gracias.*
You're very kind. *Muy amable.*
You're welcome. *De nada ("It's nothing").*
yes *sí*
no *no*
I don't know. *No sé.*
It's fine; okay *Está bien.*
Good; okay *Bueno.*
please *por favor*
Pleased to meet you. *Mucho gusto.*
Excuse me (physical) *Perdóneme.*
Excuse me (speech) *Discúlpeme.*

I'm sorry. *Lo siento.*
Goodbye. *Adiós.*
See you later. *Hasta luego* ("Until later").
more *más*
less *menos*
better *mejor*
much, a lot *mucho*
a shot of strong liquor *un cachimvaso*
very drunk *hasta el culo*
a little *un poco*
large *grande*
small *pequeño, chico*
quick, fast *rápido*
slowly *despacio*
bad *malo*
difficult *difícil*
easy *fácil*
He/She/It is gone; as in "She left" or "he's gone." *Ya se fue.*
I don't speak Spanish well. *No hablo bien el español.*
I don't understand. *No entiendo ni papas.*
How do you say...in Spanish? *¿Cómo se dice...en español?*
Do you understand English? *¿Entiende el inglés?*
Is English spoken here? (Does anyone here speak English?) *¿Se habla inglés aquí?*

TERMS OF ADDRESS

When in doubt, use the formal *usted* (you) as a form of address. If you wish to dispense with formality and feel that the desire is mutual, you can say, *"Me puedes tutear"* ("You can call me 'tu'").

I *yo*
you (formal) *usted*
you (familiar) *vos*
you (familiar) *tú*
he/him *él*
she/her *ella*
we/us *nosotros*
you (plural) *ustedes*
they/them (all males or mixed gender) *ellos*

they/them (all females) *ellas*
Mr., sir *Señor* or *Don*
Mrs., madam *Señora* or *Doña*
Miss, young, lady *Señorita*
wife *esposa*
husband *marido* or *esposo*
friend *amigo* (male), *amiga* (female)
sweetheart *novio* (male), *novia* (female)
son, daughter *hijo, hija*
brother, sister *hermano, hermana*
father, mother *padre, madre*
grandfather, grandmother *abuelo, abuela*

GETTING AROUND

Where is . . .? *¿Dónde está . . .?*
How far is it to . . .? *¿A cuanto está . . .?*
from...to . . . *de...a . . .*
highway *la carretera*
road *el camino*
street *la calle*
block *la cuadra*
kilometer *kilómetro*
north *norte*
south *sur*
west *oeste; poniente*
east *este; oriente*
straight ahead *al derecho; adelante*
to the right *a la derecha*
to the left *a la izquierda*

ACCOMMODATIONS

Is there a room? *¿Hay cuarto?*
May I (we) see it? *¿Puedo (podemos) verlo?*
What is the rate? *¿Cuál es el precio?*
Is that your best rate? *¿Es su mejor precio?*
Is there something cheaper? *¿Hay algo más económico?*
single room *un sencillo*
double room *un doble*
room for a couple *matrimonial*
key *llave*
with private bath *con baño*
with shared bath *con baño general; con baño compartido*

hot water *agua caliente*
cold water *agua fría*
shower *ducha*
electric shower *ducha eléctrica*
towel *toalla*
soap *jabón*
toilet paper *papel higiénico*
air-conditioning *aire acondicionado*
fan *abanico; ventilador*
blanket *frazada; manta*
sheets *sábanas*

PUBLIC TRANSPORT

bus stop *la parada*
bus terminal *terminal de buses*
airport *el aeropuerto*
launch *lancha; tiburonera*
dock *muelle*
I want a ticket to . . . *Quiero un pasaje a . . .*
I want to get off at . . . *Quiero bajar en . . .*
Here, please. *Aquí, por favor.*
Where is this bus going? *¿Adónde va este autobús?*
round-trip *ida y vuelta*
What do I owe? *¿Cuánto le debo?*

FOOD

menu *la carta, el menú*
glass *taza*
fork *tenedor*
knife *cuchillo*
spoon *cuchara*
napkin *servilleta*
soft drink *agua fresca*
coffee *café*
cream *crema*
tea *té*
sugar *azúcar*
drinking water *agua pura, agua potable*
bottled carbonated water *agua mineral con gas*
bottled uncarbonated water *agua sin gas*
beer *cerveza*
wine *vino*

milk *leche*
juice *jugo*
eggs *huevos*
bread *pan*
watermelon *sandía*
banana *banano*
plantain *plátano*
apple *manzana*
orange *naranja*
meat (without) *carne (sin)*
beef *carne de res*
chicken *pollo; gallina*
fish *pescado*
shellfish *mariscos*
shrimp *camarones*
fried *frito*
roasted *asado*
barbecued *a la parrilla*
breakfast *desayuno*
lunch *almuerzo*
dinner (often eaten in late afternoon) *comida*
dinner, or a late-night snack *cena*
the check, bill *la cuenta*

MAKING PURCHASES

I need . . . *Necesito . . .*
I want . . . *Deseo . . .* or *Quiero . . .*
I would like...(more polite) *Quisiera . . .*
How much does it cost? *¿Cuánto cuesta?*
What's the exchange rate? *¿Cuál es el tipo de cambio?*
May I see . . .? *¿Puedo ver . . .?*
This one *ésta/ésto*
expensive *caro*
cheap *barato*
cheaper *más barato*
too much *demasiado*

HEALTH

Help me please. *Ayúdeme por favor.*
I am ill. *Estoy enfermo.*
pain *dolor*
fever *fiebre*
stomachache *dolor de estómago*
vomiting *vomitar*
diarrhea *diarrea* or *curutaca*
drugstore *farmacia*
medicine *medicina*
pill, tablet *pastilla*
birth-control pills *pastillas anticonceptivas*
condom *condón; preservativo*

NUMBERS

0 *cero*
1 *uno* (masculine)
1 *una* (feminine)
2 *dos*
3 *tres*
4 *cuatro*
5 *cinco*
6 *seis*
7 *siete*
8 *ocho*
9 *nueve*
10 *diez*
11 *once*
12 *doce*
13 *trece*
14 *catorce*
15 *quince*
16 *dieciseis*
17 *diecisiete*
18 *dieciocho*
19 *diecinueve*
20 *veinte*
21 *veintiuno*
30 *treinta*
40 *cuarenta*
50 *cincuenta*
60 *sesenta*
70 *setenta*
80 *ochenta*
90 *noventa*
100 *cien*
101 *ciento y uno*
200 *doscientos*
1,000 *mil*

10,000 *diez mil*
1,000,000 *un millón*

TIME

While Nicaraguans mostly use the 12-hour clock, in some instances, usually associated with plane or bus schedules, they may use the 24-hour military clock. Under the 24-hour clock, for example, *las nueve de la noche* (9 P.M.) would be *las 21 horas* (2100 hours).

What time is it? *¿Qué hora es?*
It's one o'clock. *Es la una.*
It's two o'clock. *Son las dos.*
At two o'clock. *A las dos.*
It's ten to three. *Son las tres menos diez.*
It's ten past three. *Son las tres y diez.*
It's three fifteen. *Son las tres y cuarto.*
It's two forty-five. *Son las tres menos cuarto.*
It's two thirty. *Son las dos y media.*
It's six A.M. *Son las seis de la mañana.*
It's six P.M. *Son las seis de la tarde.*
It's ten P.M. *Son las diez de la noche.*
today *hoy*
tomorrow *mañana*
morning *la mañana*
tomorrow morning *mañana por la mañana*
yesterday *ayer*
week *la semana*
month *mes*
year *año*
last night *anoche*
the next day *el día siguiente*

DAYS OF THE WEEK

Sunday *Domingo*
Monday *Lunes*
Tuesday *Martes*
Wednesday *Miércoles*
Thursday *Jueves*
Friday *Viernes*
Saturday *Sábado*

Suggested Reading

A prodigious amount of literature emerged from the Sandinista years, when Nicaragua was the setting of the hemisphere's most celebrated—and criticized—socialist experiment of the century. You'll find more titles on Nicaragua in the used-book section than you will on the new releases shelf. Following is an extremely eclectic (and incomplete) list of your options.

FICTION

Sirias, Silvio. *Bernardo and the Virgin.* Chicago: Northwestern University Press, 2005. *Bernardo*'s real-life texture and ingenious use of voices and characters portrays a thick slice of Nicaragua's past and present while recounting the true story of the Virgin Mary's appearances to a *campesino* in Cuapa.

Sirias, Silvio. *Meet Me Under the Ceiba.* Houston: Arte Publico Press, 2009. Sirias's second novel is also set in small-town Nicaragua and continues the vibrant cultural portrait he began in *Bernardo.* It is based on a 1998 hate-crime murder in La Curva and addresses many issues, including homophobia and gay rights in Latin America. The narrator explains the story's importance: "Adela Rugama's murder is a chilling story. It's a sobering portrait of human frailty, of what can happen when we allow our weaknesses, our emotional flaws, to take control of our actions."

NONFICTION AND MEMOIR

Babb, Florence. *After Revolution: Mapping Gender and Cultural Politics in Neoliberal Nicaragua.* Austin, Texas: University of Texas

Press, 2001. Professor of Anthropology and Women's Studies at the University of Iowa, Babb has also published scores of academic papers on Nicaragua, mainly on issues of gender and sexuality.

Barrios de Chamorro, Violeta. *Dreams of the Heart.* New York: Simon & Schuster, 1996. A very human history of Nicaragua from the Somoza years through Doña Violeta's electoral triumph in 1990 (she served as Nicaragua's president in the early 1990s).

Belli, Gioconda. *The Country Under My Skin: A Memoir of Love and War.* New York: Anchor Books, 2003. This is a phenomenal book that provides a closeup look at various stages of *la lucha* (the struggle), written by one of the country's premier living poets. Stephen Kinzer writes, "Belli's memoir shows us a side of the Sandinista revolution we have not seen. It also introduces us to an astute veteran of two eternal wars, one between the sexes and one that pits the world's poor against its rich."

Cabezas, Omar. *Fire from the Mountain (La Montaña es Algo Más que una Grán Estapa Verde).* Phoenix: Crown, 1985. A ribald, vernacular account of what it's like to be a guerrilla soldier in the mountains of Nicaragua; one of the few books about the early stages of the revolution.

Cardenal, Ernesto; Walsh, Donald D. (translator). *The Gospel in Solentiname.* Maryknoll, New York: Orbis Books, 1979. Transcripts of the masses given by Cardenal on Solentiname that helped spawn the *Misa Campesina* and liberation theology movements.

Chomsky, Noam. *Turning the Tide: U.S. Intervention in Central America and the Struggle for Peace.* Cambridge, Massachusetts: South End Press, 1985. Succinctly and powerfully shows how U.S. Central American policies implement broader U.S. economic, military, and social aims, with Nicaragua and El Salvador as examples.

Dando-Collins, Stephen. *Tycoon's War: How Cornelius Vanderbilt Invaded a Country to Overthrow America's Most Famous Military Adventurer.* Philadelphia: Da Capo Press, 2008. This account of one of Nicaragua's most fascinating historical periods (the mid-19th century) is painstakingly researched and told in an exciting narrative. Dando-Collins weaves the stories of Vanderbilt and William Walker with a striking degree of detail. The *Wall Street Journal* said this book "reads...[like a] screenplay treatment for a hell of a movie."

Davis, Peter. *Where is Nicaragua?* New York: Simon & Schuster, 1987. Davis breaks down the revolution and Contra war, and ties them into the country's greater history; he articulates the complexity of the situation in a graspable manner.

Dickey, Christopher. *With the Contras.* New York: Simon & Schuster, 1985. Dickey was the *Washington Post* correspondent in Honduras and gives an exciting account of his experience with the secret Contra army.

Kinzer, Stephen. *Blood of Brothers: Life and War in Nicaragua.* New York: G. P. Putnam's Sons, 1991. Kinzer, the *New York Times* Managua bureau chief during the war, sensed that Nicaragua was "a country with more to tell the world than it had been able to articulate, a country with a message both political and spiritual."

Lancaster, Roger N. *Life Is Hard: Machismo, Danger, and the Intimacy of Power in Nicaragua.* Berkeley: University of California Press, 1992. Lancaster is an anthropologist and this is an ethnography studying not current events, but their effect on the Nicaraguan individual and family. It is intimate and offers details about Nicaraguan life that one can only get living with the people in their very homes. Lancaster pays attention to issues often passed over, like homosexuality, domestic violence, broken families, and the roots of machismo.

Marriot, Edward. *Savage Shore: Life and Death with Nicaragua's Last Shark Hunters.* New York: Owl Books, 2001. A curious and descriptive journey up the Río San Juan and beyond.

Pastor, Robert. *Not Condemned to Repetition: The United States and Nicaragua.* Boulder, Colorado: Westview Press, 2002. Robert Pastor was a U.S. policymaker in the period leading up to and following the Sandinista revolution of 1979. A decade later, he organized the International Mission led by Jimmy Carter that mediated the first free election in Nicaragua's history. This updated edition covers the events of the democratic transition of the 1990s and extracts lessons to be learned from the past.

Randall, Margaret. *Sandino's Daughters: Testimonies of Nicaraguan Women in Struggle.* Point Roberts, Washington: New Star Books, 1981. Explores the role of feminism in the Sandinista revolution, via a series of interviews with participants.

Rushdie, Salman. *The Jaguar Smile.* New York: Viking, 1987. Representing the pro-Sandinista Nicaragua Solidarity Campaign in London, Rushdie takes readers on a poetic, passionate jaunt through Nicaragua as part of a government cultural campaign; he offers a careful (if short) examination of their policies.

Squier, Ephraim George. *Nicaragua: Its People, Scenery, Monuments, and the Proposed Interoceanic Canal.* New York: D. Appleton, 1852. Squier remains one of Nicaragua's most prolific writers; this massive, multivolume tome is available for hundreds of dollars in rare bookstores. The discussion is divided into five parts in which he describes geography and topography; the events during the author's residence, including accounts of his explorations; observations on the proposed canal; notes on the indigenous peoples of the country, including information regarding geographical distribution, languages, institutions, religions, and customs; and the political history of the country since its independence from Spain.

Volz, Eric. *Gringo Nightmare: A Young American Framed for Murder in Nicaragua.* New York: St. Martin's Press, 2010. It is definitely every traveler's worst nightmare to end up in a filthy Third World prison, but Volz's case goes way beyond his cramped cell, and it is also much greater than the volatile social conditions in San Juan del Sur that helped lead to his arrest. This is a harrowing tale by any account, and proof that Nicaragua is *not* "the next Costa Rica." Not by a long shot. One reviewer remarked, "This story should be issued with every passport" (Bill Kurtis, A&E).

Zimmerman, Matilde. *Sandinista: Carlos Fonseca and the Nicaraguan Revolution.* Durham, North Carolina: Duke University Press, 2001. This is the first English-language biography of the legendary leader of the FSLN and arguably the most important and influential figure of the post-1959 revolutionary generation in Latin America.

PHOTOGRAPHY

Belli, Alejandro et al. *The Nicaraguans.* Managua, 2006. One of the best photography books about Nicaragua. Period. Go to www.thenicaraguans.com to learn more about this stunning collection of images celebrating the people of the country. In the foreword, Sergio Ramírez Mercado writes, "These photographs, taken by Nicaraguans observing other Nicaraguans who are simply getting through the day, reveal the multi-faceted face of peace, which today also embodies our identity."

Gentile, William Frank. *Nicaragua: Photographs by William Frank Gentile* New York: W. W. Norton & Company, 1989. These are some of the deepest, most powerful photos you'll ever see, with fantastic juxtapositions of Contra and FSLN soldiers.

Kunzle, David. *The Murals of Revolutionary Nicaragua 1979–1992*. Berkeley: University of California Press, 1995. Many murals were strictly political, but most intertwined the revolutionary process with cultural, historical, and literary themes. All are celebrated in Kunzle's book, 83-page introduction, and 100 color plates.

Meiselas, Susan. *Nicaragua* New York: Aperture, 2008. Originally published in 1981 to document both the carnage and hope of the year leading up to the revolution, this book includes some of the most iconic images of the period. This new edition comes with a DVD called "Pictures from a Revolution," in which the photographer returns to the scenes and subjects of her famous photographs.

POETRY, LANGUAGE, AND LITERATURE

Morelli, Marco, ed. *Rubén's Orphans*. New Hyde Park, New York: Painted Rooster Press, 2001. An anthology of contemporary Nicaraguan poets, with English translations.

Rabella, Joaquim and Pallais, C. *Vocabulario Popular Nicaragüense*. Managua: Hispamer. This big red linguistic bible is a wonderful dictionary celebrating Nicaraguan Spanish, complete with regional usages, sayings, and a plethora of profanities; available (hopefully) in many bookstores in Managua, and can be purchased in the airport.

Randall, Margaret. *Risking a Somersault in the Air: Conversations with Nicaraguan Writers*. San Francisco: Solidarity Publications, 1984. Just as much about literature as it is about the revolution, this is a fascinating series of interviews with Nicaraguan authors and poets, most of whom were part of the FSLN revolution and government.

White, Steven, trans. *Poets of Nicaragua: A Bilingual Anthology 1918–1970*. London: Unicorn Press, 1983.

TRAVEL

Hulme, Krekel, and O'Reilly. *Not Just Another Nicaragua Travel Guide*. Redwood, California: Mango Publications, 1990. An ebullient and fascinating guidebook for traveling Sandinista Nicaragua in the 1980s. Get it if you can find it; only 1,000 copies were printed.

Suggested Viewing

Carla's Song, a 1996 drama by Ken Loach, stars Robert Carlyle and Oyanka Cabezas. Set in 1987, Scottish bus driver George Lennox meets Carla, a Nicaraguan exile living a precarious, profoundly sad life in Glasgow. George takes her back to her village in northern Nicaragua to find out what has happened to her family, boyfriend, and country. Notable for its real and gritty location shots, in both Scotland and Nicaragua, *Carla's Song* is enjoyable and touching, and, notes its writer, Paul Laverty, "is just one of thousands of statistics, hopefully reminding the viewer that everyone in this war had a story." *Carla's Song* was awarded a gold medal at the Italian Film Festival in Venice.

Walker, a bold 1987 anachronistic biography of the infamous soldier-of-fortune from Tennessee, starring Ed Harris. Filmmaker Alex Cox (of *Sid & Nancy* fame), wanted to show that "nothing had changed in the 140-odd years between William Walker's genocidal campaign and that of Oliver North and his goons." One reviewer wrote, "What is so amazing about *Walker* is that it got made at all. It's a film condemning capitalism funded by a capitalist studio. Since it was filmed on location, its production money went straight into a country that the United States was currently at war with." Critics mostly panned the film as "sophomoric black comedy," but confirmed Nicaphiles will surely get a kick out of the familiar scenery.

The World Stopped Watching, a 2003 Canadian film by Peter Raymont and Harold Crooks, was shot in 56 mm. Nicaragua dropped from the spotlight after the end of the Contra war. This documentary, shot in late 2002 and early 2003, picks up the pieces of what happened next. Essentially, this is a sequel to *The World is Watching,* a critically acclaimed documentary from the 1980s involving many of the same characters.

Internet Resources

MOON AUTHORS
www.nomadnotion.com
Current *Moon Nicaragua* author Amber Dobrzensky's personal site and blog.

www.GoToNicaragua.com
This is the website of original *Moon Nicaragua* authors Randy Wood and Josh Berman. Chat with fellow Nicaphile travelers and expats, ask Randy and Josh travel questions, and post travelogues.

www.therandymon.com
Former *Moon Nicaragua* co-author Randy Wood's personal site.

www.joshuaberman.net
Former *Moon Nicaragua* co-author Joshua Berman's personal site and blog.

NICARAGUA NEWS
www.nicaraguadispatch.com
Nicaragua's first and only English-language newspaper, with breaking stories, cultural reports, and community news.

NICARAGUA PORTALS
www.ibw.com.ni
IBW Internet Gateway is a Spanish-language

portal that is a good introduction to the nation's print and visual media, plus links to Nicaraguan government and NGO websites.

www.lanic.utexas.edu/la/ca/nicaragua
The Latin American Network Information Center boasts a ton of Nica-sites, including many academic links.

www.nicanet.org
For more than 25 years, The Nicaragua Network, a coalition of U.S.-based nonprofits (many of them regional sister city organizations), has been committed to social and economic justice for the people of Nicaragua.

OFFICIAL

www.nicaragua.usembassy.gov
The U.S. embassy page in Nicaragua.

www.travel.state.gov/travel
U.S. State Department fact sheet for travelers in Nicaragua, including security overview.

www.voyage.gc.ca
Ditto, from the Canadians. The Canadian government has never really been politically involved in Nicaragua, so its travel warnings provide a good reality check for what you read at the U.S. State Department's site.

TRAVELING AND TOURISM

www.intur.gob.ni
www.visitanicaragua.com
Nicaraguan government tourism agency.

www.marena.gob.ni
For more information on visiting specific parks and reserves, this is the Nicaraguan Natural Resources Ministry.

www.nicaliving.com
A vibrant online community of opinionated expats and travelers.

www.nicaragua-guide.com
This thorough, diverse traveler portal is run by expats living in Granada who wanted "to show the positive side of Nicaragua and . . .community life here."

http://rightsideguide.com
A "survival guide" for travel in Nicaragua's Caribbean coast, with regularly updated information on all aquatic transport in the region, as well as lodging and eating.

www.vianica.com
Vianica is an independent, well-designed, informative overview of travel destinations throughout Nicaragua and can help you plan your trip. They even maintain updated Nicaragua bus schedules!

Index

List of Maps

$ 18.
  18.
  ___
  36.
   4
  ___
  32.

$ 28.

www.moon.com

DESTINATIONS | ACTIVITIES | BLOGS | MAPS | BOOKS

MOON.COM is ready to help plan your next trip! Filled with fresh trip ideas and strategies, author interviews, informative travel blogs, a detailed map library, and descriptions of all the Moon guidebooks, Moon.com is all you need to get out and explore the world—or even places in your own backyard. While at Moon.com, sign up for our monthly e-newsletter for updates on new releases, travel tips, and expert advice from our on-the-go Moon authors. As always, when you travel with Moon, expect an experience that is uncommon and truly unique.

KEEP UP WITH MOON ON FACEBOOK AND TWITTER
JOIN THE MOON PHOTO GROUP ON FLICKR

MAP SYMBOLS

▭ Expressway	◖ Highlight	✗ Airfield	⚲ Golf Course
▭ Primary Road	○ City/Town	✈ Airport	℗ Parking Area
▭ Secondary Road	◉ State Capital	▲ Mountain	▱ Archaeological Site
▭ Unpaved Road	❀ National Capital	✦ Unique Natural Feature	▯ Church
------ Trail	★ Point of Interest		▯ Gas Station
.... Ferry	• Accommodation	▨ Waterfall	▱ Glacier
▭ Railroad	▼ Restaurant/Bar	▲ Park	▱ Mangrove
▭ Pedestrian Walkway	▪ Other Location	▯ Trailhead	▱ Reef
▭ Stairs	Λ Campground	⚞ Skiing Area	▱ Swamp

CONVERSION TABLES

°C = (°F - 32) / 1.8
°F = (°C x 1.8) + 32
1 inch = 2.54 centimeters (cm)
1 foot = 0.304 meters (m)
1 yard = 0.914 meters
1 mile = 1.6093 kilometers (km)
1 km = 0.6214 miles
1 fathom = 1.8288 m
1 chain = 20.1168 m
1 furlong = 201.168 m
1 acre = 0.4047 hectares
1 sq km = 100 hectares
1 sq mile = 2.59 square km
1 ounce = 28.35 grams
1 pound = 0.4536 kilograms
1 short ton = 0.90718 metric ton
1 short ton = 2,000 pounds
1 long ton = 1.016 metric tons
1 long ton = 2,240 pounds
1 metric ton = 1,000 kilograms
1 quart = 0.94635 liters
1 US gallon = 3.7854 liters
1 Imperial gallon = 4.5459 liters
1 nautical mile = 1.852 km

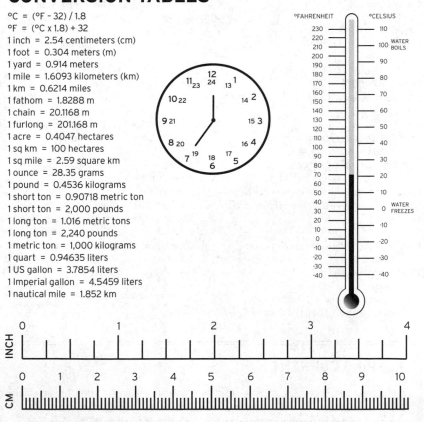

MOON NICARAGUA

Avalon Travel
a member of the Perseus Books Group
1700 Fourth Street
Berkeley, CA 94710, USA
www.moon.com

Editor: Sabrina Young
Series Manager: Kathryn Ettinger
Copy Editor: Kim Runciman
Production and Graphics Coordinator:
  Domini Dragoone
Cover Designer: Domini Dragoone
Map Editor: Mike Morgenfeld
Cartographers: Chris Henrick and Kat Bennett
Indexer: Greg Jewett

ISBN-13: 978-1-61238-356-9
ISSN: 1539-1019

Printing History
1st Edition – 2003
5th Edition – February 2013
5 4 3 2

Text © 2013 by Amber Dobrzensky.
Maps © 2013 by Avalon Travel.
All rights reserved.

KEEPING CURRENT

If you have a favorite gem you'd like to see included in the next edition, or see anything that needs updating, clarification, or correction, please drop us a line. Send your comments via email to feedback@moon.com, or use the address above.